ADVERTISING PROCEDURE

ADVERTISING PROCEDURE

6TH EDITION

Otto Kleppner
Advertising Management Consultant

with the collaboration of
Stephen A. Greyser
Harvard University
Graduate School of Business Administration

PRENTICE-HALL, INC. • *Englewood Cliffs, N.J.*

Library of Congress Cataloging in Publication Data

KLEPPNER, OTTO
    Advertising procedure.

    Includes bibliographical references.
    1. Advertising. I. Title.
HF5823.K45 1973   659.1   72–10706
ISBN 0–13–018069–6

© 1973, 1966, 1950, 1941, 1933, 1925 by Prentice-Hall, Inc.,
Englewood Cliffs, New Jersey

Printed in the United States of America

FIRST EDITION

First Printing .... May, 1925
Second Printing .... August, 1925
Third Printing .... June, 1926
Fourth Printing .... April, 1927
Fifth Printing .... January, 1928
Sixth Printing .... July, 1928
Seventh Printing .... January, 1930
Eighth Printing .... August, 1930
Ninth Printing .... June, 1931
Tenth Printing .... August, 1932

SECOND EDITION

Eleventh Printing .... July, 1933
Twelfth Printing .... September, 1933
Thirteenth Printing .... August, 1934
Fourteenth Printing .... January, 1935
Fifteenth Printing .... November, 1935
Sixteenth Printing .... September, 1936
Seventeenth Printing .... January, 1937
Eighteenth Printing .... July, 1938
Nineteenth Printing .... September, 1939
Twentieth Printing .... June, 1940

THIRD EDITION

Twenty-First Printing .... April, 1941
Twenty-Second Printing .... October, 1941
Twenty-Third Printing .... January, 1942
Twenty-Fourth Printing ... December, 1945
Twenty-Fifth Printing .... May, 1946
Twenty-Sixth Printing .... July, 1946
Twenty-Seventh Printing .... March, 1947
Twenty-Eighth Printing .... July, 1947
Twenty-Ninth Printing .... October, 1947

Thirtieth Printing .... September, 1948
Thirty-First Printing .... May, 1949

FOURTH EDITION

Thirty-Second Printing .... January, 1950
Thirty-Third Printing .... August, 1950
Thirty-Fourth Printing .... September, 1952
Thirty-Fifth Printing .... June, 1953
Thirty-Sixth Printing .... April, 1954
Thirty-Seventh Printing .... January, 1955
Thirty-Eighth Printing .... January, 1956
Thirty-Ninth Printing .... January, 1958
Fortieth Printing .... March, 1959
Forty-First Printing .... June, 1960
Forty-Second Printing .... March, 1962
Forty-Third Printing .... June, 1965

FIFTH EDITION

Forty-Fourth Printing .... May, 1966
Forty-Fifth Printing .... September, 1966
Forty-Sixth Printing .... December, 1966
Forty-Seventh Printing .... July, 1967
Forty-Eighth Printing .... January, 1968
Forty-Ninth Printing .... October, 1968
Fiftieth Printing .... May, 1969
Fifty-First Printing .... May, 1970
Fifty-Second Printing .... May, 1971

SIXTH EDITION

Fifty-Third Printing .... April, 1973
Fifty-Fourth Printing ....September, 1973
Fifty-Fifth Printing   March, 1974
Fifty-Sixth Printing .... December, 1974
Fifty-Seventh Printing ...... November, 1975
Fifty-Eighth Printing .... March, 1976

PRENTICE-HALL INTERNATIONAL, INC., *London*
PRENTICE-HALL OF AUSTRALIA, PTY. LTD., *Sydney*
PRENTICE-HALL OF CANADA, LTD., *Toronto*
PRENTICE-HALL OF INDIA PRIVATE LIMITED, *New Delhi*
PRENTICE-HALL OF JAPAN, INC., *Tokyo*

To Beatrice

Contents

V

THE ADVERTISING CAMPAIGN

strategy and theme? Meeting specific selling problems. Creating the advertisements and commercials. Selecting the media. Getting the budget and campaign approved. Preparing and scheduling the advertising. Appraising the results. Summary of the steps. Fitting the image to the times, Northwestern Mutual Life Insurance Company: a case report on a complete campaign. Bisquick: a case report on giving new life to an old product.

VI
ADVERTISING MANAGEMENT

VII
OTHER WORLDS OF ADVERTISING

Preface

THIS BOOK deals with the management, planning, creation and use of advertising, and tries to do so in as nontechnical a manner as possible. The reader who is seeking a broad view of advertising will find here a comprehensive survey. The reader whose path leads him to areas of advertising responsibility will find, I hope, insights that become ever more meaningful.

During the past decade, changes affecting advertising have been more profound than in any comparable period, including the years following the advent of television. These changes have been in response to the changes in the values of our society, such as the concern for ecology and for pollution, the impact of consumerism, and the widening role of government. Meanwhile advertising has been undergoing changes of its own—a la carte agencies, in-house agencies, media services, and upheavals in media. There have been changes, too, in the philosophy of teaching advertising, and in curricula. Mindful of all such changes, I reached into the prior edition for those things which time has proved valid and useful, and which are significant now, and then proceeded to write a fresh book on advertising as I see it today. In all instances I have tried to retain those qualities of presentation that have been so well received in prior editions.

A suggestion: For a comprehensive study, start with Chapter 1, which begins the discussion of advertising as an institution. Those who wish to proceed directly to the operation of advertising may prefer to start with Chapter 3, returning later to the prior chapters. Whichever way it is used, I hope the book will prove helpful.

OTTO KLEPPNER

Wardsboro, Vermont

Acknowledgments

I AM INDEBTED to many for their help: Sam Vitt, in the areas of television, radio and media services; Frank Vos, direct response advertising; David H. Folkman, retail advertising; David Hymes, print production; Robert La-Chance, television and radio production; Richard Briggs, outdoor and transportation advertising. For reviewing chapters in the fields of their special interest, and for their help in other ways, too, I am grateful to Roger Barton, Arthur Bellaire, Dr. Frederick Breitenfeld, Jr., Fred Dahl, Jerome Eisnitz, Franklin Feldman, Richard Manville, Alfred L. Plant, Milton Seasonwein, Fred Wittner.

For their discerning reading of the entire work, and their suggestions, I thank Professor William J. Kehoe, Marshall University, Professor S. Bernard Rosenblatt, Texas Tech University, Professor Irving Settel, Lubin School of Business, Pace College, Professor C. Raymond Swain, Jr., Lubin School of Business, Pace College, Professor Stanley Ulanoff, Baruch College of The City University of New York, Professor Stephen I. Winter, Orange County Community College. My debt is great also to the many teachers of advertising who have shared their experiences and thoughts with me.

The book has been enriched by the collaboration of Professor Stephen A. Greyser, Harvard Graduate School of Business Administration.

ADVERTISING
PROCEDURE

I
THE PLACE
OF ADVERTISING

1

Background
of Today's Advertising

*One of the oldest outdoor signs known,
this appeared over a butcher shop in Pompeii.*

THIS BOOK IS ABOUT ADVERTISING. What does the term bring to mind? TV and radio commercials? Newspaper ads? Outdoor signs? Magazine ads? Supermarket displays and packages? Certainly all of these are advertising.

Perhaps, however, you may think of all the money being spent on advertising and wonder how it affects the cost of living, or whether it couldn't better be spent on schools or in fighting poverty and pollution. Or it may bring to mind a Hollywood picture of a Madison Avenue agency, where an advertising man saves a million-dollar account by breathlessly phoning the client with a new slogan he just dreamed up. (It doesn't work that way.)

Or you may think of advertisements that you liked, or disliked. In any case, one cannot help being aware of the influence of advertising in our lives.

The fact is that over $22 billion a year* is being spent on American advertising, which in its various forms accosts us from early-morning news programs until the late shows at night. How did advertising become so pervasive in our society? We cannot find the reasons for its importance merely by studying the ads; we must rather understand the economic and social forces producing them.

* * *

The urge to advertise seems to be a part of human nature; there is evidence of it in ancient times. Of the 5,000-year recorded history of advertising right up to our present TV-satellite age, the part that is most significant to us started when the United States began emerging as a great manufacturing nation, about 100 years ago. However, the early history of advertising is far too fascinating to pass by without a glimpse of it.[1]

---

*1972 figure, which has been advancing about one billion dollars a year.

BEGINNINGS

It isn't surprising that the people who gave the world the Tower of Babel also left the earliest known evidence of advertising. A Babylonian clay tablet of about 3000 B.C. was found bearing inscriptions for an ointment dealer, a scribe, and a shoemaker. Papyrus exhumed from the ruins of Thebes showed that the ancient Egyptians had a better medium on which to write their messages. (Alas, the announcements preserved in papyrus offer rewards for the return of runaway slaves.) The Greeks were among those who relied on town criers to chant the arrival of ships with cargoes of wines, spices, and metals. Often a crier was accompanied by a musician who kept him in the right key. Town criers later became the earliest medium for public announcements in many European countries, as in England, and they continued to be used for many centuries. (At this point we must digress to tell about a promotion idea used by innkeepers in France around 1100 A.D., to tell about the fine wines served at their taverns. They would have the town crier blow a horn, gather a group—and offer samples!)

Roman merchants, too, had a sense of advertising. The ruins of Pompeii contain signs in stone or terra cotta, advertising what the shops were selling—a row of hams for a butcher shop, a cow for a dairy, a boot for a shoemaker. The Pompeiians also knew the art of telling their story to the public by means of painted wall signs. Tourism rates as one of the early users of advertising, as revealed in this advertisement on a Pompeiian wall: [2]

> Traveler
> Going from here to the twelfth tower
> There Sarinus keeps a tavern
> This is to request you to enter.
> Farewell

Outdoor advertising has proved to be one of the most enduring, as well as one of the oldest, forms of advertising. It survived the decline of the Roman Empire to become the decorative art of the inns in the seventeenth and eighteenth centuries. That was still an age of widespread illiteracy, and inns, particularly, vied with each other in creating attractive signs that all could recognize. This accounts for the charming names of old inns, especially in England—such as the Three Squirrels, the Man in the Moon, the Hole in the Wall. In 1614, England passed a law—probably the earliest on advertising—that prohibited signs extending more than eight feet out from a building. (Longer signs pulled down too many house fronts.) Another law required signs to be high enough to give clearance to an armored man on horseback. In 1740, the first printed outdoor poster (referred to as a "hoarding") appeared in London.

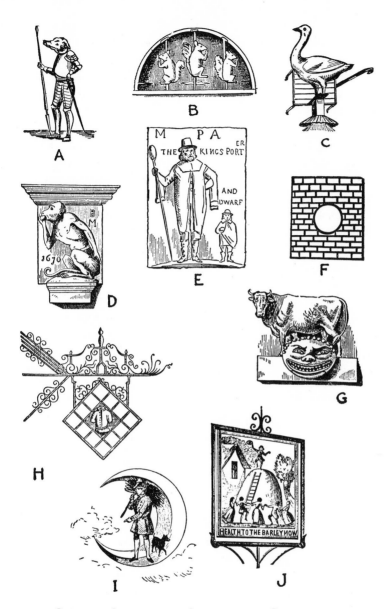

OUTDOOR SIGNS OF THE SEVENTEENTH CENTURY

These signs appeared over inns:

A. Hog in Armour
B. Three Squirrels
C. Goose and Gridiron
D. The Ape
E. King's Porter and Dwarf

F. Hole in the Wall
  "A Guide for Malt Worms"
G. Bull and Mouth
H. Harrow and Doublet
I. Man in the Moon
J. Barley Mow

THE ORIGIN OF THE NEWSPAPER

The next most enduring medium, the newspaper, was the offspring of Gutenberg's invention of printing from movable type (about 1438), which, of course, changed communication methods for the whole world. About 40 years after the invention, Caxton of London printed the first advertisement in English—a handbill of the rules for the guidance of the clergy at Easter. This was tacked up on church doors. (It became the first printed outdoor advertisement in English.) But the printed newspaper took a long time in coming. It really emerged from the newsletters, handwritten by professional writers, for the nobles and others who wanted to be kept up to date on the news, especially of the court, and other important events—very much in the spirit of the Washington newsletters of today.

The first advertisement in any language to be printed in a disseminated sheet appeared in a German news pamphlet about 1525. And what do you think this ad was for? A book extolling the virtues of a mysterious drug. (There was no Food and Drug Administration in those days.) But news pamphlets did not come out regularly; one published in 1591 contained news of the previous three years. It was from such beginnings, however, that the printed newspaper emerged. The first printed English newspaper came out in 1622—the *Weekly Newes of London*. The first advertisement in an English newspaper appeared in 1625.

"SIQUIS," THE TACK-UP ADVERTISEMENTS

The forerunner of our present want ads bore the strange name of *siquis*. These were the tack-up advertisements that appeared in England at the end of the fifteenth century. Of these, Presbrey says:

> These hand-written announcements for public posting were done by scribes who made a business of the work. The word "advertisement" in the sense in which we now use it was then unknown. The advertising bills produced by the scribes were called "Siquis," or "If anybody," because they usually began with the words "If anybody desires" or "If anybody knows of," a phrase that had come from ancient Rome, where public notices of articles lost always began with the words "Si quis."

> First use of manuscript siquis was by young ecclesiastics advertising for a vicarage. . . . Soon the siquis poster was employed by those desiring servants and by servants seeking places. Lost articles likewise were posted. Presently also tobacco, perfume, coffee, and some other luxuries were thus advertised. The great percentage of siquis, however, continued to be of the personal, or want-ad, type.[3]

Advertising in the English newspapers continued to feature similar personal and local announcements. As evidence of the high interest classified advertisements have long had in England, the *London Times,* until a few years ago, filled their first page with classified advertising.

ADVERTISING COMES TO AMERICA

The Pilgrims arrived on American shores before the *Weekly Newes of London* was first published, so they had little chance to learn about newspapers, but the colonists who followed them had, and the first American newspaper to carry advertisements appeared in 1704—the *Boston Newsletter* (note the newsletter identification). It carried an advertisement offering a reward for the capture of a thief and the return of several sorts of men's apparel—more akin to the advertisement offering a reward for the return of slaves, written on Egyptian papyrus thousands of years before, than it was to the advertising printed in the United States 250 years later. By the time the United States was formed, the colonies had 30 newspapers.[4] Their advertising, like that of the English newspapers of that time, consisted mostly of ads we describe today as classified and local.

However, neither those ads nor all the ads appearing in the millenia between them explain the role of advertising since the Industrial Revolution. The history of advertising in the United States is unique, because industrialization took hold just as the country was entering its era of greatest growth; population was soaring, factories were springing up, railroads opened the West. The United States entered the nineteenth century as an agricultural country, following European marketing traditions, and ended the century as a great manufacturing nation, creating its own patterns of distribution. A new age of advertising had begun.

We pick up the story around 1870, when this era of transition was crystallizing.

THREE MOMENTOUS DECADES—1870–1900

Transportation. Here was a country 3,000 miles wide. It had sweeping stretches of rich farmland. It had minerals and forests. It had factories within reach of the coal mines. It had a growing population. But its long-distance transportation was chiefly by rivers and canals.

Railroads today are fighting for their survival, but 100 years ago they changed a sprawling continent into a land of spectacular economic growth. In 1865, there were 35,000 miles of railroad trackage in the United States. By 1900, this trackage was 190,000 miles. Three railroad lines crossed the Mississippi and ran from the Atlantic to the Pacific. Feeder lines and networks spread across the face of the land. Where railroads went, people went, founding farms, settlements, and cities across the continent, and not limited to the waterways. The goods of the North and the East could be exchanged for the farm and extractive products of the South and the West. Never before had a country revealed such extensive and varied resources. Never since has so vast a market without a trade or language barrier been opened. This was an exciting prospect to manufacturers.

The people. In 1870, the population of the United States was 38 million. By 1900, it had doubled. In no other period of American history has the population grown so fast. This growth in population, which included those now freed from slavery, meant an expanding labor force in the fields, factories, and mines; it meant a new consumer market. About 30 percent of this growth was from immigrants. But all the European settlers before them had been immigrants, or descendants of immigrants, who had had the courage to pull up stakes and venture to the "New World," a land far away and strange to them, in search of a new and better life. The result was a society that was mobile, both in readiness to move their homes and in aspirations to move upward in their life-styles.

Inventions and production. The end of the nineteenth century was marked by many notable inventions and advances in the manufacture of goods. Among these were the development of the electric motor and of AC power transmission, which relieved factories of the need to locate next to water sources, thus opening the hinterland to development and growth. The internal-combustion engine was perfected in this period; the automobile age was soon to follow.

It was the age of fast communications; the telephone, telegraph, typewriter, the Mergenthaler linotype and high-speed presses—all increased the ability of people to communicate with each other.

In 1860, 7,600 patent applications were filed in Washington. By 1870, this number had more than doubled, to 19,000; by 1900, it had more than doubled again, to 42,000.[5]

Steel production has traditionally served as an index of industrial activity. While 20 *thousand* tons of steel were produced in 1867, 10 *million* tons were produced in 1900.[6] There is also a direct correlation between the power consumption of a country and its standard of living. By 1870, 3 million horsepower were available; by 1900, this capacity had risen to 10 million.[7] More current being used means more goods being manufactured; it also means that more people are using it for their own household needs—all of which is a good economic index.

The phonograph and the motion picture camera, invented at the turn of the century, added to the life-style of people at that time.

The first telephone ad—1877.

The Columbian exhibition in Chicago, in 1893, was attended by millions of Americans, who returned home breathlessly to tell their friends about the new products they had seen.

NEWSPAPERS

Since colonial times, newspapers had been popular in the United States. In the 1830's, the penny newspaper came out. In 1846, Hoe patented the first rotary printing press, and in 1871 he invented the Hoe web press, which prints both sides of a continuous roll of paper and delivers folded sheets. By the end of the nineteenth century, about 10,000 papers were being published, with an estimated combined circulation of 10 million. Ninety percent of them were weeklies, most of the rest dailies, published in the county seat with farm and local news. By 1900, twenty of the largest cities had their own papers, some with as many as 16 pages. Newspapers were the largest class of media at this period.[8]

To save buying their own paper, many editors (who were also the publishers) bought their paper with one side of the sheet already printed with world news and items of general interest to farmers, and with ads. They would then print the other side with their own local news, and with such ads as they could obtain. Or else they would insert such pages in their own four-page papers, offering an eight-page paper to their readers.

The religious publications. Today, religious publications represent a very small part of the total media picture, but for a few decades after the Civil War, religious publications were the most influential medium. They were the forerunners of magazines. The post–Civil War period was a time of great religious revivals, marking also the beginning of the temperance movement. Church groups issued their own publications. Many of these had circulations of no more than 1,000; the biggest ran to 400,000. But the combined circulation of the 400 religious publications was estimated at about 5 million.

Religious publications had great influence among their readers, a fact that patent-medicine advertisers recognized to such an extent that 75 percent of all the religious publication advertising was for patent medicines. (Many of the temperance papers carried the advertising of preparations that proved to be 40 percent alcohol. Today we call that 80-proof whiskey.)

Magazines. Most of what were called magazines before the 1870's—including Ben Franklin's effort in 1741—lasted less than six months, and for a good reason: They consisted mostly of extracts of books and pamphlets, essays, verse, and communications of dubious value.[9] Magazines as we know them today were really born in the last three decades of the nineteenth century. Many factors were in their favor. The rate of illiteracy in the country had been cut almost in half, from 20 percent in 1870 to little over 10 percent in 1900.[10] In 1875, railroads began carrying mail, including magazines, across the country. In 1879, Congress established the low second-class postal rate for publications, a subject of controversy to this day, but a great boon to magazines even then. The Hoe high-speed rotary press began replacing the much slower flatbed press, speeding the printing of magazines. The halftone method of reproducing photographs as well as color artwork was invented in 1876, making the magazines more enticing to the public. (*Godey's Lady's Book,* a popular fashion book of the age, had previously employed 150 women to hand-tint all its illustrations.)

Costly literary magazines now appeared—*Harper's Monthly, Atlantic Monthly, Century*—but the publishers did not view advertising kindly at first.

Even when, at the turn of the century, Fletcher Harper condescended to "desecrate literature with the announcements of tradespeople," he placed all the advertising in the back of the book.[11]

Inspired by the success of popular magazines in England, a new breed of publishers came forth in the 1890's to produce magazines of entertainment, fiction, and advice—forerunners of today's women's and general magazines. Magazines brought the works of Kipling, H. G. Wells, Mark Twain, and Conan Doyle to families across the face of the land. By 1902, *Munsey's* had a circulation of 600,000; *Cosmopolitan,* 700,000; *Delineator,* 960,000; while the *Ladies' Home Journal* hit the million mark—great feats for the age.[12] The ten-cent magazine had arrived.

The number of pages of advertising that magazines carried would make some of today's advertising directors of magazines blink. *Harper's* published 75 pages of advertising per issue; *Cosmopolitan,* 103 pages; *McClure's,* 120 pages. Between 1880 and 1890, magazine advertising more than doubled. Magazines made possible the nationwide sale of products; they brought into being nationwide advertising.

Patent-medicine advertising. Patent-medicine advertisers had been around for a long time, and by the 1870's they were the largest category of advertisers. After the Civil War, millions of men returned to their homes, North and South, many of them weak from exposure; many needed medical aid, and the only kind available to most of them was a bottle of patent medicine. As a result, patent-medicine advertising dominated the media toward the end of the nineteenth century—incidentally, with its fraudulent claims, giving all advertising a bad name.

NATIONAL ADVERTISING EMERGES

Meanwhile, legitimate manufacturers saw a new world of opportunity opening before them in the growth of the country. They saw the market for consumer products spreading. Railroads could now carry their merchandise to all cities between the Atlantic and Pacific coasts. The idea of packaging their own products, carrying their own trademarks, was enticing, particularly to grocery manufacturers; for now they could build their business upon their reputation with the consumer, and not be subject to the caprices and pressures of jobbers who, in the past, had been their sole distributors. Now magazines provided the missing link in marketing—that of easily spreading word about their products all over the country, with advertising. Quaker Oats cereal was among the first to go this marketing route, followed soon by many others.

This was the development of national advertising, as we call it today, in its broadest sense, meaning the advertising by a producer of his trademarked product, whether or not it has attained national distribution.

LEADERS IN NATIONAL ADVERTISING IN 1890's

A. P. W. Paper
Adams Tutti Frutti Gum
Æolian Company
American Express Traveler's Cheques
Armour Beef Extract
Autoharp
Baker's Cocoa
Battle Ax Plug Tobacco
Beardsley's Shredded Codfish
Beeman's Pepsin Gum
Bent's Crown Piano
Burlington Railroad
Burnett's Extracts
California Fig Syrup
Caligraph Typewriter
Castoria
A. B. Chase Piano
Chicago Great Western
Chicago, Milwaukee & St. Paul Railroad
Chicago Great Western Railway
Chocolat-Menier
Chickering Piano
Columbia Bicycles
Cleveland Baking Powder
Cottolene Shortening
Cook's Tours
Crown Pianos
Crescent Bicycles
Devoe & Raynolds Artist's Materials
Cuticura Soap
Derby Desks
De Long Hook and Eye
Diamond Dyes
Dixon's Graphite Paint
Dixon's Pencils
W. L. Douglas Shoes
Edison Mimeograph
Earl & Wilson Collars
Elgin Watches
Edison Phonograph
Everett Piano
Epps's Cocoa
Estey Organ
Fall River Line
Felt & Tarrant Comptometer
Ferry's Seeds
Fisher Piano
Fowler Bicycles
Franco American Soup
Garland Stoves
Gold Dust

Gold Dust Washing Powder
Gorham's Silver
Gramophone
Great Northern Railroad
H–O Breakfast Food
Hamburg American Line
Hammond Typewriter
Hartford Bicycle
Hartshorn's Shade Rollers
Heinz's Baked Beans
Peter Henderson & Co.
Hires' Root Beer
Hoffman House Cigars
Huyler's Chocolates
Hunyadi Janos
Ingersoll Watches
Ives & Pond Piano
Ivory Soap
Jaeger Underwear
Kirk's American Family Soap
Kodak
Liebeg's Extract of Beef
Lipton's Teas
Lowney's Chocolates
Lundborg's Perfumes
James McCutcheon Linens
Dr. Lyon's Toothpowder
Mason & Hamlin Piano
Mellin's Food
Mennen's Talcum Powder
Michigan Central Railroad
Monarch Bicycles
J. L. Mott Indoor Plumbing
Munsing Underwear
Murphy Varnish Company
New England Mincemeat
New York Central Railroad
North German Lloyd
Old Dominion Line
Oneita Knitted Goods
Packer's Tar Soap
Pearline Soap Powder
Peartltop Lamp Chimneys
Pears' Soap
Alfred Peats Wall Paper
Pettijohn's Breakfast Food
Pittsburgh Stogies
Pond's Extract
Postum Cereal
Prudential Insurance **Co.**
Quaker Oats

From Frank Presbey, *History and Development of Advertising* (Garden City, N.Y.: Doubleday & Co., 1929), p. 361.

The words "chauffeur," "limousine," "sedan," remind us that the earliest motorcars were made in France. In the United States, as in France, they were practically handmade at first. But in 1913, Henry Ford decided that the way to build cars at low cost was to make them of standardized parts, and bring the work to the man on the assembly-line belt. He introduced to the world a mass-production technique, and brought the price of a Ford down to $265 by 1925. But mass production is predicated, in a free society, upon mass selling—another name for advertising. Mass production makes possible countless products at a cost the mass of people can pay, and about which they learn through advertising. America was quick to use both.

THE ADVERTISING AGENCY

We have been speaking of the various media and their advertising. Now a word about how the media got much of that advertising—through the advertising agency, which started out as men selling advertising space for out-of-town newspapers on a percentage basis; later they also prepared the ads. The story of the advertising agency is deeply rooted in the growth of American industry and advertising. Later in the book, we devote a whole chapter to the American agency, from its beginnings to its latest patterns of operation. Until then, we need keep in mind only that the advertising agency has always been an active force in developing the use of advertising.

AS AMERICA ENTERS THE NEW CENTURY . . .

The moral atmosphere of business as it developed after the Civil War reflected laissez-faire policy at its extreme. There was corruption of high government officials by the railroads, swindling of the public by flagrant stock-market manipulations, shipment of embalmed beef to soldiers in the Spanish-American War. Advertising contributed to the immorality of business, with its patent-medicine ads offering to cure all the real and imagined ailments of man. There was a "pleasing medicine to cure cancer," another to cure cholera. No promise of a quick cure was too wild, no falsehood too monstrous.

The Pure Food and Drug Act (1906). As early as 1865, the *New York Herald-Tribune* had a touch of conscience and eliminated "certain classes" of medical advertising—those that used "repellent" words. In 1892, the *Ladies' Home Journal* was the first magazine to ban *all* medical advertising. The *Ladies' Home Journal* also came out with a blast by Mark Sullivan, revealing that codeine was being used in cold preparations, and a teething syrup

ELECTRIC BELTS.

Try it and be Convinced.

DISCOUNT, ONE-THIRD.

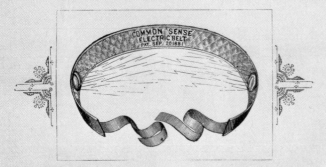

THIS BELT CURES

PARALYSIS,	LUMBAGO,	MALARIA,
NEURALGIA,	DYSPEPSIA.	LAME BACK,
RHEUMATISM,	FEVER AND AGUE,	LIVER COMPLAINT,
SPINAL IRRITATION,	SEMINAL WEAKNESS,	KIDNEY DISEASES,
NERVOUS EXHAUSTION.	FEMALE COMPLAINTS,	GENERAL DEBILITY.

FAC-SIMILE OF LABEL.

COMMON SENSE ELECTRIC BELT,
THE BELT FOR THE MILLION.

Warranted Equal to any of the High Priced Belts and Sold at a REASONABLE Price.

Manufactured by the

Common Sense Electric Belt Co.

Pat. Sept. 20, 1881.   CHICAGO, ILL.

Price, according to quality, $3.00, $4.00 and $5.00 each.

Sent by mail on receipt of price. Address your orders to our agents,

CHAS. TRUAX & CO.

ONE OF THE MILDER
PATENT MEDICINE ADS

"Electricity" was the new magic power of the 1890s, here offered in the form of a curative belt.

Reprinted from Adelaide Hechtlinger, *The Great Patent Medicine Era* (New York: Grosset & Dunlap, Inc., 1970). Copyright © by Grosset & Dunlap, Inc.

had morphine as its base. Public outrage reached Congress, which in 1906 passed the Pure Food and Drug Act—the first federal law to protect the health of the public, and the first to control advertising.

The Federal Trade Commission Act (1913). But in addition to passing laws protecting the public from unscrupulous business, Congress passed a law protecting one businessman from the unscrupulous behavior of another, in the form of the Federal Trade Commission Act, which said, in effect, "Unfair methods of doing business are hereby declared illegal." John D. Rockefeller, founder of the Standard Oil Company, got together with some other oilmen in the early days of his operation and worked out a deal with the railroads over which they shipped their oil. They arranged not only to get a secret rebate on the oil they shipped, but also to get a rebate on all the oil their *competitors* shipped. Result: They were able to undersell their competition, and drive them out of business. What was considered smart business in those days would be a violation of the antitrust laws today.[13]

In time, the FTC, as it is known, extended its province to protecting the public against misleading and deceptive advertising—a matter of which all who are responsible for advertising today are very much aware.

Of this period of exposure and reform, James Truslow Adams, the historian, said, "America for the first time was taking stock of the morality of everyday life."

ADVERTISING COMES OF AGE

Around 1905, there emerged a class of advertising men who recognized that their future lay in advertising legitimate products and in earning the confidence of the public in advertising. They gathered with like-minded men in their community to form advertising clubs.

Advertising gets organized. They subsequently formed the Associated Advertising Clubs of the World (now the American Advertising Federation). In 1911, they launched a campaign to promote "Truth in Advertising." In 1916, they formed vigilance committees; these developed into today's Better Business Bureaus (now an autonomous organization), which continue

From Ernest Elmo Calkins, *And Heavy Not* (New York: Charles Scribner's Sons, 1946), p. 171.

The FIRST ANNUAL
EXHIBITION OF
ADVERTISING ART
To be held in the Galleries of The
NATIONAL ARTS CLUB
14 Gramercy Park, New York
February 19 to March 1, 1908

to deal with many problems of unfair and deceptive business practices, and which, in 1971, became a part of the Advertising Review Council, an all-industry effort at curbing misleading advertising. The main constituency of the American Advertising Federation continues to be that of the local advertising clubs. On its board are also officers of the other advertising associations.

In 1910, the Association of National Advertising Managers was born. It is now known as the Association of National Advertisers (ANA), and has about 500 members, including the foremost advertisers. Its purpose is to improve the effectiveness of advertising from the viewpoint of the advertiser. In 1917, the American Association of Advertising Agencies was formed to improve the effectiveness of advertising and of the advertising-agency operation. Over 75 percent of all national advertising today is placed by its members, both large and small.

In 1911, *Printers' Ink,* the leading advertising trade paper for many years, prepared a model statute for the state regulation of advertising, designed to "punish untrue, deceptive or misleading advertising." The Printers' Ink Model Statute has been adopted in its original or modified form in 44 states, where it is still operative.

Up to 1914, many publishers were carefree in their claims to circulation. An advertiser had no way of verifying what he got for his money. But in that year, a group of advertisers, agencies, and publishers established an independent auditing organization, the Audit Bureau of Circulations, which conducts its own audits and issues its own reports of circulation. Most major publications belong to the ABC, and an ABC circulation statement is highly regarded in media circles. The ABC reports of circulation are fully accredited in most areas. (Today, similar auditing organizations are operating in 25 countries throughout the world.)

In June 1916, President Woodrow Wilson addressed the Associated Advertising Clubs of the World convention in Philadelphia—the first president to give public recognition to the importance of advertising. Advertising had come of age!

ADVERTISING IN WORLD WAR I

When the United States entered World War I in 1917, a number of advertising agency and media men offered their services to the government but were turned down, for, as Woods reports, "Government officials, particularly Army chiefs, believed in orders and edicts, not persuasion." [14]

But when these groups offered their services to the Council of National Defense, they were welcomed and became the Division of Advertising of the Committee of Public Information—the propaganda arm of the government.

Their first job was to help get all eligible men to register. By their efforts, 13 million men registered in one day without serious incident. The committee also succeeded in having advertisers use their own paid space to advertise Liberty Bonds, the Red Cross, and the messages of the Fuel Administration, to use less fuel, and the Food Administration, to observe its meatless and wheatless days.

THE 1920's

The 1920's began with a minidepression and ended with a crash.

When the war ended, makers of army trucks had been able to convert quickly to commercial trucks. Firestone spent $2 million advertising "Ship by Truck." With the industry profiting by the good roads that had been built, truck production jumped from 92,000 in 1916 to 322,000 in 1920. Trucking spurred the growth of chain stores, which led, in turn, to supermarkets and self-service, because of door-to-door delivery from manufacturer to retailer.

The passenger-car business boomed, too, and new products appeared in profusion—electric refrigerators, washing machines, electric shavers, and, most incredible of all, the radio. Installment selling made hard goods available to all. And all the products needed advertising.

Radio arrives. Station KDKA of Pittsburgh was on the air broadcasting the Harding–Cox election returns in November 1920, even before its license to operate had cleared. That didn't come through until 1921.[15] Many other stations soon began broadcasting. There were experimental networks over telephone lines as early as 1922. The first presidential address to be broadcast (by six stations) was the message to Congress by President Coolidge in 1923. The National Broadcasting Company started its network broadcasting in 1926 with six stations and had its first coast-to-coast football broadcast in 1927. That was the year, too, that the Columbia Broadcasting System was founded, and the Federal Radio Commission (now the Federal Communications Commission) was created.

The making of radio sets proved to be a boon to industry. According to Settel,

Radio created one of the most extraordinary new product demands in the history of the United States. From all over the country, orders for radio receiving sets poured into the offices of manufacturers. Said *Radio Broadcast Magazine* in its first issue, May 1922:

"The rate of increase in the number of people who spend at least a part of their evening listening in is almost incomprehensible. . . . It seems quite likely that before the market for receiving apparatus becomes approximately saturated, there will be at least five million receiving sets in this country." [16]

(Author's note: In 1970, there were over 330 million radio sets in use.)

Everything boomed in the mid-twenties—business boomed, advertising boomed. The issue of the *Saturday Evening Post* of December 7, 1929, is historic. It was the last issue whose forms closed before the stock-market crash in the fall of 1929. The magazine was 268 pages thick. It carried 154 pages of advertising.[17] The price: 5¢ a copy. Never again would the *Saturday Evening Post* attain that record. Never again has any magazine approached it. It was the end of an era.

THE DEPRESSION YEARS—THE THIRTIES

Much has been written about the tragedy that descended on the land in the 1930's; these reports are not exaggerated. Out of this debacle, three factors emerged that directly relate to advertising today.

The *first* of these was the emergence of radio as a major advertising medium. In March 1933, President Franklin D. Roosevelt made the first inaugural address ever to be broadcast by radio, giving heart and hope to a frightened people. His line, "We have nothing to fear except fear itself," spoken to the largest audience that had ever heard the voice of one man, became historic. In one broadcast, radio showed its power of moving a nation. Radio had arrived as one of advertising's major national media.

During all the depression years, radio programs gave cheer with their newly developed art of the soap opera, with their music, and with their star comedians, such as Fred Allen and Jack Benny. The Sunday night radio network shows gave a troubled people something to which they could look forward each week. Radio maintained its status as a prime medium until television came along.

Second was the passage of the Robinson-Patman Act (1936) to help protect the little merchant from the unfair competition of the big store, with its huge buying power. This law is operative today, especially in regard to cooperative advertising and deals.

Third was the passage of the Wheeler-Lea Act (1938), giving the Federal Trade Commission more direct and sweeping powers over advertising; and the Federal Food, Drug and Cosmetic Act (1938), giving the administration authority over the labeling and packaging of these products, and still effective today. These laws were in response to public reaction against the abuses of advertising, spurred by the intense competition of the time.

With the coming of World War II, industry turned to war production. Goods were rationed even to old customers. Why tease the customers with advertising? Yet many advertisers held that although they might be out of merchandise, they were not out of business. They wanted to hold the goodwill of their customers. Many used advertising to explain their conversion to war work. Others suggested ways to stretch the supply of their goods.

The government turned to the advertising community to help sell its war bonds, and in other public-relations problems arising from the war. A group of advertisers, publishers, and agencies created the War Advertising Council. So successful was this pooling of advertising effort that the organization, now the Advertising Council, continues its public service to this day.

TELEVISION ARRIVES

In 1939, television had its public debut, when President Franklin D. Roosevelt formally opened the New York World's Fair by telecast from Washington. It was a thrilling experience for viewers at the World's Fair. This was also the year of the first telecast of a baseball game, a football game, a boxing match. Station WNBT, New York, received the first grant for regular television operation in 1941.[18]

During the war, manufacture of consumer TV sets was suspended; then after the war, there was a freeze on television while the government decided upon which circuit would be the standard one, and also on questions of frequency allocations. The freeze was lifted in 1952.

At this point we let these figures tell the story of television:

TV Advertising Expenditures

1950	$ 171 million
1955	1,025 million
1960	1,590 million
1970	3,665 million [19]

And here is what happened to radio, the medium most affected:

Radio Advertising Expenditures

1940	$ 216 million
1950	605 million
1955	545 million
1960	692 million
1970	1,278 million [20]

From these figures, we see that radio was slowed in its growth when TV came along, but that within the past decade it has doubled its previous peak. How it did so is one of the many reports of advertising about which we shall be reading.

In keeping with our basic interest in understanding the forces outside advertising that affect it, here are some of the facts that have manifested themselves since the 1950's and that reach toward the 1980's:

1950–1970 AND INTO THE EIGHTIES

—The population of the United States grew from 151 million in 1950 to over 204 million in 1970. By 1985 it is predicted to be 245 million. One third of the expected total increase in the population by 1985 will be in the 25–34 age group. The years through 1985 represent the era of the young marrieds.[21]

—Up to 1920, most of America lived on farms and in small towns, with modest changes in living standards. By 1920 the tide had turned; most Americans now lived in cities. But the population continued to be mobile; one fifth move each year. In 1970, the largest segment of the population lived in the suburbs.[22]

—In 1950, two million students were enrolled in American colleges. In 1970, the number was seven million—a rate of increase ten times that of the total population. By 1980, the number is anticipated to be eleven million.[23]

—Young adults today are better educated, more involved with social problems, and more articulate than the preceding generations. They are more concerned with the fundamental beliefs of our society, its goals, and its values. Advertising faces a more critical audience.

—In 1950, 19,000 trademarks were filed for registration in Washington. In 1970, the number was 33,000, each representing a new product.[24] Many of these products will never reach the market, but among those that do will be the important advertised products of the future.

—Fifty-two percent of the 1970 dollar sales in supermarkets was generated by products that were nonexistent ten years before.[25] Two thirds of the products people will buy in 1985 are still to be developed. What's more, of all the children in grades one through six, about one half will be employed in occupations that do not yet exist.[26]

—The four-day workweek and longer vacations are upon us, giving more freedom for leisure pursuits.

This is the environment in which advertising operates today—in the words of Morison, "promoting the revolution of rising expectations." [27]

Review Questions

1. Can you name some of the earliest places where advertising was used? Describe what it was like and what it was used for.

2. About what year was printing invented? About what year did the first newspaper appear in England? Briefly, what were the highlights in the use of advertising between those two dates?

3. The American colonies, and the early United States cities, had newspaper advertising along the same lines as the early English newspapers. What was the chief kind of advertising they carried?

4. How did the Industrial Revolution affect advertising?

5. Comment briefly on the causes and nature of the growth of the United States between 1870 and 1900 in respect to:
   —population
   —expansion
   —transportation
   —productivity
   —media
   —advertising

6. What was the effect of the railroads on the sale of merchandise? magazines? national advertising?

7. What kind of problems led to the Pure Food & Drug Act of 1905?

8. Name some of the major advertising organizations started between 1900 and 1917, and their purposes.

9. What gave impetus to mass production in the 1920s; what was the effect on advertising?

10. What effect did radio have on advertising in the 1930s and 1940s?

11. After World War II the government put a freeze for several years on licenses for TV broadcasting. Why?

12. What have been the major changes in marketing and advertising that you can remember?

Reading Suggestions

Two definitive books on the history of advertising are:

Presbrey, Frank, *History and Development of Advertising.* Garden City, N.Y.: Doubleday, Doran & Co., 1929.

Wood, James Playsted, *The History of Advertising.* New York: Ronald Press Co. 1958.

Other books of interest:

Calkins, Earnest Elmo, & Ralph Holden, *Modern Advertising.* New York: Appleton-Century Co. 1905.

Calkins, Earnest Elmo, *"And Hearing Not."* New York: Charles Scribner's Sons, 1946.

Hotchkiss, George Burton, *Milestones of Marketing.* New York: The Macmillan Company, 1938.

Jones, Robert W., Journalism in the United States. New York: E. P. Dutton & Co., 1947.

Larwood, Jacob, and John L. Hotten, *The History of Signboards from the Earliest Times.* London: Chatto & Windus, 1875.

Morison, Samuel Eliot, *The Oxford History of the American People.* New York: Oxford University Press, 1965.

Mott, Frank L., *History of American Magazines.* Cambridge, Mass.: 1957.

Sampson, Henry, *A History of Advertising from the Earliest Times.* London: Chatto & Windus, 1875.

Turner, Ernest Sackville, *The Shocking History of Advertising.* New York: E. P. Dutton & Co., Inc., 1953.

Footnotes

1 Sources:

Frank Presbrey, *History and Development of Advertising* (New York: Doubleday and Company, Inc., 1929).

James Playsted Wood, *The History of Advertising* (New York: The Ronald Press Company, 1958).

Jacob Larwood and John Camden Hotten, *The History of Signboards from the Earliest Times,* new ed. (London: Chatto & Windus, 1898).

Henry Sampson, *A History of Advertising from the Earliest Times* (London: Chatto & Windus, 1875).

Erwin Paneth, *Entwicklung der Reklame vom Altertum Bis Zur Gegenwart* (Munich: von R. Oldenbourg, 1926).

2 Presbrey, *History and Development of Advertising,* p. 8.

3 *Ibid.,* p. 17.

4 Robert W. Jones, *Journalism in the United States* (New York: E. P. Dutton & Co., Inc., 1947), p. 21.

5 *The Story of the United States Patent Office,* 4th ed. (Washington, D.C.: U.S. Department of Commerce, 1965), p. 36.

6 Samuel Eliot Morison, *The Oxford History of the American People* (New York: Oxford University Press, Inc., 1965), p. 743.

7 Fred Albert Sharwen, *Economic History of the People of the U.S.* (New York: The Macmillan Company, 1934), p. 442.

8 Alfred McClung Lee, *The Daily Newspaper in America* (New York: The Macmillan Company, 1937), pp. 711–13.

9 Jones, *Journalism in the United States,* p. 296.

10 *Historical Statistics of the United States, Colonial Times to 1957,* A Statistical Abstract Supplement, Series H 407–411 (Washington, D.C.: Bureau of the Census, 1960), p. 104.

11 Earnest Elmo Calkins, *And Hearing Not* (New York: Charles Scribner's Sons, 1946), p. 28.

12 Earnest Elmo Calkins and Ralph Holden, *Modern Advertising* (New York: Appleton-Century-Crofts, 1905), p. 76.

13 Ida M. Tarbell, *History of the Standard Oil Company* (New York: McClure, Phillips & Co., 1904).

14 Wood, *The History of Advertising,* pp. 354–55.

15 Federal Communications Commission, INF Bulletin No. 213, issued February 1970.

16 Irving Settel, *A Pictorial History of Radio* (New York: Citadel Press, Inc., 1960), p. 41.

17 Hand count by author.

18 Federal Communications Commission, Bulletin No. 2–B, October 1970, p. 3.

19 *Printers' Ink* compilation.

20 *Ibid.*

21 Estimate by Dr. George H. Brown, director, Bureau of the Census, in a speech at Downtown Economics Club, New York, October 7, 1970.

22 Report, Bureau of the Census, 1970.

[23] Report, Department of Health, Education, and Welfare, Office of Education, OE 10030–68 (1970, Series II, pp. 383–94).

[24] Commissioner of Patents, Annual Report, 1970. Department of Commerce, U.S. Patent Office, Washington, D.C.

[25] Gordon Ryan, vice-president, General Mills, Inc., in *Progressive Grocer,* May 1971, p. 191.

[26] Scientists of National Aeronautics and Space Administration, *Sponsor Magazine,* March 1, 1965, p. 30.

[27] Samuel Eliot Morison, *The Oxford History of the American People,* p. 892.

2

Economic and Social Aspects of Advertising

NOW LET'S TAKE UP some questions about advertising that are asked by economists, sociologists, and consumers. And you yourself may have wondered about many of these questions.

THE CREATIVE IMPACT OF THE COMPETITIVE SYSTEM

In the United States, we operate basically within the system of private competitive enterprise. Advertising is a part of that system.

This system gives a man a wide opportunity to make products that he thinks others will buy, and provides the consumer a wide choice of products from which to choose. If a man undertakes the risk of creating and launching a new product, he will, if he is prudent, make sure the article works, will gauge the need for it, and will only then launch it on the market. Such men are the product leaders, who start things with their inventiveness and resourcefulness. Others will be watching the sales of his product, and if it seems to be "taking," the following may be expected to happen: (1) Followers will come out with an imitation of the product cheaper in price and probably lower in quality, for quick sale through mass merchandisers. (2) As the sales of the product continue to rise, he may expect competition from substantial manufacturers who will seek to improve on his product, and who have the resources to do so. (3) He will continue his own development work to better his own product, and to overtake the improvements offered by others. The battle of improvements, or differentials, is on.

The question now arises: At which point, if at all, should the originator stop trying to improve his product? Would you also try to stop competition from doing so, provided patents do not already stop them? If for some reason the leader in the field fails to keep up with competitive improvements, he is headed for trouble. In the drug trade, for example, McKie points out that "the period of dominance of one product is short—four or five years at most—and a firm which fails to bring out improvements or new substitutes will find its share of the market rapidly passing to others." [1]

However, among the many questions and views about advertising that this process generates are those we consider here.

THE BIG SWAPPING GAME

As long ago as 1927, Stuart Chase said, "Advertising transfers purchasing power from A to B. It makes people buy Moggs soap and stop buying Boggs Soap." [2] According to this view, advertising is a big game of swapping customers, at the consumer's expense.

Forty-five years later, Kotler reported that "consumerism will lead to legislation that limits promotional expenditures which primarily affect market shares rather than aggregate markets" [3] . . . all with a view to saving the consumer the cost of such advertising.

Both the foregoing observations are based on the assumption that markets are composed of a fixed body of people who will buy a fixed quantity of goods within a given period of time. Yet how can you think in terms of fixed markets in a country whose population grew from 151 million in 1950 to over 204 million in 1970, with an estimate of at least 245 million by 1985? How can you speak of limited markets when one third of the increase in population by 1985 will be in the 25- to 34-year age group, providing a vast new market of young marrieds? [4] How could you reach this market if not by advertising?

Since a market is constantly changing in both composition and number, the potential market for a product is constantly subject to change, especially since the people in it may also change their life-style and their tastes.

Coffee is widely considered a staple on the American scene, but in the past sixteen years, the *per capita* consumption has been dwindling, especially among the under-30 generation, which has gone in heavily for cold soft drinks—with *that* market expanding.[5] The Department of Agriculture expects per capita citrus consumption to be 20 to 25 percent higher in 1980 than

---

[1] James W. McKie, *Administrated Prices,* Hearings before the Senate Subcommittee on Advertising and Monopoly, cited by Jules Backman in *Advertising and Competition* (New York: New York University Press, 1967), p. 63.

[2] Stuart Chase, *The Tragedy of Waste* (New York: The Macmillan Company, 1927), p. 35.

[3] Philip Kotler, "What Consumerism Means to Markets," *Harvard Business Review,* May–June 1972, p. 45.

[4] See p. 121.

[5] Report of Pan-American Coffee Bureau, 1971

it was in 1969, while milk consumption, which has been declining sharply over the past few decades, is expected to drop 15 to 20 percent in that period. Per capita consumption of poultry has been going up, while per capita consumption of dairy products has gone down. Processed fruits and vegetables have increased in per capita consumption, while fresh fruits and vegetables have been going down. These changes in the per capita use are compounded by the changes in the size of the population itself.[6]

The public changes its taste in many other fields as well. Stainless steel has replaced table silver in many households. Knitted fabrics are attracting much of the market formerly given to woven goods. Synthetics have done the same to all natural fibers—wool, cotton, linen, silk. Even these historic old industries had no "fixed markets."

Now, how about a product of derived demand—tires, for example, which basically depend for their sale on the number of cars on the road? The advertising is aimed for the replacement business; it does so by offering a better price or better tire or both. This is not the same as swapping customers, but is a competition to attract customers in an expanding market of more automobiles on the road each year, by virtue of better tire value.

THE "TRIVIAL DIFFERENTIAL"

The constant effort to make a product more desirable than its competitor's by offering some product improvement is often criticized as wasting money in advertising "trivial differentials."

Those who evaluate the worth of advertising competitive products by the measure of differences between them are looking at a still photograph of a living process; they compare the size of plants standing in a row of flowerpots and say they are all about the same size. They fail to compare the growth in value of all products in a field today with the values of the same products some years ago. The continuous succession of improvements that may have appeared trivial when they came out may have led to the big improvements in the whole class of products that the buyer takes for granted today.

The General Foods coffee story provides an interesting study in this connection. Many years ago, ground roast coffee was sold to consumers in paper sacks, then cardboard boxes, then cylindrical fiber cans, then unbreakable metal cans with screw lids. Finally came the vacuum can, which provided real protection and indefinite shelf life. In recent years, General Foods developed a special blend and roast of coffee for brewing in electric percolators, in response to the growing number of homemakers who "live electrically."

From this kind of effort to make even minor improvements, new

---

[6] "A View of Food and Agriculture in 1980," in *Agricultural Economics Research,* Vol. 22, No. 3 (July 1970), 61–68, published by the Department of Agriculture.

Holds twice as much as a 20 year old refrigerator but costs $88.00 less today

1952

$467.00 *

TODAY

$379.00 *

*Manufacturer's Suggested Retail Price

1952 Model NH-8J		TODAY Model TBF-21D
8.7	CAPACITY (cu. ft.)	20.8
52	FREEZER (lbs.)	243 (4½ times as big)
Fresh Food only	DEFROSTING	100% frost free
NO	SHELVES (adjustable)	YES
NO	WHEELS	YES
NO	COLOR AVAILABLE	YES
Not Available (at any cost)	AUTOMATIC ICE	Optional (at extra cost)

Product improvements as revealed in a GE ad.

products may also emerge. General Foods now offers the Max-Pax, pre-measured coffee packed in disposable filter rings. The company also reported that 20 percent of the total net sales for 1971 were for products that had been developed in the past ten years, all because of the search for improvements.[7]

Procter & Gamble told of its continuing program of product improvements in this advertisement addressed to the grocery trade:

We keep on checking, testing and questioning our best sellers, even *after* they're on your shelves . . . looking for ways to improve their performance.

---

[7] Direct communication, General Foods Corporation.

AIR CONDITIONER 1952

This Frigidaire model sold for $320 in 1952. Capacity was 5,100–5,500 BTUs. Manual control. Net weight 178 lbs.

From *Appliance* magazine, July 1967.

Downy, for instance, has been improved six times in ten years . . . to add brightening and freshening, among other things. (And you know what this did to your fabric softener business.)

We constantly look for ways to improve packaging. Like the moisture-preventive wrapping and easy-pull tape we pioneered with Cascade.

Or we'll incorporate other new wrinkles your customers tell us they want. Like offering a choice of flavors with Crest.[8]

Dan Gerber came from a family that for three generations had been in the canning business in Fremont, Michigan. His first formula for baby food was a porridge prescribed by the doctor for his new baby, while his wife was in the hospital. When he had mastered making the baby food in quantity to sell to other parents, the chief question raised by the family was "whether there were enough babies in the world to consume enough baby food to pay a canning company to go into baby foods commercially?" . . . The rise of the baby-food industry, with many firms in it, is now history.

Today, Gerber Products Company offers over 160 varieties of strained and junior foods, meats, cereals, juices, and related items. "An unseen, but no less important value," they report, "is the incorporation by Gerber of all the latest findings in infant health and nutrition and latest food processing methods." Approximately 25 percent of their sales for 1972 came from products introduced in the last ten years.[9]

The Goodyear Tire & Rubber Company offers this report:

Undoubtedly the biggest single factor contributing to improved tire performance and consumer value since 1965 has been the introduction

---

[8] *Supermarketing,* May 1972, p. 10.
[9] Direct communication, Gerber Products Company.

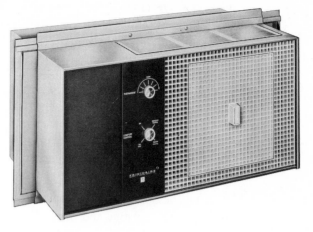

AIR CONDITIONER 15 YEARS LATER

This model sold for about $174. Cooling capacity of 6,000 BTUs. Two fan speeds and thermostatic operation. Weight: 190 lbs. A screwdriver handles mounting. Who can say that any of the steps that led to these improvements were "inconsequential"?

From *Appliance* magazine, July 1967.

of Polyglas bias-belted tires with fiberglass belts by Goodyear in 1967. This new type of construction combined with improved materials has provided the consumer with tires which give better road hazard resistance, improved handling, traction and as much as 50% increase in tread life mileage—*all* at a *lower* cost per mile than previous conventional tires.

Still further advances have been made with the Goodyear introduction of Polysteel bias-belted tires with steel belts in 1971. These tires provide additional improvements in mileage and road hazard resistance.[10]

What producers seek, in order to create a differential in value for their products, is not merely "something different" but "something better." In each instance, any improvement by one producer in a field soon becomes a standard offering to the public by all producers in the field. The differences in competing products may seem little enough at any one moment, but they serve to bring about major improvements in the entire product class.

When all competitive products in a field are "about the same," as often they are said to be, that fact may also mean that in choosing any one of them at random, the consumer is assured of a better product than he would have been able to get if that trade rivalry for a product advantage had not taken place.

THE "IMAGINARY DIFFERENTIAL"

Some writers draw a distinction between a "real difference" in a product and an "imaginary" or "fanciful" one. By real differences they mean those values

---

[10] Direct communication, Goodyear Tire & Rubber Company.

that are tangible and utilitarian, and provide a rational basis for judgment; they are products of "good utility." All others enter the "bad utility" realm of fanciful and imaginary claims, by their standards, and do not provide the basis for making rational comparisons and decisions.

A product is a want-satisfying device. Consumers buy products for many reasons, including whatever emotional satisfaction they may offer. Such reasons can be more important to a person than the composition or construction of the product. A woman will buy a particular foundation cream, not because of its chemical formula or price, but because the last time she used it she got many compliments. A man may buy a car without looking under the hood, and if he does look, he may not even know what he is looking at; but he does know that this is the year's "hot" car, and he buys it to enhance his own prestige and life-style.

"Vanity of vanities, all is vanity," said the preacher in Ecclesiastes; there are those who might regard all differences in products other than functional and utilitarian as vanity and fictitious, but that is a value judgment of an individual, not an objective standard of judgment. As Moran said, "A

How Small Improvements Lead to Big Benefits

The Eureka vacuum cleaner of 1952 (on the left) weighed 14½ lbs., had a three-quarter hp motor. Price: $69.95. The recent model (below) has a low silhouette, weighs 12 lbs., and has a 1½ hp motor. It also has a retracting cord, hose storage right within the cleaner, extra bag storage inside unit, whistle signal when the dust bag is full, and construction of nonmarring materials. Price: $69.95.

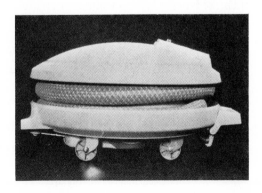

From *Appliance* magazine, July 1967.

great presumption of some economists is that they can differentiate between 'good' and 'bad' utility. The untenable notion that goods or services can be classified as 'utilitarian' and 'non-utilitarian' presumes a universal, invariant value system. Such a set of uniform values certainly does not exist in our heterogeneous culture and never likely did exist anywhere outside of theology.[11]

Isn't a lot of advertising false and misleading?

Advertising is too effective a technique to have escaped being used unscrupulously against the consumer.

The federal government has done much to curb false advertising. Many states likewise have bureaus of protection against consumer frauds, one of whose special targets is deceptive-bait advertising. Media also exercise considerable control over the advertising they accept. In 1905, the organized forces of advertising created the first vigilante committee to guard against dishonest advertising—giving birth to what is now the Better Business Bureau. In 1971, the National Advertising Review Council was formed—an industry-wide organization to curb misleading advertising, showing that the problem is a persistent one. The fact remains that by far the greatest amount of advertising must have made good on its representations; otherwise the public long ago would have learned to ignore it, making it unprofitable to use, and causing its use to dwindle. This has not been the case.

In addition to his own morality, there are functional reasons why an advertiser who hopes to stay in business seeks to deserve the buyer's confidence. First of all, advertising depends on the degree to which it is believed and accepted. Second, most consumer advertising is for repeat items. Such advertisers could not afford to persuade a buyer to try the product once, if there were not a reasonable hope that he would buy it over and over again; and he certainly won't if he feels deceived. Third, in the case of costly consumer durable goods (refrigerators, washing machines), the more a person has to spend for such products, the more he will rely upon the reputation of the makers, and ask around for the experience of others with the products of that firm. Hence, the maker has every practical pressure upon him to say and do those things that create satisfied customers.

There is much criticism of advertising for its exaggerations. The public appears sophisticated enough to discount the advertiser's exaggerated enthusiasm for his own product, however, even as it discounts the exaggerations of everyday speech, such as, "My feet are killing me," or, "You could have knocked me down with a feather." In this connection, the 4A *Study on Consumer Judgment of Advertising* reports:

[11] William T. Moran, "Marketing-Production Interaction," in Martin Kenneth Starr, ed., *Production Management Systems and Synthesis,* 2nd ed. (Englewood Cliffs, N.J.: Prentice-Hall, Inc., 1971), Sec. 1, p. 4.

What "defenses," if any, do consumers have against the expert blandishments of advertising? In the judgment of the research team, *the myth of the defenseless consumer can be laid to rest.*

In addition to having built-in resistance to being sold by advertising or in person, he views sales messages through a filter of doubt, prior experience—and not a little boredom and disinterest. *He "protects"* himself from the blind acceptance of advertising as he does from other promises and panaceas he is proffered.[12]

Drug advertising has always been a special problem. The Food and Drug Administration is alert to drugs that are unsafe for general use, and can stop their sale without prescription. It can publish its report of the effectiveness of other drug products, and can curb the advertising that makes claims that are not consistent with these findings or cannot otherwise be substantiated. There is much activity on drug advertising.

In the fiscal year 1970, the Federal Trade Commission examined for misrepresentation approximately 238,000 pages of newspaper and magazine advertisements and television scripts—the most extensive examination of advertising yet made. Of these, 13,500 were referred for legal review.[13] Thus, only about 6 percent of all advertising had even some doubt about it. Even that number is far too many, but it is far less than is the impression some may have about the prevalence of misleading advertising.

Isn't advertising a "costly armament race"?

It has been held that "as in an armament race, the more one company spends [in advertising], the more others feel impelled to spend." As in an armament race, such expenditures are said to neutralize each other, all at a cost that "society has to bear."

Whenever one speaks of the "neutralizing" effect of matching advertising dollars by competing members of an industry, one must also keep in mind that the competition among producers is being carried right into all aspects of the business, including research and development efforts, which may lead to new and better products. Seldom is a voice raised against the "neutralizing" effect of such research expenditures. Then would it not appear reasonable that telling people about the fruits of the research is an equally useful economic function? That is the role of advertising.

Doesn't the consumer have to pay for the advertising?

Yes, because whoever buys a product pays for all the costs inherent in its making, selling, financing, and delivery; he pays for the raw materials,

---

[12] *Study on Consumer Judgment of Advertising* (New York: American Association of Advertising Agencies, Inc., 1965).

[13] Communication from the Federal Trade Commission.

the wages, the taxes, and the research activities; he also pays for the salesmen and for the advertising. (If the cost of all these weren't covered by the final price that the consumer pays, where would the money come from?) The cost of advertising invites questioning more than do the costs of many other activities of business, because advertising by its very nature calls attention to itself. *But to say that the consumer pays for advertising does not necessarily mean that he is paying more because of the advertising.* Whether the consumer pays more or less, in a particular case, depends on:

1. The effect of advertising on the production costs of a product

2. The effect of advertising on the selling costs

3. The effect of the value goals of the business

The effect of advertising on production costs. Where the costs of making a product are reduced by large-scale production, and where advertising has helped produce the volume of sales needed to effect the savings of mass production, it is legitimate to say that advertising has helped make possible the reduction in the cost of *producing* those goods.

Does mass production always reduce production costs?

No. A point may be reached in mass production at which the unit costs remain constant. In fact, costs may even go up as an operation becomes bigger, because of less-efficient workmen or looser management control. The job of advertising, however, is to help create the volume of orders needed to produce the optimum level of production for a given capacity, serving to reduce the unit cost of each product. Whether that reduction in cost is passed on to the buyer, and in what form, depends upon the value goals of management, which we will come to shortly.

The effect of advertising on selling costs. Although we speak of "advertisers," the advertisers do not speak of themselves that way except at advertising conventions. They refer to themselves as being in the food business, or being in electronics, or as being drug manufacturers, as the case may be. Their concern is to sell as much of their product as they can at the lowest selling expense. Their goal is profit. To them, advertising is just one of the alternate methods of marketing a product. A reason so many manufacturers of consumer products use advertising is that they have found that:

> *advertising is the way
> to tell many people about a product
> in the fastest time
> at the lowest cost
> per message.*

If producers found a less costly way to market their product, they would use it.

Does this necessarily mean that advertising always reduces the cost of a product to the consumer?

Here again, the answer is no. The price at which a product is sold is a decision of management, which depends on its value goals.

The effect of the value goals of the business. The value goal of a business represents the value it plans to offer in the product and the form that value is to take. It is the reason for the product's existence. The value goal may be to produce a dependable product at the lowest possible price, as in the case of Timex watches, which begin at $7.95. Here the whole business was dedicated to that low-price goal—the mechanism of the works, its design, the choice of materials, the planning of production without changes in fashions to assure the best production-line economy—all with the one goal in mind of producing the lowest-cost dependable watch. But it took advertising to create the sales to amortize the cost of the special machinery needed, and to get the volume of business necessary to keep that production line busy at its cost-saving level. In this event it is legitimate to say that advertising helped reduce the cost of the product to the consumer.

Or the value goal of the business may be to offer the most luxurious product in its field regardless of cost, like the Piaget watch, which at $1,690 is advertised as "the most expensive watch in the world." Here everything will be planned with one goal in mind—to make it the finest watch possible, regardless of cost. The purpose of the advertising is to make people appreciate why the watch is worth the money. Certainly, in such a case, advertising is not an instrument for reducing cost. The same applies to the luxury or premium end of most product lines—for example, Chivas Regal Scotch Whisky, a most expensive brand.

Because of the differences in the value goals of different enterprises, it is not possible to make a single sweeping statement about the effect of advertising on the cost of a product to the consumer. The fact does remain that for most products designed for widespread consumer use, the value goal of management is *to produce a better product at a lower cost to the consumer.* For example, in 1924 the first box of Kleenex tissues, of approximately 200 9-by-10-inch sheets, cost 65¢. In 1972, a box of 200 tissues, 8.5 by 9.33 inches, greatly improved in texture and strength, and with distinctive packaging and decorator colors and prints, cost about 32¢ (in 1972 dollars).[14]

In 1954, Proctor-Silex steam iron with a cumbersome detachable reservoir retailed for around $18.95. In 1972, their steam-and-dry iron, more compact, with an internal tank, was generally available at $7.99. In 1954, the lowest-price Proctor-Silex two-slice toaster carried a regular retail price of

---

[14] Direct communication from the Kimberly-Clark Corporation.

$15.95. In 1972, a greatly improved model with modular parts that could easily be removed for cleaning and replacement was generally available at $7.99.[15] *Advertising in the United States is a part of the competitive free-enterprise system that makes better products and lower prices possible.*

Isn't the fact that the manufacturers' nationally advertised brands cost more than the distributors' brands good evidence of how much advertising costs the consumer?

A shopper is offered an unfamiliar brand of a product at less cost than a well-known advertised brand. "It's just the same," says the clerk, "and it costs less because you don't have to pay for the advertising." True or false?

When you mention "advertised brands" to a housewife, she usually thinks of the well-known brands extensively advertised by the maker. She then lumps all other products as being "not advertised." This calls for some definitions:

Nationally advertised brands. Those owned and advertised by the producer, usually on sale through many outlets.

Nationally advertised private brands. Those brands owned and controlled by the distributor and sold through his own outlets only. The outstanding example is Sears, one of the largest of all advertisers. Most of their advertising is done through their many local stores. However, they do some advertising in national magazines. Hence they are a national advertiser of private brands. The prices of their offerings, if lower, are not so because their products are not advertised, but because of their method of doing business.

Locally advertised private brands. These are owned by chains or department stores, or by independent outlets—with the merchandise confined to their respective outlets. They too are very large advertisers. Hence, here also, whatever lower prices they offer are not because "they don't advertise," but because of their operational patterns.

Private brands owned by wholesalers. Drug and hardware, grocery and liquor wholesalers, will often put up and sell their products under their own label, to local retailers. These are seldom advertised except locally in a price ad.

When a clerk says a product is "just the same," the shopper may well ask "How do you know?" If, as in the case of the largest stores and chains, there is adequate quality control for all the products they buy, there may be some basis for the statement. Some of the largest retailers even own and operate their own production facilities. But many retailers have no such facility. They can never be sure that the product is uniform in quality. When a clerk says that a private brand is made by the same manufacturer as the advertised brand, even when true—and that is always a question—there is no assurance

---

[15] Direct communication from the Proctor-Silex Corporation.

that the product is made to the same specifications as the nationally advertised brand. But most consumers rely on the consistent quality of the nationally advertised brand for a majority of the everyday products they buy.

The more a man has invested in advertising his trademarked product, the more he will protect this asset by guarding its quality. The public knows merely that on the whole it is better satisfied buying a product with a reputation behind it than it is in buying one that does not have such a reputation. With each purchase, therefore, a buyer has his choice of *risks,* not merely of products. *It is not accurate to say that two products are just the same to the buyer, if they differ in the insurance of satisfaction they offer at the time of purchase.*

If national advertisers had not created and launched new types of products and improved them constantly, the private labeled brands might not even exist. Private brands, however, constantly remind the owners of national brands that it isn't enough to keep in line with each other's prices, for as the prices of nationally advertised goods go up, the number of private brands at lower prices increases. Private-label brands serve as a countervailing force, to use Galbraith's term, to the price of nationally advertised brands.

Doesn't advertising foster monopolies?

Advertising is held to breed monopolies, restricting open competition in a field. The focal point of the monopoly power of a national advertiser is held to be his trademark. The minute a man plucks his product from anonymity by affixing his trademark, he acquires the exclusive rights over it; if people want *his* product, they must come to *him* for it.

The reputation attached to a trademark does not necessarily involve advertising, although advertising can be important. For example, Wedgwood chinaware became world-famed without the benefit of advertising. If a woman has her heart set on a piece of Wedgwood china, she must pay a price based on what the owners of the Wedgwood "monopoly" ask when they sell it to a store. The holders of the Wedgwood "monopoly" have no monopoly on her heart, however; she may decide to buy Spode china, or American Castleton china, or for that matter, use her old china and buy draperies instead. Or she can forget the whole thing and save the money.

To do away with monopolies with their "useless differentiation," Chamberlin proposed that:

> . . . the exclusive use of a trademark might be granted for a limited period, under the same principle as that of the patent laws, say for five years, after which anyone could make the identical product, and call it by the same name. The wastes of advertising about which economists have so often complained would be reduced, for no one

could afford to build up goodwill by this means only to see it vanish through the unimpeded entrance of competitors.[16]

That there would be less advertising is quite true. It is a question, of course, whether a man would be willing to risk his capital and effort in developing new and better products if he knew in advance that he had only a few years in which to recover his costs and to profit by his risk.

Among others who view advertising as monopolistic, making it difficult for someone to enter a field, is the Federal Trade Commission, as described by Backman:

> Ease of entry into a market long has been regarded as one of the key indicia of a competitive market structure. The courts have given this factor considerable emphasis in judging the legality of mergers. Heavy advertising expenditures have been viewed by some critics as creating barriers to entry because present producers develop such goodwill for their products that newcomers must spend large sums on advertising to compete effectively. Thus, it allegedly limits entry in two ways: (1) The volume of resources required to compete is very great; this limits the entry of small firms into the market; and (2) it is difficult to overcome existing brand loyalties; this acts as a deterrent to larger firms.[17]

The large national advertiser has many things going for him besides his volume of advertising. He has had ample opportunity to perfect his product; he has established dependable resources for buying his raw materials; he has an experienced organization, used to working together; he has the benefit of years of effort in getting distribution, and probably enjoys excellent shelf position in many stores; he has the finances to make needed capital expansion. His products are already widely known and used by many. All these assets he has earned over the years. However, he also gets better advertising rates than does the smaller advertiser, because of his quantity discounts. (This has been a sore point with the Federal Trade Commission.)

None of the foregoing advantages would keep out of the field another experienced competitor if he had a superior product that he thought could overcome the other's head start. Example: For generations, Colgate's was the leading toothpaste. Procter & Gamble came along with Crest, with stannous fluoride (Fluoristan), were the first to get the approval of the Council on Dental Therapeutics, American Dental Association, and are now the leaders in the field.

---

[16] Edward Chamberlin, *The Theory of Monopolistic Competition,* 6th ed. (Cambridge, Mass.: Harvard University Press, 1950), p. 274.

[17] Jules Backman, *Advertising and Competition* (New York: New York University Press, 1967), p. 40.

The greatest competition facing national advertisers who sell through stores is the price competition of the private brands owned or controlled by the very distributors on whom the advertiser depends for his shelf display and business.

America is not one market; it is many. The big advertiser may be top dog in some markets, but just one of the pack in others. Even though an advertiser may do extensive national advertising, there will be many markets —especially in the food field—where some local or regional producer will have the most popular product. In time, the popularity of that product may spread, and lo and behold, the advertiser may become a national competitor and a national advertiser. That's the story of the Oscar Mayer meat business, which began locally and today does annually over a half billion dollars in business nationally. There was no barrier to entry here.

New small advertisers have also successfully competed with the giants in their field, not by trying to match advertising dollars, which they do not have, but through ingenuity in their product design, by good timing, and by imaginative advertising, or by all three. The entry of a foreign car—and a compact, no less—the Volkswagen, into a country that prided itself on its automotive industry, is a good example of how a small advertiser shook an entire industry. And in the face of the mammoth General Electric Company and Westinghouse Electric Company, which dominated the household-appliance field at the time, a small manufacturer in Philadelphia, now known as the Proctor-Silex Corporation, came out with the first practical toaster thermostat that would make the toast pop out when it was ready, and the first electric iron with a practical adjustable thermostat control. That company now does an estimated 40 percent of the total toaster business and 25 percent of the total electric-iron business in the United States.

Galbraith, however, points out:

> . . . in an established industry, where the scale of production is considerable, there is no such thing as freedom of entry: On the contrary, time and circumstances bar the effective entry of new firms. . . . In fact the present generation of Americans, if it survives, will buy its steel, copper, brass, automobiles, cigarettes, whisky, cash registers, and caskets from one or another handful of firms that now supply these staples. As a moment's reflection will establish, there hasn't been much change in the firms supplying these products for several decades.[18]

---

[18] John Kenneth Galbraith, *American Capitalism* (Boston: Houghton Mifflin Company, 1962), pp. 38–39.

This is the reverse of the argument that advertising creates monopolies. The United States, with its industrial capacity, produces each day thousands of different products with their own variations in models, colors, styles, and sizes, to meet the varied needs and tastes of a widespread population. The number of different products in a field depends not upon advertising, but upon the nature of the business; you hear few women complain about the number of dresses on a department-store rack, but only a small proportion of these are nationally advertised brands.

In many villages throughout the world, Thursday is the market day, when all who have something to sell come from far distances and spread their wares on the ground of the village square, and all who wish to buy come from far distances to look over these offerings. In our society, manufacturers present their wares through advertising, so that the shopper can learn about the different offerings right at home.

The effort by a consumer of deciding which product among many to select is the price one has to pay for the privilege of being able to make a selection.

Isn't advertising making us a nation of conformists?

According to modern anthropology, all societies impose on their members the desire to conform; and they punish deviates from cultural norms in various ways. (In our society, we call them "odd" and avoid them.) When the majority of the society is subjected to the same influence much of the time, the tendency to conform becomes more pronounced.

Advertising is only one of the many forces in American life that tend to encourage conformity. It is one aspect of the impact of mass media in general—television, radio, magazines, newspapers, movies—which spread ideas and styles simultaneously to millions of people. Other institutions in our society have that effect, too—for instance, schools, and the urbanization of American life with its look-alike housing.

The very idiom "mass production" implies a huge output of identical goods.

Advertising, however, thrives on the diversity of its goods; it extols differentiations. The advertisements in a single issue of a national magazine featured the following varieties of the respective products advertised, as revealed in their headlines:

Ford	17 Fords to choose from
Coty	42 beautiful colors
Chevrolet	Choose from 15 Chevrolets in four beautiful series
du Pont	This fall—more styles, more colors with Dacron
Jarman Shoes	See our wide selection of shoes for every occasion

Within one year, Detroit car makers offered 323 different models. With the possible variations of trim, color, and options, the industry is reportedly able to run its assembly line for a year without producing two identical cars.

This variety *within a product* does not take into consideration the great variety *among the products* advertised, serving to encourage people to express their own individuality.

Doesn't advertising make people want things they can't afford?

No doubt it does in many ways. If it spurs a man to work harder to earn the money to buy those things, that is a good effect. Advertising seeks to show people what else is going on in the world; it seeks to point ways to "health, wealth, and happiness." Books do this. A TV travel program may do this. Newspapers and magazines do this. The schools do this. A visit with a friend may do it. All these influences may serve to make us restless in our desire to attain what we may consider a better standard of living. Under our system of government, every man has the responsibility of deciding for himself how he wants to spend what remains of his money after taxes, what things are necessary or important to him, and what he wants to work for. Would it be right to withhold information about products from those who can afford them, in an effort to avoid arousing those who might not be able to afford them today? Or who might have more important priorities for the use of their money?

A great service is performed by the man who shows people how they can live better, enjoy better things in life, get better satisfaction by improving their way of living. This is not the exclusive province of advertising. But advertising not only tells about these things; it is forever telling how they may be attained more easily, more quickly, and at less cost—the favorite words of advertising headlines.

The selfsame advertising that encourages people to want things they can't afford at the moment helps make the luxuries of today become available tomorrow at a price people can afford. The exposure to such ideas does not exempt a man from having a philosophy of life about what values are most important to him and to his family.

This question is often linked to the one asking, "Doesn't advertising make people buy things they do not need?" The basic needs of man are for food, clothing, and shelter. Even primitive man had his ideas of what his needs were, and sought to improve himself on these counts; the caves of primitive man still show the paintings on the walls. All "needs" above the subsistence level are acquired tastes, which today we call the standard of living, and each man sets that for himself as best he can.

Often, one man will pass judgment on another for buying things he does not "need" within his apparent income level. But how would that man passing judgment react if he were told someone had said the same about him? If a man buys something that he later decides he does not need, that experience is a reflection on his judgment, and not on advertising.

What about advertising and imperfect competition?

Among the broad categories economists use to describe the various forms of competition in their study of pricing systems are *perfect competition* and *imperfect competition*. Advertising is often discussed in relation to these.

Perfect competition exists when a product is exactly like all other products in its class, in a field where there are many small sellers—such as wheat, cotton, corn. Here, a man's product is indistinguishable from the others in its class. The price he gets for his crop is the one determined by an auction of all products like his on that day. There is no way or reason for him to advertise his own output to get a better price for it.

Imperfect competition exists when a number of producers make the same type of product, but each is distinguished in some way from the others. It may have a trademark, which automatically gives it a differential. It may also differ in design, construction, formula, quality of ingredients, or workmanship, or in some other respect vary from others in that field. We are now speaking of products such as electric razors, television sets, refrigerators, cosmetics, and the host of packaged goods on the supermarket shelf. The owner of the differentiated product can control the price at which he offers it; he has every inducement to advertise it. Most advertising is devoted to products sold under imperfect competition.

Writers of economic texts clearly point out that the terms *perfect competition* and *imperfect competition* are used in a special sense in discussing certain theories of price behavior. But often, writers on the subject use the terms loosely, referring to advertising as one of "the imperfections of competition," or as an "impediment to perfect competition," making advertising appear as an economic villain. They also overlook that price is only one part of the equation representing value (the other being the quality of the product), as revealed in the statement, "It [advertising] takes the eye off price, putting it on some alleged product differential." [19] The real charge here seems to be

---

19 George W. Stocking and Myron W. Watkins, *Monopoly and Free Enterprise* (New York: Twentieth Century Fund, 1950), p. 11.

that product differentials and the advertising of them interfere with the workings of a theory. The regret is in the lack of development of a theory and terminology that meet the real-life situation.

What does the public and business think about advertising?

Just about everyone has something to say about advertising, usually based on experiences with the ads he or she sees and hears every day. Seldom, though, had any systematic effort been made to find out the attitudes of the public as a whole toward advertising, or toward its specific economic and social impacts. It was for this reason that a massive and comprehensive survey, planned and supervised by an impartial academic review committee of Harvard and M.I.T. professors, was undertaken in the mid-1960's. Although the research was supported financially by the American Association of Advertising Agencies, the content and conduct of the study, and the analysis and interpretation of the data, were totally in the hands of the committee.

The large-scale study was conducted, with a nationally projectable sample, throughout the United States. Over 60,000 ads were involved, and 9,000 were examined in lengthy in-home interviews by the researchers. Among its goals were:

1. To gather the public's attitudes toward advertising overall and to its particular economic, social, and aesthetic aspects
2. To find out how consumers react to advertisements themselves
3. To learn why consumers react to ads the way they do

Many of the same attitude questions were also asked of over 2,500 executives from all types and sizes of business in separate studies conducted by the *Harvard Business Review*.[20] Thus we can examine the views of both the public and the business community on the same issues.

These studies of public and business opinion reveal an interesting combination of attitudes—on the whole, very favorable to advertising in terms of its economic functions, but critical of its social impacts and questioning with regard to aspects of its content. What the public seems to be saying is that they like what advertising does *for* them, but dislike what advertisements do *to* them.

---

[20] The basic study of public attitudes is Raymond A. Bauer and Stephen A. Greyser, *Advertising in America: The Consumer View* (Cambridge, Mass.: Harvard Business School Division of Research, 1968); also see the Gallup Organization study of attitudes toward advertising conducted for *Reader's Digest* (1970). The basic studies of executives' attitudes are Stephen A. Greyser, "Businessmen Are Advertising: Yes, But . . . ," *Harvard Business Review,* May–June 1962; and Stephen A. Greyser and Bonnie B. Reece, "Businessmen Look Hard at Advertising," *Harvard Business Review,* May–June 1971.

Let us first look in detail at the attitudes and reactions of the American public to ads and advertising.

Overall attitudes. Americans' basic attitudes toward advertising are generally favorable. Those classified as favorable (41 percent) far outnumber those whose attitudes are classified as unfavorable (14 percent). A considerable proportion of Americans take a mixed position (34 percent) or are indifferent (8 percent) toward advertising overall. Surprisingly, this picture holds relatively constant across the usual demographic groupings: Support or criticism of advertising on the whole is little related to classifications of age, sex, income, and education. Strong general support for advertising is also shown by the 78 percent who agree that advertising is essential; only 18 percent disagree.

Economic issues. It is in the economic area that advertising receives its broadest and strongest endorsement from the public. Some 71 percent of the public agrees that advertising raises our standard of living, and 74 percent that it results in better products for the public. In the area of advertising's impact on prices, opinion is more nearly divided. Some 40 percent say the effect is lower prices, 45 percent say higher prices, 15 percent can't say.

Social impacts. It is in the area of advertising's social impacts and its impact on the individual that Americans express some reservations about advertising. For example, a considerable majority (65 percent) believe advertising often persuades people to buy things they shouldn't buy.

Advertising's ethics and standards. When asked whether they think advertising presents a true picture of the products advertised, 53 percent of the public disagrees, while 41 percent agree. Nonetheless, when asked to compare the standards of today's advertising with that of ten years ago, 58 percent of the public responds "higher," and only 10 percent say "lower." It seems that as the standards of advertising have improved, people expect even more of it.

Advertising content. When it comes to individual advertisements, Americans exercise strongly their rights to their individual opinions. The same ads that annoy and offend some people are cited as enjoyable or informative by others. Ads that generate a strongly favorable or unfavorable reaction from some people are ignored by others. In the study of the public's reactions to specific advertisements, one principal finding was that people do indeed "screen out" a considerable proportion of the ads to which they are potentially exposed. Only a small proportion of ads, among the many to which his media habits expose him, actually capture the conscious attention of the average consumer. Further, even among those ads to which the average consumer *does* pay conscious attention, well under half (the percentage varies from 16 to 40 percent) make any special impression upon him. But in this study, only 16 percent of the ads that did so went on to make a particularly favorable or unfavorable impression.

What were those favorable and unfavorable impressions? First, and most important, those ads the public considered enjoyable (36 percent) or informative (36 percent) far outweighed those viewed as annoying (23 percent) or offensive (5 percent). (Of course, a relatively small proportion of objectionable ads can be enough to generate concern.)

Not surprisingly, the major reason that people regard certain ads favorably is that the people think they have learned something from them—about the product, its price, and so on. The two other principal reasons offered are that the ad created a personal involvement with the situation or product, and that the ad accurately portrayed their own experience with the product.

When Americans consider ads annoying, it is more because of the ads' direct irritation as unpleasant events than because they fail to give accurate marketing information or give rise to moral concern. In other words, it is the intrinsic qualities of the ads, more than their roles as selling instruments, that predominate in this event. Among the annoying intrinsic qualities are their intrusiveness, with unpleasant people, voices, music; their silliness, their exaggeration, their misrepresentation.

What distinguishes the offensive ads from all others is the moral concern that respondents express about products that they think should not be advertised (and in some cases, not sold) and advertisements that they think should not be seen or heard by children.

What about the ads that weren't in any of these categories? Consumers reported that such ads just weren't of interest. Either the product itself had no interest, or the ad was considered dull or unimaginative. This finding presents further proof of consumers' ability to be selective about advertising.

However, people's reactions to ads are also closely tied to their use of and preference for the products and brands involved. People react much more favorably to ads for products they use and for brands they prefer.

On the whole, then, the public shows considerable ability to identify those aspects of advertising that it likes and dislikes. Advertising's social and esthetic dimensions are the ones most criticized, even by those who are generally favorable to advertising. On the positive side, in its economic role, and as a carrier of informative and enjoyable messages, advertising is praised. Even those who are most generally unfavorable to advertising view very positively these economic contributions.

Businessmen's views. In most respects, businessmen echo the reactions of the public. As might be expected, they are somewhat more favorable to advertising in general. But they demonstrate the same ability as does the public, on the same issues, to discriminate between those aspects of advertising they favor and those they question or criticize. However, between 1962 and 1971, executives grew somewhat more critical of advertising as a whole. A partial explanation lies in their strong agreement that broader criteria than traditional business and selling effectiveness alone should be applied to assessing advertising.

In terms of an overall appraisal of advertising, executives almost unanimously agree that advertising is essential to business (even if not necessarily for every individual firm). They also agree very strongly (90 percent) that the public places more confidence in advertised products than in unadvertised ones. On specific economic dimensions, businessmen strongly believe that advertising makes a distinctive contribution in speeding the development of markets for new products. They also agree strongly that advertising helps raise our standard of living and results in better products.

Still in the economic area, although a majority of executives think too much money is spent on advertising, they acknowledge that large reductions in advertising expenditures would decrease sales—for business in general as well as for their own companies. Further, if advertising were eliminated, businessmen claim, selling expenses would have to go up.

Turning to social issues, executives are more critical of advertising. For example, they agree that advertising has an unhealthy influence on children. They strongly believe that it persuades people to buy things they do not *need,* although they split 50-50 as to whether advertising can persuade people to buy things they do not *want.* Executives single out elimination of untruthful and misleading ads as the most important form of self-improvement that advertising should undertake.

The results of this study of businessmen's image of advertising can be characterized as "Yes, but. . . ." Although this is a simplification, it still seems to serve as a convenient summary of *both* public and business views. The "but" lies in the realm of advertising's social impacts, and to some extent in its content. The strong "yes" is the reaction to advertising's primary role as an economic contributor to business and to the public.

Kleenex Facial Tissues

A case report on product improvements

FACIAL TISSUES IS ONE of the largest consumer product industries in existence today. Over 300 different brands make up this industry. The primary contributing factor to the growth of the facial tissue industry has been Kleenex facial tissue.

HISTORY OF KLEENEX FACIAL TISSUES

First introduced in 1924, Kleenex facial tissues were designed as a substitute for the "cold cream towel." The first product, a small package consisting of 100 sheets, sold at retail for 65¢. Because of the high price, the product had limited usage. Until 1930, it was estimated that less than 5 percent of the households in the United States used any facial tissue.

Several years after the product's introduction, the company started receiving letters from consumers, stating that they were using Kleenex facial tissues as a substitute for handkerchiefs, rather than strictly as a cold cream remover. To determine the extent of the product's use as a substitute for handkerchiefs, Kimberly-Clark ran a test in Peoria, Illinois. Results of this test showed that over 60 percent of the people purchasing Kleenex facial tissues were using them as handkerchiefs.

The results of this test caused a complete change in advertising and marketing strategy. The advertising started to stress the use as a handkerchief. Results of this new campaign were outstanding: In the first year, sales doubled and continued upward until the depression leveled them out.

In the late '30s and early '40s, two other features were developed for Kleenex facial tissues which set this product apart from its competition. After considerable testing and manufacturing innovations, the famous pop-up feature was introduced. It became a "first" and exclusive. Today, over 90 percent of the housewives identify the pop-up feature with Kleenex facial tissues.

It was also during this period that the quadrant package design was first introduced. This same design has been retained on today's packages. In

Courtesy, Kimberly-Clark Company, Inc.

a market research test conducted in 1966, one of the leading research firms in the United States reported that the Kleenex facial tissues package quadrant design was one of the most recognizable packages in the United States today. It ranked in the top three with the Coke bottle and the Hershey candy bar.

Another new manufacturing innovation was introduced in the late '50s and early '60s. This was the Space Saver concept. Prior to this time, manufacturers had been using larger size packages for their product. Kimberly-Clark reversed this trend. The result of this innovation has meant not only considerable dollar savings to Kimberly-Clark, but also to the retail trade.

Today, Kleenex facial tissues remains the leader of the facial tissue industry. It represents over 40 percent of the total retail dollar sales volume for facial tissue. It has also retained its leadership as the primary innovator in the business.

PRODUCT LINE

Kleenex' product line innovations have segmented the facial tissue market. Basically, Kleenex products are divided into three groups. These groups are specialty products which include Little Travelers, Man Size, and Pocket Pack. The second group can be classified as commodity or high volume put-ups. This group includes the 125's, 200's and 280's. The third group is classified as the decorative segment. This group includes the Boutique deep color and printed facial tissue.

Review Questions

1. What is meant by the creative impact of the competitive system and how does it relate to advertising?

2. "Advertising is a big game of swapping customers at the consumer's expense." Discuss.

3. "Most advertising is devoted to advertising trivial differences between products, hardly worth the expense." Discuss.

4. What are your views on "the neutralizing effect of most advertising"?

5. Explain how advertising can serve to decrease the cost of a product? Under what circumstances can it increase the cost?

6. If advertising were not used to bring products before the public, what alternatives would there be? How would their cost compare?

7. Select any two of the following four common criticisms of advertising and discuss:

    It creates monopolies.

    It confuses people with too many products.

    It leads to a nation of conformists.

    It makes people buy things they do not need.

8. What do economists mean when they speak of "perfect competition" and "imperfect competition"?

9. Based on the consumer study cited, how do most consumers regard advertising? Favorably? Unfavorably? Indifferently? By what percent? What are the common causes of annoyance about advertising?

10. As head of a major advertiser, what instructions would you issue as to the standards your advertising must meet?

Reading Suggestions

Backman, Jules, *Advertising and Competition.* New York: New York University Press, 1967. Excerpted in Kleppner and Settel, *Exploring Advertising,* p. 33.

Bauer, Raymond A., and Stephen A. Greyser, *Advertising in America: The Consumer View.* Boston: Harvard University, 1968.

Becker, Boris W., "The Image of Advertising Truth: Is Being Truthful Enough?" *Journal of Marketing,* July 1970, pp. 67–68.

Borden, Neil H., *The Economic Effects of Advertising.* Chicago: Richard D. Irwin, Inc., 1942.

Chase, Stuart, *The Tragedy of Waste.* New York: The MacMillan Company, 1927.

Doyle, P., "Economic Aspects of Advertising," *The Economic Journal,* September 1968, pp. 570–602.

Edwards, Corwin D., "Advertising and Competition," *Business Horizons,* February 1968, pp. 59–76.

Galbraith, John K., "The Economic Theory of Advertising," in *Exploring Advertising,* ed. by Kleppner and Settel. Englewood Cliffs, N.J.: Prentice-Hall, Inc., 1970.

Goldman, Marshal L., "Product Differentiation and Advertising: Some Lessons from the Soviet Economy," *The Journal of Political Economy,* Vol. 68, No. 4 (August 1960).

Greyser, Stephen A., "Advertising: Attacks and Counters," *Harvard Business Review,* March–April, 1972, pp. 22–28ff.

Greyser, Stephen, and Bonnie B. Reece, "Businessmen Look Hard at Advertising," *Harvard Business Review,* May–June 1971, pp. 18–26.

Howard, John A., and Spencer F. Tinkham, "A Framework for Understanding Social Criticism of Advertising," *Journal of Marketing,* October 1971, pp. 2–7.

Levitt, Theodore, "The Morality (?) of Advertising," *Harvard Business Review,* July–August 1970, pp. 84–92.

Marketing Science Institute, *Appraising the Economic and Social Effects of Advertising.* Cambridge, Mass., 1971.

Petit, Thomas A., and Alan Zakon, "Advertising and Social Values," *Journal of Marketing,* October, 1962, pp. 15–17. Also in Kleppner and Settel, *Exploring Advertising,* p. 100.

Simon, Julian L., *Issues in the Economics of Advertising.* University of Illinois Press, Urbana, Ill., 1970.

Trowbridge, Alexander, "Challenges of Advertising," in *Exploring Advertising,* ed. by Kleppner and Settel. Englewood Cliffs, N.J.: Prentice-Hall, Inc., 1970.

3

The Roles
of Advertising

THE VALUE GOAL

THE CHIEF ROLE OF advertising is that of selling goods and services. Advertising is only one part of a marketing program, which begins at the inception of the product. This is the time when the makers decide upon the goal of values the product will offer.

The value goal may be to produce the lowest-priced product in its class—as the Pinto car. Or the value goal may be to produce the finest product in its class, such as the Lincoln Continental car. It may be to come out with an altogether new product, like the original Polaroid camera; to produce an improvement in an existing product, such as the Instamatic camera by Kodak; to make a new type of biodegradable package; or to provide a new style of the product. The goal may be to make a new product formulation, as with instant iced tea that is presweetened and preflavored with lemon. In brief, what is the value goal of the makers for the product they plan to offer, to give their product a place in the sun?

As time goes on, the management may change its set of value goals to meet changing conditions. The company may offer a special guarantee, such as American Motors' offer of the free use of a car while overnight repairs are being made. Volkswagen first featured its small-size, single "Beetle" model and lowest price; it has since come out with more models, larger in size.

With the decision as to what the value goal is to be, all efforts for production and for marketing the product begin.

THE MARKETING MIX

In making plans for marketing a product, many elements are involved, including brand policy, pricing, distribution, sales representatives, and advertising—referred to collectively as the *marketing mix*.[1] A number of these elements go into every marketing plan, each affecting the others.

---

[1] A term coined in the 1930's by Professor Neil H. Borden of the Harvard Business School.

An understanding of key factors in the marketing mix may help explain why advertising is more important in some industries than in others, why it varies in use between members of the same industry, and how the total marketing mix affects the role of advertising.

Product and brand policy. Here is a new product. Should the manufacturer have it bear his own trademark? Or should it bear the private labels of the chain stores, mail-order houses, and other distributors to whom he sells it? In the latter case, the manufacturer has no advertising problem. (He may have other problems, but that's another story.) If the product is made by a well-known company, should it come out under the company name (*Kellogg's* cornflakes, *Kraft* cheese) or just under its own brand name, as in the case of Procter & Gamble products (*Cheer, Dreft, Tide*)? If the product is for a new company, will it be one of a line? If so, that must be anticipated in the choice of trademark and packaging design. Is it a style product that calls for continuous change, or will the style stay constant? One home-furnishings manufacturer demonstrates continuous innovation, another is proud of the stability of his design. These are among the product and brand policy questions that affect the rest of the marketing mix.

Pricing. The price at which a product is to be offered affects its entire marketing program. A frozen-food manufacturer needs supermarket distribution, but he can decide whether to offer a high-quality, higher-priced product, or one that meets a lower-price market. Most consumer goods are made in different price ranges: Stockings are made to sell for 39 cents a pair; they are also made to sell for $2.50 per pair, or higher. The price at which a manufacturer offers his stockings may affect his entire marketing pattern and advertising plans.

The subject of pricing is more complex than is appropriate for extended discussion here, but is cited as a major element of the marketing mix.

Distribution. One of the important decisions that has to be made in marketing a product is that of selecting the channels for distributing it.

There has been a change going on for many years in the so-called traditional channels of distribution. Watches were traditionally sold in jewelry stores, till Timex came along and sold them through stationery and drug stores.

A manufacturer may decide to sell through house-to-house salesmen, to sell by mail, to sell through the trade via his own salesmen or through a sales agency.

A television manufacturer can decide whether to seek broader distribution with relatively more promotional support via advertising; in the TV industry this has traditionally been done by RCA, GE, and other "mass marketers," using department stores and discount houses. Or he may seek more selective distribution with relatively more support at the exclusive-dealer level; this has been pursued by Magnavox and Stromberg Carlson.

A foundation-garment manufacturer may follow a marketing strategy of prefitted merchandise, sold at low prices through department stores aimed at the mass market, as Playtex did. Or he may provide more fashion-oriented, higher-priced merchandise, sold on a custom-fitted basis primarily through the women's apparel shops, as has been more traditional in the industry.

The decision on the distribution method is one of the important elements in the marketing mix.

Sales representatives. Personal selling was here before advertising. Some concerns still depend on sales representatives for their consumer operation, as does Avon Products with its large staff of women who sell in the home; some businesses do not use salesmen at all—for instance, mail-order houses. Between these two extremes, the salesman represents varying degrees of importance and is used at varying junctures in a marketing plan. In the consumer field of self-service products, the salesman is not called upon directly to initiate consumer sales; that is chiefly the burden of the advertising. He is, however, of most importance in getting distribution through the trade, in presenting the company's deals and offers, and, wherever allowed, to see that the goods are well displayed. As a product gets more expensive or technical, the sales representative plays a more important role in the buyer's final decision-making process, as in the case of household appliances and cars in the consumer field, and of all marketing in the field of selling to industry.

All these elements of the marketing mix are usually decided before the question of advertising arises. Although this book deals with advertising, it is always well to remember when the use of advertising is being considered, that it is only one variable in the marketing mix.

VARIATIONS IN THE IMPORTANCE OF ADVERTISING

Advertising may be the most conspicuous element in the marketing picture, but it is not equally important in all situations. In some instances it can work well; in other instances it is ineffective. What are some of the conditions under which it is useful, and when is it not useful?

Conditions Conducive to the Use of Advertising

Among the conditions favorable to the use of advertising are the following:

1. *A good product.* This is the single most important factor in the

success of advertising. This point was demonstrated by Preston Townley, marketing director of General Mills, in his 1971 remarks to the Federal Trade Commission. He described the fate of Clackers, a graham-flavored ready-to-eat cereal introduced in 1968. Consumer research had indicated high initial enthusiasm for the idea of a graham cereal, and consumer taste-testing research was positive. Gaining proper distribution and determining an appropriate price did not prove difficult. The main burden of success was thus thought to rest on the advertising. The advertising approach scored well in consumer tests and in the marketplace; initial sales were high. Yet after six months, sales began to decline, and continued to do so, despite the obvious consumer willingness to try the product. What went wrong? In Townley's words, "The major culprit was the product; few people bought it more than once! . . . Perhaps the porous disc form of the product was too hard; perhaps graham is not a sustaining flavor for a dry cereal, or perhaps . . . it should have been made sweeter . . . [for] children." Townley's conclusion: "The product can completely cancel advertising's potential." [2]

2. *The product should have a significant differential.* When a new product appears on the scene, it should offer something that existing ones do not have. If it is identical with others already in the field, why should anyone select it?

Furst and Sherman point out that "Some marketing men are misled by thinking that they can get away with giving a product a 'new look' through promotional advertising. These methods may prove to be very arresting but they fail most dramatically because they do not give the product a meaningful social value." [3] But in addition to the differential being *significant;* it should also be *conspicuous* or *demonstrable.* Just being of a better quality is seldom enough; quality is one of the most difficult things to prove. For example, if Maxwell House coffee were improved in quality and an ad were to say, "Buy the Improved Maxwell House Coffee," people could not see the differential; they would have no way of telling how significant was the improvement until they tasted it, and then wouldn't be sure they liked it better. However, when Maxwell House came out with their Freeze-Dried Coffee, for instant coffee-making, people could see the different granules in the glass jar; the differential was effective. The same was true in their introduction of the Max-Pax filter, with its added convenience, which people could see. A differential is a good asset also if it can be demonstrated on TV, as is done for some paper towels to show their absorbency and strength.

---

2 Remarks at the FTC's Hearings on Modern Advertising Practices, Washington, D.C., October 29, 1971.

3 "National Food Situation," published by Economic Research Service. U.S. Department of Agriculture, NFS-107, January, 1964, p. 10.

The condition of a product category as having little or no product differential is not necessarily permanent. For example, small batteries (for flashlights, transistor radios, etc.) represent a product category where for many years there was relatively little brand-versus-brand differentiation, and advertising was of only modest importance. With the development of the longer-lasting battery, Mallory aggressively advertised this differentiating feature, and with the competitive response, advertising became a more important factor in the marketing program of the entire battery industry.

3. *The product should be identifiable by a trademark.* Of what avail is it to advertise a product if people cannot ask for it? If the trademark cannot be applied to the product itself, perhaps it can be applied to the package. The producers of Chiquita bananas developed a way of putting a label on the banana without squashing it, and made Chiquita bananas advertisable.

4. *The standard of quality must be maintained.* When people buy something, they buy on faith. If they buy an advertised product and they like it, they expect the same quality next time. If they are disappointed, advertising can never bring them back again. This is one of the reasons that the larger the advertiser, the more he invests in quality control. People selected Chiquita bananas because they could count on their good quality.

5. *The price should fit into a market price bracket.* Often, trade practice in an industry establishes different price categories for products of similar quality. Scotch whisky that is bottled in Scotland generally sells at a higher price than does Scotch whisky that is shipped in in barrels and bottled in the United States. If a firm planned to come out with a domestically bottled Scotch whisky at a price between the two levels, it would be in trouble.

6. *The product can be sold impersonally to a mass market.* Advertising is at its peak of effectiveness in impersonal selling to a mass audience, as in self-service shopping. Here it has the chief burden of preselling shoppers on a product before they enter the store. At the store, the product calls for quick selection, with little time for deliberation. And if the product is sold on a frequent repeat basis, so much the better, for the shoppers have the opportunity to change their choice of purchase to your brand (and away from it too, but you hope to win more customers than you lose). Conversely, if there is only a limited market for a product, or if all its prospects are in the same territory, sales representatives may be the important element in the marketing mix, rather than advertising.

The following figures show how much is spent for advertising in industries where the favorable conditions exist:

INDUSTRY	AVERAGE ADVERTISING EXPENDITURE IN RELATION TO SALES *
Bottled soft drinks and flavors	5.36%
Soaps, cleansers	10.06%
Toilet goods, drugs	9.25%

* *Advertising Age (1968–1969 figures), April 10, 1972, p. 48.*

Where there is no product differentiation, price will often be the prime consideration, and advertising expenditures will be low, as shown in the following table:

INDUSTRY	AVERAGE ADVERTISING EXPENDITURE IN RELATION TO SALES *
Iron ore	0.00%
Coal mining	0.08%
Stone–sand–gravel	0.22%

* *Ibid.*

When manufactured goods become higher priced, when the product has technical features and the prospect wants to have demonstrations and questions answered, the salesman becomes more important in the total marketing mix. Automobile advertising, a modest factor in the manufacturer's total sales budget (less than 1 percent of sales for most cars), is dwarfed by the percentage devoted to the network of dealers and their salesmen, even though the total of dollars spent for car advertising is large.

When a product is sold on a competitive price-bid basis for a given set of specifications, as in the case of government contracts for raw materials, advertising has little place in the picture. *Forbes* magazine made an analysis of the American corporations whose money was best managed, based on return of stockholders' equity over a long period. It reports:

> Is there, then, any single characteristic that all of the Top Ten share? Only one, but it is highly important: Each of these companies sells clearly identifiable, branded products with high reputations in their field— . . . The products are backed in every single case, by an image of quality, the kind of image that can be created only by superior products backed by superior advertising and promotion.[4]

Variations in Importance of Advertising
Within an Industry

Not only is there a difference in the role of advertising from industry to industry, but within an industry there will be a big variation in the per-

---

[4] *Forbes,* January 1, 1969, p. 74.

ADVERTISING AS PERCENT OF SALES

Covering Total 1970 Ad Expenditures,
Including Measured and Unmeasured Media

Ad Rank	Company	Advertising	Sales	Adv. as % of Sales
Cars:				
4	General Motors Corp.	$129,764,000	$18,752,354,000	0.7
9	Ford Motor Co.	90,250,000	14,979,900,000	0.6
24	Chrysler Corp.	57,764,100	6,999,675,655	0.8
70	Volkswagen of America	25,500,000	1,100,000,000	2.2
92	American Motors Corp.	18,460,000	1,089,787,000	1.7
Food:				
2	General Foods Corp.	170,000,000	1,975,583,000	8.6
19	Kraftco	65,000,000	2,751,129,000	2.4
25	Standard Brands Inc.	57,500,000	1,119,762,299	5.1
29	General Mills	54,000,000	1,120,000,000	4.8
34	Campbell Soup Co.	49,000,000	964,754,000	5.1
35	Kellogg Co.	48,000,000	614,411,901	7.8
41	Norton Simon Inc.	45,000,000	1,099,459,000	4.1
45	Pillsbury Co.	40,000,000	696,675,000	5.7
48	Nabisco	38,000,000	868,900,000	14.1
53	CPC International	33,500,000	684,400,000	4.9
54	Ralston Purina Co.	32,000,000	1,567,009,384	2.0
61	Carnation Co.	28,130,000	1,053,358,436	2.7
65	Borden Inc.	27,000,000	1,827,341,000	1.5
70	Quaker Oats Co.	25,500,000	597,652,000	4.3
73	McDonald's Corp.	25,000,000	587,041,000	4.3
75	Nestle Co.	24,500,000	391,500,000*	6.3
Soaps, cleansers (and allied):				
1	Procter & Gamble Co.	265,000,000	3,178,081,000	8.3
6	Colgate-Palmolive Co.	121,000,000	540,133,000	22.4
19	Lever Bros.	65,000,000	525,000,000	12.4
50	S. C. Johnson & Son	36,000,000	220,000,000*	16.4
96	Clorox Co.	15,000,000	98,212,000	15.3
Drugs and cosmetics:				
5	Warner-Lambert Pharmaceuticals	126,000,000	803,624,000	15.6
7	Bristol-Myers Co.	117,000,000	981,155,000	11.9
8	American Home Products Corp.	100,000,000	1,050,039,000	9.5
13	Sterling Drug Inc.	76,900,000	405,084,000	19.0
27	Richardson-Merrell Inc.	57,000,000	380,620,000	15.0
33	Alberto-Culver Co.	52,000,000	170,062,591	30.6
35	Miles Laboratories	48,000,000	296,495,000	16.2
46	Johnson & Johnson	39,000,000	705,427,000	5.5
46	Pfizer Inc.	39,000,000	458,900,000	8.4
49	Schering-Plough Inc.	37,500,000	402,239,000	9.3
56	Carter-Wallace Inc.	30,750,000	129,660,000	23.7
59	Smith Kline & French	29,100,000	347,023,000	8.4
62	Morton-Norwich Products	28,000,000	320,723,000	8.7
65	J. B. Williams Co.	27,000,000	75,000,000*	36.0
68	Chesebrough-Pond's	26,000,000	260,986,000	10.0
68	Revlon Inc.	26,000,000	371,335,106	7.0
76	Merck & Co.	23,540,000	747,562,000	3.1
78	Block Drug Co.	23,000,000	75,667,000	30.4
83	Mennen Co.	20,500,000	95,000,000*	21.6
88	Noxell Corp.	19,000,000	64,262,000	29.6
Gum and candy:				
80	Wm. Wrigley Jr. Co.	22,749,500	176,832,000	12.2
100	Mars Inc.	10,875,000	140,000,000*	7.8

Note: All ad totals are domestic. Wherever possible, AA has reported the company's domestic sales figure in this table, although for some companies only a worldwide sales total was available.

* Domestic sales estimated by AA.

centage of sales different companies spend on their advertising. For example, in 1970, in the food field, Nabisco spent 14.1 percent of its sales on advertising, General Foods 8.6 percent, Campbell's Soup 5.1 percent, Borden Company 1.5 percent. We do not have the figures available regarding how much these companies spent on other sales expenses, or how much they invested in product research or in other company expansion programs. All we can say is that each company sets its own goals for the way it wishes to invest its income in advertising. In the drug field, there are similar big differences: J. B. Williams spent 36 percent, American Home Products 9.5 percent, Revlon 7 percent.[5] On the other hand, Avon Products, whose sales are twice those of Revlon, spent so little on advertising that it is not listed among the 100 largest advertisers; the key to their marketing mix is the in-home women representatives. They invested their sales expenditure chiefly in their field-force operation.

In the home vacuum-cleaner industry, Electrolux has for years made door-to-door selling (direct distribution) the major part of its marketing program. Its advertising expenditures have been virtually nonexistent. In marked contrast, General Electric and Hoover spend much more on advertising their vacuum cleaners, which are sold through retail outlets.

ADVERTISING AS AFFECTED BY SOCIAL TRENDS

Basic trends in consumer living styles and habits can affect the importance of advertising for an entire product category. Convenience food products became popular during the 1950's and 1960's; their advertising budgets grew also. In contrast, advertising became less effective for calorie-laden foods in that time. The "no deposit, no return" glass bottle, a heavily advertised feature in the 1950's and 1960's became far less "advertisable" in the ecology-oriented 1970's.

The current concern for ecology has had a direct impact on the advertisability of nonreturnable bottles. Nonphosphate detergents have emerged as a meaningful product category. By late 1971 a national survey showed that 34 percent of women reported use of a nonphosphate household cleaner, and 8 percent a nonphosphate detergent for dishes.[6]

65 years ago, three million dozen felt hats were manufactured; the figure for 1970 was only about 20,000 dozen.[7] Chief among the reasons, according to hat men, are automobiles and the growth of the suburbs. More men were driving regularly, with their cars providing a substitute head covering. Longer hair styles were also a factor. (College men were the originators of the hatless movement, decades ago.) And more informal living also hurts

---

[5] *Advertising Age,* August 30, 1971, p. 22.

[6] Venet Advertising Inc. survey, reported in *Marketing News,* Vol. V, Number 11, Dec. 1, 1971.

[7] Leonard Sloane, New York Times News Service, *Boston Herald-Traveler,* February 6, 1972.

men's hats, seen as a symbol of older, more formal times. Even a costly advertising campaign could not overcome these social factors.

The widespread popularity of home sewing among women (18–35) has caused a growth in the industries supplying fashion and sewing materials from three billion dollars in 1960 to ten billion dollars in 1970. (Another sign of the boom: the number of books published on home sewing.)

Technical changes may also affect the desirability of a product and the potency of its advertising. Until about 1967 aerosol starch was one of the fastest-growing products on the shelves of supermarkets. But then along came wash-and-wear clothes and permanent press and double knit garments, and the business has been sliding ever since. No amount of advertising can reverse such trends.

OTHER WAYS OF VIEWING ADVERTISING

Advertising according to who does it. Most advertising is that of firms to increase the sales of their products or services. But much advertising is also done by trade associations to help the entire industry. The Dairy Association advertises "Drink milk at bedtime—sleep better tonight"; the Wool Council uses advertising to popularize wool; the Wallpaper Council advertises "Wallpaper a room and give it vivid new color," while the American Wood Council advertises the advantages of building with wood. Such efforts by trade associations are to expand the total market for the products of their members, to meet the competition of other materials or of adverse trends, and otherwise to meet the public relations problems facing the industry. (Illustration on page 69.)

Advertising according to the subject advertised. Most advertising in the United States is for *products*—foods, soft drinks, detergents, beauty aids, cars, tires, paint. There is much advertising also for *services*—airlines, car rentals, banks, insurance companies, travel agencies. Then there is the form of advertising called *institutional,* which does not try to sell a specific product of a company, but rather is devoted to the company as a whole, telling of its policies or ideals, or ways of handling a problem, seeking to generate a favorable attitude that will redound to the benefit of its products and services at such time as people are in the market for them.

Advertising according to the stage of the marketing journey to which it is applied. Think of a product in terms of its journey through the distributing process, from the point at which it is made to the point at which it is bought by its final user. Advertising is used to move that product along in its journey, and differs in its immediate objective at various parts of the trip; it is identified as follows:

1. National advertising
2. Retail advertising
3. Trade (and professional) advertising
4. Industrial advertising
5. End-product advertising
6. Direct-response advertising

1. *National advertising.* The term *national advertising* has a special meaning. It is the advertising by a producer aimed directly at consumers, asking them to buy his trademarked product, at whatever store they wish. National advertising, as the term is commonly used, refers not to the extent of the advertising, but to its purpose, which is to leave the consumer favorably disposed toward buying the product. It is through national advertising that we have come to know the vast lexicon of brand names, such as *Colgate* toothpaste, *Brillo* steel-wool pads, *Heinz* chili sauce, *Hotpoint* washers, *Toyota* cars, *Ked* shoes—the list is endless—sold through many outlets. When most people speak of "advertised products," they usually refer to nationally advertised products. (Illustration on page 62.)

2. *Retail advertising.* Retail advertising is also aimed directly at consumers. It is that advertising of a merchant or dealer that is designed to cause the consumer to visit and to buy at his store. Chief among the retail advertisers are department stores, discount stores, chain stores, and supermarkets. (Illustration on page 64.)

National advertising says, "When you want good sheets, buy Wamsutta sheets." Retail advertising says, "Select your Wamsutta sheets here, from our large white-goods assortment." Moreover, much retail advertising deals with products that are not nationally advertised, particularly style products, as well as the retailer's own branded goods.

3. *Trade (and professional) advertising.* We think of the man who runs a store as one who is always occupied in selling his wares, but a great part of his work is buying the things he is going to sell. He is an important buyer of goods in quantity. When a manufacturer who hopes to sell to and through such retailers advertises to them, explaining why they should buy and sell his particular wares, his advertising is called *trade* advertising. Trade advertising is addressed not to the consumer of the product advertised, but to the retailer who is to sell that product to the consumer. Closely related is *professional* advertising, the advertising directed by the maker or seller of a product to someone who can either recommend its use to others or who specifies or buys it for use by those whom he advises. Manufacturers advertise to physicians, dentists, and architects, not in the expectation that the physician or dentist or architect will consume the product personally, but that he will prescribe, recommend, or specify it to those who will buy it on his recommendation. (Illustration on page 63.)

4. *Industrial advertising.* A manufacturer is a buyer of the machinery, equipment, and raw materials used in producing the goods he sells. He is also a buyer of the materials and components that go into the making of his product. Those who have machinery, equipment, or material to sell to other producers will address their advertising especially to them. It is quite unlike consumer advertising (as we discuss later) and is referred to as *industrial* advertising. (Illustration on page 67.)

5. *End-product advertising.* Cluett, Peabody have a patented process called *Sanforizing,* to prevent the shrinkage of fabrics. They sell it to mills, which use it in the fabrics they weave; these mills sell their fabrics to garment manufacturers who make the shirts the consumer buys. Although Cluett, Peabody sells its product to the mills, it advertises to the consumer, telling the advantage of Sanforizing, and urging him to look for the Sanforized tag or label in the shirt he buys. The process of a manufacturer's advertising to the end users of his product, rather than to those to whom he sells, is called *end-product* advertising. Much consumer advertising of men's and women's wear is the end-product advertising of the mills that produce the fabrics of which the garments are made.

Du Pont makes Teflon II for lining pots and pans, selling it to manufacturers of such products. To encourage women to ask for pots and pans so lined, du Pont advertises to the end user, the housewife, telling her of the advantage of pots and pans marked with a Teflon II tag. The customer asks for such pots and pans at the store. The store seeks them from the manufacturer. The manufacturer has to order Teflon II from du Pont. Everybody is happy—or should be. (Illustration on page 66.)

6. *Direct-response advertising.* Yet another kind of advertising is the one that seeks direct response from the consumer—either by mailing in an order for the product advertised, or by returning a coupon for a catalog or for more information (or for a salesman to call) or else doing so by phone or cablevision. Mail-order advertising is, of course, a form of total selling, not merely advertising. Direct-response advertising differs from retail advertising in that the latter tries to get the consumer to come into the store; direct-response advertising wants an immediate response from the ad. It differs from national advertising in that the latter tries to get people to ask for a particular trademarked product wherever it is convenient to buy it; direct-response advertising seeks an immediate reply. (Illustration on page 65.)

Comparison of forms of advertising by marketing function. The various forms of advertising mentioned here may be characterized by the way in which they seek to encourage the transfer of goods from the maker to the user. Much of our economy is devoted to branded consumer goods that are widely advertised by the manufacturer to get the consumer to buy them at a store. Hence, in this book we view advertising chiefly from the point of view of its use by the producer, referred to as national advertising. Later we shall have special discussions of retail, trade, industrial, and direct-response advertising.

OTHER PURPOSES OF ADVERTISING

Advertising in the United States is used for many purposes other than to sell goods and services. It is used to fight drug addiction and to battle pollution. It is used to raise funds for research against diseases. It is used to elect men to office, and then to oppose the laws they are proposing. It is used by groups to oppose the way things are being run. It is used by unions to tell why they are striking, and by employers to tell how unreasonable the unions are. It is used to raise funds for community chests and to help the afflicted in far-off countries and for other public service causes. Most of such advertising is done by nonprofit groups dedicated to a cause. Often, public-service advertising is sponsored by a corporation that is public-spirited and sees a consistency with their own long-range goals in supporting the cause sponsored. In brief, advertising represents a technique and a facility open in the United States to all who have a message to spread before the public.

Although this book speaks of the advertising of products and services, we are really discussing a technique for delivering a message, at low cost per message, to a lot of people—whatever the message may be.

**PUBLIC BROADCASTING CONTRIBUTIONS
BY INDUSTRY**

Support of at least $50,000 and up to as much as $1,500,000 has been individually granted by these leading corporations for national public television program underwriting:

Celanese—The Great Teachers
Ciby-Geigy—The Restless Earth
Coca-Cola—General Programming
Faberge—General Programming
General Electric—International Performance
General Foods—Sesame Street repeats
General Telephone & Electronics—Helen Hayes Special; Joan Sutherland, opera plus other dramatic specials
IBM—Hanzel & Gretel

Martin-Marietta—Boston Pops
Minnesota Mining & Manufacturing—The Quiet Epidemic, "V.D."
Mobil Oil—Masterpiece Theatre
Polaroid—French Chef
Quaker Oats—Sesame Street repeats
Schlitz—July 4 Parade
Sears, Roebuck—Mister Rogers
Standard Oil (New Jersey)—Vibrations & Age of Kings
Trans-World Airways—EEN Newsfront
Xerox—Civilisation *

* Source: Initiatives in Corporate Responsibility, report prepared by Honorable Frank E. Moss, Chairman, Consumer Subcommittee, for the use of the Committee on Commerce of the United States Senate (Washington, D.C.: U.S. Government Printing Office, 1972), p. 10.

Some Examples

"The best to you each morning"®

© Kellogg Company © 1972 by Kellogg Company

When you're eight years old, Mornings are long and full of sunny hours and it seems like a year till lunch—but they're never long enough for all you want to do. Which means that the 8-year-old engine is a very busy one. It better start that long morning with a good breakfast.

Like one built around his favorite cereal, Kellogg's Sugar Frosted Flakes with milk. He won't mind stopping for that. (And it's a good idea for grown-ups too.)

SUGAR
FROSTED FLAKES®

NUTRITIONAL FACTS

One ounce of Kellogg's Sugar Frosted Flakes provides these percentages of an adult's officially established minimum daily requirements (MDR): Percent MDR in—

NUTRIENT	Sugar Frosted Flakes 1 oz. (1¼ cup)	Sugar Frosted Flakes with ½ cup Whole Milk*
VITAMIN A	33%	37%
VITAMIN D	33%	45%**
VITAMIN C	33%	37%
NIACIN	33%	34%
THIAMINE (B₁)	33%	37%
RIBOFLAVIN (B₂)	33%	50%
IRON	7%	7%
PHOSPHORUS	—	15%
CALCIUM	—	19%
***VITAMIN B₆	0.6 mg	0.65 mg
***VITAMIN B₁₂	1.6 mcg	2.1 mcg
***MAGNESIUM	2.0 mg	17.9 mg

TYPICAL NUTRITIONAL COMPOSITION

	SUGAR FROSTED FLAKES % of Total Weight	Amount in 1 oz.	SUGAR FROSTED FLAKES With ½ cup Whole Milk*
Protein	4.8%	1.4 gm	5.7 gm
Fat	1.2%	0.3 gm	4.6 gm
Carbohydrates	88.6%	25.1 gm	31.1 gm
Calories		109 calories	189 calories

*Whole Milk values derived from USDA Handbook No. 8 and USDA report No. 36.
**Vitamin D fortified milk at 400 USP units/quart.
***Minimum daily adult requirements have not been established.

NATIONAL ADVERTISING

This is the advertisement of a producer telling consumers of the values of the product bearing his trademark. Purpose: to get them to ask for it at any store where it is available.

62

TRADE ADVERTISEMENT

This advertisement by Kellogg's is addressed to the trade, telling of the profit of stocking and selling this highly advertised brand. Purpose: to get retailers to order it.

RETAIL ADVERTISEMENT

The purpose of this discount store advertisement is to get readers to come to the store for these nationally advertised watches, and for other items advertised; also to establish the store as a low-price place to buy.

DIRECT-RESPONSE ADVERTISING

Within the space of this one advertisement, the advertiser hopes to induce the reader to order the books by sending in the coupon—characteristic of all direct-response advertisements.

How you can tell that the cookware you're giving is really a gift.

You won't be doing anybody a favor by giving them cookware that just looks good. If food sticks to it and it has to be scoured and scoured, it isn't a gift.

If it comes with the TEFLON II* Quality Seal, it's really something to give. The TEFLON II Quality Seal is your assurance of a no-stick, easy-clean finish that's been tested and approved by Du Pont.

TEFLON II. It tells you the cookware you're giving is really a gift.

DU PONT
REG. U.S. PAT. OFF.

*TEFLON is Du Pont's registered trademark for its non-stick finishes. TEFLON II is Du Pont's certification mark for scratch-resistant TEFLON-coated cookware which meets Du Pont Standards.

END-PRODUCT ADVERTISEMENT

A du Pont advertisement addressed to the housewife telling of the advantages of cooking ware lined with Teflon II, which it sells to the manufacturers of such goods. Purpose: to induce manufacturers to use Teflon II in their pots and pans.

66

See it at the Machine Tool Show

The largest MOORE Jig Grinder ever built

Moore Model G-48
Precision Jig Grinder (No. 5)
with travel of
24 inches x 48 inches
(600 mm x 1200 mm).

Introducers of jig grinding to industry 30 years ago and pioneers of *every major improvement* in jig grinding since then, Moore Special Tool Company will exhibit at the International Machine Tool Show — and for the first time anywhere — its new Model G-48 Jig Grinder (No. 5).

The machine — with a travel of 24 inches x 48 inches (600 mm x 1200 mm) — will be demonstrated under power, jig-grinding a jumbo-size workpiece.

Built into the G-48's large capacity and its capability of jig grinding in the largest size range is the Moore tradition of extremely close precision. Repeatability of settings is 5 millionths inch (0,15 μm). In longitudinal and cross travel the greatest error in any inch is 30

millionths inch (0,8 μm). Total accumulative error in the longitudinal travel is 150 millionths inch (3,8 μm), and in the cross travel, 90 millionths inch (2,3 μm).

Like the Moore No. 3 jig grinders, jig borers and measuring machines, the G-48 carries a 10-year guarantee of accuracy.

Don't miss the inaugural performance of this machine at McCormick Place—Moore Booth No. 2412. It promises to be among the most talked-about new developments there.

If you'd like advance information and literature on the G-48 Jig Grinder, write R. W. Kuba, World Sales Manager, Moore Special Tool Co., Inc., 800 Union Avenue, Bridgeport, Conn. 06607.

MOORE Special Tool Co., Inc.
Bridgeport, Connecticut 06607
European Technical Center: 8005 Zurich, Switzerland
Far East Technical and Training Center:
International Machine Co., Ltd., Tokyo, Japan

PRECISION TOOLS

Manufacturers of Jig Borers, Jig Grinders, Universal Measuring Machines, Rotary Tables, Tool Room Products, and High Precision Measuring Instruments and Physical Standards.

INDUSTRIAL ADVERTISING

An advertisement by one machine tool manufacturer to other manufacturers who could use such equipment. Purpose: to get manufacturers to buy this equipment.

Easy Avis.

Now renting a car is as easy as signing your name.

Now Avis has an easy new way to rent a car. The Wizard® Golden File.℠

With it, you call for a reservation, give us your Golden File number, and your rental form will be waiting for you by the time you get to the counter.

Then simply show your driver's license and charge card, sign your name, and you're away in your sparkling new Plymouth or other fine car.

Nothing could be faster.

We recently introduced The Wizard of Avis, the most advanced computer system in the travel business, to make it easier to rent a car. And now The Golden File makes things even easier.

The Avis Golden File.

Call 800-231-6000* for an application or send in this one to get your Golden File identification card.

LAST NAME   FIRST NAME   MIDDLE INITIAL

HOME ADDRESS

CITY   STATE   ZIP CODE

COMPANY NAME

COMPANY ADDRESS

CITY   STATE   ZIP CODE
SEND BILLS TO HOME ☐ OR COMPANY ☐ ADDRESS

DRIVER'S LICENSE NO.

STATE OF ISSUE

EXPIRATION DATE   MONTH   DAY   YEAR

PLEASE ENTER AID NUMBER (IF APPLICABLE)

Card to be used:
(Please select only one.)   (Include all letters.)
- ☐ Avis   No._____
- ☐ Air Travel   No._____
- ☐ American Express   No._____
- ☐ Diners' Club   No._____
- ☐ Other (Specify)
          No._____

Usual car preference:
- ☐ Luxury (Chrysler, Imperial, or Equivalent)
- ☐ Standard (Fury, Polara, or Equivalent)
- ☐ Intermediate (Satellite or Equivalent)
- ☐ Economy (Duster, Demon, or Equivalent)

Do you normally purchase the collision damage waiver as part of your rentals? ☐Yes ☐No

Do you normally purchase safe trip insurance as part of your rentals? ☐Yes ☐No

☐ If you want an Avis Charge Card application, check here.

Mail to: Avis, 900 Old Country Rd.
Garden City, N.Y. 11530
Attention: Wizard Golden File, Dept. 115

Avis. We try harder.

® ℠ WIZARD IS A REGISTERED TRADEMARK AND GOLDEN FILE IS A SERVICE MARK OF AVIS RENT A CAR SYSTEM, INC
*IN TEXAS CALL 800-392-3966   ©AVIS RENT A CAR SYSTEM, INC

AN ADVERTISEMENT BY A SERVICE

An increasing proportion of our national economy deals with the rendering of services. Much of the same technique used in advertising products applies to services. Purpose of the advertising: to reach those people who could use the service; induce them to do so.

How to get
more house out of your next house.

Your next house may well be the biggest and the best investment you'll ever make.

So, naturally, you'll want to get the most for your money.

Which means you'll want to think about where it's built. How it's built. And what it's built out of.

We think one of the best things to build with is wood.

Because wood gives lasting value.

Take a house with a roof of wood shingles or shakes.

Sure they're beautiful. But they're also wind resistant. Durable. And insulate against cold and heat better than any other material.

If your next house has wood siding – plywood, boards, shingles or hardboard – you'll have added value.

Many wood sidings need no finishing or maintenance at all.

Others can be stained to bring out all the beauty of wood's natural grains or sawn textures. Or painted with new acrylic or latex finishes that'll stay fresh up to six years.

All wood sidings have

great weathering qualities. Which means they'll last the lifetime of your house.

Inside, wood adds still more value.

Prefinished or textured wood paneling not only looks warm and beautiful. It also never needs painting. And is easy to clean.

New wood floor systems of finished hardwood on plywood glued to supporting beams are quiet and comfortable to walk on. And unlike carpeting, a hardwood floor is permanent.

What makes wood even more valuable is the strength it adds to your house.

In the 1964 Alaskan earthquake and hurricane Camille, wood frame houses with wood sheathing held up much better than other kinds of construction.

No wonder 8 out of 10 homes in America

are built with wood.

By now we hope we've whetted your appetite for more facts.

Just send for our House-Hunter's Guide (with free mortgage calculator). Or our Home Improvement Guide. Both are crammed full of facts and come with a free guide to wood products.

When you're making the biggest investment of your life, you need all the facts you can get.

American Wood Council

Box 4156T, Chevy Chase, Md. 20015

Please send
—House Hunter's Guide 50c each
—Home Improvement Guide 50c each
—Send both Guides $1.00

Name

Address

City   State   Zip

ASSOCIATION ADVERTISING

Trade associations frequently advertise to meet the problems facing the entire industry. Here the American Wood Council presents the advantages of wood, to meet the competition of other materials used in home construction.

69

Last year, Nicky K., age three, drank a bottle of furniture polish. A telephone number saved his life.

The poisoning took place in Tyringham, Mass.

The number belonged to a poison control center 135 miles away.

But what if Nicky's parents didn't know it existed?

What if they had to waste precious minutes frantically searching through phone books before they could even attempt to reach it?

And what if they needed something more than advice over the telephone — like a doctor or ambulance?

At Metropolitan Life, we are working to keep all those "what if's" from becoming "if only's."

In many communities, we're distributing emergency kits with lists of numbers that can make the difference between life and death.

It's part of a 44-year-long effort on our part to show people how to avoid emergencies, and how to handle those that are unavoidable.

Because accidents will happen.

And when they do, what people don't know <u>can</u> hurt them.

Institutional Ads for a Public Service

On these pages are two ads which are institutional, in that they seek the public good will for their entire company; they are also public service ads in the message they convey. Examples of two goals meeting in one advertisement.

Save a watt

(it's wise to conserve energy)

Save a watt. Because New York and Westchester, and perhaps other places too, may face power emergencies this year. Because now and in future years protection of the earth's environment requires we use <u>all</u> kinds of energy wisely and not wastefully.

Save a watt. Because if we start conserving electricity now, *especially in day time,* we may avoid more serious problems later. Con Edison is doing everything possible to end power shortages. If new facilities can be completed on schedule, we will have one of the nation's most modern electric systems in just a few years. But even when power is plentiful it should be conserved.

Save a watt. Because with your help there's less chance of serious disruptions of electric service this summer. And using <u>all</u> energy wisely is essential to keeping the earth a good place to live.

10 ways to save a watt

1. During the day, when no one is home, turn the air conditioning off.

2. When using air conditioners, select moderate or medium settings rather than turning your unit on high. During the day keep windows closed and adjust blinds and shades to keep out the sun so that air conditioners won't have to work so hard.

3. Whenever possible, plan to run major appliances — and smaller appliances as well — before 8 am and after 6 pm.

4. If possible, use dishwashers just once a day — after the evening meal.

5. If possible, plan washer and dryer loads for evenings and weekends. Do one full load instead of many small loads.

6. Keep lights off when it's daylight except for safety, health and comfort reasons (the heat from lighting requires more air conditioning).

7. Never leave a kitchen range or oven on when not actually in use.

8. Turn off television and radio sets when you are not looking or listening.

9. If you can, save once-in-a-while jobs like vacuum cleaning or working with power tools until the weekend.

10. When buying an air conditioner, look for the right size unit for your needs. Select one that gives you the maximum amount of BTU's of cooling for every watt used.

Con Edison conserve energy

The Advertising Council shakes up a lot of people. Thank God!

We shake 'em up with tough, factual, thought-provoking advertising on drug abuse. We jar 'em with picture-stories of drunks on the highways and what happens to some people who forget safety belts. We're tough where we have to be. Reassuring and gentle where we can be. We try desperately to make people alert and aware. Because we believe that people who are aware are better able to cope with the problems around them.

Our product is action-oriented advertising campaigns in the public interest, conducted by The Advertising Council for over twenty-nine years.

We get a lot of help in our job. Business people, advertising agencies and advertising media. People and companies who volunteer their space, time, talent and facilities, free! Last year, the value of their services totaled over $450 million for campaigns created and donated in the public interest. Campaign subjects range from Drug Abuse

- Highway Safety
- Pollution
- Crime
- Education
- Minority Business Enterprise
- The Handicapped
- United Funds
- Jobs For Veterans
- to Smokey Bear.

We work together quietly, efficiently and effectively. It doesn't bother us at all that most of the people we help, don't even know our name!

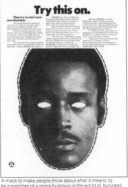

Try this on.

A mask to make people think about what it means to be a member of a minority group in the world of business. One ad in the **Minority Business Enterprise** campaign.

Daddy, what did you do in the war against pollution?

People start pollution. People can stop it.

A highly emotional appeal aimed at broadening the **Keep America Beautiful** campaign to include the overall environmental pollution situation.

ADVERTISING COUNCIL

A pictorially devastating graphic, this award winning poster was created for the **Drug Abuse Information** campaign. Its message is clear!

Advertising Contributed For The Public Good

PUBLIC SERVICE ADVERTISING BY ADVERTISING GROUPS

The Advertising Council represents an advertising industry contribution to helping public service projects.

72

AN ORDINARY DOG IN AMERICA EATS BETTER THAN SHE DOES.

Cristina eats whatever she can find in the garbage. And that is far less than some prowling dog would find in your garbage can.

For just $12 a month, you can save such a child.

Through our Children, Inc. "Adoption" program you can help provide a child with a better diet, new clothes and medical attention. Even an education.

But there's not a moment to lose. Every 60 seconds, five or six more children will die from starvation.

Write direct to Mrs. Jeanne Clarke Wood, Children, Incorporated, Box 5381, Dept. A-3, Richmond, Va. 23220.

I wish to "adopt" a boy ☐ girl ☐ in _____.
Name of Country

I will pay $12 a month ($144 a year). Enclosed is my gift for ☐ a full year ☐ the first month. Please send me the child's name, story, address and picture.

I understand that I can correspond with my child, and continue the "adoption" longer than one year if I wish. Also, I may discontinue the "adoption" at any time.
☐ I cannot "adopt" a child, but want to help $_____
☐ Or, I will pledge $_____ per month.
☐ Please send me further information.
☐ If for a group, please specify_____
Church, Class, Club, School, Business, etc

Name_____
Address_____
City_____State_____Zip_____

You can "adopt" a child from any of the following countries: Bolivia, Chile, Colombia, Guatemala, Honduras, Hong Kong, India, Iran, Japan, Korea, Lebanon, Mexico, Nigeria, Paraguay, Peru, Syria, Thailand, U.S.A.—Appalachian children or American Indians. (Or a child of greatest need.) All gifts are fully tax deductible.

CHILDREN, INCORPORATED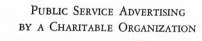

PUBLIC SERVICE ADVERTISING
BY A CHARITABLE ORGANIZATION

This advertisement appealing for funds to help children is typical of others which have raised much money for such social problems.

1. What is meant by the "value goal for a product"? Selecting three products with which you are familiar, what would you judge the value goals were in producing them?

2. What is the "marketing mix?" What are some of the elements that go into it?

3. Cite the conditions that are conducive to advertising.

4. Here are two companies each with the same volume. One sells packaged goods to the consumer. Another sells plastics to industry. What are the reasons the former does so much more advertising than the latter?

5. What lesson is to be learned from the General Mills experience with Clackers?

6. Why may two firms in the same business, doing the same volume, differ so much in their advertising expenditure?

7. Can you cite some products whose sales have been affected by social trends? In which respect?

8. What is meant by the "product differentials"? What is its role in advertising?

9. Define and give an example of:
    National advertising
    Retail advertising
    End product advertising
    Trade advertising
    Direct response advertising
    Industrial advertising
    Advertising of services
    Institutional advertising
    Public service advertising

Reading Suggestions

Barton, Roger, *The Handbook of Advertising Management.* New York: McGraw-Hill Book Company, 1970.

Bogart, Leo, *Strategy in Advertising.* New York: Harcourt, Brace & World, Inc., 1967. Excerpted in Kleppner and Settel, *Exploring Advertising,* p. 63.

Borden, Neil H., "The Concept of the Marketing Mix," *Journal of Advertising Research,* June, 1964.

Buell, Victor (Editor), *Handbook of Modern Marketing.* New York: McGraw-Hill Book Company, 1970.

Business Week, "How to Get Salesmen Through the Doorway," June 4, 1966, pp. 84, 89. Also in Kleppner and Settel, *Exploring Advertising,* p. 67.

Buzzell, Robert D., "The Role of Advertising in the Marketing Mix," Marketing Science Institute Special Report, October 1971.

Buzzell, Robert, Robert Nourse, John Matthews, and Theodore Levitt, *Marketing: A Contemporary Analysis.* New York: McGraw-Hill Book Company, 1972.

Davis, Kenneth R., *Marketing Management,* 3rd edition. New York: The Ronald Press, 1972.

Dougherty, Philip H., "Ma Bell a Swinger," *The New York Times,* April 7, 1968, p. 77. Also in Kleppner and Settel, *Exploring Advertising,* p. 45.

Kotler, Philip, *Marketing Management,* 2nd edition. Englewood Cliffs, N.J.: Prentice-Hall, Inc., 1972.

Kuehn, Alfred A., "How Advertising Performance Depends on Other Marketing Factors," *Marketing in Progress,* Hiram C. Barksdale, ed. New York: Holt, Rinehart & Winston, Inc., 1964.

McCarthy, E. Jerome, *Basic Marketing,* 4th edition. Homewood, Ill.: Richard D. Irwin, Inc., 1971.

McGinniss, Joe, *The Selling of the President: 1968.* New York: Trident Press, 1969.

II
PLANNING
THE ADVERTISING

4

The Advertising Spiral

THE FOLLOWING ADVERTISEMENT APPEARED in a New York newspaper. The name of the product is omitted. What would you guess the product to be?

HAVE YOUR _____ SENT HOME
BEFORE THANKSGIVING DAY

Add one more source of delight for the children and pleasure for the grown-ups. No home is at its best until you have a _____. Nothing else makes the home so bright and cheerful; nothing else keeps the children so lively and happy; nothing else serves so well to keep the older folks from being dull and the time from dragging. There is pleasure for all in a house that possesses a _____.

Isn't it an addition well worth having sent home before Thanksgiving Day comes with its holiday for the children and the friends who will visit you?

What product would you say was being advertised?
A videocassette? No.
A color television set? No.
A hi-fi set? A tape recorder? A radio? A phonograph? No.
It was the predecessor to all these, a mechanical music box, by Regina, advertised by the John Wanamaker store in 1901.

THE ADVERTISING STAGES

Yet there is an unmistakable similarity between the Regina music box ad and those used to introduce more recent inventions, because from the time a *new type* of product first appears on the market to the time various brands of that product are household words, the product faces similar advertising stages. These are:

—The pioneering stage
—The competitive stage
—The retentive stage

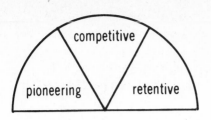

A clear understanding of these stages is essential in planning basic advertising strategy.

The Pioneering Stage

An inventor may have been working for many years on a useful new device. When he finally succeeds, does the public arise in elation and clamor for it? Not in most cases, because it may never have occurred to consumers to seek such a device. Until people recognize that this is something they want, the product is in the first, or *pioneering* stage.

The advertising of products in the pioneering stage (or *pioneering advertising,* as we call it) must show that previous conceptions of that field are now antiquated. Methods accepted as the only ones possible are now shown to have been improved; satisfactions never before thought of are now shown to be attainable; limitations tolerated as "normal" are now demonstrated to have been overcome safely. The safety razor supplanted the straight-edge razor and the advertising said, "If you are still depending upon the barber or old-fashioned razor, you are in the same category as a man who climbs ten flights of stairs when there is an elevator in the building. With the Gillette Safety Razor the most inexperienced man can remove without cut or scratch in three to five minutes any beard that ever grew." And when the electric shaver came upon the scene, its advertising proclaimed "no bother or fuss of old-fashioned soap and brush . . . no more shaving cuts with the new electric shaver." And when Remington introduced the new removable-blade electric shaver, the advertising said, "With the new Remington you won't have to start searching for a repair shop when your blade gets dull. Instead, you pop in a new set of blades, and start getting the kind of shaves you got when the shaver was new."—all pioneering advertising.

Even color television was launched by the pioneering advertising of RCA Victor in the 1950's, which said:

> See World Series Baseball in Living Color. . . . Rarely in a lifetime can you share a thrill like this. . . . You can see baseball's greatest spectacle come alive in your own home in color . . . you'll sense a new on-the-spot realism in every picture of the crowd, the players, the action. . . . Made by RCA—the most trusted name in electronics.

Mazda presents the "Elegant" engine.

It started a Rotary Revolution on the West Coast that's sweeping the nation.

Here you see the basic bits of a 2-rotor, rotary engine. Many call it, "The Engine of Tomorrow." To a mathematician or engineer, it's "Elegant"—meaning, it represents the simplest solution to a problem.

For compared to an ordinary piston engine, a rotary has about 40% fewer parts, weighs less by anything from a half to a third and it's only half the size of a Six. In addition, because of its inherent characteristics, compact shape and small size, the rotary's emissions can be controlled to meet the most stringent standards.

Perhaps a more remarkable feature of "The Engine of Tomorrow" is that for once it is indeed "Here Today!", a viable, reliable reality. And all this thanks to a company called Toyo Kogyo that got its start making machine tools, rock drills and 3-wheel trucks.

Why so remarkable? Because, if the rotary's simplicity is elegant, it is also incredibly sophisticated—a 3-lobe rotor turning through 360° within a figure-8 shaped epitrochoidal chamber, the rotor apexes in constant contact with the walls.

And although since 1958 some 20 international companies have bought licenses to develop a rotary,

Basic elements of Mazda Rotary Engine

Mazda RX-2 Coupe—whirling up a storm of smooth, silent, rotary power.

Mazda is still the only one that has managed to mass-produce thoroughly proven and utterly reliable rotary engine cars at a reasonable price. All other things being equal, the reason why Mazda succeeded where the Giants failed must be a matter of old-fashioned determination and enthusiasm. An enthusiastic auto maker. Unusual.

So much for facts. For fun, a Mazda RX-2 Rotary belts out big horsepower from only 70 cu. in. Power that's smooth and silent to an almost unbelievable degree. Because the rotary's moving mass spins in the same direction as the driveshaft—no jiggling up and down with pistonitis.

The fun and excitement of driving a Mazda Rotary is better experienced than described. See your Mazda Dealer and give it a whirl. There's just nothing else like it on the road. The Mazda Rotary is licensed by NSU/Wankel.

MAZDA
Toyo Kogyo Co., Ltd.

THE WANKEL ENGINE IN THE PIONEERING STAGE

The Wankel engine is not a mere improvement in the details of a present car engine, but a revolutionary design, possibly "The Engine of Tomorrow." Before it is accepted, however, pioneering advertising is needed to make the people understand the great advantage of this engine.

Man might conquer disease, stop crime and save his environment with the help of this little machine.

THE VIDEOCASSETTE IN THE PIONEERING STAGE

"It's a revolutionary new means of communication—instead of printed words, the Sony U-matic Videocassette Player-Recorder uses television pictures and sound." With these words heralding a new age of communication, Sony presents its color videocassette system.

It's a revolutionary new means of communication.

And if you wonder whether that's enough to change the world —remember the invention of the printing press.

Instead of printed words, the Sony U-matic Videocassette Player-Recorder uses television pictures and sound.

It's television you program yourself. Television you play back at will.

If you have something to say or demonstrate, it records your program" on a color videocassette the size of a book.

To receive a program, you just insert the programmed cassette, and plug the U-matic into any TV set. At once, your program appears on the screen.

The uses of this little machine boggle the mind. It could, for instance, solve one of the biggest problems in the conquest of cancer.

Getting new developments out to doctors—fast.

Today, 1 out of 3 cancer patients is saved. It could be 1 out of 2, if doctors just had access to all the present knowledge.

With this little machine, they can.

Suppose a cancer specialist has some valid success with a new form of treatment.

He doesn't wait to present a paper at some future medical convention.

Right then and there, he records his technique on a U-matic color videocassette. Thousands of copies are made and mailed out.

Within days, thousands of doctors in hospitals and private offices have seen the technique on their U-matic, and can put it to use.

Knowledge snowballs.

You can see the possibilities: Long-distance teamwork among police in different cities. Among ecologists all over the world.

A communications explosion in education, business, industry.

What makes the U-matic so especially useful is that a program can come from many sources.

It could be something shot "live" right on the spot.

Existing tape. Film. Anything you can see or hear.

You can also buy or rent pre-programmed cassettes.

On hundreds of subjects, from riot control to golf technique.

Perhaps, some day, there'll be a U-matic in every living room.

But right now, as fast as Sony can turn them out, these little machines head for laboratories, schoolrooms, conference rooms, showrooms and factories.

Already, by the thousands, they are changing our world.

THE SONY® U-MATIC*
color videocassette system

For more information, write Sony Corporation of America, Video Products Dept., 47-47 Van Dam St., Long Island City, N.Y. 11101

"Perhaps some day, there'll be a U-matic in every living room." Before that time comes, however, a lot of pioneering advertising will be needed to explain just what a videocassette is, how it works, how it can change the life style of the user. Expect to see much more pioneering advertising in this vein.

Saab vs. Audi

1972 Saab 99E, 4-door	Model	1972 Audi 100 LS, 4-door
4 cylinders, in-line, water-cooled	Engine Design	4 cylinders, in-line, water-cooled
Yes	Overhead Cam	No
95 hp (SAE) at 5200 rpm	Maximum Engine Output	90 hp (SAE) at 5200 rpm
113.1 cubic inches	Displacement	114.2 cubic inches
Yes	Electronic Fuel Injection	No
4-speed manual/3-speed automatic OPTIONAL	Gearbox	4-speed manual/3-speed automatic OPTIONAL
Yes	Front Wheel Drive	Yes
0 to 60 in 12.5 seconds	Acceleration	0 to 60 in 12.7 seconds
197 feet	Stopping Distance Maximum Load at 60 mph	222 feet
99 mph	Top Speed	105 mph
97.4 inches	Wheelbase	105.3 inches
172 inches	Overall Length	182.6 inches
66.5 inches	Overall Width	68.1 inches
34 feet	Turning Circle Diameter	36.7 feet
3.5	Steering Wheel Turns, Lock to Lock	3.94
23.3 cubic feet	Trunk Space	23 cubic feet
2550 lbs.	Curb Weight	2467 lbs.
Yes	Electrically Heated Driver's Seat	No
Yes	Heating Controls for Rear Seat Passengers	No
Yes	Fold-down Rear Seat	No
Yes	Impact Absorbing Bumpers	No
Yes	Rack and Pinion Steering	Yes
Yes	Disc Brakes On All Four Wheels	No
Yes	Dual-Diagonal Braking System	No
Between rear wheels	Fuel Tank Location	Behind rear wheels
1 year/unlimited mileage	Factory Warranty	2 years/24,000 miles
$3,795	Base Price	$3,855

Before you buy theirs, drive ours. Saab 99E.

All information compiled from manufacturers own printed material wherein it states, all specifications subject to change without notice. Prices listed exclude dealer preparation, transportation, state and local taxes if any. For the name and address of the dealer nearest you, call 800-243-6000 toll free. In Connecticut, call 1-800-882-6500.

ADVERTISING IN THE COMPETITIVE STAGE

Here the specifications of the Saab and the Audi are directly compared by the makers of the Saab, to show its advantages over the competitive car.

Although the music box and color television were over half a century apart, and although the advertising techniques of their day were worlds apart, yet both products attacked their common problem the same way: "Add one more source of delight" . . . "rarely in a lifetime a thrill like this." These themes, of new satisfactions in life that are now attainable, are recurrent in the pioneering advertising of new types of products.

By new types of products, we refer to those that represent a technical breakthrough leading to innovations, such as were Xerox reproduction, Wankel engines, one-piece disposable diapers, video telephones, video cassettes; also products that apply a new principle or technique to existing types of goods, such as *transistorized* products, *freeze-dried* coffee, *tuning-fork* electric watches. These are more than minor model improvements; each called for a new set of tools and dies and production facilities—and pioneering advertising.

The Competitive Stage

By the time the public accepts the idea of using the new category of product, competitors undoubtedly will have sprung up. When the public no longer asks, "What's that product for?" but rather, "Which make shall I buy?" the product enters the *competitive* stage. We speak of the advertising for a product in the competitive stage as *competitive advertising.* (This is a restrictive meaning of that term, not to be confused with the looser usage that holds that all advertisements are competitive with each other.)

Most products in everyday use are in the competitive stage: cars, tires, detergents, toothpaste, cereals, razor blades, soft drinks, shampoos. The purpose of advertising in the competitive stage is to show how the brand being advertised will satisfy the buyer better than will other brands, usually because of its unique features or *differentials.*

The advertising may do so by direct comparison with other brands:

Tasters Choice makes   Our competition
fresh coffee in seconds   is still boiling
————Tasters Choice Freeze-dried Coffee

The $3,900 Audi has the same steering system as the $38,400 Ferrari
————Audi Car

The advertising may stress its special advantages, as reported in these headlines:

Toro mows more safely
—Rear safety shield   —Deflector bar
—Blade guard   —Safety stop switch
————Toro mowers

The quiet one. It doesn't whoosh. It doesn't whine. It whispers.

——Kodak Carousel Projector

None of these advertisements tells you why you should use its type of product; that is taken for granted. But each sets out to tell you why you should select that particular brand from among the others in its field.

General Electric Ranges with Total-Clean Ovens clean parts of an oven others expect you to clean.

All ovens that claimed to clean themselves aren't created equal. What's the difference? One works by heat. While the other, called "continuous cleaning," depends upon a dark-colored porous enamel. This porous surface is designed to soak up splatter and grease as you use the oven. But since many parts of the oven can't be made with this porous finish, you're expected to lend a hand.

The General Electric Total-Clean self-cleaning system is completely automatic. It cleans the entire oven interior. All you do is latch the door and set the control. Spills, greasy spots and oven soil are decomposed by the heat. General Electric pioneered the Pyrolytic self-cleaning oven, so it's probably no surprise that we have the largest selection of Total-Clean Ovens.

P-7 plus double ovens
The J797 Americana® The lower oven has the P-7® Total-Clean System. Removable panels and shelves in the upper oven can be cleaned in the P-7 Lower oven. Other features include: dependable solid-state oven temperature control, Sensi-Temp™ automatic surface unit with griddle, automatic rotisserie, meat thermometer, infinite heat surface units, two picture window doors. Available in Harvest, Avocado or White.

P-7 free-standing models
The J757 is a free-standing 30″ model. In addition to the P-7 Total-Clean Oven, you get a solid-state oven temperature control, no-drip cook-top, with Sensi-Temp automatic surface unit and griddle, automatic rotisserie, meat thermometer, infinite heat surface units and picture window oven door. Available in Harvest, Avocado or White.

P-7 top and bottom wall ovens
The JK29 is a 27″ built-in double-oven with two Total-Clean Ovens. Other features: dependable solid-state oven temperature control, picture window door in both ovens, easy-set oven timer, rotisserie, and automatic meat thermometer. Counter top surface units with matching exhaust hoods are available. All in Harvest, Avocado or White.

Customer Care Service Everywhere.
This feature goes with every P-7 Total-Clean range we sell. This is our pledge: that wherever you are or go you'll find an authorized GE serviceman nearby. Should you ever need him.

GENERAL ⓖⓔ ELECTRIC

Advertising in the Competitive Stage

General Electric offers an automatic oven-cleaning system, which it calls Total Clean, as the distinctive advantage for selecting this oven.

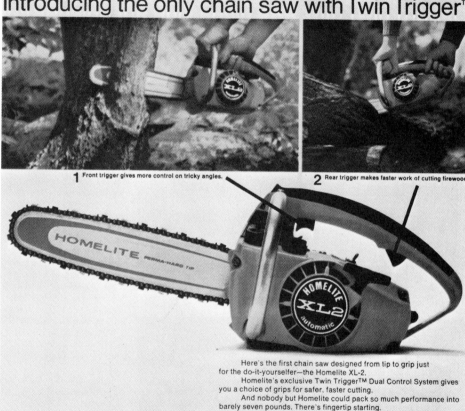

HOMELITE JUST MADE CUTTING TWICE AS EASY!

Introducing the only chain saw with Twin Trigger™

1 Front trigger gives more control on tricky angles.

2 Rear trigger makes faster work of cutting firewood.

Here's the first chain saw designed from tip to grip just for the do-it-yourselfer—the Homelite XL-2.

Homelite's exclusive Twin Trigger™ Dual Control System gives you a choice of grips for safer, faster cutting.

And nobody but Homelite could pack so much performance into barely seven pounds. There's fingertip starting.

Rugged two-cycle engine. And, automatic chain oiling is standard—not an expensive option.

Use the XL-2 to cut firewood, trim, prune, or for almost any outdoor construction. In just a few weekends you'll probably have saved yourself the price.

HOMELITE® XL2 With Twin Trigger™ $119.95*

™ Trademark of Homelite *Suggested Retail Price

HOMELITE • A textron DIVISION • PORT CHESTER, N.Y. 10573

ADVERTISING IN THE COMPETITIVE STAGE

This advertisement does not tell you why you should use a chain saw; it focuses on the competitive advantage of its differential—the Twin Trigger—as the reason you should get this particular one.

85

The Retentive Stage

There is a third stage through which a product *might* pass—the *retentive stage*. When a brand of product is used by a large share of the market, the chief goal of the advertising may be to hold on to those customers. All over the world, for example, there are signs saying *Drink Coca-Cola*. They do not say what Coca-Cola is; they give no reason why you should drink it or why Coca-Cola is better than any other drink. That advertising is addressed to people who know Coca-Cola; the company just wants to retain its patronage at the minimal cost per customer.

COCA-COLA IN THE
RETENTIVE STAGE

Not a word about the merits of Coca-Cola in the ad; it assumes the readers already know that. Its entire thrust is to keep users from switching to other soft drinks.

Retentive advertising is often referred to as "name advertising," for that is often its chief feature. However, retentive advertising embraces other problems of a product in the retentive stage, such as staving off imitators—an experience faced by every highly successful advertiser. The retentive advertising will say, "Don't be fooled by imitators," or, "Get the real thing," or words to that effect. In World War II there was rationing; old customers couldn't get their orders filled, but companies nevertheless wanted to hold their goodwill. Manufacturers used retentive advertising to show how people could stretch the supply of the product. It is used today whenever a company's production has temporarily been curtailed, as by strikes or floods or fires.

SHIFT OF STAGE WITHIN ONE MARKET

Since people may change their attitudes toward a product gradually, the shift of a product from pioneering stage to competitive stage may also be gradual. Half the space of a movie-camera ad may be pioneering, telling of the joy of having moving pictures of children as they grow up; the other half may be competitive, explaining the special features of this particular camera.

PRODUCT IN DIFFERENT STAGES IN DIFFERENT MARKETS

In considering the advertising stages of a product, we think of it in terms of specific markets. A product may be in different stages in different markets at the same time. For example, typewriters are in the competitive stage in the business-office market, but are largely in the pioneering stage for use by teenagers.

TWA advertises its new Ambassador coaches and first-class flights to regular air travelers (competitive advertising). In different ads, it features its "Getaway Program" of comprehensive vacation plans, encouraging people who "want to go, but there are so many reasons why you don't" (pioneering advertising). Kleenex advertising speaks of its new "Boutique tissues in a variety of colors" (competitive advertising) in women's magazines, but for the general public reached by car cards, the message is "There's only one Kleenex" (retentive advertising). As a business grows, there is a greater need to segment its markets, and to prepare advertising suited to the stage of each.

PRODUCT IN THE COMPETITIVE STAGE:
DETAIL IN PIONEERING STAGE

Not all products presented as "new" are new *types* of products. Many are familiar products in the competitive stage, with a feature representing a new principle that requires pioneering advertising to get acceptance. Change is a continuum.

The new Remington.
It's designed for changing blades so you don't have to keep changing shavers.

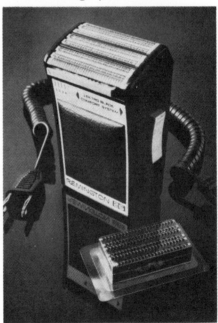

Almost any good electric shaver can give you a clean shave when it's new. But the <u>Remington</u>® <u>Lektro Blade</u>® Shaver is designed to keep giving you good shaves when it's no longer new.

No shaver is any better than its blades, since it's the blades themselves that do the shaving.

So we gave this new Remington the sharpest shaver blades we've ever made.

And we made these new blades replaceable.

In fact, we designed a completely new shaver around them. With a big, Hideaway™ trimmer, adjustable comfort controls, and a slant-head design for easier, more comfortable handling.

When you notice this new Remington losing sharpness, in 6 months or so, the importance of replaceable blades will come home to you.

Because you won't have to start searching for a repair shop.

Or looking at new models.

Instead, you pop in a new set of blades and start getting the kind of shaves you got when the shaver was new.

If you have a shaver that doesn't change blades, maybe you should change your shaver.

REMINGTON®
LEKTRO BLADE SHAVER

⬧ SPERRY RAND

PRODUCT IN THE COMPETITIVE STAGE—DETAIL IN THE PIONEERING STAGE

Often a competitive product will come out with a feature so new that it requires pioneering advertising to get acceptance, as in the case of the Remington replaceable blades.

When Ford came out with a new station wagon tailgate, it used pioneering advertising to introduce "something new from the Ford Motor Company. . . . A station wagon tailgate that's a door that's a tailgate," with its secret of the unique feature—the Ford-developed patented hinges . . . "doubles the pleasure of owning a wagon." In such instances, the advertising focuses on the product's new feature that is in the pioneering stage; the product continues in the competitive stage.

Before long, competitors come out with their version of that new feature, and it becomes accepted as the standard for that type of product, as has the tailgate door. The company must then find some other rationale for being selected.

DIFFERENCE IN POLICIES

The stage of a product may be determined readily enough, but two advertisers may follow different policies in interpreting the facts. The first may recognize that there is still a large public that buys neither his article nor any like it. He will continue to stress pioneering appeals, bringing more customers into the field, and to himself. The second advertiser will take advantage of the pioneering work already done in creating a market, and will use competitive advertising only, to get his brand selected.

WHY BE A PIONEER?

Since the pioneering advertiser has the expense of educating the public to the advantages of his type of product, and since he can expect others then to take advantage of his work, he may well ask what benefits, if any, will compensate him for his investment. In most instances he has little choice; either he comes into the market at the outset, with pioneering efforts, or allows someone else to step in as the first in the field. He may then have to pay more to enter the market later, when he has to compete with the advertising and distribution of many others.

The only advantage of which a pioneering advertiser can be sure is a *time* advantage; he has a head start over the followers. His name will be the first to come to mind for that type of product. People will know his trademark better than that of the followers; they will have more confidence in his product because they will feel that he has had more experience with it than his competitors. He will have the choice distributors for his product.

For five years, the B. F. Goodrich Company worked to perfect the tubeless tire, which was then a revolutionary idea. After all the expense and travail on the part of Goodrich in producing such a tire and getting the public to accept tires without inner tubes (a radical proposal!), competitors jumped into the field with their brands of tubeless tires. Goodrich sought to stop them through patent suits—and lost! *Nevertheless, the B. F. Goodrich Company had sold over one million tubeless tires before their competitors got into the act.*[1] This lead over their followers was their payback for their pioneering effort.

COMPARISON OF STAGES

There is much less advertising of products in the pioneering stage than in the competitive stage, because new *types* or categories of products, not mere minor improvements on old ones, do not appear on the scene too often.

Most advertising is for products in the competitive stage. Often such advertising introduces a new feature that is in the pioneering stage, and that, for a time, gets the advertising spotlight.

The least amount of advertising is for products in the retentive stage. This stage, however, represents a critical moment in the life cycle of a product, when important management decisions must be made; hence it is important to understand the retentive stage.

AFTER THE RETENTIVE STAGE?

It appears only logical that the life of a product does not end when it reaches the retentive stage, for here it is at the very height of its popularity, where, if allowed, it can coast along. But a business that coasts can only coast downward—deceptively slowly at first, then nose-diving suddenly as the impact of more aggressive competition makes itself felt.

No business can rely for its continuity on old customers only. They die off, their patterns of living change, they are lured away by the offerings of competitors. Just when a product is enjoying its peak years of success—when its name is the most prominent in the field—the advertising usually takes a new turn. It shows people who are already familiar with the product new ways of using it, and reasons for using it more often. It enters a new pioneering stage.

The Singer Company, whose name is synonymous with sewing machines throughout the world, is again advertising to get women to make their own clothes, showing the ease of doing so, the money they can save, and the creative enjoyment it affords. Reynolds, a name familiar to housewives for

---

[1] Sidney Furst and Milton Sherman, eds., *Business Decisions That Changed Our Lives* (New York: Random House, 1964), p. 147.

aluminum wrap, introduced the new idea of "Freezer-to-Table Cooking" and advertised "How to cook frozen meat, fish, poultry, without thawing." Johnson & Johnson, whose Band-Aid bandages can be found in medicine chests throughout the country, is continuously advertising a warning to watch out for small scratches, as they may lead to infections, in order to get the bandages out of the medicine chest more often.

In time, other advertisers may move into the new market created by the pioneer. Other sewing-machine companies are going after the new sewing-machine prospects generated by Singer. Besides Johnson & Johnson's Band-Aids, other adhesive bandages are advertised to the public that is aware of such bandages—and the product enters a new competitive stage in that market.

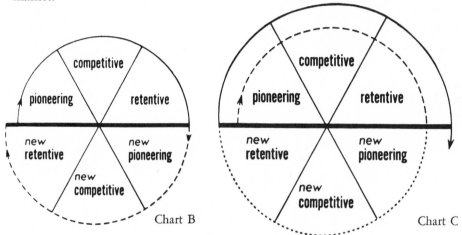

Chart B   Chart C

The product does not actually return to the point at which it first started its career, however; instead, the market stretches out to include the additional buyers now embraced (Chart B). After it has gone through the stages in this field, the product may repeat the movement in other fields, or with new generations, with every turn enlarging the total market of buyers, the process represented by a spiral (Chart C).

MANAGEMENT DECISIONS AT THE RETENTIVE STAGE

As a product approaches the retentive stage, management must make some important marketing decisions.

> —Can it make some significant improvement in the present product so that it virtually represents a new type of product? That's what Gillette did when it came out with its continuous-band-shave razor.

How do you put fresh tomato flavor into a meatloaf, a stew, a sauce, a casserole or a soup bowl? With Campbell's Tomato Soup.

Campbell's Tomato Soup makes it easy to enjoy fresh tomato flavor all year round. Our tomatoes are sun-ripened on the vine. And that sunny flavor, seasoned with a touch of real butter, has made Campbell's Tomato Soup America's favorite. Great as soup! And great for cooking, too! Campbell's Tomato gives you fresh tomato flavor in every can and an easy-to-prepare, kitchen-tested recipe on every label.

M'm! M'm! Good!

Yankee Noodle Bake: For a terrific casserole, begin by browning 8 frankfurters (sliced) with ¾ cup chopped onion. Combine in 1½-qt. casserole with 2 cups cooked medium noodles, 1 can (10¾ oz.) Campbell's Tomato Soup, ½ cup water, 1 tsp. prepared mustard. Top with ¼ cup buttered bread crumbs. Bake at 350°F. for 30 min. 4 servings.

Tomato Meatloaf: When you make your favorite meatloaf (1½ to 2-lb. size) substitute one half cup undiluted Campbell's Tomato Soup for the liquid you normally use. Bake as usual. Pour remaining soup over meatloaf for last 5 min. of baking.

Souper Stew: For a great new flavor, add Campbell's Tomato Soup to stews—beef, chicken or lamb.

Instant Sauce: Want a delicious pour-over sauce? Check the back of Campbell's Tomato Soup label for the recipe. Add parsley, if desired.

CAMPBELL'S SOUP IN NEW PIONEERING STAGE

The name "Campbell's" is almost synonymous with soup. Yet the company continues advertising in the new pioneering stage showing other uses of Campbell's soup. Other advertisements encourage the more frequent serving of soup, as something hot to have in the summer with cold sandwiches.

—The company may come out with a related item—the first step in creating an expanded line? The makers of Clairol first came out with a hair rinse, then with other hair preparations, then with an ever-expanding line of cosmetics. First there was the Frigidaire refrigerator; today there are also the Frigidaire washer, Frigidaire dryer, Frigidaire food-waste disposal, Frigidaire air-conditioners, among their other products. Each shares the prestige of the original product in the line, as well as sharing the company's production resources and marketing skills.

—The company may buy another concern and put all the products under one corporate umbrella. (The handling of a company with diversified products is a separate decision of corporate identity, which we discuss in the trademark chapter.)

—Sometimes a company is a leader in a field, but the whole field is shrinking. That's what happened to Ronson, famed for its table cigarette lighters. The solution of that company was to reach out for other products they could make, with their technical competence. In one full-page ad they subsequently featured the Ronson broiler oven, the Ronson blender, the Ronson hair dryer, and the Ronson electric knife.

These are some typical alternatives. There are, of course, others.

Thus we see that the life cycle of a product may be affected by many conditions. If, however, the product is to continue to be marketed, its own advertising stage must be identified before its advertising goals are set.

USING THE ADVERTISING SPIRAL TO SET POLICY

The advertising spiral is a graphic representation of the advertising stages of products. It provides a point of reference for determining which stage or stages a product has reached at a given time with a given audience, and what the thrust of the advertising message should be. In many respects, the advertising spiral is the advertising parallel to the life cycle of a product, except that it shows where the product can go when it reaches a new high level of success.

A product may not necessarily go through all these stages. It may begin in the competitive stage, and spend its life fighting for a larger share of an expanding market. But the advertising spiral forces one to answer the important questions: In which stage is the product in a given market? Do we need to do pioneering work to create a market? Competitive work to get a larger share of the existing market? What proportion pioneering? What proportion competitive? As we approach the retentive stage, is it time to see whether we can expand the total market for this product, or come out with a new product? These are not just advertising decisions, but marketing decisions.

The Singer Spiral Saga

Nothing to Watch....
but the Flowing Seam

SINGER, always the pioneer, has created a new sewing machine. You sit at ease before it, press a lever ever so gently with the knee, and while you merely guide your material, you watch a perfect seam flow forth, ruffles form like gathering foam or a tiny hem fall into place.

Tucking, shirring, binding, all those deft details of trimming and decoration, you do more perfectly than by hand—and in a tenth the time. Such is the versatile magic of this new Singer Electric that its very presence is a temptation to sew, and the creation of lovely things becomes a fascinating joy.

There is an easy way to prove to yourself what a modern Singer will do. The nearest Singer Shop will gladly send one to your home that you can use for thirty days, in doing your own sewing. You may have your choice of the widest variety of models—electric, treadle and hand machines. Any one of them may be yours on a convenient plan by which you will receive a generous allowance for your present machine, and your new Singer will pay for itself as you save.

The Famous Singer "S"

is one of the oldest of trade-marks. You will find it on the windows of 6,000 Singer Shops, in every city in the world. It is the identifying mark of sewing machines of enduring quality. It means, too, that every Singer Shop is ready always with instruction, repairs, supplies and courteous expert service.

When the Singer representative comes to your home let him tell you about this service Singer maintains in your neighborhood, wherever you live.

"Short Cuts to Home Sewing"—*Free*

This interesting practical book shows you how to save time in a hundred ways on your sewing machine— how to do all the modish new details of trimming. It will help with your sewing no matter what make of machine you may have—or even though you have none now. The book is free. Simply phone or call at the nearest Singer Shop (see telephone directory) or send for a copy by mail, postpaid.

Singer Sewing Machine Company, Dept. 32A, Singer Bldg., N. Y.

SINGER
SEWING MACHINES

Entire contents of this advertisement copyright 1926-7 by The Singer Manufacturing Co.

THE SINGER ELECTRIC
SEWING MACHINE
IN THE PIONEERING STAGE

The electric sewing machine was introduced by Singer with this advertisement of 1927 in true pioneering fashion—explaining the "versatile magic" of this new way of sewing.

As electric sewing machines became widely accepted, with different brands on the market, Singer came out over the years with improvements, providing product differentials to give it an advantage over competitors, as exemplified by this advertisement of the late 1960s.

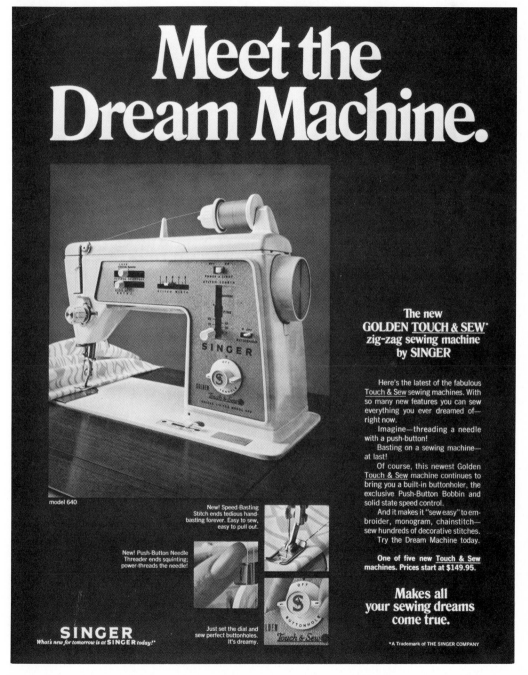

Make the most of yourself—

Fit to Flatter—exclusive Speed Basting gives you stitches up to 2 inches long! Ends tedious hand-basting.

Show-Off Buttonholes are simple to make with the Built-in Buttonholer. Just set the dial—it's sew easy!

Push-Button Bobbin winds right *in* the machine. It's exclusive! So's the whole threading system that keeps stitching smooth, even.

Happy Ending: zig-zag your way to stronger, smoother seam finishes with The Dream Machine. Ideal for knits, synthetic fabrics.

make it with The Dream Machine.

Go ahead—cover yourself with glory! Discover how easy it is to sew up the great clothes you've dreamed of—with The Dream Machine. The newest Golden Touch & Sew® sewing machine by Singer. This fabulous zig-zag has all the special features we've shown here—and lots more! Sew on it today at the Singer Center near you.

See all 5 Touch & Sew machines. There's one priced at only $149.95. Other Singer sewing machines are priced from $69.95 at your Singer Center. And Singer has a credit plan to fit *your* budget.

What's new for tomorrow is at SINGER *today!**

*A Trademark of THE SINGER COMPANY

Model 640

The SINGER SEWING MACHINE IN A NEW PIONEERING STAGE
—THE ADVERTISING ANSWER

Instead of basking in the retentive stage with something like "Singer for Sewing," Singer went off in two directions: From the advertising viewpoint, it went into a new pioneering stage, encouraging women to sew their own clothes—"Discover how easy it is to sew up the great clothes you've dreamed of."

Now Singer is "riding on its name" by also going into the vacuum cleaner business.

Give everyone our best

Give the **Stylist** zig-zag portable sewing machine by Singer with case. Makes buttonholes and embroiders. **$139.95.**

Choose a **Singer Vacuum:** Golden Power Master upright **$89.95.** Golden Glide canister **$99.95.** Power Sweeper **$29.95.**

Colorful Array of sewing boxes and baskets at Singer from **$1.49** to **$14.98.**

Give the **Fashion Mate** zig-zag portable sewing machine by Singer with case. **$88.00.**

Give **One Touch Sewing** on the newest Golden Touch & Sew sewing machine by Singer in the handsome Bakersfield desk. Features the exclusive Push-Button Bobbin, a built-in button-holer, plus a choice of nine stretch stitches.

Give the **Little Touch & Sew** sewing machine by Singer to the little girl on your list; really sews lockstitches. **$16.95.**

FREE INSTRUCTIONS show you how to use your new Singer sewing machine.
FREE GIFT WRAP all bright and be-ribboned — to save you Christmas tie-ups.
FREE DELIVERY anywhere in the U.S.A. including Alaska and Hawaii.
GIVE A SINGER GIFT CERTIFICATE to the friend who's hard to shop for.

The Singer 1 to 36 Credit Plan helps you keep Christmas **within your budget**... or you may defer monthly payments till Feb., 1971. Or — use the Singer Lay-Away Plan — deposit holds any item till Dec. 19.

Get the **SINGER** spirit!

For address of the Singer Sewing Center nearest you, see White Pages under SINGER COMPANY.   *A Trademark of THE SINGER COMPANY.

1. What is the "advertising spiral"?

2. Can you give an example of a product chiefly in (a) the pioneering stage, (b) the competitive stage, (c) the retentive stage, (d) a new pioneering stage?

3. What is the essence of the advertising message in presenting a product at each stage? What concepts must be stressed?

4. Can you cite two situations where a product's advertising can be at more than one stage at a time?

5. What are the major advantages and the major risks of doing the pioneering advertising for a product?

6. Why is the retentive stage a critical one for a product?

7. Cite several examples of important marketing and advertising decisions that might be considered as a product approaches the retentive stage.

8. Can you explain why some products that are new do not begin in the pioneering stage?

9. Why is it important for an advertiser to decide the stage of the spiral his product is in?

10. Different advertisers in the same product category may see their products at different stages of the spiral. Explain how this can happen.

Reading Suggestions

Brink, Edward L., and William T. Kelley, *The Management of Promotion,* Chapter 7. Englewood Cliffs, N.J.: Prentice-Hall, Inc., 1963. Excerpted in Kleppner and Settel, *Exploring Advertising,* p. 70.

Durkee, Burton R., *How to Make Advertising Work.* New York: McGraw-Hill Book Company, 1967.

Forrester, Jay W., "Advertising: A Problem in Industrial Dynamics," *Harvard Business Review,* March–April 1959, pp. 100–110. Also in Kleppner and Settel, *Exploring Advertising,* p. 47.

Levitt, Theodore, "Exploit the Product Life Cycle," *Harvard Business Review,* November–December 1965, p. 81ff.

Wasson, Chester R., *Product Management: Product Life Cycles and Competitive Marketing Strategy.* St. Charles, Ill.: Challenge Books, 1971.

Weilbacher, W. M., "What Happens to Advertisements When They Grow Up," *Public Opinion Quarterly,* Summer 1970, pp. 216–223.

5

Target Marketing

Procter & Gamble has long been well known for its marketing capabilities in the detergent and food-products fields. In the late 1950's, P & G entered the paper-products field. By the early 1970's, P & G's Bounty paper towels and Charmin toilet tissues were market leaders, and Pampers disposable diapers had captured the bulk of that product's sales.

P & G's ability to market new products effectively to the housewife was again a dominant factor in its success. The company was demonstrating not so much its skill in manufacturing paper-goods as its skill in creating products for a market, and in creating markets for a product. This approach to advertising via marketing is the subject of the present chapter.

What Is a Product?

To those who are buying it, any product represents a bundle of satisfactions. Some of these satisfactions are purely functional—a car is for getting places, a watch is for telling time, a camera is for taking pictures. Some of the satisfactions are psychological—a car may be for showing what a sporty person the owner is, a watch may represent a beautiful piece of jewelry, a camera may be used to show how up to date the owner is. Different people have different ideas about the satisfactions that are important to each of them when they consider a product. Although some may want a sporty car, others may want a family car. Some men want transportation at as low a price as possible, and others may want all the luxury in driving that money can buy.

Products are designed with satisfactions to match the interests of a particular group of consumers. That is why every car company makes a wide range of cars, each with many variations. Within the product class of cameras, there is equipment that is simple to operate and geared to nonexperts, and there is also sophisticated, controls-laden equipment for the serious photographer. (Note that cameras are not strictly divided by price, since some simple equipment can be more expensive than some of the complex devices.)

Yankelovich defined three groups of consumers in the watch field on the basis of values each sought from the product. These are:

1. People who want to pay the lowest possible price for any watch that works reasonably well. If the watch fails after six months or a year, they will throw it out and replace it.

2. People who value watches for their long life, good workmanship, good material, and good styling. They are willing to pay for these product qualities.

3. People who look not only for useful product features but also for meaningful emotional qualities. The most important consideration in this segment is that the watch should suitably symbolize an important occasion. Consequently, fine styling, a well-known brand name, the recommendation of the jeweler, and a gold or diamond case are highly valued.[1]

Hence, when we look at a can of coffee or a Cadillac car, for instance, we do not see just a tin can holding coffee, or an expensive car with a big wheelbase. We try to picture the kind of person enjoying a mildly stimulating and warming drink, or we try to picture the owner of the Cadillac. Target marketing means focusing on groups of people who seek similar satisfactions from a product.

Changing product styles. Few products are static in the wake of product development. For generations after the fountain pen had become a standard writing instrument, no up-and-coming young man would be without his Waterman pen. But after World War II, a new writing marvel appeared on the scene—the ballpoint pen, which was advertised as a pen that would write under water (even though no one explained why you should want to write under water). People stood on line to buy them at five dollars. By the 1960's, prices of ballpoint pens had come way down, and they were being sold more like long-lasting pencils than as pens. But meanwhile, fountain pens had entered a new life; they were offered as luxury items, often in gold and set in expensive desk stands, providing a different set of consumer satisfactions than those of the ballpoints. A pen is not just a pen; markets change with the product, and products change with the market.

WHAT IS A MARKET?

"Almost all advertising and marketing men could answer this question," said Sissors, "and yet many would give different answers to the same question." He then offered eight definitions commonly used.[2]

---

[1] Daniel Yankelovich, "New Criteria for Market Segmentation," *Harvard Business Review,* March–April 1964, p. 133.

[2] Jack Z. Sissors, "What Makes a Market," *Journal of Marketing,* July 1966, p. 17.

Lest we be accused of making life still more complicated by trying to combine all those eight definitions into one, or by coming out with still another definition, we shall rephrase the question: "What is the first step in describing a market from the viewpoint of advertising?" As a starter, we view a market as a group of people (1) who can be identified by some common characteristic, interest, or problem; (2) who could use our product to advantage; and (3) who could afford to buy it. Examples of potential markets: mothers of young children, teen-age girls, skiers, fathers worried about financially protecting their families, or people suffering from corns.

We will pursue the question of defining a market throughout the book.

The *majority fallacy* is a term applied to the assumption once frequently made that every product should be aimed at, and acceptable to, a majority of all consumers. Kuehn and Day have described how successive brands all aimed at a majority of a given market will tend to have rather similar characteristics, and will neglect an opportunity to serve consumer minorities. They offer an illustration from the field of chocolate cake mixes: Good-sized minorities would make a light-chocolate cake and a very dark chocolate cake, respectively, their first choice over the competitive medium-chocolate cakes, even though the latter would be the majority choice of the whole market. So while several initial entrants into the field would do best to market a medium-chocolate mix to appeal to the broadest group of consumers, later entrants might well gain a larger market share by gaining the first-choice preference among a minority of the market.[3]

WHAT IS THE COMPETITION?

We speak of competition in the broadest sense, to include all forces that are inhibiting the sales of a product. They may be products in the same subclass as your product, or the same product class, or forces outside the category of your product.

Does the "small cigar" primarily compete with other brands of small cigars (subclass), with full-sized cigars (product class), or with cigarettes (beyond product class)?

Does instant iced tea compete with non-instant iced tea, iced coffee, or soda pop? With hot tea or coffee? With beer? With alcoholic beverages? In short, is the competitive array that of tea, of cold nonalcoholic beverages, or of refreshment generally?

The competitive array can widen even further as the basic price of the product increases. For example, in terms of the suburbanite's family budget,

---

[3] Alfred A. Kuehn and Ralph A. Day, "Strategy of Product Quality," *Harvard Business Review,* November–December 1962, pp. 100ff.

the real competition for a brand of riding mower (garden tractor) may well *not* be other brands. Rather, for such a purchase, involving over $1,500 in some instances, the competition could be central air conditioning or a family vacation.

The immediate competition for a product already in the market is that of other products in its class. How does this product compare with the others in differentials? In total sale? In share of the market? In the sales of this particular brand? What do consumers like and dislike about the products being offered, including the one under consideration?

MARKET SEGMENTATION

In speaking of marketing trends in the twentieth century, Frank, Massy, and Wind say:

> . . . Improvement in transportation and communication made it possible to define markets broadly, often in terms of national boundaries and beyond. Thus the concept of the mass market emerged and came to dominate much business thought. By standardizing products and selling them to a broad range of customer types, it was possible to reduce production costs. . . . But the last twenty years have seen at least a partial reversal of these trends. For many products the mass market has become larger than necessary to achieve economies of scale. Improved production techniques have made diversity of product offerings technically possible. . . . Consumers were willing to embrace standardized products only as the costs of diversity remained high.[4]

As the production "costs of diversity" have come down, the variety of new products has proliferated, each for a special segment of the population. Market segmentation is the process of focusing market effort on the group most interested in the particular service or values a product offers. Its premise is that an effort focused on a selective market may prove more fruitful than a broad appeal to a broad market. The fact that a market is selective does not preclude it from being, or becoming, a very large one.

The idea behind market segmentation is not new. In fact, the first person to discover that mass production alone was not the answer to marketing problems was the man who developed mass production—Henry Ford.[5] For

---

[4] Ronald E. Frank, William F. M. Massy, and Yoram Wind, *Market Segmentation* (Englewood Cliffs, N.J.: Prentice-Hall, Inc., 1972), p. 4.

[5] All cars made at the beginning of the century when Ford began were costly to make. Fords were, too. They were considered "rich men's toys." Ford perceived that there was no future in making automobiles for that market. The industry would have to sell cars to the masses, and it never could unless the price came down. It was this marketing perception that launched Ford into his creation of mass-production techniques.

many years he used his new mass-production techniques with spectacular success, producing and selling millions of his low-priced, completely standardized Model T cars—all one model, all one color (black). Any change, he felt, would increase the cost of the car, with consequent loss of buyers. Meanwhile, others came out with different model cars in different colors to meet the varying tastes of the public. The Ford Motor Company went through a business crisis before it recognized that people have varying needs and tastes, and are willing to pay for them. Now every car company offers such a range of models and colors that cars are almost custom-made.

Market segmentation has loomed into importance in recent years, not because industry is producing such huge volumes of goods, but because of diversity. It has also been fostered by the increased purchasing power of many who can now afford to choose from the greater variety of products available. Another great influence has been the pressure on business concerns to come out with new products to spur the company rate of growth, and to offset products whose peak of sales has passed. (As this is being written, *Advertising Age* reports that the Ralston Purina Company is going to market a line of health foods—the first major company to do so.)[6]

Segmentation can be brought about by creating a product variation to meet the needs of a focused market, or by positioning the product through an appeal to attract a focused market, or by both.

Creating a product for focused interests. One of the principal ways that marketers attract a focused interest group is through variations in the conventional product. These variations are based on research, observation, or intuition that suggests a large enough submarket with an interest in the product offering. Thus, in refrigerators, the development of small apartment refrigerators and smaller office refrigerators, as well as small decorator-designed refrigerators for the living room or family room, came about because of a growing group of consumers interested in, and believing they would like, such a product variation. Similarly, beers for those who prefer a lighter or stronger taste, facial and toilet tissues in decorator colors or floral designs—all these are product variations based on the existence of some prospectively interested and large enough group of consumers.

To meet the needs of the one-person household, foods are being packed in small-size packages; Hunt's Reddi-Bacon, for example, can be cooked in a toaster without any mess, and comes four slices to the packet, four packets to the box. On the other hand, the Swanson Frozen Foods division of the Campbell Soup Company offers the Hungry Man's Dinner, which includes a second helping of meat. It was created as a result of research showing that many men felt that frozen-food dinners did not provide big enough portions. Crest toothpaste was the first to be recognized by the American

---

[6] *Advertising Age,* July 21, 1972, p. 2.

It's almost too good to believe – new 8-ounce Philadelphia Brand Imitation Cream Cheese has only 432 calories in the whole package! That's only 54 calories an ounce* (or 42 calories less than regular cream cheese). Give it your own taste test. Spread it on bagels, toast or muffins. Blend it in a dip. Melt it in a cream sauce. Bake a cheese cake with it. It looks, cooks and tastes like regular cream cheese. It's lower in fat, higher in protein, too.

PRODUCTS CREATED FOR
MARKET SEGMENTS

Philadelphia Imitation Cream Cheese was created for those who are watching their calories.

The Hamburger Helper was packaged for a family of five. Each of these products is targeted at a special group.

Dental Association for using stannous fluoride, and has been stressing its ability to prevent cavities, while conversely, Ultra-Brite toothpaste was formulated primarily to help teeth look brighter. A mail-order company has built a large national business selling wearing apparel for tall men only.

There is much segmentation in the coffee market. Regular coffee, first of all, differs among brands in price, taste, and the way it is ground to suit different ways of brewing it (for electric percolators, filter devices, drip pots, and so on). Instant and freeze-dried coffees are offered for those who want the convenience of just adding water. Then there is decaffeinated coffee, appealing to the large group who, for health reasons, want to avoid caffeine. Each type of coffee is designed to satisfy a different market of people who drink coffee. The introductions of a low-acid coffee (Kava) and of a chicory-flavored coffee (Luzianne) were both made to attract a small but steady group of consumers.

Whit Hobbs reports an experience with the S.C. Johnson Company (furniture wax) when the account was first assigned to his agency. The product had clear advantages over competition, but sales had been sliding. Instead of embarking on a campaign to stress product differentials, the agency conducted research to find out why the sales were declining. He reports:

> It wasn't a healthy market. . . . What was the problem? The problem was that women hated to wax their furniture. It was a chore and a bore. They did it once or twice a month and wished it were even less often than that. On the other hand, research pointed out that women *dust* their furniture nearly every day. And this fact led to a strategic question: What would happen if you could get that once-a-month furniture wax onto the dust cloth?
>
> What happened was a remarkable sales success. The creative team took this get-it-on-the-dust-cloth creative strategy and came up with the promise of "waxed beauty instantly as you dust." The Johnson product, Pledge, did not merely stop the decline; it doubled the market.[7]

How different interest groups of consumers in the home-gardening market can be attracted by product variations in lawn mowers designed specifically for them is illustrated by Boyd and Levy. They examine three major types of gardeners—small casual, small careful, and large casual.

—The first is characterized by intermittent gardening work on a random schedule, and interest in grass primarily for cover. This kind of gardener is seen as wanting a lawn mower that is simple, rugged, inexpensive, and easy to use.

---

[7] Whit Hobbs, "Copy Strategy," in *The Management of Advertising,* ed. Roger Barton (New York: McGraw-Hill Book Company, 1970), p. 14–4.

A Product Created Through Positioning

—The second is characterized as working in the garden extensively on a planned-care basis, and is seen as near-compulsive in the desire for perfection. This gardener's interest in lawn mowers is for special attachments and adjustable blades, for which he is willing to pay a premium price.

—The large casual gardener is characterized as being interested in making a "big production" of his work on great sweeps of lawn. In his "mini-estate" view of his lawn, this kind of gardener wants a big fancy lawn mower, with gadgets, and will pay a premium for these features.[8]

---

[8] Harper Boyd and Sidney Levy, "New Dimension in Consumer Analysis," *Harvard Business Review*, November–December 1963, p. 129.

In many product fields today, there are so many sets of particular consumer needs and interests that a single standardized product with some appeal to many people may fare less well than, or have the market nibbled away by, products tailored to appeal strongly to a segment of the market.

Positioning by choice of appeal. Sometimes you can position, or reposition, a product without making any physical changes, just by changing the advertising appeal. Kleenex tissues, as cited in an earlier chapter, came out as a paper handkerchief, but changed its positioning to a facial tissue, which launched a new industry. Noxzema was repositioned from a skin medication to a beauty treatment. It is now the largest-selling skin cream in the world.

SEGMENTATION—GOING AFTER PARENTS OF KIDS

Crest is directing pioneering advertising toward parents to get their children to brush their teeth, with a minor competitive plug for Crest.

How to get your kids to brush.

Truth, not tricks.

Little people are very smart people. Smart, and curious, and enthralled with the answers to "why." So, rather than offering them money or something for each time they brush, which doesn't tell them the answer to "why," offer them the truth.

Tell them all about their teeth and how they're living things (kind of like toes, or eyes, or skin) and can be hurt. That there are many shapes of teeth, some for chewing, some for biting, some for grinding.

Tell them that even though food is good for their bodies, some food, particularly if it's sweet, can cause cavities if it stays on their teeth very long. But if they brush their teeth soon after eating, brush well, up and down, back and around, they can remove the food. And take care of those teeth that are alive and belong to them.

Explain what cavities are. (Holes in teeth might be enough of an explanation.)

And by all means, let them see you brush, too. What you do is more believable than what you say.

A little help from your friends.

If your kids are going to do their job (brushing after every meal), the toothpaste they use ought to do its job. And Crest with fluoride does.

Crest fights cavities. Crest is accepted by the American Dental Association.*
And, on top of all that, it tastes good.
Regular flavor tastes a little like bubble gum, and mint tastes a lot like mint.
Tell your kids all about their teeth and about Crest. We honestly feel that's the way to get them to brush.

Fighting cavities is the whole idea behind Crest.

QT suntan preparation had been promoted as a suntan oil that also tanned the skin indoors. But the advertising was repositioned to stress its special cosmetic usefulness. "QT makes the imperfect tan perfect," said its new advertising, which showed girls how QT could match up the gaps in the tan, such as those left by strap marks from bathing suits. QT's market share in the field was the only one to show growth.[9]

Kikkoman soy sauce is best known as a special seasoning. In order to popularize its use as a general seasoning, the maker advertised its other specific applications, and urged housewives to make Kikkoman sauce an on-the-table partner of salt and pepper.

Elsewhere in this book we speak of going after the younger generation, but Johnson & Johnson reversed the play by appealing to the older generation to use their baby powder and baby oil for themselves. "It's not just for baby; it's good for adults," with separate campaigns for men, women, teenagers. The product remained the same; but the positioning was changed and sales doubled.[10]

THE PROFILE OF THE MARKET

We now address ourselves to the overall market for the product. First we ask, What is the overall usage of this type of product? This might be defined in terms of dollar sales, percentage of households who use such a product, or the total number of units. Has the field been growing or dwindling? What is the share of the market enjoyed by those in the business, by territories? What change has taken place in the past few years in their ranking? What is the chief product advantage featured by each brand?

Where are the best markets? In which territory are most products of this type sold? For example, only 25 percent of the homes in St. Paul use instant coffee, but 52 percent of the homes in Milwaukee do; baked beans are almost twice as popular in Omaha (83 percent of the households are users) as in Pensacola (42 percent). In Wichita, 34 percent of the homes use instant tea, but in Duluth-Superior, only 7 percent do; 66 percent of the households in Indianapolis have electric shavers, but only 34 percent of those in West Palm Beach do.[11]

Another breakdown used is by location in terms of metropolitan center city, metropolitan suburb, and non-metropolitan territory.

---

9 *Advertising Age,* November 18, 1971, p. 3.

10 *Ibid.* August 14, 1972, p. 3.

11 *19th Annual Consumer Consolidated Analysis,* 1964, published by 13 newspapers, including the *Milwaukee Journal,* 1964.

**Recommended Standard Breakdowns For Demographic Characteristics
In Surveys of Consumer Media Audiences**

I. DATA FOR HOUSEHOLDS:

	Minimum Basic Data	Additional Data Highly Desired
A. **County Size:** (see Note 1)	A County Size B County Size C County Size D County Size	

B. **Geographic Area:**
(see Notes 2 & 3)

Minimum Basic Data:
Metropolitan Area
Non Metropolitan Area
  Farm
  Non Farm

Additional Data Highly Desired:
Urban
  Urbanized Areas
    Central Cities
    Urban fringe
  Other urban
    Places of 10,000 or more
    Places of 2,500 to 10,000
    Rural places of 1,000 to 2,500
  Other rural

Metropolitan Area:
1,000,000 and over
500,000 - 999,999
250,000 - 499,999
100,000 - 249,999
50,000 - 99,999

C. **Geographic Region:**
(see Notes 4 & 5)

Minimum Basic Data:
New England
Metro New York
Mid Atlantic
East Central
Metro Chicago
West Central
South East
South West
Pacific

Additional Data Highly Desired:
North East
North Central
South
West

D. **Ages of Children:**

Minimum Basic Data:
No Child Under 18
Youngest Child 6-17
Youngest Child Under 6

Additional Data Highly Desired:
Youngest Child 12-17
Youngest Child 6-11
Youngest Child 2-5
Youngest Child under 2

E. **Family Size:**
Minimum Basic Data:
1 or 2 members
3 or 4 members
5 or more members

F. **Family Income:**

Minimum Basic Data:
Under $5,000.
$5,000 - 7,999.
$8,000 - 9,999.
Over $10,000.

Additional Data Highly Desired:
Under $3,000.
$ 3,000 - 4,999.
$10,000 - 14,999.
$15,000 - 24,999.
$25,000 and over

G. **Home Ownership:**

Minimum Basic Data:
Own home
Rent home

Additional Data Highly Desired:
Residence Five Years Prior to Survey Date
  Lived in same house
  Lived in different house
    In same county
    In different county

H. **Home Characteristic:**
Minimum Basic Data:
Single family dwelling unit
Multiple family dwelling unit

I. **Race:**
Additional Data Highly Desired:
White
Non-White

J. **Household Possessions:**
Additional Data Highly Desired:
Data on household possessions or purchases will presumably be governed by the medium's particular selling needs.

II. DATA FOR INDIVIDUALS:

	Minimum Basic Data	Additional Data Highly Desired
A. **Age:**	Under 6 6-11 12-17 18-34 35-49 50-64 65 and over	18-24 25-34
B. **Sex:**	Male Female	

C. **Education:**
Grade school or less (grades 1-8)
Some high school
Graduated high school (grades 9-12)
Some college
Graduated college

D. **Marital Status:**
Married
Single
Widowed
Divorced

E. **Occupation:**
Professional, Semi-Professional
Proprietor, Manager, Official
Clerical, Sales
Craftsman, Foreman, Service Worker
Operative, Non-Farm Laborer
Farmer, Farm Laborer
Retired
Student
Unemployed

F. **Individual Possessions:**
Data on individual possessions or purchases will presumably be governed by the medium's particular selling needs.

III. DATA FOR HOUSEHOLD HEADS:

	Minimum Basic Data	Additional Data Highly Desired
A. **Sex:**	Male Female	
B. **Age:**	34 and younger 35-49 50-64 65 and older	18-24 25-34

C. **Education:**
Grade school or less (grades 1-8)
Some high school
Graduated high school (grades 9-12)
Some college
Graduated college

D. **Occupation:**
Professional, Semi-Professional
Proprietor, Manager, Official
Clerical, Sales
Craftsman, Foreman, Service Worker
Operative, Non-Farm Laborer
Farmer, Farm Laborer
Retired
Student
Unemployed

IV. DATA FOR HOUSEWIVES:

	Minimum Basic Data	Additional Data Highly Desired
A. **Age:**	34 and younger 35-49 50-64 65 and over	18-24 25-34

B. **Education:**
Grade school or less (grades 1-8)
Some high school
Graduated high school (grades 9-12)
Some college
Graduated college

C. **Employment:**
Not employed outside home
Employed outside home
  Employed Full Time (30 hours or more per week)
  Employed Part Time (Less than 30 hours per week)

Demographic breakdowns, as recommended by the American Association of Advertising Agencies, Inc.

PROFILE OF THE BUYER

When a seller meets a buyer face to face, he soon knows much about the buyer and his family, and how they live. A national advertiser speaking to thousands or millions of prospective buyers cannot hope to attain such a relationship. The most he can hope to do is formulate a picture based on a statistical average of where and how they live, their economic and social backgrounds, and other demographic data. A list of these significant demographic characteristics of the buyer of a product, which each advertiser has to develop for himself, is referred to as a *buyer profile*. For example, the basic facts all advertisers want to know about the users of their products are sex and age.

An advertiser then seeks other information about the consumer, relevant to the sale of his product. If it is food, he will want to know the size of the family. A demographic profile of heavy users of hot cereals showed them to be young housewives, 30–39 years of age, in the upper income group, with three or more children. For heating equipment, an advertiser will want to know whether or not a person owns his own home. A car advertiser will want to know which car or cars a person owns now, his approximate income, occupation, education, and size of family. In each case the advertiser has a profile to describe the buyers of his product. This will be important to him when he is scheduling media and determining what to say in advertisements.

The foregoing demographic breakdowns are recommended to media in making their demographic surveys. Advertisers can then compare their demographic profile with those of any media they are considering.

Heavy users. For any product, there will always be a small percentage of users who are responsible for a vastly disproportionate share of the product's sales. According to Simmons, 17 percent of the total male users of beer accounted for 48 percent of beer consumption; 13 percent of male laxative users accounted for 59 percent of laxative consumption; among women, 22 percent use 47 percent of the cake mixes, 30 percent use 57 percent of the peanut butter, and 26 percent use 56 percent of the instant coffee consumed.[12]

For the advertiser, "heavy users" are obviously prime prospects to try to reach.

Psychographic characteristics. Between two groups of buyers who have the same social and economic demographic characteristics, there will still be a big difference in the nature and extent of their purchases. This fact has led to an inquiry beyond demographics to try to explain the reason for such differences, and in turn to further sharpening of the view of a buyer in terms of *psychographic characteristics—personality traits*, chiefly in willingness to try something new. The group more willing to do so is referred to as *creative consumers,* in contrast to *passive consumers*. In connection with this study, Demby reports:

---

[12] *Simmons Marketing Digest,* W. R. Simmons & Associates, New York.

HEAVY USERS
Female Heads Reflecting Household Usage

PRODUCT CLASS	HEAVY USER DEFINITION	% TOTAL USERS	% TOTAL USAGE
American cheese	1 lb+ /wk	34	64
Baby food	15+ jars/wk	33	63
Biscuit mixes	3+ pkgs/mo	27	63
Breakfast mixes	11+ glasses/wk	23	47
Butter	1 lb+ /wk	48	75
Cake mixes	4+ pkgs/mo	22	47
Catsup	2½ bottles/mo	30	67
Cereal, cold			
Unsweetened	11+ portions/wk	21	40
Presweetened	8+ portions/wk	30	55
Cereal, hot	5+ portions/wk	38	70
Colas (soft drinks)			
Regular	5+ glasses/wk	45	78
Low calorie	5+ glasses/wk	37	69
Coffee			
Regular ground	7+ cups avg/day	35	60
Instant	5+ cups/day	26	56
Corn snacks	8+ pkgs/mo	14	41
Crackers			
Flavored snack	4+ pkgs/mo	16	45
Other salted	5+ pkgs/mo	29	67
Flour—all-purpose	4+ bags/mo	32	68
Frosting, mixes	3+ pkgs/mo	39	71
Frozen dinners	7+ pkgs/mo	22	44
Gelatin dessert	8+ pkgs/po	21	47
Ice cream	20+ pkgs/mo	21	45
Margarine			
Regular/whipped	2+ lbs/wk	21	49
Diet	1+ lb/wk	40	67
Mayonnaise	8+ jars/mo	20	51
Mayonnaise salad dressing	8+ jars/mo	18	47
Nondairy cream subs			
Liquid or frozen	4+ pkgs/mo	34	71
Powder	2+ pkgs/mo	19	53
Noodles	6+ pkgs/mo	15	43
Orange juice—frozen	5+ glasses/day	25	52
Pancake/waffle mixes	2½+ pkgs/mo	28	63
Peanut butter	4+ jars/mo	30	57
Potatoes, instant	6+ pkgs/mo	23	61
Potato chips	8+ pkgs/mo	49	31
Pudding or pie filling	8+ pkgs/mo	39	70

Courtesy: W. B. Simmons & Associates Research, Inc. ©.

An interesting lesson in the study of the acceptance of new products . . . those which changed a person's life-style, and those which did not. Those which did not change a person's life-style had a good chance of reaching the mass market. Those which did change a person's life-style, or cooking style, or serving style, would be more quickly purchased by the creative consumer, those who are constantly looking for new products.[13]

---

[13] Address to the Media Research Group, American Marketing Association, at the Americana Hotel, New York, March 17, 1970.

SOURCES OF USAGE AND DEMOGRAPHIC DATA

Advertisers and agencies making marketing and media plans rely heavily on the syndicated services to which they subscribe for their research information on the users of the product. The *Simmons Reports,* as an outstanding example, are based on personal interviews on a year-round basis. The annual total sample for magazines includes 27,000 interviews with 15,000 respondents, with 12,000 supplying a full bank of marketing and behavioral information, and 7,000 keeping two-week diary entries in the fall. Readership and viewership information is gathered for 65 magazines, as well as major TV time periods, newspapers, and radio stations. The report gives the heavy-user demographics for 250 different products, and compares this usage with the audiences of different media. Such information is invaluable in media planning.

Another source of information about a market is the special surveys made by individual media, for the purpose of providing the advertiser such information and thus pointing up the desirability of the medium in reaching his markets. The following profile of new small-car buyers, prepared by *U.S. News & World Report,* comes from such a survey. This is followed by a report of research made by the American Sheep Producers Council regarding the market for lamb; the report was a basis for a campaign to encourage the use of lamb.

PROFILE OF NEW SMALL-CAR BUYERS

The accompanying profile of 1971 new-car buyers of six small cars distributed by U.S. manufacturers is based on responses from some 4,500 owners of these six cars to a survey conducted by *U.S. News & World Report.* (The respondents represent about 52% of those surveyed.)

Note how the profiles differ. Cricket, for example, is stronger among those in the 35–49 age brackets, and with $10,000–$24,999 incomes. Vega is more popular with younger car buyers (18–34 age brackets), and Hornet with those over 50. Capri, in contrast, shows up strongest among those over $15,000 in income, with college education or beyond, and—particularly—with one-person families. Gremlin has more appeal to those with somewhat larger families.

New Car Buyers by Education of Household Head

	TOTAL	HORNET	GREMLIN	COLT	VEGA	CAPRI	CRICKET
High school or less	38.1%	42.5%	41.0%	41.1%	37.2%	26.6%	42.3%
Some college	29.4	24.9	32.5	32.3	27.6	31.3	27.8
Graduated college	14.1	12.4	13.6	11.7	16.8	19.3	10.3
Postgraduate college study	15.1	14.4	8.9	11.5	17.1	20.8	15.7
No answer/Don't know	3.4	5.7	4.0	3.5	1.4	1.9	4.0
Total *	100.0%	100.0%	100.0%	100.0%	100.0%	100.0%	100.0%

* *May not add to 100.0% due to rounding.*

By Age of Household Head

	TOTAL	HORNET	GREMLIN	COLT	VEGA	CAPRI	CRICKET
Under 18	.1%	—	.3%	—	.1%	.1%	—
18–24	17.1	5.9%	20.1	19.8%	19.2	21.6	15.8%
25–34	25.6	23.6	26.7	25.0	29.9	26.3	22.6
35–44	16.8	16.0	17.3	14.0	17.5	14.2	22.2
45–49	12.0	9.7	13.0	13.3	10.6	11.9	13.2
50–64	22.1	29.5	17.9	23.0	18.9	22.3	20.3
65 and over	4.4	12.7	1.8	3.5	3.4	1.8	3.3
No answer	1.9	2.6	2.8	1.3	.4	1.8	2.4
Total *	100.0%	100.0%	100.0%	100.0%	100.0%	100.0%	100.0%
Median age	38.7 yrs.	46.6 yrs.	35.9 yrs.	38.3 yrs.	35.3 yrs.	35.7 yrs.	39.7 yrs.

* May not add to 100.0% due to rounding.

New Car Buyers by Total Yearly Household Income

	TOTAL	HORNET	GREMLIN	COLT	VEGA	CAPRI	CRICKET
Under $8,000	18.4%	20.9%	21.0%	23.2%	19.4%	11.5%	15.9%
$8,000–$9,999	13.1	14.5	13.2	13.8	14.4	10.8	12.7
$10,000–$14,999	28.7	31.0	28.7	27.5	26.6	27.8	30.6
$15,000–$24,999	24.8	19.0	24.4	23.7	26.7	28.3	26.0
$25,000 and over	8.9	6.3	7.0	6.2	8.8	15.2	8.7
No answer/Don't know	6.1	8.3	5.8	5.6	4.1	6.5	6.0
Total *	100.0%	100.0%	100.0%	100.0%	100.0%	100.0%	100.0%
Median income	$12,692	$11,688	$12,252	$11,862	$12,658	$14,408	$12,994

* May not add to 100.0% due to rounding.

New Car Buyers by Size of Household

	TOTAL	HORNET	GREMLIN	COLT	VEGA	CAPRI	CRICKET
One	10.8%	10.7%	8.2%	10.5%	12.0%	14.4%	8.1%
Two	25.5	26.9	25.5	28.1	23.6	26.1	22.5
Three	21.6	18.3	24.4	23.5	21.0	20.6	22.2
Four	20.7	20.9	22.1	19.5	21.5	19.1	21.6
Five	10.1	9.3	7.2	8.3	11.7	10.0	13.6
Six	4.1	5.2	4.3	3.7	4.2	3.6	4.1
Seven	3.1	2.8	3.4	3.4	2.8	2.7	3.3
No answer/Don't know	4.1	5.8	3.1	3.1	3.6	4.5	4.5
Total *	100.0%	100.0%	100.0%	100.0%	100.0%	100.0%	100.0%

* May not add to 100.0% due to rounding.

New Car Buyers by Occupation of Household Head

	TOTAL	HORNET	GREMLIN	COLT	VEGA	CAPRI	CRICKET
Professional, Technical, Official/Proprietor	46.7%	42.1%	43.7%	41.4%	47.3%	58.5%	44.6%
Clerical/Sales	10.5	9.6	10.4	10.1	10.9	10.4	11.4
Craftsman/Foreman/ Factory worker/ Service worker/ Laborer	25.3	24.2	29.8	30.2	24.6	17.7	27.5
Retired/Unemployed	5.5	13.3	3.5	5.8	4.2	2.6	4.0
Student	2.9	1.7	2.8	2.4	4.2	3.0	3.2
Housewife (not employed outside home)	1.3	2.3	.6	1.1	1.7	.9	1.0
Other	3.9	2.2	4.0	6.5	4.3	3.9	2.8
No answer	3.9	4.7	5.2	2.5	2.8	3.0	5.4
Total *	100.0%	100.0%	100.0%	100.0%	100.0%	100.0%	100.0%

* May not add to 100.0% due to rounding.
Courtesy U.S. News & World Report, 1972.

The following research was conducted by the American Sheep Producer's Council, Inc. to determine the best market for lamb. From this information, how would you describe the best market?

CLASSIFICATION	TOTAL USERS %	MORE FREQUENT USERS %	LESS FREQUENT USERS %	NONUSERS %
By region:				
Mid Atl. & New Eng.	54	29	25	46
East-North Central	32	N.A.	N.A.	68
West-North Central	17	7	10	83
East South Central &				
S. Atl.	23	8	15	77
West-South Central	25	9	16	75
Mtn. & Pacific	52	29	23	48
By type of family:				
Adults only	37	20	17	63
With children	37	16	21	63
By age:				
Under 25	30	9	21	70
25–34	33	15	18	67
35–44	37	17	20	63
45+	40	20	20	60
By income:				
Under $3,000	23	11	12	77
$3,000–5,999	32	14	18	68
$6,000–9,999	42	18	24	58
$10,000+	60	35	25	40
By location:				
City center	48	27	21	52
Suburban	43	19	24	57
Nonmetropolitan	23	8	15	77
By educational level:				
Grammar school	29	14	15	71
High school	36	16	20	64
College	51	26	25	49
Total respondents	37	17	20	63

Source: The American Sheep Producers Council, Inc., "Lamb & the Consumer," 1964.

The Marketing Strategy
behind French Line Advertising
A case report on positioning
by John S. Nussbaum

THE S.S. *France,* the longest, largest ship afloat, is the flagship of the French Line. During the summer season it is in transatlantic service, sailing between New York and Southhampton/Le Havre. On a limited number of crossings, it goes to Bremerhaven. In the winter it has a Caribbean cruise program from New York, and usually has a Mediterranean cruise in the spring from Cannes.

In recent years, all transatlantic carriers have been reducing the number of their crossings by cutting sailings in the spring and fall, and transferring them to cruise schedules. This has eliminated the transatlantic crossings with the lowest load factors.

Most lines have decided that they would prefer not to gamble on a long transatlantic season (with its higher profits), and prefer to opt for a longer cruise season, where there is a better passenger potential, even though at a lower total profit.

Over this same period, competition has lessened as various lines have eliminated transatlantic service completely or have gone out of business.

Today, the principal competitor crossing the Atlantic is Cunard's *Queen Elizabeth II,* and, naturally, the airlines.

In assessing the position of the French Line with the client, sales figures were broken down geographically to determine the origins of revenue. It was found that six territories accounted for almost 80 percent of the passenger dollars. These were New York, Boston, Chicago, Washington, Philadelphia, and Los Angeles—with New York by far the largest contributor, since it is the port of call.

Past experience had shown that the best travel prospects were men and women with the demographics of higher education, upper income, and mature age. It was decided, however, to broaden the concept of the audience to include a slightly younger group of persons who are good cruise prospects.

Because the trend in ocean travel continues to move in the direction of cruises (rather than straight transportation), it was decided to promote the *France* as a distinctly special cruise ship—as a floating vacation resort, a distinctively French resort—whether on the Atlantic, in the Caribbean, or in the

Courtesy: French Line. Advertising Agency, N. W. Ayer/New York. Account Executive, John S. Nussbaum.

Mediterranean. The advertising would have to attract people to it as a very special kind of vacation in itself, rather than just as transportation.

It was also decided to put the bulk of the advertising investment in geographical areas where the revenue potential is most promising. Beyond those markets, it was decided to use selective magazines to reach travel prospects nationally in the most efficient manner.

In newspapers, the advertisements appeared in the Sunday travel sections. Newspapers used were the *New York Times, Boston Globe, Chicago Tribune, Washington Post, Baltimore Sun, Philadelphia Inquirer,* and *Los Angeles Times.* Because of their audience characteristics, the *New Yorker,* the *Saturday Review, Gourmet,* and *Réalités* were used for magazine insertions.

(See layouts and ad on pages 389–392.)

Review Questions

1. Discuss how the same product can have more than one set of values.

2. What is meant by "the majority fallacy"?

3. Give an example of competition (a) within the same subclass, (b) within a product class, and (c) beyond the product class.

4. "Seven-Up" advertised itself as "the Uncola." What does this tell us about its view of its competition?

5. Explain the basic premise of market segmentation. Discuss several examples.

6. Give examples of the two major ways of achieving segmentation.

7. What is meant by "positioning"? Can you give examples?

8. Can you name some products which have changed their marketing approach by re-positioning?

9. Explain what is meant by a "buyer profile."

10. What is meant by demographic data? Who gathers it and how do advertisers use it?

11. Discuss what an advertiser of a particular brand of small American cars would be looking for in *The U.S. News & World Report* profile data.

Reading Suggestions

Barnett, Norman L., "Beyond Market Segmentation," *Harvard Business Review,* January–February 1969, pp. 152–166.

Barton, Roger, *The Handbook of Advertising Management.* New York: McGraw-Hill Book Company, 1970.

Bogart, Leo, "Youth Market Isn't All That Different," *Advertising Age,* April 12, 1971, p. 37ff.

Frank, Ronald E., and William F. Massy, *Market Segmentation.* Englewood Cliffs, N.J.: Prentice-Hall, Inc., 1972.

Gibson, D. Parke, *The $30 Billion Negro*. New York: The Macmillan Company, 1969.

Greenland, Leo, "Is This the Era of Positioning?" *Advertising Age,* July 10, 1972, p. 43ff.

Haley, Russell I., "Benefit Segmentation: A Decision-oriented Research Tool," *Journal of Marketing,* July 1968, pp. 30–35.

Leezenbaum, Ralph, "The New American Woman . . . and Marketing," *Marketing/Communications,* July 1970, pp. 22–28.

Martineau, Pierre, "Social Class and Spending Behavior," *Journal of Marketing,* October 1958, pp. 121–130.

Mayer, Lawrence A., "New Questions about the US Population," *Fortune,* February 1971, p. 80ff.

Rotzoll, Kim, "The Effect of Social Stratification on Market Behavior," *Journal of Advertising Research,* March 1967, pp. 22–27. Also in Kleppner and Settel, *Exploring Advertising,* p. 81.

Silberman, Charles E., "Identity Crisis in the Consumer Markets," *Fortune,* March 1971, p. 92ff.

Sissors, Jack Z., "What is a Market?" *Journal of Marketing,* July 1966. Also in Kleppner and Settel, *Exploring Advertising,* p. 187.

Trout, Jack, and Al Ries, "The Positioning Era Cometh," a three-part series in *Advertising Age.* April 24 (p. 35), May 1 (p. 51), and May 8 (p. 114), 1972.

Twedt, Dik W., "How Important to Marketing Strategy is the Heavy User," *Journal of Marketing,* January 1968, pp. 71–72.

Wasson, Chester R., "Is It Time to Quit Thinking of Income Classes?" *Journal of Marketing,* April 1969, pp. 54–57.

Ziff, Ruth, "Psychographics for Market Segmentation," *Journal of Advertising Research,* April 1971, pp. 3–9.

6

Basic Media Strategy

MEDIA STRATEGY REFERS TO the overall media plan for implementing the marketing strategy of a company by means of advertising. We have many media available for delivering the message—television, radio, newspapers, magazines, outdoor signs, transportation advertising, and direct mail, among others. In each category we have hundreds, if not thousands, of individual media from which to select. This calls for a plan.

Advertising expenditure is often the greatest variable expense in marketing. The media expenditure represents the largest money risk in advertising, since there can be a tremendous difference in effectiveness between two programs. So a plan must be a composite of many factors, including the answers to the following:

1. Whom are we trying to sell?
2. Where is the product distributed?
3. How much money is available?
4. What is the competition doing?
5. What is the nature of the copy?
6. Reach vs. frequency vs. continuity
7. What about timing?
8. Is there a tie-in with a merchandising plan?
9. What combination of media is best?

WHOM ARE WE TRYING TO SELL?

The impulsive response to this question is, "Everyone!"—but that may not be the wisest. In creating a product in the first place, the maker may have had in mind some specific type of buyer for whom it was intended. The U.S. Time Company decided to make a watch, not for everybody, not for those who bought a watch as a lifelong possession or for those who planned to give it as a gift, but for those who wanted to pay the lowest possible price for a watch that worked reasonably well. Accordingly, the media strategy for the Timex watch was geared to reach as wide a *nonluxury* market as possible, even though watches are usually regarded as luxury items. *Market segmentation* can begin with the making of the product itself, as in the instance above. At other times, it means reviewing a product's total market and going after different segments of it in different ways as parts of an overall campaign.

A second approach in defining a market is to go after those consumers who use a product in the largest quantity—the *heavy users*—as we discussed in the previous chapter.

WHERE IS THE PRODUCT DISTRIBUTED?

Advertising is a part of a total marketing program that prescribes the areas in which the product is sold. We now seek to coordinate the circulation of the advertising with the geographical distribution of the market. Three basic media plans are used: a *local* plan, a *regional* plan, and a *national* plan. There is also a fourth plan, which we shall discuss separately—a *selective* plan.

Local plan. A local plan is used when the product is on sale only in one town or community, and its immediate trading zone. This might be the case with a new product, or when a product is being tested in different and distant markets. Furthermore, manufacturers often build their business town by town, or city by city.

For a local plan, the criterion for selecting a medium is that its circulation be confined to the specific geographic area in which the advertiser has distribution. This applies no matter which media are used: newspapers, spot television and spot radio, outdoor advertising, transit advertising, or direct mail.

Regional plan. As the sales of a product spread to larger areas, the advertiser seeks to employ media that reach that region. He uses a regional plan, which is a local plan grown larger. The region may cover several adjoining markets, or an entire state, or several adjoining states. Regional plans are also used when the sale of a product varies with sectional differences in taste or local requirements. More households buy tea in New England than in the Middle West. More blended whisky is sold in the Middle Atlantic states than on the Pacific Coast. Most low-calorie soft drinks are sold in the Northeast and East Central regions. Hence, an advertiser whose product reflects such regional differences in taste will seek media whose circulation coincides with the territories in which his product is sold. The media can include regional editions of national magazines and regional network television and radio—in addition to the media for a local plan.

ADVERTISING VOLUME 1960 AND 1970

| MEDIUM | 1960 | | 1970 | | % CHANGE, '70 vs. '60 |
	MILLIONS	% OF TOTAL	MILLIONS	% OF TOTAL	
Newspapers total	$ 3,703	31.0%	$ 5,745	29.3%	55.1%
national	836	7.0	1,014	5.2	21.3
local	2,867	24.0	4,731	24.1	65.0
Magazines total	941	7.9	1,323	6.7	40.6
weeklies	525	4.4	617	3.1	17.5
women's	184	1.5	301	1.5	63.7
monthlies	200	1.7	374	1.9	8.7
farm, national	32	0.3	31	0.2	−3.1
Television total	1,590	13.3	3,665	18.7	130.5
network	783	6.6	1,712	8.7	118.6
spot	527	4.4	1,247	1.8	136.6
local	281	2.3	706	3.6	151.2
Radio total	692	5.8	1,278	6.5	84.7
network	43	0.4	58	0.3	34.9
spot	222	1.8	355	1.8	59.9
local	428	3.6	865	4.4	102.1
Farm publications (regional)	35	0.3	31	0.2	−11.4
Total farm publications *	(66)	(0.6)	(62)	(0.4)	(−6.1)
Direct mail	1,830	15.3	2,734	13.9	49.3
Business papers	609	5.1	740	3.8	21.5
Outdoor total	203	1.7	234	1.2	15.3
national	137	1.1	154	0.8	12.4
local	66	0.6	80	0.4	21.2
Miscellaneous total	2,328	19.6	3,850	19.7	65.8
national	1,368	11.5	2,148	11.0	56.4
local	960	8.1	1,702	8.7	77.2
Total:					
national	7,296	61.1	11,485	58.6	57.3
local	4,636	38.9	8,115	41.4	75.0
Grand Total	$11,932	100.0%	$19,600	100.0%	64.3%

* *Included in other media totals—not to be added.*
Estimates include media and production.
Source: 1960 data: Printers' Ink, *Aug. 10, 1962*
      1970 data: Marketing/Communications, *July, 1971.*
      % change: '70 vs. '60: Prepared for Advertising Procedure.

National plan. We now jump many millions of dollars ahead to the point at which the product is in widespread distribution all over the country—in every city, town, and hamlet; Coca-Cola, for example, or Colgate toothpaste, or Chevrolet cars. Here the task is that of reaching as many different buyers of our product all over the country at the lowest cost per thousand (CPM), and we embark on a *national* plan for using media. We can now consider network television, network radio, and full-circulation national magazines, along with the nationally syndicated Sunday supplements. Newspaper, outdoor, and transit advertising are also very much in the running.

Selective plan. We now come to a fourth plan, based not on the geographical distribution of the product, but on the special interest of the users of the product *wherever they may happen to be*—as in boating and yachting, art, and antiques, along with other crafts and hobbies whose partisans may be scattered all over the country. The problem in such an instance is not the cost per thousand for reaching these people, but how the greatest number of them can be reached. The media most useful here are the magazines published for these respective fields, direct mail, and possibly the special sections of any Sunday paper that are devoted to such interests. Also special radio and TV programs.

A selective plan is often combined with a geographical plan. For example, if you wanted to reach all homeowners in a certain part of the country, you might take a sectional edition of a national shelter magazine. The local, sectional, and national plans, along with the selective plan, provide a good media framework within which to work. But of course, there is always a question of money. . . .

How Much Money Is Available?

The smaller the budget, the greater the need for resourcefulness in order to do an adequate job. The small advertiser looks for media that are not commonly being used in the field. One looks for special space units. Another shops intensively for television and radio spots off prime time. Such resourcefulness is good at any level; it is particularly necessary for the small advertiser. (The term *small advertiser* means small in comparison with others in his field.) The larger the budget, the greater the risk in making decisions that usually entail large investments; there is no escape from the financial day of reckoning. The first judgment to make in connection with a budget, therefore, is to see whether its size permits one to think in terms of the most costly media—television networks and magazine color pages, for example—assuming that one would want to consider them. Many advertisers hold that good intermedia planning calls for doing a good job in one important medium, which becomes the *primary* medium. There may be some areas in which the primary medium could use increased frequency and support because of competitive reasons, at which time a *secondary* medium may be used. A goal in selecting the secondary medium is to create an interplay with the primary medium that will enhance the impression made by each (referred to as the *synergistic effect,* or $2 + 2 = 5$).

WHAT IS THE COMPETITION DOING?

In media planning, we are very much interested in what our competition is doing, especially if their expenditure is bigger than ours (as it usually seems). One popular guide is not to compete with them in media that they already dominate. Instead, it might be better to pick a medium in which you can dominate or hold your own among the advertising of products of the same class. There are numerous media in which your advertisement will not be overshadowed by others in your field. However, where the campaign is based on unusual copy that would be unique in any medium, there may be no reason for denying the schedule to any medium, regardless of competition. Furthermore, there may be "sleepers" among media, reaching markets that competition has been overlooking.

The David and Goliath story has its counterpart today among those who use the anti-competitive-media approach. Holton C. Rush, president of the advertising agency of Greenshaw & Rush, Inc., reports the following experience:

> When our agency started handling Omega Flour, a regional brand, we faced strong competition from two national flours with multimedia programs. A careful survey showed that in outdoor and in Negro radio there was an opportunity to outadvertise our competitors. We concentrated on those media and Omega now had more sales volume in the market than either of the two big-name flours. Both we and the client give primary credit to the media strategy.[1]

WHAT IS THE NATURE OF THE COPY?

At times, the nature of the copy suggests the type of medium in which it could best be presented. If the chief point of the advertising is to stress the beautiful color of a fabric, that fact might point to magazines with fine color

---

[1] Holton C. Rush, "Some Important Things I Believe a Young Account Representative Should Know About Media" (American Association of Advertising Agencies, Inc., December, 1963).

work or Sunday supplements, or possibly to color television. Does the copy call for a demonstration? That would probably suggest television. Can the message be compressed into a simple, sharp statement? Then let's consider radio. Can the story be communicated in five seconds? Outdoor advertising might then be a possibility. Is it to be the announcement of a new product? That might point to newspapers. Thus we look to the nature of the copy to see if it suggests any particular medium, and build our schedule around that. However, it does not necessarily follow that the advertising message of every product is best told in only one medium.

REACH VERSUS FREQUENCY VERSUS CONTINUITY

Reach refers to the total number of people to whom you deliver a message; *frequency,* the number of times it is delivered within a given period (usually figured on a four-week basis for ease in schedule planning); *continuity* refers to the length of time a schedule runs. Only the biggest advertisers can afford all three at once, and even they seek to spread their money most efficiently.

The advantage of going for reach as the prime goal is that you get a message before the greatest number of people. A disadvantage is that you may not have enough money to reach them impressively enough or often enough to make a meaningful impression.

Next arises the question, How often do you have to tell people your story to get them to act on it? We do not have enough scientific data to make any generalizations. Admittedly, you can reach a point with an audience when just telling the story more often in order to make customers costs more than it is worth in terms of sales. But in mass media, the fifth impression on one person may be the first impression on someone who has not been exposed to that medium or program. By the law of averages, every time the advertisement appears, it reaches some people when they are ready to buy. Furthermore, it may reach some people who had not been interested in the product before.

The third ball in this juggling act is continuity. Among the clearest examples of those who make this the prime factor are the companies that engage in long-range institutional campaigns to establish favorable attitudes toward themselves.

In the absence of more scientific data, many media directors apply the rule for competitive products. "Match competition and then some." If there is not enough money to match competition on a national scale, you may be able to pick out a market where competition has spread itself thin, and outshine it in that territory.

There is much research being done and to be done on the criteria for evaluating reach, frequency, and continuity in a given situation. One such study, by Pomerance and Zielske, reached the following conclusions:

1. Advertising is quickly forgotten if the consumer is not continuously exposed to it.

2. Numerous exposures are needed to impress a message upon the memory of a large proportion of target prospects.

3. Both the number of different persons who can be made to remember a message and the length of time it can be remembered increase as the number of exposures is increased.

4. An intensive burst of exposures is more effective in making a maximum number of different persons remember advertising, at least temporarily, than spreading 13 exposures throughout the year.

5. To achieve this same goal, fewer exposures per prospect among a relatively large group is preferable to 13 exposures per prospect among a smaller group.

6. In achieving this goal, dollar efficiency of advertising decreases as additional exposures are purchased.[2]

We will go further into this subject in the chapters on television and radio.

WHAT ABOUT TIMING?

A decision as to *when* to spend the money in advertising is one of the key elements of media strategy. Among the chief patterns for using media, and the reasons for them, are the following:

Seasonal program.   First of all, we meet those products whose sales have seasonal fluctuations; for instance, cough drops in the winter, suntan lotion in the summer, and watches at graduation time and at Christmas. In such instances, the advertising is scheduled to reflect the seasonal peaks, appearing in concentrated dosage with the approach of the appropriate season. The advertising usually begins ahead of the consumer buying season—when people might first begin thinking of such products.

Steady program.   When the sale of a product is quite uniform throughout the year (toothpaste, for example), the advertising could be maintained steadily. The chief reason for not doing so might be that such a schedule would be too thin when spread over twelve months; hence it might be concentrated in fewer months, permitting more impressive advertising during that period. Other reasons for concentrating advertising are that money

---

[2] Eugene Pomerance and Hubert Zielske, "How Frequently Should You Advertise?" *Media/scope,* September 1958, pp. 25–27.

may be needed to meet competitive promotional efforts during the year or to provide for special local campaigns. The drop in reading and viewing habits in the summer may also affect the continuity of the schedule during that season. Many television network advertisers take a hiatus during the summer months, returning in the fall. However, radio listening goes up then.

Pulsation.   Pulsation refers to the technique of having several short but intensive bursts of advertising during the year, each series of advertisements lasting, for example, three weeks to three months at a time.

The process of going in and out with a schedule is also referred to as *waving.* According to Herbert Zeltner:

> Waving in this context is not normally the result of adjusting levels of activity to seasonal activity, but rather the somewhat arbitrary building of heavy periods of activity interspersed with hiatuses. The wave can be only two or three weeks—or it can be for several months of intensive effort before withdrawal from activity for a more or less sustained period.

One of the conclusions from Zeltner's study is:

> Wave scheduling is not necessarily a good thing—and of itself . . . it represents a lesser of two evils—when a more consistent pattern of effort is either unaffordable or may lack effectiveness.[3]

As an illustration of circumstances in which pulsation may be desirable, Kuehn offers the following instances:

> In allocating advertising dollars to regional metropolitan markets, planners frequently must decide whether to allocate extra funds to some areas at the expense of others. Generally, however, they find it difficult to temporarily withdraw funds from areas in which a brand is doing poorly, since they see the problem as one of survival. Under such circumstances, *pulsation* in advertising or promotion, coordinated with sales-force efforts, offers better prospects of profits and gains in distribution than a continuous dribble of advertising. In many such cases, it would also appear desirable to withdraw funds from some territories to concentrate on others, a result contrary to that suggested by most advertising models. By concentrating on a few markets, a brand frequently has a better chance of forcing distribution and increasing its overall short-term profitability, thereby obtaining the means for subsequent investment expenditures in other territories. It

---

[3] Herbert Zeltner, "Are Waves Worthwhile?" *Media/scope,* November 1964, pp. 10–18.

can be expensive to hold one's own in every market simply as a matter of principle, especially if this prevents the brand [from] becoming firmly established and profitable in any one region.[4]

In addition to the foregoing patterns of timing, we have the campaigns of the automobile companies, where the chief advertising effort is concentrated at the time of the annual presentation of the new models. In the first six weeks of the new-car introduction, 20 percent of the total annual budget will be spent, *half of that—10 percent—in the first week alone!* The timing and cadence of the advertising thus has its birth in the annual marketing cycle of the product itself. In such instances, there may also be a preliminary teaser campaign to whet curiosity and excitement for the Big Moment.

IS THERE A TIE-IN WITH A MERCHANDISING PLAN?

The role of the dealer in the marketing of the product may influence the media strategy. The advertiser may wish to run an extensive cooperative campaign that would call for local media tie-ins (newspaper ads, television spots, radio spots, and outdoor posters and bulletins). He may plan a coupon or sampling campaign in different markets in connection with intensive advertising in local media. If such plans are in the offing, provisions for them must be in the media program.

These are among the problems that enter into the formulation of a media program. They add up to one thing: There is great opportunity for creative thinking in planning the use of media. And with the use of the computer, the challenge has become even greater.

WHAT COMBINATION OF MEDIA IS BEST?

The usual bench mark for comparing costs of comparable media is the cost per thousand circulation, or audience. This is determined by the following formula:

$$\frac{\text{amount of money}}{\text{number of people (in thousands)}} = \text{cost per thousand (CPM)}$$

This is a simple yardstick of costs when you are considering a choice between, say, two alternate women's magazines of equal editorial stature. But when you

---

[4] Alfred A. Kuehn, "How Advertising Performance Depends on Other Marketing Factors," *Journal of Advertising Research*, II, No. 1 (March 1962), 7.

expand the schedule to include many magazines or television programs or both, the problem of getting the best spread for your money with minimum unplanned duplication gets a bit complicated. Fortunately, the computer is a big help on such problems, and we move on into the world of computer thinking.

COMPUTER THINKING

By *computer thinking,* we mean the thought of the *user* of the computer, not the supposed thinking of the computer itself; computer thinking is thereby distinguished also from the incredible task of computer programming and operation. The greatest contribution of the computer to media planning— even to those who do not use it—is the necessity that it imposes to think in precise terms, to state problems in precise form, and to base decisions on accurately gathered information.

Uses of Computers

Basically, the computer speedily coordinates into a meaningful form a given set of facts from a larger set of facts. Hence the first requirement in the use of the computer for making media decisions is to define the "facts" that are fed into it. There is a familiar phrase in the computer world: GIGO (garbage in, garbage out). If you speak of "users of a product," do you mean households or individuals? If individuals, does it include children? What constitutes a user? A person who has once used the product? A person who has some on hand right now?

A second characteristic of the computer is that it deals with numbers, not adjectives. All factors for a computer, therefore, must be put in numerical form, or *quantified.* As an example: Suppose you plan to put all the data of a set of magazines on a computer—their circulation, the number of readers in different age groups, and so on. These are data already offered in numerical form. However, in evaluating magazines you also want to consider their editorial tone, their prestige, and the environment in which the advertisement appears. Because of this, someone must go over the different magazines and form a judgment on such qualities. He must then quantify that judgment by giving each magazine a rating for "editorial tone"—let us say, from 1 to 5. The computer will then be able to give an end figure in which a magazine rated 4 for its editorial tone would get twice the weight of a magazine rated only 2.

Iteration

As one example of the use of the computer, we consider *iteration.* Iteration is a trial-and-error method of getting a mathematical solution to a problem that cannot be reduced to a formula in advance. It has been applied to determine how to get the biggest reach in a list of media at the lowest cost per thousand. Assume we use only one medium, A, reaching one million households. We then add Medium B, which also reaches one million households. But we find there is duplication of 600,000 households reached by the two media, represented as follows:

	CIRCULATION	
	TOTAL	EXCLUSIVE
Medium A	1,000,000	700,000
Medium B	1,000,000	700,000
	2,000,000	1,400,000

Thus we are reaching a total of only 1,400,000 different households. Then we add Medium C, which also reaches one million households. However, because of the duplication among the three media, this is now the picture:

	CIRCULATION	
	TOTAL	EXCLUSIVE
Medium A	1,000,000	600,000 *
Medium B	1,000,000	600,000 *
Medium C	1,000,000	500,000
	3,000,000	1,700,000

* 100,000 of the former 700,000 is duplicated by Medium C.

We are paying to reach 3,000,000 households, but we are only reaching 1,700,000 *different* households. Then we begin wondering if we would be better off to

Keep A and B, but drop C
Keep A and C, but drop B
Keep B and C, but drop A

As more media are added to the list, the job of picking the most efficient combination becomes even more complex. This is the problem for which iteration is used. Instances are commonplace in which a medium with smaller total circulation provides greater exclusive circulation within a given list.

The instant-coffee example (on next page) shows how a list of 22 media was reduced to 10 media, with a loss of only 5.6 percent of the households reached. The details are provided for those who may be interested in how such problems are handled.

A Media Problem

Reaching heavy users of instant coffee

The problem was to determine which combination of media used can reach the largest number of different households that are heavy users of instant coffee. This represents a problem for which iteration is used. You begin with the *maximum* possible list of media and whittle it down in successive steps till you get a list that gives optimum reach per dollar (in contrast to the usual

This case study courtesy SRDS Data, Inc.

PRELIMINARY RUNS A and B
MEDIA EXPOSURE AMONG HEAVY INSTANT COFFEE
USING FEMALE HOUSEHOLD HEADS (in thousands)
NATIONAL

	RUN A	Exclusive Fem. Head Heavy Instant Coffee	RUN B Network Daytime TV Shows	Exclusive Fem. Head Heavy Instant Coffee
	Magazines			
A	General - mass	233	TV Show - A	35
B	General - mass	198	TV Show - B	95
C	General - mass	125	TV Show - C	128
D	General - mass	543	TV Show - D	176
E	Shelter	---*	TV Show - E	---*
F	Shelter	75	TV Show - F	26*
G	Women's - mass	185	TV Show - G	35*
H	Women's - mass	110	TV Show - H	52
I	Shelter	14*	TV Show - I	130*
J	Shelter	41*	TV Show - J	164
K	Women's - mass	103	TV Show - K	60
L	Women's - mass	240	TV Show - L	730
M	General - mass	620	TV Show - M	60
N	Women's - mass	82*	TV Show - N	371
		2,569	TV Show - O	17*
			TV Show - P	373
			TV Show - Q	26
				2,478

Chart I

* Eliminated for first iteration

Total Heavy Instant Coffee Using
Female Household Heads 15,234

Magazines & Network Daytime TV Shows	Total Audience (All Inds.)	Heavy Using Fem. Head Aud.	First Iteration Exclusive Heavy Using Fem. Head Aud.	Second Iteration Exclusive Heavy Using Fem. Head Aud.	Third Iteration Exclusive Heavy Using Fem. Head Aud.
A General – mass	29,336	3,199	176	248	319
B General – mass	24,668	2,835	213	304	375
C General – mass	22,604	2,516	74*	Dropped	Dropped
D General – mass	20,759	2,805	216	378	455
F Shelter	15,380	2,340	71	91*	Dropped
G Women's – mass	13,467	2,570	112	112*	Dropped
H Women's – mass	14,758	2,771	152	223	304
K Women's – mass	13,164	2,505	41*	Dropped	Dropped
L Women's – mass	18,038	3,259	142	294	446
M General – mass	36,356	4,518	477	649	812
TV Show – A	4,006	809	10*	Dropped	Dropped
TV Show – B	4,597	997	71	101*	Dropped
TV Show – C	5,838	1,366	20*	Dropped	Dropped
TV Show – D	11,146	2,339	177	319	461
TV Show – H	8,522	1,616	51*	Dropped	Dropped
TV Show – J	9,273	2,244	51*	Dropped	Dropped
TV Show – K	6,279	1,140	41*	Dropped	Dropped
TV Show – L	21,521	2,673	345	436	507
TV Show – M	5,328	988	61	132	183
TV Show – N	13,570	1,771	81	223	315
TV Show – P	7,521	979	20*	Dropped	Dropped
TV Show – Q	4,507	566	--*	Dropped	Dropped
Total (Exclusive Reach)			2,602	3,510	4,177
Total Unduplicated Reach			12,815	12,354	11,958
Total Goal			15,234	15,234	15,234
Per Cent Coverage			84.1%	81.1%	78.5%

Chart II

* Eliminated for next iteration

way of beginning with one medium and building upon that). In computer language, each round of eliminations represents an *iteration*.

Chart I (Preliminary Runs A and B) lists 14 eligible magazines and 17 desirable television programs, each of which might be suitable for advertising instant coffee. Alongside each medium is the number of female heads of households who are heavy users of instant coffee and whom that medium reaches exclusively (that is, who are reached by no other medium on the list).

We review the media to see which contribute the fewest number of households not reached by other media. As a result, we drop four magazines and five television shows from this preliminary list. That leaves 10 magazines and 12 television shows that we now combine on Chart II.

Chart II reports on the total number of female household heads who are heavy users of instant coffee; this is our goal of   15,234,000

The total number reached exclusively by each medium in the first iteration, consisting of 22 media, is now   2,602,000

The total unduplicated number reached by all the media (that is, if a household is reached by more than one, it is counted only once) is   12,815,000

The percentage of the goal covered by the list is   84.1%

In looking over Chart II, we again weed out those media that contribute the smallest share of exclusive households (households not reached by others, marked by *). We drop nine. That leaves 13 media.

In the second iteration, with only 13 media, the percentage coverage of goal is now   81.1%

Again, we mark for elimination the media that contribute the fewest number of households not reached by other media (marked by *); this time we drop three. In the third iteration, we have 10 media whose reach of the total goal is   78.5%

MEDIA EXPOSURE AMONG HEAVY INSTANT COFFEE
USING FEMALE HOUSEHOLD HEADS (in thousands)
NATIONAL
FINAL SCHEDULE

Total Heavy Instant Coffee Using
Female Household Heads 15,234

Magazines & Network Daytime TV Shows	Total Audience (All Inds.)	Heavy Using Fem. Head Aud.	Exclusive Heavy Using Fem. Head Aud.
A General - mass	29,336	3,199	319
B General - mass	24,668	2,835	375
D General - mass	20,759	2,805	455
H Women's - mass	14,758	2,771	304
L Women's - mass	18,038	3,259	446
M General - mass	36,356	4,518	812
TV Show - D	11,146	2,339	461
TV Show - L	21,521	2,673	507
TV Show - M	5,328	988	183
TV Show - N	13,570	1,771	315
Total (Exclusive Reach)		4,177	
Total Unduplicated Reach		11,958	
Total Goal		15,234	
Per Cent Coverage		78.5%	

Chart III

The final list developed by this series of iterations consisted of 10 media reaching 78.5 percent of the goal of female household heads who are heavy users of instant coffee, in contrast to the original list of 22 media reaching 84.1 percent of such households. A reduction of the media list by 55 percent resulted in a loss of only 5.6 percent of households.

There are other elements in a media discussion besides the choice of media, such as the frequency of appearance, size of advertisement, and the copy message. But the use of the computer for iteration helps answer the question, Which combination of media provides the widest reach per dollar? And more sophisticated methods for using the computer are constantly being developed.

Review Questions

1. The strategy of creating a media plan for a product is based on a variety of factors. The text lists nine. Can you name them?

2. Discuss the local, regional, national, and selective media plans. What type of media might be used for each plan?

3. What media strategies might best be employed by advertisers whose budget is much smaller than that of their competitors?

4. What is the significance of reach, frequency, and continuity in planning media schedules?

5. The chapter describes three different patterns of timing in media scheduling. What are they?

6. What is the usual benchmark for comparing costs in relation to circulation in comparable media?

7. In what respects do you think the computer can be most helpful in media scheduling?

Reading Suggestions

Barton, Roger, *Media in Advertising.* New York: McGraw-Hill Book Company, 1964.

——, *The Handbook of Advertising Management.* New York: McGraw-Hill Book Company, 1970.

Bogart, Leo, "Is It Time to Discard the Audience Concept?" *Journal of Marketing,* January 1966, pp. 47–54. Also in Kleppner and Settel, *Exploring Advertising,* p. 217.

Cook, Harvey R., *Selecting Advertising Media: A Guide for Small Business.* Washington, D.C.: U.S. Government Printing Office, 1969.

Friedman, Lawrence, "Constructing a Media Simulation Model," *Journal of Advertising Research,* August 1970, pp. 33–39.

Gensch, Dennis H., "Media Factors: A Review Article," *Journal of Marketing Research,* May 1970, pp. 216–225.

Greenberg, B., and B. Dervin, "Mass Communication among the Urban Poor," *Public Opinion Quarterly,* Summer 1970, pp. 224–235.

Jones, Richard P., "Quiet Revolution in Media Planning," *Media Decisions,* September 1967, p. 36ff. Also in

Kleppner and Settel, *Exploring Advertising,* p. 209.

Pomerance, Eugene, and Hubert Zielske, "How Frequently Should You Advertise?" *Media/Scope,* September 1958, pp. 25–27.

Ray, Michael L., and Alan G. Sawyer, "Repetition in Media Models: A Laboratory Technique," *Journal of Marketing Research,* February 1971, pp. 20–29.

Roth, Paul M., *How to Plan Media.* Skokie, Ill.: Standard Rate & Data Service, 1968.

Sissors, Jack Z., "Matching Media with Markets," *Journal of Advertising Research,* October 1971, pp. 39–43.

Twedt, Dik W., "How Can the Advertising Dollar Work Harder?" *Journal of Marketing,* April 1965, pp. 60–62. Also in Kleppner and Settel, *Exploring Advertising,* p. 197.

Vitt, Sam B., "How Media Are Selected," *Madison Avenue,* August 1966, p. 8ff. Also in Kleppner and Settel, *Exploring Advertising,* p. 183.

Wolfe, H. D., J. K. Brown, G. C. Thompson, and S. H. Greenberg, *Evaluating Media.* New York: National Industrial Conference Board, Inc., 1966.

Zeltner, Herbert, "Are Waves Worthwhile?" *Media/Scope,* November 1964, pp. 10–18.

III
MEDIA

Rank	Company	Total in Millions	Newspapers	Magazines*
1.	Procter & Gamble Co.	$188,417.5	$ 751.2	$ 7,362.8
2.	General Foods Corp.	121,509.7	9,140.3	11,858.8
3.	General Motors Corp.	119,164.2	20,096.0	23,856.4
4.	Bristol-Myers Co.	110,872.0	1,872.2	20,381.2
5.	Colgate-Palmolive Co.	101,480.7	3,169.3	5,018.4
6.	American Home Products	90,544.3	3,322.8	7,334.1
7.	R. J. Reynolds Industries	83,986.5	1,661.8	9,731.8
8.	Ford Motor Co.	79,745.5	11,220.9	14,544.9
9.	Sterling Drug Inc.	73,212.5	1,169.8	10,003.3
10.	Warner-Lambert Pharmaceuticals	73,123.7	223.1	3,108.5
11.	Lever Bros.	67,019.8	2,009.1	3,734.9
12.	Philip Morris Inc.	66,703.8	532.6	13,745.7
13.	American Brands	58,572.7	7,397.8	15,438.9
14.	Coca-Cola Co.	52,965.8	2,276.3	6,064.6
15.	Sears, Roebuck & Co.	52,685.0	253.7	13,399.1
16.	Gillette Co.	51,805.5	304.6	5,383.6
17.	General Mills	51,777.5	1,752.0	7,004.1
18.	Kraftco	50,073.0	6,307.7	8,897.4
19.	Chrysler Corp.	48,714.1	7,034.2	9,366.4
20.	Distillers Corp.-Seagrams Ltd.	46,986.7	11,883.0	25,825.0
21.	Brown & Williamson Tobacco Co.	46,700.4	2,800.0	11,457.3
22.	Loew's Corp.	46,413.0	3,535.9	5,364.9
23.	PepsiCo Inc.	46,060.2	1,566.6	2,896.5
24.	American Telephone & Telegraph Co.	45,889.9	4,036.0	9,568.9
25.	Miles Laboratories	42,136.5	906.8	1,845.8
26.	Kellogg Co.	38,855.0	1,979.8	2,906.0
27.	Rapid-American Corp.	38,807.9	4,767.9	10,811.7
28.	Liggett & Myers Inc.	36.016.6	3,230.6	12,198.2
29.	Norton Simon Inc.	35,887.7	4,748.7	8,075.2
30.	International Telephone & Telegraph	34,938.2	1,699.8	5,435.5
31.	Goodyear Tire & Rubber Co.	34,409.5	20,599.1	3,320.2
32.	Campbell Soup Co.	33,179.7	2,533.2	6,859.7
33.	S. C. Johnson & Son	32,193.2	489.6	541.1
34.	RCA Corp.	31,662,4	8,317.6	10,729.6
35.	Firestone Tire & Rubber Co.	31,243,4	18,676.4	3,164.3
36.	Alberto-Culver Co.	30,278.5	46.3	2,604.3
37.	Ralston Purina Co.	29,942.4	922.6	980.4
38.	Schering-Plough Inc.	29,595.9	756.3	3,234.7
39.	Johnson & Johnson	27,174.2	116.0	7,312.4
40.	Eastman Kodak Co.	26,637.4	2,445.1	7,241.4
41.	Richardson-Merrell	26,253.6	1,990.6	3,591.0
42.	Pfizer Inc.	26,156.8	46.3	5,119.1
43.	J. B. Williams Co.	25,476.0	797.5	1,885.9
44.	Heublein Inc.	24,736.3	2,093.2	5,720.4
45.	American Cyanamid Co.	24,543.3	57.4	4,879.8
46.	Volkswagen of America	24,335.7	2,950.0	6,510.5
47.	Carnation Co.	24,218.3	1,222.9	958.4
48.	Standard Oil of New Jersey	24,061.0	2,598.4	2,933.8
49.	Block Drug Co.	23,844.0	———	3,647.9
50.	Westinghouse Electric Corp.	23,771.7	4,327.3	8,209.0

Farm Publica- tions	Business Publica- tions	Spot Television	Network Television	Spot Radio	Network Radio	Outdoor
$ 2.0	$ 769.2	$50,796.7	$128,444.5	$ 278.0	$ 4.1	$———
135.0	270.6	49,259.2	44,642.0	5,263.0	502.0	438.8
457.3	4,180.3	8,961.1	32,972.3	20,906.0	2,804.3	4,930.5
———	4,287.2	23,351.1	57,078.6	2,843.0	599.8	458.9
———	43.3	36,860.9	46,507.8	8,141.0	1,690.0	50.0
78.9	347.7	26,355.8	40,791.8	10,731.0	1,360.0	222.2
254.3	176.8	14,401.2	52,405.9	4,304.0	804.7	246.0
1,214.8	1,797.5	7,544.6	31,345.8	7,430.0	1,676.3	2,970.7
162.0	442.8	12,940.1	41,324.0	4,195.0	2,975.5	
———	4,334.1	17,853.4	46,200.3	1,087.0	315.6	1.7
———	———	20,893.2	38,554.9	1,331.0	496.6	1
	81.5	11,491.5	36,685.8	2,500.0	833.7	833.0
5.4	661.7	2,092.0	31,365.6	899.0	15.6	706.7
———	474.3	16,944.6	15,527.8	10,239.0	———	1,439.2
———		18,960.9	15,273.5	4,306.0	59.5	432.3
	114.3	16,320.3	27,479.3	1,817.0	382.9	3.5
16.6	395.1	17,940.0	24,152.4	117.0	386.7	13.6
40.7	1,844.2	13,181.1	18,359.3	1,025.0	108.8	308.8
106.9	491.9	3,926.7	21,341.6	4,869.0	930.5	646.9
	751.2	254.3	———	202.0	150.3	7,920.9
	51.6	7,657.6	21,881.9	261.0		2,591.0
	46.1	15,536.2	15,903.6	3,319.0	1,127.6	1,579.7
69.7	390.7	13,797.7	16,864.3	9,194.0	468.0	812.7
7.3	2,308.2	11,110.1	12,928.3	4,806.0	64.1	1,071.0
	614.2	9,594.3	28,937.6	69.0	168.8	
64.1	145.9	8,490.3	24,934.7	———	———	334.2
	761.3	1,788.7	16,210.6	127.0		4,340.7
5.8	271.6	3,957.3	13,842.6	635.0	247.0	1,628.5
———	390.4	10,169.0	9,150.7	1,792.0		1,561.7
	3,870.0	13,434.9	9,707.5	330.0	18.0	442.5
465.9	973.0	2,778.3	6,067.9	108.0	———	97.1
———	525.0	6,388.1	13,590.4	1,897.0	1,293.8	92.5
———		2,111.9	28,803.7	110.0	135.2	1.7
	1,365.0	3,953.7	6,367.2	480.0	35.3	414.0
390.9	576.6	1,833.0	5,681.1	861.0	53.9	6.2
	152.7	14,472.8	12,971.0	31.0	———	4
448.0	50.0	7,905.9	18,739.1	523.0	246.2	127.2
10.1	2,056.1	5,172.2	13,966.2	1,368.0	2,171.4	860.9
11.5	530.6	9,807.5	7,737.2	1,659.0		
6.2	2,898.0	2,208.3	10,994.4	798.0	———	46.0
38.1	850.5	6,039.7	13,220.9	508.0	———	14.8
737.6	1,010.5	2,005.4	14,921.6	1,388.0	536.2	392.1
———	60.0	138.4	22,425.0	47.0	122.2	———
	83.4	6,040.4	6,486.9	2,374.0		1,938.0
1,072.3	3,498.1	3,265.4	11,250.6	390.0	118.4	11.3
	233.4	3,841.0	8,859.1	453.0	———	1,488.7
69.8	569.2	9,510.1	11,562.1	207.0	102.2	16.6
165.0	898.1	6,617.7	6,620.4	3,026.0	———	1,201.6
———	73.6	3,152.9	15,971.6	998.0		
33.9	2,500.0	5,335.4	3,211.6	74.0	———	80.5

Crain Communications, Inc.

7

Using Television

SINCE THE ADVENT OF the automobile, nothing has changed American family life so much as television. Nothing else has had such an impact on advertising. Over 96 percent of all American households, representing 62 million homes, have television sets. Many have two or more. The average family has its set on for 6 hours and 20 minutes a day [1]—to which many fathers would say, "In *my* house, that's an understatement!"

Television accounts for 45 percent of all media expenditures for national advertising. The use of television by local advertisers represents the fastest-growing segment of all the advertising media; between 1960 and 1970, it grew over 150 percent. [2]

FEATURES AND ADVANTAGES

Television provides the most spectacular way in which an advertiser can reach the greatest number of people at one time. The average nighttime television network program reaches between one sixth and one fifth of all of the television homes in the country, and some of the very highest-rated programs reach one fourth of them. Eighty percent of all adults view TV at some time during the average day, and 95 percent during the average week. [3]

---

[1] *Broadcasting Yearbook for 1972*, p. 11.
[2] *Television Bureau of Advertising Index*, February 1970.
[3] See p. 121.

The number of households using television nationally increases steadily throughout the day, then jumps sharply during after-work hours, reaching a peak between 8 and 10 P.M. There is a higher morning viewing level for Los Angeles, and a higher late evening level for New York.

Courtesy, A. C. Nielsen Company

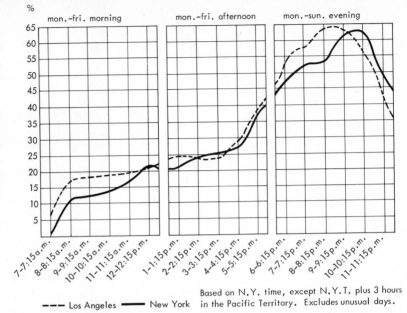

--- Los Angeles   ——— New York   Based on N.Y. time, except N.Y.T. plus 3 hours in the Pacific Territory. Excludes unusual days.

What makes television so attractive to advertisers, and what makes the total audience that can be reached through television so huge, is the diversity of TV programming. Almost everybody, no matter what his taste, has a few favorite programs he watches fairly regularly.

TV is an intimate medium. It is a great medium for demonstrating how to do something, or how something works, or how a product performs. Through choice of time and programs, an advertiser can reach a great proportion of listeners who are of the sex and age group he is seeking.

LIMITATIONS AND CHALLENGES

Time for the commercial message on television is fleeting. Most commercials are for 30 seconds; a one minute commercial is considered a long one. The challenge is to hold the attention of the viewer and leave with him a message that will cause him to remember the name of the product favorably. We have seen many commercials do this in an informative, often entertaining way. We have seen many commercials that are dull and, even in 30 seconds, boring.

The biggest problem facing television is clutter—the playing of credits for all personnel involved in a program, station-break announcements, public-service notices, "billboards" (just the name of a product or a slogan), in addition to the commercials crowded upon each other three or even four in a minute. The viewer comes away from this kaleidoscope with a high degree of annoyance and confusion about which product was advertised; the misidentification rate is high, and the number of commercials being offered is constantly increasing.

Forms of Television Usage

An advertiser can buy television time through a network (*network TV*). Or he can buy time as he sees fit from individual stations (*spot TV*). If a national advertiser buys spots, it is, strictly speaking, national spot TV, but is generally referred to as just *spot TV*. When a local advertiser uses spots, it is, strictly speaking, local spot TV, but is referred to as just *local TV*. In 1971, 48 percent of all television expenditure was for network; 34 percent, spot; 18 percent, local.[4] In the present discussion we deal with network and spot chiefly; we discuss local television in the retailing chapter.

Network Television

A television network consists of a number of interconnected stations capable of transmitting simultaneously the same program originating at one

---

[4] Annual Report. *Federal Communications Commissions,* 1972 (1971 figures).

THE TELEVISION STRUCTURE

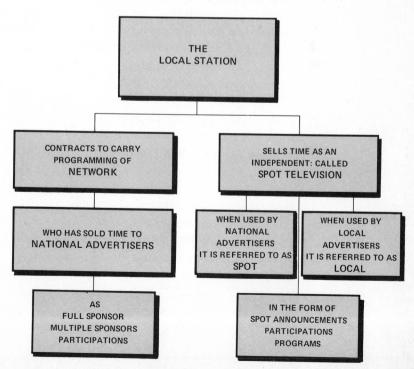

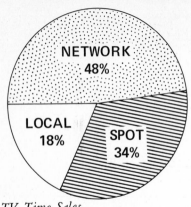

TV Time Sales
Source: Annual Report of The Federal
Communications Commission, 1972
(1971 figures).

of their stations. (Because of difference in time zones across the country, some stations may show a network program as a *delayed telecast.*) There are three national networks, ABC, CBS, and NBC. Each has arranged affiliations with stations throughout the country whereby these stations will carry the network's programs and commercials at certain times. The stations sell the rest of the time independently. An advertiser placing a schedule with a television network is obliged to use a prescribed minimum number of affiliated stations from their total list, and expand his list from their other stations as he sees fit. Networks can give an advertiser the largest nationwide audience for his message.

Commercial time on network television is sold in units of 30 seconds and 60 seconds. A single minute of commercial time in a nighttime network program generally runs in the range of $35,000 to $70,000, with "specials" costing much more (bowl games and world championship games cost close to $200,000 for a commercial minute).

But network coverage has its problems and challenges. In the first place, we are speaking of large sums of money, for both time and production. These costs rule out any but companies that have a product or line of products with widespread distribution. Most network advertisers have a whole range of corporate divisions, or products, to share the time and costs. Then, too, there is great competition for good programming. This means not only a program that in itself is good, but one that can get on at a time in which a program on a competitive station won't cut too deeply into its rating; also at a time when it can get a good carry-over from the preceding program.[5]

Each station on the network lineup is different in the composition of the market area and its competitive TV programming. An advertiser's message on a network, therefore, may not always be distributed across the country in ideal proportion to the distribution of his market. For this reason, an advertiser will often supplement his use of network television in certain markets with spot television. An advertiser can buy time on a network as a single, multiple, or participating sponsor.

Single sponsorship. With single sponsorship, advertisers can develop an extensive collateral advertising program with the trade. However, single sponsorship represents the biggest cash commitment in television. Singly sponsored programs are generally so costly that they are seldom used by manufacturers of a single product only, except to make one outstanding splash that will receive great attention from the public and earn prestige with

---

[5] Based on the assumption that networks continue to control the programming of their facilities.

TV Control Room   Courtesy, CBS Television Network

This is a production control console at the CBS Television Network Center in New York City. The bank of picture monitors are in the background. Seated from left to right are the technical director, script girl, program director, assistant program director, and audio operator.

the trade. The chief users of singly sponsored programs are the large companies interested in developing a favorable corporate image (AT&T, Xerox) or companies selling seasonal product lines (Hallmark cards).

Multiple sponsorship.   Programs are sold on a multiple-sponsorship basis in different ways, such as quarters of a football game or alternate weeks of a nighttime half hour. Usually, the advertisers cooperating in a multiple sponsorship are seeking some of the advantages of single sponsorship—identity with a prestigious program, promotional opportunities, and merchandisability to their dealers—but at reduced cost and risk. Many sports events, such as the World Series and the bowl games, are sold on this basis, and frequently prestigious prime-time evening programming will have multiple sponsorship.

Participating (network) advertiser.   Most network television commercial time is sold on a participating basis; that is, a number of advertisers each pay for 30 seconds or 60 seconds of commercial time in a program. Advertisers may participate in a program one time only, or they may participate

143

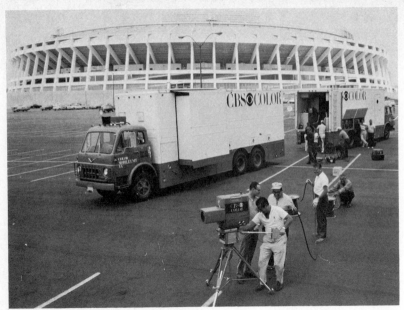

A CBS MOBILE UNIT

—getting ready to film a sports event.

Courtesy, CBS Television Network

in it a number of times on either a regular or irregular schedule. Through *participations,* an advertiser can have his message delivered to network audiences at the lowest cost and least risk. By spreading his budget over a number of different network programs, he can reach a greater variety of audiences. This method of network-time buying is known as a *scatter plan.*

The use of participations in network television advertising has greatly increased; that of single and multiple sponsorships has steadily declined. In 1970, 88 percent of network commercials were participating, 7 percent alternate or multiple, and 5 percent single.[6]

Buying Network Time

Buying single or multiple sponsorship of television network programming requires long-range planning. The advertiser's time buyer has to shop around among the networks to see what time slots or programs are available for the next season; study the programs that will be competing on other networks for the audience during the same time periods; consider the preceding or lead-in programming to determine what kind of audience it is likely to make available for the beginning of the show, and the ever rising cost.

Buying network participations is somewhat simpler. Here the buyer asks, "What's available?" He will generally be offered several "packages" of participations by each of the networks, from which he can select the combination of participations that he believes will best reach the audience he is after.

---

[6] *Advertising Age,* January 19, 1970, p. 6.

Spot television, in contrast to network television, is the time sold by an individual station to an individual advertiser.[7] Spot television gives the national advertiser complete flexibility in choice of markets, the number and length of the spots he uses in each market, and the manner in which they are scheduled in each market. Spot television can be used by itself; it can also be used to supplement a national network television schedule in markets where the local affiliate is not the strongest station, or in markets of above-average importance to the advertiser. Or it can be used to reinforce a newspaper or magazine campaign.

Buying Spot Time

Spot time is most often sold in 10-, 20-, 30-, and 60-second lengths, but chiefly 30 seconds. The 10-second spot—just long enough for a short selling message identifying the product—is often referred to as an *ID* (short for identification), referring both to product identification and to the early practice of scheduling these announcements in conjunction with station call-letter and channel-number identifications. Most commercial ID's are actually only 8 seconds long, allowing 2 seconds for station identification. The 20-second spot is sometimes referred to as a *chainbreak,* from its frequent scheduling in the breaks between network programs.

Rates on a station vary according to the time of day or night selected, reflecting the differences in the size of the audiences at the various hours. Rates are usually grouped by time classifications, most often beginning with Class AAA or AA (rates for the choicest and most costly time periods), through Class A, Class B, Class C, and so on, in descending order of size of audience and cost. Each station has its own classifications, and lists them on its rate card. Some are simple, as the following:

> Class A—7:30 P.M. to 11:00 P.M.
>
> Class B—All other times

Most stations, however, have four or five time classifications, as in this instance:

> Class AA—Daily 7:30–11:00 P.M.
> Class A —Daily 7:00–7:30 A.M.; Sun. 5:30–7:30 P.M.
> Class B —Mon. thru Sat. 4:30–6:00 P.M.; Sun. 2–5:30 P.M.
> Class C —Sat. sign-on–4:30 P.M.; Mon. thru Fri. noon–4:30 P.M.
> Class D —Mon. thru Fri. sign-on–noon; Sun. sign on–2 P.M.

---

[7] The term "spot" is another of those words in advertising that are used in two senses: (1) *time-buying use*—a way of buying time on a non-network show; and (2) *creative use*—"We need some 30-second spots."

WQXI-TV

(Airdate September 30, 1951)

METRO TV SALES

Data verified/revised for June '71 issue

Media Code 6 211 0185 6.00

Pacific & Southern Company, Inc., 1611 W. Peachtree St., N. E. Atlanta, Ga. 30309. Phone 404-892-1611. TWX 810-751-8360.

1. PERSONNEL

President—Arthur H. McCoy.
Vice-Pres. & Gen'l Mgr.—George Hagar.
General Sales Manager—James Thrash.
Sales Manager—Steve Halpern.
Station Manager—Sid Pike.
Promotion Manager—Tony Visk.

2. REPRESENTATIVES

Metro TV Sales.

3. FACILITIES

Video 316,000 w., audio 63,200 w.; ch 11.
Antenna ht.: 1,040.6 ft. above average terrain.
Operating schedule: 7-1:15 am. EST.
Transmitter: 110 Arizona Ave., N. E., Atlanta, Ga.

4. AGENCY COMMISSION

15% to recognized agencies on time charges; no cash discount.

5. GENERAL ADVERTISING See coded regulations

General: 1a, 2a, 2b, 3a, 3b, 3c, 3d, 4a, 5, 6a, 8.
Rate Protection: †10i, 11m, 12m, 13m, 14c, 16.
Contracts: 21, 22a, 22c, 23, 25, 26, 29, 32b.
Basic Rates: 41c, 42, 44b, 45a.
Comb.; Cont. Discounts: 60f.
*Cancellation: 70a, 70f, 73a, 73b.
Prod. Services: 84, 85, 86, 87c.
   (*) Announcement contracts subject to cancellation on 14 days prior written notice.
   (†) Prime time designations of AA1, AA2, AA3 28 days.
Affiliated with ABC Television Network.
All contracts with the same advertiser may be combined for determining rate of discount.

Multiple Product Announcements

Station does not accept commercials of any length containing advertising messages of two separate corporations; nor one minute announcements containing more than two selling messages or more than two products (or services); or announcements of less than one minute in length which urge the viewer to purchase more than one product (or service). Service charge for splicing and/or editing piggyback announcements will be 15.00.

Product Protection

Station will attempt to provide 10 minutes separation of directly competitive products, where scheduling is under control of station. Rebates, credits, and makegoods will not be issued on any product conflict other than those occurring back-to-back.

6. TIME RATES

No. 5 Eff 1/18/71—Rec'd 1/25/71.
Rev. 3/8/71—Rec'd 3/15/71.

7. SPOT ANNOUNCEMENTS

A—Mon thru Fri 6-7:30 pm; Sat & Sun 5-7:30 pm.
B—Mon thru Fri 4:29-5:59 pm; Mon thru Sun 11-11:30 pm; Sat & Sun 3:29-4:59 pm.
C—Mon thru Sun noon-4:29 pm.
D—Mon thru Sun sign-on-noon & 11:30 pm-sign-off.
(30/20 seconds unless otherwise specified)

MON PM:	Fixed	(*)	(†)
8:00	300	250	225
8:30	300	250	225
9-concl, rotates to Sun thru Tues Movie.			
30/20 sec.	600	500	450
TUES:			
7:30-8:30, rotates to Welby/Eddie's Father.			
30/20 sec.	600	500	450
8:30-10, rotates to Sun & Mon Movie.			
30/20 sec.	550	450	400
10-11, rotates to Mod Squad/Eddie's Father.			
30/20 sec.	600	500	450
WED:			
8:00, rotates to Welby/Mod Squad.			
30/20 sec.	600	500	450
8:30-10:30	290	250	.....
10:30-11	250	225	200
20 sec.	210	190	170
THURS:			
8:00	250	200	250

CLASS B	Fixed	(*)	(†)
60 sec.	160	140	120
30/20 sec.	95	85	70
10 sec.	50	45	35

CLASS C			
60 sec.	100	85	70
30/20 sec.	60	50	35
10 sec.	30	25	15

CLASS D			
60 sec.	80	70	60
30/20 sec.	50	40	35
10 sec.	25	20	15

(*) Preempt.
(†) Immediately preemptible.

8. PARTICIPATING ANNOUNCEMENT PROGRAMS

(60 seconds unless otherwise specified)

MON THRU FRI:	Fixed	(*)	(†)
Morning Funnies—7-7:30 am	50	40	30
30/20 sec.	30	25	20
10 sec.	15	13	10
Tubby & Lester—7:30-9 am.			
60 sec.	100	80	60
30/20 sec.	50	40	30
10 sec.	25	20	15
Romper Room—9-10 am.			
60 sec.	80	60	40
30/20 sec.	50	40	30
10 sec.	25	20	15
Morning Movie—10-11:30 am.			
60 sec.	100	80	60
30/20 sec.	50	40	30
10 sec.	25	20	15
Day ROS—10 am-4:30 pm.	100	85	70
30/20 sec.	50	45	35
10 sec.	25	20	15
Free for all Movie—4:30-6 pm.			
60 sec.	220	200	180
30/20 sec.	110	100	90
10 sec.	55	50	45
Dick Van Dyke/Hazel/What's My Line—6-7:30 pm, rotates thru Hazel/Line 6:30-7:30 pm Sat.			
60 sec.	360	300	270
30/20 sec.	180	150	135
10 sec.	90	85	70

SUN THRU THURS:			
Dick Cavett—11:30 pm-concl.			
60 sec.	100	80	60
30/20 sec.	50	40	30
10 sec.	25	20	15

NEWS BLOCKS

	Fixed	(*)	(†)
Eyewitness News—6:55-7 am Mon thru Fri.			
60 sec.	50	40	30
30/20 sec.	25	20	15
10 sec.	15	10	.....
Eyewitness Midday News—12:30 -1 pm Mon thru Fri.			
60 sec.	120	100	80
30/20 sec.	60	50	40
10 sec.	30	25	20
Eyewitness News—11-11:30 pm Sun thru Fri.			
60 sec.	200	180	150
30/20 sec.	100	90	75
10 sec.	50	45	40
Eyewitness News—approx 1-1:30 am Mon thru Fri.			
60 sec.	50	40	30
30/20 sec.	25	20	15
10 sec.	15	10	.....
SAT:			
Best of Hollywood—11:30 pm-concl Sat thru Fri, rotation.			
60 sec.	120	100	80
30/20 sec.	60	50	40
10 sec.	30	25	20
Saturday Cartoon Rotation—7:30 am-noon.			
60 sec.	100	80	60
30/20 sec.	60	40	30
10 sec.	30	20	15
Saturday Afternoon Movie—3-4:30 pm.			
60 sec.	100	55	70
30/20 sec.	50	45	35
10 sec.	25	20	15
Wide World of Sports—5-6:30 pm.			
30/20 sec.	250	225	200
10 sec.	125	110	100
Championship Sports—10:30-11:30 pm.			
60 sec.	400	360	300
30/20 sec.	200	180	150
10 sec.	105	90	75
SUN:			
John Wayne Theatre—noon-2 pm.			
60 sec.	100	85	70
30/20 sec.	50	45	35
10 sec.	25	20	15
Movie Matinee—2-4 pm.	100	85	70
30/20 sec.	50	45	35
10 sec.	25	20	15
Sunday Free for all Movie—5-7 pm.			
60 sec.	450	400	360
30/20 sec.	225	200	180
10 sec.	115	100	90

(*) Preempt.
(†) Immediately preemptible.

The hours from 7:00 P.M. to 11:00 P.M. EST (6:30 P.M. to 10:00 P.M. CST) attract peak audiences, are called *prime time,* and are the most expensive time in television. On network-affiliated stations, 2½ hours of this time are programmed by the networks, with stations selling "spots" early in the breaks between programs. The network stations have 7:00 to 7:30 P.M. E.S.T. for their own programming and sale.

The hour or so adjacent to prime time is called *fringe time. Early fringe* precedes prime time; *late fringe* follows prime time. These rank next to prime time in costliness.

The Standard Billing week is Monday through Sunday. The Standard Billing month ends on the last Sunday.

THE RATE STRUCTURE

Stations offer a variety of discounts.

Frequency discounts. These are offered to advertisers usually in the form of a *plan rate* for a given number of spots within a week's time—that is, *5 plan* or *10 plan.*

Package rate. The package rate is generally a total price for a schedule of spots at different time belts that costs less than the total of the rates for the individual spots making up the package.

Preemptible rate. A considerable proportion of spot television advertising time is sold on a preemptible (lower-rate) basis, whereby the advertiser gives the station the right to sell his time slot to another advertiser if he will pay a better rate for it, or if it is part of a larger package deal. If the station has the right to sell to another, higher-rate advertiser any time up until the time of the telecast, the rate for the preemptible advertiser is called the *immediately preemptible* (IP) rate. If the station can preempt only if it gives the original advertiser two weeks notice, the rate is designated as *preemptible with two weeks notice.* An advertiser can buy a nonpreemptible time slot by

EXAMPLES OF WEEKLY SCHEDULES IN THE TOP 100 MARKETS

Number of 30 sec. Announcements and Daypart Used	Weekly Cost	Gross Audience (000)			Cost Per (000)		
		Homes	Men	Women	Homes	Men	Women
10 Daytime M-F	$ 43,030	34,230	8,170	28,190	$1.26	$5.27	$1.53
5 Early Evening	50,565	34,835	19,080	25,085	1.45	2.65	2.02
5 Nighttime	142,610	48,730	32,485	42,005	2.93	4.39	3.40
5 Late Evening	35,345	19,720	12,735	16,160	1.79	2.78	2.19
5 Weekend Day	39,025	21,300	15,225	12,590	1.83	2.56	3.10

Source: TvB's Spot TV Planning Guide
Feb. 1971

Spot TV CPM'S

Courtesy, Batten, Barton, Durstine, & Osborn, Inc.

paying the highest rate; the *two-weeks preemptible* rate is the next highest, and the *immediately preemptible* rate is the lowest. The moving of a preemptible spot elsewhere on a schedule (with the advertiser's approval) is one of the major causes of confusion in billing and paying for spot television schedules.

Participations. Every station carries its own regularly scheduled non-network shows in which spot advertisers can buy *participations*. Some are built around a popular local personality. Most are half-hour or hour-length films created by independent producers and rented (or *syndicated*) to local stations for scheduling to attract certain types of audiences. They may also include reruns of popular old network offerings.

Special features. News telecasts, weather reports, sports news and commentary, stock-market reports, and similar programming are called *special features*. Time is generally sold in connection with special features at a premium price.

Run of schedule (ROS). An advertiser can earn a lower rate by permitting a station to run his commercials at its convenience whenever time is available, rather than specifying the station-break positions, participating programs, and special features in which it must appear. This is called an ROS (run of schedule) basis.

Negotiation. There is a wide practice, especially on large schedules, of negotiation for rates better than the published card rates. We discuss this matter in Chapter 25.

Piggybacks and integrated commercials. Until the late 1960's, most television time was sold in units of 10, 20, or 60 seconds. Sometimes an advertiser would buy a 60-second spot and run commercials for two products on it, called *piggybacking*. Since then, time has been sold in 30-second units; the 20-second spot is fading from use; hence the need for piggybacking is likewise fading out.

OTHER TRADE PRACTICES

Closing time. Tapes and films that are to be part of a commercial must be in the station's hands 72 hours in advance. Stations are usually capable of accommodating a request for a shorter closing time in special instances.

Certificate of performance. Station invoices for spot television time include a *Certificate of Performance* (station affidavit) attesting to the fact that the commercials were run on the days and times enumerated. (A similar statement appears on network bills, too.) Unfortunately these statements are not always submitted on time for prompt payment, nor are they always accurate. A system for electronically coding TV commercials has been developed that, by the help of computer tape, provides an exact record.

Station representatives.   Men with offices in the main advertising centers act as sales agents for stations around the country. They provide the time buyer with data about the market, the station's programming, and the audience of the station; they find out for the time buyer what times are available on the various stations they represent (mostly by long-distance telephone or teletype). The station representative submits his list of *availabilities* to the time buyer, who selects the announcement positions he regards as the most desirable. Some representatives handle both television and radio stations; others specialize in television only or radio only.

Product protection.   Advertisers do not want to have a commercial for a competitive product appear close to their own; they would prefer to have a 15-minute, or at least a 10-minute, separation. This spacing of commercials in relation to those of competitive products, or to an undesirable type of product, is called *product protection,* and is subject to negotiation between advertisers and stations.

The paper problem.   Ask any media man what the biggest headache is in the handling of spots (both for television and radio), and he will reply, "Paper work!" There is a lot of paper work involved in assembling the availability of spots for a schedule, in gathering the demographic information for making choices. There is paper work involved in placing orders under the various discount plans and deals. There is a tremendous amount of paper work involved in trying to get records of the appearances of spots, particularly when the bulk of them are bought on a preemptible basis. Then comes the question of keeping track of the *make-goods* (running of commercials which were skipped in schedule), before paying the bills for them. As a result, payments are often held up till some open-billing matters on it are resolved; meanwhile, the next month's bill comes along.

ELEMENTS OF TV PLANNING

In making plans for a television effort in a market, the advertiser keeps asking, "How can I reach the greatest number of people who may buy my product? On what station? At what time? On what program? At what cost?" The advertiser himself has to define the type of person who may buy his product. Man? Woman? Child? But then he can turn to the audience-measurement research services to learn what stations or programs reach each of these groups, and what their age brackets are.

The figure under "Nielsen Avg. Audience %" is the "Nielsen Rating." "This week" is compared with "Last week," as advertisers are very concerned about a program's staying power. Note difference in ratings per program.

Courtesy, A. C. Nielsen Company

NATIONAL Nielsen TV RANKING
(Estimates supplementing National Nielsen TV Ratings Report)

SECOND REPORT FOR MAY 1972
(TWO WEEKS ENDING MAY 21, 1972)

Rank NAA	Program Name	Prog. Type	Dur. Ntwk. Freq.	NAA % This Report	NAA % Last Report	Share % This Report	Share % Last Report	Prog. Covg.
	EVENING							
	AVERAGE FOR ALL 95 PROGRAMS	AC1	20C1	13.5		52		
1	MISS USA BEAUTY PAGEANT	AC1	35C1	25.2	25.1	54	51	99
2	*24TH ANNUAL EMMY AWARDS	AC1	35C1	23.6	27.9	49	39	99
3	ALL IN THE FAMILY	CS	30C1	23.1	21.1	40	31	98
4	GUNSMOKE	EW	60C1	21.8	16.1	40	31	98
5	SONNY & CHER COMEDY HOUR	CV	60C1	21.2	23.6	44	42	99
6	FLIP WILSON SHOW	CV	60C1	20.9	18.5	44	40	99
7	HERE'S LUCY	CS	30C1	20.4	18.2	43	40	99
8	MANNIX	MS	60C1	19.7	16.3	40	28	99
9	DORIS DAY SHOW	CS	30C1	19.7	18.2	36	38	99
10	IRONSIDE	MS	60N1	19.6	20.8	36	38	99
11	MARY TYLER MOORE SHOW	CS	30C1	19.0	21.9	39	40	98
11	MEDICAL CENTER	GD	60C1	19.0	20.1	34	34	99
13	*AMERICA'S JR-MISS PAGEANT	AC	60N1	18.7	20.2	29		98
13	ROWAN & MARTIN LAUGH-IN	CV	60N1	18.7	20.2	32	35	98
15	NEW DICK VAN DYKE SHOW	CS	30C1	18.2	19.9	32	36	97
16	SANFORD AND SON	CS	30N1	17.9	21.2	38	37	92
17	ADAM 12	MS	30N1	17.9	18.6	33	34	99
17	*ELECTION'72 :NEB-W.VIR.	N	5A1	17.8		33		99
19	ARNIE	CS	30C1	17.8	18.6	33	34	99
19	BONANZA	EW	60N1	17.6	23.6	32	39	99
21	MISSION:IMPOSSIBLE	MS	60C1	17.6	16.5	36	33	99
21	NBC MYSTERY MOVIE	MS	90N1	17.6	23.8	32	39	97
23	MARCUS WELBY, M. D.	GD	55A1	17.5	17.7	35	38	97
23	PARTRIDGE FAMILY	CS	30A1	17.5	21.1	35	32	96
25	HAWAII FIVE-O	MS	60C1	17.4	19.0	29	30	97
26	MOVIE OF THE WEEK	FFVARA1		16.7	17.4	29	33	98
27	CANNON	MS	60C1	16.6	17.7	30	34	97
28	NBC MONDAY NIGHT MOVIES	FFVARN1		16.4	19.0	30	34	96
29	LOVE, AMERICAN STYLE	CS	30C1	16.3	17.6	30	34	99
30	ODD COUPLE	CS	30A1	16.1	18.7	31	36	95
30	ROOM 222	CS	30A1	16.1	19.4	31	34	95
32	DEAN MARTIN SHOW	GV	60N1	15.9	18.3	29	36	97
33	MOD SQUAD	MS	60A1	15.6	16.5	29	30	97
34	*SECRETS-AFRICAN BAOBAB	DO	60N1	15.5		32		97
35	F.B.I., THE	N	30C5	15.5	17.7	30	32	97
36	NIGHT GALLERY	GD	60N1	15.2	13.5	30	28	96
37	CAROL BURNETT SHOW	CS	30N1	15.1	18.6	30	31	99
38	BRADY BUNCH	CS	30A1	15.0	18.6	26	30	99
39	WONDERFUL WORLD OF DISNEY	MS	60C1	14.8	11.9	33	37	99
40	*ANNIE:THE WOMEN-LIFE-MAN	VM	60C1	14.4	19.4	24	22	94
41	CBS SUNDAY NIGHT MOVIES	FF120C1		14.3	12.8	28	23	99
42	BOLD ONES	GD	60N1	14.1	12.8	28	38	99
42	PONDEROSA	EW	60N1	14.1	12.6	26	23	93
44	CBS EVENING NEWS-CRONKITE	N	30C5	13.9	15.1	29	29	98
44	EMERGENCY	GD	30N1	13.9	15.1	27	28	97
44	JIMMY STEWART SHOW	CS	30N1	13.8	11.9	27	31	97
47	OWEN MARSHALL-AT LAW	GD	60A1	13.7	11.9	26	24	96
48	CADE'S COUNTY	MS	60C1	13.7	12.7	24	28	94
49	ABC MONDAY NIGHT MOVIE	FFVARA1		13.6	12.7	24	23	93
49	GLEN CAMPBELL HOUR	VM	60C1	13.6	12.5	24	22	94

Rank NAA	Program Name	Prog. Type	Dur. Ntwk. Freq.	NAA % This Report	NAA % Last Report	Share % This Report	Share % Last Report	Prog. Covg.
	EVENING (cont'd)							
51	*ELECTION'72:MO-MICH.10:15	N	5A1	13.2	19.6	25	35	83
52	*ABC SUNDAY NIGHT MOVIE	FFVARA1		13.0	15.4	27	28	96
52	NBC FRIDAY NIGHT MOVIES	FF120C1		13.0	15.4	26	26	95
54	*CBS THURSDAY NIGHT MOVIES	FF110C1		12.9	14.0	26	28	96
55	NBC THURSDAY NIGHT MOVIES	FFVARN1		12.9	14.1	25	28	97
56	NEW CBS FRI. NIGHT MOVIES	FF	90C1	12.6	16.6	25	30	93
57	*ELECTION'72:MO-MICH.9:25	N	10A1	12.4		22		93
57	LONGSTREET	MS	60A1	12.4	12.3	23	21	95
59	NBC NIGHTLY NEWS	N	30N5	11.7	11.0	27	25	95
60	*MY THREE SONS	CS	30C1	11.4	12.5	23	22	98
61	*ALIAS SMITH AND JONES	EW	60A1	11.2	12.3	23	22	96
61	*CBS REPORTS-TUE.	DO	60C1	11.2		23		97
61	*O'HARA U.S. TREASURY	MS	60C1	11.0	13.1	22	24	97
64	MOVIE OF THE WEEKEND	FF	90A1	11.0	13.1	28	24	96
65	CBS SATURDAY NEWS-MUDD	N	55C1	10.6	10.3	21	27	94
65	*ESCALATION IN VIETNAM	N	30C1	10.6		25		94
67	SIXTH SENSE	MS	60A1	10.5	11.9	25		90
68	DON RICKLES SHOW	CS	30C1	10.4	12.5	21	24	90
69	ME AND THE CHIMP	CS	30C1	10.3	10.5	21	26	90
70	*MONDAY NIGHT SPECIAL	FV	60A1	10.2	7.8	18	14	90
71	JAMES GARNER AS NICHOLS	A	60N1	10.1	8.4	18	16	92
72	*STANLEY CUP PLAYOFFS	SE170C1		10.0		19		99
73	60 MINUTES	N	60C1	9.8	10.1	23	25	97
74	*ABC NEWS-SMITH-REASONER	N	30A5	9.5	8.9	23	22	95
74	*CBS NEWS-CAMPAIGN '72	N	30C1	9.5		20		85
76	*HEARTLAND U.S.A.	DO	30A1	9.5		15		92
77	COURTSHIP-EDDIE'S FATHER	CS	30A1	9.4		17		94
78	*WHO DO YOU THINK YOU ARE	GO	30A1	9.1		17		89
78	*AMERICA LIVES	DO	30A1	8.7		14		90
80	NBC SATURDAY NIGHT NEWS	CV	30A1	8.4	8.1	18	21	92
80	M. FELDMAN COMEDY MACHINE	CV	30A1	8.0	5.5	15	9	78
82	*CBS NEWS-CAMPAIGN'72	N	5C1	7.8		17		94
83	*ABC WEEKEND NEWS-SAT.	N	15A1	7.7	6.5	15	15	92
84	TONIGHT SHOW	GV	75N5	7.4	6.8	32	31	99
85	BEWITCHED	CS	30A1	6.9	7.3	14	14	91
86	*NBC SUNDAY NIGHT MOVIES	N	30N1	6.9		20	18	90
86	LATE NIGHT CBS MOVIES	FFVARC4		6.3	6.1	19	31	95
88	*CHAMPIONSHIP AUTO RACE	SE	30A1	5.8		13		90
89	*CBS SUNDAY NEWS	N	15C1	5.5	5.7	13	14	81
91	PERSUADERS	MS	60A1	5.3		10		76
92	*ABC WEEKEND NEWS-SAT.	N	30A1	4.9		11		93
93	*ABC WEEKEND NEWS-SUN.	N	15A1	3.7	5.6	7	19	92
93	SAT/SUN TONIGHT SHOW	GV	75N1	3.4		7	17	73
95	DICK CAVETT SHOW	GV	60A5	3.3	3.2	12	14	86

* Telecast one week only in this report interval. See program index for date. Programs are rated in terms of total duration. Telecasts with curtailed duration or station facilities are excluded.

Although this program was telecast both weeks of this report period, one week is excluded from this ranking due to substantial departure from normal station facilities, duration or time of telecast.

These data are confidential, subject to some permissible uses as NTI Ratings Reports.

Copyright 1972 — A. C. Nielsen Company

A National Nielsen TV Audience Estimate of Network Shows

Prepared on a daily basis.

Courtesy, A. C. Nielsen Company

NATIONAL *Nielsen* TV AUDIENCE ESTIMATES — EVE. • SUN. APR. 30, 1972

TIME	7:00	7:15	7:30	7:45	8:00	8:15	8:30	8:45	9:00	9:15	9:30	9:45	10:00	10:15	10:30	10:45	11:00

ABC TV

The F.B.I. (R) — ABC Sunday Night Movie "ASSIGNMENT: MUNICH" (9:00-11:00PM)

TOTAL AUDIENCE (Households (000) & %): 14,660 / 23.6 ... 19,440 / 31.3

AVERAGE AUDIENCE / SHARE OF AUDIENCE % / AVG. AUD. BY ¼ HR. %:
10,620 17.1 / 30 / 14.8 — 15,0* 27* / 15.3 — 19,2* 33* / 19.8 — 18.5* 31* / 18.5 — 21.1* 35* / 21.2 — 20.3* 38* / 19.8 — 18.4* 38* / 17.6 — 19.1

CBS TV

CBS Sunday Night Movies "UP THE DOWN STAIRCASE" (7:30-9:30PM) — Metropolitan Opera "SALUTE TO SIR RUDOLF BING" (taped)

TOTAL AUDIENCE (Households (000) & %): 15,710 / 25.3 ... 8,260 / 13.3

CBS TV (K)

Wonderful World of Disney (R) "LIGHT IN THE FOREST" PART II — Jimmy Stewart Show (Procter & Gamble)(R)

AVERAGE AUDIENCE:
8,290 13.2 / 24 / 11.7 — 11.5* 23* / 11.7 — 13.1* 24* / 13.5 / 12.7 — 13.3 — 13.4* 23* / 11.7 — 15.1 — 15.1* 25* / 15.1 — 9.0* 15* / 8.8 — 8.2* 15* / 8.1 — 8.3

NBC TV (1)

Bonanza (R) — Bold Ones (R)

TOTAL AUDIENCE: 16,830 / 27.1 ... 12,540 / 20.2 ... 19,690 / 31.7 ... 16,210 / 26.1

AVERAGE AUDIENCE:
11,860 19.1 / 37 / 16.1 — 17.2* 35* / 18.4 — 20.5 — 23.9* 38* / 21.3 — 18.0 — 21.4* 35* / 22.2 — 25.9* 43* / 26.1 — 20.5* 38* / 19.6 — 19.1* 40* / 19.0

EVE. • SUN. MAY 7, 1972

ABC TV

Friars Roast — The F.B.I. (R) — NBA Championship Game (NEW YORK VS LOS ANGELES, 10:00-12; 20AM)(1)

TOTAL AUDIENCE: 11,670 / 18.8 ... 16,080 / 25.9

AVERAGE AUDIENCE:
14,840 23.9 — 11,300 18.2 / 33 / 15.4 — 16.2* 31* / 17.1 — 20.3* 36* / 20.6 — 13.5 / 22 / 13.7 — 13.7* 22* / 13.7 — 13,2* 22* / 13.1 — 15.3* 27* / 15.7 — 16.0 — 15.9* 30* / 15.8

CBS TV

CBS Sunday Night Movies "ENTER LAUGHING" (7:30-9:30PM) — Cade's County (R)

TOTAL AUDIENCE: 17,700 / 28.5 ... 13,850 / 22.3

CBS TV (K)

Wonderful World of Disney (R) "JOKER, THE AMIABLE OCELOT" — Jimmy Stewart Show (Procter & Gamble)(R)

AVERAGE AUDIENCE:
7,640 12.3 / 22 / 10.3 — 10.3* 21* / 10.3 — 11.0* 20* / 11.1 — 11.5* 20* / 11.7 — 16.2 — 16.3* 27* / 14.7 — 15.1* 26* / 15.5 — 18.0 — 17.7* 31* / 17.3

NBC TV (2)

London Bridge Special (General Motors) — Bold Ones (R)

TOTAL AUDIENCE: 16,210 / 26.1 ... 12,730 / 20.5 ... 18,440 / 29.7 ... 16,700 / 26.9

AVERAGE AUDIENCE:
12,230 19.7 / 37 / 16.5 — 17.7* 35* / 18.9 — 21.7* 39* / 21.8 — 21.4* 31* / 17.4 — 13,540 21.8 / 36 / 21.2 — 21.4* 35* / 21.7 — 22.2* 38* / 22.3 — 20.1* 36* / 20.1 — 20.4 — 19.8* 40* / 19.2

TV HOUSEHOLDS USING TV

	WK 1 (See Def. 1)	WK 2															

WK 1: 42.6 — 45.1 — 47.7 — 50.9 — 53.9 — 55.9 — 56.9 — 59.0 — 60.1 — 61.0 — 60.9 — 60.4 — 55.2 — 52.0 — 49.1 — 46.6

WK 2: 45.0 — 46.3 — 48.8 — 53.9 — 56.5 — 57.1 — 59.9 — 60.7 — 61.4 — 59.9 — 58.6 — 57.2 — 56.0 — 48.0

U.S. TV Households: 62,100,000

(B) Originated in Black & White. **(R)** Repeat. See page B. **†** For Sponsorship Detail, See Audience Estimates by Sponsorship. **(OP)** Other Programs; See Pages 80-89. ***** Half-hour ratings (for immediately preceding and subject quarter-hours).

FOR REM, RATINGS, SEE OP PAGES.

37

151

4 WK TIME PERIOD AVG   SPOT BUYING GUIDE

	ADI RATINGS							TIME		TOTAL SURVEY AREA, IN THOUSANDS																
	WOMEN			MEN		TNS	CHD	ADI TV HH RTG	METRO TV HH RATING	TV HH	TOTAL PERSONS 2+	TOTAL ADULTS 18+	WOMEN					HOUSEWIVES		MEN			TEENS		CHILDREN	
DAY, TIME, AND STATION	TOT	18-49	18-34	TOT	18-49	TOT	TOT						TOTAL	18-49	18-34	25-64	25-49	TOTAL	−50	TOTAL	18-49	18-34	TOTAL	GIRLS	TOTAL	6-11
	27	28	29	32	33	35	37	1	3	5	6	7	8	9	10	11	12	14	15	16	17	18	21	22	23	24
TUESDAY																										
5.00P - 5.30P / 4.45P- 5.15P																										
WJBF	7	6	4	6	6	16	18	17	14	27	48	18	12	7	4	9	6	9	6	6	4	3	10	5	21	13
WRDW	10	8	6	8	6	15	18	16	18	25	47	28	19	10	3	13	8	17	8	10	4	3	10	4	9	5
	17	14	10	14	12	31	36	36	33	52	95	46	31	17	7	22	14	26	14	16	8	6	20	9	30	18
5.30P - 6.00P / 5.15P- 5.45P																										
WJBF	8	8	7	9	8	19	19	19	18	33	61	29	17	10	5	13	8	14	8	12	7	5	15	9	18	12
WRDW	11	9	8	8	6	13	18	17	18	27	52	29	17	9	4	12	8	16	9	12	6	3	9	4	14	6
	19	17	15	17	14	32	37	39	35	60	113	58	34	19	9	25	16	30	17	24	13	8	24	13	32	18
6.00P - 6.30P / 5.45P- 6.15P																										
WJBF	25	21	17	·26	20	21	10	29	27	47	86	58	31	17	8	25	14	28	15	27	14	8	14	8	14	6
WRDW	13	12	10	13	13	3	5	18	20	27	48	34	19	11	5	15	10	18	11	15	9	5	5	5	10	5
	38	33	27	39	33	24	15	51	47	74	134	92	50	28	13	40	24	46	26	42	23	13	19	10	24	13
6.30P - 7.00P / 6.15P- 6.45P																										
WJBF	25	23	19	28	23	21	10	38	37	59	111	89	47	24	11	37	21	42	21	43	21	13	13	7	9	5
WRDW	14	15	11	17	18	4	8	20	25	31	50	43	22	15	7	21	14	21	14	21	14	7	1	1	6	3
	39	38	30	45	41	25	18	62	61	90	161	132	69	39	18	57	35	63	35	64	35	20	14	7	15	8
7.00P - 7.30P / 6.45P- 7.15P																										
WJBF	31	31	31	28	28	48	32	39	38	61	134	94	50	30	15	39	25	44	25	44	26	17	22	12	18	13
WRDW	15	15	13	12	10	10	24	21	24	32	63	47	25	16	7	21	15	25	16	22	13	7	4	1	13	7
	46	46	44	40	38	58	56	66	63	93	197	141	75	46	22	60	40	69	41	66	39	24	26	13	31	20
7.30P - 8.00P / 7.15P- 7.45P																										
WJBF	36	39	40	31	32	48	45	43	41	70	172	109	62	40	22	48	32	53	32	47	31	21	32	19	32	24
WRDW	15	15	13	13	10	8	24	22	22	32	70	45	25	16	8	20	14	24	15	20	10	7	6	2	20	11
	51	54	53	44	42	56	69	69	64	102	242	154	87	56	30	68	46	77	47	67	41	28	38	21	51	35
8.00P - 8.30P / 7.45P- 8.15P																										
WJBF	35	38	40	31	32	48	45	47	44	78	190	119	69	45	25	54	36	58	35	50	33	20	33	21	39	27
WRDW	14	14	14	13	10	8	23	20	22	30	68	44	25	16	8	19	13	22	14	20	10	7	6	2	18	10
	49	52	54	44	42	56	68	66	66	108	258	163	94	61	33	73	49	80	49	70	43	27	39	23	57	37
8.30P - 9.00P / 8.15P- 8.45P																										
WJBF	26	30	31	24	24	25	22	41	42	67	157	102	58	39	22	47	32	51	32	45	30	17	26	14	29	20
WRDW	23	25	24	18	18	19	20	24	25	37	84	56	33	23	13	25	18	29	19	23	14	9	10	6	18	10
	49	55	55	42	42	44	42	64	66	104	241	158	91	62	35	72	50	80	51	68	44	26	36	20	47	30
9.00P - 9.30P / 8.45P- 9.15P																										
WJBF	24	28	30	21	22	24	18	30	28	53	117	82	46	32	18	38	26	41	27	36	24	12	19	8	17	10
WRDW	23	25	23	20	20	18	19	30	28	46	97	68	40	27	15	31	22	37	24	29	19	12	13	9	16	10
	47	53	53	41	42	42	37	67	66	99	214	150	86	59	33	69	48	78	51	65	43	24	32	17	33	20
9.30P - 10.00P / 9.15P- 9.45P																										
WJBF	23	29	31	20	22	23	12	30	35	49	108	77	44	32	18	36	25	38	26	33	23	12	18	7	13	8
WRDW	19	22	22	17	19	14	6	28	26	44	86	66	38	26	15	30	21	34	23	28	20	12	11	7	10	7
	42	51	53	37	41	37	18	63	63	93	194	143	82	58	33	66	46	72	49	61	43	24	29	14	23	15
10.00P - 10.30P / 9.45P-10.15P																										
WJBF	23	26	23	13	14	25	10	29	33	49	103	75	46	33	18	38	27	40	27	29	21	11	19	9	10	7
WRDW	17	19	22	16	17	8	4	25	25	39	69	58	34	24	15	28	20	31	21	25	18	11	7	4	4	3
	40	45	45	29	31	33	14	57	58	88	172	133	80	57	33	66	47	71	48	54	39	22	26	13	14	10
10.30P - 11.00P / 10.15P-10.45P																										
WJBF	24	26	24	14	15	20	9	29	31	49	92	70	47	31	16	41	27	42	26	23	16	9	15	8	8	7
WRDW	9	8	9	7	6	5		17	17	27	44	38	22	14	10	17	11	21	13	17	12	8	4	2	2	1
	33	34	33	21	21	25	9	47	48	76	136	108	69	45	26	58	38	63	39	40	28	17	19	10	10	8
11.00P - 11.15P / 10.45P-11.15P																										
WJBF	11	9	3	8	8	7		22	23	37	63	51	34	21	10	30	18	30	17	17	12	6	9	5	4	3
WRDW	5	4		3	3	3	1	10	12	16	23	20	12	6	4	10	5	12	5	8	5	3	2	2	1	1
	16	13		11	11	10	1	33	35	53	86	71	46	27	14	40	23	42	22	25	17	9	11	7	5	4
11.15P - 11.30P / 11.00P-11.30P																										
WJBF	9	8	2	7	7	6		14	14	21	31	27	17	9	2	15	8	15	8	10	7	3	4	3		
WRDW	5	4	5	3	2	1	1	8	12	12	15	13	9	4	3	8	4	8	3	5	3	2	1	1	1	1
	14	12	7	10	9	7	1	23	26	33	46	40	26	13	5	23	12	23	11	15	10	4	5	4	1	1
11.30P - 11.45P / 11.15P-11.45P																										
WJBF	6	5	1	4	5	4		11	12	17	23	20	13	7	1	12	6	12	6	7	6	3	4	3		
WRDW	5	3	4	4	5	2	1	8	11	11	14	13	8	4	1	7	3	8	4	5	3	2	1	1	1	1
	11	8	5	8	10	6	1	20	23	28	37	33	21	11	4	19	9	20	10	12	9	4	5	4	1	1
11.45P - MDNGHT / 11.30P-MDNGHT																										
WJBF	5	4	1	3	4	4		9	10	13	16	13	9	4		9	4	9	4	5	4	2	3	2		
WRDW	5	4	1	3	4	4		7	11	11	15	14	8	4		10	5	12	5	8	5	3	2	2		
	9	7	5	7	8	6	1	17	20	24	31	27	17	8	3	16	7	17	8	11	8	4	4	4		
MDNGHT - 12.15A / 11.45P-12.15A																										
WJBF	4	4	1	2	3	3		7	8	11	12	10	7	4		7	4	7	4	4	3	2	3	2		
WRDW	4	3	4	4	5	1		7	11	10	13	13	7	3	2	6	3	6	3	5	3	1	1	1		
	8	7	5	6	8	4	1	15	18	21	25	23	14	7	2	13	6	14	7	9	8	4	4	3		
12.15A - 12.30A / MDNGHT-12.30A																										
WJBF	4	4	1	2	3	3		6	6	8	9	7	6	3		5	3	5	3	4	3	2	2	2		
WRDW	4	3	4	4	5	1		7	11	10	13	12	7	3	2	6	3	5	2	6	5	3	2			
	8	7	5	6	8	4	1	13	16	18	21	19	11	6	2	10	5	13	6	6	5	4	2	2		
12.30A - 12.45A / 12.15A-12.45A																										
WJBF	4	4	1	2	3	3		5	5	7	9	7	5	3		4	3	5	3	2	2	1	2	2		
WRDW	4	3	4	4	5	1		7	10	9	12	11	6	3	2	5	2	5	2	5	5	3	2			
	8	7	5	6	8	4	1	12	15	16	21	19	11	6	2	9	5	11	6	8	7	4	2	2		
12.45A - 1.00A / 12.30A- 1.00A																										
WJBF	3	3	1	2	3	3		5	5	7	9	7	5	3		4	3	5	3	2	2	1	2	2		
WRDW	4	3	4	4	5	1	1	6	10	9	12	12	6	3	2	5	2	6	3	6	5	3				
	8	7	6	6	8	4	1	12	15	16	21	19	11	6	2	9	5	11	6	8	7	4	2	2		

!TECHNICAL DIFFICULTY

+ PARENT/SATELLITE RELATIONSHIP

TUESDAY   FEB/MARCH 1972   PAGE 17   AUGUSTA

Courtesy, American Research Bureau

A Spot Buying Guide

This shows the type of demographic information available to advertisers in buying spot television. Such reports are prepared for cities across the country; this one was for Atlanta.

A number of research firms specialize in gathering such information on a syndicated basis, which means that at their own expense (which is considerable), they gather audience viewing data all over the country, covering all markets, and publishing it. Then they sell the reports on an annual subscription basis. These serve as the basis for making media plans. These reports include the Nielsen Station Index (NSI), the Nielsen TV Local market reports; the American Research Bureau (ARB), ARB TV Local market reports, and the ARB Radio market reports. The Pulse is prominent for its reports in the radio field. The Simmons Reports go into the demographic study of TV audiences and also of magazine readers.

Principles of Audience Research

All audience research is based on established principles of sampling, culling from a carefully planned sample of the total audience information that can then be extrapolated to a larger audience. There are three principal means of getting this information:

1. The telephone coincidental method
2. The diary method
3. Mechanical recorder

1. *The telephone coincidental method.* By this method, a preselected sampling of people is called up and asked, "Do you have a television set? How many members of the family are watching it? What channels? What programs?" The advantages of this method are that it gets the information quickly and directly. The disadvantages are that the questions must be brief, that people might not be at home to answer the phone, and that one cannot call too early in the morning or too late at night. Nevertheless, it represents the most widely used method of television audience research.

2. *The diary method.* The diary is a notebook, kept next to the television set, in which members of a family can record the stations and programs they watch; they can also tell something about themselves as consumers. The research firms must arrange to get the cooperation of various families with a carefully planned sampling pattern; there is a fee in payment. These diaries are then returned to the research firm and tabulated. The advantage of the diary is that it covers all broadcast hours, it covers all members of a family, and it can include information about the listener as requested. There is always a question of the validity of self-filled-out records, but research companies have developed various statistical techniques for spotting and meeting this problem.

| When set is OFF draw line down OFF column | When set is ON put an X in ON column | Write in CALL LETTERS & CHANNEL NOS. of stations tuned in over 5 minutes | Write in NAMES OF PROGRAMS watched while tuned to each station | Place a 1 in column for MAN OF HOUSE and/or LADY OF HOUSE if watching when TV is on | Write in NUMBER of OTHERS watching TV— Men Women Teens (T) Children (C) |

TIME	SET USE		STATION TUNED IN		NAME OF PROGRAM WATCHED	PERSONS WATCHING TV					
						Men		Women		T	C
QUARTER-HOURS	OFF	ON	CALL LETTERS	CHAN. NO.		Man of House	Others Over 17	Lady of House	Others Over 17	12 Thru 17	2 Thru 11
12:00-12:14	25										
12:15-12:29	26										
12:30-12:44	27										
12:45-12:59	28										
1:00- 1:14	29	X	WBBB	5	Star Showhouse		1		1		
1:15- 1:29	30				Movie – The Crisis				2		
1:30- 1:44	31										
1:45- 1:59	32										
2:00- 2:14	33										
2:15- 2:29	34		WBBB	5					2		
2:30- 2:44	35	X	KAAA	9	KAAA – News Extra	1		1			
2:45- 2:59	36										
3:00- 3:14	37										
3:15- 3:29	38										
3:30- 3:44	39	X	WBBB	5	Lucky 7 Quiz Show		1		1		2
3:45- 3:59	40	X	WBBB	5			1		1		2
4:00- 4:14	41										
4:15- 4:29	42										
4:30- 4:44	43										
4:45- 4:59	44										
5:00- 5:14	45										
5:15- 5:29	46										
5:30- 5:44	47										
5:45- 5:59	48										

Comments: _____

A PAGE FROM A TV DIARY (Courtesy, A. C. Nielsen Company)

3. *Mechanical recorder.* A mechanical recorder is a device affixed to the television set, with the consent of the set owner, automatically registering when the set is turned on. (Nielsen calls their device the Audimeter; ARB calls theirs Arbitron.) Reports can be mailed in weekly. These recorders can also be hooked up by direct wire to the research bureau's recording center for overnight reports to the advertiser. The advantages of recorders are that they are continuous, they are not subject to human error in keeping records, and they give information swiftly. The disadvantage of the recorder is that the system is costly to install and maintain (especially the instantaneous records, which are, at this writing, operated only in New York City and Los Angeles, although additional cities may be added to the list). Also, the recorder tells when the set is turned on; but it does not tell who or how many are listening. Despite this, the information is useful to many advertisers.

The recorder in one market is often used in connection with diary or coincidental telephone reports in the same market, and with diary or coincidental telephone reports in other markets where a network program is being measured.

The audience rating services have been at the forefront in developing techniques to give better information, and are continually working to improve them.

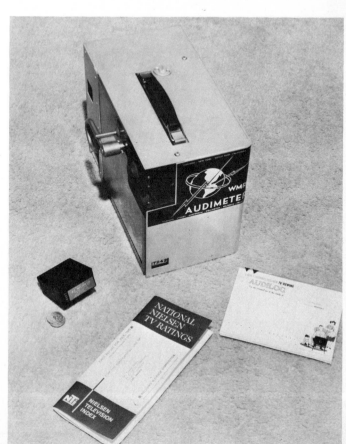

A NIELSEN AUDIMETER

Arrangements are made to have this hooked up in homes of a carefully selected sample of households. It records on tape when the set was in operation. The respondent sends in the tape weekly. The Audimeter is often used in connection with diary reporting by others in the area.

Courtesy, A. C. Nielsen Company

It would be well to be acquainted with the terms used in audience-measurement research and calculation. Roth presents them this way:

A. *TV penetration*

Start with a theoretical "universe" . . . 10 households. 9 of these 10 households own TV sets; TV *penetration* or *set ownership* in "universe" = 90 percent.

B. *Coverage*

The TV signal of a theoretical network covers 8 TV households. The *coverage area,* therefore, is defined as: 8 out of 9 TV households in the universe = 89 percent *coverage.*

C. *Sets-in-use*

At 9–10 P.M., 6 TV households are watching TV = *sets-in-use.* 6 out of 9 TV households in the universe = 67 percent sets-in-use.

D. *Share of Audience*

At 9–10 P.M., 2 TV households are watching *our* program: 2 out of the 6 with TV sets in use. Our *share of audience* is thus 33⅓ percent.

E. *Rating*

At 9–10 P.M., 2 TV households are watching our program = rating. 2 out of 9 TV households in the universe = 22 percent, spoken of as a rating of 22. A rating point, therefore, is one percent of all the households who have TV and are tuned into our program.[8]

Ratings are the units most used in planning schedules.

Gross Rating Points (GRPs)

Media schedules are often spoken of as "light" or "heavy," attributing to the schedules a sense of weight, or impact, on a market. To translate that feeling into mathematical form useful in planning media schedules, the Gross Rating Point (GRP) system has been evolved. One rating point represents 1 percent of the total TV households reached within a specified measurement area as defined by the rating service used. It applies also to radio, where the rating service also estimates the number of persons using radio.

A *gross rating point* is the rating a program gets, multiplied by the number of times the program is played. Usually this is figured over a four-week period. Thus, if a commercial ran on a program with a rating of 10

---

[8] Paul M. Roth, *How to Plan Media* (Skokie, Ill.: Standard Rate & Data Service, Inc., 1969), Chap. 4.

once a week for four weeks, it would have a GRP of 40. If it also ran four times on another program with a rating of 8, it would have a GRP of 40 + 32, or 72.

One of the principal merits of the GRP system is that it provides a common base that accommodates all size markets equally. One GRP in New York has exactly the same relative weight as one GRP in Salt Lake City.

The cost for time, of course, varies by the city. The cost per rating point in different cities has been worked out, and the following list is typical:

CITY	30 SECS. PRIME-TIME COST PER RATING POINT
New York	$225
Los Angeles	150
Washington	55
Atlanta	20
San Diego	13
Columbus, Ohio	14
Salt Lake City	6

The advertiser has to make a decision as to how much weight, or GRPs, he wishes to place in his markets, and for how long a period. This will be a uniform number of GRPs, for in each market it means he reaches the same proportion of TV households. Say he selects 100 to 150 per week as his GRP figure (considered a good working base). This still gives him great discretion in each market as to how to allocate the time: put it all on one station? divide it among all the stations? with what yardstick? This depends on whether he wants to reach as many people as possible with his message (called *reach*), or whether he wishes to reach people more often (*frequency*)—in which case he will have to limit himself to fewer people or to shorter messages (perhaps 10 seconds instead of 30 or 60 seconds). In all instances, delivery of a message is the important thing, not just reaching people. (In the next chapter we will see how the computer is used to present the various alternatives possible with a given number of GRPs.)

Important though the GRP is, however, it has its limitations: Consideration must be given to the number of prospects for the product that are being reached by a program, regardless of rating. But the GRP concept provides a unified dimension for making scheduling judgments.

Additionally, GRPs alone cannot tell how effectively a broadcast schedule is performing. If an advertiser's target audience is women aged 18 to 49, for example, it is often the case that five GRPs will deliver more women 18–49 for the advertiser than will ten GRPs. This, as would be suspected, is a function of *where* the GRPs are scheduled. Five GRPs scheduled in a "Sunday Night Movie" will almost always deliver many times more women 18–49 than will ten GRPs scheduled on a Saturday morning.

One would logically suspect that over the years, standard criteria had developed as to how many GRPs were needed for each market. Advertiser needs being as diverse and varied as they are, however, this is not as yet generally the case.

One method that appears well received among advertisers whose products have wide appeal (such as packaged goods) is arbitrarily to determine the number of GRPs required to make an impact on a market. If the budget can then not accommodate the cost of providing this number of GRPs, the schedule may be further refined as to the desirable level of frequency. Here, too, the budget must be reexamined as to how many additional dollars, if any, will be required to beef up frequency to this desired level.

Cumes

A *cume* represents the accumulated number of people who have been exposed to a commercial that ran more than once—usually figured, for convenience, over a four-week period. Say a commercial runs on a station three times a week for a four-week period. It reaches 10,000 viewers each time it appears. That does not mean that it has reached 120,000 people, for every time it appeared, some of the previous watchers were not watching, and some new viewers joined the audience. The actual cume of an audience is computed by the audience-measurement services, based on research and statistical experience, and is available to the advertiser. The cume, in the instance above, is figured at 15,000, which means that 15,000 different households listened to that program over a four-week period.

DEFINING TELEVISION MARKETS

Publishers have always reported their circulation by states—the traditional boundaries for sales territories—but for television something better was needed to define territories in terms of the stations that best reached them. As a result, two of the major audience-measurement services have each prepared such maps, based upon the reach of stations around markets. These include those counties that account for 95 percent or more of a station's audience. The A. C. Nielsen Company (Nielsen) calls its territorial locations *Designated Marketing Areas* (DMA). The American Research Bureau calls its maps *Areas of Dominant Influence* (ADI)—"an exclusive geographic area consisting of all counties in which the Home Market stations receive a preponderance of total viewing hours." Many marketing plans are made in accordance with these territorial designations.

TV schedules are made out in terms of weeks (Sunday to Saturday), not months. A program for a series of weeks is referred to as a *flight*.

In planning the use of television in a market, we ask a series of questions, including:

1. What is the budget? How does it compare with that of the competition?

2. What geographical area (DMA or ADI) do we want to cover? Over what period of time?

3. What audience do we want to reach? Sex? Age? Other qualifications, as large families, homeowners?

4. What is the weight in GRP's we want for a market (four-week plan)?

5. What is the relative importance of: *reach*—getting the message before as many people as possible; *frequency*—getting the message before the same group as often as possible; *continuity*—maintaining message delivery over a long period of time?

6. How can TV best supplement, or be supplemented by, other media?

The network buying plan. If the plan indicates the possible use of networks, we inquire:

1. What are the availabilities of each network? What programs?

2. How many people do they reach?

3. How does the lineup of stations in the network correspond to the markets in which we are most interested? How much supplementary scheduling will have to be done?

4. What is the share of market of the individual station in its respective market?

5. What is the cost per thousand viewers?

6. What is offered by way of product protection? Promotions? Other features?

Network programs must be planned well in advance—often a year ahead.

The spot buying plan. If our plan calls for spot, we check individual stations for:

1. Station's reach—What is its prime listening area?

2. Share of audience—Of all homes using television in the market, how is the share of audience distributed among stations being considered?

3. What are the station ratings, by quarter-hour periods?

4. Programming environment—How does the audience watching the program mesh with the demographic requirements of the audience we are seeking?

5. Length of schedule (flight)—How many weeks are planned?

6. Cost—What is the best deal that can be worked out to get the spots we want at the least cost?

7. Other criteria—What is the station's history of reliability in handling spots, product protection, and make-goods?

These are among the considerations in making a television spot schedule.

UHF (Ultrahigh-frequency) Stations

As you cast your eyes over the accompanying chart of the electromagnetic spectrum through which all electronic communication by air takes place, you will see that television and radio are only two of many claimants for frequency allocations. They have competition from other users. When television came along, the Federal Communications Commission (FCC), which is the responsible government authority, assigned to it what were then the best available channels, now known as Channels 2 through 13. These twelve channels are in the very-high-frequency band of the spectrum, and are referred to as VHF stations. Today they are the basic TV stations we get on the air.

But the demand for more television frequencies grew faster than had been anticipated. The FCC did not want to repeat its mistake of not allowing room for expansion. This time, they leapfrogged into the ultrahigh-frequency band, where they made room for 70 channels—channels 14 to 83, referred to as UHF. But it takes a different type of receiving set to tune in on these channels. Since May 1965, by law, all new TV sets have had to be capable of receiving UHF as well as VHF.

UHF stations usually offer programs of selective quality to attract specific audiences, rather than trying to compete with the entertainment fare of local stations. They are very popular in the Middle West.

Within five years, from 1965 to 1970, the number of UHF stations in the United States doubled, from 88 to 176.

The Electromagnetic Spectrum

Showing how frequencies are allocated for different purposes by the FCC. This chart is not in mathematical scale (no room), but in logarithmic scale. To get an idea of how much of the spectrum is assigned to AM and FM radio, and to VHF and UHF television, judge by the small (megacycle) numbers left of the bar.

2900 Mc — Radio Navigation / Meteorological (Radiosonde) / Radar

1300 Mc

1000 Mc
890 Mc — **UHF TELEVISION (CHANNELS 14-83)**

470 Mc

216 Mc — **VHF TELEVISION (CHANNELS 7-13)**
174 Mc

118 Mc — Radio Navigation
108 Mc
100 Mc — **FM BROADCAST**
88 Mc — **VHF TELEVISION (CHANNELS 2-6)**

54 Mc
45 Mc

Land transportation
Police
Industrial, Medical, Scientific
Maritime Mobile
10 Mc — International Broadcast
Maritime Mobile
Amateur
Standard Frequency (time)
Aeronautical Mobile

2 Mc

1605 Kc
1 Mc — **AM BROADCAST**
535 Kc

415 Kc — Radio Direction Finding
Aeronautical Mobile
Aeronautical Radio Navigation
Radio Navigation
0.1 Mc
90 Kc

CATV; Cable Television

CATV stands for *community antenna television,* also known as *cable television.* It is a paid subscriber system whereby one antenna serves a community of households that cannot get reception, or else get only poor reception, because of interference of the surroundings. It began in the mountains of Pennsylvania, to bring television reception to homes from which it had been blocked by those mountains. CATV spread to the cities, where residents were beset by the same problems owing to the steel structures or the hills that surrounded them. The lines, or cables, by which subscribers are connected are strung either on the telephone or light poles by leasehold arrangement, or carried through conduits in the cities.[9] An important feature of CATV is that its reception is far better than that of direct transmission, because the height of the aerial puts it above electronic disturbances from many sources.

A Short Course in Cable

That's the title of a report in *Broadcasting* magazine which said:

There are about 2,750 operating cable systems in the U.S. There are another 1,950 systems approved but not built, and 2,900 applications pending before local governments. Pennsylvania, where cable began, has the most systems: about 300. Systems currently in operation reach about 6 million homes, perhaps 18.5 million viewers. The

---

[9] As this is being written, a mini-laser system has been announced to do away with wires or cables—a cableless cable system!

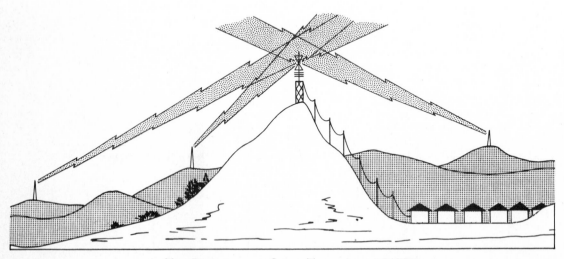

The Principle of Cable Television (CATV)

When the local systems operator originates a broadcast to subscribers via cable, it is called cable television.

CABLE TV MOVES AHEAD
Providing programs on its own channels, in addition to those from other stations.

average system has 2,150 subscribers. The largest—in San Diego—has over 51,000. Some have fewer than 100. Most systems offer between 6 and 12 channels; the average for all is 10.4. Most new systems being constructed have 20 channels. The state-of-the-art maximum is about 48 forward channels. Monthly fees average about $4.95. Installation fees range from nothing to over $100; the average is $20. Total cost of an average system is estimated between $500,000 and $1 million. The cost of laying cable ranges from $4,000 per mile in rural areas to more than $50,000 per mile in large cities. Over 400 systems have the capability of originating programs, and nearly 300 do so on a regularly scheduled basis—an average of 16 hours a week. Almost 800 have the capability of providing such automated originations as time and weather services and stock reports. Advertising is known to be carried by 53 systems which originate programs. Another 375 accept advertising with automated services. The average charge is $15 per minute, $88 per hour-long program. About 42% of the cable industry is owned by other communications interests. Broadcasters account for 30%, newspaper publishers for 7%, telephone companies for 5%. The CATV industry had total subscriber revenues estimated at $360 million in 1971.[10]

The original role of CATV was to relay to subscribers via cable the programs of stations it could receive over the air. But the stations could also be turned into local sending stations by playing their own programs over their cables to their subscribers (called *cablecasting*). In fact, the Federal Communications Commission now requires all systems with 3,500 subscribers or more to broadcast their own programs along with those received over the air. The philosophy of this is to encourage the opening of the many channels of CATV to community-oriented programs.

Two-way Cable Communication

The biggest change cable television promises to bring to our society is through its facility for having two-way communication between the subscriber and the station, by means of a double cable. The FCC reports:

Cable operators foresee their systems developing into two-way home communications centers through which subscribers may shop for merchandise shown on their screens, order facsimile newspapers, or have utility meters read. These and other potential uses of CATV are still being explored.[11]

---

[10] *Broadcasting*, May 15, 1972. © Reproduced by permission, Broadcasting Publications, Inc.

[11] *Community Antenna Television (CATV)*, Federal Communications Commission, 22–0, November 1970.

In 1965, the first communications satellite—the Early Bird—provided direct communication between North America and Europe. It was a synchronous satellite, in that it rotated around the earth, at 22,550 miles above the equator, at the same rate as the earth; it was "geostationary." It served as a relay, transmitting its message in a straight line of vision one-third the way around the earth.

In 1970, there were five synchronous satellites providing full-time global service, with 40 earth stations located in 28 countries to receive and to relay their messages. (They also act as relays for telephonic messages.) They cover Europe, Africa, the Near East, Latin America, and countries in the Pacific. The United States has seven satellite earth stations. In 1970, 947 hours of television time were transmitted or received in the United States.[12] These were news events of wide importance; they would be received by the satellite earth station, transmitted to the networks, and rebroadcast, with time sold at the end.

The biggest impact of satellites in the United States is still ahead.[13] We soon may expect three domestic satellites capable of transmitting from coast to coast without relays or lines, potentially changing the entire system of television communication methods.

TRENDS IN TELEVISION

Between 1960 and 1970, expenditures for television advertising grew by 130 percent—making it the fastest-growing of all media.[14] In 1972, the U.S. Department of Justice filed an antitrust suit against the three networks, designed to sever their control of the production of shows from the broadcasting operation. The fact that the networks financed and produced these shows, which cost far more than a single advertiser might care to invest, has been one of their chief contributions to making network television viable. The suit may take years to adjudicate. Should the views of the Department of Justice prevail, there will be a great reorientation of network broadcasting.

Meanwhile, improvements in videotape recordings, and reduction in their cost, will permit an increasing amount of the programming now on networks to be handled directly by the local stations. A strength of the networks will continue to be in their news programming.

---

[12] Federal Communications Commission, *Annual Report,* 1970.

[13] There are TV stations called *satellites* that have nothing to do with objects in orbit. A satellite station is a smaller station connected by tie line to a larger one whose telecasts it can transmit.

[14] See p. 121.

The biggest change within TV will be brought about by cable television, which could affect all media. To the public it represents an expanded form of service; to the advertiser it represents a possibility for better market targets, and also more audience fragmentation. There is much political pressure and financial turmoil taking place regarding the control of these stations and the range of services they will be allowed or required to render, reminiscent of the problems radio and TV had in getting established.

> Will cable television develop into a mere conduit for over-the-air broadcast signals, or will it assume the competitive position of an alternate medium of communication?
>
> —FCC Chairman Dean Burch, in *Broadcasting Magazine,* May 22, 1972, p. 22.

The advent of television cassettes, by means of which people can play their own choice of movies or old TV shows from cartridges they can buy or rent, can have an impact on TV viewing.

Domestic satellite broadcasting promises to affect the entire method of station intercommunication. It may transmit directly to the home—in time.

Three problems wait to be resolved: mounting costs, clutter, and paper work on schedules. These wouldn't be so important if television were not so important.

*   *   *

We will discuss the creation and production of television commercials in the next section of this book. Meanwhile, we continue the discussion of media.

Alpo Dog Food

A case report on the use of television

by James V. O'Gara

ROBERT F. HUNSICKER, who started the Alpo Dog Food Company in 1936, in a rented garage, on a $200 bankroll, tells the story:

> In 1959, we knew that only one out of every four households had a dog. We also knew that most of these dogs were in the suburbs, so we were after people with some money to spend on a product that cost more than the others.
>
> Spot TV could offer good selectivity and flexibility. The cost was moderate. Pets, like babies, are a "natural" for viewer involvement. Our Alpo selling idea of 100% meat, no cereal filler, was well suited for demonstration. And television could be effectively used to sell supermarket chain buyers.

Alpo put 61 percent of its ad budget into daytime and fringe-time newscasts, personality shows, and spots in and around shows geared to dog-owning audiences. In 1960, sales increased by 30 percent, by 36 percent in 1961, and by 47 percent, in 1962. These spectacular gains were registered while pet industry sales as a whole were advancing about 5 percent annually.

In 1964, when Alpo still lacked national distribution, it bought into the "Today" and "Tonight" shows. The result was a 40 percent sales increase and the opening of a number of new markets. Then Alpo bought spots on all three networks, backing them with heavy local spot drives. By this time, 90 percent of the Alpo ad budget was going into TV.

When the smoke cleared," according to Mr. Hunsicker, "dogs were eating Alpo in all fifty states. Our total sales gain, over the past five years, climbed to 510 percent—while all pet-food sales had gone up 60 percent." In the ten years beginning in 1959, Alpo sales dollars increased about 1,500 percent, and its total advertising dollars were ahead about 1,400 percent.

Today, 80 percent of the $8,000,000 Alpo ad budget goes into television, including "Today" and "Tonight," nighttime westerns, news broadcasts, and daytime serials like "The Doctors" and "Secret Storm." In one recent quarter, Alpo ran 4,102 spots in 36 markets, 375 commercials on national programs, and 167 regional spots. Sales for the period were up 21 percent over the corresponding quarter in the previous year.

Excerpted from a report by James V. O'Gara, from the May 10, 1971 issue of *Advertising Age.* Reprinted with permission. Copyright 1971 by Crain Communications, Inc.

1. What are the chief advantages of television for the national advertiser? Its chief limitations?

2. What is network TV? Spot TV? Local TV?

3. What are the advantages and limitations of network TV? Spot TV?

4. When an advertiser wishes to go on a network program, he has a choice of three buying formats. What are they?

Full Sponsor — Multiple Sponsor Participant

5. What is a scatter plan? What is a package of participations?

6. What is the difference between spot television and a television spot?

7. Why does a station have different time classifications? How do their rates compare?

8. When an advertiser is concerned with the product protection offered by a station, what does he mean?

9. Describe the telephone coincidental, diary, and mechanical recorder methods of television audience research. What are the advantages and limitations of each?

10. What do the following terms mean?
   a. TV penetration
   b. coverage
   c. sets-in-use
   d. share of audience
   e. rating
   f. cume

11. What are the chief questions you would ask in (a) buying network TV and (b) in buying spot TV?

12. What is cable TV? What is cablecasting?

13. For Alpo Dog Food, what were the advantages of television generally? Of network TV in 1964? Of network TV in 1970?

Reading Suggestions

Advertising Age, "Broadcast Advertising: 1970," a special section, November 2, 1970, p. 19ff.

Barton, Roger, *The Handbook of Advertising Management.* New York: McGraw-Hill Book Company, 1970.

Blank, David M., "Television Advertising: The Great Discount Illusion, or Tonypandy Revisited," *The Journal of Business,* January 1968, pp. 10–38.

Everson, George, *The Story of Television.* New York: W. W. Norton, 1949.

Forbes, "TV: Is the Bloom Off the Old Rose?" October 15, 1970, p. 28ff.

Friendly, Fred W., "Television and the First Amendment," *Saturday Review,* January 8, 1972, pp. 46–47ff.

Hoffman, Robert M., "Awareness Change in TV," *Media/Scope,* May 1968. Excerpted in Kleppner and Settel, *Exploring Advertising,* p. 202.

Lessing, Lawrence, "Stand By for the Cartridge TV Explosion," *Fortune,* June 1971, p. 81ff.

Mayer, Martin, *About Television.* New York: Harper & Row Publishers, 1972.

Thompson, T., "How a Network Boss Picks Shows," *Life,* September 10, 1971, pp. 46–50ff.

8

Using Radio

RADIO HAS BEEN CALLED the ubiquitous medium—it seems to be everywhere. There are over 336 million radio sets in the United States; that's five per household, including plug-in sets, car sets, portable transistors, sets in combination with phonograph-TV sets, AM–FM combinations, and clock radios. Ninety-nine percent of all homes have radios. 71 percent have a radio in the bedroom, 56 percent in the kitchen, 47 percent in the livingroom, 40 percent in the study or den, 22 percent in the dining area, and 22 percent in the laundry room. The radio plays in the householder's workshop, and many a farmer drives his tractor with a radio slung from its chassis.

Eighty-five million cars have radios. Riders in them listen to the radio more than 60 percent of the time they are traveling, a figure that peaks up in the morning and evening trips to and from work; 82 percent of commuters travel by car.

The radio is the companion on all trips—to the seashore, to the mountains, and to wherever travel plans take a devotee. Transistor sales alone in 1970 were over $31 million (compared with $11 million in 1962).

In the course of a week, 90 percent of all adults enjoy the programs coming from 4,500 AM and 2,200 FM stations, planned to serve and entertain every sector of the population.

FEATURES AND ADVANTAGES

Radio is a personal medium. When you listen to a voice on the radio, someone is speaking directly to you in the first person. Many people have a close rapport with a radio personality to whom they listen faithfully. Eighty percent of adults rely on radio for weather news; 75 percent of teenagers, 50 percent of adult men, and 56 percent of adult women have transistor sets for their own use. Nine out of ten listeners rate radio as a source of relaxation and pleasure in their daily lives, to which they can listen as they go about their chores.[1] Radio brings a wide range of sound effects to involve

---

[1] Sources: *Radio Facts,* Radio Advertising Bureau, 1971; *Radio Today,* the National Association of Broadcasters, 1971; *Broadcasting 1971 Yearbook.*

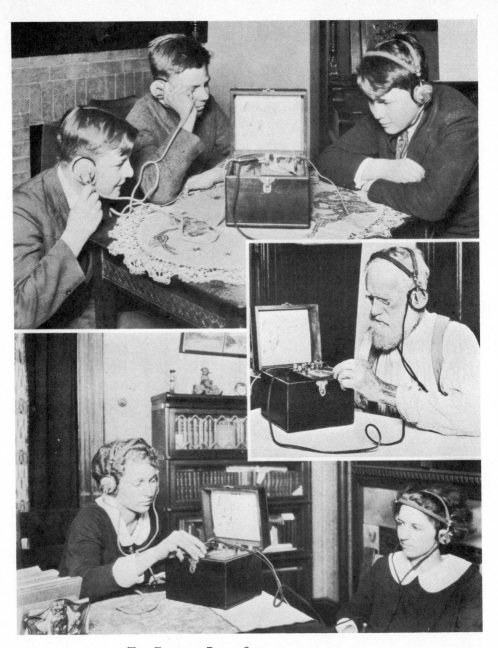

THE EARLIEST RADIO SETS

The Aeriola, Jr., got heavy use in the early 1920's. Rural listeners particularly turned to their sets for farm information, weather reports, and even for church services. (From *A Pictorial History of Radio*, Irving Settel (New York: Grosset & Dunlap, 1960). © Irving Settel, 1960.)

the reader's imagination in the script. You can hear a plane leave the airfield as vividly as if you saw it off. Radio listening goes way up in the summer time, when people are outdoors.

Radio is broadly selective. An advertiser can pick the markets in which he is interested. He can reach broad demographic groups, such as housewives, men, women, teenagers, farmers, ethnic groups, by virtue of the station programming and by time selection.

Radio is flexible. Time can be bought for a day, a week, a month, or longer. Many advertisers place orders for short-term schedules (called *flights*) several times a year. Orders may even be placed to run when the weather reaches a certain temperature—cold for antifreeze, hot for soft drinks —or when the pollen count reaches a certain number, for hay-fever preparations.

LIMITATIONS AND CHALLENGES

There has been a great proliferation of radio stations, with many cities of under 300,000 population having eight radio stations each. The total number of radio stations is nine times that of television stations. The audience is highly fragmented; it may take a number of stations to cover a market. Radio audience research is costly and expensive.

Radio is an aural medium. Its use is limited in the case of products that are sold because of style or appearance. It cannot be used for advertising requiring coupons.

The chief complaint about radio is that it has too many commercials per hour. This lessens the impact of all commercials and makes it that much more difficult to space a commercial away from that of a competing product, even though stations try to do this. The competition for attention in commercials, however, has inspired some of the most imaginative writing in the field of mass communication.

The paper work in putting through a schedule of national radio spots, as in television, can be quite overwhelming, involving planning, confirming clearances, ordering, checking appearances and make-goods due and make-goods delivered, approving bills for payment, and billing to clients with proper credits. The industry is working to simplify this labor.

Yet, with all these drawbacks, radio expenditures grew 84.7 percent between 1960 and 1970.[2] compared with an increase for all media of 64.3 percent; radio is a friendly, warm way of delivering a message, at a low cost per thousand.

---

[2] See p. 121.

There are about 4,500 Amplitude Modulation (AM) radio stations, and about 2,200 Frequency Modulation (FM) radio stations.[3] Each system offers different values to the advertiser. It's all a question of waves, and a brief understanding of this subject will help explain many things in radio.

The way of waves. All waves have two attributes: They have height, spoken of as *amplitude,* like the difference between an ocean wave and a ripple in a pond; and they have speed, measured by the *frequency* with which a succession of waves pass a given point per minute, or per second. If a radio station operates on a frequency of 1580 kilocycles, for example, it means that 1,580,000 of its waves pass a given point per second.

Based upon these two dimensions—amplitude and frequency—two separate systems have been developed for carrying the sound waves. The first system carries the variations in a sound wave by corresponding variations in its amplitude; the frequency remains constant. This is the principle of *amplitude modulation* (AM).

The second system carries the variations in a sound wave by corresponding variations in its frequency; the amplitude remains constant. This is the principle of *frequency modulation* (FM). These differences affect what the advertiser can expect from each type of station.

We first discuss AM radio, the most familiar form.

AM RADIO

In AM broadcasting, the radio waves are primarily *ground waves,* which travel along the surface of the earth and are relatively unaffected by obstacles or even the earth's curvature. They lose energy to the ground as they travel, finally fading out. Good ground-wave reception can extend up to 200 miles, so that the listening area could be a circle 400 miles in diameter. Certain antennas, called *directional antennas,* can be arranged to direct ground waves to certain areas, to prevent interference.

AM waves also shoot out to the sky (*sky waves*). They can reach the ionosphere—the deep curtain of electric particles that surrounds the earth's atmosphere. In the daytime, the ionosphere has no effect on the AM waves, but when the sun does down, the ionosphere forms an electronic ceiling that bounces the AM waves back to earth, landing at a point far removed from their point of origin. That is why you might receive stations from a thousand miles away on your AM set at night, but not in the daytime.

---

[3] *Annual Report,* Federal Communications Commission, 1972 (1971 figures).

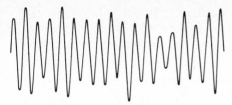

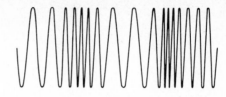

Amplitude Modulation (AM). Here the wave varies in its size (amplitude). The frequency is constant.

Frequency Modulation (FM). Here the wave varies in its frequency. The size is constant. There are differences in what AM and FM can do.

Comparative Sizes of AM and FM Waves

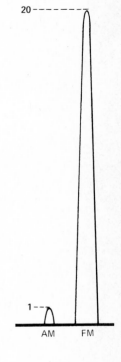

Allocation of AM stations. To make the best use, without interference, of the frequencies within the limited confines of the AM band (535 kc. to 1605 kc.), the Federal Communications Commission established four classes of stations:

Class   I—clear channel, 50,000 watts (maximum power AM radio) (These are the giant stations, able to send skywaves at night.)

Class II—clear channel, 250 to 50,000 watts

Class III—regional channel, 500 to 5,000 watts
A regional-channel station shares its frequency with other stations far enough away so as not to interfere.

Class IV—local channel, 1,000 watts maximum daytime to 250 watts at night, sharing their frequencies with distant local stations.

Most stations are in Classes III and IV. Almost half operate during daytime only, to prevent nighttime interference.

THE STRUCTURE OF RADIO ADVERTISING

Radio time is sold in three broad categories—network, spot, and local—like television time, but the percentages are different. In radio, networks do approximately 4 percent of the business, spots 29 percent, local 67 percent.[4]

Radio Networks

The three national AM radio networks are CBS, NBC, and ABC. Each offers a long list of stations with which it is, or can be, interconnected, in combinations designed to reach all parts of the country, and flexible

---

[4] *Ibid.*

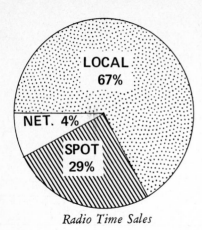

Radio Time Sales

LOCAL 67%
NET. 4%
SPOT 29%

enough to meet the advertiser's marketing map, at a low cost per thousand. About two thirds of network radio programming is worldwide news and information; one third is for entertainment programs, chiefly daytime, for the audience of housewives. The network commercials appear within the total network time period assigned to the network by the stations.

There are also regional and state networks, interconnected but not part of a national network. Many separate stations are sold as a group, sometimes called a *transcription network,* on a one-order, one-bill basis.

Spot Radio

When an advertiser buys time on an individual station, the usage is called *spot radio.* The program originates at the station from which it is broadcast; that is, it is not relayed from a network broadcast. As in television, when a national advertiser uses spot radio, it is, strictly speaking, *national spot radio;* however, by trade custom it is called simply *spot radio.* Similarly, when a local advertiser uses spot radio, it is, strictly speaking, *local spot radio;* but by trade custom it is referred to as *local radio.* (We discuss local radio in the Retailing chapter.)

Spot radio represents the height of radio flexibility. An advertiser has about 6,500 stations from which to tailor his choice to fit his markets. He can go on as often as he wants, for as long or short a flight as he wants. The schedule can be pinpointed to the weather (for antifreeze), to the pollen count (for hay-fever preparations), or to the season (for gift suggestions).

Spot radio is often used to amplify the reach and frequency of a campaign running in radio network, newspapers, television, magazines, and/or outdoor advertising.

Many stations have programs directed to the farm markets; others are directed primarily to black or Spanish audiences. Over 500 stations broadcast in 58 different languages to reach the various ethnic groups.[5]

An advertiser can move fast with spot radio. Although some stations ask for two weeks closing, most specify 72 hours closing for broadcast materials. When asked his closing time, one candid station manager replied, "Thirty minutes before broadcast!"

---

[5] Standard Rate & Data Service, September 1972.

THE RADIO STRUCTURE

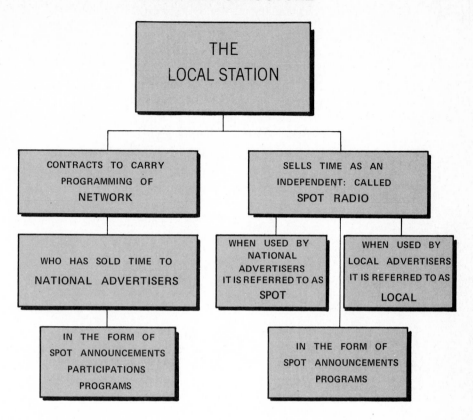

TIME CLASSIFICATIONS

The broadcast day is divided into time periods, whose rates reflect the size of their audience. These periods generally are:

NAME	TIME	INDEX OF COST
Drive or Traffic time	6–10 A.M.	100
Daytime, or Housewife	10 A.M.–3 P.M.	60
Afternoon, Drive time	3 P.M.–7 P.M.	83
Evening	7 P.M.–midnight	50 *

Based on Katz Spot Radio Estimate #14, *1971.*

Weekend rates are regarded as a separate time classification.

Stations often refer to the time periods as classes, as Class A, B, C, D; rates vary accordingly. Each station defines its classes on its rate card.

Time is sold in units of 1 minute, 30 seconds, or 10 seconds. The formerly popular unit of 20 seconds has largely given way to the 30-second spot.

RATE CLASSIFICATIONS

Drive time.   This is the most desired and costly time on radio.

Preemptible vs. nonpreemptible time.   As in TV, radio time is preemptible by the station unless it has been ordered nonpreemptible at extra cost. Of course, the total time of any station is preemptible for any public announcement of major importance.

Run-of-station (ROS).   This means the station has a choice of moving the commercial at will, wherever it is most convenient to the station. Preemptible ROS time is the lowest on the rate card.

Special features.   This refers to time adjacent to weather signals, news reports, time signals, or traffic or stock market reports, for which a premium is charged.

Participations.   Some stations have outstanding-personality shows or community events in which an advertiser can buy time called *participations,* at a special rate.

WEEKLY PACKAGE PLANS

Originally, stations offered frequency discounts based on 13-, 26-, 39-, or 52-time usage—a holdover from magazine days. This type of discount has been replaced by weekly package plans (also called *Total Audience Plans*), in which a station offers a number of time slots divided in different proportions over the broadcast day, at a special flat price. The advertiser must buy the package to get the special price. As typical examples of such package plans, we have these actual cases.[6]

STATION A

PACKAGE PLANS PER WK. EA.:	1 MIN.	30 SEC.
20 ti (8 Drive, 12 all other times)	$55	$44
15 ti (5 Drive, 10 all other times)	57	46

---

[6] From *Spot Radio Service* of Standard Rate & Data Service, September 1972.

WIND .5M/VM DAYTIME COVERAGE AREA

COPYRIGHT—American Map Company
Release #14010

A contour map showing the areas reached by the station with its strongest signal and less strong signal.

STATION B

TOTAL AUDIENCE PLAN

PER WK.:	12 TI	18 TI	24 TI	30 TI
(⅓ TRAFFIC, ⅓ HOUSEWIFE, ⅓ WEEKEND)				
1 min.	$26	$24	$22	$20
30 sec.	21	19	18	16

STATION C

TOTAL AUDIENCE PLAN	8 TI	16 TI	24 TI	32 TI
1 min.	$17	$15	$13	$11
30 sec.	13	12	10.40	8

¼ ea. 6–10 A.M., 10 A.M.–3 P.M., 3–7 P.M., 7 P.M.–midnight.

INDIANA

Indianapolis—Continued

WIBC
1938

 RAB

Subscriber to the NAB Radio Code

Media Code 4 215 4465 1.00
Fairbanks Broadcasting Co., Inc., 2835 N. Illinois
St., Indianapolis, Ind. 46208. Phone 317-924-2661.
TWX 317-634-3906.

STATION'S PROGRAMMING DESCRIPTION
WIBC: Programmed for adults and young adults.
MUSIC: middle-of-the-road, familiar album product.
Current top selling singles complimentary to format
are aired, along with gold records from past fifteen
years. Music presented by personalities, who's comments are geared to community involvement. FARM:
farm news, weather and market reports with farm
director 5-6 am & 12:15-1 pm. NEWS: 10 man
staff and mobile units, plus UPI audio. 10 min reports at 7-8 am & 4-5-6 pm. 5 min reports at 6:30-
7:30-8:30 am & 4:30-5:30 pm. Balance of day 5 min
reports on hour. Community service: regular schedule
of public affairs and religious programming. Contact
Representative for further details. Rec'd 12/23/68.

1. PERSONNEL
President—Richard M. Fairbanks.
Vice-Pres. & Gen'l Mgr.—James Hilliard.
Vice-Pres. & Gen'l Sales Mgr.—Richard Yancey.

2. REPRESENTATIVES
Blair Radio.

3. FACILITIES
50,000 w. days, 10,000 w. nights; 1070 kc.
Directional—separate patterns day and night.
Operating schedule: 24 hours daily. EST.

4. AGENCY COMMISSION
15/0 time only.

5. GENERAL ADVERTISING See coded regulations
General: 1a, 2a, 3a, 3b, 3c, 3d, 4a, 4d, 5, 6a, 7b, 8.
Rate Protection: 10c, 11c, 12c, 13c, 14c, 15a, 16.
Basic Rates: 20b, 21a, 21d, 22a, 23a, 24c, 25a,
  26, 27, 29b, 30, 33a.
Contracts: 40a, 41, 42b, 44b, 45, 46, 47a, 51a.
Comb.; Cont. Discounts: 60b, 60e, 60i, 61a, 61b, 62d.
Cancellation: 70a, 70e, 71a, 72, 73a, 73b.
Prod. Services: 80, 82.
Affiliated with Blair Represented Network.
FM facilities: WNAP (FM).
Sold in combination with WNAP (FM). See that
listing for rates.

TIME RATES
No. 11 Eff 2/15/71—Rec'd 2/15/71.
AA—Mon thru Fri 6-10 am, noon-1 pm & 3-7 pm.
A—Mon thru Sat 5-6 am; Mon thru Fri 10 am-noon
& 1-3 pm; Sat 6 am-7 pm; Sun 5 am-7 pm.
B—Mon thru Sun 7 pm-midnight.
C—Mon thru Sun midnight-5 am.

6. SPOT ANNOUNCEMENTS

CLASS AA

PER WK:	1 ti	6 ti	12 ti	18 ti	24 ti	30 ti
1 min	60	55	50	48	46	44
20/30 sec	48	44	40	38	36	34
ID's	36	33	30	29	28	27

CLASS A

	1 ti	6 ti	12 ti	18 ti	24 ti	30 ti
1 min	50	44	40	38	36	34
20/30 sec	40	35	32	30	28	26
ID's	30	26	24	23	22	21

CLASS B

1 min	25	23	22	21	20	19
20/30 sec	20	19	18	17	16	15
ID's	16	15	14	13	12	11

CLASS C

1 min	16	15	14	13	12	11
20/30 sec	13	12	11	10	9	8
ID's	11	10	9	8	7	6

Minutes, station breaks and ID's may be combined
for maximum frequency.

WIFE
1941
A Star Station
Independent

RAB

Subscriber to the NAB Radio Code

Media Code 4 215 4560 9.00
Star Stations of Indiana, Inc., 1440 N. Meridian
St., Indianapolis, Ind. 46202. Phone 317-637-1375.

STATION'S PROGRAMMING DESCRIPTION
WIFE: Programmed for young adults.
MUSIC: Current hits, album selection and past hits.
Air personalities each segment. NEWS: 24 hours
in 5 min segments at :55, headlines at :28, sports
at :20. Local, national & international using 7 man
news staff, 2 mobile units. AP, UPI audio
service. Program features include weather twice per
hour, high school reports twice nightly. Comedy phone
calls done by morning personality. Household hints.
Frequent contest and station promotions. Contact
Representative for further details. Rec'd 3/29/71.

1. PERSONNEL
Chairman of the Board—Don W. Burden.
Vice-Pres. & Gen'l Mgr.—Robert D. Kiley.
Chief Engineer—Murray Smith.

2. REPRESENTATIVES
HR/Stone Radio Representatives, Inc.

3. FACILITIES
5,000 w. days, 1,000 w. nights; 1310 kc.
Directional—night only.
Operating schedule: 24 hours daily. EST.

4. AGENCY COMMISSION
15/0 time only; 10th of following month.

5. GENERAL ADVERTISING See coded regulations
General: 2a, 3a, 3b, 4a, 4d, 5, 6a, 8.
Rate Protection: 10b, 11b, 12b, 13b, 14b.
Basic Rates: 20a, 22a, 23a, 28b, 29a.
Contracts: 40a, 45, 46, 47a, 48.
Comb.; Cont. Discounts: 60a, 60k, 61a, 61b, 62b.
Cancellation: 70e, 71c, 73a.
Rotating Plan Packages and programs, in all cate-
gories, are combinable. 1-min and 30-sec spots may
earn frequency discounts on 10-second spots. Rate
holders are not available.
Combines with AM to earn higher FM frequency,
however, FM is not combinable with AM for higher
AM frequency.

TIME RATES
Eff 8/1/70—Rec'd 7/30/70.
AA—Mon thru Sat 5:30-10 am & 3-7 pm.
A—Mon thru Sat 10 am-3 pm & 7-11 pm; Sun 6-10
pm.
B—All other times.

7. PACKAGE PLANS

1-MINUTE TOTAL AUDIENCE PLANS

PLANS:	I	II	III	IV
5:30-10 am		6	4	3	2
10 am-3 pm	12	8	6	4
3-7 pm		6	4	3	2
7 pm-midnight and/or wknd	12	8	6	4

PER WK, EA:	36 ti	24 ti	18 ti	12 ti
1 min	35.00	37.00	38.50	40.00

30 sec or less: 80% of 1-min.
10 sec or less: 50% of 1-min.

1-MINUTE ROTATING PLAN

PER WK:	(*)	12 ti	18 ti	24 ti	36 ti
AA	56.00	50.00	49.00	48.00	47.00
A	45.00	44.00	43.00	42.00	41.00
B	25.50	25.00	24.50	24.00	23.50

(*) 6 or less ti.
Specified position, extra 10%.

AM/FM COMBINATION
(Based on TAP disbusement)

PLAN:	I	II	III	IV
PER WK:	72 ti	48 ti	36 ti	24 ti
1 min (1/2 am, 1/2 FM)	1620	1152	900	648

8. PROGRAM TIME RATES
10 min—200% of 1-min.   2 min—125% of 1-min.
5 min—150% of 1-min.

WIFE/KISN, VANCOUVER, WASH./KOIL,
OMAHA, NEBR.
5% for a 3 station buy.

Extract of a
page of radio
rates from
Standard Rate
& Data Service.
Here all rate
cards are
published in
full, giving
information in
standardized
numerical
sequence for
each medium.

Courtesy SRDS

6A.M.-10A.M.

STATIONS	MEN RTG	MEN (00)	WOMEN RTG	WOMEN (00)	TEENS RTG	TEENS (00)	TOTAL RTG	TOTAL (00)	MEN 18-24 (00)	MEN 25-34 (00)	MEN 35-49 (00)	MEN 50-64 (00)	WOMEN 18-24 (00)	WOMEN 25-34 (00)	WOMEN 35-49 (00)	WOMEN 50-64 (00)
WAIT	1.2	278	1.4	376	.2	21	1.0	675	4	94	36	128		46	152	119
WBBM	1.7	399	2.0	531			1.5	997	12	34	103	144		33	126	192
WBBM-FM	.2	57	.2	40	.3	25	.2	122		24	33		29		11	
WBEE			.1	15				15					15			
WCFL	1.2	290	.9	229	3.8	340	1.4	977	198	68	18	2	83	28	82	36
WDAI-FM	.3	66	.2	52	.1	7	.2	125	53		13		52			
WDHF-FM			.2	41			.1	41						4	37	
WFMF-FM	.7	157	.3	87	.1	5	.4	261			30	9		31	27	12
WFMT-FM	.3	67	.4	103			.2	170			58	8	6	25	42	30
WGN	5.4	1277	6.1	1580	.9	82	4.3	2949	139	176	468	339	74	296	467	495
WGRT	.5	120	.8	208	.7	64	.6	392	91	5	24		41	49	64	54
WIND	1.7	407	1.8	463	.5	41	1.4	944	44	137	53	81	16	145	104	114
WJJD	.8	197	1.3	340			.8	537	10	6	104	34		62	76	183
WJJD-FM	.1	19	.1	33			.1	52		3	'16		9	14	10	
WJOB	.1	30	.5	122			.2	152		7	3	11			90	32
WKFM-FM	.2	55	.2	45			.1	100		46		3	18	11		22
WLS	2.2	528	2.6	688	5.6	508	2.8	1906	301	121	52	30	211	141	172	164
WMAQ	.7	162	1.6	420			.9	607	8	9	65	33	25	56	172	118
WNUS	1.1	268	.5	122			.6	423		29	121	'79	11	72	18	21
WNUS-FM X																
WSDM-FM	.4	105	.1	14			.2	119	37	66	2		9	5		
WVON	1.8	415	2.0	524	1.4	127	1.6	1093	104	130	93	54	213	159	113	39
WWCA	.4	89		11			.1	100			89			11		
WWEL-FM	.2	49	.2	50			.1	99			32	11		4	13	33
TOTAL	21.9	5151	24.1	6282	14.3	1292	19.5	13271	1019	973	1425	973	801	1199	1881	1656

THE PULSE, INC.   CUMULATIVE AUDIENCE ESTIMATES IN-HOME & OUT-OF-HOME

STATIONS	MEN RTG	MEN (00)	WOMEN RTG	WOMEN (00)	TEENS RTG	TEENS (00)	TOTAL RTG	TOTAL (00)	MEN 18-24 (00)	MEN 25-34 (00)	MEN 35-49 (00)	MEN 50-64 (00)	WOMEN 18-24 (00)	WOMEN 25-34 (00)	WOMEN 35-49 (00)	WOMEN 50-64 (00)
WAIT	6.8	1588	8.0	2097	1.1	100	5.7	3852	34	362	437	570	72	304	782	578
WBBM	12.1	2852	9.5	2488	1.6	148	8.5	5798	58	258	612	1326	59	230	742	877
WBBM-FM	3.0	701	1.7	446	3.3	299	2.1	1446	157	275	133	136	231	173	42	
WBEE	.3	73	.6	145	1.0	89	.5	307	73				59	51	35	
WCFL	11.7	2760	8.0	2090	34.5	3118	14.3	9721	1841	598	244	31	955	412	491	232
WDAI-FM	1.6	365	1.1	288	1.5	136	1.2	789	272		93		211	63	14	
WDHF-FM	.1	34	.3	72			.2	106			34			16	56	
WFMF-FM	2.7	624	2.2	567	.5	41	2.0	1332	'22	55	197	125		163	103	66
WFMT-FM	1.1	267	1.7	433			1.0	700		37	176	31	100	63	96	174
WGN	23.6	5539	17.5	4573	6.0	543	16.3	11093	368	1136	1733	1692	325	731	1120	1365
WGRT	6.2	1451	6.3	1658	5.5	494	5.5	3748	531	220	530	170	712	430	336	180
WIND	13.8	3242	9.4	2443	5.0	448	9.6	6533	470	967	652	900	321	497	515	682
WJJD	3.9	923	6.2	1620	.2	18	3.8	2561	40	264	341	198	171	425	451	372
WJJD-FM	.6	146	1.7	434			.9	580		23	123		18	123	140	153
WJOB	1.2	284	2.6	689			1.4	973		28	119	68	118	71	280	220
WKFM-FM	1.1	250	1.2	323			.8	573		147	38	42	72	47	84	86
WLS	17.3	4064	14.8	3861	39.7	3586	21.5	14604	1851	1186	420	504	1507	927	865	528
WMAQ	4.9	1144	6.1	1595	1.0	94	4.5	3033	78	125	392	343	54	166	537	524
WNUS	6.8	1594	3.6	947			3.9	2674		186	646	538	148	342	208	182
WNUS-FM																
WSDM-FM	1.8	433	.6	160			.9	593	73	206	154		18	41		
WVON	11.6	2734	12.2	3189	9.3	843	10.2	6911	512	765	983	328	1064	834	922	369
WWCA	1.9	456	1.0	254			1.0	710			293	94	45	39	120	50
WWEL-FM	1.6	368	1.6	420			1.2	788			37	131	177	70	92	124
TOTAL	84.9	19936	81.3	21240	66.4	6001	75.3	51201	3242	4063	5746	4567	3524	4109	5747	4948

TOTAL INCLUDES MEN, WOMEN, TEENS + CHILDREN

Courtesy, The Pulse, Inc.

A page from an audience radio report, which estimates how many people were reached during the week by the different stations. It divides men and women by age groups, and lists teens separately.

In the purchase of spot time, there is often much negotiation of rates between stations and time buyers. We discuss this later in the book.[7]

The Standard Billing Week is Monday through Sunday. The Standard Billing Month ends on the last Sunday.

Types of Station Programming

Most radio stations select a particular demographic group or groups and plan their programming to reach these groups. Most provide a consistent recognizable sound throughout the broadcast week. Station formats in general use are:

Format A—*Contemporary "Top 40"*
Record-sales charts provide the basis for the music selection. Geared to a younger target audience.

Format B—*Middle of the Road*
Popular music, bright, bouncy, but not as briskly paced as Format A. Limited playing of contemporary music, except for major hits.

Format C—*Standard*
A wider selection of music than Format B. Tends to be the "standards" of this and other years.

Format D—*Good Music*
A lush, largely instrumental sound, with vocal selections mainly ballads.

Format E—*Classical/Semiclassical*
Ranges from light classical to complete opera. Quartettes, symphonies, concertos, etc.

Format F—*Modern Country Music: "The Nashville Sound"*
Ballads and American folk music, performed in basic rhythms with a wide range of orchestrations.

Format G—*Talk*
Both "two-way" and personality talk programming. Adult oriented.

Format H—*News*
All or virtually all news programming. This does *not* refer to capsule newscasts as found on almost any station.

Format I—*Black*
Programming directed primarily to a black audience in terms of both music selection and talk.

(There is no need to memorize these classifications; just be aware they exist.)

Some stations utilize a mixture of formats, playing one kind of music in one part of the day, and featuring entirely different programming in other parts. Each portion of the programming is planned to reach a specific target audience, as revealed in these excerpts of rate cards:

---

[7] P. 588.

WDVH, Gainesville, Fla.

Programmed with emphasis on 25–55 age group. *Music:* country and western, primarily Nashville-produced modern country hits and polished versions of all-time familiar favorites.

WPAT, Paterson, N.J.

Programmed for young adults and adults. *Music:* 85% popular standards to jazz, show tunes to light classics, film music to folk, vocals and instrumentals mixed, edited and blended on tape to achieve a distinctive sound.

WXYZ, Detroit

Programmed for adults and young adults. 6 air personalities introduce popular music comprised of middle-of-the-road and current hit selections.

KXA, Seattle

Music: show tunes, popular concert, film tunes, and light concert. Symphonic treatment of standard melodies, and familiar tunes. Large popular choral groups and concert orchestras with instrumental soloists.[8]

FM APPEARS

Up to now we have been speaking chiefly of AM radio, which has been on the scene for over 50 years. FM arrived on the scene around 1940. It was just beginning to become known to music lovers, because of its fine tonal qualities, when World War II came along and stopped production. In the late 1940's, FM resumed its growth, retarded, however, by the fact that it needed a separate, costly FM set. But it grew.

The secret of the fine tonal reception of FM lies chiefly in the fact that the FM wave is twenty times as wide as the AM wave; that fact alone makes for better reception. To accommodate a wave of that width, however, a wide band on the spectrum was needed, and FM was assigned one so high that its frequency is measured in megacycles (mgs.), rather than kilocycles (kcs.) as in the case of AM. At that height, the FM wave is above the static, fading, and background noises that prevail at the lower levels. The result of all this is sound pure enough for stereophonic reception of music.

The range of FM. However, FM has its limitations. Unlike AM waves, FM waves travel in straight lines only. They cannot go around obstacles, or follow the curvature of the earth over the horizon. Their transmission has been likened to a "line-of-sight" path.

Furthermore, FM waves are not reflected back to earth at night, as are the AM waves; they continue to go right through the ionosphere. That is why you never get FM stations at night from as far away as some AM stations. FM antennas are erected at the highest terrain in the area, so that they can have their signal reach as far as possible within the limits set by the FCC.

---

[8] Standard Rate & Data Service, January 1972.

At first, AM programs were often duplicated by FM "sister" stations: these duplicated programs were called *simulcasts*. But in the 1960's, the FCC required that no more than half of the broadcast day could be simulcast on FM. FM stations had to originate programming of their own, and now offer as much variety as is found on AM stations. Independent FM stations, with no AM affiliation, have of course always originated all their own programming. Originally largely programmed with fine music, classical and semiclassical, FM today runs the entire gamut from "underground rock" to classical. A survey in 1970 showed that most of the programming (24 percent) was "Middle of the Road." Then came Beautiful Music (14 percent), Modified Contemporary (9 percent), and Modified Middle of the Road/Beautiful Music (9 percent). Only 3 percent of the programming was for classical music.[9]

The Recent Growth of FM

The growth of FM since 1965, when it was unhooked from its "little sister" role, has been spectacular.

—In 1965, 6.5 million FM sets were sold; in 1970, 93 million.

—In 1965, 8 percent of portable radio sets sold were AM–FM sets; in 1970, 59 percent.

—In 1965, 630,000 FM car-radio sets were sold; in 1970, 1,430,000 sets were sold.[10] Legislation is afoot to require all new radio receivers to be able to receive FM as well as AM.

PLANNING THE REACH AND FREQUENCY SCHEDULES

When we plan to go into a market, the question arises in radio, as in television: Shall we try to reach as many people as possible a few times with a given message, or shall we try to reach fewer people more often? What is our message, what is our target, and what is the optimum balance? (As a matter of unifying comparisons, frequency is measured in terms of a four-week period, although a schedule can be much longer or shorter.)

A great step toward getting a mathematical base for making a decision was made under the auspices of the Radio Advertising Bureau, where 10,000 different radio schedules were fed into a computer, and the range of

---

[9] Report, National Association of FM Broadcasters, 1970.

[10] *RAB Instant Background FM Radio,* published by the Radio Advertising Bureau, 1971.

reach and frequency of exposure was determined at different levels of exposure. Reach and frequency curves were then developed and have been published in book form by the Bureau.[11]

The Westinghouse Broadcasting Company also developed a computerized program with its Numath System (since improved by its Numa System), as per the following example published through their courtesy:

---

[11] *Radio's Fourth Dimension: 4-Week Reach & Frequency* (New York: Radio Advertising Bureau, 1970).

Numa Programming

Radio planning by computer

An advertiser has a budget of $500,000 for advertising. He is interested in reaching women in the 25- to 49-year-old age group. He has determined that his copy is most adaptable and effective in a one-minute form. He also wants to confine his advertising to weekdays and Saturday before 7:00 P.M. to coincide with shopping hours; therefore he will spread his advertising over the period of 6:00 A.M. to 7:00 P.M., Monday through Saturday. What is the best pattern of reach and frequency?

These are oversimplified decisions for the sake of illustration, but they do reflect the kinds of choices that are made.

Four factors have to be established . . . namely, reach, frequency, number of markets, and number of weeks of advertising. Each of these is directly related to the others; and the choice of one will greatly affect the other. Using a computer program, it is possible to establish a variety of criteria and then make a selection from the alternatives, depending upon which element is most important.

Choice 1. The advertiser wants to *reach* at least 75 percent of the target group in any market over the course of four weeks. He then has a choice of these alternatives:

REACH	FREQUENCY	NUMBER OF MARKETS	NUMBER OF WEEKS
75	6.8	Top 10	13
75	4.2	Top 20	13
75	Cannot be achieved	Top 50	13
75	11.2	Top 10	8
75	7.6	Top 20	8
75	4.2	Top 50	8

Choice 2. The advertiser wants an average *frequency* of 8.0 over a four-week period. In this case the alternatives would be as follows:

Frequency	Reach	Number of Markets	Number of Weeks
8.0	68.8	Top 10	13
8.0	51.5	Top 20	13
8.0	33.2	Top 50	13
8.0	89.9	Top 10	8
8.0	71.4	Top 20	8
8.0	51.5	Top 50	8

Choice 3. The campaign must cover the *top 20 markets for a period of 13 weeks.* The advertiser then can select from the four-week reach and frequency alternatives available.

Number of Markets	Number of Weeks	Reach	Frequency
Top 20	13	17.5	31.7
Top 20	13	42.9	10.4
Top 20	13	65.8	5.6
Top 20	13	78.2	3.9

To demonstrate how any of the alternatives in Choice 3 can be implemented, the summary table below shows the average number of stations per market to be used and the average number of announcements to be used on each over a period of time, depending on the degree of importance of reach, frequency, number of stations, and frequency in each situation.

Reach	Frequency	Average Number of Stations	Average Number of Announcements per Station
17.5	31.7	1 or 2	100
42.9	10.4	3 or 4	27
65.8	5.6	7 or 8	11
78.2	3.9	12 to 15	5

This system does not tell you which plan to use. That depends on your own judgment of what is most important to you—reach, frequency, number of markets. But under this system, rather than buying an arbitrary number of stations and number of announcements in each market, the program provides a far more precise figure, which indicates the number of stations to be used in each specific market, and the number of announcements to be made per station, once the buying policy has been established.

The Radio Market Area (RMA)

A local advertiser has little problem in selecting the best stations to use; he lives right in the territory; he knows through which station or stations he can best reach his prospects. But a national or regional advertiser planning to use radio in a wide geographical spread has a more complex problem, particularly when stations from neighboring larger cities overlap the local stations of the adjacent territories, which often represent important markets. In 1972, the first Radio Market Area report was published, permitting an advertiser to determine which stations to use to get the optimum spread per dollar in all the markets in a territory.

As a typical example, we have the case of an advertiser who is using radio in two metropolitan markets 100 miles apart. Between them lie three smaller cities, A, B, and C; each, however, represents an important market. Question: To cover those markets, should he also use the local stations in each? That is an obvious way. The RMA report showed, however, that he should use the local stations in cities A and B, but he did not have to do so to get good coverage in city C. To a national advertiser planning a widespread radio schedule, such information can make a big dollar difference.

The Radio Market Area concept, by Vitt Media International, is parallel in radio to Nielsen's Designated Market Area (DMA) and the Area of Dominant Influence (ADI) of the American Research Bureau, used for television planning.

Gross Rating Points for Radio

A rating point is an estimate of the size of a radio or television audience, expressed as a percentage of a total audience. The system used in television is also used in radio, applied to its special needs. The difference between a radio rating point and a television rating point relates to the group being measured. In television, we measure homes and people, while in radio we measure only people 12 years old and over. Therefore we can equate radio and television only against people 12+ years old who use either medium.

One GRP (Gross Rating Point) is 1 percent of the total population group under evaluation, whether it is homes or people.

A national advertiser planning to enter metro markets across the country can determine how many GRP's he plans to buy in each market, and use that as a yardstick in actually scheduling stations and programs in a city.

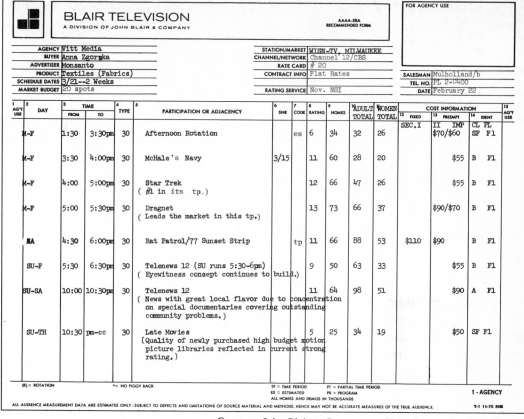

AG'Y USE	DAY	FROM	TO	TYPE	PARTICIPATION OR ADJACENCY	SNR	CODE	RATING	HOMES	ADULT TOTAL	WOMEN TOTAL	FIXED	PREEMPT (II IMP)	IDENT (CL PL)	AG'Y USE
M-F		1:30	3:30pm	30	Afternoon Rotation	es		6	34	32	26	SEC.I	$70/$60	SF F1	
M-F		3:30	4:00pm	30	McHale's Navy	3/15		11	60	28	20		$55	B F1	
M-F		4:00	5:00pm	30	Star Trek (#1 in its tp.)			12	66	47	26		$55	B F1	
M-F		5:00	5:30pm	30	Dragnet (Leads the market in this tp.)			13	73	66	37		$90/$70	B F1	
SA		4:30	6:00pm	30	Rat Patrol/77 Sunset Strip	tp		11	66	88	53	$110	$90	B F1	
SU-F		5:30	6:30pm	30	Telenews 12 (SU runs 5:30-6pm) (Eyewitness concept continues to build.)			9	50	63	33		$55	B F1	
SU-SA		10:00	10:30pm	30	Telenews 12 (News with great local flavor due to concentration on special documentaries covering outstanding community problems.)			11	64	98	51		$90	A F1	
SU-TH		10:30	pm-cc	30	Late Movies (Quality of newly purchased high budget motion picture libraries reflected in current strong rating.)			5	25	34	19		$50	SF F1	

(R) = ROTATION   * = NO PIGGY BACK

TP = TIME PERIOD   PT = PARTIAL TIME PERIOD
ES = ESTIMATED   PR = PROGRAM
ALL HOMES AND DEMOS IN THOUSANDS

1 - AGENCY

ALL AUDIENCE MEASUREMENT DATA ARE ESTIMATES ONLY-SUBJECT TO DEFECTS AND LIMITATIONS OF SOURCE MATERIAL AND METHODS, HENCE MAY NOT BE ACCURATE MEASURES OF THE TRUE AUDIENCE.

T-1 11-70 50M

Courtesy, John Blair & Company, and Vitt International Media, Inc.

How Recommended Availabilities are Presented

Planning and Buying Radio Time

We begin with a budget for a given time, a list of markets, a reach–frequency pattern, and a decision as to length of commercial.

In buying spots, we ask:

1. What is the station's rating?
2. Does the programming attract our target audience?
3. What is the station's share of the total audience we seek?
4. What is the power of the station? If we are out for reach, that might be important.
5. What is its reptuation on preemptions and make-goods?
6. What is the best deal that can be negotiated?

In the case of a radio network, we ask about:

187

1. *Physical facilities.* How many stations comprise the network? How strong are the network affiliates in the markets most important to us?

2. *Special-event availability.* What programs are available? Ratings? What kind of demographic audience do they attract, and how large is it?

3. *Cost.* What are the comparative rate advantages and disadvantages of the networks being considered, in reaching the best potential customers? The goal is to reach the greatest number of the people *you want to reach* at the lowest cost per message. What is the best price that can be negotiated?

4. *Programming environment.* Does the audience attracted by the programs mesh with the demography of the product profile? Is it compatible with the message to be delivered?

5. *Other considerations.* Is it desirable to have the same advertising pressure in all markets, or does the product sell better in large cities, in rural areas, etc.? If so, it may be desirable to consider using spots to supplement a network schedule.

TRENDS IN RADIO

Between 1960 and 1970, radio network increased 35 percent; spot, 60 percent; local, 102 percent.[13] Local radio will continue to zoom ahead, because it is so readily available to local merchants, there is no (or little) production cost, an advertiser can go on with short notice, it reaches out to specific audiences in the advertiser's market, and it has proved highly effective. The pricing of spots has become more realistic for the national advertiser, and the ability to reach specific audiences will increase their usage. Networks are being largely reduced to five-minute newscasts on the hour, and most of their other programs are by transcription.

FM radio, which shot up so fast since AM and FM stations were unhooked in broadcasting, promises to be one of the great growth sectors in radio.

* * *

We will discuss the creation and production of radio commercials in the next section of the book. Meanwhile, we continue the discussion of media.

---

[13] See pp. 136-137.

Travelodge

A case report on the use of radio

by Carl J. Short

The appropriateness of any medium for any client involves one basic task. That is matching the characteristics of a given medium with the communication objectives of a given client. In this particular instance, the client was Travelodge International, one of the largest motel/motor-hotel chains in the world.

Travelodge's objectives were:

1. To communicate the availability and convenience of Travelodge's one-number reservation system.

2. To communicate the availability of Travelodge's directories (rate, facility, and location guides which had proved to be effective in increasing business once in the hands of a traveler).

3. To communicate to the traveler the convenience of availability offered by a nationwide network of over 450 properties and 27,000 rooms.

4. To communicate the dual personality of Travelodge, for there no longer existed a typical Travelodge product (in addition to their traditional two-story motels, Travelodge has added in recent years a number of high-rise motor hotels).

To meet these objectives, we needed a medium which could offer:

1. National coverage of Travelodge's target audience at a low cost-per-thousand.

2. High frequency of exposure to this target audience because of the number of subjects we had to communicate.

3. Great flexibility—the flexibility of inserting copy changes on rates or special events at a moment's notice, tagging a corporate announcement with reference to an individual property, or placing the greatest advertising support in areas particularly important as origination or destination centers or cities where Travelodge motor hotels are located.

We conducted a review of media possibilities, beginning with a study of Brand Rating Index data as it applies to the print and broadcast

Excerpted from *Matchmaking the Message with the Medium* by Carl J. Short, Vice-President, Dailey & Associates. *Broadcasting*, August 9, 1971. Reprinted with permission, Broadcasting Publications, Inc.

media. Magazines were the first to be eliminated, because we felt they couldn't deliver sufficient frequency. Television was eliminated because of its cost. Newspapers went because we felt that on a national basis they were an inefficient buy.

That left radio, which could fulfill all of the needs outlined above. It could also provide us with flexibility (Travelodge could "move around"— change messages on short notice to suit seasonal or special situations). It would provide a personal contact with the prime target audience—the male adult with a college education and better-than-average income, and the businessman who would make Travelodge his business address, would influence a decision for using Travelodge motor hotels for sales meetings, and would think of Travelodge when planning personal or family vacations.

Next came the decision of which type of radio to buy. First we reviewed the availabilities on all networks and then the facilities of all networks —particularly in major markets and markets of special interest to Travelodge.

We also looked at the possibilities of using spot radio only. This drew a negative response, because it was felt that it would not offer enough cohesiveness through the peak travel season—markets would vary so much with format and personality that there would be no Travelodge "feel."

Standing there at attention was network radio. But which network?

The stature of CBS Radio, its strength in the major markets, as well as its nationwide coverage with over 240 stations (reaches over 21,000,000 different adults in a given week), made it the most desirable. This, plus the availability of *"Walter Cronkite Reporting,"* a five-a-week news analysis series produced by CBS News, and the willingness of CBS to work with us in building a 26-week program—13 weeks of Cronkite in peak summer travel time (July–August) and a scatter plan of 60-second announcements preceding and following the Cronkite schedule.

Also affecting the decision were the efficiency of CBS Radio (our buy delivers in excess of 1,300 adult listeners per dollar) and the merchandisability of Walter Cronkite and CBS to the Travelodge owners and operators —i.e., the immediate rapport established through such a spokesman.

To increase our frequency and flexibility, we added spot-radio flights in 17 major markets. There we could supplement our corporate spots with "live" tags for individual Travelodge properties; we could concentrate our efforts in those metropolitan markets important as origination and destination centers (generally paralleling population rankings); and those areas where Travelodge had motor hotels or large clusters of motel properties (not always paralleling population rankings); and we could greatly expand our frequency of exposure, thus increasing our chances that a large segment of Travelodge's target audience would hear each of Travelodge's communication messages.

The final problem faced—capturing the rural/city dual personality of the client's product—demonstrates the close relationship between the medium and the message. In this case the use of sound permitted an effective translation of this duality. Voice casting and music selection were chosen on the basis of combining just the right balance of "down-home" and "down-town" sounds.

. . . After three months, this program has aided Travelodge in increasing the participation and enthusiasm of individual co-owners and managers, in placing a larger percentage of their business through the one-number reservation system, and in increasing the overall occupancy rate of the chain.

Review Questions

1. What are the major advantages of radio for the national advertiser? Its limitations?

2. Why is radio called the "ubiquitous" medium?

3. About how many radio stations can you get on your set? How does the number of radio stations in a market affect the use of radio as a medium?

4. Why are radio stations assigned to different classes? What are they?

5. Why is FM reception better than AM reception? You can hear AM stations from far distances at night. Why not FM stations?

6. Into what time periods is the broadcast day usually divided? Rank them as to size of audience.

7. Define or describe the following:
   a. weekly plan
   b. preemptible time
   c. radio participations

8. Explain why radio stations have different program formats. Can you name five formats in general use? How would you characterize the formats of major stations in your area?

9. What are the four factors that were considered in Westinghouse's Numa analysis, presented in this chapter, and what value does this analysis have for the advertiser?

10. Discuss the major considerations involved in buying radio network time and radio spot time.

11. In the case of Travelodge, what were the major reasons the company chose radio? What were their reasons for choosing it the way they did?

Reading Suggestions

Advertising Age, "Broadcast Advertising: 1970," a special section, November 2, 1970, p. 19ff.

Barton, Roger, *The Handbook of Advertising Management.* New York: McGraw-Hill Book Company, 1970.

Broadcasting Yearbook, published annually by *Broadcasting* (magazine), Washington, D.C.

Chester, Giraud, Garnett Garrison, and Edgar Willis, *Television and Radio,* 3rd edition. New York: Appleton-Century-Crofts, 1963.

Coddington, Robert H., *Modern Radio Broadcasting.* Blue Ridge Summit, Pa.: Tab Books, 1969.

Media Decisions, "Radio Turns the Tables," March 1971, p. 44ff.

Radio Corporation of America, *The First 25 Years of RCA.* New York: Radio Corp. of America, 1944.

9

Using Newspapers

THINK OF THE UNITED STATES not as one big market, but as 1,503 individual markets. The focal point of each market is a city or town where one or more newspapers are being published. At the editorial desk of each paper sits a man who has lived in that community for many years; he was probably born in that region. He knows its people, their ethnic background, where they live, how they make a living, how they live, and what kind of news interests them most. No wonder 78 percent of the population over the age of 18 read a daily newspaper.

More money is invested in newspaper advertising than in any other medium. Of that advertising, 80 percent is local; 20 percent national.*

BACKGROUND

In the United States there are about 1750 newspapers. Of these, about 80 percent are evening papers; 20 percent morning papers. This number includes about 200 newspapers that are both morning and evening papers. There are also 600 Sunday newspapers. These are aside from the weekly papers, which we consider separately.

The number of daily papers has been shrinking over the years, as has the number of cities with two or more papers, but the total newspaper circulation has been rising, as follows:

YEAR	NO. OF PAPERS	CIRCULATION
1920	2,042	27,790,656
1940	1,878	41,131,611
1960	1,763	58,881,746
1970	1,748	62,107,527

There has also been a change in the geographical sites where the newspapers are being published, reflecting the population shift. While a

---

* See pp. 121.

number of metropolitan papers have closed shop or merged with others, many "outside," or suburban, papers have sprung up. Within twenty years, the total circulation of the central-city papers went up by 1 percent; that of the suburbs increased by 150 percent.

Newspaper Reading

The average newspaper is read by more than two people per issue (it makes the author unhappy to use the statistician's figure of 2⅓ readers per paper). Of the readers, 42 percent spend over 40 minutes with their paper; 23 percent spend 30 to 39 minutes; and 30 percent spend up to 30 minutes.

Newspaper readership goes up with education, from 75 percent of those who attended high school to 87 percent among college graduates. Readership also goes up with household income, from 75 percent of those with income of $5,000 to $8,000, to 86 percent of those with income of $15,000 to $25,000.

However, the reading of newspapers is not uniform throughout the country, as revealed by these figures showing the ratio of circulation to the number of households in different markets:

Kansas City, Mo.	1.32	San Francisco, Calif.	.90
Richmond, Va.	1.26	Salt Lake City, Utah	.82
Springfield, Mass.	1.25	El Paso, Tex.	.80
Wichita, Kans.	1.17	Los Angeles, Calif.	.73 [1]

This means that if you wanted to cover a market, you would do better with newspapers in Kansas City than in Los Angeles. In the latter case you would have to supplement newspaper advertising with other local media.

Features and Advantages

To the national advertiser, the newspaper offers great *geographic flexibility in selecting definable local markets* in which to advertise. He can concentrate his advertising in territories in which his type of product is being sold, as in the case of hard-water soap, or confine it to those territories in which his product is well distributed. He may concentrate in those markets enjoying good economic conditions, avoiding those that are going through a bad time. He may wish to test different advertising programs in various cities, to see which program works best before embarking on a more extensive campaign. He can adapt the copy to the market. If he has a seasonal product, he

---

[1] Source of foregoing statistical data: Bureau of Advertising, 1971.

may readily plan his advertising by weather; the advertising of an antifreeze was scheduled to appear first in the North, then move with the cool weather toward the South.

Because they are printed, newspapers can *picture styles of products*. The fact that newspapers are issued daily permits the advertiser to move fast in meeting a sudden marketing opportunity; they are a *timely* medium. The papers are also full of advertisements featuring the latest daily offerings on sale. Hence advertisers meet an audience receptive to learning "What's new?" Newspapers are the *preferred medium for cooperative advertising* placed by national advertisers through the local stores.

Limitations and Challenges

Every medium has certain limitations that may prove to be disadvantageous for a given program. Some limitations are beyond the control of the advertiser. There may be some limitations, however, which the advertiser can offset, and even turn into advantages. For example:

—*The life of a newspaper is very short; it is read hurriedly*. This is a challenge to prepare ads that will compete with news headlines, as well as with other ads.

—*The local advertisers get all the front pages; national advertisers are pushed to the back*. This is a challenge to make your ad so striking that it will stand out anywhere. (Even an ad on page 3 will be skipped if it's dull.)

—*Newspapers are printed on high-speed presses on rough, porous wood pulp paper, resulting in comparatively poor reproduction, especially of photographs*. But you can design black-and-white art work that will reproduce well on newsprint, with deep-etched plates, and end with the best-looking ad in the paper.

—*Newspapers are overcrowded on Wednesdays, Thursdays and Fridays with supermarket ads*. But people read the papers earlier in the week too, and are always interested in learning about products that can be helpful to them.

—*Newspapers reach everybody, but we are interested only in a certain limited demographic group*. This calls for a review of other media.

At all times, a newspaper is in competition with other local media, especially television and radio, on a cost-per-thousand basis of delivering an effective message.

Two new studies show

Newspaper-TV mix produces twice the increase in market share compared to TV alone.

And at <u>no extra advertising cost.</u>

Two of America's largest food advertisers recently completed tests that prove that newspapers—in combination with television—produced share of market increases that were *twice as large* as those generated by TV alone.

And with no increase in advertising costs.

There were two separate tests. One for a canned and frozen food advertiser. The other for a dog food advertiser. Each test was conducted by the advertiser, not by us. We simply paid for the measurement of sales.

In both cases, the test markets were carefully matched. Each advertiser used network TV as a base in both markets. Spot TV was added to one market. An equal dollars' worth of newspaper advertising was added to the other market.

• In both tests the newspaper and television mix delivered *twice the increase* in market share as the "TV only" schedule—and for the same advertising cost.

• In one test the newspaper combination produced a larger number of new *customers*.

• In both tests, *brand loyalty* increased most in the newspaper market.

What do these tests mean to you?

There is dramatic new evidence that newspapers can play a major role in your marketing strategy by increasing both market share and total sales at no extra advertising cost.

Certainly, a similar test for your own product would be well worth the effort.

The research procedure is simple, inexpensive, accurate, yet it is proven and highly regarded. The method used actually washes out unwanted market variables which plague many tests.

If you would like more details, contact any of our office managers or Joe Chamberlin, President.

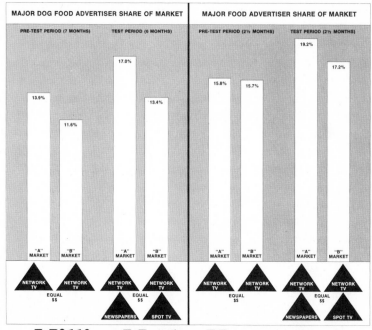

MAJOR DOG FOOD ADVERTISER SHARE OF MARKET

PRE-TEST PERIOD (7 MONTHS) — "A" MARKET 13.9%, "B" MARKET 11.6%
TEST PERIOD (6 MONTHS) — "A" MARKET 17.0%, "B" MARKET 13.4%

MAJOR FOOD ADVERTISER SHARE OF MARKET

PRE-TEST PERIOD (2½ MONTHS) — "A" MARKET 15.8%, "B" MARKET 15.7%
TEST PERIOD (2½ MONTHS) — "A" MARKET 19.2%, "B" MARKET 17.2%

Million Market Newspapers INC.

SIX EAST FORTY-THIRD STREET, NEW YORK, N.Y. 10017 212-986-3434

BOSTON GLOBE • MILWAUKEE JOURNAL AND SENTINEL • PHILADELPHIA BULLETIN • ST. LOUIS POST-DISPATCH • SAN JOSE MERCURY & NEWS • WASHINGTON STAR

ENCOURAGING INTER-MEDIA USE

This advertisement, addressed to advertisers and their agencies, goes after some of the money being spent in television by showing the advantages of using newspapers along with television.

Display advertising covers all advertising in the newspaper other than *classi-fied*. Display advertising is divided into *local* (or retail) advertising, and *national* (or general) advertising. Some newspapers have a division, Classified Display, for advertising which falls between local and national, as Real Estate, Amusements, Hotels, Restaurants.

Local (or retail) advertising. This refers to the advertising of local business establishments. Largest of these are the department stores and the supermarkets. Included also are the local banks, furniture stores, service stations, and all other merchants and institutions of the community. About 83 percent of newspaper advertising is local. This includes classified advertising.

National (or general) advertising. This represents chiefly the world of nationally advertised trademarked goods sold through many outlets; also services, such as the airlines and other non-locally oriented advertisers. (The term "general" is a vestigial term, seen chiefly on rate cards.) About 17 percent of newspaper advertising is national.

Local rates vs. national rates. Different sets of rates prevail for local advertising and for national advertising; each has its own rate card. National rates are higher than local rates by as much as 60 percent in the largest cities. The difference is rationalized by the fact that retail advertisers have traditionally been the steadiest and largest newspaper advertisers, and that their advertising is placed directly, without agency commission and the need for special representatives in the major advertising centers. But the difference in rates exceeds these costs, and there has been great pressure by national advertisers to get their rates reduced. Some newspapers have uniform rates for national and local advertising.[2]

HOW NEWSPAPER SPACE IS BOUGHT

Measuring space. The width of newspaper space is measured in terms of *columns*. The depth from top to bottom is measured in terms of agate lines per column, referred to just as *lines,* of which there are 14 to the inch. The size of an ad is specified in terms of lines × columns. An advertisement five inches deep by two columns wide is written as 70 × 2, spoken of as "70 on 2," and is a 140-line ad. The width of the column varies from paper to paper, but has no bearing on the line rate. And the number of lines of type set up in a display ad likewise has nothing to do with the measurement of

---

[2] Bureau of Advertising, 1970.

space in terms of lines. Rates are quoted just by the line. (In small-town papers of low circulation, space may be sold by the inch.) Just remember: 14 lines to the column inch.

The rate structure.   Each publisher sets his own rates. About 75 percent of the papers offer a uniform *flat rate* to all national advertisers. Other newspapers offer a *quantity* discount or an alternative *time* or *frequency* discount. The advertiser elects whichever discount structure is best for him.

The highest rate, against which all discounts are figured, is called the *open rate*, or *basic* rate, or *one-time* rate, as illustrated in the following rates from a newspaper rate card:

QUANTITY DISCOUNTS		TIME DISCOUNTS	
Open rate .... 39¢		Open rate .... 39¢	
2,500 lines within one year 37		13 times within one year 37	
5,000 " " " " 34		26 " " " " 34	
10,000 " " " " 31		52 " " " " 29	
20,000 " " " " 28		156 " " " " 28	

ROP and preferred-position rates.   The basic rates quoted by a newspaper entitle the advertisement to a *run-of-paper* (abbreviated *ROP*) *position* —anywhere in the paper that the publisher places it, although he will be mindful of the advertiser's request and interest in getting a good position. An advertiser may buy a choice position by paying a higher, *preferred-position rate*—similar to paying for a box seat in the stadium instead of general admission. A cigar advertiser, for example, may elect to pay preferred-position rate to be sure that he gets on the sports page; a cosmetic advertiser may buy preferred position on the society page. There are preferred positions on the page itself. An advertiser may pay to have his advertisement appear at the top of a column, or else top of column next to news reading matter (called *full position*). Each paper specifies its preferred-position rates; there is no great consistency in this practice. (A familiar position request for which you do not have to pay extra is "Above fold urgently requested.")

Combination rates.   In a number of cities, the same publisher issues a morning paper and a separate evening paper, in which you can buy space individually or at a better combination price for both. In some instances, the advertiser has no choice—the papers are sold on a *forced combination basis*. The same space and copy must be used in both papers. Such publishers require the ads be run the same day, but you may be able to get them to run the ads a few days apart, to get the advantage of a wider time spread.

THE RATE CARD

A publisher's rate card contains all the information that an advertiser needs to place an order, including all his rates, copy requirements, and mechanical requirements. In 1920, the American Association of Advertising Agencies recommended a Standard Form Rate Card, which is followed to this day. It is folded to 6 × 3½ inches, and calls for the information to be given in a standard numbered sequence.

Most advertising offices subscribe to the Standard Rate & Data Service, which publishes in full all the rate-card information in monthly volumes, kept up to date during the month by supplements. Having all the information standardized in sequence proves its special advantages here. A computerized service is also available. (A separate service is published for each medium.)

Published Morning, Evening, Sunday
Publication Address
Telephone Number

NAME OF NEWSPAPER

Rate Card Number
Issue Date
Effective Date

1—PERSONNEL

a. Name of publisher.
b. Names of advertising executives.
c. Name of production supervisor.

2—REPRESENTATIVES

a. Names, addresses, and telephone numbers of advertising representatives.

3—COMMISSION AND CASH DISCOUNT

a. Agency commission.
b. Cash discount.
c. Discount date.

4—GENERAL

a. Policy on rate protection and rate revision notice.
b. Regulations covering acceptance of advertising.
c. Policy regarding advertising which simulates editorial content.

5—GENERAL ADVERTISING RATES

a. Black and white rates for standard space units. Bulk and/or frequency discounts.
b. Starting date if sold in combination.

6—COLOR — ROP

a. Color availability – days of week and number of colors available.
b. Minimum size for ROP Color advertisements.
c. Rates for standard units – 1 page, 1500 lines, 1000 lines – with black and white costs as base for comparison.
d. Rates for non-standard units–black and white line rate plus applicable flat or % premium.
e. Closing dates for reservations and printing material.
f. Cancellation dates.
g. Leeway on insertion dates, if required.

h. Number of progressive proofs required.
i. Registration marks on plates and mats.
j. Full page size for direct casting, in inches.
k. Number of mats required for direct casting.
l. Running head and date line for direct casting, if required.
m. Bulk or frequency discounts on color.

7—MAGAZINE SECTIONS
(Name of Section and when issued)

a. Rates for letterpress – black and white, color.
b. Rates for rotogravure – monotone, color.
c. Minimum depth and mechanical requirements.
d. Closing and cancellation dates.

ANATOMY OF A RATE CARD

This is a model rate card, as widely used by newspapers, based on the Recommendation of the American Association of Advertising Agencies. The chief features of the card is that all information is given standardized numbers, and is listed in standardized sequence. All newspapers follow the same numbering system and sequence for such information as they have to give. If they have no information under some particular numbered classifications, they just skip the number, but do not change the numbering of the rest of the card.

8—COMIC SECTIONS (When issued)

a. Rates for color units.
b. Minimum depth and mechanical requirements.
c. Closing and cancellation dates.

9—CLASSIFICATIONS

a. Rates for special classifications (amusements, financial, political, etc., and special pages.)

10—SPLIT RUN

a. Availabilities and rates.

11—POSITION CHARGES

a. Availabilities and rates.

12—DAILY COMIC PAGES

a. Rates.
b. Minimum requirements.
c. Regulations covering acceptance of advertising.
d. Closing and cancellation dates.

13—CLASSIFIED

a. Rate per word, line or inch; number of words per line.
b. Minimum requirements.

14—READING NOTICES

a. Available pages.
b. Rates and requirements.

15—CONTRACT AND COPY REGULATIONS

a. Regulations not stated elsewhere in rate card.

16—CLOSING AND CANCELLATION DATES
(Black and White)

17—MINIMUM DEPTH ROP

18—MECHANICAL MEASUREMENTS

a. Type page size before processing — inches wide by inches deep.
b. Depth of column in lines.
c. Number of columns to page.
d. Number of lines charged to column and to page.
e. Number of lines charged to double-truck and size in inches.
f. Requirements as to mats, originals and electros.

g. Screen required.
h. Address for printing material.
i. Other mechanical information.

19—CIRCULATION INFORMATION

a. Circulation verification (details in Publisher's Statement and Audit Report).
b. If unaudited, basis for circulation claim.
c. Milline rates, if desired. Daily................, Sunday................ .

20—MISCELLANEOUS

a. Year established.
b. Subscription price; single copy price.
c. News services, e.g. AP, UP.
d. Other information not listed elsewhere.

(Standard Form Rate Card recommended by the American Association of Advertising Agencies, Inc.).

OAKLAND

Alameda County—Map Location B-6
See SRDS consumer market map and data at beginning of the State.
Corporate city population (1970 govt. census) 361,561

	Households	Population
ABC city zone ('70 census)	242,595	646,215
ABC retail tr. zone ('70 census)	295,449	985,358
*Metro Area 1-71, see state table	1,093,510	3,148,800

(*) San Francisco-Oakland.

TRIBUNE

P. O. Box 509, Oakland, Calif. 94604.
Phone 415-273-2000. TWX 910-366-7227.

Media Code 1 105 4875 7.00
EVENING MONDAY THRU FRIDAY.
MORNING SATURDAY, SUNDAY.

1. PERSONNEL
Pres. & Editor—W. F. Knowland.
Advertising Director—Roy E. Boody.
General Adv. Mgr.—John W. Carnahan.
Production Manager—Paul McIntosh.
2. REPRESENTATIVES and/or BRANCH OFFICES
Cresmer, Woodward, O'Mara & Ormsbee, Inc.
3. COMMISSION AND CASH DISCOUNT
Agency commission 15%; 2% 20th following month.
4. GENERAL RATE POLICY
30-day notice given of any rate revision.
Alcoholic beverage advertising accepted.

ADVERTISING RATES
Effective October 1, 1970.
Received September 11, 1970.

5. BLACK/WHITE RATES

	Flat per line	1 page	1,500 lines	1,000 lines
Daily	.77	1,854.16	1,155.00	770.00
Sunday	.81	1,950.48	1,215.00	810.00

FULL PAGE R.O.P. DISCOUNTS
Full page units within 1 year:
10 pages.......... 10%   30 pages.................. 17%
20 pages.......... 15%   40 pages.................. 19%
Discounts apply to pages of 1 product or multiple products under 1 brand name. Discounts applicable to space and color premium charges. Contract required.
7. COLOR RATES AND DATA
Spot color available daily and Sunday. *Full color daily and Sunday with 2-day leeway required. Minimum 1,000 lines.
Use b/w line rate plus the following extra cost:

	b/w 1 c	b/w 2 c or 3 c
1,000 to 1,499 lines	35%	600.00
1,500 to Full page	35%	850.00

(*) Sunday multiple color available only in Society, (standard); "Entertainment Week," "California" (tabloid sections).
Closing dates for multiple color: Complete material in Tribune Plant 4 working days before publication.
Special inks, other than standard colors, 30.00 extra (non-commissionable).
Fluorescent inks 200.00 per color.
8. CLASSIFICATION AND OTHER RATES
Automobile and Accessories, Financial, Transportation & Travel Services, etc., general rates apply. Political —local, state and national candidates and issues.
R.O.P. position—general rates apply; on or facing radio or TV pages daily .82; Sunday .86.
STRIP ADVERTISING—R.O.P.
Daily per agate line .77; Sunday .81.
POSITION CHARGES
Next to reading 12-1/2%; full position, (42 line min.) 25%. Editorial page not sold.
Radio & TV Programs on or facing radio or TV pages per line, daily .82; Sunday .86.
9. SPLIT-RUN
Available. Minimum 1,000 lines. Flat charge 75.00 (non-commissionable). For additional information, contact general advertising manager.
10. CLASSIFIED AD RATES
15% agency; 2% 15th following month; cash with order unless credit established.
.94 per line, daily. 1.07 per line, Sunday. Minimum 2 lines. Blind box charge 3.00. 1 col. width 1-1/2" before processing.
Deadline 4:30 p.m. day preceding Tues., Wed., Thurs.; 4:30 p.m. Wed. for Friday; 4:30 p.m. Thurs. for Sat. and Sun. Sunday Real Estate Section 4:30 p.m. Wednesday; Thursday Auto Section 4:30 p.m. Tuesday. Classified Display deadline—contact publisher.
Regulations (see Contents)—C 1, 2, 5, 6, 8, 9, 10, 11, 13 thru 17, 19, 22, 23, P 1 thru 6. T 1, 2, 4.
11. SPECIAL PAGES, FEATURES
Food Day: Wednesday.
Fashion, Thursday; Automotive, Thursday Classified; Teen Pages, Wednesday and Saturday; Travel, Sunday; Real Estate, Sunday Classified.
12. MINIMUM DEPTH R.O.P.
As many inches deep as columns wide. Over 280 lines deep charged full col. 301 lines).
13. CONTRACT AND COPY REGULATIONS
See Contents page for location of regulations—items

CALIFORNIA

	Total	CZ	TrZ	Other	flat
*ExSat	193,036	100,780	85,866	5,518	3.92
†SatM	191,959	98,239	88,749	4,856	3.94
‡Sun	224,530	113,990	102,420	7,966	3.55

(*) Includes 872—Transportation Terminals.
(†) Includes 115—Transportation Terminals.
(‡) Includes 154—Transportation Terminals.
For county-by-county and/or metropolitan area breakdowns, see SRDS Newspaper Circulation Analysis.

OCEANSIDE

San Diego County—Map Location G-11
See SRDS consumer market map and data at beginning of the State.
Corporate city population (1970 govt. census).. 40,494

	Households	Population
ABC city zone ('70 census)	18,362	55,438
ABC retail tr. zone ('70 census)	46,955	163,575

BLADE-TRIBUNE

1722 S. Hill St., Oceanside, Calif. 92054.
Phone 714-722-8222.

Media Code 1 105 4950 8.00
EVENING (except Saturday) AND SUNDAY.
Member: Bureau of Advertising, A.N.P.A.
1. PERSONNEL
Publisher—Thomas F. Missett.
Advertising Manager—Dave Oxley.
Advertising Sales Mgr.—Gary Nelson.
Class. Adv. Mgr.—Pete Doughtie.
2. REPRESENTATIVES and/or BRANCH OFFICES
Ward-Griffith Company, Inc.
3. COMMISSION AND CASH DISCOUNT
15% to agencies; 2% cash discount 15th following month.
4. GENERAL RATE POLICY
60-day notice given of any rate revision.
Alcoholic beverage advertising accepted.

ADVERTISING RATES

CAUTION: NEW RATES
EFFECTIVE MAY 1, 1972
SEE "FUTURE RATE PAGE"

Effective January 1, 1968.
5. LINE RATE
Flat (daily or Sunday), per line......... .14
6. COMBINATION RATES
Effective November 1, 1971:
OCEANSIDE BLADE TRIBUNE AND
ESCONDIDO TIMES-ADVOCATE UNIT

	Flat per line	1 page	1,500 lines	1,000 lines
Comb. rate	.30	722.40	450.00	300.00

Combination rate applies when same size unit appears within 2 week period in both papers. Send separate printing material to each paper and insertion orders to Joe Anthony, Nosadico Newspapers, P. O. Box 1477, Escondido, Calif. 92025 showing group rate or indicate to run ad in both newspapers.
COLOR RATES AND DATA
Available daily or Sunday in combination. One day leeway requested on Wednesday and Thursday insertions. Minimum 1,000 lines.
Use b/w line rate plus the following applicable flat costs:

	b/w 1 c	b/w 2 c	b/w 3 c
Page units, extra		105.00	210.00
Less than Page	160.00	265.00	370.00

Net Paid—Audited Combined 9-30-71

	Total	CZ	TrZ	Other	Max flat	Min flat
ExSat	36,773	25,460	10,746	527	8.02	
Sun	37,378	26,036	10,813	549	7.89	

Also sold in combination with Blade Tribune Tri-City Advertiser (Wednesday) pick-up from daily (same copy) extra .07 per line.
Circulation Sworn 9-30-69, free 15,397.
7. COLOR RATES AND DATA
Available daily. Minimum 1,000 lines.
Use b/w line rate plus the following flat costs:

	b/w 1 c	b/w 2 c	b/w 3 c
Extra	95.00	135.00	175.00

Closing dates: Reservations 3 days before publication; printing material 2 days before publication.
8. CLASSIFICATION AND OTHER RATES
Amusements, per inch 2.10. Political, per inch 2.40.
POSITION CHARGES
Extra 25%.
10. CLASSIFIED AD RATES
15% agency; 2% 15th following month; cash with order unless credit established.
.30 per line; 6 line min. (6 pt.); 5 words per line; 12 lines per inch.
11. SPECIAL PAGES, FEATURES
Best Food Day: Wednesday, Entertainment page, Friday; TV Section, Sunday; Auto page, Sunday; Real Estate, Sunday.
12. MINIMUM DEPTH R.O.P.
As many inches deep as columns

Extract of a page of newspaper rates from Standard Rate & Data Service. Here all rate cards are published in full, giving information in standardized numerical sequence for each medium.

Courtesy, S.R.D.S.

The space contract.　Placing an advertisement in a newspaper usually involves two steps: first, agreeing upon the rate terms (the *space contract*); and second, forwarding the advertisement with an order definitely requesting insertion (the *insertion order*). The two steps may be taken at one time, but each step serves a separate function.

A space contract between an advertiser and a publisher is not necessarily an agreement to buy and sell a fixed amount of space; it is an agreement to abide by the prevailing rate card for the contract period for *such space as the advertiser actually uses.*

The insertion order.　When the advertiser is ready to place his advertisement, he forwards an insertion order giving the date or dates upon which the advertisement is to appear, the size in lines and columns, the position request, and the rate; he also advises how the plates or mats are being forwarded. The space contract may be made a part of the first insertion order. In either case, the two steps—contract and order—still serve separate functions.

THE MILLINE RATE

In comparing the cost of newspaper space, two variables enter: the rate per line and the circulation. To provide a clear basis for computing comparative costs, a hypothetical figure called the *milline* rate is used. *A milline is what it would cost per line to reach a million circulation of a paper, based upon its actual line rate and circulation.*

Since virtually all newspapers have either more or less circulation than an even million, the milline was created to put them on a comparable basis.[3] The formula is:

$$\frac{1{,}000{,}000 \times \text{rate per line}}{\text{quantity circulation}} = \text{milline}$$

as shown in these examples:

A. What is the milline rate of a newspaper with 2,000,000 circulation and a rate of $2.00 per line?

$$\frac{1{,}000{,}000 \times \$2.00}{2{,}000{,}000} = \$1.00 \text{ milline rate}$$

B. What is the milline rate of a newspaper having 350,000 circulation and a rate of 95¢ per line?

---

[3] The milline was the brainchild of Benjamin Jefferson, then advertising manager of the Lyon & Healy Piano Co., Chicago, in the early 1920's.

$$\frac{1,000,000 \times \$.95}{350,000} = \$2.71 \text{ milline rate}$$

You cannot buy a *milline of advertising*. It is merely an index figure for comparing the cost of circulation of different newspapers.

The milline rate at the maximum discount level is called a *maxiline,* and at the lowest discount level, a *miniline*. But *milline rate* is the basic unit of comparison.

THE SHORT RATE

If the newspaper charges a flat rate, the advertiser pays that rate for whatever space he uses. If the newspaper offers space discounts, the advertiser estimates the amount of space he will use during the next twelve months, and enters a contract to pay the corresponding rate for whatever space he uses, subject at the end of the year to adjustment.

For example, let us assume that a newspaper has the following rates:

Open rate	39¢
2,500 lines	37
5,000 lines	34
10,000 lines	31

An advertiser estimates (not guarantees) to run 5,000 lines during the current year, and enters a contract at the 5,000-line rate of 34 cents. He is billed each month for space used at the 34-cent-a-line rate. However, he runs only 3,500 lines during the year, and is entitled only to the 2,500-line rate of 37 cents; there is no 3,500-line rate. There is then an end-of-the-year reckoning, as follows:

3,500 lines @ 37¢	$1,295
Paid 3,500 lines at 34¢	1,190
Short rate due	$105

If the advertiser under such contract earns a better rate at the end of the year, he gets a *rebate* for the sum due him.

Some newspapers bill at the open rate only, and give rebates for lower rates when earned.

NEWSPAPER SIZES AND MAKEUP RESTRICTIONS

In newspapers, we have the *tabloid-size page* and the *large* or *standard-size page*. The tabloid is usually five or six columns wide and 200 lines deep,

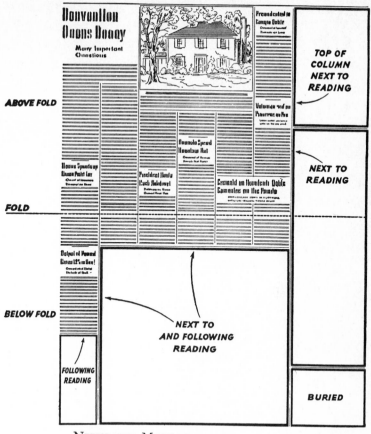

NEWSPAPER MAKE-UP

This diagram has been arranged to show different page positions.

making a full page of 1,000 or 1,200 lines. Most standard-size papers have eight columns to the page, and a column depth of between 280 and 330 lines.

Each newspaper will have its own restrictions regarding the size and shape of the ads it will accept. To prevent the use of freak-shaped advertisements, many publishers require the advertisement to be a *minimum depth* in ratio to the column width. The average restriction requires an advertisement to be 14 lines deep for every column of width. This would not apply to special strip positions across the bottom of the page, sold by some newspapers.

Another example: If a tabloid page is 200 lines deep, it may say that any ad over 170 lines deep will be charged for the full 200 lines. (If the ad were 190 lines deep, the paper would have a hard job selling the other ten lines to other advertisers.) Likewise, a standard-size paper 300 lines deep might place the upper limit at 270 lines, before being charged for a full page.

With this in mind, some advertisers, contemplating a full-page ad in a standard-size paper of eight columns and 300 lines, will instead plan an ad 7 columns by 270 lines. They feel they will be dominating the page, and in fact welcome having some news items in the adjacent columns to attract more interest to that page. They therefore save the cost of one whole column (300 lines) plus 30 lines on each of the remaining seven columns their ad occupies, or 210 lines. Total: 510 lines.

In connection with mats: the rule of thumb is that they shrink in depth 1 line in 50, in the course of newspaper production. A 100 × 2 ad might end up 98 × 2, a loss of four lines; a 200 × 5 ad may end up 196 × 5, or less, a loss of 20 lines. These losses are real, as the newspapers charge for space ordered, and not space filled. Best thing to do is to make mats longer so they will shrink to the correct size, or specify in the order, "not to exceed so many lines."

THE BLACK NEWSPAPERS

In 1972 there were 203 black newspapers with a total circulation of over 3,900,000, according to a study by Henry La Brie of the University of Iowa. Of that total, 11 papers have over 50,000 circulation, including the *New York Voice* (90,000), the *Black Panther Newspaper* (100,000), and *Muhammed Speaks* (625,000). Of all 203 newspapers, only 17 are audited by the Audit Bureau of Circulations. The *New York Amsterdam News* (83,000) is the top black paper of the ABC audited papers.[4] Many of the non-audited papers have small circulations. All tend to get high readership.

THE AUDIT BUREAU OF CIRCULATIONS

The basic source of information about the circulation of a publication is its ABC report, issued by the Audit Bureau of Circulations, an independent auditing organization, supported by advertisers, agencies, and publishers.

Over 95 percent of the daily papers belong to the ABC and issue ABC reports, as do most of the significant magazines. The ABC reports go into great detail on the quantity of circulation, how secured, and where distributed. As mentioned, these reports of statistics are accepted in all advertising circles. Among the key items to look for in such reports are:

1. What is the net paid circulation?
2. How much of it is in the city area, the wider retail area, and outside of that? If, for example, we had a new product with distribution in the city alone, that information would be important.

---

[4] *Advertising Age,* May 15, 1972, p. 24.

3. How much of the circulation is fully paid up; how much was obtained by cut prices or through contests and premiums? The latter circulation would not be as meaningful as the fully paid-up readership.

4. How much of the circulation was home or mail delivered? How much sold over the newsstand? The method of distribution varies from city to city, but within a city having home delivery such circulation is advantageous, and those figures are significant.

The ABC reports have nothing to do with the rates of a paper, or the quality of its circulation. They deal with the circulation statistics. Publishers, however, will also supply a separate demographic report of readership.

SPECIAL NEWSPAPER REPRESENTATIVES

Many publishers have their own *special sales representatives* in the major advertising centers to provide the advertiser and the agency with facts about the market and the competitive merits of a paper. The representative also provides other helpful services to the advertiser in connection with his marketing plans and schedules. One representative may handle many different newspapers, each in a different city. He is paid by the newspapers he represents.

A, B, AND C NEWSPAPER SCHEDULES

An advertiser selling in many markets will often prepare one newspaper schedule consisting of the maximum *total* linage for the largest markets and a schedule of lesser linage for the smaller markets; he may even have a third and still smaller schedule to run in the smallest towns. These schedules will be referred to as the advertiser's *A, B, and C schedules*—not to be confused with the ABC circulation statements.

There are two main reasons for A, B, and C schedules: First, the largest markets provide the largest volume of sales, hence the largest amount of money can be invested in them. The newspapers in the largest markets also carry the greatest amount of advertising and have the highest rates. Hence it may take larger advertisements and a larger part of the budget to compete against the other advertising for readership.

As the markets get smaller, the newspapers carry less advertising; therefore it does not take as vigorous a schedule to tell the message to the people in that market as it does to tell it to those in the larger markets.

CITY	CITY ZONE POPULATION	NEWSPAPER	ED.	CIRC.	SCHED.	RATE	
		NEWSPAPER SCHEDULE					
Cincinnati	1,043,900	Post Times Star	E	255,100	A	.62	
Cleveland	1,197,500	Plain Dealer	M	325,000	A	.95	1.57
Dayton	464,100	News Jrnl. Herald	M&E	252,800	B	.73	
Toledo	473,600	Blade & Times	M&E	212,300	B	.70	1.43
Akron	455,300	Beacon Journal	E	169,600	C	.50	
Canton	192,800	Repository	E	71,000	C	.27	
Youngstown	230,100	Vindicator	E	102,100	C	.32	1.09

WEEK OF	A SCHEDULE 1.57	A COST	B SCHEDULE 1.43	B COST	C SCHEDULE 1.09	C COST	
1st week	1000 li.		600		400		
2	1000		600		400		
3	1000		600		-		
4	-		-		400		
5	1000		600		400		
6	1000		600		-		
7	1000		600		400		
8	-		-		400		
9	1000		600		-		
10	1000		600		400		
11	1000		600		400		
12	-		-		-		
13	1000		600		400		
Total Lineage	10,000 lines @ 1.57 =		6,000 lines @ 1.43 =		3,600 lines @ 1.09 =		
GRAND TOTAL		$15,700.		$ 8,580.		$ 3,924.	$28,204.

AN A, B, C NEWSPAPER SCHEDULE

When a newspaper schedule is to be run in markets of different sizes, different schedules may be prepared to meet their different needs. Note differences in the population of the A, B, and C markets; also, the difference in the size of the advertisements and total investment in each market.

When a national advertisement has been run, the publisher will forward to the agency a copy of the page bearing the advertisement, torn out of the newspaper, and called a *tear sheet* or *checking copy* for magazines. To *check a tear sheet* is to examine the page and record on a form whether the advertisement ran per the instruction and standards of the agency, particularly in respect to position in paper, position on page, and reproduction. If it did not appear properly, the advertiser may be entitled to an adjustment, possibly to a correct re-run of the advertisement, called a *make-good,* without additional cost.

Most newspapers forward their tear sheets through a private central office—The Advertising Checking Bureau.

A RECORD OF THE PUBLISHED ADVERTISEMENT

After an advertisement is published, a copy of the actual page or issue containing the advertisement is sent to the advertiser. This is known as a "checking copy" or "tear sheet." A record is kept on a form like this.

Copyright 1920 American Association of Advertising Agencies	(Blank No. 4)

CHECKING RECORD

MONTH	1	2	3	4	5	6	7	8	9	10	11	12	13	14	15	16	17	18	19	20	21	22	23	24	25	26	27	28	29	30	31	TOTAL	

TO PUBLISHER OF

ORDER NO.

CITY AND STATE

DATE

PLEASE PUBLISH ADVERTISING OF (advertiser)

FOR (product)

SPACE — TIMES — DATES OF INSERTION

POSITION

COPY   KEY   CUTS

ADDITIONAL INSTRUCTIONS

RATE

LESS AGENCY COMMISSION   PER CENT ON GROSS | LESS CASH DISCOUNT   PER CENT ON NET

PER ----------------------------

MONTH	1	2	3	4	5	6	7	8	9	10	11	12	13	14	15	16	17	18	19	20	21	22	23	24	25	26	27	28	29	30	31	TOTAL	

To merchandise newspaper advertising is to enlist the store support of the retailers who sell the manufacturer's products advertised in the newspaper.[5] When the schedule is large enough, many newspapers will help the advertiser "merchandise" the advertising to his trade in that community.

Among the merchandising services most frequently rendered by newspapers are distribution of advance proofs of the newspaper advertising to retailers and trade mailings to retailers and wholesalers that call attention to the forthcoming advertising. Other services include conducting surveys to check such things as distribution, shelf position, rate of sale, dealer attitude; preparing portfolios for an advertiser's sales force; collecting market data; schedules, proofs, and route lists of retail outlets.

NEWSPAPER MARKETING DATA

Newspapers offer extensive market information about the communities they reach, including such data as:

1. *Basic statistics of the market.* This includes an economic description of the territory and demographic data on population, as to income and housing.
2. *Consumer sales and brand-purchase analysis.* Some newspapers conduct research showing the degree to which the product is used in that market and the ranking of the individual brands.
3. *Brand-distribution analysis.* Such reports show the extent to which the product is stocked in different stores, regardless of popularity or latest sales.

SELECTING THE PAPER

In about 190 cities, the advertiser has a choice of two papers. In eight cities, he has a choice of three or more. Which paper, or combination of papers, to select?

We regard each city as unique; each has its own newspaper personality. The morning paper may be best in one city, the evening paper in another. We view each city by itself.

We begin by establishing exactly whom we are trying to reach. If we are advertising, say, heating systems, is it chiefly men? housewives? homeowners? Exactly what is our market target? We then can compare each of the newspapers in terms of our target market.

---

[5] *Merchandising* is one of the many words in advertising used to express different ideas. See the Glossary.

BASIC MARKETING DATA—MILWAUKEE SMSA *

POPULATION—7/1/69

Population	1,468,400
Children, Under 5	129,200
Children, 5 Through 9	167,400
Children, 10 Through 19	308,400
Population (1960 Census)	1,278,850
(1) % Native White	88%
(2) % Foreign Born White	6%
(3) % Non-White	6%

Source: 1960 Census and The Milwaukee Journal Research Department

HOMES—7/1/69

Occupied Dwelling Units	435,100
Owner Occupied Homes (68%)	295,900
Renter Occupied Homes (32%)	139,200
Single and Two Family Dwelling Units	336,720
Multiple Units, Three Family or More	96,890
Households With Telephones	387,500
Households With Gas	338,500
Households With Electricity	432,900
Households With Television	430,700
Homes Heated With: Gas	291,500
Oil	121,800
Coal, Coke, Other	13,100

Source: The Milwaukee Journal Research Department, Consumer Analysis, Public Utilities and Metropolitan Builders' Association. 7/1/69

SALES, INCOME—1969

Disposable Personal Income ($000)	$4,890,720
Average Family Disposable Income	11,443
Retail Sales ($000)	2,832,996
Per Household Retail Sales	5,576
Food Store Sales ($000)	532,973
General Merchandise Stores ($000)	465,385
Apparel Stores ($000)	128,561
Furniture, Hsld. Appliances ($000)	124,361
Eating and Drinking Places ($000)	222,350
Drugstore Sales ($000)	73,488
Lumber, Building Material ($000)	85,620
Automotive Sales ($000)	430,952
Gasoline Station Sales ($000)	151,357

Source: Sales Management Survey of Buying Power, June, 1970

LABOR FORCE—12/31/69

Men in the Labor Force	410,400
Men Employed	398,900
Women in the Labor Force	230,800
Women Employed	221,500
Housewives Employed (40%)	174,000
Total Labor Force	641,200
Total Employed	620,400

Source: Wisconsin Employment Service, Milwaukee Journal Consumer Analysis, 1970

HOUSEHOLD PROFILE—1970
TOTAL HOUSEHOLDS: 435,100

INCOME:

Under $3,000	8%
$3,000-$4,999	8
$5,000-$7,999	18
$8,000-$9,999	22
$10,000-$14,999	31
$15,000-$24,999	10
$25,000 and Over	3

AGE (Male Head of House)

18-24	6%
25-34	20
35-49	34
50-64	28
65 and Over	10
No Man in Household	10

AGE (Female Head of House)

18-24	3%
25-34	18
35-49	33
50-64	26
65 and Over	10
No Woman in Household	2

OCCUPATION (Male Head of Household)

Prof. and Semi-Prof.	13%
Mgrs., Officials, Props.	12
Clerical	8
Sales	5
Craftsmen, Foremen	19
Operatives	17
Service Except Domestic	5
Laborers Except Farm	4
Retired	10
Other	7

EDUCATION (Head of Household)

Grade School or Less	18%
1-3 Yrs. High School	19
Graduated High School	33
1-3 Yrs. College	15
Graduated College	15

FAMILY SIZE

One Person	7%
Two Persons	28
Three Persons	18
Four Persons	19
Five or More Persons	28

Source: Milwaukee Journal Consumer Analysis, 1969-'70

MILWAUKEE JOURNAL/SENTINEL
MARKET PENETRATION and EFFICIENCY

		PENETRATION		
	Households	Jrnl./Sentl. (M&E)	Journal (S)	Jrnl./Sentl. (M&S)
Metro Area (4 Counties)	435,100	99%	79%	99%
Milw. "ADI" (9 Counties)	565,800	79%	69%	90%
ABC Retail Trade Zone (11 Counties)	620,900	72%	66%	86%

Source: ABC Audit Report, 3-31-70; NCA 1970-1971; S.M.S.B.P., June, 1970

COST EFFICIENCY Milline (5,000 Line Contr.)	$2.78	$2.45	$2.37
Rank Among Major Newspapers in 25 Largest ADIs (Lowest is 1)	6th	7th	4th

Source: NCA, 1970-1971; SRDS Newspaper Rates and Data, October, 1970; Journal/Sentinel Rates Eff. 1/1/71.

* The Standard Metropolitan Statistical Area as defined by the Bureau of the Census is Milwaukee, Waukesha, Ozaukee and Washington Counties.

SELLING A MARKET AS WELL AS A PAPER

One of the jobs newspapers have in selling their space to national advertisers is to convince them to advertise in the newspaper's market. Hence newspapers prepare market and demographic data such as this.

We have two sources of information to help us: the publisher's ABC report of circulation, and his supplementary report of the demographics of that circulation. The ABC report tells us the size of the circulation, where it is distributed, how that circulation was obtained. The demographic reports give an insight into the life styles of the readers—their home ownership, average income, ethnic background, education, and other glimpses of what their economic and social life is like.

COLOR ADVERTISING

ROP color advertising. This is run-of-paper advertising with one, two, or three extra colors printed at the same time on the same paper, and on the same presses as the rest of the paper. ROP color printing compounds all the problems that black-and-white newspaper printing has—high-speed printing on rough, porous paper, making fine reproduction and close registration of colors difficult. ROP color is used chiefly for making the ad distinctive with the aid of bold backgrounds, designs, borders, or headlines in color. It is not dependable for reproducing a product in colors or for conveying an impression of quality products. There is an extra charge for color, and papers usually have a minimum size requirement.

Preprint color pages. If, while turning the pages of your newspaper, you suddenly come upon a page with a beautiful full-page color advertisement, printed on paper slightly better than the rest of the newspaper, you are looking at a page that was preprinted by an outside color-printing plant, in gravure or by offset. (Some papers print their own.) The page was carefully printed in advance on one side of the sheet, and the other side was left blank and forwarded to the newspaper on big rolls, for its own printing of the obverse side. These are known as HiFi Color or SpectaColor pages (representing different production systems and effects). The advertiser pays for the cost of the color plates and printing, in addition to the newspaper space, at the black-and-white page rate. Because of the cost of the initial plates, preprints are usually planned for a large run to be used in many papers at about the same time. Arrangements must be made well in advance, with both the newspaper and the printing house.

NEWSPAPER-DISTRIBUTED MAGAZINE SUPPLEMENTS

How could we be sure it was a weekend if it weren't for the colorful magazine sections in our newspapers to remind us? These sections, known as *syndicated supplements,* form a unique medium unto themselves. They provide good local coverage, superior color reproduction, high and prompt family

The automatic media plan.

We're not going to tell you TV's no good—you know better and so do we—but we are saying there are too many automatic media plans being submitted these days.

The pattern is usually the same. Let's face it—your budget doesn't go very far on TV. It's a cinch you can't cover the country, so the spot TV plan probably calls for:

25 markets representing 2/3rds of your business. 50 gross rating points a week (about seven 30-second commercials) and your schedule runs for 26 weeks.

Sound familiar? Your competition probably outspends you 3 or 4 to 1—maybe higher. He's got the dollars to do the national job, plus enough left over to heavy up in key markets.

So, you wind up playing his game in his ball park where he has all the clout.

What can you do about it?

You could use network TV, but you run into the same problem.

Plus some others. If you go daytime, you get a shot at about 65% of the homes—at most. No matter how much you spend.

And on Prime Time—at $25,000 per 30-second spot—you can run out of money before you get started. And you still wind up hitting the heavy viewer—over and over.

So why don't you hit the competition where he isn't—or at least where he's weak. What you need to do is think "Prime Time" in print—Parade in particular. In Parade you can be a big frog in a big pond because Parade has all the guns.

IF I WERE A PRODUCT MANAGER FOR A PACKAGE GOODS BRAND SPENDING $1.5MM, HERE ARE SOME OF THE THINGS I'D THINK ABOUT BEFORE AUTOMATICALLY GOING TO TV.

The Fourth Major Network.

Nothing gets read like Parade...it's in 96 newspaper markets...gets into 17 million homes...has over 30 million readers...reaches 95% of them in the first week...has fantastic flexibility. The weeklies aren't even in the same league. We reach 65% or more of the homes in most of our markets. That makes us look more like a major TV network than a weekly.

And on our network you won't fight the clutter.

And you won't be outgunned.

We'd hate to tell our story in 55 words.

Enough of the numbers game. Think about this.

Maybe your product needs more than 30 seconds a few times a week. Any good writer will tell you that's about 50 to 55 words read fast.

30 seconds go by pretty quick and when they are gone, they are gone for good, only the clutter is left. But there is something permanent about an ad in Parade...it gets read.

Reading day.

The reader spends 60 seconds with each Parade page. Compare that with Reader's Digest, 38...Good Housekeeping, 29...Ladies' Home Journal, 37...McCall's, 39. It's pretty clear Parade is about the last place you can get or afford a "60-second spot."

It's because Parade arrives in 96 leading newspapers on "reading day"—Sunday, when reading the Sunday paper is as much a tradition as ham and eggs.

So, if I were a product manager with $1.5MM to spend in the package goods field, before I automatically went to TV, I'd think about running a schedule in Parade.

What do you think?

Think Parade.

readership. These supplements are printed in rotogravure or offset color either by the paper itself or at outside central printing plants, and distributed to newspapers with the newspaper's name on the masthead. These syndicated magazine sections are sold by their publishers in terms of groups of cities, to meet the advertiser's marketing pattern. Well known among these are *Family Week,* with about 270 newspapers and a national circulation of about 8 million, and *Parade,* with about 100 newspapers and a circulation of about 17 million. Metropolitan's *Sunday Newspaper Group,* or *Metro,* is totally edited with a choice of several combinations of papers in different markets; circulation is around 28 million. Some newspapers, such as *The New York Times, Philadelphia Inquirer, Chicago Tribune,* and *Los Angeles Times,* have their own local magazine supplements. Other newspapers give their readers both a syndicated magazine supplement and their own. Magazine supplements are frequently used for special drives featuring premiums and for other promotional offers.

COMICS

The Sunday comic supplement appearing as a part of most weekend newspapers is an important family institution, with a total audience estimated at 111 million readers. What may be surprising is that adults of 18 and over comprise 72.4 percent of the total audience; teenagers between 13 and 17, 11.1 percent; and children from 7 to 12, the other 16.5 percent.[6]

Space in comics can be bought through newspaper-comic groups, each representing a single weekly comic syndicated to different newspapers. Space may be bought in papers on a national or sectional basis, such as in *Puck,* with a total circulation of 15 million, and in *Metro Sunday Comics,* with a total national circulation of 23 million. An advertiser can also buy space in other syndicated comic sections, which may be purchased individually by markets. Space in the comic publications is usually sold in terms of a page or fraction of a page. Some papers now print their comics in rotogravure.

SPLIT RUNS

For advertisers who would like to test different ads for the same product, Sunday magazine supplements offer a *split run.* By this method, an advertiser prepares plates of two or more ads of the same size to be run on the same day, each representing a different appeal, each with a coupon with its key number, calling for a reply. The plate for one ad is included on the pages printed on Press A; the plate for the second ad is included on the pages printed on adjacent Press B. Both presses feed alternately into a common stacking of

---

[6] Bureau of Advertising.

newspapers—that is, newspapers that are distributed in the same neighborhood to the same type of readers. The only difference is that of the ads. The advertiser can then tell from the coupon responses which of the two ads pulled better. (We go into this matter further in the discussion of advertising testing, later in the book.)

Preprinted (Loose) Inserts

A practice that has zoomed into one of a newspaper's important sources of income is the loose, separate preprinted insert, ranging from a single eight-by-ten-inch sheet to a section of tabloid-size pages running to 32 pages, or even more. It is printed in advance of the time the newspaper is printed, by an outside printer, and delivered to the newspaper to insert loosely in the regular printed editions.

The advertiser must supply the printed inserts, bearing on the first page "Supplement to [name of paper]" for second-class postal reasons. At first, papers accepted reprints for Sundays only; now some are accepting them four days a week. In some cities, an advertiser can buy circulation in specific sections of his city, at a fixed cost per thousand.

The preprint is designed for quick response. It is being used widely by retail stores, by national advertisers in promotions with coupon redemption offers, and very largely by direct response advertisers as a reaction to increasing postal rates for direct mail. Some now have a reply card tip-in which is mechanically affixed to the advertising page.

Weekly Newspapers

America was a country of weekly newspapers before it became a daily-newspaper land, and to this day there are about 8,000 weekly newspapers with a combined circulation of about 29 million. About two thirds of the papers are urban-oriented, published in communities in the metropolitan areas, or in the suburbs and in the satellites of the suburbs; one third are in farm communities. Seventy-eight percent of the urban circulation is among homeowners, 86 percent of whom live in single-family homes. Fifty-four percent have children under 18. Their median income is almost 20 percent higher than the national average.[7]

Weekly newspapers have high readership because of their local news (if a publication has less than 25 percent news it is deemed a shopping newspaper), because they carry much local advertising, and because they are around for a whole week. National advertisers often use suburban papers to round out a promotion or campaign they are running in the dailies of a city.

---

[7] *Starch 1969 Annual Media Study of Primary Audiences.*

They are usually offered as part of a group of papers within the same geographical market. The Suburban Press of Chicago, for example, offers a flat rate for a group of 82 separate suburban papers, combined circulation 541,000. The Pickwick Publishing Company of Chicago offers its suburban papers in terms of separate groups averaging six papers each. Milline rates are higher.

Many papers are circulated on a free basis, to reach as many people in an area as possible; other papers are on a paid basis. Some papers have both kinds of circulation. The Los Angeles Suburban group, for example, with about 1.2 million circulation, has about one fourth paid subscribers, three fourths unpaid.

National advertisers usually buy weekly newspapers through special weekly newspaper representatives, representing large lists of papers. An advertiser picks his territory or territories, places one order, gets one bill, and pays one check—a great facility for handling a medium that reaches into the homes of so many different communities.

Trends in Newspapers

In 1960, total newspaper-advertising expenditures were $3,703 million; in 1970, they were $5,745 million, for a total gain of 55 percent. During this time, national newspaper advertising had a gain of 21 percent; local newspaper advertising had a gain of 65 percent.[8]

During this period also, the number of newspapers dropped, but their total circulation increased. There was a drop-off of papers in the metropolitan areas, but there was a great proliferation of papers in the suburbs and in the satellite communities.

Two conspicuous advances were made in the use of newspapers: First was the increased use of HiFi and SpectaColor advertising. The second big development has been the growth in the loose preprinted insert, for quick-response advertising, representing everything from a two-page circular to a full-page-size insert averaging 32 pages. There has been no evidence to suggest that these trends won't continue.

---

[8] See p. 121.

Why SAS Went 95% Newspaper

A case report on the use of newspapers

YOU HAVE $1.5 MILLION to spend on advertising media. Your direct competitor has over $30 million. Numerous other competitors (national and regional) join the fray in all-out battle. How do you compete?

This was the challenge that confronted Scandinavian Airlines advertising manager William H. Bender when he arrived last year in the Queens, N.Y., headquarters of the North American Division of SAS. . . .

His decisions: Stay out of TV (on the ground that there wasn't enough money to match the competition in that medium). Concentrate instead in broad-appeal media where he could look important.

Bender's reasoning: "In order to get impact, you have to concentrate your advertising messages.

"If you have a large budget . . . you can concentrate on vertical audiences and buy the media that appeal to them while you do the broad-base job.

"But if you have a small budget, you can't segment the approach because the total portions of the population you can afford to reach are too tiny. Therefore, you have to choose major media in which you *can* appear with a size and frequency sufficient to make you important."

As far as Bender was concerned, this meant newspapers and radio: "Where SAS can buy equal or greater weight locally, compared with other carriers"—and concentrated in peak selling periods. . . .

The choice of newspapers as base medium for SAS was also related to needs exposed by some hard-nosed market research. . . .

1. The bulk of the travel was coming from essentially the same people. They tended to be over 35, college educated, over $20,000 in income, in the professions or business management, and had been to Europe more than once, usually because of a Scandinavian background or related business interests.

2. Very few people seemed to know what SAS stood for.

3. On the other hand, attitudes toward Scandinavia were highly favorable. Americans seemed to like the people of the region, ranking them high in reliability, cleanliness, humor, appearance. . . .

The job ahead, then, was to expand the passenger base while retaining

---

Excerpted from *Media Decisions,* August 1971. Courtesy *Media Decisions.*

the hard-core repeat group; to go after younger people in their late twenties and early thirties, special interest groups, and especially that broad mass of American tourists who are visiting Europe for the first time.

This called for putting Scandinavia into head-on competition as a first-trip destination with the traditional tour magnets of Paris, London, Rome. A tough job because, according to an SAS spokesman, "these great capitals are part of the educational tradition of the United States, while Scandinavia remains on the periphery, despite the heavy concentration of Scandinavia stock in the midwest." He notes that there is not one full-time American news correspondent in any of the three countries—Sweden, Norway, Denmark.

Bender's second objective became: To build a public awareness of SAS, so that the letters would be immediately recognized. This meant the campaign had to have "eye appeal."

Previous advertising had been designed to appeal to the middle-income, middle-aged, repeat traveler through upper-level magazines. It had been effective for that purpose. But Bender felt it was time to put SAS into a broad-appeal medium. He sought an audience profile that would coincide with that of the broad base he was going to attempt to attract.

"The profile of the newspaper was right," he says. "The newspaper hits the whole age group. The chances are that if a person doesn't read a newspaper, he isn't a prospect for us anyway."

About 75% of Bender's first SAS budget thus went to newspapers. The remaining 25% was reserved for "opportunity buys," largely in radio.

Bender is prepared to move should an appealing TV special come along at the right price. He's interested in the possibility of obtaining "a strong, though partial, sponsorship which would allow solid merchandising down to the travel agency level." . . .

Bender admits that in magazines he could also achieve a position of equality or near-equality with the airline giants in specific publications. But newspapers and radio give him a combination of spot and operational flexibility.

"In the airline business," he points out, "you are really doing a combined national and regional advertising job." There are several SAS campaigns going at the same time, all subject to change on short notice. The national copy tells the general SAS story, while specific marketing area route and schedule promotions are geared to local sales needs.

"The North American Division is responsible for the advertising of seven great areas covering the Western Hemisphere. Each has its gateway city from which the SAS planes take off and return. And each has somewhat different advertising needs.

For example, in the East, primary emphasis is on the only daily non-stop service to both Bergen and Copenhagen, and daily direct service to Stockholm. . . .

In Chicago there is a large ethnic market to draw from. Minneapolis draws on the Scandinavian ethnic groups which feed into the Chicago gateway, and Chicago itself promotes the large Polish market. Primary destinations for promotion here are Scandinavia, Eastern Europe and the Middle East. . . .

The West Coast promotion points elsewhere. Primary emphasis is on the "shortest route," the Polar route. SAS promotes travel from Los Angeles to London, Paris, Amsterdam, and the Mediterranean via Copenhagen. There are daily flights from that city and Seattle. . . .

The basic newspaper ad size is two thirds of a page, running a little better than one per week in the gateway cities—New York, Montreal, Chicago, Seattle, Boston, New Orleans, Los Angeles—and with varying frequency in the "feeder" cities. The size permits Bender to dominate the page, he feels, and to benefit from adjacency to editorial matter. It also enables him to get a better frequency than he could with the higher-cost full page. . . .

Bender visits with each area manager, who is a member of the company's Management Council and is totally responsible for SAS operations in his area, and is informed of the manager's sales goals and plans and of the routes he wants to stress. From the input of the seven managers, Bender fashions the specifics of the media plan.

Through this system, Bender believes SAS is achieving the flexibility it needs for what is essentially a local and regional operation. Newspaper themes are varied to match local interests. And this summer a special campaign in radio was added to tap a special marketing opportunity: young people with a yen to visit Copenhagen.

Copenhagen is the current mecca for young travelers. And radio "is the most effective line of communications to today's 20-to-25 set," says SAS director of marketing services Raoul Vincent. "Naturally, we are especially interested this year in getting the attention of the 20- through 25-year-old, single, business and professional people of both sexes. They qualify for SAS youth fares."

Review Questions

1. What are the major advantages of newspapers? Limitations?

2. Give a brief definition, explanation or description of:
   a. display advertising
   b. classified advertising
   c. ROP
   d. tear sheet
   e. page make-up
   f. split run

3. How do local rates compare with national rates? What reasons are given for the difference?

4. What is the difference between volume discount and frequency discount?

5. What is the difference between a preprint color page and a syndicated color magazine supplement? Who is responsible for the printing of each?

6. What is the difference between a milline rate and a short rate? How is each computed?

7. What is the Audit Bureau of Circulations?

8. What are the important things in an ABC report for an advertiser to look for?

9. What does the newspaper *Merchandising Service* do?

10. What considerations enter the choice of one newspaper in a two- or three-newspaper city?

11. In the report of the SAS Airline experience, why were newspapers particularly appropriate?

Reading Suggestions

Advertising Age, "Newspapers: 1970," a special section, April 20, 1970, p. 43.

Advertising Research Foundation, *A Study of the Opportunity for Exposure to National Newspaper Advertising.* New York: Audits & Surveys Co., 1964.

Barton, Roger, *The Handbook of Advertising Management.* New York: McGraw-Hill, 1970.

Bureau of Advertising, *What Can One Newspaper Ad Do?* New York: Bureau of Advertising, 1969.

Ferguson, James, *The Advertising Rate Structure in the Daily Newspaper Industry.* Englewood Cliffs, N.J.: Prentice-Hall, Inc., 1963.

McClure, Leslie, and Paul C. Fulton, *Advertising in the Printed Media.* New York: Macmillan Company, 1964.

Petrof, John V., "Newspaper Advertising and the Negro Market," *Journal of Retailing,* Spring 1970, pp. 20–31.

Stewart, John B., *Repetitive Advertising in Newspapers.* Boston: Harvard University Graduate School of Business Administration, 1964.

10

Using Magazines

MAGAZINES FIRST MADE NATIONAL advertising possible in the 1870's, and in all the years since, have continued to be a major medium. But changed life styles, the impact of television, the computer, and target marketing have completely changed the role of magazines as a marketing tool. However, that's getting a bit ahead of our story.

FEATURES AND ADVANTAGES

Magazines are a selective medium. Most magazines are written for specific people who have certain tastes and interests in common, and who will provide an identifiable market for the advertiser. Just to name a few publications will immediately bring to mind the different type of person for whom each is published: *Playboy, Atlantic Monthly, Good Housekeeping, Seventeen, Popular Mechanics, Sports Illustrated, Field and Stream, Fortune, Ebony. Reader's Digest* is an example of a mass general magazine—edited, however, within a recognizable editorial framework. Every editor has a pile of proposed manuscripts that he reads with one question uppermost: "Is this for *our* readers?"

Magazines are designed to be read in a leisurely manner. The advertiser has a chance to tell an informative selling story of his product. Since weekly magazines are around the house for at least a week, and monthly magazines for at least a month, the advertisement has a good chance of being read and reread.

Magazines are outstanding for controlled color and black-and-white reproduction. Some of our most beautiful contemporary color and graphic work appears in the magazines, with their fine plate and press work. To the advertiser to whom color is important in depicting his product, and to all advertisers who want to enhance their advertising with exquisite color work, this is significant. The color reproduction in magazines is among the finest available in any medium.

Geographical and demographic editions. Most large-circulation magazines are available in *geographic/demographic editions* to meet the advertiser's target marketing goals. This represents a departure from the former monolithic national circulation concept, which for a long time had characterized nationally circulated magazines. *Time* offers 136 city and state editions (aside from its international editions). *National Geographic* has ten

TIME DEMOGRAPHIC EDITIONS

Covering 185 countries in 113 U.S. Metropolitan editions.

sectional editions. The *Ladies' Home Journal* offers its magazine in 60 separate markets—a local magazine in each. These are referred to as *geographical editions*—virtually regional or local magazines. They permit market-by-market programming, local testing, and listing of local dealers in the respective editions.

Time has separate *demographic editions* for doctors, educators, and college students. Some magazines select subscribers living in the affluent parts of the communities, as identified by their zip codes, and offer that as a *demographic buy. House & Garden* has a "Home Movers" edition, representing subscribers who have moved in the past month (culled from its own notices of address changes).

Many magazines offer split-run editions whereby an advertiser can test different ads in the same issue in the same size space, in different press runs of the same edition.

LIMITATIONS AND CHALLENGES

But magazines, like other media, have their limitations. Even large-circulation magazines do not reach many people whom the advertiser may want to reach. Magazines prove costly per thousand in reaching broad masses of people where selectivity is not of the essence. Magazines have early closing dates—sometimes two months for color plates in a monthly (although weekly magazines often have a fast closing date). But of course, not every advertiser has to have his advertisement appear immediately.

Special editions have limitations, too. The number of pages per issue available for special editions is limited; plans must be made well ahead. The forms close before the regular ones do. The cost per thousand is higher than for the full run in the main book. Some publishers have regional editorial matter to go with the regional editions; many do not. The result is that all the regional advertising for that edition is bunched together in the book, with ad facing ad, placement that does not help the readership of the advertisements.

MAGAZINE ELEMENTS

Magazine sizes. The *page size* of a magazine is the type area, not the size of the actual page. Advertisements that cover the entire page area out to its very edge, with no margin, are called *bleed pages* (opposite). An advertisement can also bleed on three sides only. These are used by advertisers to gain extra attention and impressiveness. Bleed pages usually cost more than non-bleed pages. For convenience, the sizes of magazines are characterized as

What makes Brown Jordan furniture expensive is what makes it Brown Jordan.

What makes Brown Jordan? Exquisite designs like Classic II. Durable elegance that springs from a no-compromise attitude toward construction. Our hand-cast aluminum is hand-welded for smoothly invisible joints. Table tops are individually cut and fitted. Even the prime coat is hand-rubbed. That's what makes it Brown Jordan—and inexpensive at the price. Don't settle for anything less.

BROWN JORDAN
A SUBSIDIARY OF SCOTT PAPER COMPANY

You'll find Brown Jordan at leading stores and interior designers. For color brochure and nearest dealer, write Brown Jordan, El Monte, Cal. 91734. Plant also in Newport, Ark.

BLEED ON THREE SIDES

A bleed advertisement is one where the background runs right off the edges. A full bleed advertisement runs off all four sides. This advertisement is bled on only three sides, allowing margin at the bottom where this type is set. An advertisement can also be bled on two sides.

large size (about 9" × 12", like *Better Homes & Gardens*), *standard size*
(about 8" × 10", like *Time*), and *small size* (about 4⅜" × 6½", like *Reader's
Digest*). When it comes to ordering plates, it is necessary to get the exact
sizes from the publisher's rate card.

Space designations. The front cover of a magazine is called *first
cover page*. This is seldom, if at all, sold in American consumer magazines.
The inside of the front cover is called the *second cover* page; the inside of the
back cover is the *third cover* page; the back cover is the *fourth cover* page.
Cover pages are highly desirable positions for national advertising. There is a
premium for back cover position.

Space in magazines is usually sold in terms of full pages and fractions
thereof, as half page, three columns, two columns, or one column. There is
also a line rate for smaller units.

A half page in a magazine may be vertical or horizontal. Some magazines do not accept horizontal half-page advertisements or, when they do, may
make an extra charge. This difference in shape is important in planning and
designing half-page magazine advertisements. Large-size magazines also offer
space to be used in various ways, as indicated on the accompanying diagram.

Junior units. Some ingenious publisher of a large-size magazine
discovered he could get more business if he accepted the plates already appearing in a standard-size magazine (saving plate costs). However, it was
an odd unit of space for which to set a price. It wasn't a half page, and it
wasn't two thirds of a page; actually it was about 61 percent of a page. But
someone with a fine sense of semantics and merchandising came to the rescue.
"Let's call this a *Junior unit*," he said, and a special flat rate was set for that
unit of space; and that's how a full page of a smaller-size magazine when
placed on a full page in a larger-size magazine is known today.

The Junior unit is usually placed on a page with no other advertising;
therefore, it is an economical way of dominating a page. Some advertisers still
prefer to run full pages in the belief that the additional prestige is worthwhile.
Not all magazines sell Junior units. To give an idea of comparative costs, the
rates for the *Ladies' Home Journal* are as follows:

1 page, 4 color	$37,000
Junior size	27,000
½ page	19,000

Gatefolds. Perhaps you have turned to a page in a magazine only to
discover that it is an extended page, folded over to fit into the magazine. This
folded-over area may range from a fraction of a page to two or more pages,
and is called a *gatefold*. You can also have a gatefold *cover*. Gatefolds provide
advertisers with the most elaborate use of magazine space, useful in making a

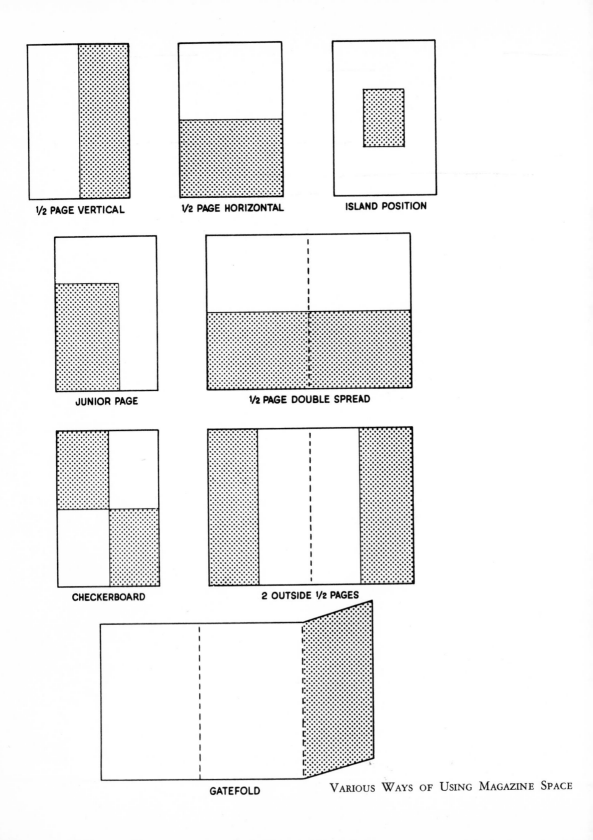

½ PAGE VERTICAL

½ PAGE HORIZONTAL

ISLAND POSITION

JUNIOR PAGE

½ PAGE DOUBLE SPREAD

CHECKERBOARD

2 OUTSIDE ½ PAGES

GATEFOLD

Various Ways of Using Magazine Space

spectacular announcement. Not all magazines offer gatefolds; when available, they are sold on a premium basis.

Cards and detachable inserts.   You may have come across a mailing card or a coupon, bound between the pages of a magazine, that is good for a sample, or perhaps you have found a whole booklet of helpful hints or recipes that you could readily tear out. These devices are effective in getting direct responses, also in distributing booklets or samples at low unit cost. One magazine carried a thin plastic phonograph record. Now there is a "microfragrance" coated overlay, which can be scratched to give forth the fragrance of the product. The use of inserts in connection with page advertising must be planned well in advance.

Magazine dates.   There are three sets of dates of which to be aware in magazine scheduling: the *cover date,* the date appearing on the cover; the *on-sale date,* on which a magazine is issued (the January issue of Esquire is on sale December 3, important to know in scheduling); and the *closing date,* on which all material must be in the hands of the publisher to be included in a given issue. All dates are expressed in relation to the cover date.

How Space Is Sold

Magazine rate structure.   Each publisher issues a rate card quoting the costs of advertising space in his magazine. The rate card of one weekly reads like this:

Black/White	
1 page (3 columns)	$3,700.00
Double column (⅔ page)	2,700.00
Single column	1,350.00
½ column	675.00
Agate line	9.25

The listing above is the one-time rate. The card continues to give the rate for 13, 26, 39, and 52 insertions. (The units for giving discounts in weeklies is 13). The card gives comparable rates for color.

Whereas in newspapers, rates are compared in terms of millines, in magazines they are compared in terms of *cost per page per thousand circulation.*

Ordering magazine space.   The purchase of space in a magazine usually entails two steps: a space contract and an insertion order. A space contract is an agreement on the rates to be paid for *whatever space is used* in the coming year. As with newspapers, it is an agreement on the rate schedule; it

Playboy

Media Code 8 468 0900 2.00
Published monthly by Playboy Enterprises, Inc.,
919 N. Michigan Ave., Chicago, Ill. 60611. Phone
312-642-1000.
Advertising Office— 405 Park Ave., New York, N. Y.
10022. Phone 212-688-3030.
For shipping info., see **Print Media Production Data.**

PUBLISHER'S EDITORIAL PROFILE
PLAYBOY is a magazine of entertainment—offering
fiction, serious and satirical articles, cartoon, and
picture stories of pretty girls; including service features such as: monthly articles on male fashion,
food and drink, gifts and other merchandise, travel,
and, less regularly, apartment and office furnishings,
automobiles, sports, and other leisure and avoca-
tional interests. The editors review books, records,
movies, legitimate plays, restaurants, night life.
Approximately one third of the editorial pages is
purchased nonfiction, including one interview or panel
discussion in every issue. Fiction comprises one sixth,
picture stories another sixth, and service and regular
departments the remaining third.

1. PERSONNEL
Ed. & Pub.—Hugh M. Hefner.
Advertising Director—Howard W. Lederer. (N.Y.).
Assoc. Advertising Manager—Jules Kase. (N.Y.).
Assoc. Advertising Manager—Joseph B. Guenther,
Jr. (N.Y.)
Production Manager—John Mastro. (Chicago).

2. REPRESENTATIVES and/or BRANCH OFFICES
New York 10022—Jules Kase, 405 Park Ave. Phone
212-688-3030.
Chicago 60611—Sherman Keats, 919 N. Michigan
Ave. Phone 312-642-1000.
Detroit 48202—William F. Moore, 818 Fisher Bldg.
Phone 313-875-7250.
Atlanta—Pirnie & Brown.
Los Angeles, San Francisco—Perkins, Stephens, Von
Der Lieth and Hayward.
London—Joshua Powers Ltd.

3. COMMISSION and CASH DISCOUNT
15% to agencies; 2% 10 days from invoice date.
Net 30 days. Bills rendered on the 1st of month
preceding date of issue.

4. GENERAL RATE POLICY
Orders beyond 3 months at rates then prevailing.
No conditions, oral or printed on the contract, order,
or copy instructions, or elsewhere, other than those
set forth in, or incorporated by reference into, publisher's rate card, will be binding on the publisher.

ADVERTISING RATES
Rates effective October, 1971 issue.
Rates received April 12, 1971.

5. BLACK/WHITE RATES

STANDARD UNITS
1 page................ 27,500.	1/3 page................	9,985.
2/3 page............. 19,665.	1/6 page................	5,080.
1/2 page............. 15,265.	1 inch................	1,045.

HALF CIRCULATION
Half-Circulation Run for ads appearing in every 2nd
copy throughout national print run, for any given
issue. Orders for half circulation runs non-cancellable
after 90 days prior to closing date. One page Half-
circulation counts as 1/2 page for Bulk and Renewal
discount.

Rates:	b/w	2 color	4 color
1 page................	15,815.	19,765.	22,400.

Circulation: Effective October, 1971 issue, rates based
on circulation of 2,625,000.

SPACE DISCOUNTS
Discounts apply to aggregate space used within 1
year from date of 1st insertion.

	Discount		Discount
6 pages...............	5%	18 pages...............	15%
12 pages.............	10%		

4th covers and special units not subject to discount,
but may be counted within a schedule to earn discount on other space.
Spreads— Entitled to either 10% discount from the 1
time rate, or to earned space discount, whichever is
larger. Not applicable to spreads off inside covers.
Spreads count as two pages when computing discounts.

RENEWAL DISCOUNTS
Available to advertisers whose aggregate corporate
space in any calendar year equals or exceeds space
run in previous calendar year. Minimum 2 pages
or equivalent in previous calendar year.

1st renewal year..................	2%
2nd renewal year.................	3%
3rd renewal year.................	4%
4th renewal year.................	5%
Additional renewal years	5%

Renewal years must be consecutive. Renewal discounts
apply after deduction of Space discounts. Back covers
and special units not subject to Renewal discounts
but count toward earning Renewal discounts on other
space.

5a GEOGRAPHIC and/or DEMOGRAPHIC EDITIONS

EASTERN EDITION
States: Maine, New Hampshire, Vermont, Massa-
chusetts, Rhode Island, Connecticut, New York, New
Jersey, Pennsylvania, Delaware, Maryland, District
of Columbia, Virginia and West Virginia.

Rates:	b/w	2 color	4 color

1 page................	10,850.	13,560.	16,275.

Circulation: A.B.C. 6-30-71—1,526,044.

CENTRAL EDITION
States: Ohio, Indiana, Illinois, Michigan, Wisconsin,
Kentucky, Minnesota, Iowa, Missouri, North Dakota,
South Dakota, Nebraska, Kansas.

Rates:	b/w	2 color	4 color
1 page................	8,815.	11,025.	13,225.

Circulation: A.B.C. 6-30-71—1,328,407.

WESTERN EDITION
States: Washington, Oregon, California, Montana,
Idaho, Wyoming, Colorado, New Mexico, Arizona,
Utah, Nevada, Alaska, Hawaii.

Rates:	b/w	2 color	4 color
1 page................	8,280.	10,350.	12,420.

Circulation: A.B.C. 6-30-71—1,192,250.

SOUTHEAST EDITION
States: North Carolina, South Carolina, Georgia,
Folrida, Tennessee, Alabama, Mississippi.

Rates:	b/w	2 color	4 color
1 page................	3,725.	4,655.	5,590.

Circulation: A.B.C. 6-30-71—543,361.

SOUTHWEST EDITION
States: Arkansas, Louisiana, Texas, Oklahoma.

Rates:	b/w	2 color	4 color
1 page................	2,900.	3,625.	4,350.

Circulation: A.B.C. 6-30-71—410,204.

DISCOUNTS
Advertisers who run in 3 or more Regional Editions
of the same issue are entitled to a 5% discount on
such advertising in addition to regular space, spread
and renewal discounts.

• • •

6. COLOR RATES

	2 color	4 color
1 page................	34,375.	38,950.
2/3 page.............	25,135.	28,735.
1/2 page.............	19,600.	22,795.
1/3 page.............	13,110.	....

7. COVERS

4th cover (4 color)................	48,685.

9. BLEED

Extra	10%

No charge for gutter bleed on spreads.

10. SPECIAL POSITION
Orders specifying positions on request basis only,
however, specified position not guaranteed unless approved by Advertising Director in letter separate
from acknowledgment.

11. CLASSIFIED and READING NOTICES
DISPLAY CLASSIFICATIONS
Mail Order—regular rates apply. Details available.
National and Regional Edition advertisers whose retail over-the-counter sales exceed 50% of their gross
business receive a 20% discount in lieu of all other
discounts.

14. CONTRACT AND COPY REGULATIONS
See Contents page for location—items 1, 2, 4, 7, 8,
10, 11, 12, 14, 19, 20, 21, 24, 25, 27, 30, 34, 35, 36,
37, 39.

15. MECHANICAL REQUIREMENTS
For complete, detailed production information, see
SRDS Print Media Production Data.
Trim size: 8-3/8 x 11-1/8; No./Cols. 3.
Binding method: Saddle Stitched.
Colors available: Matched; 4-Color Process (AAAA/
MPA); Simulated Metallic.
Cover colors available: 4-Color Process (AAAA/
MPA).

DIMENSIONS—AD PAGE
1	7-1/16 x 10	1/2	7-1/16 x 4-15/16
2 col.	4-11/16 x 10	1 col.	2-1/4 x 10

16. ISSUE AND CLOSING DATES
Published monthly.

		Closing	
		B/W	4-color &
Issue:	On sale	2 color	regional
Oct/71	9/14	7/20	7/10
Nov/71	10/12	8/20	8/10
Dec/71	11/11	9/20	9/10
Jan/72	12/10	10/20	10/10
Feb/72	1/12	11/20	11/10
Mar/72	2/11	12/20	12/10
Apr/72	3/16	1/20	1/10
May/72	4/13	2/20	2/10
June/72	5/13	3/20	3/10
July/72	6/15	4/20	4/10
Aug/72	7/13	5/20	5/10
Sept/72	8/12	6/20	6/10

Cancellations or changes in orders not accepted after
closing date and none may be considered executed
unless acknowledged by publisher. Orders for back
covers, special units and half circulation runs non-
cancellable after 90 days prior to color closing date.

17. SPECIAL SERVICES
A.B.C. Supplemental Data Report received 11/25/70.

18. CIRCULATION
Established 1953. Single copy 1.00 (except December
and January 1.50); per year 10.00.
Summary data—for detail see Publisher's Statement.
CPM—B/W 4.63.
A.B.C. 6-30-71 (6 mos. aver.—Magazine Form)

Total	Non-Pd	Paid (Subs)	(Single)	[Assoc]
5,939,968	31,785	5,908,183 1,402,089	4,506,094	....

TERRITORIAL DISTRIBUTION 2/71—5,977,278
N.Eng.	Mid.Atl.	E.N.Cen.	W.N.Cen.	S.Atl.	E.S.Cen.
319,577	944,485	959,748	347,741	730,633	171,071
W.S.Cen.	Mtn.St.	Pac.St.	Canada	Foreign	Other
396,317	256,468	971,986	351,806	327,501	199,945

Publisher states: Effective October, 1971 issue,
"Rates based on circulation of 5,250,000."

(S-C)

Extract of a page of magazine rates from Standard Rate & Data Service. Here all rate cards are published in full, giving information in standardized numerical sequence for each medium.

Courtesy, S.R.D.S.

is not a commitment for any given amount of space unless it is specifically noncancellable. It serves also to protect the advertiser against rate increases during the year.

Whenever the advertiser is ready to order space, he sends an *insertion order* for the space he wants. A space contract is often combined with the first insertion order.

A publisher might give a *frequency* discount, to reward those who advertise more often during a twelve-month period; thus:

13 times	5%
26 times	10%
39 times	12%
52 times	16%

As an alternate to a frequency discount based on the number of times space is used, a publisher may allow a discount based on the total amount of business placed in a year, called a *bulk discount,* as follows:

13 pages or more	7%
26 pages or more	12%
39 pages or more	16%
52 pages or more	20%

The foregoing discounts, *frequency* and *bulk,* are the most common.

Publishers are continually devising special discounts to entice the large advertisers. The discounts are called by terms such as *corporate discount, renewal reinvestment discount, brand discount,* and so on. There is no need to memorize these terms; they are not standardized. Just remember that such discounts exist. Would you like a nice 36 percent discount in one of our magazines? Just spend $1,527,750!

All magazine rates are based upon the guarantee that a certain number of copies will be distributed, a number known as the *circulation rate base.* Most large magazines supply circulation statements verified by the Audit Bureau of Circulation (the ABC reports). These statements also supply much data about the distribution of the circulation, and most important, how that circulation was obtained—e.g., at regular or special subscription prices.

The magazine short rate.   As we have mentioned, a space contract is an agreement on the scale of rates to be charged for *such space as is used,* unless it is a noncancellable contract (possibly for a special position). An advertiser's rate is finally computed at the end of the year, based upon what he actually ran, regardless of the rate, based on his original estimate, at which he was billed during the year. For example, let us assume that the following are the rates for a black-and-white page in a monthly magazine:

1-time rate	$1,000
6-time rate	950
12-time rate	850

The advertiser starts off believing he will run twelve times during the year, entitling him to the $850 rate, and enters upon a space contract accordingly. Every time the advertisement runs, he is billed $850. However, he decides to skip the last two insertions that he had previously planned, and runs only ten times. Therefore, he did not earn the 12-time rate. The rate he earned was the next best rate, or the 6-time rate of $950 (there is no 10-time rate). The arithmetic, therefore, is as follows:

$$
\begin{aligned}
\text{Should have paid} \quad & 10 \times \$950 = \$9,500 \\
\text{Paid} \quad & 10 \times \$850 = \underline{8,500} \\
& \text{Short rate} \quad \$1,000
\end{aligned}
$$

If an advertiser earns a better rate than the one to which he originally agreed, per the space contract he signed, he gets a cash rebate. Failure to keep short rates in mind when there is a reduction in an original schedule can lead to unwelcome surprises.

MAGAZINE CIRCULATION

Primary and pass-along circulation. *Total* circulation is the actual number of copies sold by a publication, as revealed by its Audit Bureau of Circulation statement or other verified reports. *Primary* circulation represents the number of households who paid for the magazine, on newsstand or by subscription. *Pass-along circulation* is aptly termed to represent the readership of a magazine by people who had asked, "When you're through with that magazine, could I have it?" Such circulation may be quite extensive. Pass-along circulation also includes magazines read in the waiting rooms of physicians and dentists, and in beauty shops and barber shops.

The difference in desirability between primary readership and total readership (which includes pass-along readership) may vary with the product. For a hair-coloring advertisement, the fact that a woman sees it in a beauty shop rather than at home may be an advantage; hence *total* readership may be a useful criterion. Similarly, *total* readership might be meaningful for selling any everyday household item of modest cost—canned foods, toothpaste. For high-priced household appliances—a refrigerator or washing machine—the advertiser might be interested in primary readership only.

MPA *Magazine Publishers Association, inc.*

Magazine Center / 575 Lexington Avenue, New York, N.Y. 10022 / 212 752-0055

CIRCULATIONS OF ALL A.B.C. MAGAZINES
GENERAL AND FARM (EXCLUDING COMICS)

First Six Months Averages

Year	No. of Magazines or Groups	Combined Circulation Per Issue			U.S. Adult Population (Add 000)	Circulation per 100 Adults
		Single Copy	Subscription	Total		
1945	214			116,444,141	97,903	118.9
1946	225	66,371,816	60,903,481	127,275,297	104,966	121.3
1947	235	62,761,163	69,126,824	131,887,987	106,783	123.5
1948	238	63,711,508	77,374,676	141,068,184	108,085	130.5
1949	242	61,406,473	81,119,610	142,526,083	109,288	130.4
1950	249	63,610,284	83,069,191	146,679,475	110,471	132.8
1951	251	62,879,392	87,758,612	150,638,004	111,111	135.6
1952	250	69,617,481	89,224,072	158,841,553	111,889	142.0
1953	251	70,152,155	93,336,015	163,488,170	112,870	144.8
1954	259	64,173,653	98,766,250	162,939,903	114,112	142.8
1955	260	66,466,568	99,820,290	166,286,858	115,505	144.0
1956	275	71,280,594	111,664,048	182,944,642*	116,743	156.7
1957	281	71,673,064	109,292,364	180,965,428	118,208	153.1
1958	278	62,980,836	118,016,642	180,997,478	119,854	151.0
1959	269	61,962,679	120,347,382	182,310,061	121,438	150.1
1960	269	61,043,613	126,870,013	187,913,626	123,890	151.7
1961	270	58,875,504	133,349,584	192,225,088	125,304	153.4
1962	269	58,840,661	137,954,198	196,794,859	127,692	154.1
1963	275	60,978,115	141,793,745	202,771,860	129,797	156.2
1964	282	62,723,889	142,650,050	205,373,939	132,005	155.6
1965	279	63,9 2,905	147,736,636	211,659,541	133,909	158.1
1966	277	65,911,477	154,340,580	220,252,057	135,798	162.2
1967	283	67,562,389	161,580,510	229,142,899	137,877	166.2
1968	283	70,401,711	166,280,774	236,682,485	140,200	168.8
1969	298	69,039,195	167,985,665	237,024,860	142,600	166.2
1970	303	69,760,900	175,545,155	245,306,055	145,200	168.9

* In 1956 Reader's Digest became an ABC magazine

SOURCE: Circulation - ABC records covering the <u>first</u> six months of each
                  year.
              Population - Bureau of the Census, midyear estimates of population
                  aged 15 years and older, excluding members of the
                  armed forces overseas.

Courtesy, *Magazine Publishers Association, Inc.*

MAGAZINE MERCHANDISING SERVICES

Every national advertiser seeks to have as many retailers as possible stock his
goods prior to the appearance of his advertisement, thus selling more goods
to the dealer by virtue of that advertisement. In fact, he uses the forthcoming
advertising as a sales incentive for the dealer to order the goods. The <u>pro-
cedure of telling a dealer about a forthcoming campaign designed to help him
sell the product</u> is called *merchandising the advertising.*

BEER – HOUSEHOLD USAGE BY AMOUNT AND BRANDS
AVERAGE-ISSUE AUDIENCE
TOTAL ADULTS

(IN THOUSANDS)

		U.S. TOTAL	AMERICAN HOME	AMERICAN MAG. / TWA AMBASSADOR	ARGOSY	BARRON'S	BETTER HOMES & GARDENS	BUSINESS WEEK	CAR CRAFT	COSMOPOLITAN	DUN'S REVIEW	EBONY	ESQUIRE	FAMILY CIRCLE
TOTAL		130326	9320	1590	4175	641	22724	4349	1516	4814	680	4238	7306	14516
	PCT. MARKET COVERAGE	100.0	7.2	1.2	3.2	.5	17.4	3.3	1.2	3.7	.5	3.3	5.6	11.1
01 USED ANY BEER IN HOME														
IN PAST MONTH		64050	4834	952	2606	353	11762	2770	757	3037	439	2516	4597	7910
	PCT. COMPOSITION	49.1	51.9	59.9	62.4	55.1	51.8	63.7	49.9	63.1	64.6	59.4	62.9	54.5
	INDEX	100	106	122	127	112	105	130	102	129	132	121	128	111
	PCT. MARKET COVERAGE	100.0	7.5	1.5	4.1	.5	18.4	4.3	1.2	4.7	.7	3.9	7.2	12.3
NO. GLASSES USED PAST WK														
02 9 GLASSES OR LESS		40516	3037	696	1342	266	7542	1804	427	2149	270	1432	3135	5225
	PCT. COMPOSITION	31.1	32.6	43.8	32.1	41.5	33.2	41.5	28.2	44.6	39.7	33.8	42.9	36.0
	INDEX	100	105	141	103	133	107	133	91	143	128	109	138	116
	PCT. MARKET COVERAGE	100.0	7.5	1.7	3.3	.7	18.6	4.5	1.1	5.3	.7	3.5	7.7	12.9
03 10 – 19 GLASSES		14660	1094	142	729	**35	2785	615	**175	595	*120	483	986	1695
	PCT. COMPOSITION	11.2	11.7	8.9	17.5	5.5	12.3	14.1	11.5	12.4	17.6	11.4	13.5	11.7
	INDEX	100	104	79	156	49	110	126	103	111	157	102	121	104
	PCT. MARKET COVERAGE	100.0	7.5	1.0	5.0	.2	19.0	4.2	1.2	4.1	.8	3.3	6.7	11.6
04 20 OR MORE GLASSES		8875	703	114	536	***51	1435	350	*155	294	***49	601	476	990
	PCT. COMPOSITION	6.8	7.5	7.2	12.8	8.0	6.3	8.0	10.2	6.1	7.2	14.2	6.5	6.8
	INDEX	100	110	106	188	118	93	118	150	90	106	209	96	100
	PCT. MARKET COVERAGE	100.0	7.9	1.3	6.0	.6	16.2	3.9	1.7	3.3	.6	6.8	5.4	11.2
05 10 OR MORE GLASSES		23535	1797	256	1264	86	4220	966	*329	889	169	1084	1462	2685
	PCT. COMPOSITION	18.1	19.3	16.1	30.3	13.4	18.6	22.2	21.7	18.5	24.9	25.6	20.0	18.5
	INDEX	100	107	89	167	74	103	123	120	102	138	141	110	102
	PCT. MARKET COVERAGE	100.0	7.6	1.1	5.4	.4	17.9	4.1	1.4	3.8	.7	4.6	6.2	11.4

W. R. SIMMONS & ASSOCIATES RESEARCH, INC.
1972

Courtesy, W. R. Simmons & Associates, Research

A DEMOGRAPHIC ANALYSIS OF MAGAZINE CIRCULATION

Showing percentage of beer drinkers among readers of different magazines. Similar
reports are made up for other products, as an aid in selecting magazines.

Magazines offer a variety of services to help advertisers merchandise
their advertising. The service may consist of mailings prepared for the advertiser to notify the dealer of the forthcoming advertising, along with counter
display cards for use by the stores, saying in substance, "As advertised in
_____ Magazine." The service may extend to elaborate department store
promotions: *Esquire* has a fashion promotion with 1,000 department stores
four times a year, featuring spring, fall, and back-to-campus styles, and Father's
Day. The August issue of *Mademoiselle* is famous for its back-to-school
fashion predictions, and the magazine holds a fashion show in New York in
June, attended by store buyers and fashion coordinators. *Reader's Digest* has
a computerized marketing service that helps readers find local outlets via a
single nationwide phone number. The success of many magazine campaigns

EBONY'S Total-Selling Plan: We don't just sell ad space, we sell your product.

That's why 80 out of the 100 largest magazine advertisers use EBONY.

Most publications just run your ads. Not *Ebony*. We have a slew of sales specialists who see to it your ads get results.

First, there's our team of crack *Ebony* salesmen who are actually trained marketing men. Any one of them can sit down with you and discuss any problem of marketing to that big 36.4 billion-a-year Black consumer market. They'll be able to offer sound, objective advice based on scientific research data, and supplemented by on-the-spot daily reports of the *Ebony* merchandising staff.

These "Men-on-the-Move" form a second set of specialists. They're in 12 major

PERCENT OF WOMEN WHO PURCHASED BUSINESS AND STREETWEAR IN PAST YEAR		
	U.S. Total	EBONY Women
BOUGHT 1 or MORE	69.8	75.5
BOUGHT 3 or MORE	49.3	54.0

SOURCE: DANIEL STARCH

Our salesmen are supremely knowledgeable of the Black consumer market, and can offer insights that might have escaped the manufacturer himself.

markets, and have a great rapport with big-volume, downtown retailers, your whole-salers and distributors.

They help restock shelves, arrange for product demonstrations, check competitors' brand facings, schedule that hard-to-get floor space, and set up P.O.P. materials. They'll even recruit and supervise additional personnel for door-to-door sampling, in-store give-aways or couponing.

Retailers want to cooperate because they know the pulling-power of ads in *Ebony*.

They know that *Ebony* readers are the cream of the affluent Black consumer market.

The facts: 39.1% of *Ebony* households

The EBONY merchandising men swing a lot of weight with "Central City" retailers.

earn $10,000 or more, and 58.4% own their own homes. The median *Ebony* family income ($8,594) is nearly $1,200 *more* than the median U.S. family income ($7,421).

Our readers believe in *Ebony*. They trust in its journalistic integrity. For good reason. Our award-winning editorial staff is all-professional: dedicated, competent and involved.

And the trust our readers have in our journalism spills over to a belief in the ads we run.

Read *Ebony* and see for yourself. Then perhaps you'll agree with L. J. Evans, President of the Grumman Corporation:

"I am opening my own subscription to *Ebony* in order to get a broader view of all America. From time to time, I have noticed in *The New York Times*, the cogent text of your page advertisements. In the future those advertisements will have more significance to me."

For further information, please call: (New York) William P. Grayson, Exec. V.P., 1270 Avenue of the Americas, 586-2911. (Chicago) Lincoln Hudson, V.P., 1820 South Michigan Avenue, 225-1000.

EBONY
is where
4.2 million smart people do their shopping.

MERCHANDISING THE ADVERTISING

Ebony tells what it does to help its advertisers get retail support.

has been helped by the ability of the manufacturer's salesmen to present the advertising to a store and show the buyer the advantage of building his merchandising efforts around it.

Merchandising services vary from magazine to magazine; their scope depends also upon the size of the advertiser's schedule.

FARM MAGAZINES

We have a farm population of about ten million people who have their own special magazines and other periodicals. These may be classified as *general farm magazines, regional farm magazines,* and *vocational farm magazines.* Because a good number of the larger magazines have geographical and demographic splits, these classifications overlap.

General farm magazines. The largest of these—*Farm Journal,* with a circulation of about 3 million—reported that two thirds of its editorial content is devoted to farm production, management, and news, and one third to the needs of women and their families. It is published in a series of regional editions.

Regional farm magazines. These are publications specifically aimed at the total problem of farmers in different regions of the country, including problems relating to their chief crops, their general welfare, and governmental activity affecting that area. Here we have publications such as *Ohio Farmer, California Farmer,* and *Dakota Farmer.*

Vocational farm magazines. Many farm publications are devoted to certain crops, or forms of farming. They are really vocational papers relating to specific types of farming, and include such publications as *The Dairyman, American Fruit Grower, Poultry Press,* and *Better Beef Business.* There is an overlapping in these classifications, and we have the *New England Dairyman, Washington Cattleman,* and *Gulf Coast Cattleman.*

Whatever the farmer's interest may be, there are a number of publications edited for him. Many farm homes get several publications.

Farm-publication advertising dropped between 1960 and 1970, from $66 million in 1960 to $62 million in 1970, reflecting the drop in farm-publication circulations, which in turn reflects the reduction in the number of individual farm households. This field as a whole may be slowly shrinking, but nevertheless represents a basic part of our total population, and continues to be a large market.

TRENDS IN MAGAZINES

The final issue of *Life* magazine, in December, 1972, marked the demise, within a four-year span, of the last of the three one-time giants of the mass weekly field: *The Saturday Evening Post* (1968), *Look* (1971), *Life* (1972).

For generations *The Saturday Evening Post* had been the preeminent mass magazine and advertising medium, strong on fiction, as well as articles and editorials of national interest. *Life* came out in 1936, introducing photographic journalism; *Look* followed in *Life*'s footsteps, first as a weekly, then as a bi-weekly. Soon their circulation soared. *The Saturday Evening Post* was hurt and began a long checkered course trying to create a new, viable editorial image to meet the times. There were changes in editors, changes in policies, changes in management, changes in ownership, which began a new round of changes to attract and hold a meaningful market for advertisers—all to no avail.

During this time, despite their success, *Life* and *Look* were aware of what was to become their nemesis—television. "After all," the public seemed to say, "why buy a magazine to see news pictures when we can see them live, on TV, along with other programs?" TV attracted the mass audiences and the large advertising budgets. The general weeklies were hurt.

Yet there were many advertisers who still looked with favor on magazines, spurring intense competition among them for the largest circulations in their fields, hoping thereby to become the magazine of choice for advertisers. But this "numbers game," as this drive was called, proved prohibitively costly to magazines whose income was declining. Instead of being impressed by the big weeklies' large figures, advertisers questioned the diluted quality of the circulation.

Magazines tried a different gambit. They announced they would concentrate their circulation in the major markets only, where advertisers did most of their business, and prune their circulation elsewhere by redirecting circulation efforts. They dropped millions in their outlying circulation. They reduced their page rates. They divided their circulation into regional and local editions. This brought in much welcome business, but did not stay the overall downward trend.

Meanwhile production costs of all magazines had been going up. This most affected the big weeklies with their large page size, their costly color plates, and their frequency of publication. Postal rates had gone up, too. *Life* faced 1973 with the prospect of a 127 percent increase in mailing costs over the next five years, if it continued. That was the coup de grace.

Increased postal rates and production costs will encourage large-size magazines to reduce their page sizes, and to find ways to distribute their magazines other than by mail.

The death of all these weeklies was presaged by issues which became thinner and thinner, both in advertising pages and in substance. Each publication had lost the editorial distinction which would attract an identifiable market for advertisers. Each had lost its reason for being . . . Thus ended the age of the large-size weekly magazines addressed to the general public.

How to make an investment in carpeting you won't regret.

Most carpets, even synthetics, look great when they're new, but a wool carpet looks newer longer. Why?

As recent tests of wool vs. a comparable acrylic showed, a wool carpet comes cleaner by vacuuming, comes cleaner by shampooing. Here's proof.

TELLING A STORY IN A DOUBLE SPREAD

The left side of this magazine ad was in black and white, the right side in full color, giving the entire advertisement an impressive appearance. Magazines give an advertiser an opportunity to tell a story that can be read fully at leisure.

The vacuum test:

Wool and acrylic carpets were laid at a cafeteria entrance for 3 months and walked on by 48,000 people. The samples were alternated every day and vacuumed every day. On the last day of the test an electron microscope studied the carpets.

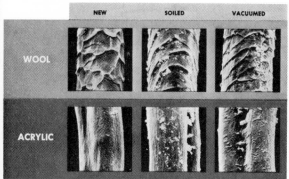

Result: Before vacuuming less dirt adhered to the wool fiber—with its scale-like surface—than to the acrylic. After vacuuming, wool had shed dirt more. **Conclusion:** Wool's scaly fiber tends to reject dirt. <u>Wool cleans better.</u>

The shampoo test:

Wool and acrylic carpets were laid on the floor and shampooed after every 20,000 steps until 100,000 footsteps had been recorded—the equivalent of 2 to 3 years' wear in an average home. Photographs show how wear changed the color of the carpets.

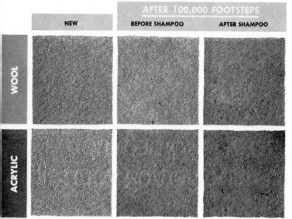

Result: After the first shampooing, the wool had shed soil about 4 times better than the acrylic...its color was still bright. As the heavy traffic on both carpets continued, the acrylic carpet soiled from four to five times more than the wool—and kept collecting soil faster than wool after each subsequent shampooing. **Conclusion:** Wool carpet stays newer looking than acrylic. <u>Wool cleans better.</u>

A wool carpet cleans better. By test. Ours. And yours.

Which carpet cleans better, wool or acrylic? Wool's the one. The winner twice over. Rejects dirt better. Cleans better. And looks newer longer.

We've proved it in test situations and you'll prove it at home. Every time you vacuum your wool carpet or shampoo it.

And all the credit goes to the scaly wool fiber. Hedged all around by hard shingles very much like the shingles on your roof, wool's uncopyable structure is the real reason a wool carpet does not attract and hold dirt.

To sum up. Acrylic carpeting gets dirtier faster than wool. And wool gets cleaner easier by the two methods you use in your own home.

Wool. It's got life. And it looks it.

PURE WOOL PILE®

The Woolmark label on carpeting means it has passed a battery of tests in the Wool Bureau laboratories, for fiber content, pile weight per square yard, mothproofing, backing construction. Look for the Woolmark label. It means you've got a quality-tested carpet made of pure wool pile.

Wool. It's got life.

While these magazines were going through terminal pains, other magazines were flourishing. They had one thing in common: Their editors had a sharp editorial picture of whom they were trying to reach and a clear editorial direction as to how to reach such readers. *Reader's Digest*—the largest magazine published in terms of copies sold—stated its editorial goals this way:

> *Reader's Digest* is a general interest non-fiction reading magazine for the entire family. It aims for simplicity, brevity, clarity, putting the heart of the story within the reader's easy grasp.

Other magazines with sharply defined editorial points of view will continue to thrive—*National Geographic, Playboy, Cosmopolitan, Good Housekeeping, Time, Sports Illustrated*. The age of giants in the magazine field is not over, except they will be specialized giants. Newer magazines which have a sharply defined point of view, such as *Psychology Today, Money, Ms.,* will continue to appear.

A growing category in the magazine field will be "store books"— volumes containing articles on specific subjects, largely compiled from the magazines whose names they carry.

There will be greater use of magazines to carry insert and merchandising units.

The General Foods magazine study (1971), showed the power of magazines to deliver a message that people remembered, in comparison to the misidentification of television commercials. This may mark a turning point in restoring to magazines some of the advertising volume which has been going to television.

The biggest change in the magazine picture may come from cable television, which promises to have programs targeted to groups with special interests, affecting even the magazines of special interests; and TV cassettes, which may represent one more influence to turn people away from reading.

CRITERIA FOR PICKING MAGAZINES

Does the publication reach the type of reader to whom we are trying to sell our product? How does the distribution of its circulation compare with that of our product? How was the circulation obtained? What is the cost of reaching a thousand *prospects,* not merely the cost per thousand readers?

How do the readers regard the magazine? How thoroughly do they read it? Will the advertisement be in acceptable company? How important are merchandising aids, and what is available? If there are gaps in the coverage the magazines supply, it might be time to look at other media.

OTHER MAGAZINES

In addition to the foregoing magazines, we also have magazines used as trade papers and for industrial audiences. Because of the specialized nature of these publications, we treat them separately in a later chapter, "Business Advertising."

Case Reports
on the Use of Magazines

7 facts about learning to fly.

Read how you can enjoy the exhilarating
and adventurous world of flight.

1. Can Anyone Learn To Fly?
Almost anyone can be taught to take off
and land, but becoming a well-rounded
pilot is a different thing. It takes the kind
of person who likes a challenge and can
apply himself. The 750,000 people in the
U.S. who fly—and the thousands who are
taking it up right now—are people who rel-
ish the satisfaction of accomplishing something out of the ordinary.

2. What Are The Physical Requirements?
You just have to be in general good health.
Common sense and mature judgment are
the basic elements of a safe pilot. Only a
simple physical examination is required.
Eyeglasses are no deterrent. There is no
maximum age limit. (Sixteen is the minimum
age for solo.)

3. How Long Does It Take To Get A License?
The government requires a minimum of 35
hours of flight time for a Private License.
Since you are flying while learning, the required hours are enjoyable and exciting.
You learn at your leisure, and pay on a
lesson-to-lesson basis.

4. How Complicated Is It To Learn?
You are introduced to the basic elements
of flying one at a time. First, the effect of
the controls...ease back on the wheel to
climb, ease forward to descend...make
turns by turning the wheel left or right to
establish a bank. After several hours of
practice you can handle the airplane in-
stinctively—you'll move confidently in the
three-dimensional realm of flight.
Take-offs and landings are much simplified with modern tricycle landing gear.

Landings are even easier with low wing
design, as in the Piper Cherokee, because
an invisible pillow of air builds up under
your wing to cushion the touchdown.
When you start using an airplane for its
real purpose—straight, swift transportation
—you are amazed at the miraculous but
simple-to-use electronic navigation aids
that tell you exactly where you are.

5. What About All Those Instruments?
Sort them out and you find most are the
same as on a car or boat—a clock, a compass, a speedometer, and engine instruments, plus an altimeter. The additional
instruments provided in most modern panels include, for example, a dial that shows
your rate of climb or descent, an artificial
horizon that shows whether you're level,
and a gyroscopic compass that remains
steady in flight...all there to simplify your
handling of the airplane.

6. Do You Have To Own An Airplane To Enjoy Flying?
Not necessarily so. It's very practical for
you and two or three friends to share
ownership in a new, over 130 mph Piper
Cherokee. Since flying can be enjoyed all
year round, a share can be a very sound

investment. Many pilots join clubs or rent
airplanes as you would a car.

7. Where Should I Learn To Fly?
You'll learn best at a Piper Flite Center,
which offers programmed aviation training
with a complete 30-step system. Modern
training equipment is used and every in-
structor is a government-rated professional.

$5 For Your First Lesson
The first introductory lesson at a Piper
Flite Center costs only $5. The Special
Flying Start Course, available exclusively
at Piper Flite Centers, offers four lessons,
log book, and preliminary ground school
instruction for only $88. Actually getting
your pilot's license costs about the same
as taking up golf or skiing. And when you
can fly, it's something the whole family
can enjoy with you.

Act Now
Use the coupon below to get a complete
Flight Information Kit which includes:
Let's Fly! 20-page illustrated booklet on
learning to fly / Piper Partnership book-
let / Piper Pilot Magazine / Special money-
saving first flight lesson coupon. Visit your
Piper Flite Center (listed in the Yellow
Pages) for your first flight lesson. See if
you're up to this exciting challenge.

PIPER Aircraft Corporation, Lock Haven, Pa. 17745

Gentlemen:
    Please send me my free FLIGHT INFORMATION KIT

PIPER
Flite Center

Name_____
Address_____
City_____
State_____ Zip_____ Phone_____

We label it fresh-fruit good, and it is.

KRAFT

pure
Strawberry *preserves*

STORE COUPON

Save 7¢
Good on any size, any flavor
Kraft Jellies or Preserves

Redeem This Coupon Promptly

Nothing but good fresh fruit goes into
Kraft Pure Strawberry Preserves. The
same kind of sweet, ripe, plump berries
you'd pick out yourself if you made
your own preserves. Want a taste?
Just pluck the coupon.

See Kraft Music Hall, Wednesday Nights, NBC-TV.

"Kraft increased their share of market by 65%."

THE SALES IDEA: "This ad was the focal point of a total marketing effort behind a Kraft Strawberry Preserves promotion, and was supported by announcements on the Kraft Music Hall which ended with a reference to the 7¢ coupon appearing in magazines. A copy of the ad and a montage of the magazines were also included in the TV commercials.

THE RESULT: "Reprints of the ad served as a sales tool for the Kraft sales force in arranging for features tying in with this promotion. During the time this program was in effect, Kraft increased their share of the Strawberry Preserves market by 65%."

J. R. Johnson, Account Executive, Needham, Harper & Steers, Inc.

AGENCY: Needham, Harper & Steers, Inc.

This box is trying to tell you something!

NEW IDEA!
one-pot main dish-complete with tender beef

Lipton.
beef stroganoff
new main dish complete with beef!

Save 15¢ on any new Lipton Main Dish

STORE COUPON · STORE COUPON

15¢ · 15¢ · 15¢ · 15¢

There's an exciting new kind of dinner inside.

Imagine! A delicious main dish for two—complete with meat—ready in 15 minutes, in just one step! Choose Lipton Beef Stroganoff, Chicken La Scala, Turkey Primavera or Chicken Baronet. Each lavish with tender meat.

vegetables, golden egg noodles and its own savory sauce and zesty garnish. You've never served—he's never tasted—anything like them. **Tonight! Don't just set the table, set the mood.**

"Successfully pioneered new market segment."

THE SALES IDEA: When Lipton introduced the first complete-with-meat packaged dinners, they tell us they had to build a market from scratch. They literally had to establish a whole new concept in family eating. To do this, they acknowledge, they had to reach those families most likely to try new and innovative products—the better-educated, higher-income families.

THE RESULT: "We had to reach the taste-makers in communities across the country, and we did. With the introduction of Main Dishes, Lipton successfully pioneered an entirely new market segment. Now there is an expanded line of Lipton Main Dishes—ranging from Beef Stroganoff to new Chicken Supreme with sherry —in national distribution."

Ted Labiner, Product Manager—Lipton Main Dishes

AGENCY: SSC and B, Inc. Advertising

"We sold 50,000 Tuborg drinking horns on an advertising budget of less than $200,000."

"By taking advantage of magazines' ability to portray beautiful merchandise, we sold 50,000 Tuborg drinking horns on an advertising budget of less than $200,000. It is doubtful whether any other medium would have pulled as well, because magazines enabled us to combine the message, a beautifully reproduced photograph and a response mechanism (coupon) in one neat package called a one page, four-color bleed insertion."

Mel Roth, Account Executive, Gilbert Advertising Agency, Inc.

AGENCY: Gilbert Advertising Agency, Inc.

1. What are the major advantages and limitations of magazines for the national advertiser?

2. Give a brief definition or explanation of:
   a. geographical editions
   b. demographic editions
   c. bleed pages
   d. second cover
   e. junior unit
   f. gatefold
   g. primary circulation
   h. circulation guarantee

3. What is the standard unit of cost on which magazines are compared?

4. Explain the difference between primary and pass-along circulation. Under what conditions might an advertiser be more interested in one or the other?

5. What are the major considerations an advertiser should use for selecting a consumer magazine?

6. Describe the differences among general, regional, and vocational farm magazines.

7. What are some of the chief trends in magazines?

Reading Suggestions

Barton, Roger, *The Handbook of Advertising Management.* New York: McGraw-Hill, 1970.

Ford, James L. C., *Magazines for Millions: The Story of Specialized Publications.* Carbondale, Ill.: Southern Illinois University Press, 1969.

Howard, Pamela, "Ms. and the Journalism of Women's Lib," *Saturday Review,* January 8, 1972, pp. 43–45ff.

Mott, Frank Luther, *A History of American Magazines,* three volumes. Cambridge, Mass.: Harvard University Press, 1930–1938.

Tebbel, John, "Time to Change Your Page Size," *Saturday Review,* October 9, 1971, pp. 68–70.

Wood, James Playstead, *Magazines in the United States,* 3rd edition. New York: The Ronald Press Company, 1971.

11

Outdoor Advertising
Transit Advertising

OUTDOOR ADVERTISING

MUCH OF AMERICA IS on wheels today, going to and from work, shopping and visiting, touring all parts of the country. In metropolitan areas, 83 percent of all families own cars; in nonmetropolitan areas, 79 percent own cars. Fifty-two percent of all families own one car; 25 percent own two cars, and 4 percent own three or more cars; [1] and as they drive they are greeted by outdoor advertising.

FEATURES AND ADVANTAGES

Outdoor advertising provides the advertiser with the largest colorful display of his trademark, product, and slogan. It offers the most spectacular use of lights and animation and color to attract attention.

It is geographically flexible, available in any of 9,000 markets across the country. An advertiser can reach his market nationally, regionally, or even in local spots, and in those areas he can reach out for ethnic groups or demographic groups. Outdoor advertising offers frequency of impression. Its cost of appearing before a large audience is therefore low per thousand. It is widely used in connection with other media.

When we speak here of outdoor advertising, we speak only of that advertising placed by plant operators organized as an industry to place advertising in markets all over the country. We do not speak of the multitude of signs announcing the businesses along the roads—the bowling alleys and car washes, motels, discount stores, eating places. The signs of organized outdoor industry represent only 5 percent of all outdoor signs. In terms of dollars, however, these members represent a $350-million industry.[2]

---

[1] W. R. Simmons & Associates Research Study, 1970.
[2] Report, *This is Outdoor Advertising,* Institute of Outdoor Advertising, 1971.

Outdoor signs are passed quickly; this is the greatest challenge to create a design that can tell its story in rapid, crisp form. Not all messages are suited to such compression. Outdoor advertising reaches a wide audience—a factor that is an advantage for a product in widespread sale, but is a limitation if the target of the market is a thin demographic group. Its use is also limited by zoning laws, but even those living in neighborhoods where its use is not allowed will be greeted by outdoor signs where allowed on the roads leading to and from their homes. Although the outdoor industry has done much to limit the use of outdoor advertising to compatible environments, many people object to outdoor advertising as a whole.

It takes time to print and post outdoor signs; their use must be planned well ahead of appearance dates.

The industry is still in the process of getting adequate reach and frequency reports.

PLANT OPERATORS

The basic business unit in the outdoor-advertising industry is the local plant operator. He studies the traffic flow in his market and seeks suitable outdoor sign locations along these routes. It may be an empty lot or the side or roof of a building. As long as the location is exposed to traffic and the zoning law permits the erection of a sign, the plant operator is interested in it. He leases from the owner of the property the right to erect an outdoor sign structure (or he may buy the site itself). He then "sells" space to the individual advertiser for a period ranging from one month to five years. He is responsible for physically placing the advertisement on the sign as well as for its lighting and maintenance.

In large markets, there may be several competitive plant operators, each offering his own set of locations.

FORMS OF OUTDOOR ADVERTISING

The chief categories of outdoor advertising used by national advertisers are:

1. Posters
2. Painted bulletins
3. Spectaculars

Briefly, posters represent the form of outdoor advertising that is the least costly per unit; they are the "bread and butter" use of outdoor adver-

tising. Painted bulletins are costlier signs, and are usually placed in better locations only; they are the "cake" of outdoor advertising. Spectaculars are the
largest, the costliest, and the most flamboyant of all forms of outdoor advertising, and are for locations whose traffic warrants such expense; they are
the cake-with-icing-plus-ice-cream of outdoor advertising.

Posters

The term *poster* in the outdoor advertising world is used in a special
and restricted sense. It is the trade term for a structure or a blank panel of
standardized size and border that is affixed in the ground, to a wall, or on a
roof. The advertisement to appear on the poster is printed at a lithography
plant on large sheets of paper, which are then mounted by hand on the face
of the panel.

Poster sizes. Poster sizes are referred to in terms of sheets. The term
originated in the days when it took 24 of the largest sheets that the presses
could hold to cover a sign 12 by 25 feet. The presses have changed, but the
designation has stuck. Today, all posters are still mounted on a board of that
size, but the actual sizes of the posters themselves are as follows:

1. 24-sheet poster (8'8" × 19'6"). The rest of the board area is a
   margin of blank paper.
2. 30-sheet poster (9'7" × 21'7"). The rest of the board is a margin
   of blank paper. 25% more copy than the 24-sheet.
3. Bleed poster, which extends the artwork right to the frame. It
   averages 40% larger than the 24-sheet poster.

The 30-sheet poster is the most widely used by advertisers today.

There is also a 3-sheet poster size, 90 inches high by 46 inches wide,
mounted on panels on walls adjacent to a store in which the product is sold.
Approximately 230,000 poster panels span the country. In markets of
100,000 and over, 64 percent of panels are illuminated at night, to take advantage of night traffic, including the many who shop then. The percentage
drops to 3 percent in markets of 5,000 to 10,000.

Poster showings. Posters are not sold individually, but as a preselected assortment called a *showing*. The number of boards in a showing is
referred to on a comparative scale, in terms of showings. A #100 showing
represents a selection of panels the number and distribution of which is designed to do an excellent job of covering that market. In each instance, the
plant owner specifies the number of boards included in his showings, and the
cost per showing. The number of a showing has nothing to do with the number of posters included, nor are showings to be read as 100 percent or 50

STANDARD POSTER

The poster is a standardized structure, 12′ high and 25′ long, on which outdoor advertisements are pasted. The poster is the most widespread form of outdoor advertising.

On the 12′ by 25′ poster panel, advertisements of three sizes can be mounted. The differences in their sizes depend upon how much white space is left in the margins. The sizes are referred to in terms of "sheets."

THREE-SHEET POSTER   Courtesy, Criterion Advertising, Inc.

This size poster is used extensively outside stores in
which the product is being sold; also used at train
stations.

percent. A #50 showing is about half a #100 showing. In larger markets,
there are also #75 and #25 showings. An advertiser can also buy a
#150 or a #200 showing, usually for a short intensive drive. The most fre-
quently used showing is the #50 showing.

Each plant operator decides how many boards are in his showings, and
how they are distributed in his market—for example, approach roads, business districts, neighborhood shopping centers. All boards in a showing will
have the same distribution values in a market as other boards of the same size
showing. The number of boards in a #100 showing varies from market to
market, depending on the population, the area, and the traffic pattern.*

According to studies on the subject by Ted Bates & Company, the
average #100 showing provides a four-week reach of almost 90 percent of all
men in a given market, with exposure of 31 during that period.

Painted Bulletins

For the more important traffic sites, a larger and more elaborate form
of outdoor sign, called a *painted bulletin,* is used. These structures have a
prefabricated steel facing with a standardized border trim. The advertisement
is painted on the face of the bulletin. In some markets, lithographed sheets
are being used. The proportions of painted bulletins are standard, even
though actual sizes may vary. The most common size for bulletins is 14 by
48 feet.

---

* In 1973, the GRP began replacing the showing. One outdoor GRP represents the
number of boards that in one day provides exposure equivalent to 100% of the market population.

OUTDOOR ADVERTISING UNITS

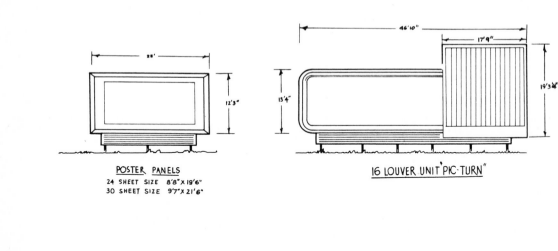

POSTER PANELS
24 SHEET SIZE 8'8" X 19'6"
30 SHEET SIZE 9'7" X 21'6"

16 LOUVER UNIT "PIC-TURN"

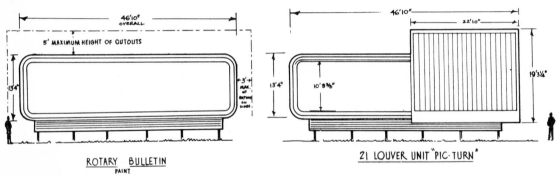

ROTARY BULLETIN
PAINT

21 LOUVER UNIT "PIC-TURN"

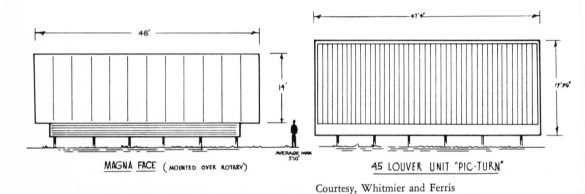

MAGNA FACE (MOUNTED OVER ROTARY)

45 LOUVER UNIT "PIC-TURN"

Courtesy, Whitmier and Ferris

Painted bulletins are illuminated for the night traffic. They often have extending from them clocks, thermometers, or an electric time and temperature unit known as a *jump clock*. They may also have enlarged cutouts, such as a package or trademark, displayed in brilliant lights, extending beyond the board itself, as well as three-dimensional structures made of Styrofoam.

Of the combined totals of poster panels and painted bulletins now on display, painted bulletins constitute 38 percent, posters, 62.[3]

---

[3] Institute of Outdoor Advertising, 1971.

PAINTED BULLETIN

Courtesy, Foster and Kleiser

This is a special construction placed in areas of heavy traffic, illuminated at night. The advertisements are painted on the face of the panel.

PAINTED BULLETIN
WITH SPECIAL CONSTRUCTION

Note the simplicity of the message.

Courtesy, Foster and Kleiser

A painted poster with a specially constructed louvre, which turns to show another illustration.

The other side of the louvre—an effective way of getting attention and telling a two-faced story quickly.

Courtesy, Lamar Dean

Buying painted bulletins. Painted bulletins are bought individually, in contrast to posters, which are bought by showings. Contracts run for a year or more, especially with extra construction. Copy changes usually take place three times a year. The advertiser, or his representative, will visit a territory, personally inspecting each location offered by the local plant operator. He will judge its circulation, the distance from which it is visible, the amount of traffic, competing signs and distractions, and any special features affecting its visibility. The price quoted for the individual painted bulletin may be subject to negotiation. The advertiser supplies the design and art work to the plant operator, who is responsible for reproducing it and maintaining the sign in good condition.

Rotary plans. Instead of having one painted bulletin in the same location for a year, an advertiser in many markets can buy a *rotary plan,* whereby the whole face of the bulletin bearing his advertisement is moved every 30, 60, or 90 days to a different preselected location—thus getting the message before different audiences. It may even be moved to a different market. The advertiser selects in advance those locations he considers best for his purpose. The board itself is painted, or the advertisement mounted, in the shop.

There has been a great increase lately in the use of rotary showings. It's the "in" thing in outdoor advertising buying.

Spectaculars

In an industry with its own special jargon, it is refreshing to come upon a word that literally means what it says—the outdoor *spectacular* sign. Spectaculars are the most conspicuous of all outdoor advertisements, placed and designed to attract the greatest number of passersby. They are built of steel beams, sheet metal, and plastics, and utilize bright lights, flashing lights, animation movies, waterfalls in the background, rising steam, and smoke— designs representing the height of the technical ingenuity of outdoor-sign construction. Great nighttime brilliance, along with daytime value, is obtained for many signs through the use of the newest techniques in painting and lighting.

Spectaculars are the costliest of outdoor signs, erected at the heaviest traffic spots. The price ranges from $25,000 to a third of a million dollars per year. They are individually designed, and the cost of space and construction is individually negotiated. They represent a large capital investment in the structure, which is amortized over a three- to five-year space contract. Changes are costly because they may entail reconstruction of steel work and neon lighting.

An advertiser may often use all three forms of outdoor advertising in a market: a spectacular at a particularly advantageous location from the viewpoint of heavy traffic, and some painted bulletins on the main arteries, supplemented by 24-sheet posters in the neighborhood areas during peak months.

OUTDOOR SPECTACULAR   Courtesy, Douglas Leigh, Inc.

This sign uses brilliant animated illumination to catch the eyes of passers-by.

In about 1,000 shopping centers in 230 markets, an advertiser can get display panels suspended from the lightposts in the parking area. Average national showing includes 6,000 displays in 1,000 centers.

Outdoor Advertising Circulation

Circulation in outdoor advertising is spoken of as "effective circulation," which is interpreted to mean the number of people who may pass a given sign and have a reasonable opportunity of seeing it. This number is measured as half the pedestrians, half the automobiles, and one fourth of the surface-transportation passengers who pass the sign. (As the reader will observe, the term *circulation* means different things in different media.) The chief value of such figures is to provide a comparative basis of the worth of different locations.

The chief source of information of such data has been the *Traffic Audit Bureau,* composed of members of the industry. In 1971 it restructured its operation to provide the modern type of information that advertisers seek. Their program now is:

—To publish circulation data that can be used for planning of outdoor advertising campaigns, market by market.

—To reflect circulation that can be delivered.

—To obtain data that over the years can be used for trend information.

—To detail the audited information in its simplest form, so that the information may apply to what the advertiser or agency desires to buy and what the plant operator offers to sell.

—To report information *only* for markets and companies audited. In markets where some companies do not audit, lack of audit will be reported.

—To distribute the Plant Operator's Statement of effective circulations in a manner similar to that of ABC and BPA statements—to supporting advertisers and agencies.

Buying Outdoor Advertising

In buying a poster showing, the outdoor space buyer will ride through the area with a plant operator or his representative, to examine the sites included in a showing. He may suggest one or two alternative choices, but on the whole he buys the preplanned package of locations designated by the plant owner as a showing.

OUTDOOR RATES AND MARKETS

Indiana

PLANT	MARKET-COUNTY		POP.	EFF. DATE	#	NON ILL.	ILL.	COST PER MONTH	DISC.	CROSS REF. NO.
						COVERAGE — POSTERS				
0255.0	EVANSVILLE (090)	VANDERBURGH	145.0	01-01-0	100	10	14	1680.00	D	0690
					75	7	11	1305.00	D	
					50	5	7	930.00	D	
					25	2	4	495.00	D	
0255.0	EVANSVILLE GREATER METRO MKT IND-K (090) POSEY VANDERBURGH WARRICK IND HENDERSON KY		248.6	01-01-0	100	20	20	2570.00	D	
					50	12	10	1490.00	D	
7965.2	EVANSVILLE SUBURBAN MKT (090) POSEY WARRICK	GIBSON	7.6	05-01-0	100	8		336.00	D	
					50	4		168.00	D	
9162.4	FAIRMOUNT (018)	GRANT	3.1	01-01-1	100	2		90.00	D	1355
					50	1		45.00	D	
8270.2	FARMERSBURG (104)	SULLIVAN	1.0	01-01-0	100	1		36.00		
6575.0	FARMLAND (041)	RANDOLPH	1.1	01-01-9	100	1		42.00	D	2425
4785.0	FERDINAND (090)	DUBOIS	1.4	01-01-9	100	1		40.00		
9162.0	FISHERSBURG (018)	MADISON	.1	01-01-1	100	1		45.00	D	0040
5685.2	FLORA (018)	CARROLL	1.7	01-01-1	100	1		48.00		
7965.2	FORT BRANCH (090)	GIBSON	2.0	01-01-0	100	1		42.00	D	
9162.0	FORTVILLE (018)	HANCOCK	2.2	01-01-1	100	1		45.00	D	0040
0965.0	FORT WAYNE MKT (089)	ALLEN	249.1	01-01-0	100	7	15	1430.00		0747
					75	5	12	1105.00		
					50	4	10	910.00		
0965.0	FORT WAYNE METRO MKT (089)	ALLEN	267.7	01-01-0	100	13	15	1760.00		
					75	9	12	1335.00		
					50	7	10	1075.00		
6265.0	FOUNTAIN CITY (041)	WAYNE	.8	10-01-9	100	1		45.00	D	
9147.0	FOWLER (018)	BENTON	2.5	01-01-0	100	2		90.00	D	
					50	1		45.00	D	
9147.0	FRANCESVILLE (088)	PULASKI	1.0	01-01-0	100	1		45.00	D	
9162.2	FRANKFORT MKT (018)	CLINTON	30.7	01-01-1	100	4	2	300.00	D	
					50	3	1	200.00	D	
9162.0	FRANKTON (018)	MADISON	1.4	01-01-1	100	1		45.00	D	0040
3825.2	FRENCH LICK-WEST BADEN (038)	ORANGE	2.8	01-01-0	100	3		126.00	D	
					50	2		84.00	D	
5685.2	FULTON (088)	FULTON	.4	01-01-1	100	1		48.00		
9168.0	FURNESSVILLE (003)	PORTER	.4	01-01-0	100	1		47.00	D	1410
7420.0	GALVESTON (018)	CASS	1.1	01-01-0	100	1		41.00		
0965.0	GARRETT (089)	DE KALB	4.7	01-01-0	100	2		96.00		
					50	1		48.00		
7167.2	GARY METRO MKT (003)	LAKE	223.7	01-01-1	100	10	8	1236.60	D	0347
					75	8	6	961.80	D	
					50	5	4	618.30	D	
9162.4	GAS CITY-JONESBORO (018)	GRANT	7.7	01-01-0	100	3		135.00	D	1355
					50	2		90.00	D	

POSTER RATE LIST

Note the difference in the number of posters in a showing. Compare the showings in Evansville and Fort Wayne.

From *The Buyers' Guide to Outdoor Advertising,* Institute of Outdoor Advertising

Buying painted bulletins is a different matter. Here each sign is handpicked and bought separately. The plant owner will supply a *traffic-flow map* showing the location of his signs in relation to the main arteries and traffic routes of his market.

The outdoor space buyer will then ride out and personally inspect all the promising available locations before selecting any. He does the same for spectaculars.

He may find room for negotiation on some bulletins and spectaculars.

The plant owner will submit a separate estimate of the cost of special construction for bulletins and spectaculars. This cost may be included in the monthly bill and amortized over the contract period (a three- to five-year period).

Inspecting the outdoor sign. When the outdoor signs are up, the agency is notified. A man from the outdoor department will inspect the signs (called *riding a showing*) to make sure that all boards are in proper working order. The boards will then again be inspected regularly to make sure the traffic flow has not changed, that no obstruction—such as the foliage of a tree —or new construction, impedes the view of the sign, and, in the case of posters, to make sure that the posters are not peeling, and that all flashing and lighting arrangements are working properly.[4]

Just what may be involved in an inspection of outdoor signs was revealed by Richard Briggs, who handled the outdoor-advertising account of Old Charter Bourbon at the McCann-Erickson agency:

> We insisted on a number of quality controls. We reviewed materials and construction, elevation of structure, spacing and individuality, lumen output, pictorial reproduction, size of display as related to impact, copy flexibility as related to repaints, space costs as related to circulation, and audience demographics of traffic passing the location.[5]

CRITERIA FOR SELECTING OUTDOOR SIGNS

Among yardsticks besides circulation to take into consideration in picking a location are:

—*Length of unobstructed approach*—the distance from which the location first becomes fully visible to people driving.

---

[4] Many agencies work through the National Outdoor Advertising Bureau (NOAB), a cooperative outdoor-advertising facility, which handles the mechanics of ordering and inspecting the boards of its members.

[5] Report of Richard L. Briggs, *Media Decisions,* August 1971, p. 62.

COMPARISON OF STANDARDIZED OUTDOOR ADVERTISING

	DESCRIPTION	CHIEF CHARACTERISTICS	HOW BOUGHT	SPECIAL FEATURES	OTHER COMMENTS
Posters	Permanent structure (generally 12' x 25') on which pre-printed advertisements are mounted.	1. The least costly form of outdoor advertising, per unit. Standard size nationwide.	1. By *showings*—a ready-made assortment, bought as a unit. Can be bought on monthly basis.	1. Illuminated in better night traffic locations.	1. Most popular standard sizes, 24-sheet, 30 sheet. Other sizes 3-sheet, 9-sheet. 2. Showing sold as #50 showing, #100 showing, depending upon number of boards. Number of boards in showing differs by markets. 3. Copy changeable monthly.
Painted Bulletins	Permanent structure (usually 14' x 48') on which the message is painted.	1. Placed in higher traffic locations. 2. No uniform size.	1. Individually. 2. Price individually negotiated. Bought on one- to three-year basis.	1. Illuminated. 2. Many extra construction features: clocks, oversize bottles; neonlit trademarks, etc.	1. Some uniformity in frame appearance; otherwise quite individualistic in treatment. 2. Costlier per unit than posters. 3. Usually repainted every four or six months.
Spectaculars	Special steel construction, built to order.	1. Placed in the busiest night urban locations. 2. The most costly form. 3. Each one specially fabricated. 4. The most conspicuous of all forms of outdoor advertising.	1. Individually. 2. Price of construction, rental, and maintenance individually negotiated.	1. Everything is built to order.	1. The costliest form of outdoor advertising. 2. Usually bought on a three- to five-year basis because of high cost of construction. 3. Change of copy costly.

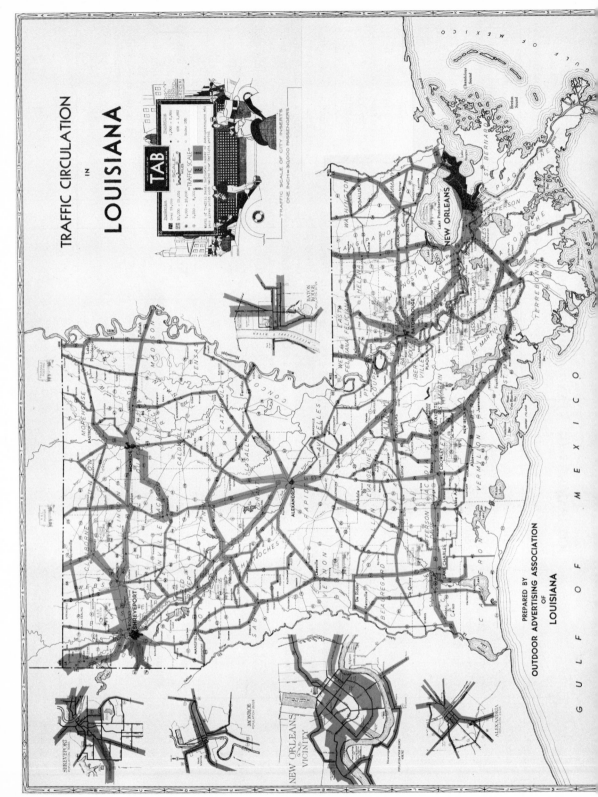

A Traffic-Flow Map

—*Type of traffic*—the slower the better. Is it all auto, or is it also pedestrian, bus, or a combination of these? Is the traffic toward the location or away from it, as on a one-way street?

—*Characteristics of placement*—angled, parallel to line of traffic, or head-on. *Angled* is easily seen as cars approach in one direction; *parallel* can be viewed by traffic traveling in both directions, but better by people sitting in the car at the near side; *head-on* is viewed by traffic approaching a location on the outside of a curve or where traffic makes a sharp turn.

—*Immediate surroundings*—Is it close to a shopping center? What competition from surrounding signs? Is it by a traffic light? Red lights give people more chance to read the sign.

—*Size and physical attractiveness of the bulletin.*

—*Price*—an area of comparative values and negotiation.

ADAPTING COPY FOR OUTDOOR ADVERTISING

The outdoor advertising of a national advertiser is usually a part of a campaign also appearing in other media. The problem is to create an effective tie-in with the total campaign theme. It is recommended that outdoor advertising contain not more than three elements:

1. *Clear product identification.* The trademark can be alone or on a package. Can it be immediately recognized? How clear is it at a distance?

2. *Large illustration size.* Size gets attention. The picture should tell the story. Colors should be bold, no pastel effects. Figures should be distinct and silhouetted. Backgrounds usually interfere with illustrations.

3. *Short copy.* The copy, if any, should be concise, the words short, the message unambiguous. Read the copy out loud. If it takes more than eight seconds, it's too long. The typography should be large. Best to use heavy sans-serif type, spaced liberally.

The great art of outdoor advertising design is simplification.

THE HIGHWAY BEAUTIFICATION ACT OF 1965

Outdoor advertising has been severely criticized by those who feel that natural scenery was made to be enjoyed by the public and not to act as a backdrop for advertising. The organized outdoor plant owners had long been withdrawing such signs, and concentrating their placements in the business and shopping centers, where permitted by zoning.

In 1965, Congress passed a Highway Beautification Act, in connection with the many highways being built with federal assistance. This law banned the erection of outdoor signs within 650 feet of the right-of-way of a highway built with such funds, but permitted such signs within that area if it is locally zoned for business and industrial use. If this law is not enforced by the state governments, their federal highway subsidies are withheld. The result has been not only a reduction in the number of signs which had already been built along Federally financed highways—the big interstate roads —but the prevention of the erection of these signs on interstate roads built since the law went into effect.

TRENDS IN OUTDOOR ADVERTISING

In 1960, $203 million was invested in outdoor advertising; in 1970, the figure was $234 million, an increase of 15 percent in dollar volume. The national advertising increased 12 percent; the local, 21 percent.[6] During this time, there was a decrease in the number of signs, and a general withdrawing to the shopping areas, which were zoned for outdoor signs and concentrated where the markets were. There is no evidence, however, to suggest that the public criticism of outdoor advertising is decreasing.

Meanwhile, the quality of the poster structures has improved. The use of painted board has increased, as have rotary showings. The big effort of the industry is to gather more definitive data about circulation, reach and frequency, and impact, and this effort promises to continue.

---

[6] See p. 121.

TRANSIT ADVERTISING

THE TERM *transit advertising* embraces all the advertising carried by buses, subways, and streetcars, as well as in their stations, on their platforms, and in their terminals. It includes advertising in commuter trains and stations, and on their platforms. The signs and displays at air terminals, too, are a part of transit advertising.

Transit advertising is a rapidly growing medium, having risen from $22 million in 1960 to $35 million in 1969—a gain of over 60 percent.[7]

Of all transit advertising, 42 percent is national, 58 percent local. Among the long-time national users of transit advertising are Procter & Gamble (47 years), Best Foods (45 years), and American Home Products (25 years). Chiefly responsible for the growth of the medium in recent years is the extensive use of the outsides of buses, the development of better displays, and the standardization of industry practices (only in recent years has the Standard Rate & Data Service included transit advertising in its reports). Also helpful in the use of the medium have been research findings about the effectiveness of transit advertising in the total advertising plans.

Bus advertising represents two separate media—that on the inside (also called *car card advertising* or *interior advertising*), and that on the outside (called *exterior advertising*). Each offers its own dimensions and values to the advertiser. Interior transit advertising represents 22 percent of the total transit dollar volume; exterior transit advertising represents 78 percent.

INTERIOR TRANSIT ADVERTISING

Features and Advantages

More than 40 million people per month ride in public transit vehicles in the United States. In markets of over one million, 46 percent of all white-collar workers and 50 percent of all blue-collar workers, 31 percent of all adults with $10,000 or more annual income, and 24 percent of all adults in households of two or more automobiles travel in public vehicles. This is aside from the teenagers and other children who ride to and from school regularly. The average length of the ride is 22 minutes, and the average rider takes 24 rides a month.[8]

---

[7] The Transit Advertising Measurement Bureau.

[8] *U.S. Transit Volume,* 1968. Transit Advertising Measurement Bureau, Inc.

This regular mass movement of people in public transit vehicles provides the following advertising opportunities:

—It is a flexible medium geographically, available in over 380 major markets. It is flexible timewise: It can be bought just on a monthly contract in the winter for cough preparations, and it can be peaked in the summer for soft drinks.

—It is a sharply definable local medium. In some markets, the advertiser has a choice of routes, from which he can choose the one that passes through the neighborhoods of the ethnic or other demographic groups he is anxious to reach, or the shopping center.

—Because of the length of the ride, the passenger has a chance to read the ads within viewing distance. Because of the number of times he goes back and forth on the same route, the different ads get a double chance of being seen, and also the advantage of frequency.

—Bus advertising can carry the theme being run in other media at the same time, magnifying the total frequency (this applies to exterior advertising too) of impression of the entire advertising effort.

—It allows for many special constructions, lighting, and color effects.

—Transportation advertising literally rides on the already-existing facilities that provide the audience, without additional circulation or programming costs—one of the chief factors of its comparatively low cost.

MONTHLY AUDIENCE COMPOSITION BY USE OF TRANSIT
AVERAGE DAY/WEEK
("A" MARKETS)

TOTAL

AVERAGE MONTH: 19,942,000 RIDERS

RIDE AVERAGE WEEK
14,223,000
71.3%
OF MONTHLY TOTAL

RIDE AVERAGE DAY
6,837,000
34.3%
OF MONTHLY TOTAL

MEN

AVERAGE MONTH: 8,444,000 RIDERS

RIDE AVERAGE WEEK
6,085,000 MEN
72.1%
OF MONTHLY TOTAL

RIDE AVERAGE DAY
3,477,000 MEN
41.2%
OF MONTHLY TOTAL

WOMEN

AVERAGE MONTH: 11,498,000 RIDERS

RIDE AVERAGE WEEK
8,138,000 WOMEN
70.8%
OF MONTHLY TOTAL

RIDE AVERAGE DAY
3,360,000 WOMEN
29.2%
OF MONTHLY TOTAL

Chart to be read: In the average week, 14,223,000 "A"-market adults ride Transit. This is 71.3% of the monthly "A" markets Transit audience. In the average day, 6,837,000 "A"-market adults ride Transit, 34.3% of the monthly total. (Data presented are the results of an electronic data processing procedure where percentages and projections derived from the base have been rounded to the nearest tenth for percentages and nearest thousand for projections.)

Courtesy, The Transit Advertising Association, Inc.

On the whole, interior transit advertising provides pleasant companionship for the traveler, with time for him to study carefully those cards within his view, and a low-cost opportunity to the advertiser to get his message before a wide audience.

Limitations and Challenges

—Transit advertising does not reach that large segment of the population that does not travel on public transportation. This number varies with the community.

—It reaches a wide nonselective audience, which may meet the needs of some advertisers, but not of those seeking a sharply defined market.

—Most travel is in the peak morning and evening rush hours. The crowded buses at those peak hours limit the opportunity and ease of reading.

Circulation

The first questions an advertiser asks of a medium are, "How many people can I reach with my message? How much will that cost me per thousand?" As the first step toward answering these questions about interior transit advertising, the industry has established a rigid system of measuring inside audience by a fare-box count, defined as "one person riding a display-carrying vehicle for one trip." The Standard Rate & Data Service, which publishes all transit-advertising information in a special edition, reports whether or not it has received certified or notarized figures from the different transit operations. All references to circulation are in terms of "estimated monthly rides." This does not mean that all riders see every card, or that they represent different people each trip. Special research facilities are available in some markets to judge how many riders saw and remembered specific advertisements.

Standard Sizes

The standard size of interior transit advertising is for the overhead racks, 11 by 28 inches, and most cards are sold in that size. (Other size units available are 11 by 42 and 11 by 56 inches.) A large unit, 21 by 22 inches, is available near the doors of many vehicles, at a premium.

Special Effects

Transit advertising offers great flexibility in the use of colors, printing processes, light, and materials, and invites ingenuity of design and construction. In some markets, signs are offered on backlighted transparencies. The Reynolds Metals Company was able to print its signs in aluminum, while Gordon's Gin had its bottle realistically reproduced on the card in three-dimensional plastics.

A special card called a *Take One* has a pad of direct-response return cards attached. The rider is invited to take one and mail it in, either for further information, or else for an application blank to join something—like the Diners' Club. These special effects entail an extra charge.

In some markets, an advertiser can rent a bus converted into a traveling showroom, to which he can invite the store buyers in a given area; this is called a *merchandising bus.*

Buying Interior Transit Space

The unit of sale of interior transit advertising is the *showing,* also referred to as a *run* or *service.* In interior transit, the word *showing* has a special meaning. A 100 showing usually means one card in each vehicle; a 50 (or *half*) showing means one card in every other vehicle; a 25 (or *quarter*) showing means one card in every fourth vehicle. Every operator specifies the number of showings in his line. The advertiser must supply the cards two weeks in advance. The cost of the cards is an important factor to consider in planning a transit budget. Contracts are made by the month, with discounts for three-, six-, and twelve-month periods. Cards can be changed monthly, without cost. Many advertisers run off extra cards for distribution as dealer displays.

A Standard Car Card

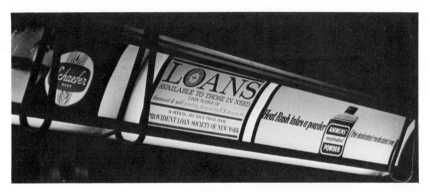

A Back-lighted Car Card

A Side-Position Car Card

An Over-the-door Car Card

Columbus—Continued

8. MECHANICAL REQUIREMENTS
Outside
Poster Requirements:

		Showing		
Size:	100	75	50	25
Queen	120	90	60	35

MECHANICAL SPECIFICATIONS
Queen Size posters should be produced on 70 or 80 lb. waterproof opaque poster paper or on 14 or 16 ply waterproof cardboard. Margin of 1-1/2" on all sides.

Inside
Card Requirements:
Full service 280; half service 140; quarter service 75.

MECHANICAL SPECIFICATIONS
Inside cards to be screened on 4- or 5-ply stock, grain horizontal.

Shipping Information
Shipping dates: To arrive prepaid at least 10 days in advance of showing date.
Ship to: Buckeye Transit Advertising, c/o The Columbus Transit Co., Cleveland Ave., Equipment Dept., 832 Cleveland Ave., Columbus, Ohio 43201.

9. MONTHLY ESTIMATED RIDES
SRDS—3/31/71
Monthly rides (12 month average)....................1,633,439

DAYTON

The City Transit Co., St. John Transportation, Miami Valley Bus Lines, D & T Bus Lines.
Operated by Rolco Advertising Co., Dayton Municipal Airport, Rm. 212, Terminal Bldg., Vandalia, Ohio 45377. Phone 513-898-1339.

1. PERSONNEL
President—Gaylord A. Gourley.
Executive Vice-Pres.—William S. O'Neill.

2. REPRESENTATIVES
Mutual Transit Sales.
New York, N. Y. 10017—230 Park Ave. Phone 212-682-9100. Telex 1-2321.
Chicago, Ill. 60611—410 N. Michigan Ave. Phone 312-467-5200. Telex 253-852.
Detroit, Mich. 48202—500 Fisher Bldg. Phone 313-874-5100. Telex 235-425.
Philadelphia, Pa. 19103—19th & Walnut Sts. Phone 215-561-5950. Telex 84-52-95.
Los Angeles 90057—2233 Beverly Blvd. Phone 213-384-3161. Telex 674-919.

3. AREAS SERVED
Dayton, Kettering, Oakwood, Shiloh, Trotwood, Brookville, Englewood, Union, Page Manor, Knollwood, Xenia, West Milton, Vandalia, Ohio.
Number of vehicles operating: 193.

4. AGENCY AND CASH DISCOUNT
Agencies 15%; cash discount 0%. Terms: Payable at the end of each month during the term aforesaid.

5. ADVERTISING RATES
Eff 4/15/70.
Outside Rates
Showing values:
100 showing—30 units.
75 showing—23 units.
50 showing—15 units.

KING SIZE POSTERS (left and right)
30" x 144":

Showing	1 mo.	3 mos.	6 mos.	12 mos.
100	1,200.00	1,140.00	1,080.00	960.00
75	920.00	874.00	828.00	736.00
50	600.00	570.00	540.00	480.00
Unit rate	40.00	38.00	36.00	32.00

HEADLIGHTS (front and rear)
11" x 42":

Showing	1 mo.	3 mos.	6 mos.	12 mos.
100	214.50	203.70	193.20	171.60
75	164.45	156.17	148.12	131.56
50	107.25	101.85	96.60	85.80
Unit rate	7.15	6.79	6.44	5.72

TRAVELING DISPLAY (left and right)
20" x 44":

Showing	1 mo.	3 mos.	6 mos.	12 mos.
100	214.50	203.70	193.20	171.60
75	164.45	156.17	148.12	131.56
50	107.25	101.85	96.60	85.80
Unit rate	7.15	6.79	6.44	5.72

TRAVELING WRAP-AROUND (TROLLEY BUSES ONLY)
(left and right rear)
Showing values:
100 showing—64 units.
75 showing—48 units.
50 showing—32 units.
25 showing—16 units.
22" x 17":

Showing	1 mo.	3 mos.	6 mos.	12 mos.
100	640.00	608.00	576.00	512.00
75	480.00	456.00	432.00	384.00
50	320.00	304.00	288.00	256.00
25	160.00	152.00	144.00	128.00
Unit rate	10.00	9.50	9.00	8.00

Inside Rates
Service values:
Full 193 vehicles.
Half 96 vehicles.
Quarter 48 vehicles.
Service:
11" x 14":
60% of 11" x 28" rate.

MECHANICAL SPECIFICATIONS
King Size and Queen Size posters must be produced on 70 or 80 lb. waterproof opaque poster paper. A margin of 1-1/2" should be allowed on all sides. For long term showings of same copy, messages may be silk screened directly on masonite for durability. Traveling Displays, Front-end and Rear-end posters must be produced on 10-ply waterproof stock, with grain running horizontally, and varnished after printing.
Inside
Card Requirements:
Full service 50; half service 25.

Shipping Information
Shipping dates: Ship cards prepaid to arrive at least 10 days in advance of showing.
Ship to: Marvin F. Davis, Rolco Advertising Co., 2027 Leo St., Dayton, Ohio 45404.

9. MONTHLY ESTIMATED RIDES
SRDS—3/31/71
Monthly rides (12 month average)............... 1,370,902

TOLEDO

TAA

Toledo Area Regional Transit Authority.
Operated by The Batchelder Co., 502 E. War Memorial Dr., Peoria, Ill. 61614. Phone 309-688-8508.

1. PERSONNEL
Regional Manager—Bruce Holland.

2. REPRESENTATIVES
Mutual Transit Sales.
New York, N. Y. 10017—230 Park Ave. Phone 212-682-9100. Telex 1-2321.
Chicago, Ill. 60611—410 N. Michigan Ave. Phone 312-467-5200. Telex 253-852.
Detroit, Mich. 48202—500 Fisher Bldg. Phone 313-874-5100. Telex 235-425.
Philadelphia, Pa. 19103—19th & Walnut Sts. Phone 215-561-5950. Telex 84-52-95.
Los Angeles 90057—2233 Beverly Blvd. Phone 213-384-3161. Telex 674-919.
Branch Offices
Covington, Ky. 41015—Rt. No. 5, Box 415. Phone 606-356-7560.
Toledo, Ohio 43610—1127 W. Central Ave. Phone 419-243-1241.

3. AREAS SERVED
Toledo, Rossford, Perrysburg, Maumee, Ottawa Hills.
Number of vehicles operating: 150.

4. AGENCY AND CASH DISCOUNT
Agencies 15%; cash discount 0%. Terms: Bills issued monthly.

5. ADVERTISING RATES
Eff 7/1/71.
Outside Rates
Showing values:
100 showing—60 units.
50 showing—30 units.
25 showing—15 units.

KING SIZE POSTERS
30" x 144":

Showing	1 mo.	3 mos.	6 mos.	12 mos.
100	2,400.00	2,280.00	2,160.00	1,920.00
50	1,380.00	1,311.00	1,242.00	1,104.00
25	750.00	712.50	675.00	600.00
Unit rate	50.00	48.00	45.00	40.00

QUEEN SIZE POSTERS
30" x 96":

Showing	1 mo.	3 mos.	6 mos.	12 mos.
100	1,680.00	1,596.00	1,512.00	1,344.00
50	945.00	897.75	850.50	756.00
Unit rate	35.00	33.25	31.50	28.00

TRAVELING DISPLAYS
22" x 42":

Showing	1 mo.	3 mos.	6 mos.	12 mos.
100	600.00	570.00	540.00	480.00
50	300.00	285.00	270.00	240.00
Unit rate	10.00	9.50	9.00	8.00

21" x 72" (Rear):
22.00 per space per month on firm 12 months contract only.
21" x 36" (Front):
12.00 per space per month on firm 12 months contract only.

Inside Rates
Service values:
Full 140 vehicles.
Half 70 vehicles.
Quarter 35 vehicles.
Service:
11" x 28":

	1 mo.	3 mos.	6 mos.	12 mos.
Full	315.00	299.25	283.50	252.00
Half	157.50	149.50	141.75	126.00
Quarter	78.75	74.75	70.75	63.00

11" x 56":

	1 mo.	3 mos.	6 mos.	12 mos.
Full	469.00	445.55	422.10	375.20
Half	243.50	231.25	219.15	194.80
Quarter	117.25	111.25	105.50	93.80

Special Transit Advertising Promotions
Take-One charges per month: .50 per card, non-commissionable.
Kleen-Tear Service: .35 per card monthly charge, non-commissionable.

Extract of a page of rates for outside bus posters from Transportation Section of the Standard Rate & Data Service. All rate cards are given in full, in standardized numerical sequence for each medium.

Courtesy, S.R.D.S.

EXTERIOR TRANSIT ADVERTISING

The chief form of exterior transit advertising is that carried on the outside of buses. They pass through the neighborhoods where people live, shop, work. They provide great reach for any message. In larger cities, the advertiser can select the routes that best reach the demographic group he seeks. These signs are virtual traveling outdoor signs, reaching pedestrians at eye level and telling their stories to riders of passing cars, even to the riders of other buses. They reach many who never travel inside the bus, and reach out to a wide unselected audience at a low cost per thousand.

How Exterior Bus Space is Sold

The sizes of space units in most widespread use are the following:

King Size	30″ x 144″	(for side of bus)
Queen Size	30″ x 88″	"
Traveling Display	21″ x 72″	"
Taillight Spectacular	21″ x 72″	(for rear of bus)
Headlights	17″ x 21″	(in front)
	21″ x 44″	

Of those above, the *King Size, Traveling Display Size,* and *Headlights signs* are most widely used.

A handful of lines also offer a *Bus-O-Rama* sign, a fully colored backlighted, transparency roof sign, running the length of the bus, 21⅜ by 144¾ inches.

Space is sold usually by the showing, or by the unit, by the month, with time discounts at the three- six- and twelve-month levels. *Showing* in outside bus advertising has a meaning different from that for interior bus

Exterior Bus

advertising. It is an arbitrary number of units that the line operator sets. The usual 100 showing in the largest cities is 400 units. This goes down to 25 units in the smaller cities. Based on this figure, proportionately there are also 75, 50, and 25 showings, which are sometimes called *full service, half service,* and *quarter service* (just to bewilder the beginner, no doubt).

How transit rates are quoted. The rates for the outside of buses are published in the Standard Rate & Data Service. The rate card covers:

—the average monthly rides (twelve-month average)

—the sizes and number of units for different sizes (King, Queen)

—whether for left side, right side, or both

—the number of units in a 100 or other showing. Sometimes the rates are just quoted by number of units.

—the cost per month at rates from one to twelve months

For example, here are how the rates for a King Size Display 30" by 144" are quoted in different cities:

Long Beach, California:
    No. of rides—twelve-month average, 937,997
    Position—left only
    Quantity—quoted by units 20–50
    Basis of charging—number of units
    Costs—20 units–$23 per unit for one month

Indianapolis:
    Number of rides—twelve-month average, 1,755,448
    Position (right & left)
    Quantity of units—100 showing = 80 units
    Basis of charging—By showing
    Cost—100 showing (80 units) $3,200 for one month

Baltimore:
    Number of rides—twelve-month average, 9,851,240
    Position—both sides
    Quantity of units—100 showing = 120 units
    Cost—$4,800 for one month

In most larger cities the cost for a King Size outside poster averages around $40 per display per month on a 100 showing basis, and $20 to $30 in smaller ones, subject to lower rates for longer contracts.[9]

The Basic Bus

The basic bus represents one of the newer developments in bus advertising, whereby one advertiser can buy all the cards inside a bus. He can

---

[9] Source: Standard Rate & Data Service, November 1972.

use it for one product, or for his line of products. He can have a long display covering several of the display panels, for variety. This means that for the duration of the bus ride—about 22 minutes, on the average—the rider is surrounded by the massive presentation of one advertiser.

An advertiser gets the exclusive run of basic advertising as against competitors for the duration of the contract run. The cost per bus is low, but the order is usually based on a large number of buses.

An advertiser can also buy all the advertising space on the exterior of a bus—front, back, sides, and top. This is called a *total bus*. This too is on an exclusive basis per industry. Elgin Industries, Inc., scheduled 800 total buses in Chicago, Los Angeles, and New York, for a one-month preholiday campaign for its watches, sailboats, hi-fi sets, and washing machines, exposing their entire line to riders who were not aware of its diversity of products. If the advertiser combines a basic-bus buy with a total-bus buy, he is said to have bought a *total total bus*. You can't buy more on a bus than that.

Basic buses are not available in all cities, but the number of cities no doubt will increase.

Station and Platform Posters

Poster space is available on the walls of many bus, subway, and train stations. Since the passenger has time to read while waiting for his transportation, there is opportunity to have more copy on these posters read. Since suburbanites visit the stations regularly, there is more opportunity for frequency.

The posters here are of standard sizes, of which the *one sheet* (30 inches high by 46 inches wide) and the *two sheet* (60 by 46 inches) are most common. There is also a *three sheet* (90 by 46 inches).

The New York subways—the largest users of station posters—are reducing the number of one-sheet posters, replacing them with a fewer number of two-sheet posters, reducing the clutter, and improving the quality of the frames. This wider two-sheet poster permits the adaptation of art work from television and magazine advertising, providing continuity to the advertising.

The Basic Bus

Displays in Grand Central Station in New York City

In the sale of station and platform advertising, the number of posters is identified in terms of showings, but here they speak of them as *intensive showings, representative showings,* and *minimum showings*. In each instance, the plant operator announces how many posters are involved in each bracket.

Trains and Air Terminals

One sector of the transit advertising industry specializes in commuter trains and train terminals. There are such train stations in about 50 cities, serving over 400 communities.

In New York, Philadelphia, and Chicago, two out of three executives commute from home to office by train. The level of affluence of commuters is higher than that of riders in subways and buses. The average length of rides is 44 minutes; usually passengers have seats and plenty of opportunity to see the signs in the trains, and on the stations while waiting for the trains. There is also the advantage of frequency of exposure of the signs.

Airports and terminals provide another opportunity for reaching a special audience. Eighty-six percent of all flights are for business trips by executives, business men, or professionals. And to the airports come not only those who are flying, but those who want to see them off or await their arrival.

A characteristic of major train and airline terminals is the variety of advertising forms available to the advertiser: floor exhibits, two-sheet posters, dioramas (three-dimensional scenes), island showcases, illuminated signs, and clocks. If ever you find yourself in an air terminal with time on your hands (that does happen), you can make good use of it by seeing how many different forms of advertising you can spot.

TRENDS IN TRANSIT ADVERTISING

In 1960, $22 million was spent in transit advertising. In 1969, the figure was $35 million, an increase of 61 percent.[10] During this time, the industry

---

[10] Transit Advertising Association, 1971.

established a firm base for figuring circulation and attained continuing recognition as a standard advertising medium by its special section of the Standard Rate & Data Service.

The basic bus made its appearance. The full use of the interior and exterior of a bus by an advertiser will become increasingly popular.

New transit systems, like the BART (Bay Area Rapid Transit) system in San Francisco and the Washington, D.C., subway system, will increase the total audience exposed to transit advertising, as will the increase in riders on the present public transportation routes. There is increasing pressure on the government to put more funds into mass transportation efforts.

Continued progress will be made to give the advertiser more definitive information about the effectiveness of transit advertising in delivering its messages to riders.

There will be an increase in the use of transit advertising in connection with other media being used within a market.

Review Questions

1. What are the major advantages and limitations of outdoor advertising?

2. What is meant by:
   a. 24-sheet poster
   b. #100 showing (outdoor)
   c. rotary plan
   d. plant owner
   e. riding a showing

3. Identify the three main forms of outdoor advertising and describe their distinguishing characteristics.

4. How did the 24-sheet poster get its name? What is its size?

5. How is outdoor advertising circulation computed?

6. What considerations besides circulation should enter the advertiser's decision to buy a particular location?

7. Discuss the three main copy considerations involved in developing outdoor advertising.

8. What is a full showing, and a half showing, in interior bus advertising?

9. What are the major advantages and limitations of transit advertising?

10. Define interior and exterior transit advertising, and describe their relative share of transit advertising volume.

11. How is interior transit advertising circulation computed?

12. What is the "basic bus"?

13. At a nearby bus, train, subway, or air terminal, list the variety of advertising forms available to advertisers.

Reading Suggestions

Barton, Roger, *The Handbook of Advertising Management.* New York: McGraw-Hill, 1970.

Houck, John, ed., *Outdoor Advertising: History and Regulation.* Notre Dame, Ind.: University of Notre Dame Press, 1969.

Litka, Michael P., "Aesthetic Standards and the Regulation of Outdoor Advertising," *Business Perspectives,* Fall 1968, pp. 17–21.

Media Decisions, "Outdoor: It's Full of Surprises," September 1970, p. 40.

12

Supplementary Media

THERE ARE A NUMBER of supplementary media that may prove useful in rounding out an advertising campaign. True to the meaning of the word "supplementary," they serve to "reinforce and extend the whole." Among the forms of such advertising are specialty advertising, films, directories, and programs. Often the use of such media overlaps the efforts of the sales and public relations department, but since the materials used are forms of advertising, we include them in our media discussion.

ADVERTISING SPECIALTIES

An advertising specialty is a useful object bearing the advertiser's name or message, given to a carefully defined audience as a goodwill offering, without any cost or obligation to the recipient. The category includes calendars, pens, matchbooks, memo books, key rings, can openers, bottle openers, measuring cups, shop aprons, shopping bags, golf balls, car windshield scrapers . . . anyone who tries to make a fuller list will be prepared to accept the industry statement that there are 10,000 advertising specialties.

An advertising specialty differs from a premium in that a premium requires a proof of purchase, often accompanied by a charge. There is no limit to the amount charged for a premium. The advertiser's name, as a rule, does not appear on the premium, which is a merchandising inducement rather than an advertising medium. An advertising specialty is an advertising medium; it carries a name and/or a message; it is given free; it is usually quite inexpensive. Few reach the $4 maximum allowed by law as not subject to the business gift tax rules. The great advantages of the specialty are that it is a useful goodwill gift, and that it keeps the advertiser's name before the recipient for a long time.

Limitations of the advertising specialty are the shortness of the message it can deliver, and the problem of getting it into the right hands. Advertising specialties are not a substitute for advertising in the mass media; each of these serves different functions.

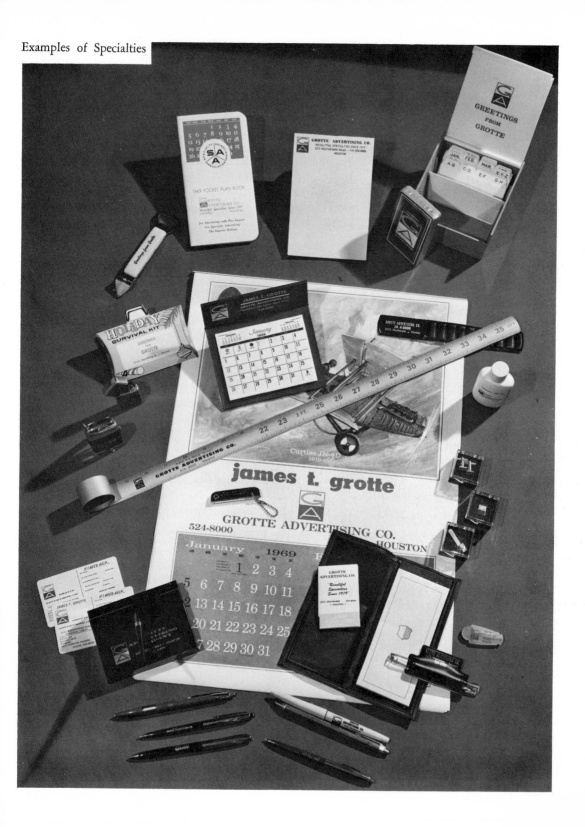

Forms of Specialties

Calendars. One of the oldest and most widely used forms of specialty is the calendar, and we give them this special mention. Gaw reports surveys showing that 75 percent of all calendars produced are kept by the recipients. One firm, making a special study, found 87 percent of the homes to which it had distributed the calendar had kept them on the walls. One company, which had distributed 250 calendars with a reorder page attached to each, received 248 unsolicited requests for calendars the following year.[3]

Writing instruments. The second largest class of specialties sold are writing instruments for office, home, and pocket. The flow of ballpoint pens seems endless, but how many are resting unused and unusable in desk drawers we'll never know. Nevertheless they are popular.

Matchbooks. Matchbooks continue to be a highly popular form of advertising, especially for restaurants and hotels. Matchbooks come in different sizes and forms, to give distinctiveness. We have a particularly apt use of matchbooks in the case of the Phifer Wire Products Corporation soon to be discussed.

A personal test. Here's something interesting. Make a list of every specialty you have on your person, in your study, office, home, or car. Put down first the number you think you have. Compare it with the final number.

The Distribution of Specialties

The industry is divided into supplier, distributor, and direct selling houses.

A *supplier* manufactures, imports, converts, imprints, or otherwise processes advertising specialties, calendars, or business gifts for sale through specialty-advertising distributors.

The man who buys from the supplier and sells to the user is technically the *distributor.* Actually he is better known as a *specialty advertising counsellor,* for he acts not only as a distributor for suppliers, but as counsel on the promotion or campaign, providing the ideas and the copy, as well as the items.

A *direct selling house* combines the functions of supplier and distributor within one organization. It primarily manufactures its own products and sells them directly to advertisers through its own sales force. Many firms handling specialty advertising also handle business gifts not bearing the advertiser's name, but sometimes the name or initials of the recipients; also merchandise suitable as incentive prizes for salesmen and distributors.

---

[3] Walter A. Gaw, *Specialty Advertising,* 2nd ed., Specialty Advertising Association, 1970.

The Use of Specialties

Specialties may well be considered when there is a specific and limited group of people whose goodwill you wish to incur and develop. It may be a defined group of prospective customers, it may be present customers, it may be those in a position to influence important sales—like architects, physicians, and certain corporate officials. The use of the specialty should be part of an organized plan for reaching these defined audiences.

Specialties are widely used by local stores and institutions for specific periods of time to reach specified audiences. They are used by national advertisers to reach distributors and salesmen. They are used by industrial advertisers to reach those who are in the decision-making area involving the selection of their equipment. They are used by advertisers to commemorate some important events, such as a significant anniversary, the launching of a new model, or the opening of a new branch.

The qualities desired of a specialty are that it be useful, durable, used often, and if possible unique and apropos. If it is easily mailable, so much the better.

The following guidelines for an effective specialty promotion are recommended by the Specialty Advertising Association:

1. Define the objectives—know what the program is expected to accomplish.
2. Identify the target audience.
3. Develop a suitable distribution plan.
4. Choose an advertising theme that will reflect the product or service being offered.
5. Develop a message to support the theme.
6. Select the specialty advertising article, preferably one that bears a natural relationship to the product, service, or advertising theme.[1]

The advertiser can distribute his specialty in a number of ways: He can hand it out directly, as might a bank giving calendars to its depositors. He can mail it along with a letter, which may get more attention because of the gift. National advertisers usually distribute their specialty through the sales departments, in conjunction with an advertising campaign or promotion taking place at that time. They may distribute the specialty to the wholesaler for distribution to his customers. This is often done on a cooperative basis, which not only reduces the cost to the advertiser but, more important, enlists the vigilance of the wholesaler in seeing that the gifts are not wasted. Handing

---

[1] Specialty Advertising Association, 1971 reports.

out an inexpensive gift is standard practice at most business conventions and trade shows.

In each instance, the distribution of a specialty is to a preselected target audience. The biggest problem in the use of specialties is controlling the distribution and checking the results.

Some Cases in the Use of Specialties

Perhaps the quickest way to get an insight into the effective use of specialties is to cite some cases from the group of prize winners at an annual competition of the Specialty Advertising Association: [2]

Gateway National Bank, Fort Worth, Texas

PURPOSE: To increase traffic and generate new accounts by acquainting newcomers to the area with the bank.

SOLUTION: Managers of apartment complexes were called on by a bank officer with coaster sets in cellophane for distribution to new tenants, together with a letter of welcome to the bank.

RESULTS: Deposits increased approximately 30 percent during campaign.

---

[2] Courtesy Specialty Advertising Association.

PURPOSE: To increase sales of the company's cutting fluid and grinding wheels.

SOLUTION: As an annual promotion, Cincinnati Milling offered its distributor salesmen a complete specialty advertising program—on a cooperative cost basis—for quantity distribution to customers and prospects. Advertising specialties included in the program were a golf tee pack, ice scraper, bottle opener with plastic caps, ballpoint pen, and mechanical pencil; all were provided with the corporate advertising message as well as the imprint of the local distributor.

RESULTS: Cincinnati Milling was very pleased with the program. Distributors participated heavily and advertising specialties bearing the company message received especially widespread distribution.

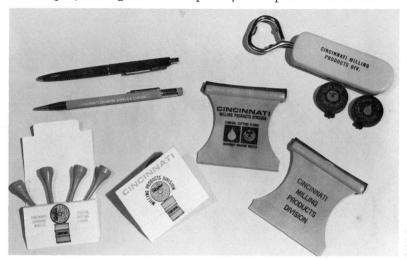

Trans World Airlines, Inc.

PURPOSE: To increase awareness, in the commercial travel market, of the worldwide points served by TWA.

SOLUTION: The target audience consisted of executive secretaries, who are in a position to influence the travel plans of top executives for whom they book travel arrangements. Secretaries received, first, a charm bracelet with one charm attached. Succeeding mailings each included a charm depicting a different faraway location. Each charm was accompanied by a letter.

RESULTS: A marked increase in commercial boardings by executives whose secretaries received the mailing. TWA representatives who made follow-up calls enjoyed excellent receptions.

Phifer Wire Products, Inc.

PURPOSE: To develop customers for a new aluminum insect solar screening.

SOLUTION: To selected window screen fabricators went a test mailing of giant matchbooks and a personal letter. The Sun Screen story was spelled out on the matchbook cover, and specific features of the product were outlined on the oversized individual matches. A swatch of the screening was inserted behind the rows of matches, and fabricators were invited to light a match, hold it behind the screening and see for themselves how the product blocked out glare without obstructing the view.

RESULTS: None of the 250 prospective fabricator customers had ever been approached by the company before. Of these, 83 ordered test rolls, 67 of whom later placed substantial repeat orders. The company attributed sales of more than $100,000 to the promotion.

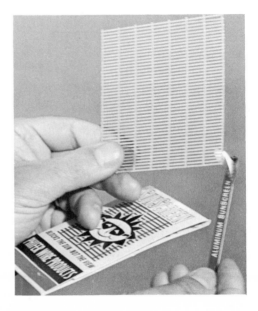

Many companies use films to good advantage in getting different aspects of their story to various markets.

We have films sponsored by advertisers that are of sufficient interest to be run as shorts between features at movie houses; these are called *theatrical films*. We have other films designed to be shown before selected groups; these are broadly referred to as *sponsored films*. If prepared to be shown before business, technical, or professional groups, they are called *business films*.

Theatrical Films

About 12,000 theaters in the United States, both "hardtops" and drive-ins, show advertisers' shorts between their features.

These showings provide an advertiser with a mass audience in selected territories. Their length is usually ten minutes or less. A single print can reach an average audience of 50,000 viewers annually; a single print is good for three to four years, with a total potential viewing in its lifetime of 1,500,000 to 2,000,000 people. Advertisers order between 20 and 200 prints of a picture.

To be acceptable in film houses, the film must be entertaining, without commercials in the TV sense, and with high pictorial quality. The favorite pictures are sports and travel, in which the role of the advertiser's product can be naturally but not obtrusively shown.

Theater film procedure. When embarking on a film operation, the advertiser will select one of the many film producers specializing in producing sponsored films. Most of them are located in the large metropolitan centers—especially Los Angeles, Chicago, and New York. These firms will prepare the script, shoot the picture, and make the necessary prints. The advertiser will then turn his film over to a film distributor. In the case of theater films, these distributors work through the various film exchanges through which all motion pictures are exclusively distributed to movie houses. The costs per booking depend upon the length of the film, and are billed at the end of the month, when the advertiser receives a report of the theaters where his film was shown, and their attendance.

Sponsored Films

Millions of children have seen a ten-minute, colored, animated Disney cartoon, *How to Catch a Cold,* dramatizing ways of preventing a cold. The movie was sponsored by the makers of Kleenex tissues, supplementing their regular advertising program with an educational goodwill selling message.

"THE VIEWING MILLIONS"

are seeing such films as these (promoted, serviced and distributed by Association Films):

"FIRESTONE FILM LIBRARY"

Sponsor: The Firestone Tire & Rubber Company
Films in Release: 10
Period of Distribution: 29 months average per subject
16mm showings: 118,407
16mm audience: 6,795,790
Telecasts: 1,546
TV Audience: 98,027,366

"UNCLE JIM'S DAIRY FARM"

Sponsor: National Dairy Council
Period of Distribution: 10 years
16mm showings: 35,301
16mm audience: 3,935,499
Telecasts: 562
TV Audience: 49,977,314

"THE KING WHO CAME TO BREAKFAST"

Sponsor: National Biscuit Company
Period of Distribution: 9 years
16mm showings: 88,635
16mm audience: 7,102,643
Telecasts: 927
TV Audience: 69,361,685

"YOUR SAFETY FIRST"

Sponsor: Automobile Manufacturers Association
Period of Distribution: 2 years 10 months
16mm showings: 15,152
16mm audience: 928,505
Telecasts: 415
TV Audience: 31,615,654

"WASHINGTON —SHRINE OF AMERICAN PATRIOTISM"

Sponsor: Baltimore and Ohio Railroad
Period of Distribution: 10 years 9 months
16mm showings: 64,784
16mm audience: 4,796,224
Telecasts: 558
TV Audience: 50,226,724

"THE LIVING CIRCLE"

Sponsor: United Fruit Company
Period of Distribution: 3 years 7 months
16mm showings: 24,310
16mm audience: 1,598,786
Telecasts: 497
TV Audience: 38,594,037

Non-Theatrical Films

This film is typical of 150,000 other sponsored business films—for example, *Athletic Injuries—Their Prevention and Care,* issued by the Kendall Company; *Beauty in the Making,* issued by Avon Products; and *Jet Freighters Move at Night,* issued by American Airlines—that are free for group showing. Such films are known as sponsored films (as distinguished from the theatrical films previously discussed). They are also called *business films.*

The essence of a good sponsored film is that it be educational and otherwise interesting, that it not attempt to compete with films that just entertain, nor, on the other hand, rely on merely a "trip through the factory."

Sponsored film procedure. As in the case of the theater film, the advertiser is responsible for having his film produced, and he can do this through the professional film-producing houses. For the distribution and showing of his film, he can turn to one of the film-distributing houses. These firms have built up extensive lists of groups who are receptive to showing sponsored films to round out their programming needs. From their lists, the advertiser can select groups that meet the demographic audience he is trying to reach. The distributing firm handles all the details, such as arranging for the booking, physically getting the film into the right hands, providing publicity material to help the program chairman get the crowd out, checking performance, and billing. The charge for this service is a fixed fee per showing.

To give an idea of how comprehensive and resourceful film distributors are in finding audiences for the advertiser's film, we quote from the report of the Modern Talking Picture Service, Inc., one of the large firms in the field:

The community audience

This is the primary audience for sponsored films. It includes clubs, churches, men's service clubs, women's clubs, fraternal societies, and other community clubs that bring people together; in fact any audience that owns or has access to a 16-mm. sound projector. The audiences are receptive, because they ask for films of particular interest to them (from an extensive catalog).

The airport audience

In major airports throughout the country, we operate free movie lounges for waiting travelers. About half the viewers see three or more sponsored pictures while they are waiting.

The resort audience

During summer months, sponsors can reach affluent vacationing families through a special distributing operation that serves over 1,500 resorts, with a different sponsored film each night.

The television audience

Almost all TV stations use sponsored films. Though not all films are suitable, those that are reach millions of viewers with their message.

Sixteen percent of the films are shown during evening hours. Most daytime films are shown weekends.

The college audience

We have created a network of free campus movie lounges to reach 3 million college viewers a year.

Videotape audience

This consists primarily of high schools, colleges, business organizations, medical groups that have access to video playback machines.[4]

The charges for distributing films are a fixed fee per booking or showing. The initial cost of a film is high, not only in direct expense, but in the time it takes to go through the meetings with different company officials to clear all technical and policy questions. Furthermore, films are for firms that wish to venture with a part of their budget on paths other than the straight dollar competition in the mass media. Films can be a valuable supplementary medium.

CONSUMER DIRECTORIES—THE YELLOW PAGES DIRECTORY

The Yellow Pages telephone directory is a unique institution in advertising. It is published in over 5,000 cities; it is published also all over the world. An advertiser can specify the exact territory he wants to reach. The directory is a separate volume in the larger cities, and a part of the white-page directory in smaller sections. It is published in uniform type style and size throughout the world. It is widely used by local merchants and service organizations. It is extensively used by national advertisers in connection with a "Where to buy it" listing, giving the names of their dealers; often this is a cooperative deal, or they may list their own branch offices or factory service branches. The system provides uniform control by the advertiser of the distributors' listings in the county. National advertisers of products that are bought in showrooms, or on home or office demonstration, frequently say in their ads, "See Yellow Pages for nearest dealer."

The Yellow Pages has its own extensive rate book. Rates are quoted by the month, and billed annually. A national advertiser can place all his business on a one-order basis.

PROGRAMS

Advertisers may reach target audiences for their product through the programs of the events they attend—sports events, plays, concerts, the opera.

---

[4] Courtesy, Modern Talking Picture Service, Inc.

For example, an advertiser can reach most theatergoers in New York City through *Playbill,* a miniature magazine issued with the particular program and notes relating to each theater, and dependably operated.

Programs may be effective for products that are already well known. Their cost per thousand must be compared to alternate media for reaching the same audience. Their cost per thousand is usually high; the homogeneity of the audience may be worth it. A problem in the use of most programs is that of verifying circulation.

. . . . AND OTHER FORMS OF SUPPLEMENTARY MEDIA

In addition to the media discussed here, there are other forms of communication—shopping bags, shirt boards, movable lighted signs projected on the sides of buildings, textbook covers and ads inside notebooks, skywriting, and whatever other ways the ingenuity of man develops for delivering an advertising message. The important points to keep in mind at all times about the media are that their use should begin with a plan; yardsticks should be established for determining the value of any of them; steps should be taken to assure receiving the circulation, distribution, or audience for which one is paying; goals should be established as to what is expected; and procedures should be established for appraising the results.

Review Questions

1. What is an advertising specialty? How does it differ from premiums?

2. What are the major uses and limitations of specialty advertising?

3. Discuss several ways in which an advertiser may distribute a specialty advertising article.

4. List the specialties in your own possession, on your person, in your room, or at home.

5. Define and explain the differences between theatrical and sponsored (or business) films.

6. What are some of the major audiences for sponsored films?

Reading Suggestions

Anny, "A Premium User's Nightmare," May 10, 1968. Also in Kleppner and Settel, *Exploring Advertising,* p. 258.

Gaw, Walter A., *Specialty Advertising,* 2nd edition. Chicago: Specialty Advertising Association, 1970.

Herpel, George L., and R. A. Collins, *Specialty Advertising in Marketing.* Homewood, Ill., Dow Jones-Irwin, 1972.

IV
CREATING
THE ADVERTISING

13

The Behavioral Sciences
in Advertising

DRIVING ON A HIGHWAY overlooking the modest-sized backyards of a ten-year-old development of middle-class homes, one is struck first by the similarity of the houses and lots. But a second and third look are more illuminating. For behind the similarity in size and shape of the backyards lie differences, differences that reflect the individual interests, personalities, and family situations of those who live in the homes. One backyard, for example, has been transformed into a carefully manicured garden. Another includes some shrubs and bushes, but most of the yard serves as a relaxation area, with outdoor barbecue equipment and the like. A third yard is almost entirely a playground, with swings, trapezes, and slides. A swimming pool occupies almost all the space in another yard. Still another has simply been allowed to go to seed, and is overgrown and untended by its obviously indoor-oriented owners.

If you wanted to advertise to this community of people, you would be speaking to people with different interests, different tastes. The study of these differences among people is where the behavioral sciences make their contribution to advertising.

WHAT ARE THE BEHAVIORAL SCIENCES?

The decision of someone to buy a product is the end effect of many influences. Some of these may reach back to his cultural heritage (as might his food preferences). The study of man's cultural heritage is the province of the *anthropologist*. A man's decision may have been shaped by "the right thing to do" among his friends (see how alike they are in dress). The study of man as part of a group is the field of the *sociologist*. A man's action may be a direct result of his own goals and desires (as in buying a particular car). Man's reaction to his drives is the *psychologist*'s zone of study. These disciplines often overlap, but they are all part of the behavioral sciences. The field of consumer behavior represents the coming together of all the behavioral sciences in the study of how and why we buy as we do. In addition to reviewing the contributions of these disciplines, we shall look at some other approaches to understanding and explaining consumer behavior. We do not presume to offer a comprehensive survey of the behavioral sciences, nor do we venture to join a discussion as to where to draw lines among them. We merely touch upon some highlights of these fields to show their relevance and usefulness to advertising.

ANTHROPOLOGY AND ADVERTISING

When one says "anthropology," the first thing that comes to most people's minds is the study of primitive societies. But anthropologists study the cultures of *all* societies, and from their work they have found certain needs and activities that are common to man wherever he is. One such list includes 73 items, among them bodily adornment, cooking, courtship, food taboos, gift giving, language, marriage, status, sex, and superstition.[1] Each society attaches its own values and traditions to such considerations. In some societies, to this day the marriages are arranged by parents.

The anthropologist sees the United States as a pluralistic society made up of an array of subcultures, each representing a different way a group of people live and the values, customs, and traditions its members have in common. That some 500 radio stations broadcast programs in 50 languages bears witness to the strength of cultural identification in the United States. Every man is born into a society and is taught its culture. It has a permanent influence on him, even if he moves into another culture.

Anthropologists make major contributions to advertising through their study of the distinctive living patterns of cultural groups and subgroups. Ethnic, religious, and racial subgroups all have their identities. These can affect food preferences, language, customs, styles of dress, roles of men and women—all of which may in turn affect the advertiser.

A major exploration of comparative household expenditures by black and white families showed some distinct differences, amounting to 6.6 percent of all spending. For example, black families spent more on clothing, personal-care products, household furnishings, and alcoholic beverages than did whites. The pattern suggested by the researchers was that black families spend more than do comparable white families on maintaining appearances and immediate gratification.[2]

Some ethnic groups prefer highly spiced foods (like Polish or Italian sausage) or distinctively flavored foods (such as Louisianan chicory-flavored

---

[1] George Peter Murdock, "The Common Denominator of Cultures," in *The Science of Man in the World Crisis,* ed. Ralph Linton (New York: Columbia University Press, 1945), pp. 123–42.

[2] Raymond A. Bauer and Scott M. Cunningham, *Studies in the Negro Market* (Cambridge, Mass.: Marketing Science Institute, 1970), p. 22.

Does an Italian wine go with Noël, La Navidad, Hanukkah and Weihnachten?

Bolla does.

It has a gift for celebration.

A handsome wooden-rack filled with 6 bottles of delightful Bolla wine imported from Italy.* About $20. Feel free to give the Bolla Gift Selection to anyone, any time. It will be the nicest compliment a holiday ever had. No matter what language you feast in.

Bolla
Gift Selection

*2 bottles each of Soave and Bardolino, 1 each Valpolicella and Rosé.

ANTHROPOLOGY IN ADVERTISING

An advertisement which recognizes that people have different cultural backgrounds.

coffee). Indeed, many dishes favored in certain parts of the country are a direct identification of people in that area with their cultural past. Pennsylvania Dutch cookery, with its fastnachts and shoofly pie, has its roots mainly in the valley of the Rhine. In North Carolina, the serving of lovefeasts (sugar cake, Christmas cookies, and large white mugs of coffee) is its Moravian (Czechoslovakian) heritage, while in Rhode Island, tourtiere (meat pie) reflects the French-Canadian influence. We have Cornish pasties (meat and vegetable pie) in Michigan, the Norwegian julekake in North Dakota, and Swedish kaldomar (cabbage rolls) in Illinois. The heavy influence of Mexico is revealed in the tamale pie and other Mexican-style foods of southern California and the Southwest.

There are regional variations in the American language, too. For example, creamed cottage cheese is known as *schmierkase* around Cincinnati, while what is cottage cheese to most Americans is *cream cheese* in New Orleans. A *snap bean* in Virginia is a stringbean elsewhere; *salad* in Virginia means kale and spinach, which are called *greens* in other parts of the country. In Kentucky, green or regular garden peas are called *English peas,* while mashed or whipped potatoes are called *creamed potatoes.* When citizens of Indiana speak of *mangoes,* they refer to sweet green peppers. In Key West, evaporated milk is referred to as *cream,* and sweetened condensed milk is *milk.* Pancakes in Texas are called *battercakes,* while cakes are known as *sweetbreads.*

Milestones of life. There are certain points in everyone's life when he passes from one stage of life to another, such as coming of age and marriage. In any society these are deeply significant times. In our society, these milestones usually have products associated with them as symbols. For example, a girl's becoming a young woman (her first bra or high-heel shoes), a child's going off to school (new clothes or first lunchbox), one's marriage (bridal gifts), one's first child (baby gifts or family insurance).

An advertiser of "training bras" would be interested in knowing about the product's meaning as a symbol of "growing up" to both daughter and mother. This in turn might affect the extent to which the advertising would be oriented to the daughter herself ("now you're growing up"), to the mother as a mother ("when a daughter needs her mother"), or to the mother as the girl she once was ("remember when"). Likewise, the appearance of facial hair is part of a boy's coming of age. His first razor or shaver is usually a big event for him as well as for his father. Insights help make clear the symbolism of such events and help make it easier to understand the deeper meaning of products associated with them.

The roles played by the sexes. In different cultures and in different eras, the sexes may play different roles; this is another area of anthropological study that is relevant to advertising. Winick gives a Canadian example from

The Changing Role of Women

The phone company wants more installers like Alana MacFarlane.

Alana MacFarlane is a 20-year-old from San Rafael, California. She's one of our first women telephone installers. She won't be the last.

We also have several hundred male telephone operators. And a policy that there are no all-male or all-female jobs at the phone company.

We want the men and women of the telephone company to do what they want to do, and do best.

For example, Alana likes working outdoors. "I don't go for office routine," she said. "But as an installer, I get plenty of variety and a chance to move around."

Some people like to work with their hands, or, like Alana, get a kick out of working 20 feet up in the air.

Others like to drive trucks. Some we're helping to develop into good managers.

Today, when openings exist, local Bell Companies are offering applicants and present employees some jobs they may never have thought about before. We want to help all advance to the best of their abilities.

AT&T and your local Bell Company are equal opportunity employers.

the experience of an advertiser trying to address the French-Canadian house-wife. The advertisement showed a woman in shorts playing golf with her husband. Winick points out that in the French-Canadian culture the wife would not be wearing shorts and would not be playing golf with her husband.[3]

The changing roles of women and men in the United States—particularly in the work force—are reflected in the AT&T advertisement above. "Woman's work" at the telephone company had traditionally been regarded as chiefly sitting at switchboards. Now not only do women act as installers, but the telephone company reports that it also has several hundred male switchboard operators. All this reflects a basic cultural change in our society. Anthropology helps sharpen our insights into such changes taking place around us.

---

[3] Charles Winick, "Anthropology's Contributions to Marketing," *Journal of Marketing,* July 1961, pp. 53–60.

Society's changing values.   Another example of how society's chang-ing values and cultural norms can affect advertising is our attitude toward *debt,* important to firms selling products with large price tags and to companies making loans to consumers.

For many years after the depression of the 1930's, most Americans believed that personal debt for product purchases was something to work one's way out of, that to pay off one's installment bills and to be free of debt was an important goal. The only long-term debt viewed as "normal" was a home mortgage. This attitude toward debt persists in the seventies with many families. However, many other families, particularly among younger Ameri-cans, look upon such debt differently. For them, installment debt has become part of their way of life—not just for home mortgages, but for cars, appli-ances, home furnishings, vacations, and the like. (An interesting reflection of the traditional attitude is linguistic: the German word for debt is the same as that for "guilt"!) Household Finance Company tries to link its advertising for consumer-loan services to the older tradition: "Never borrow needlessly" is part of their basic message.

SOCIOLOGY AND ADVERTISING

The sociologist views man in relation to others. He observes man's identifica-tion with a group—its influence on him, and his on it. Whenever a consumer asks himself, "What will *they* think?" he is behaving according to one or more reference groups. These "reference groups" can be face-to-face groups (friends, family) or impersonal groups with which an individual may identify himself. For example: An Oldsmobile television commercial serenaded a happy man riding about town in his new car with the theme, "If your friends could see you now." A *Wall Street Journal* ad for a major Southern utility company asked and answered:

> What do a Boston banker, a New Orleans bottler, a California in-surance executive, and planters from Arkansas and Mississippi all talk about when they get together? Middle South Utilities in the year 2000.

Social class and stratification.   One characteristic of an industrial so-ciety such as that of the United States is that it is clustered into many classes. The standards around which these classes form may be wealth, income, occu-pation, achievement, or learning, among others. Each person senses where he fits into this pattern; he identifies himself with others in his class ("these are my kind of people") and generally conforms to its standards.

An understanding of social-class structure helps explain why data on income, occupation, and other demographic categories sometimes fail to provide meaningful insights into consumer characteristics. For example, a

SOCIOLOGY IN ADVERTISING

An advertisement based upon the drive to be identified with a group.

young professional and his working wife may have the same family income as a senior factory foreman—but their interests in products will be worlds apart. Martineau points out that a rich man is not simply a poor man with more money, and given the same income, the poor man would not behave exactly like the rich man. He cites studies that revealed that the lower-class person is profoundly different in his mode of thinking from someone in the middle class. Where and what he buys differs not only in economics but in symbolic value.[4]

Our knowledge of social-class behavior is based on the pioneering work of W. Lloyd Warner and his colleagues. In their studies of American communities, they have identified six groups of Americans, each group seeming to share similar ways of looking at life. Warner's associate, Richard Coleman, drew these pictures of six social classes:

1. *Upper-Upper.* This small (less than 1 percent of a community) group of people comprises locally prominent families who live graciously and are concerned with reflecting their good breeding.

2. *Lower-Upper.* Another small (2 percent) group, this one comprises more recently arrived wealthy families and very successful executives and professional people. Their goals are a mix of gracious living and the pursuit of success.

3. *Upper-Middle.* This 10 percent of the population comprises successful managers and professionals, plus those younger people in these fields who anticipate such success by dint of upbringing or education. Career success tastefully reflected at home is the common goal. For most advertising purposes, Coleman says, the three uppermost classes can be viewed as a single category.

4. *Lower-Middle.* This third of the public are white-collar workers, small businessmen, and some high-status blue-collar families. Respectability is a goal in their home, clothes, and neighborhood; striving characterizes their orientation to work and to a good education for their children.

5. *Upper-Lower.* This 40 percent of our people is the other part of the "average man's world" along with the lower-middle class, comprising largely semiskilled workers. This group, even when earning good money, is less concerned with respectability and more with enjoying life. They do want comfortable living, away from the bad part of town, but middle-class views are not theirs.

6. *Lower-Lower.* The remaining 15 percent constitutes the unskilled and underemployed. Their very modest purchasing power has not been of much interest to marketers.[5]

---

4 Pierre Martineau, "Social Classes and Spending Behavior," *Journal of Marketing,* 23 (October 1958), 122–23.

5 Richard Coleman, "The Significance of Social Stratification in Selling," in *Marketing: A Mature Discipline,* ed. Martin Bell. Proceedings of the American Marketing Association Conference, Chicago, 1961, pp. 171ff.

Social-class analysis is important, since advertising that seems to be oriented to upper-class Americans may turn off those in the middle majority (lower-middle and upper-lower) groups, and vice versa.

An interesting example of social analysis was reported by Jay M. Kholos, whose agency handled the advertising of an independent clothier with but one store and no street traffic. The trade was a lower-middle-class market, "where the purchase of a suit is usually a special occasion." "In selecting television spots for this client," he reports, "the best audiences are the fans of the roller derby (not baseball). Spots in such programs are fitted to the audience." And there you have a class distinction between roller derby fans and baseball fans! [6]

Innovators. There are people who like to be among the first to try new products and services. They represent a good source of sales at the critical early stage of a product's existence. In addition, many of them, but not all, may help to spread the word about the product. Every advertiser of a new product would like to identify and reach such people.

Extensive research has been done on the ways people learn about new products and accept them. Rogers divided them into five groups, differing in the point of time at which they accepted a product.

1. *Innovators* (2.5%). These people are highly venturesome and are cosmopolitan-oriented; they are eager to try new ideas, and are willing to accept the risk of an occasional bad experience with a new product.

2. *Early Adopters* (13.5%). These people, more than the innovators, are those in the community with whom the average man or woman checks out an innovation; a successful and *careful* innovator, the early adopter is more influential with those who follow.

3. *Early Majority* (34%). This group tends to deliberate before adopting a product; they are seldom leaders but are important in legitimatizing an innovation.

4. *Late Majority* (34%). This cautious group adopts ideas after most people, when the bulk of public opinion is already in favor of an innovation.

5. *Laggards* (16%). These past-oriented people are suspicious of change and those who bring it; by the time they adopt a product, it may already have been replaced by yet another.[7]

It is helpful to try to understand the nature of those who are among early buyers. Among their personal characteristics are venturesomeness, cos-

---

[6] Jay M. Kholos, president, Jay M. Kholos Advertising, Encino, Calif., in *Broadcasting*, August 28, 1972, p. 11.

[7] Everett Rogers, *Diffusion of Innovations* (New York: The Free Press, 1962), pp. 168–71. The percentages are based on the statisticians' "normal" distribution.

mopolitanism, social integration within the community, financial well-being, and self-confidence in problem solving.[8]

Advertising appeals to the innovator to be the *first* in his group to have a particular product. This is typified by urging a consumer to "be the first on your block" to own a particular new product. Fleischmann's Yeast personalized the attraction:

> Make your husband glad he's yours. Be the only wife on your block to make a beautiful whole wheat bread loaf. . . . Let him brag about you.

The same kind of advertising approach is used for much more expensive products: American Airlines' advertisement for its four-week Pacific Islands tour ($1,185 plus air fare) called the consumer's attention to "the last great area to explore. Before everybody else does."

Influentials. Not every early buyer of a new product is in turn looked to by others as a reliable source of new-product ideas. But those particular people whose ideas and behavior do serve as models to others are of special interest to advertisers. These opinion leaders, or *influentials,* can speed the pace of new product sales by their own purchases and discussion of them. Despite efforts to pinpoint these "generalized opinion leaders," it seems that different people serve as sources of product information and use in different fields. The doctor who is influential with colleagues in adopting new drugs may not lead in consumer-goods adoption. Housewives who are fashion influentials may not be food-product influentials.[9]

The spread of new-product information from influentials to others is principally through word of mouth. Advertisers naturally try to stimulate favorable word-of-mouth comment, sometimes using direct appeals along this line. For example, Peugeot's 1972 ad campaign was built around a word-of-mouth network, with the theme, "One Peugeot owner leads to another." The ads stated that the buyer had learned about the car from a friend who owned one, and showed him in turn telling his friends about it.

One of the most traditional uses of the opinion leader in advertising has been in the use of testimonials—using status figures or experts in a field to endorse products, such as movie stars endorsing cosmetics and star athletes endorsing breakfast cereals.

An ad may seek status for the product through association of products to the establishments that use them. Advertisements for Sweet 'N Low low-calorie sugar substitute devoted half its space to asking consumers, "What do

---

[8] Lyman C. Ostlund, "Identifying Early Buyers," *Journal of Advertising Research,* April 1972, pp. 25ff.

[9] Elihu Katz and Paul Lazarsfeld, *Personal Influence* (New York: The Free Press, 1955).

you have in common with . . ." a number of airlines and major hotels. (The answer: the use of Sweet 'N Low.) Similarly, ads for Open Pit prepared barbecue sauce featured "Edgar Herrmann, chef at a leading Chicago hotel" to tell housewives why a chef who could make his own great barbecue sauce used Open Pit.

Sometimes the "expert" is just an ordinary citizen, but with a relevant background for the product. Television commercials for Ragú spaghetti sauce featured a man who characterized himself as Italian and *not* famous . . . "but I do know spaghetti sauce, and Ragú is the best." A Volkswagen commercial asked—and showed—"How does the man who drives the snowplow *get* to the snowplow?" (All testimonials fall under the Federal Trade Commission rulings, as described in our legal chapter later in the book.)

Reducing risk in purchasing. Spending money always involves some risk. The first question one asks himself about a product is, "Is it worth it?" Beyond this, two distinctive kinds of risk have been identified in consumer purchasing. One is summarized by the question, "Will the product work?" The other has to do with "Does the product fit with me?" Bauer calls these *performance* risk and *psychosocial* risk, respectively.[10]

Testimonials are only one of the ways advertisers try to reduce the amount of risk a consumer may feel he is taking in buying a particular product. They often try to reduce psychosocial risk by showing the product and people using it in situations with which prospective consumers can identify themselves. The so-called slice-of-life commercials, which show "ordinary people" using a product in realistic situations, reflect this. Thus it is not surprising that an important reason consumers consider certain ads informative and others enjoyable is that the ad made them "feel in the situation."[10]

Advertisers try to reduce performance risk in several ways. One is to show the product in use and the happy results of that use. Another is the statement of the money-back guarantee. Usually this is in the form of a "money refunded if you are not satisfied" pledge—or sometimes double your money back.

Even *after* a person has bought a product, he often asks himself, "Did I make the right decision?" This kind of post-purchase anxiety is particularly likely in the case of major-product purchases, such as a car. One role that advertising can play in such situations is to reassure the consumer by providing information supporting the decision, and hence reduce the anxiety. This may explain why recent purchasers of a high-price product are often among the more avid readers of its ads. It may also explain why consumers in fact consider ads for brands they prefer and for products they use to be far more

---

[10] Raymond A. Bauer, "Consumer Behavior as Risk-Taking," in *Dynamic Marketing for a Changing World*, ed. R. S. Hancock (Chicago: American Marketing Assn., 1960), pp. 389-398.

informative and enjoyable than those for products they don't use or brands they don't prefer.[11]

When a person receives new information that is contrary to his present belief or behavior, there is a conflict. Most people try to reduce this kind of inconsistency either by modifying their beliefs or behavior, or by rejecting the new information. For example, faced with a report that artificial sweeteners may be dangerous, a person using them may pooh-pooh the report, or he may stop or reduce his use of the product.

Both these reactions are explained by what behavioral researchers call *dissonance theory,* which explores how we psychologically attempt to maintain or restore consistency in our beliefs and actions.[12] When an advertiser seeks to reassure buyers through the advertising message, or when he employs a repetitive advertising schedule to aim his ads at present users, he is making use of these ideas about consumer behavior.

PSYCHOLOGY AND ADVERTISING

One of the most effective tire advertisements in recent times showed a woman on a lonely road gazing forlornly at the flat tire on her car. "When there's no man around, Goodyear should be," said the caption of the advertisement, which went on to say:

> She'll never have to change tires with Goodyear Lifeguard Safety Spare. Stranded. Helpless. Alone. You'd help her if you were there—but you're not. . . .

A psychologist could explain why the advertisement did so well. First, there was a sense of *self-identification* by women readers with the woman in the advertisement; a woman could easily picture herself in such a predicament. Second, there was a clear understanding of the woman's feelings and *motivation*—the desire to avoid danger. A man reading the advertisement could see his wife or daughter in that predicament, so that he, too, is compelled to identify with it. It makes him aware of his responsibility toward them; he is motivated by his *desire to protect those he loves.* These interpretations represent insights that advertising has gained from psychology. In fact, the language of psychology has become a part of the advertising man's vocabulary—self-identification and motivation, status symbol, ego-involvement, self-image, appeals.

---

[11] Raymond A. Bauer and Stephen A. Greyser, *Advertising in America: The Consumer View* (Cambridge, Mass: Harvard Business School Division of Research, 1968), Chap. 7.

[12] Leon Festinger, "Cognitive Dissonance," *Scientific American* (October 1962), p. 93.

The nature of motivation. Psychology is the branch of the behavioral sciences that is particularly interested in motivation—what makes a person act as he does. Motivation represents all the inner strivings variously described as wishes, desires, needs, urge, and all the drives that initiate the series of events known as "behavior." Just what are these drives? The question is enormously complicated. Students of clinical psychology have compiled many different lists of drives. One classification speaks of *physiological* motives and *secondary* or *social* motives—physiological motives referring to those whose satisfaction is essential to survival, as hunger, thirst, mating, while the secondary or social motives are those not involved in this function, as the desire to be socially accepted, to win a tournament, to get a promotion. Another lists motives in terms of 28 attitudes, including the *acquisitive* attitude (to gain possession of property), *conserving* attitude (to protect against damage), *constructive* attitude (to organize and build), *achievement* attitude (to overcome obstacles), *recognition* attitude (to excite praise and commendation), and *dominative* attitude (to influence or control others).

Bayton describes motives in terms of man's needs, grouped as follows:

1. Affectional needs—*the needs to form and maintain warm, harmonious, and emotionally satisfying relations with others*

2. Ego-bolstering needs—*the needs to enhance or promote the personality; to achieve; to gain prestige and recognition; to satisfy the ego through domination of others*

3. Ego-defensive needs—*the needs to protect the personality; to avoid physical and psychological harm; to avoid ridicule and "loss of face"; to prevent loss of prestige; to avoid or to obtain relief from anxiety* [13]

Other lists, according to Berelson and Steiner,[14] contain as many as 60 separate motives.

No single set of classifications has been recognized as a standard in the field. At all times, man is crying (even though the world does not often hear him), "Please understand me!" The advertising man needs to *understand the buyer,* not merely the product; to have insight and empathy with *his* goals, *his* wishes, *his* desires, *his* drives, *his* problems. Highway signs warning drivers that it is "unsafe to pass" are likely to have more impact than do warning that it is "illegal to pass." "No headache seems small when it's yours" was Bufferin's way of recognizing this fact.

Differences in motivation. The reason a man *says* he buys a certain product may have nothing to do with his real reason for buying it. If asked

---

[13] James A. Bayton, "Motivation, Cognition, Learning—Basic Factors in Consumer Behavior," *Journal of Marketing,* 22, 3 (January 1958), 289.

[14] Bernard Berelson and Gary A. Steiner, *Human Behavior* (New York: Harcourt Brace Jovanovich, Inc., 1964), Chap. 14.

"You can actually be rediscovered by the man in your life simply by changing your mode of dress."

Dr. Joyce Brothers,
Nationally known psychologist

Judy Gibbs styled
this suit for the woman who
loves being rediscovered by the man
who matters. The multi-colored stripes with
black accent will open
his eyes with a click. Made of
easy-care 100% Trevira® polyester
knit. Sizes 3 to 15.
Wear it, and he'll act
like he met you yesterday.

**About $48 at Abraham & Straus, all stores;
Jacobson's, Michigan; Jordan Marsh, Boston.**

Trevira
makes it easy

Hoechst Fibers Incorporated, 485 Lexington Avenue, N.Y. 10017, Licensee of the Internationally Registered TM

Sex appeal, so labeled by psychologists, is effectively used in this advertisement for an end-product advertiser.

for the reason he made a specific purchase, he will give an explanation that will make him sound like a thoughtful, rational man. The real reason may be different. A middle-aged man will say he bought a car because he likes its looks; the real reason may be that he likes the youthful way it makes *him* look. A woman will buy a dress because, she says, she needs it; perhaps she really bought it because she felt she needed a "lift." A man may say he does not like tea because of the taste; his real reason may be that he regards it as a "sissy" drink.

A product may mean different things to different people. Take the matter of a shampoo for men. Dichter reports that there are three major attitudes of men toward shampoos. First, there are men who might be described as masculine rebels. Shampoo has such feminine associations for these men that they will not use it; they wash their hair with bar soap. Second, there are the resentful conformists. Such a man washes his hair with whatever brand of shampoo his wife uses, but he feels vaguely—or in some cases, acutely—uncomfortable about it. Third, there are the secure males. By and large, their selection of a shampoo is determined on the basis of practical considerations rather than psychological needs. "They are likely to use whatever is handy, as long as it will do the job quickly and thoroughly." [15]

Tietjen cites examples of the extremes in the beneath-the-surface attitudes of different people toward the same product: [16]

Housecleaning Products

"INVOLVED HOUSEKEEPER"	"FUNCTIONAL HOUSEKEEPER"
Buys products to help her—she is doing the cleaning and enjoys it.	*Buys products to do the work for her —she seeks the quick and easy way to do the job.*

Foods

"DEVOTED COOK"	"CASUAL COOK"
Likes to be in kitchen—enjoys cooking as a means of self-expression.	*Likes to spend time with family in other ways—cooking represents a chore.*

Home Improvement Products

"OWNER"	"DWELLER"
Buys house for long-range habitation and is constantly changing and improving it.	*Buys a house for short-term use— makes few, if any, improvements, moves on when family increases or decreases.*

---

[15] Ernest Dichter, *Handbook of Consumer Motivations* (New York: McGraw-Hill Book Company, 1964), p. 183. Used by permission.

[16] Karl H. Tietjen, "New Directions for New Product R&D," *Printers' Ink*, February 12, 1965, p. 14.

Self-images and roles. Our motivations are closely related to how we see ourselves—our self-images and the different roles we play. Products are one of the ways we tell the world how we would like to have it think of us. In this way, products serve as symbols of who and what we think we are. A Drexel furniture advertisement dwells on the symbolic significance that furniture may have, by saying, "In subtle ways it can speak volumes about you and your taste . . . reflect who you are and where you are going."

Sometimes the advertising for a product needs to be changed to help change the consumer's view of himself or herself. For example, psychological research showed the importance of such self-images in the early days of instant coffee. Researchers showed housewives comparable shopping lists, differing only in listing instant coffee and regular coffee, and asked for descriptions of the kinds of women whose lists they were. The findings showed that housewives saw the image of the woman who used instant products as that of a lazy homemaker.[17]

What was done? The copy was repositioned from an emphasis on ease and time-saving alone, toward the benefits of using that time. More broadly, in the product formulation of some products, work for the housewife was "left in" as part of the product-usage process. For example, cake mixes called for the housewife to add eggs to the mix, so that she would have more feelings of participating in the making of the cake.

All of us have a number of *roles*—even at the same time. Thus, the same 25-year-old man is a husband, a father, and a son. In each of these roles, he may be addressed by advertising for different products—insurance for the family, labor-saving appliances for his wife and the home, gifts for his parents.

CONSUMER LIFE-STYLES

Each of the behavioral sciences we have touched upon has its own contributions to offer. They can also work in combination, as is the case in the study of "consumer life-styles." *Life-style* is the term for the "distinctive or characteristic mode of living . . . of a whole society or segment thereof." [18] Advertisers are interested in life-styles as they reflect the ways individuals see themselves and their living patterns. Life-style research is very much linked to social trends, and how people fit themselves into them. The future of virtually any consumer product is affected by one or more of these trends. They can also affect the direction and tone of advertising.

---

17 Mason Haire, "Projective Techniques in Marketing Research," *Journal of Marketing,* April 1950, pp. 649ff.

18 William Lazer, "Life Style Concepts and Marketing," in *Toward Scientific Marketing,* ed. Stephen A. Greyser. Proceedings of the American Marketing Association Conference, Winter 1963, Chicago, 1964, p. 130.

Daniel Yankelovich has extensively studied American life-styles and has identified 31 social trends that he believes can change the overall patterns of American life and of buying behavior.[19] These are *not* pushing in a single direction, and do *not* affect all people. They have been categorized into five major groupings:

1. Trends that are effects of the psychology of affluence, particularly felt among consumers who seek fulfillment beyond economic security. Included are trends toward personalization (expression of one's individuality through products), new forms of materialism (deemphasis on money and possessions), and more meaningful work (work satisfactions aside from money).

2. Trends that reflect a quest for excitement and meaning beyond the routines of daily life. Included are trends to novelty (constant search for change), to sensuousness (emphasis on touching and feeling), and to mysticism (new spiritual experience).

3. Trends that are reactions against the complexities of modern life. Included are trends toward life simplification, toward return to nature (rejection of artificial and chemical in dress and foods), toward stronger ethnic identification (new identification in one's background), and away from bigness.

4. Trends that reflect new values pushing out traditional ones. Included are trends toward pleasure for its own sake and living for today, toward blurring of the sexes (and their roles), and toward more liberal sexual attitudes.

5. Trends reflecting the personal orientations of those now in their teens and twenties. Included are trends toward tolerance of disorder (such as against fixed plans and schedules, affecting shopping and eating habits), toward rejection of hypocrisy (affecting attitudes toward exaggeration in communication), and toward female careers (away from traditional home-and-marriage as sufficient for women).

Effects of life-style trends. To reflect these changing trends and values, *and* their effect on marketing and advertising, Yankelovich offers three vignettes:

An older married couple whose children are grown move from their big home to a smaller, brand-new apartment. With fewer home repairs, with more labor-saving appliances, they have more time and money for leisure pursuits. Their efforts at "life simplification" are relevant to marketers of such products as home appliances, prepared and frozen foods, and travel.

---

[19] "What New Life Styles Mean to Market Planners," *Marketing/Communications,* June 1971, pp. 38ff.

He lives with his parents and I live with mine. And so to be alone to talk, to dream, to scheme, we take aimless drives to no place special.

Then he said "isn't it time we stopped driving nowhere and started our lives going somewhere."
And I said yes.

Photographed for De Beers Consolidated Mines, Ltd. by Peter Vaeth.

The Traditional Life-style

A diamond is forever.

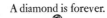

"The Day You Buy a Diamond," a free booklet with the answers to any questions you may have about buying an engagement diamond, is available at many retail jewelers, or you may write for a copy to: The Diamond Information Center, 260 West Lehigh Ave., Philadelphia, Pa. 19133.

An unmarried secretary has reacted to the "return to nature" trend by going bra-less when not at work. She has also changed her hair-style, lipstick, and perfume, and she buys some of her food at a small natural food store. She and those like her are of relevance to marketers of foundation garments, clothing, and cosmetics.

A young professional, about 30 and married with two children, wonders about how meaningful his job really is, how important the traditional home-family-job "ratrace" is. With longer hair and side-burns, he has experimented with marijuana, bought new stereo equipment, traded in his American sedan for a more functional foreign car, and is an avid reader of publications that tell about how people are changing their lives. His attempt to "personalize" his life and to seek

The
"Live Today"
Life-style

For only $168*a week you can lay aside the things that clutter your life. You're at Club Méditerranée/Martinique. Friendships form quickly. Last names, job titles and related trivia couldn't matter less.

You live all day in a bathing suit. At night, you need only wear a bit of super-casual finery. Ties and jackets, never.

Everything but the bar and boutique is absolutely free: The sailing, tennis, scuba diving, picnics, water skiing, yoga, snorkeling, spearfishing, dancing, three French meals every day, and the free-flowing wine with lunch and dinner.

Best of all, the whole atmosphere is free, and the people are free with each other.

A bank president and bank teller, without the usual wall of pinstripe between them, make real contact. Human being to human being.

Sometimes, one of the most fascinating people you meet here is someone you've been too busy to get in touch with at home.

Yourself.

*From $168 to $245 a week depending on season (slightly higher Christmas and New Year's). Air fare not included.

Here we do not impress each other with our money, our status or our clothes.

We impress each other with each other.

Club Méditerranée

Please send me your free 4 page booklet with further information on vacations to Caribbean, Tahiti, Mexico, Morocco and Ski Villages. BGM-07092-M

Name ____ Mr. Mrs. Miss

Address ____ City ____ State ____ Zip

My travel agent is ____

Michèle, Club Méditerranée
Service Center
P.O. Box 515,
Farmingdale, N.Y.
11735.

"pleasure for its own sake," is of relevance to marketers of such products as expensive liquor, music equipment, and cars.

Multiple directions. Obviously, these trends are not all moving in the same direction. And further, many Americans are not caught up in patterns of change at all. Wells' research on a broad sample of married middle-class Americans shows that this "large segment of U.S. society portrays itself as happy, home-loving, clean, and square." More specifically, "mod youth have not had much impact on the central values of the average man. . . . For most Americans it is indeed a Wyeth, not a Warhol, world." [20]

---

[20] William D. Wells, "It's a Wyeth, Not a Warhol, World," *Harvard Business Review,* January–February 1970, p. 26.

Dramatically different life-styles are reflected in the two accompanying advertisements appealing to young, single people. One (the De Beers diamond ad) is still oriented to the traditional pattern of finding the ideal mate and a happy marriage. Although the couple is pictured with the hairstyles and rather informal attire of the seventies, the text evokes the traditional life pattern: "He lives with his parents and I live with mine. And so to be alone to talk, to dream, to scheme, we take aimless drives to no place special. Then he said 'isn't it time we stopped driving nowhere and started our lives going somewhere.' And I said, yes."

How different an orientation to life from the advertisement in behalf of Club Méditerranée, a vacation resort emphasizing an informal, anti-status, manner of living. "Last names, job titles and related trivia couldn't matter less. . . . Ties and jackets, never . . . the whole atmosphere is free, and the people are free with each other . . . We impress each other with each other."

The difference between the two ads is not mere advertising technique; it is in the life-styles pictured.

Views vs. facts in consumer trends. Although advertisers are greatly concerned with changes and trends in consumer behavior, overconcentration on change may obscure some realities of that behavior. *Grey Matter* listed a number of widely held views about markets and changing consumer trends—along with the corollary facts. Among them:

"Flying is a way of life."
— Only 17% of the U.S. population took an airplane trip in 1971.
— Only 16% of adults had traveled outside the U.S. in the 1965–70 period.
"America is living on credit."
— Only 8% have one of the three major national credit cards.
— Only 24% have bank credit cards.
"Hardly anyone prepares food from scratch."
— Only 10% of eating occasions were at a restaurant in 1970, including working people's lunches out.
— Three-quarters of vegetables are bought fresh.
— 82% of housewives bake cookies and cake from scratch in the course of a year.[21]

These items were cited not to suggest that changes are unimportant. Rather, to point to the importance of watching change.

---

[21] *Grey Matter,* published by Grey Advertising Agency, New York, June 1972.

Those who have studied how the human mind works in making buying decisions have long sought to identify a single predominant factor that explains buying behavior. So far, however, no one pattern has been found that can be applied to all—or even most—buying situations. But many of these schools of thought have ideas to contribute to our understanding of the workings of the consumer mind as it "processes" ideas and information about products in the course of making buying decisions. These approaches to how the consumer's mind works are often called "models" of consumer behavior. Kotler has conveniently classified them into the following five categories: [22]

1. Marshall's *economic* model portrays man as responding chiefly to economic cues, with emphasis on careful, rational deliberation of costs and available income in making all buying decisions. From the advertiser's perspective, emphasis in this model on so-called "rational" choices is overdone, especially for most low-cost products. Experience shows that most people buy some products for many other reasons than price alone. But there are some applications of it, especially in advertising reduced prices and in understanding what competitive products might be seen as substitutes for the advertiser's.

2. Pavlov's *learning* model is described by Kotler as portraying man as a creature of habit more than of careful consideration of each action. Particular cues and past experiences prompt consumer reactions. From the advertiser's perspective, this helps explain why a person may form a habit of always buying the same one or several brands in a product category (called "brand loyalty"), or of always buying the lowest-price brand. For example, in a particular product category where existing loyalties are strongly entrenched, a new entrant or brand with a low market share would have to break through a much tougher barrier of habit, even to get consumers to try the brand. This might call for dramatic changes in the pricing or presentation of the product.

3. Freud's *psychoanalytic* model is characterized by Kotler as portraying man's choices as influenced by deeply buried motives, many of which are sexually related. These motivations are difficult to understand, even by the individual himself. In Kotler's view, the most important marketing implication of the Freudian model is its emphasis on the symbolism of products—for example, that convertible cars serve men as a substitute mistress. Another major outgrowth from this model has been extensive consumer research seeking to probe into the subconscious—"motivational research." Such research can provide useful ideas for advertisers, especially by linking products to

---

[22] Philip Kotler, "Behavioral Models for Analyzing Buyers," *Journal of Marketing,* October 1965, pp. 37ff.

consumers' hopes and ambitions for themselves, such as feeling more masculine through smoking strong cigars.

4. Veblen's *social-psychological* model portrays man's behavior as very much linked to his group associations. This kind of emphasis on social influences on our behavior has resulted in extensive research into our group memberships by sociologists and cultural anthropologists. We have already explored some of this research and its implication for advertisers. At this point, it is useful to review what two major kinds of group associations are involved. Of these, one kind is *face-to-face* groups, such as families, neighbors, working colleagues, and friends. The *non*-face-to-face associations include cultural and subcultural groups (national, regional, ethnic, and religious identifications), social class (identification in terms of economic circumstances, background, and occupation), and reference groups (those whose activities or roles in society people identify with or want to imitate). Any of these group identifications, depending on the particular product or advertising circumstances, can have an impact on a particular consumer's behavior.

5. An *organizational-buying* model tries to describe how people make their decisions when they are buying for business purposes; for example, a purchasing agent in an industrial plant. This kind of buying differs from that done for personal consumption. In organizational-buying situations, the model tries to reflect the buyer's concerns with the organization's goals—such as low price and good service—and with his personal goals—such as enhancing his reputation as a good buyer, and getting along with others in the organization. For us, it is important to recognize that not all organizational-buying decisions are exclusively "rational" on behalf of company interests; these purchases can also be affected by the buyer's personal motives, as recent research has confirmed.[23]

UNDERSTANDING PEOPLE— A CONTINUING STUDY FOR ADVERTISING

All advertising seeks to influence people's behavior. Sometimes the goal is simply to reinforce a consumer's existing patterns, such as the repurchase of his present brand of a frequently bought product. Sometimes the goal is to modify a consumer's behavior, such as getting him to switch brands or to replace an older model of a product with a newer one. Sometimes, especially in the case of truly new products, it can be to change a behavior pattern—to convince someone to substitute a new way of doing something for an old one.

All this points up one of the most important elements of effective advertising—understanding people.

---

[23] Wallace Feldman and Richard Cardozo, "Industrial Buying as Consumer Behavior," in *Marketing for Tomorrow . . . Today,* eds. M. S. Moyer and R. G. Vosburgh. Proceedings of the American Marketing Association Summer 1967 Conference, Chicago, 1967, pp. 102ff.

Consumer Attitudes Toward Beer and Beer Advertising

A case report illustrating
the use of a behavioral-sciences concept
in beer advertising

THE STUDY [24] WAS UNDERTAKEN to determine the real underlying attitudes and motives people have toward beer, to determine any differences in these attitudes by social-class levels, and to measure the impact of typical beer advertising on these different classes. Why do people drink beer? When? With whom? What advertising can cause them to switch brands?

METHOD

The findings in the study were based on over 350 psychological depth interviews with men and women of all social classes. The research question was basically, "*Why* do people do this?" rather than, "*How many* do this?" Typical quotations revealing fundamental attitudes toward beer and beer advertising are cited in the report summary.

SOCIAL CLASS

This study accepts the concepts of social class in America developed by Dr. Lloyd Warner, based on studies of typical American communities. Social classes are not economic classes. Social status is determined by education, family background, type of occupation, type of home, and neighborhood, not just amount of income.

The two major social-class groupings important to the advertiser are the Upper-Middle and Upper classes (15% of the population—the quality market), and the Middle Majority (65% of the population—the mass market). . . .

With most products, the upper middles react most positively to advertising that caters to their higher-status positions in society—which indicates through sophisticated language, prestige objects, and well-to-do settings that the advertiser feels that those who appreciate the finer things of life will use his product. In terms of copy and layout, they prefer ads that are reserved, do

_____

[24] Material is based on a study for the *Chicago Tribune* by Social Research, Inc. Courtesy Social Research, Inc.

not make extravagant claims, and are often playful in their treatment of the product.

The middle majority, on the other hand, often react quite negatively to advertising that appeals to the upper middles. They feel that such advertising is too high-flown, and they prefer advertising that is realistic in terms of settings and people, that sticks to practical details. They react most positively to advertising catering to their needs and interests, giving them information of use, and showing respect for the common man.

There is no real proof that middle-majority families fall all over themselves to imitate high society. Some scientists have said that the greatest single motivation for an American is fear of being different from his own class.

By far the largest group of beer drinkers is in the middle majority, and the middle majority consumes the largest amount of beer per capita as well.

HIGHLIGHTS

Up and down the social ladder, we find beer a well-liked drink. People have clear attitudes toward beer and its uses. They know what they want from beer; they get basic social and psychological satisfactions in drinking it.

When Do People Drink Beer?

Beer is a congenial drink. It oils the wheels to make a social gathering enjoyable, relaxing, and refreshing; it breaks down social barriers and lets people be democratic. ("A good drink for a get-together.") "After a couple of drinks of beer, you feel like talking more.")

Solitary beer drinking is meaningful too. Men drink it as an adjunct to other activities—puttering, reading, watching TV, working. Fewer women drink alone, but some find beer enjoyable while they are doing housework or for a break in the day's routine.

When Is Beer an Appropriate Social Drink?

Beer fits best where equalitarian relaxing is in order. People drink beer in all social classes and for similar reasons. Beer is considered to mark the absence of authority; it is an invitation to informality. Most drinking is done to be socially proper. What is appropriate differs from class to class.

In the upper middle class (the UMC): People often speak, act, and dress to mark themselves off from the way of life of the middle majority. In drinking habits, the mark of UMC status is the mixed drink or the fine wine, not beer. Only when the UMC person is emphasizing his commonality with others does he drink beer to show that he is a good fellow. When he wants to emphasize his membership in a higher-status group, as is more often the case, he drinks something else.

In the middle majority (MM): There are fewer occasions when people wish to be formal, to "put on the dog." Most MM people take their "in-between" status for granted and have few needs to appear classier. They consider beer the drink of the Common Man. They insist that when those above them drink beer, they are bringing themselves down to the "like-me" level. Only on formal occasions (few in middle-majority society) do they bring out the high-status mixed drinks or wine. Cost also makes beer the drink of the middle majority.

Guides to Beer Drinking

Middle-majority members often express hostility at the suggestion in beer advertising that they should be guided by the upper classes. (Said a 28-year-old clerk: "Those 'man of distinction' ads make me mad. My money will buy just as good liquor as anybody else's.") This feeling manifests itself toward testimonials too. While snob appeal is effective for some prestige items recognized as such, beer is not a prestige item.

What Makes Beer a Good Drink?

At the most universal level, the pleasure of beer drinking lies in the throat. Words used to describe beer are more descriptive of how it feels than how it tastes—e.g., "smooth."

Beer is disliked when the flavor interferes with the feel. Beers are disliked because they taste bitter, sour, biting, or when they are "watery" and without texture.

Beer is just alcoholic enough to give the drinker a feeling of relaxation and lack of inhibitions. In socializing, this enables him to feel more at home and more willing to be spontaneous. At the same time, there is little likelihood of losing control completely. Middle-majority people, especially, are attracted to this quality; they fear drunkenness but need something to make them relax in social situations. ("I can drink beer for hours on end and still not overdo it.")

A thirst quencher. There is almost complete agreement that beer is a good cooling drink, noticeably more thirst-satisfying than whisky or wine.

How Do People Feel About Brands?

For most people, there is "my brand," "the brand that let me down," *and "all those others."* And people describe their favorite beer(s) with all the good words advertisers have taught them to apply to what a beer should be. With bad words, they describe the beer that let them down—e.g., the beer they were drinking "that time the party was no fun." People usually know three or four good and bad beers; all the rest are just beers. Beer drinkers generally stick to a brand for an extended period; few people will drink *any* kind.

Generally speaking, many people feel that nationally advertised brands are more trustworthy than brands with less advertising or less extensive distribution. A large majority of the people do not believe beers from one city are better than those from another. ("Just because it's from Milwaukee doesn't make it a good beer.") Most people are quite willing to accept a less well-known beer once they've tasted it.

The consumer rationalizes his reasons for preferring a brand. There is no general consumer agreement as to the meaning of terms used to describe beer. The terms used to justify brand preferences are actually the emotional symbols expressing pleasure in beer drinking. The same positive admiring characteristics are applied to different beers that middle-majority people like, and common negative descriptions are applied to those they do not like.

What Are the Common Appeals in Beer Advertising?

Most beer advertisers don't make use of favorable attitudes toward beer. In place of advertising that harnesses these attitudes most successfully, much beer advertising falls into these main categories:

The prestige endorser theme—perhaps the most popular theme among beer advertisers. This approach seeks to influence the beer drinker through endorsements by some prominent persons. There are at least three disadvantages:

—People do not believe it; they believe the endorsers are "insincere."

—The situation is usually impersonal; it has few connotations of a friendly relation.

—Many of the figures chosen are not meaningful to the audience, such as theater stars only vaguely known to the middle majority, or sports stars who people believe should not endorse beer because they're in training and heroes to the young. ("Those big shots don't drink beer; you can't kid me.")

The high-class theme—in advertising communicates to the audience by dress, setting, and tone of copy that beer is a "high-class" drink. To the MM (and even the UMC) people, this idea is distinctly inappropriate. For them, beer is a universal drink, not the formal beverage of the wealthy or prominent. Typical reactions of ordinary beer drinkers indicated disbelief of and resentment toward this theme. (A 21-year-old Italian laborer said, "Looks like they might be drinking highballs instead, in a real ritzy place.")

The scientific-proof theme—emphasizes technical phrases, information to prove that one brand of beer is better than others. People do not use technical reasons for their beer preferences. Most beer drinkers judge beer more by the satisfaction they get from it—simply by using it—and have little interest in technical information. (A 52-year-old housewife commented, "I don't care how beer is made as long as it tastes good.") Also, this theme is essentially impersonal and does not have the attention-holding power of ads that tie in with the social and personal meanings of beer. The scientific theme has reassurance value but is not a good attentiongetter as a major ad appeal.

The average-man theme—is not widely used, but where it is, it receives a good deal of favorable attention from the audience. Such ads emphasize people who look "average" or slightly better in dress and surrounding and who are doing things middle-majority people commonly do or want to do. People feel that such ads "fit" with beer and the meanings it has for them. The ad is much more likely to arouse interest and a desire to have a beer. ("I get relaxed just looking at this—because I feel that way myself with a glass of beer in my hand, nice and relaxed.")

Appeals that Elicit Response

Appeals recalling, suggesting, and demonstrating pleasure are those to which people respond most. Beer is bound up with social and personal feelings—what it is used for, what pleasure it can give.

We Recommend that Advertising:

Should be directed primarily at the middle majority, since this is the mass market and the market in which more beer is consumed per capita.

Should take into account that men are probably the major market in terms of both consumption and brand selection, but that women are important and apparently increasing in importance.

Should embody and emphasize:

—Family and friends in informal gatherings

—Relaxation and refreshment after work or exercise

—Refreshment of spectators at appropriate sports gatherings

—Equalitarian festivities such as lodge meetings and Fourth of July

—Beer with meals

Should use these kinds of people:

—Hearty, active men of middle majority and upper-middle class in informal clothing

—"All-American girls," with emphasis on wholesomeness, not sexiness

Should talk about beer as:

—A cool, refreshing drink

—A friendly, hospitable drink

—A drink for equals, "for people like you"

—A drink that *feels good*

—A drink consistent in quality, clean, and carefully made

Do's and Dont's of Beer Ads

People should be:

—Either man or woman at middle-majority level

—Interesting to middle majority

—Someone who represents activity, "he-man" achievement, spectacular or romantic work

People should not be:

—Intellectuals or artists

—Businessmen with a formal "man of distinction" manner

—Merely sexy or glamorous

Settings should be:

—Casual and informal

—Nice, clean but modest. Not a Hollywood version of an upper-class home, party, or table setting

—Believable in terms of the kinds of people shown and the kinds of occasions at which beer is served

Settings should not be:

—Loaded with high-status symbols in location, furnishings, or activities

—Unbelievable in terms of either people or serving beer

—Extremely stiff or formal

Review Questions

1. How does the anthropologist view man's behavior? How is this viewpoint applicable to advertising? Cite an example from current advertising.

2. Find and discuss an example of current advertising illustrating two of the following: subcultural differences, a milestone of life, sex roles.

3. How does the sociologist view man's behavior? How is this viewpoint applicable to advertising? Cite an example from current advertising.

4. Find and discuss an example of current advertising illustrating two of following: reference group, social class, innovators, reducing risk in purchasing.

5. How does the psychologist view man's behavior? How is this view-point applicable to advertising? Cite an example from current advertising.

6. Explain the differences a) between physiological and social motives, and b) among affectional, ego-bolstering, and ego-defensive needs.

7. Find and discuss an example of current advertising illustrating any three of the items in Question 6.

8. Define life styles and find two examples of current advertising reflecting different life styles.

9. Explain what models of consumer behavior are, and the pros and cons of their usefulness to advertisers.

10. Using examples of from current advertising, discuss the applicability of the social class case report of today's beer advertising.

Reading Suggestions

*313
The
Behavioral
Sciences in
Advertising*

Barach, Jeffrey A., "Advertising Effectiveness and Risk in the Consumer Decision Process," *Journal of Marketing Research,* August 1969, pp. 314–320.

Bauer, Raymond, and Robert Buzzell, "Mating Behavioral Science and Simulation," *Harvard Business Review,* September–October 1964.

Berelson, Bernard, and Gary Steiner, *Human Behavior: An Inventory of Scientific Findings.* New York: Harcourt, Brace & World, Inc., 1964. Excerpted in Kleppner and Settel, *Exploring Advertising,* p. 90.

Bliss, Perry (ed.), *Marketing and the Behavioral Sciences.* Boston: Allyn and Bacon, Inc., 1967.

Boyd, Harper W., Jr., and Sidney J. Levy, *Promotion: A Behavioral View.* Englewood Cliffs, N.J.: Prentice-Hall, Inc., 1968.

Cohen, Joel B (ed.), *Behavioral Science Foundations of Consumer Behavior.* Riverside, N.J.: The Free Press, 1972.

Day, George S., *Buyer Attitudes and Brand Choice Behavior.* New York: The Free Press, 1970.

Dichter, Ernest, "How Word-of-Mouth Advertising Works," *Harvard Business Review,* November–December 1966.

Engel, James F., David T. Kollat, and Roger D. Blackwell, *Consumer Behavior.* New York: Holt, Rinehart and Winston, Inc., 1968.

Glock, Charles Y., and Francesco M. Nicosia, "Uses of Sociology in Studying 'Consumption' Behavior," *Journal of Marketing,* July 1964, pp. 51–54. Also in Kleppner and Settel, *Exploring Advertising,* p. 93.

Kangun, Norman, "How Advertisers Can Use Learning Theory," *Business Horizons,* April 1968, pp. 29–40.

Kassarjian, Harold, and Thomas Robertson, *Perspectives in Consumer Behavior.* New York: Scott-Foresman and Co., 1968.

Katz, Elihu, and Paul Lazarsfeld, *Personal Influence.* Glencoe, Ill.: The Free Press, 1955.

Lessig, V. Parker, *Personal Characteristics and Consumer Buying Behavior.* Pullman, Wash: Washington State University Press, 1971.

Martineau, Pierre, "Social Class and Spending Behavior," *Journal of Marketing,* October 1958, pp. 121–130.

McNeal, James V. (ed.), *Dimensions of Consumer Behavior.* Appleton-Century-Crofts, New York, 1969.

Myers, James H., and William H. Reynolds, *Consumer Behavior and Marketing Management.* Boston, Mass.: Houghton-Mifflin Co., 1967.

Myers, James H., Robert R. Stanton, and Arner F. Haug, "Correlates of Buying Behavior: Social Class vs. Income," *Journal of Marketing,* October 1971, pp. 8–15.

Packard, Vance, *The Status Seekers.* New York: David McKay Company, Inc., 1959.

Robertson, Thomas, *Consumer Behavior.* Glenview, Ill.: Scott, Foresman and Company, 1970.

Rogers, Everett, *Diffusion of Innovations.* New York: Free Press of Glencoe, 1962.

Westfall, Ralph, "Psychological Factors in Predicting Product Choice," *Journal of Marketing,* April 1962, pp. 34–40. Also in Kleppner and Settel, *Exploring Advertising,* p. 100.

14

The Search
for the Appeal

THE REMARKABLE THING ABOUT advertising is that it can prompt people to buy a specific, advertised product voluntarily. It has no authority to compel a person to buy anything; it exercises no mystical power. To the most vigorous exhortation of an advertiser, the meekest of men can yawn and say, "No, thank you!" Apparently, however, people are buying goods as a consequence of advertising. Since it has neither the power nor the authority to compel a person to do anything, one may ask just how does advertising do its work?

NOT MILLIONS, JUST ONE

In discussing advertising we deal with big numbers: billions of dollars spent on advertising, millions of television sets, thousands of radio stations on the air . . . billions, millions, thousands. But an advertisement deals with only *one* person at a time—whether reader, viewer, or listener. If he feels the ad is speaking directly to him, he pays attention; otherwise he does not. In either case, he is indifferent to the fact that the advertisement is addressing millions of others at the same time. His interest depends upon the degree to which the ad speaks to him about *his* interests, *his* wants, *his* problems, *his* goals.

THE APPEAL

An appeal is any statement designed to motivate a person to action. When a three-year-old says, "Please carry me, Daddy," he is appealing to his father's love (and is sure to get action). In seeking to move a person towards buying a product, the advertiser likewise must appeal to some of the manifold motives that prompt a man to act—as a desire to fulfill a hope, ambition, need, interest, or goal. The central premise of the advertising appeal is its promise of a benefit the product will render to the buyer.

For example, the National Oil Fuel Institute planned a campaign to urge householders who were not using oil heating to convert their heating system to oil fuel. It listed 11 different appeals to the homeowner which might persuade him to choose oil heat over any other forms, as follows:

Comfort	Cleanliness
Convenience	Dependability
Service from supplier	Adequate hot water
Economy of installation	Safety
Economy of operation	Modern features
Trouble-free performance	

The question arose as to which of these advantages meant the most to home-owners, for obviously it would be better to dwell on that one subject than on less significant ones. A research revealed that one stood out—Adequate hot water. A whole campaign was successfully built on that theme as shown in the opposite ad.

In the case of a watch, the appeals might be:

—It is a stylish watch.

—It is an inexpensive watch.

—It is a dependable watch.

Similar lists can be made for any product, if you look at it through the eyes of the prospective buyer. For example, take a *checking account.* To a bank, a checking account is a specific kind of financial arrangement. But to a customer, a checking account can represent:

Safety

Convenience
    —of paying bills
    —of keeping records
    —of transferring funds

Accuracy

Status

Availability of funds instantly

Any of these, or some combination of them, may serve as effective bases for appeals by banks to increase checking account customers. Similarly numerous appeals may be made for any product. In this chapter we discuss how to arrive at that appeal which is most significant for a given product at a given time.

How many times do you have to run out of hot water before you switch to Oil heat?

We don't know what kind of heating system you have now. But if it isn't dependable Oil heat, chances are you've run out of hot water more than once. And it's no fun taking a cold shower. Or waiting around until the hot water builds up so you can do dishes, or the laundry.

That doesn't happen when you heat with Oil. Why?

Because Oil heats water at least three times faster than any other fuel. Faster than your family can use it up.

That in itself should be a good enough reason for heating your house with Oil. But if it takes more to convince you, consider this.

Oil heat is comfortable. It's dependable. It's safe. It's economical. And it's clean. In fact, there's no cleaner way to heat your home.

If you still want one more reason, your Fuel Oil Dealer should be it. He's a neighbor, in business to serve you, so your family's comfort is pretty important to him. That's why he works harder to keep you happy.

So why don't you get in touch with him? He'll be glad to give you the facts.

And do it soon.

Before you run out of hot water again.

National Oil Fuel Institute, Inc., 60 East 42nd Street, New York, N.Y. 10017.

A CAMPAIGN THEME BASED ON RESEARCH

Courtesy, National Oil Fuel Institute, Inc.
Advertising Agency: Fuller & Smith & Ross, Inc.

The three characteristics that an appeal should have are that it be *meaningful, distinctive, believable.*

What makes an appeal "meaningful"? When we ask this question, we mean "What makes it most meaningful *to the buyer?*" There is only one way to find out; go out and ask the kind of people who may become buyers. The way you ask the question is a matter of research technique, but out among the consumers lies the answer.

What makes an appeal "distinctive"? An appeal should present a product in a distinctive light. If it is a new type of product, in the pioneering stage, that news alone makes it distinctive. But if it is in the competitive stage, as are most products, the first question to arise is, "What does it have to offer that the others in the field don't have?" That differential, to be worth consideration, should also be meaningful; in addition, it should preferably be conspicuous and demonstrable. If it lacks any such quality, perhaps it is time that it be improved or restyled before any more advertising money is invested in it.

What makes an appeal "believable"? This really means "believable to a skeptical prospect." If the product is a new, low-priced one put out by a reputable company, that fact may be enough for a person to try it. If it is a high-priced product, or if the claim exceeds the prospect's experience with similar products, or if indeed it is a new type of product in the pioneering stage with which the consumer has had no experience, the burden of the advertising is to corroborate its claims with the most desirable type of evidence— demonstration; accreditation by a recognized, competent authority (as Crest toothpaste did by getting the American Dental Association's endorsement for its Fluoristan toothpaste when it first appeared); by trial offers, guarantees, money back offers; or similar steps of assurance.

THE SEARCH WITHIN

Where does one begin looking for the appeal of a product? Right in the product itself. The chief appeal of a product may lie in its whole reason for being (its value goal), such as Calgon's Cling Free, an anti-static fabric softener, or Maclean's toothpaste, the toothpaste that fought its way into a highly competitive market by being the first advertised brand to be formulated for brightening teeth, while Close-Up toothpaste was formulated to emphasize its mouthwash qualities. Or, there is Liquid Gold, which provides natural oils to dried-out wood paneling and furniture, restoring their surfaces.

Sometimes a product has a distinctive characteristic which it must try to make more meaningful to consumers. For example, du Pont's Zerex antifreeze said, "Leaks are the #1 radiator problem, and Zerex stops leaks."

The built-in uniqueness may be the distinctive capability of a firm offering a service. For example, at a time when airlines were advertising with a wide variety of appeals, such as tours with attractive destinations, on-the-ground curbside check-in service, more comfortable seating, choice meals, in-flight entertainment, smiling stewardesses, Pan Am advertised, "Chances are you choose an airline exactly wrong," as a way of stressing the importance of its own differential—its capability and experience in travel planning.

On the other hand, the Dutch government, which owns KLM airlines, recognized that it could not pretend that Amsterdam had the glamor and excitement of Paris, London, or Rome. Research by the Ogilvy & Mather advertising agency showed that Amsterdam was considered to be lacking in things to do. The resulting advertising program focused on "Surprising Amsterdam," listing many specific activities taking place there, and under-scoring the pleasant nature of the Dutch people and the high percentage of them who speak English. This is a good example of the principle: "Sell what you've got."

The Greyhound advertising reveals another example of a unique appeal. All intercity buses have competition from the airlines, and to a limited extent from the railroads. The competition became particularly acute on the Boston to New York run, because of the airline shuttle service, and the newly launched high-speed Turbotrain between the two cities. But the one advantage the Greyhound buses had was their lower price, and they advertised the saving as the big reason for going Greyhound. Another example of finding the appeal in "selling what you've got."

Establishing distinctive image. For all products, it is important to have distinctive advertising. But for some products, the importance is even greater. Beer, for example. Beers differ in taste, but often the difference is so subtle that when a man cannot get his favorite brand he will seldom reject an alternate choice. Research, however, may reveal that different beers appeal to different groups within the beer market, and the advertiser can direct his efforts toward the type of beer-drinkers who would like his beer. For example, Schaefer's theme, "the one beer to have if you're having more than one" (directly appealing to heavy users) employed scenes of active men engaged in athletics. In contrast, Miller's advertising emphasized not activity, but relaxation—"when it's time to relax"—as the occasion to enjoy Miller's; both the setting and the music complemented the theme of relaxation. For Schlitz, the emphasis was on gusto—with scenes of "rugged-individualist" type men in strongly masculine and adventuresome settings. Each beer advertiser was attempting through his advertising to reach people whose personality patterns matched those presented in the ads. The decision on the image to project was an appeals decision.

SAY WHAT THEY WILL ABOUT THE TURBOTRAIN TO NEW YORK, WE'VE STILL GOT THE LAST WORD.

Greyhound has more than twice as much service, and usually gets you to New York sooner than Amtrak.

Greyhound has more daily service than any airline. But here's the last word:

Greyhound's Shuttle saves you $12 round trip to New York, over Amtrak Turbotrain coach fares. ($19.44 over Parlor Car. $28.70 over air Shuttle fare).

Also, Greyhound's non-stop Shuttles leave for New York every-hour-on-the-hour, from 8 am to 8 pm every day. (Plus 2 other non-stops).

Also, they take you from Park Square to mid-town Manhattan in as little as 4 hours and 15 minutes. Even quicker from MBTA Newton.

Also, you don't need a reservation—you get a seat for sure! So much for the last word. When do you want to go?

Non-stops leave Greyhound Terminal:
AM 8:00 9:00 10:00 11:00
PM 12:01 1:00 2:00 3:00 4:00 5:00 6:00 7:00 8:00
10 St. James Ave. Phone 423-5810
MBTA, Riverside (Rte. 128, Exit 53) • Phone 969-8660

SAVE $12*

*Greyhound One Way	$ 9.65
Greyhound Round Trip	19.30
Turbotrain Round Trip	31.30
Amtrak Parlor Car	38.74
Air Shuttle	48.00

GO GREYHOUND SHUTTLE
Every-hour-on-the-hour, non-stop.

Meeting Competition by Featuring Advantages

THE RESEARCH APPROACH

Finding out what the consumer considers most important and attractive about a product, or least attractive, may help not only in selecting the best appeal to use, but may also lead to improvements in the product itself—even to a new product. Research for one of these questions often ends up with answers for the other. The two main types of such research are: (1) structured, and (2) unstructured research. Sometimes they are used in connection with each other.

Structured research is designed to get specific answers to specific questions, presented in the form of a questionnaire. Its great advantage is that everyone is asked the same questions the same way: by scientifically planning the sample of people you question, the results can be "quantified"—used as a basis for advertising to a vast number of people. The limitation is that the questionnaire may not be asking the right questions. (We will discuss later how this can be overcome.) Whoever has answered a questionnaire has participated in a structured research. It is the most widespread form of research.

The chief elements of a structured research are:
1. Selecting the sampling pattern
2. Deciding on the method of interviewing
3. Preparing the questionnaire
4. Carrying out the interview
5. Tabulating results

1. Selecting the Sampling Pattern

Advertising deals with large numbers of people; it would never be feasible to learn their opinions if it were not for the principles of sampling. Crisp described them this way:

> If a small number of items or parts (called a *sample*) are chosen at random from a large number of items or a whole (called a *universe* or *population*) the sample will tend to have the same characteristics and to have them in approximately the same proportion, as the universe.[1]

The principles of sampling are used in many fields, such as when the doctor draws a small amount of blood from your arm to get a reading on your overall count of red and white cells, or when you take a sip of wine from a bottle to judge what the whole bottle is like.

"But how many people do you have to reach to get a fair sample of a big market?" is often asked. Statisticians have tables showing the possible degree of inaccuracy for any given number of people chosen as samples. The number needed is much smaller than most people would think. The principle is that after a certain number of responses, all additional responses make only an insignificant difference in the total result. After a time, it takes a fourfold increase in the size of the sample to double the accuracy of the result, at a cost that is hardly worthwhile.

---

[1] Richard D. Crisp, *Market Research* (New York: McGraw-Hill Book Company, 1957), p. 95.

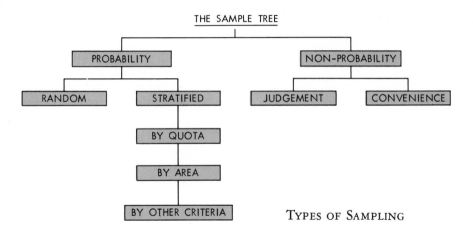

THE SAMPLE TREE

PROBABILITY

NON-PROBABILITY

RANDOM STRATIFIED

JUDGEMENT CONVENIENCE

BY QUOTA

BY AREA

BY OTHER CRITERIA

TYPES OF SAMPLING

Most research samples can be identified as either *probability* samples or *nonprobability* samples.

Probability samples. A probability sample is one in which each member of the group (universe) among whom the research is being conducted has *known* probability of inclusion. The essential characteristic of a probability sample is that each member of the universe has an *equal chance* of being drawn and was selected at random by a method that could not predict whether any given name would be included. There are two types of probability samples: *random* and *stratified.*

RANDOM (PROBABILITY) SAMPLE. If you were to pick every tenth name from a phone list (beginning anywhere at all), you would have a fair sample of people whose characteristics are similar to those of all the people in the rest of the phone book. Statisticians even have tables that will tell you the degree of probable error in such a sample, which is known as a random sample. When used in this sense, random does not mean a haphazard method of sampling; it refers to a rigid mathematical approach to selection.

STRATIFIED (PROBABILITY) SAMPLE. Another type of probability sample is the stratified sample, designed to sharpen the representations of the sampling universe. We can stratify it by any criterion we want; for example, quota, age, or city size. A stratified quota sample (referred to just as *quota sample*) is one drawn with certain predetermined restrictions as to the characteristics of the people to be included. That is to say there is a fixed quota of various types of respondents to be included. For example, the quota may be 75 percent men, 25 percent women, or 30 percent homes with no children, and 70 percent homes with children (representing the proportion of homes buying the product).

In stratified area sampling (referred to just as *area sampling*) one geographical unit is selected as typical of others in its environment. It may be a few streets selected as typical of other streets in that section, a few parts of a city as representative of the whole city, or a town in each of several states as typical of its respective area. The sampling effort will be confined to this area. The advantage of area sampling is its accuracy. But it is costly.

In some major national samples, such as those used by Gallup, *random* (probability) sampling is combined with *area* (probability) sampling. Dr. Gallup explained:

> . . . What we've had to do is break the country down by election districts—precincts. And we've picked those precincts, literally, out of a hat, so to speak. We just line them up and pick every *x* number of precincts, taking the various sizes into account. We do this right across the country. So we end up with a random selection of geographical areas.
>
> Now, having chosen the districts at random, we send an interviewer in and he follows a set pattern. He can't just go and pick people by himself. We actually give him a block assignment. He may be instructed to start with the third house from the northeast corner and then go to other dwelling units that assure a random selection. The selection of those interviewed is out of his hands. . . .[2]

Nonprobability samples. For certain purposes it may not be necessary to go to the expense and time of gathering a probability sample as we have just discussed; we can use *nonprobability* samples. For example, an expert can choose what he considers to be representative cases suitable for study, based on his experience and knowledge of the field. This is referred to as a *judgment* sample. Another form of nonprobability sample is the *convenience* sample—selecting whoever happens to be handy. A research man can show an advertisement to the first ten men he meets on the street to find out if its headline is clear and correctly understood. He will learn fast enough if it isn't absolutely clear.

2. Deciding on the Method of Interviewing

The chief methods of interviewing are by mail, telephone, personal interview, with a panel and, before long, through cablecasting.

Mail interviewing. A questionnaire is mailed to the prospective respondent along with a letter inviting cooperation and usually a reply card or a stamped reply envelope.

The advantages of a mail questionnaire are: It is inexpensive—cost per questionnaire mailed out is probably the lowest of any method. It enables you to reach either a widely diversified geographical spread of people or a relatively small group of people in widely scattered places.

---

[2] "Do Polls Tell the Whole Story?" From a copyrighted interview in *U.S. News & World Report*, October 5, 1964, p. 53.

Among the *disadvantages* of a mail questionnaire are these: A major problem in any mail survey is the question of "representativeness." Are those who respond the same kinds of people as those who do not respond? Mail surveys are also limited as to the kind of questions you can ask.

It is always desirable to pre-test a mail questionnaire by sending it out on a small scale in order to make sure the questions are clear.

Telephone interviewing. In telephone interviews the interviewer asks for the correct party and asks the questions from a prepared questionnaire. Check-off boxes or pre-listed answers are also printed on the interviewer's form to encourage response.

The *advantages* of telephone interviewing are: It is selective; it enables one to pinpoint specific types of people; one gets the information almost instantly; and the costs of the telephone interview are lower as a rule than those of personal interviews.

The *disadvantages* of telephone interviewing are: The length of questioning time is usually limited; people who do not have telephones cannot be reached; and others that do may have calls screened by their secretaries. A major problem is that information in depth may not be obtainable.

Personal interviewing. The personal interview is probably the most widely used approach to getting information. Here, a trained interviewer calls upon people in accordance with predetermined sampling methods and enlists their cooperation in giving the desired information. The great advantages of the personal interview lie in the number of questions that the interviewer might be able to get answered, and in the ability to record respondents' comments that may prove very revealing of attitudes. The big problem in using this technique lies in the caliber, training, integrity, and supervision of the interviewer, on whom everything then depends. Also, there is always the possibility that the interviewer lets his or her own bias influence the answers, albeit unconsciously. Personal interviewing costs the most per interview but tells you the most per dollar.

A panel. A panel is a group of people gathered as representative of a larger group, with whom arrangements are made to send regular reports of their purchases or listening habits. This is one method used by TV research companies who supply those in a panel with a device which records their TV listening, along with a diary they keep of the stations tuned in. Often matched groups of panelists are selected for conducting comparison tests of ideas.

Small panels are often used in unstructured research, as we discuss next, for guided discussions on problems of most interest to the advertiser.

Thus the panel is used for watching trends among a fixed group of people, for getting spontaneous responses of occasional groups and for comparing the impact of ideas among matched sets.

LOUIS CHESKIN ASSOCIATES
MARKETING RESEARCH

105 WEST ADAMS STREET • CHICAGO 3, ILLINOIS • Phone: 332-5362

CONFIDENTIAL REPORT

ASSOCIATION TEST: FIVE MARKETING THEMES

Sample: 204 Mothers

Area: Urban - Los Angeles

Theme No. 1 - The cereal with the natural goodness of whole grains.
Theme No. 2 - The different hot cereal for flavor, nutrition, economy.
Theme No. 3 - The hot cereal that dares to be different.
Theme No. 4 - The satisfying hot cereal for natural nutrition.
Theme No. 5 - The natural whole grain cereal with the nut like flavor.

Number of Associations

FAVORABLE	Theme No. 1	Theme No. 2	Theme No. 3	Theme No. 4	Theme No. 5
highest quality	79	33	8	38	46
most adequate breakfast	61	51	7	50	35
best for daily use	61	77	6	35	25
most costly ingredients	64	14	21	17	88
most flavorful	48	29	8	8	111
most appetizing	54	30	12	25	83
most appealing	61	32	12	18	81
Total	428	266	74	191	469

UNFAVORABLE	Theme No. 1	Theme No. 2	Theme No. 3	Theme No. 4	Theme No. 5
lowest quality	9	39	113	25	18
least adequate breakfast	9	29	119	25	22
not best for daily use	12	30	114	31	17
cheapest ingredients	12	71	78	29	14
least flavorful	21	28	98	48	9
least appetizing	18	34	93	45	14
least appealing	8	48	97	40	11
Total	89	279	712	243	105
Grand Total	517	545	786	434	574

SELECTING THEMES

Which of these advertising themes mean most to women in connection with a cereal? The above is an analysis of the reactions of mothers. Themes #5 (Score 469) and #1 (Score 428) proved best. Courtesy, Louis Cheskin Associates

Cablecasting. The newest entrant to the research field is cablecasting, with two-way communication. A series of research questions can be asked at the local CATV station, and the subscriber can state a choice by pushing a button (still pending).

3. Preparing the Questionnaire

The tool of the structured interview is the questionnaire to which the interviewer must adhere. In preparing a questionnaire, it is important to have clearly in mind the information one is trying to learn, and to include only questions that will gather facts towards this objective, eliminating "interesting" questions that will not add information to the problem at hand.

Questions must be clear to the person interviewed; they must have the same meaning for everyone. The person questioned should not be put in the position of trying to impress the interviewer that he is on a higher socio-economic or cultural level than he really is. One should try to avoid personal questions, such as those dealing with race, politics, and religion. A questionnaire that can be checked off is better than one that must be filled in.

The questionnaire for a telephone survey should be relatively short. A mail survey might be somewhat longer, and could include more "open end" information (inviting a person to express himself) since the respondent can take his time writing the answer. A personal interview may be fairly long —usually ranging between 15 and 45 minutes.

A questionnaire should be pretested to check for ease of interpreting instructions, for question clarity, for logical sequence of questions, for length, and for any unanticipated problems.

4. Carrying Out the Interview

In the case of a mail research, the problem is a purely mechanical one of mailing out the questionnaire to the selected list and tabulating the replies. Much of this is done by computer, as revealed in the little numbers that are affixed to the questions in many such questionnaires. Many questionnaires often leave room for further comment, and these are very important and deserve intensive review by some competent person to pick out significant statements, and not be left to mass summary alone.

In the case of personal interviews, everything depends upon the interviewer's personality and diligence in getting responses, and most of all, upon the interviewer's integrity. Research companies whose reputations depend upon the accuracy of the field reports have check-up systems whereby a supervisor will phone a sampling of names on the reports handed in to make sure the interviews actually took place.

5. Tabulating Results

Once the questionnaires are sent in, the replies are reviewed. Additional comments noted on the questionnaires are grouped into categories as "other favorable comments" or "other unfavorable comments." The results are tabulated and summarized. At this point, the conclusions are presented to management for their interpretation and use.

Criteria for Structured Research

By way of brief review—the Advertising Research Foundation uses the following criteria for judging research studies:

1. Under what condition was the study made—including period of time, definition of terms, methodology?
2. Has the questionnaire been well designed?
3. Has the interviewing been adequately and reliably done?
4. Has the best sampling plan been followed?
5. Has the sampling plan been fully executed?
6. Is the sample large enough?
7. Was there systematic control of editing, coding, tabulating?
8. Is the interpretation forthright and logical?

UNSTRUCTURED RESEARCH

In unstructured research an interviewer, by appointment, spends a lot of time with one person, or a small group of people. He will have only a list of topic areas to cover, rather than a set of specific yes or no questions. The person interviewed is invited freely to express his feelings and attitudes toward a product. He is not given a questionnaire. The unstructured interview is usually conducted early in the research process. It is also known as a *depth interview* or *motivation research* or a *projective study*. Dichter comments:

> Many of the aspects of depth interviewing are borrowed from the approaches used in psychiatry. We employ these techniques continuously in our daily lives. When the hostess keeps urging us to stay a little longer, but yawns at the same time, most of us don't need any knowledge of depth interviewing or of psychology to detect a discrepancy between her statement and her actual feelings. We leave.
>
> Basically a depth interview is a nondirective interview. The respondent is being urged to talk about a subject rather than to say yes or no to a specific question. No questionnaire, in the usual sense, is used.[3]

---

[3] Ernest Dichter, *Handbook of Consumer Motivations.* Copyright © 1964 McGraw-Hill, Inc. Used by permission of McGraw-Hill Book Company, New York, p. 414.

In another form of unstructured technique designed to get a person to tell what he really thinks about a given subject, he is asked to complete a sentence, such as,

The thing I like best about my car is . . .

The kind of men who use electric shavers are . . .

Unstructured research also uses cartoons which will be shown to a person who is asked to describe what is going on, or else to complete within a balloon a sentence in the cartoon. The whole purpose of this approach is to get an individual to reveal his real attitude towards the subject being studied without the influence of the interviewer. The research director of one agency, commenting on the role of such research, stated that "some of the subheads and even headlines have come directly out of the mouth of consumers." [4]

The unstructured technique is used to ask a woman, or a panel of women, to give their opinion on different products or ideas. They may be requested to rank them from one to ten, or compare them as "superior," "inferior," and if so why, or "about the same." Or they may tell in their own

---

[4] Dr. Alin Gruber, of Norton Simon Communications, *Madison Avenue,* April 1972, p. 16.

A Projective Cartoon
Designed to get a person to express his own attitudes about fences.

Courtesy, Anchor Post Products
Advertising Agency: VanSant, Dugdale and Company, Inc.

words what they really think of the products they are using, or have used, and why they changed, or what their idea is of a dream product in the advertising field. It's an invitation to open up and talk freely in some area of interest which relates to their experience and attitude in relation to a product, service, or firm. It has to be done on a personal basis, either alone or in a small group, under a discussion leader, at which time tapes may be made to be studied more carefully later.

There are several schools of thought about unstructured research. One group holds that unstructured research relies too much on the competence and personality of the interviewer, that it takes a lot of time per interview, and that the feasible number of interviews does not represent a sample that can be "quantified," hence does not meet the criterion of a scientific methodology. Proponents of the unstructured school hold that full free-flowing expression from fewer people provides greater insights than precise but superficial answers to compartmentalized questions from many people; that such research provides new hypotheses that can then be validated, if desired, by quantitative research.

The various forms of unstructured research are particularly helpful in generating new ideas for products and advertising appeals, in exploring general reactions to product categories, and in providing directions that can be followed up in structured research.

At a later point in the book we again take up the subject of research to appraise which of a series of advertisements most effectively presents that appeal, and finally to appraise the whole campaign built around this important decision.

STRATEGY PROBLEMS AND DECISIONS

Balancing importance and distinctiveness. An important product characteristic makes for a meaningful appeal. But, as Overholser points out, "the more important an attribute is to a large number of consumers, the less likely it is that any brand . . . will have a unique advantage. The strategist must often face a difficult choice between emphasis on an important but generic quality or on a somewhat less important but differentiating quality." [5]

Target market considerations. While target market considerations always affect appeals decisions, sometimes they are of particular importance. This was so when Northwestern Mutual Life Insurance Company examined its image in conjunction with a campaign very much aimed at non-owners of the company's insurance.

---

[5] Charles Overholser, "Advertising Strategy from Consumer Research," *Journal of Advertising Research,* October 1971, p. 9.

Its research examined the desirability of ten characteristics of insurance companies, and the image of Northwestern in relation to them.

1. Is an old and large life insurance company.
2. Offers insurance at a lower cost.
3. Is very selective about whom it will insure.
4. Has a high return on investments.
5. Holds its overhead costs to a minimum.
6. Has among the best agents in the insurance business.
7. Is a mutual company.
8. Has agents that sell you the correct amount of insurance for your needs and resources.
9. Pays high dividends to its policyholders.
10. Gets much of its business from old customers.

A research was conducted among the company's current policyholders, and among non-owners. All respondents were from the same demographic groups of prime insurance buyers. The research pointed to three particular characteristics:

—"an old and large insurance company"
—"has among the most knowledgeable agents in the business"
—"agents help you decide on the correct amount of insurance for your needs and resources."

All three of the selected characteristics were rated very strongly by policyholders as representing what the Northwestern was like—in fact—as a company. Second, these three were all characteristics which *non*-owners very much did *not* see the company possessing. Advertising's job was to communicate believably to non-owners what owners knew to be strengths. Separately, for owners, the advertising would serve to reinforce the known positive elements of the company's image. (The complete report on the campaign which followed is presented in Chapter 23.)

The reward for not following competition. Every responsible manufacturer in any field will seek to find out what the public wants most in a product such as his, and the answer in almost every case case will be the same. Most manufacturers will proceed, therefore, to give the buyer what he seeks, as best they can. Because all manufacturers are competing by using the "most wanted" quality, that may leave the market clear of competition for a manufacturer who specializes in the so-called "less wanted" quality. That's what Motorola did.

The Motorola Company started with consumer research in the mid 1960s on what attributes people wanted most in color television sets. This investigation showed that picture quality was most important (about 50 percent), then ease of tuning (about 30 percent), and then service (about 15 percent). Here is where management judgment entered: The company decided to aim heavily at the 15% service group, *because competition was not focusing on this area.* This was the main appeal and target market. (At the same time, attention was paid to the other areas, but the focus was on service.)

From this decision came the product development efforts, leading to an accessible chassis with plug-in modules. In turn, the chassis was built in slide-out form, for its distinctive advantage. The slide-out feature was dubbed "works-in-a-drawer" as the "communication key"—the term used to describe how technical features are presented to the public.

A Guide for Action

As we have observed, a person may buy a product for many reasons, each representing a different appeal. We have discussed research methods to find the most effective appeal for a given product in a given market at a given time. But first we have to understand the nature of appeals—why people buy the way they do. This calls for constant observation; this calls for intuition. Unless a person is willing to sharpen his talents in these directions, reports are cold statistics, which can lead to costly errors of operation. In the foregoing Motorola case, although research showed that "service" was 'way down the list of importance to the TV set buyer, it was management's *judgment* to develop this feature because competition was not doing so.

We have support for the role of intuition in this scientific age from Lord Brain, late President of the British Association for the Advancement of Science, who said,

> The contributions which science can make to the interpretation of something as complex as human nature are at present limited, and in unscientific theories, as in art, there may be insights, intuition, and illuminations, which are of value for practice as well as for theory.[6]

It is good that we begin our creative work with the "insights, intuitions and illuminations" of which we are possessed, and which "are of value for practice"—especially in translating research findings into warm advertisements.

---

[6] Lord Brain, F.R.S., "Science and Behavior," *The Listener,* LXXII, No. 1848 (August 27, 1964), p. 294

Consumer Research on Banking Services

A case report on consumer questionnaires

A SUBURBAN BANK IN a metropolitan area was interested in learning about consumer attitudes toward banking services generally, and reserve-credit accounts in particular. The latter was then a relatively new service in the area. It gave consumers the opportunity to write checks for more than their balance —in short, make a loan whenever they wished. The research was built around the accompanying questionnaire.

Objectives. The questionnaire was designed to explore reactions to the reserve-credit service, get reactions to a proposed single monthly statement, and to link that information to people's behavior regarding other banking services. Further, it could reveal the benefits most likely to attract a new reserve-credit account. It also helped identify the kinds of people most interested in the bank's services and get information on consumer reactions to prospective advertising appeals.

Procedure. The questionnaire was mailed on a predetermined sampling basis to a cross-section of homes randomly selected in the several communities served by the bank. Respondents were not asked to give their names. In a brief cover letter they were asked to give their "thoughts about banking services . . . to help create new and better banking services for everyone in this area." To encourage response, the questions called mostly for checkmarks or very brief answers. A postage prepaid envelope was enclosed. The return address was not that of the bank itself, to avoid prejudicing responses.

Detailed analysis. The initial questions help to identify whether respondents are at present actively involved with bank services, especially minimum balance and no-charge checking accounts (Question 2). Question 3 identifies those who have bank-issued credit cards, how they have used them, and the banks involved. Those with such a bank-issued charge card presumably would be more interested in the new reserve-credit service. Questions 4–9 are the core of the questionnaire. First, the respondent's familiarity with the reserve-credit service is probed. Questions 5 and 6 explore *how they have used the account* and *why they like it.* This information can be used to develop basic appeals in the advertising. This can be in terms of showing particular uses which consumers make of the service, as for travel, shopping, taxes, insurance, and the like. Or it can be in terms of reasons for liking the service— for example, ability to write one's own loan, low payments, or ease of use.

Note that these questions are answered only by those who *already have such an account.* Thus, a bank already offering the service can learn about the actual behavior of users.

Question 6 permits a direct comparison of the appeals of a reserve-credit account and a bank-issued charge card.

Questions 7 and 8 explore the reasons for *not* having an account and which financial benefits of one might attract the consumer.

Question 10 is addressed to a new banking service in the community, namely a single monthly statement with checking, savings, and reserve credit, plus transfer privileges. In addition to getting basic reactions to the service, the question sought reasons for lack of interest in it. From the latter information, executives could better assess the strength of negative reactions and perhaps judge how they could be overcome.

Questions 11 through 14 gather statistical information, which permits identification of those who represent the best potential market for the new services. It also allows special analyses of the reactions of particular consumer groups.

Findings. In terms of the focus of the advertising, achieving awareness of the reserve-credit account was shown not to be a problem. Many consumers were aware of "reserve-credit" 'accounts (over 75 percent of respondents), but relatively few actually had such accounts (about 20 percent). Thus, advertising would not have as much a task of pure information as would be the case if awareness were low. Rather, the advertising would have to overcome the reservations expressed by the "aware but don't have" group about borrowing at all.

Clues of specific appeals came from the responses of non-holders of the account and also from present users. Among respondents who were aware of reserve-credit accounts, but had not opened one, about 30 percent listed at least one benefit that would interest them in applying for an account. This showed there was an opportunity to try to convince people to open a reserve-credit account.

Holders of reserve-credit accounts reported that they most liked the service because they were able to write their own loans, and that the account was nice for emergencies. These replies provided direct appeals for future advertising.

Please indicate your response by placing a check mark in the appropriate space. It will take just a few minutes to complete the questionnaire; thank you for your help.

1. Do you have a savings account? (Please answer for your *main* account, if more than one.)

    ( )¹ yes, with _____ 5,6,7
    (please enter name of bank)

    Please name other banks where you have savings accounts:

    _____ 8,9,10
    _____ 11,12,13

    ( )² no

2. Do you have a checking account?

    ( )¹ yes   ( )² no   14

    If "yes", what type of account do you have? (Please answer for your *main* account, if more than one.)

    ( )¹ "Regular" or "Special"—pay service charges
    ( )² Minimum Balance Required—but no service charges
    ( )³ Free—but must pay for checks   15
    ( )⁴ Free—no charges at all
    ( )⁵ Free—savings account required

    Which bank is your main checking account bank? _____ 16,17,18
    (please enter name of bank)

    Please name other banks where you have checking accounts.

    _____ 19,20,21
    _____ 22,23,24

3. Do you have a *bank* charge card?

    ( )¹ yes   ( )² no   25

    If you have one or more cards, please check the one you use most often.

    ( )¹ Master Charge   ( )² BankAmericard   ( )³ other   26

    Which bank issued that card? _____ 27,28
    (please enter name of bank)

    Please indicate below ways you have used your bank charge card in the past Year:

    ( )¹ for travel and/or entertainment
    ( )² for shopping   29
    ( )³ for a major purchase (over $100)
    ( )⁴ for an emergency expense
    ( )⁵ to take advantage of a bargain
    ( )⁶ for taxes and/or insurance premiums
    ( )   other (please specify) _____ 30
    ( )⁷ I have not used my card in the past year

4. Are you familar with "reserve credit" type accounts, such as Evergreen, First Check Credit, Check-Loan, or "The Long Green Line", which allow you to write a check for more than your checking account balance, or to "make your own loan" by writing a special check?

( ) yes, I have this type of account with _____ 31,32
(please enter name of bank)

Please check the type of account you have:

( )^1 write checks for more than checking account balance
( )^2 write special checks to make a loan 33
( )^3 both of the above

( )^1 yes, I know of this service, but don't have it.) Please
) go to
( )^2 no, I am not familiar with this service) Queston 7 34

5. Please indicate ways you have used your "reserve credit" account during the past year:

( )^1 for travel and/or entertainment
( )^2 for shopping 35
( )^3 for a major purchase (over $100)
( )^4 for an emergency expense
( )^5 to take advantage of a bargain
( )^6 for taxes and/or insurance premiums
( ) other (please specify) _____ 36
( )^7 I have not used my account in the past year

6. Please indicate below features of your "reserve credit" account (and bank charge card, if you have one) that you like best:

	Reserve Credit	Charge Card
			37,38
easy to use	( )^1	( )^1
convenient to carry	( )^2	( )^2
widely accepted by stores	( )^3	( )^3
nice for emergencies	( )^4	( )^4
ability to "write my own loan"	( )^5	( )^5
low monthly payments	( )^6	( )^6
overdraft privilege	( )^7	( )^7
other (please specify below)	( )^8	( )^8

_____

(please go to question 9)

7. ' If you do not have a "reserve credit" account, please indicate why.

( )^1 I am unfamiliar with the service
( )^2 my bank doesn't offer it 39
( )^3 I don't need it because I have a bank charge card
( )^4 my application for reserve credit was refused
( )^5 I don't like to borrow
( )^6 other (please specify) _____ 40

8. If you do not have a "reserve credit" account, would the benefits listed below interest you enough to apply for one?

        Reduced interest rate   ( )^1

        Up to 36 month repayment   ( )^2 41

        Two "no-payment" months per year   ( )^3

        Courtesy check cashing privilege   ( )^4

        Opportunity to purchase merchandise at special

        low prices using "reserve credit"   ( )^5

    ( )^1 yes (please check the benefits which interest you most)   ) Please

) go to   42

    ( )^2 no   ) Question

) 10

9. Would the benefits listed in question 8 interest you enough to switch your "reserve credit" account to a bank that offered them?

    ( )^1 definitely yes ⎤ Please check the benefits in question 8 above that interest

    ( )^2 probably yes ⎟ you most   43

    ( )^3 maybe   ⎟

    ( )^4 probably no ⎦

    ( )^5 definitely no ⎬ Please describe why not _____ 44

10. If your bank offered a new service based on a single monthly statement detailing your checking, savings and credit accounts (which would also enable you to transfer funds between accounts automatically), would you use this service?

    ( )^1 definitely yes

    ( )^2 probably yes   45

    ( )^3 maybe

    ( )^4 probably no   Please describe why not _____

    ( )^5 definitely no   _____

                                      _____ 46

Please answer the next few questions for statistical purposes only:

11. In what city or town do you live? _____ 47

12. What is the occupation of the head of the household? Please indicate profession or type of occupation, not place of employment._____ 48

    In what city or town does he (she) work? _____ 49

13. In which age group is the head of the household? (check one)

    ( )^1 under 21   ( )^3 30–39   ( )^5 50–59   50

    ( )^2 21–29   ( )^4 40–49   ( )^6 60 and over

14. In which category is your total family income? (check one)

    ( )^1 under $5,000   ( )^3 $10,000–$14,999   ( )^5 $20,000–$24,999 51

    ( )^2 $5,000–$9,999   ( )^4 $15,000–$19,999   ( )^6 $25,000–over

Sodaburst

A case of consumer research for advertising appeals
and product development

SODABURST IS A FROZEN homemade ice cream soda product—a combination of ice cream, syrup, and frozen carbonated water. By the addition of tap water to the combined unit, the carbonated water would release and mix with the syrup to make a homemade ice cream soda ready to serve in a minute.

Research areas. Some consumer research was undertaken during the product development period, chiefly to aid in the product's physical and taste formulation and in estimating the size of its potential market. Later a week-long home use test in 400 households was conducted, including a number of follow-up questions oriented to developing advertising appeals and message strategy for Sodaburst's initial test marketing. From this information, and the earlier product research, the basic advertising premise and advertising message on behalf of the product were to be developed.

The questions covered housewives' reaction to: (a) the eating occasions for which they saw Sodaburst as appropriate (such as snacks or dessert); (b) the appeal of the product among adults, teens, or children; (c) specific product appeals (such as flavor, convenience, and nutrition).

Findings. The main findings in each area were:

(a) Children's and teen parties and snacks, rather than desserts, were the occasions seen as most suitable for the product's use. "Very appropriate" scores were children's parties 81 percent, teens' parties 71 percent, evening snacks 68 percent, afternoon snacks 54 percent, dessert at lunch 23 percent, dessert at dinner 19 percent, and serving to adult guests 22 percent.

Separately, housewives also said that they saw the product helping to promote "family sociability" at snack time. The product was not viewed as a direct substitute for fountain ice cream sodas because the latter also carried with it the experience of "going out."

(b) Young children and teenagers were seen about equally by the housewives as groups to whom the product would appeal, with ratings of 75 percent and 72 percent respectively in terms of "a great deal" of appeal.

Source: Adapted with permission from Sodaburst (A) and (B) cases in Stephen A. Greyser, *Cases in Advertising and Communications Management* (Englewood Cliffs, N.J.: Prentice-Hall, Inc., 1972).

Adults were not considered a major prospective consuming group, with only a 29 percent rating.

(c) Flavor and taste mentions of the product dominated the specific "likes" expressed by housewives about the product itself. This area was mentioned by 67 percent of the housewives—and by 78 percent of those who (separately) indicated a "high intent" to buy the product. Within the flavor-taste areas the two most important particular positives cited were "tastes like a real ice cream soda" and "good ice cream taste." Convenience and ease of preparation were the two areas mentioned next most frequently. In a separate question, 68 percent of all housewives—and 80 percent of those with high intent to buy—rated Sodaburst as "very" or "fairly" nutritious.

Decisions. The Sodaburst product management and advertising agency group drew from this information (from the 400 housewives in the use test) as they developed the basic claim and message for Sodaburst. The statement of the message strategy included:

> The principal objective of the advertising will be to announce that all the familiar taste enjoyment of an ice cream soda is now quickly and conveniently available at home with Sodaburst. A secondary objective will be to convince housewives of the product's quality/wholesomeness that makes it suitable for all-family consumption. The copy will dramatize the interest and excitement inherent in the totally new product concept SODABURST represents.

The basic advertising premise built on the latter point about the new concept represented by the product: "A real ice cream soda that makes itself at home in one minute cold." The initial ads put primary emphasis on the product being consumed by children with a mother in a "family at snacktime" setting.

Review Questions

1. What is meant by an advertising appeal? On what is it based? What is it supposed to do?

2. From current advertising of different specific appeals, see how many you can find being used for different brands in the same field.

3. Thinking about the most expensive item you bought in the past six months, what was the basic reason you bought the product? The particular brand?

4. What are the qualities recommended for an effective advertising appeal?

5. What are the differences between structured and unstructured research? What is the chief use of each?

6. What are the basic steps of a structured research?

7. Give a brief definition, description or explanation of:

a. random sampling
b. probability sampling
c. area sampling
d. panel
e. stratified sample
f. depth interview

8. What are the chief methods of getting information in a consumer survey by interviewing? What are the principal advantages and disadvantages of each?

9. As an advertising manager reviewing a large-scale consumer research proposal, discuss the guidelines you would use in judging it.

10. In the consumer research conducted by Sodaburst, how were the findings in each of the three main question areas used in the decisions made about the product's ads?

Reading Suggestions

American Marketing Association, "Sampling in Market Research," 1958.

Axelrod, Joel, "Reducing Advertising Failures by Concept Testing," *Journal of Marketing,* October 1964, p. 41.

Boyd, Harper W., Michael L. Ray, and Edward C. Strong, "An Attitudinal Framework for Advertising Strategy," *Journal of Marketing,* April 1972, pp. 27–33.

Boyd, Harper, and Ralph Westfall, *Marketing Research.* Homewood, Ill.: Richard D. Irwin, Inc., 1964.

Business Week, "Why Business Is Spending Millions to Learn How Customers Behave," April 18, 1964. Also in Kleppner and Settel, *Exploring Advertising,* p. 260.

Dichter, Ernest, *Handbook of Consumer Motivation.* New York: McGraw-Hill Book Company, 1964.

Long, Durwood, "Selectivity: Key to Effective Sampling Techniques," *Advertising & Sales Promotion,* November 1971, pp. 38–41.

Overholser, Charles, "Advertising Strategy from Consumer Research," *Journal of Advertising Research,* October, 1971, p. 9.

Stefflre, Volney, "Market Structure Studies: New Products for Old Markets and New Markets for Old Products," in *Application of the Sciences in Marketing Management.* New York: John Wiley and Sons, 1968.

Twedt, Dik W., "How to Plan New Products, Improve Old Ones, and Create Better Advertising," *Journal of Marketing,* January 1969, p. 53.

Wells, William D., Seymour Banks, and Douglas J. Tigert, "Order in the Data," in *Changing Marketing Systems,* ed. by Moyer, Reed. Chicago: American Marketing Association, 1968. Also in Kleppner and Settel, *Exploring Advertising,* p. 289.

15
Copy

FROM APPEAL TO TOTAL CONCEPT

WE ARE NOW AT the point of translating the appeal into a printed advertisement that could, if we desire, provide the theme of an entire campaign. This is the great moment of complete detachment from all the stereotypes by which the product has been described in the past; the moment to view it afresh in terms of a person who asks, "What can this mean to me?" The sharpest form of answering is with a headline, alone or with a visualization, representing a complete concept on which the copy [1] can be built.

The importance of thinking in terms of a total concept was revealed in a help-wanted advertisement for two art directors, run by an advertising agency in *Advertising Age*. It said:

> We want total concept people who believe they can write as good a headline as some of our writers (because our writers, more often than not, have great visual ideas).

We therefore want to think of an idea in terms of both copy and illustration as a unit. As most printed ideas are first expressed with words, we discuss copy first, in this chapter, and then visualization, in the next.

THE STRUCTURE OF AN ADVERTISEMENT

Beginning with the promise held forth by the appeal, the advertisement may develop along these lines:

---

[1] The term *copy* is a carry-over from those days in printing when a compositor was given a manuscript to set in type and told to *copy* it. Before long, the manuscript itself became known as *copy*. In the creation of a printed ad, *copy* refers to all the reading matter in the ad. In the production of printed advertisements, *copy* also refers to the entire subject being reproduced—words and pictures alike. This is one of the instances in advertising of the same words being used in different senses—a practice that all crafts and professions seem to enjoy as a way of bewildering the uninitiated.

An advertisement begins with	*Promise of benefit*
If called for, it then offers	*Amplification*
If called for, it then offers	*Proof*
It ends with	*Action requested or implied*

For those who like acronyms, it's PAPA.

Promise of Benefit (The Headline)

Usually, the promise of a benefit, or an idea leading directly to it, is expressed at the outset. Sometimes this tells the whole story. But frequently, more needs to be said, in which case the first statement can serve as a headline. The headline is the most-read part of the ad. It is the part that causes a person to decide whether or not to read further. It is the part on which writers labor the hardest. The chief forms of headlines are:

—Direct promise of benefit
—News (of product)
—Curiosity and provocative
—Selective
—Command

Direct-promise headlines. These make a direct promise of the way the product will benefit the reader, thus:

Stop Sunburn Pain	*Solarcaine*
Wash after Wash, Hanes Fits	*Hanes T Shirts*
How to Cook Frozen Meats and Poultry Without Thawing	*Reynolds Wrap*

Any factual promise made within an advertisement must be supportable by evidence.

News headlines. People are interested in "what's new" in products affecting their families or themselves, as in these examples:

New Westinghouse "Heavy Duty 15" Washer: Engineered to prevent costly repair bills	*Westinghouse Washer*
New Kleenex towels absorb 50% more because they're 2 layers thick—not 1	*Kleenex Towels*
Bye Bye Yellow . . . Hello Clear . . . A new "Scotch" Brand Tape is here.	*Scotch Tape*

Facts about a product are new as long as a substantial number of prospective buyers are not aware of them. This period is longer than those close to the product believe it is.

Curiosity and provocative headlines.   As a change of pace from the direct-promise headline, an advertiser may use a headline to arouse the curiosity of the reader, or provoke him to read the copy. The headline promises that what follows will be of interest to him. The promise that the product holds forth can then be presented in the copy. As examples:

How many times do you have to run out of hot water before you switch to oil heat?	*National Oil Fuel Institute*
How much should a young man tell his wife?	*Phoenix Mutual Life Insurance Co.*
Does your child know why it doesn't hurt when his hair is cut? Do you?	*Book of Knowledge*

An advertisement that gets the reader's interest by arousing his curiosity should proceed immediately to satisfy it; otherwise the reader will feel he has been tricked.

Selective headlines.   A reader scanning a publication is much more likely to read an advertisement if it seems to concern him particularly. For this reason, we have the *selective* headline, addressed to a particular segment of the total readership of a publication.

To illustrate this principle, we have here four headlines:

To All Men

To All Young Men

To All College Men

To All College Seniors

The first of the foregoing headlines is addressed to the greatest number of readers, but would be of least interest to any one of them. As the series progresses, each headline reduces the size of the audience it addresses, but improves the chances of attracting that particular group.

Headlines can reach out to select particular groups of readers either by addressing them directly, or else by the nature of the problem discussed, as:

How to Cook for a Man	*Birds Eye Chicken*
Troubled with Deafness?	*Zenith Hearing Aids*

The best reason for going to Europe this summer is because you're not getting any younger	*Pan Am Airlines*

Command headlines. In another category are headlines that directly urge the reader to use or buy the product, usually holding forth a reward if he does so, as:

Use an Evinrude; get more fish	*Evinrude Outboard Motors*
Seal the cylinder; save the oil	*Sealed Power Piston Rings*
Give him an electric blanket; he'll feel warm all over	*Pacific Gas & Electric Co.*

Different types of headlines can often be combined. Based on a lifetime of mail-order experience in the testing of headlines, which provides the most scientific data there is, Schwab writes:

> There are two principal attributes of good headlines. They select, from the total readership of the publication, those readers who are (or can be induced to be) interested in the subject of the advertisement. And they promise them a worthwhile reward for reading it.[2]

The subcaption. The most important thing about a headline is that it should say something important to the reader. The actual number of words is not of the essence—the fewer the better, of course, but a long message can be constructed with a main headline and with a *subcaption* (also called a *subhead*). The subcaption can spell out the promise of the product, stressing its unique features. It can invite further reading. As examples:

POLAROID INTRODUCES
THE $19.95 BIG SHOT

An amazing camera for goof-proof close-ups

(*Polaroid Cameras*)

* * *

THE TIMEX QUARTZ WATCH
$125

A micro-computer with over 300 transistors
controls its accuracy
to within 15 seconds a month.

(*Timex Quartz Watches*)

* * *

---

[2] Victor O. Schwab, *How to Write a Good Advertisement* (New York: Harper & Row, Publishers, 1962), p. 5.

Read how you can enjoy the exhilarating
and adventurous world of flight

(*Piper Aircraft*)

Amplification

Before buying a high-priced, once-in-a-long-time product, a person may wish to get all the specific facts about it that he can, so that he can compare specifications with those of other sellers. An advertisement for such a product will proceed from the headline and subheadline to amplify and support the claims made with details. Since you can seldom put all the technical facts into one advertisement, you pick out a few of the more cogent ones and present them in terms of the benefits the buyer can expect as a result, as was done in the following Westinghouse Heavy Duty 15 Washer advertisement (italics by author):

> Take a look at that heavy duty suspension system securely bolted to its massive steel base. *No shimmy, shaky antics here.* It's designed *to take the strain of heavy family use, and to prevent vibrations caused by extra-heavy washloads.*

The amount of detail in an advertisement should be sufficient to answer the questions that a person considering the product might ask at that time. If there are more facts needed to make a buying decision than can be presented in that space, the reader can be invited to go to the dealer for a demonstration, or to write for further information.

Proof

There comes a point in the consideration of a new or costly product when the prospective buyer wants proof or evidence that the product will perform as claimed. He wishes to reduce the risks of purchase before he buys the product. Among the forms of evidence used to allay his doubts are:

Proofs of quality control. Westinghouse reported that it checked and rechecked its washing machine "from its porcelain top right down to its massive steel bottom, for 138,000 hours."

Demonstration. Reports of timely demonstrations and unusual experiences are often used, as in the case of Firestone Tires, which said:

First time in history, winner of Indianapolis auto race goes full 500 miles without a tire change. . . . Now the same Sup-R-Tuf rubber in durable Firestone race cars is in Firestone tires for *your* car.

Duofold 2-Layer underwear reported:

This is the two-layer underwear that conquered Mt. Everest [worn by leader of American Expedition].

Performance. Sometimes such an experience offers such dramatic proof of the virtues of a product that a whole advertisement is built around it, as was done by Accutron Watches, which reported:

> How An Accutron Watch
> Helped Me Set The American Record
> For The Fastest Single-Handed Sailing
> Across The Atlantic

—followed by the details of this saga.

It is important that proof be available for any factual claims made in behalf of the product.

Before Closing . . .

We are now in the homestretch. We still have to face the fact, however, that a person who has been favorably impressed by the product may be inhibited from buying it for any of a number of reasons.

Berelson and Steiner speak of:

> . . . common ambivalence toward the purchase of an expensive item (cost versus desire), especially in the case of luxury items. Repeated approaches (window-shopping, inquiries, price haggling) often stop just short of purchase—perhaps because the pain or guilt associated with the expenditure rises more sharply as the point of commitment is approached than does the attractiveness of the item.[3]

To meet such attitudes, advertisements often seek to rationalize purchases by offering justifications, as in these instances:

> A North Star Blanket will cost you between $25 and $80. The best things in life are frequently expensive. And who deserves it more?
>
> (*North Star Blankets*)

> Go ahead. Spend the extra $2. It's Christmas, isn't it?
>
> (*Chivas Regal Whisky*)

The closing passages may also be devoted to removing doubts or prejudices against the use of such a product:

---

[3] Bernard Berelson and Gary A. Steiner, *Human Behavior* (New York: Harcourt Brace Jovanovich, Inc., 1964), p. 274.

Concentrated Janitor has no phosphates and is biodegradable so it will not pollute water.

(Janitor in a Drum Cleaner)

Action

The chief action that many national advertisers hope their ads will inspire is a strengthening of the reader's determination to buy, or continue buying, the advertised product. But as a product gets more costly and calls for inspection and demonstration, or for greater explanation (which can best be done by a salesman), there are a number of suggestions that may spur the reader to take the next step toward purchase and do what the advertiser hopes to have him do. Among these are:

Visit a showroom for a demonstration:

See it in action at your Westinghouse dealer's.
For location of your nearest Kelvinator dealer, telephone free 800- 343–6000.

Send for further information or sample (usually a lead for a salesman):

Send for free 24-page booklet containing sample pages from the Book of Knowledge.

Invite representative to call:

Call your local Gold Band Rock Wool Applicator for a free demonstration.

Mail in order or coupon:

Whenever a direct order is sought (in direct-response advertising).

Sometimes two methods are combined:

Visit your dealer or send for booklet.
Look in the Yellow Pages for your Kitchen Aid dealer. Or send the coupon.

Since the chronic foe of all decision making is inertia, the final words of the advertisement may urge the reader to *do something now,* preferably with some advantage for doing so:

Try this recipe tonight and delight the family.
Mail coupon now and get extra bonus offer.

•   •   •

The foregoing represents the structure of copy when a full selling story is to be presented. But many advertisements do not require amplification and proof to make their point; they can tell their story tersely, as in the case of the accompanying Arm & Hammer advertisement, which is the total substance of a newspaper ad occupying five-eighths of a page. But if an explanation of a claim is called for, and proof is needed to establish its validity, the foregoing structure will be helpful: Promise of Benefit—Amplification—Proof—Action.

**Give your kids a gift for their future.
Clean water.**

Arm & Hammer Laundry Detergent. It's free of water-polluting phosphates.

A SHORT COPY AD

Some advertisements can tell their story in a few words.

New Westinghouse Heavy Duty 15 washer

engineered to prevent costly repair bills

Next time your automatic quits and you're left with loads of dirty laundry, don't go to your neighbor's...Go to your Westinghouse dealer instead. He now has a new heavy duty washer engineered to avoid washday breakdowns and prevent annoying repairs.

new trouble-free transmission

It's half again as large as those found in other automatics. And the only one designed for heavy duty washloads. All its working parts are tested and completely checked. It should actually last twice as long as the transmission found in ordinary washers. Westinghouse engineered it that way to minimize the chance of costly repair bills.

new vibration-free suspension system

Take a look at that heavy duty suspension system securely bolted to its massive steel base. No shimmy, shaky antics here. It's designed to take the strain of heavy family use, and to prevent vibrations caused by extra-heavy washloads.

new Giant-Action agitator

Its special built-in ramps pull your clothes deep down into the center of the tub. While the agitator moves backward, the ribbed basket moves forward creating a double-cleaning action unmatched by any other washer.

Big 15 pound capacity

To handle today's big washloads, you need a solid, work-loving automatic washer like the new Heavy Duty 15. It's designed to tackle any load from a big 15 pounds to the smallest family size. Year after trouble-free year.

Proof: tested 138,000 hours

From its porcelain top right down to its massive steel bottom, this new "Heavy Duty 15" has been checked, re-checked and tested—for 138,000 hours—to minimize the chance of costly repairs. So don't worry about giving it too much use. It's built for extra long life. See it in action at your Westinghouse dealer's.

You can be <u>sure</u> if it's Westinghouse

A LONG COPY AD

To sell some products, advertisements must tell a complete story, as did this Westinghouse washer ad, analyzed above.

THE STYLE OF COPY

Advertisements, like people, have personalities all their own. Some say what they have to say in a fresh way. They make an impact. Others, trying to say the same thing, are dull. You may be polite to a dull man, but no one is polite to a dull ad. You just pass it by.

Up to now we have been discussing how the building blocks of copy are put together. We now discuss how to lift what we have to say out of the humdrum by the way we say it. That's style.

The copy approach. The creative essence in writing copy is to see a product in a fresh way; to explore the possible effects of the product upon the reader; to explain things in a way that causes the reader to view the product with new understanding and appreciation.

Most advertisements end by asking or suggesting that the reader buy the product. The difference between a fresh advertisement and a dull one lies in the *approach* to the message at the outset of the advertisement.

The lens through which a writer sees a product may be the magnifying glass of the technician, who sees every nut and bolt and can explain why each is important. It may be the rose-colored glasses of the romanticist, who sees how a person's life may be affected by the product. Therefore we speak of approaches of ads, rather than types of ads. The chief approaches in describing an article may be characterized as:

—The factual approach

—The emotional approach

The factual or rational approach. In this approach we deal with reality—that which really exists, to quote the dictionary. We talk about the product—what it is, how it's made, what it does. This approach calls for more than a list of engineering specifications, unless the ad is talking to engineers. It focuses on the facts about the product that are of most importance to the reader, and then explains their advantages.

Here, for example, is the Goodyear Polyglas Tire ad. Note how each set of technical features is followed by an explanation of its advantage to the reader (set in italics by the author).

THE INSIDE SECRET OF THE GOODYEAR POLYGLAS TIRE
IT'S THE POLYESTER CORD BODY

You see it here—it's the very heart of this Custom Wide Tread Polyglas tire.

What makes polyester unique is that it combines the strength of nylon with the smooth ride of rayon.

So you get a tire that softens the hard knocks—and rolls over the bumps while absorbing the shocks.

In this Goodyear Polyglas tire, we've securely bonded the polyester cord body to two tough fiberglass cord belts—using a special polyester adhesive known only to Goodyear.

These belts help to hold the rugged tread firm and flat on the road for mileage and traction.

TRACTION, STRENGTH, AND MILEAGE

A polyester cord body, two fiberglass belts, a big wide tread—that's the vital combination that goes into the construction of the Goodyear Custom Wide Tread Polyglas tire.

As a result, you get a combination of advantages . . . traction, strength, and mileage. And they all add up to value.

An interesting thing about a fact is that it can be interpreted in different ways, each launching different lines of thinking. Take, for example, a fact like the date—Friday, January 15.

It is the day estimated tax payments are due (*must get check out*).

It is payday (*now you can buy that item*).

It is the last day of midterms (*hurray!*).

It is someone's birthday (*call up*).

Hence we see that a fact is not necessarily a single statement. It has many facets. The most familiar example is that of the eight-ounce glass holding four ounces of water, of which it could be said:

This glass is half full.
This glass is half empty.

Both statements are factually correct. The difference is in the interpretation of the reality, and in the viewpoint they project. The skill in presenting a fact is to present that aspect of it that means most to the person you are addressing, and to translate it into his life experience.

For example, the Economic Development Department of Memphis, Tennessee, ran an advertisement to encourage industries to move there. The writer could have said:

Memphis—a city of 650,000

But he interpreted that fact, and said:

Memphis—city of manageable size

A Polaroid camera ad could have said:

Here is a useful gift

Sears reveals 7 good reasons to put a radio on your wall.

1. It's out of the way. Won't clutter up a table top, counter top or anything else. Who couldn't use more space?

2. You can have music wherever you go, because you can put this radio in any room: even places you haven't put a radio before—a basement, or even a garage.

3. It's so safe and shock-proof you can use it in a bathroom, dripping wet, since it's battery-operated.

4. It sounds good. It's solid state, has a 3-inch speaker, gets both AM and FM and has an electronic device to lock FM stations in. It's easy to operate, too.

5. It looks good, as you can see from the picture at the top of the page. For a slight extra charge, you can get a cabinet to match your decor: Classic, Colonial or Mediterranean.

6. It's so easy to install, you don't even need a screwdriver. Just take off the covering from the adhesive on the back, press it in place—and that's it.

7. Sears sells it. Which means you can get it at a reasonable price. (Batteries are extra.) Available through the Christmas catalog or at any Sears retail store. Drop in and play it some time.

New and only at

SEARS, ROEBUCK AND CO.

THE FACTUAL APPROACH

Here the advertisement presents the technical features of the Sears radio as the reason for buying it.

But the writer presented that fact in a new light:

The gift you never stop opening

An advertisement for the John Deere snow blower could have said:

Blow heavy snow away quickly with a John Deere

Instead it said:

Blow away a blizzard before breakfast . . . behind a John Deere

This ability to present a fact in a meaningful way extends even to classified ads. A man had a house for sale. He described his grounds this way:

Not too much grass to cut

A fact is no less a fact if it is described and interpreted from a fresh viewpoint that stirs the reader's imagination. Because of the many ways of presenting a product, there is never an occasion to say, "There's nothing new to say."

With that approach as a start, the rest of the ad flows along readily enough.

The emotional or imaginative approach. In the factual approach, we seek facts that are real, existent, demonstrable. But there is a world of values that have no yardstick, that can never be weighed, that can only be experienced. People often buy products for the satisfaction and joy to be experienced from their use. We cannot find these qualities by cutting the product apart and seeing what is inside it. Rather we must look into the reader's life to perceive how his life, or that of someone in whom he is interested, somehow, somewhere, will be enriched through this product. That launches us on an imaginative exploration of the emotional possibilities. We call this the *emotional approach*.

Here, as an example, we have an advertisement of a Suzuki motorcycle, with enough technical specifications to fill many pages. Yet the motorcycle was not presented as an engineering feat, but in this imaginative way, describing its effect to the reader:

SUZUKI
conquers
BOREDOM

Life has always been what you make it. Excitement or just routine.
And the line between freedom and feeling trapped can be as simple as two wheels.

Salton Hotray® enables a woman to do an unheard of thing at mealtime.

Sit down.

Every day at mealtime the American woman becomes a ping pong ball.

Bouncing back and forth between the kitchen and the dining room with remarkable speed.

Well, we think a woman shouldn't act like a waitress unless she's paid to be one.

So we recommend every home have a Salton Hotray electric food warmer.

It keeps fresh cooked food in a state of suspended animation for hours. Tasting exactly as it does when it comes out of the oven or off the stove.

A woman need simply place her dinner on a Hotray® food warmer near or on the dinner table. And serve her entire meal. Without ever leaving the table.

And while no woman can afford to be without a Hotray food warmer, any woman can afford to buy one. They're priced anywhere from $7.50 to $59.50.

If you drop a line to Salton, Inc., 521 East 72 St., N.Y. 10021, we'll send you all the details about the Salton Hotray brand of food warmer. For heavens sake, write.

As every husband has been pleading with every wife, "Will you sit down and eat!"

HOTRAY AND HOTABLE ARE TRADEMARKS REGISTERED IN THE U.S.P.O. BY SALTON, INC., THE SOURCE OF THE FOOD WARMERS DESCRIBED.

Available at: Abraham & Straus, B. Altman & Co., Bloomingdale's, Macy's, Hammacher Schlemmer, Gimbels, Bamberger's, stores throughout the country.

THE EMOTIONAL APPROACH

This advertisement begins by discussing the effect of the product on the life of the reader, before swinging into an explanation of the Salton Hotray.

Something like getting on a Suzuki and breaking away. Getting out to see the rugged land you never see from inside your car. . . .

. . . It's your life. And you can make it anything you like.

A phone call to your nearest Suzuki dealer can be a whole new beginning.

Emotional approach backed by factual copy. Although a person may become interested in an advertisement because of its emotional approach, he may nevertheless want to know the specifics of a product before deciding to buy it. Often, therefore, we have an advertisement whose approach to the subject is emotional, but that swings into a factual portrayal, as in the accompanying Salton advertisement.

Some of the most effective ads have been those with an emotional headline and picture, backed up directly with factual copy, or else a factual statement interpreted imaginatively, backed up by factual copy. We avoid speaking of *factual advertisements* or *emotional advertisements,* but only of ads using a factual *approach* or an emotional *approach.*

SLOGANS

The word slogan comes from the Gaelic *slugh gairm,* meaning "battle cry." Today, a slogan is used as the sales battle cry of the advertiser, trying to impress his main claim to its readers' acceptance. The use of slogans as a tool of copy has varied with the years. But it is still a potent instrument in certain situations. It is useful in advertising a low-priced item (like chewing gum), which calls upon no deep deliberation. It is useful for epitomizing the theme of a campaign. It may be helpful in providing a corporate theme, telling the public the service or standard the company represents.

Slogans seek to explain, exhort, extol. Most slogans fall into these classes:

1. Describing the uses of a product:

    For upset stomachs (PEPTO-BISMOL)

2. Suggesting the special advantage or importance of the product:

    Once in the morning does it (SCOPE MOUTHWASH)

3. Suggesting the product be used:

    Long Distance is the next best thing to being there (BELL SYSTEM)

4. Creating an overall uniform image of the company:

    You're in good hands with Allstate (ALLSTATE INSURANCE COMPANY)

5. Guarding against substitutes:

    It's the real thing (COCA-COLA)

Slogans are also potent weapons in political campaigns, and in crusading for public causes. They are usually emotionally charged.

The way to create a slogan is not to set out to create a slogan; but rather to discuss the most important theme of the product. In the course of the discussion, someone with a keen ear will say, "That's it; that's our slogan!"

Elements of a Good Slogan

A slogan differs from all other forms of writing because it is designed to be remembered and repeated over and over again word for word. This makes it imperative that the slogan say something meaningful to the listener. It should be short, easy to understand and to repeat. Rhyming helps: *A title on the door rates a Bigelow on the floor.* Alliteration helps: *Save the surface and you save all.* Parallelism helps: *Total cereal watches your vitamins while you watch your weight.* Of course, brevity and aptness help, and having the name in the slogan is most desirable, as in *Close-Up is for closeups.*

The purposes of slogans are as varied as the purposes of advertising itself and *should derive from the current advertising goals for a product.* Should the campaign theme for a product be changed to meet changing marketing conditions, its accompanying slogan can be placed to rest—*The King is dead; long live the King!*

REVIEWING THE COPY

After the copy has been written, it may be well to review it with these questions in mind:

> —Is it arresting?
> —Is it clear?
> —Is it simple?
> —Does it give the information that the reader would expect at this point of decision making?
> —Are all factual claims supportable?
> —Is it believable?
> —Does it deliver the message about the product it was meant to deliver?

If a piece of copy can pass this test, it may do even better when we add visualization to it, as we shall discuss in the next chapter.

1. Advertising copy, especially for a new product, generally has a basic structure. What are the elements of that structure? Many advertisements do not contain all these elements. Can you explain?

2. What two major purposes can be served by a headline?

3. Under what product or buying conditions is proof important in copy?

4. How many different forms of proof or substantiation can you find in current ads?

5. Can you find examples that show: (a) a news headline, (b) a selective headline, (c) a promise headline?

6. What are the differences between the factual and emotional copy approaches?

7. The book speaks of advertising employing an emotional approach backed by factual copy. Can you find an example?

8. Describe the situations where slogans are particularly useful tools.

9. What are the five major types of slogans?

10. List some slogans you remember from advertising and discuss why you think you remember them.

11. From current advertising find and analyze the copy approaches used by two different brands of the same product.

Reading Suggestions

Barton, Roger, ed., *Handbook of Advertising Management.* New York: McGraw-Hill Book Co., 1970.

Bernbach, William, "Some Things Can't Be Planned," in *Exploring Advertising,* ed. by Kleppner and Settel. Englewood Cliffs, N.J.: Prentice-Hall, Inc., 1970.

Burnett, Leo, *Communications of an Advertising Man.* Chicago: Leo Burnett Company, Inc., 1961. Excerpted in Kleppner and Settel, *Exploring Advertising,* p. 138.

Burton, Philip Ward, and G. Bowman Kreer, *Advertising Copywriting,* 2nd edition. Englewood Cliffs, N.J.: Prentice-Hall, Inc., 1962.

Dichter, Ernest, "Creativity Based on Facts," in *Exploring Advertising,* ed. by Kleppner and Settel. Englewood Cliffs, N.J.: Prentice-Hall, Inc., 1970.

Flesch, Rudolf, *The Art of Readable Writing.* New York: Harper & Row, 1949.

Glatzer, Harold, *The New Advertising.* New York: The Citadel Press, 1970.

Higgins, Denis, *The Art of Writing Advertising.* Chicago: Advertising Publications, Inc., 1965.

Norins, Hanley, *The Compleat Copywriter.* New York: McGraw-Hill, Inc., 1966.

Ogilvy, David, *Confessions of an Advertising Man.* New York: Atheneum Publishers, 1964.

Politz, Alfred, "The Dilemma of Creative Advertising," *Journal of Marketing,* October, 1960, pp. 1–6. Also in Kleppner and Settel, *Exploring Advertising,* p. 157.

Reeves, Rosser, *Reality in Advertising.* New York: Alfred A. Knopf, Inc., 1961. Excerpted in Kleppner and Settel, *Exploring Advertising,* p. 124.

Schwab, Victor O., *How to Write a Good Advertisement.* New York: Harper & Row, 1962.

16

Visualization, Layouts

VISUALIZATION

WHOEVER HAS LEAFED THROUGH the pages of a magazine, or scanned the pages of a newspaper, has been aware that certain advertisements stood out in a way that attracted his attention, while his eye just swept by other advertisements. That difference, in getting attention or not getting it, is the most critical moment in the life of an advertisement.

There are many elements that may cause a person to stop and look at an advertisement. Among these is his interest in the product as a whole. If he is seriously interested in buying something, he will be on the alert for all advertisements dealing with the subject. But even for such products, he may notice some advertisements and overlook others. The chief reason a person looks at an advertisement is because it says something that interests him.

In the copy discussion, we paid much attention to interesting a person in an advertisement through its headline. We now seek to relate that headline with the visualization that helps project a whole concept.

To visualize an idea is to *think* in terms of pictures, and you don't have to be an artist to do that. For example, how would you visualize "golfing"? Perhaps you might suggest showing a man teeing off. You might suggest a twosome in a golf cart, or a golfer blasting out of a sandtrap. This is visualizing, and it can be done without drawing a picture—just by describing it. (Just for fun, how would you visualize "success"?) Having thought of a visual way to express an idea, you can always transmit it to an artist verbally, or with matchstick drawings, or in any way you can best express what you had in mind. But the *idea* of what is to be drawn is the important thing in visualizing.

Not all advertisements need a visualization. The message might be expressed just in a few words that can be set in large type. Or the message may be in the form of a long statement, in which case the only problem will be to set it in readable type. But for those messages that can be enhanced by a pictorial presentation, we explore visualization.

In actual creative work, it is hard to say which comes first, the headline or the visual version; but that is not important—often they are created in the same mental breath. However, since we have already discussed headlines, we study here how a visualization and a headline might work together as a basic unit. (In speaking of headlines here, we include those captions that stand by themselves, and are not followed by supporting copy.)

RELATING HEADLINE AND PICTURE

A visualization of an idea may relate to the headline in the following ways:

1. The headline and the visualization need each other to complete a thought.
2. The visualization imaginatively dramatizes what the headline says.
3. The visualization literally portrays the product, people, or action that the headline talks about.

The approaches above are not offered as a definitive classification of visualizing methods, which is limited only by man's imagination, but as a stimulus to thinking about pictures and headlines as a single entity in getting attention to the advertisement.

Since this is a section on visualizing, we will let the exhibits on the following pages do most of the talking.

You do not need full pages to do a good visualizing job, as this Easy-Off oven cleaner ad reveals.

The headline and the picture need each other.

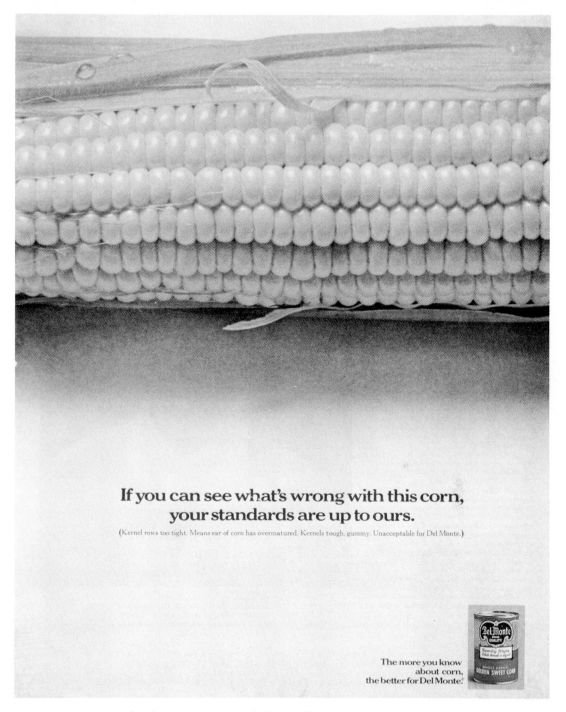

If you can see what's wrong with this corn, your standards are up to ours.

(Kernel rows too tight. Means ear of corn has overmatured. Kernels tough, gummy. Unacceptable for Del Monte.)

The more you know
about corn,
the better for Del Monte.

It takes both the picture and the headline to complete the concept.

Drive as far as you like for a week. $99.

We've created a special rate that'll let you travel literally thousands of miles on your vacation at no extra cost.

In most of our U.S. and Canadian offices, we'll rent you an intermediate or standard Ford or a similar sedan for seven days for $99. You can drive as far as you like without paying us a penny over the $99 as long as you return the car to the city from which you rented it. Insurance is included, gas is not.

If you rent the car in Florida or in California, the rate is the same, but you can return the car to any city in the state. And regardless of where you rent, if you want to pick up the car in one city and leave it in almost any other, we have a plan to cover that, too.

Our $99 rate is an excellent deal if you're going more than 500 miles. If you're driving less, we have a special rate at most Hertz offices that's even better: The Hertz 747.

We'll rent you an intermediate or standard Ford or a similar sedan for a minimum of seven days, for a weekend, or over a two-day holiday for $7.47 a day and 10 cents a mile. Insurance is included, gas is not. (Since the $99 and 747 rates are not available at all Hertz locations, call us for details.)

If you'd like some suggestions on what to do with the car once you've got it, we've motoring and touring guides for almost every part of the country.

No matter which rate you choose, the company comes at no extra cost.

Hertz

@HERTZ SYSTEM, INC., 1970

You don't just rent a car. You rent a company.

The picture is a dramatic visualization of the headline.

It's a lot easier to do push-ups when you're 25.

It's easier to get life insurance, too.

Another nice thing, it's easier to pay for because, as a young man, your premium is lower.

And best of all, when you start young you get more years of satisfaction knowing you are providing financial security for the ones you love at the time they need it most.

Remember, he who hesitates pays more for family protection in many ways.

Think it over, young man, then get in touch with your New York Life Agent.

He's a good man to know.
New York Life Insurance Company
51 Madison Ave., New York, N.Y. 10010
Life, Group and Health Insurance,
Annuities, Pension Plans.

For a happier life

The picture, with its headline, imaginatively interprets what the copy headline says.

Don't forget to feed your camera this weekend.

Pick up several rolls of your favorite kind of Kodak film at your supermarket. And have a memorable weekend.

Kodak makes your pictures count.

Another advertisement built on an imaginative interpretation of a factual statement: "Be sure you have enough film this weekend."

Warm is going barefoot in January.

The colder it is outside, the more you need the gentle, even warmth of clean gas heat. Gas heat makes you feel cozy and taken care of. No cold spots and it's always there when you need it. Gas heat is thrifty. And gas is the clean heat that doesn't dirty the air indoors or out. It helps you have a clean, comfortable home —and a cleaner world for babies to grow up in.

Gas, clean energy for today and tomorrow

AMERICAN GAS ASSOCIATION

The factual advantages of gas heat are imaginatively presented in the headline and illustration.

Put this in your pot and perk it.

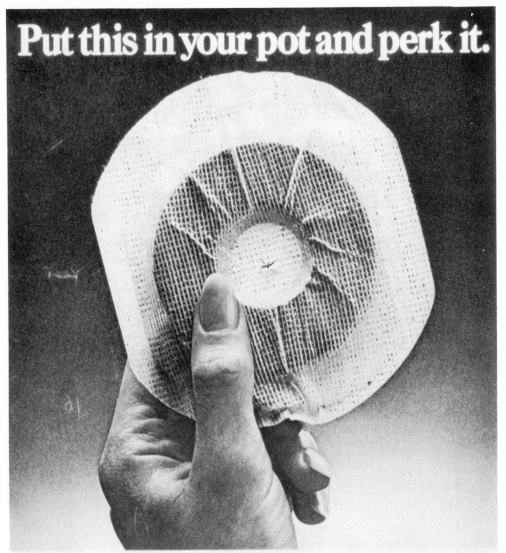

New Max-Pax Ground Coffee Filter Rings. Great tasting coffee in a throw-away filter.

It's new! Ground coffee packed in its own filter. The Max-Pax filter actually traps grounds and sediment that can make coffee taste bitter. So every cup of Max-Pax tastes great. Right down to the bottom of the pot.

Just put one or more filter rings in your regular coffeepot and perk. Each ring makes about 4-6 cups of coffee, depending on the strength you like.

And with Max-Pax, there's no measuring, no spilling, no messy grounds to clean up. Afterwards, just throw the filter away.

The new Max-Pax Ground Coffee Filter Ring.

It's the difference between good coffee and great coffee.

When the product represents something newsworthy, especially if it looks different, the product itself can provide the visualization idea.

364

100% washable

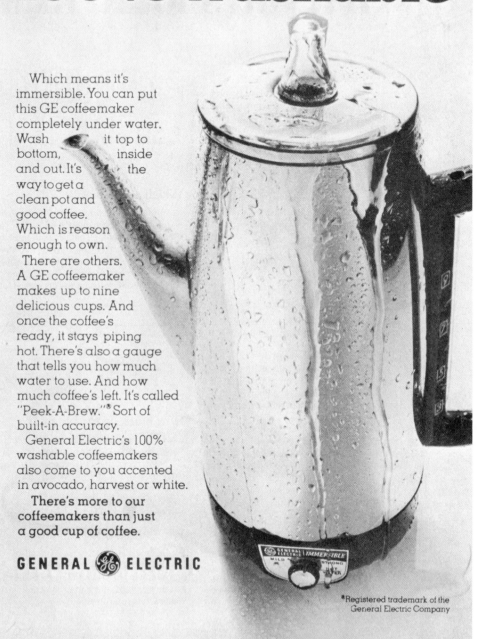

Which means it's immersible. You can put this GE coffeemaker completely under water. Wash it top to bottom, inside and out. It's the way to get a clean pot and good coffee. Which is reason enough to own.

There are others. A GE coffeemaker makes up to nine delicious cups. And once the coffee's ready, it stays piping hot. There's also a gauge that tells you how much water to use. And how much coffee's left. It's called "Peek-A-Brew."* Sort of built-in accuracy.

General Electric's 100% washable coffeemakers also come to you accented in avocado, harvest or white.

There's more to our coffeemakers than just a good cup of coffee.

GENERAL ⊛ ELECTRIC

*Registered trademark of the General Electric Company

The purpose of this illustration is to attract every woman who has ever used an electric percolator.

What you should know

First, what _are_ radial tires?

They're very different from the bias-ply tires you're used to. Compare the constructions shown on the right...the direction of the body plies especially. Radial body plies go straight (radially) away from the bead. On other tire types they go at an angle. It makes a big difference.

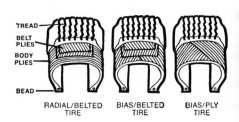

RADIAL/BELTED TIRE   BIAS/BELTED TIRE   BIAS/PLY TIRE

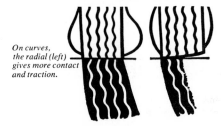

On curves, the radial (left) gives more contact and traction.

What are their advantages?

Quite a few. For example, the track marks above show one big radial advantage at a glance: _more contact with the road._

Why? The radial ply sidewalls of the tire _flex_ — much more than conventional constructions. Result — the tread won't "lift off" on a turn — it stays on the road. Your car has more stability at high legal speeds; in passing situations; on slippery surfaces.

Now add a tremendous advantage in mileage — long, long mileage — 30-35-40,000 miles and better. The belts hold the tread of a radial in a way that limits the "erasing" action — so the tread lasts longer...additionally, the belt and radial plies lower the rolling resistance, and you will get better gas mileage than on bias-ply tires.

Any disadvantages?

Frankly, yes. At low city speeds, you may feel the bumps a little more — but this is offset by the extra smoothness at turnpike speeds.

Also, because the radial must be built on special complex and expensive equipment, radials cost more.

Which cord is best?

Rayon makes fine tires but lacks nylon's strength. _Nylon_ is very strong but flat-spots when cooling. _Fiberglass_ is light, strong, doesn't stretch — great for belts and maybe someday for the body. _Polyester_ provides the smooth ride of rayon with increased strength. _Steel_ is most expensive, but very strong and resistant to cuts — ideal for belts.

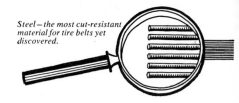

Steel — the most cut-resistant material for tire belts yet discovered.

How much do radials cost?

Expect to pay $50 to $90 each depending on size. They cost more than conventional tires, but on a _per mile_ basis, they're cheaper. Driving 1,000 miles on a standard-size bias-ply tire costs about $1.85; a radial about $1.60 per 1,000 miles. Your General Tire retailer can estimate comparative mileage costs for _your_ car.

Who should buy radial tires?

Putting radials on a car you intend to keep for a while will save money in the long run. But anyone interested in a smooth turnpike ride, excellent steering control and cornering traction will also want radials regardless.

Some ideas can best be visualized with the aid of charts and diagrams. In the above instance they were used to advantage in this long explanatory advertisement.

about Radial Tires.

Vhat you should know about the

General Dual-Steel Radial™

Now that you know why a *regular* radial can give you so much, imagine what you'd get from our radial with two *steel* belts in it. We've built our new *General Dual-Steel Radial* with the uncompromising *quality* of the famous General Dual-90®...a combination that lets us *guarantee* our Dual-Steel Radial for 40,000 miles.

The first polyester and steel radial delivered for Detroit's new prestige cars.

There's something else you should know about our radial. It's quiet. It should be, because it's *Calibrated*®...a General Tire exclusive. It's designed for *American* cars, proved by our tests to be quieter-running than the most popular European brand.

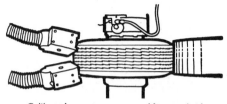

Calibrated...computer-processed for smooth ride.

Your General Tire retailer is receiving Dual-Steel Radial tires now. Check him for your size ...and join our safe-driver customers for 40,000 miles...guaranteed.

GENERAL TIRE

The safe-driver tire company.

To create advertisements in terms of total concepts, learn to think in terms of a picture which would present in a fresh way the words you have in mind, and to think of the words that would best help a picture deliver your message.

LAYOUTS

WE HAVE DISCUSSED COPY. We have discussed visualization. We now discuss putting these together in an orderly form, called the *layout* of the advertisement. The term *layout* is one of the many used in advertising in two senses: First, it means the total appearance of the advertisement, its design, the composition of its elements; you will hear it said, "That is an attractive layout." The term *layout* also means the physical rendering of the design for the ad—its blueprint for production purposes. You will hear a man say, "Here's the copy and the layout," as he hands another man a typed page and a drawing. Right now we are talking about the layout as the overall design of an advertisement.

Here the story is told chiefly in picture form.

THE LAYOUT MAN AS EDITOR

Although the man who created the visual idea may be the same as the man who makes the layout, the two functions are different. As a visualizer, he designs the furniture to go into a room; as a layout man, he arranges it. As a visualizer, he translates an idea into visual form; as a layout man, he takes that illustration and all the other elements that are to go into the ad, and arranges them in orderly form, similar to planning a blueprint.

Before he puts pencil to paper, the layout man—usually an art director—reviews all the elements before him. His first task is to decide what is most important. Is it the headline? The picture? Both? Is it essentially an ad to tell a fast story with a picture and headline, or is it a long copy ad with the illustration only an incidental feature? The importance of the element determines its size and placing within the advertisement. The layout man picks the most important feature and builds his ad around that.

Here the story is told chiefly in copy.

Choose a pot like you choose a husband.

Don't get one you'll have to replace every few years. Look for durability. Farberware makes its pots and pans of the finest stainless steel. So they'll be strong enough to last through years of use. The bottoms are aluminum-clad to give you evenly distributed heat with no hot spots to burn what you're cooking. You wouldn't want to keep cookware around that didn't do its job right.

Avoid the flashy type. Farberware is good-looking. But not too good-looking, if you know what we mean. It's handsome, but rugged and functional. So you don't have to treat it with kid gloves for fear of marring its great beauty. And it's easy to clean. Which makes Farberware easy to live with.

Look out for the troublesome kind. We were brought up never to do anything that would harm a lady. So we use a material for our handles that won't retain heat and burn delicate fingers. And we design our pots and pans with a smooth lip that curves under, so they couldn't possibly cut anybody. Our covers have rolled edges for exactly the same reason. And you can even put Farberware in the oven.

Be sure you get something steady and well-balanced. Good construction is important. So we gently curve the inside of our pots' bottoms and raise them slightly at the center. When you heat the metal, it expands a bit, the center flattens down, and the aluminum-clad bottom lies securely on the burner.

Ask your friends what they think. But only the ones with experience on the subject. Some of them may have chosen unwisely the first time. They're probably older and wiser now and know about Farberware. One thing they'll tell you for sure. No matter what the old song says, you won't find a million-dollar baby in a 5 & 10¢ store. **FARBERWARE**
S.W. Farber Division of Walter Kidde & Company, Inc.

It's tough on your beard. Not on your face.

Gillette
Techmatic.

©1972, The Gillette Company, Boston, Mass.

(LEFT)
An advertisement that tells its whole story quickly. The copy is most important, the illustrations supportive——telling what the ad is all about.

(BELOW)
Picture, headline, and copy get about equal attention in this advertisement, based on a factual approach (accuracy) interpreted in fresh, human terms. Observe the simplicity of presentation and the dramatic touch of having the watch band set on a slight diagonal, with a difference in the shading of background.

HAVE YOU BEEN LIVING ON BORROWED TIME?

With a dishonest watch you go around begging people for the time.

Trying to spot a clock.

And getting dirty looks from the lady sitting next to you, when you were only trying to see her wrist.

But with an Accutron* watch you mind your own business.

It doesn't have a mainspring or a balance wheel that can make ordinary watches fast or slow.

It has a tuning fork movement that's guaranteed honest to within a minute a month.*

So never again will you have to beg anyone for the time.

Or try to spot any clocks.

And though you may still get dirty looks from the lady sitting next to you, it won't be for staring at her wrist.

ACCUTRON® BY BULOVA
The faithful tuning fork watch.

Shown: Accutron "263". Combination brushed and polished stainless steel case. Applied silver markers. Sunray silver dial. Grey napped strap with silver lamé inserts. $125. Ask your dealer to show you the many other styles from $110.
* Timekeeping will be adjusted to this tolerance, if necessary, if returned to Accutron dealer from whom purchased within one year from date of purchase.

Every advertisement in a publication is in direct competition for attention with every other advertisement and with the editorial matter.

It is axiomatic in advertising that a person has first to pay attention to your advertisement if it is to be read. Many sins have been committed in the name of this oversimplified directive, because you can use an odd device or freak drawing that will catch a person's eye—long enough for him to discover that it was only a lure to get him to read something of no concern to him. The real art in getting meaningful attention to an advertisement is to say something significant to the reader, and to do so with words or pictures in a striking way. The attention will then be directed to an idea involving the reader; it is not merely an optical trick that leads to resentment.

COMPOSING THE ELEMENTS

A layout consists of parts. A layout man thinks in terms of these parts as the main illustration, headline, copy, other illustrations, trademarks if needed. The skill is to assemble all these elements into one pleasing arrangement. Here are some guides in the creation of a layout that may be helpful.

Unity. All creative work begins by seeing a subject as a whole unit; a face is more than eyes and nose and mouth; it is a complete expression of personality. A man smiles not only with his mouth but with his eyes. Thus a layout must also be conceived in its entirety, with all its parts related to each other, to give one overall, unified effect.

Balance. By balance, we mean the relationship usually between the right-hand side and the left.

When objects to the right and left of the vertical center of the page are of equal optical weight and placed opposite each other, the balance is called *formal* balance. This balance is the easiest to secure. It makes the easiest reading. It tends to be static.

In *informal* balance, the objects are not arranged so that the right side of the page is the same as the left side; the objects are placed seemingly at random on the page, but in such relation to each other that the page as a whole *feels* in balance. Informal balance is more difficult to attain than formal balance, but it can prove more interesting.

Flow. We speak now of that quality in an ad that causes the reader's eyes to flow naturally through the advertisement. In formal balance, that is no problem; he begins at the top and goes toward the bottom. But in informal balance, the art is to attract attention at the head of the page, and by having optical stepping-stones leading from there to the end, hold the ad together and lead the reader through the copy. Flow may also be helped by the line of direction of the artwork, sweeping across the page. It may be helped by *gaze motion,* that is, having the people in the picture look toward or, perhaps along with other elements of the ad, lead the eye to the center of attention.

UNITY THROUGH FLOW

The plates of beans seem to be coming right to you, holding the advertisement together.

GAZE MOTION AT WORK

Everything in this ad focuses on the baby's head.

Formal Balance   Informal Balance

COLOR IN ADVERTISING

With most full-page advertisements in magazines these days in color, as are many half-page ones, there is a great pressure from the competition of other ads—and from the advertiser's own trade—to be in color also, for those ads that can be enhanced by color. Yet while virtually all liquor advertisers were using full color in the magazine advertisements, the makers of Jack Daniels whiskey used black-and-white ads, in keeping with their rustic story. They not only stood out in contrast, but saved color rates, and production costs.

  Products in which color is an important part of the selling story clamor for color reproduction—fabrics, carpeting, rugs, cosmetics. Color is eloquent in picturing appetizing dishes of food. Color may be used for the sheer beauty with which it brings attention to an advertisement.

  Color talks its own psychological language: To make a drink look cool, there will be plenty of blue in the background; to make a room look warm (for heating advertisements), there will be plenty of red in the background; springtime suggests light colors, and autumn the dark tones. Thus a clue to the choice of the dominating color may often be found in the mood in which the product is being shown.

374

Maybe if you spend a little more for the vegetables, you can spend less for the meat.

For years, steak has been the hero of the American table. But the hero has become a very expensive hero.

Birds Eye® International Recipe Vegetables have a way out. Next time you serve them chicken or some other less expensive (but nutritious) cut of meat, serve them Birds Eye Spanish style Vegetable Medley.

The chicken dinner won't be just another chicken dinner.

Not when they dig into that zucchini squash and those carrot strips, and pearl onions and sweet red peppers in a special Birds Eye orange-flavored sauce.

All at once, your less expensive meal will be as interesting as your more expensive meal.

And you won't only be a good cook, you'll be a smart cook.

Birds Eye International Recipe Vegetables
Japanese, Danish, Mexican, Spanish, or Bavarian style

There's nothing like color to make food look appetizing.

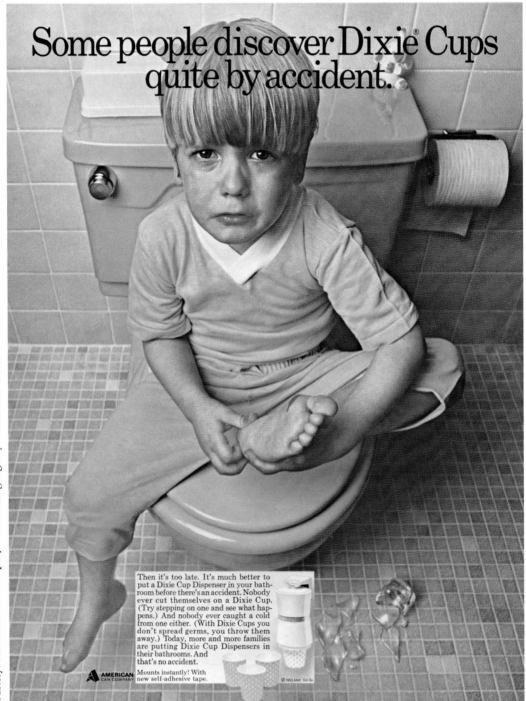

Some people discover Dixie® Cups quite by accident.

Then it's too late. It's much better to put a Dixie Cup Dispenser in your bathroom before there's an accident. Nobody ever cut themselves on a Dixie Cup. (Try stepping on one and see what happens.) And nobody ever caught a cold from one either. (With Dixie Cups you don't spread germs, you throw them away.) Today, more and more families are putting Dixie Cup Dispensers in their bathrooms. And that's no accident.

AMERICAN CAN COMPANY. Mounts instantly! With new self-adhesive tape.

© 1969 Amer. Can Co.

A whole story is quickly told in this picture, enhanced by the deft use of color.

Small advertisements refers particularly to one-column ads up to four inches deep, which will be found in many magazines and with which many businesses have been built. Successful small advertisements usually have a strong promise in a selective headline. The eye takes in all of a small advertisement at one time, so that a liberal part of the space is used merely to get notice. A small advertisement is not a big advertisement reduced; it is created by abstracting the one or two most essential elements of a big advertisement (if one had already been created) and emphasizing one of them.

28 LINES TO 50

Advertisements of this size are the backbone of many advertising campaigns. You have to think in terms of copy and layout at the same time. Notice the strong promise headlines, the variety of illustrative effects used, the ingenuity and simplicity of layouts, the clarity of typography.

"Give a camera for Christmas" is the message of this advertisement, which interprets a fact about a camera in a fresh way, under an appropriate picture of a child. Gives an abundance of "catalogue copy" in a well-organized, readable way.

The gift you never stop opening.

With a Polaroid Land camera, it's one set of goose bumps after the next.

Beautiful color pictures, a minute after you take them. Black-and-white in seconds.

Just seeing how much camera you can give may be a surprise in itself.

The Colorpack II, under $30.

Beautiful color pictures in a minute, at a beautiful price. Electronic shutter and electric eye for automatic exposures. Sharp 3-element lens. Drop-in pack film loading. Built-in flash for 4-shot flashcubes.

The Model 320, under $60.

The most economical in our popular line of folding cameras. Coupled rangefinder-viewfinder lets you focus as you shoot. Electronic shutter and electric eye read and set exposures automatically—even for flash. Detachable camera cover and carrying strap.

The Model 330, under $80.

A lot more gift for a little more money. Built-in mechanical timer automatically tells you when your picture's ready. Transistorized electronic shutter. Precise triplet lens that can use optional filters. Double-image rangefinder-viewfinder for easy focusing.

The Model 340, under $100.

One of the most sophisticated cameras you can give for under $100. Takes indoor black-and-white shots without flash. Built-in development timer. Foldaway rangefinder-viewfinder. Four film speed settings. Handles a whole list of optional accessories such as close-up and portrait attachments.

The Model 350, under $160.

How automatic can you get? Built-in electronic timer "beeps" when your picture is perfectly developed. Takes automatic time exposures up to 10 seconds. Electronic shutter and electric eye. Single-window Zeiss Ikon rangefinder-viewfinder. Handsome all-metal body with brushed chrome finish.

The Model 360, under $200.

The most self-sufficient camera in the world. Snap-on electronic flash. (At 1/1000th of a second it can stop the action at a teenage party.) Recharges on ordinary house current. Electronic development timer. Triplet lens and Zeiss Ikon rangefinder-viewfinder. Four exposure ranges: Two color, two black-and-white.

Polaroid Land Cameras

We mentioned earlier that the term *layout* also refers to the physical drawing of the design of the ad, its blueprint. Layouts come in various degrees of completion. They may begin with a series of thumbnail sketches. The best ones are selected for the making of *roughs* (full size), showing the placement of the major features, several different rough layouts being made as experiments to see which arrangement is most satisfactory. The one selected is then carried out in more definite and precise form, called a *finish* or *comprehensive* layout. All these layouts are designed to get the approval of someone up the corporate ladder, and much depends upon the experience of that someone as to how far up the scale of finality a layout has to go before the ad is approved for production. (See pp. 381-397.)

A WELL-ORGANIZED AD

Showing how a lot of copy with numerous pictorial elements can be organized in a way which invites reading. Note the use of a selective headline to reach women interested in cooking, narrow columns of type to make long copy readable. Note also the position of the pots and knives. The pot handle leads the eye upwards, holding the layout together.

A good cook's guide to better cooking.

Cooking — really cooking — has become very fashionable again.

That means, of course, a good cook can no longer rely on hearty meals — you're expected to serve creative, nutritious meals.

Which makes us delighted. Because the more serious you get about cooking, the more likely you are to buy Ekco Flint pots, pans and knives.

Perhaps that sounds immodest. But consider the following.

A piece of Ekco Flint cookware will actually help you do a better job of cooking. The food will taste better and be better for you.

That's partly because every Flint pot and pan is made with three layers of metal. The outside layers (the ones you see) are gleaming stainless steel — for easier cleaning and greater durability.

The inside layer (which you can't see) is carbon steel. It's a radiant heat core that distributes the heat and cooks food evenly, all around, like an oven.

The special rims on Ekco Flint cookware also contribute to better cooking. When you lower the heat, a vapor seal is formed between the rim and the cover.

You can then cook with less water and lower heat.

This is helped along by Flint's self-basting lids. They let foods simmer in their own rich, natural juices.

The result with Ekco Flint, you don't boil away the vitamins and flavor you pay for.

We said earlier that Flint cookware is durable. That's more than a claim. It's a guarantee.

In fact, we guarantee Ekco Flint cookware for 15 years against defects in materials and workmanship. The same is true for our Flint cutlery. For your money back, just return to Ekco.

Flint stainless steel cookware won't chip or crack or discolor. The handles stay tight. The lids fit snugly year after year.

And stainless steel is one of the easiest things there is to keep sparkling.

Of course, there's more to good cooking than cooking. Fixing meals calls for a lot of cutting, slicing, peeling, chopping, coring, boning and/or trimming.

And no single knife can do them all.

So Ekco cutlers design special blades for each job — each properly balanced for that job. Then they go a step further.

For all 7 different blade types, they've engineered special grinds and edges to make each Ekco Flint knife as perfect a tool as possible.

They all have one thing in common. They're crafted (that's the right word) from high-carbon vanadium stainless steel. That's so they hold a keen edge and so they won't rust or discolor.

Our handles are carved, instead of molded. And they're grooved to give you a firm grip even with wet or greasy hands.

What's more, our handles are made from Pakkawood®, real wood treated to make it impervious to burns, stains, acids and even dishwashers.

One more thing about our Ekco Flint knife handles. They have a riveted tang (that's the part of the blade that extends into the handle). With inferior knives, the tang is driven into the handle, like a nail, and usually comes loose. A riveted tang holds forever.

As we said in the beginning, we're offering this guide out of enlightened self-interest.

Which leads us to this final, helpful word. Both our cookware and our cutlery are available in money saving sets or in open stock.

For the name of your nearest Ekco dealer and our free booklets, "How to Carve" and "How to Choose and Use Cookware," call free 800-631-1972 (800-962-2803 in New Jersey). Ask for Operator Five.

Or write us, care of Dept. NGC.

EKCO

Ekco Housewares Company
Franklin Park, Illinois 60131

When a layout is ready for production, a duplicate will be made and marked up with instructions for the typographer, to whom it will be sent along with the copy to be set in type. It is also used as a guide for ordering plate sizes. This layout is referred to as the *mechanical*.

THE ARTIST'S MEDIUM

The *artist's medium* refers to the tools and background material an artist uses to render his illustration, the term *medium* being used in a different sense than in speaking of an *advertising medium* (as TV or magazines). The most popular artist's medium used in advertising is photography. Other popular ones are pen and ink, pencil, crayon, and wash. Advertisers will use different artists' media as a way of making an advertisement stand out, particularly when most are using photographs. Sometimes art of different media will be used in one advertisement. Perhaps a photograph will be used as the main illustration, but for the smaller secondary illustration, pen and ink will be used for clarity and contrast. The choice of the artist's medium depends upon the effect desired, the paper on which it is to be printed, the printing process to be used, and, most important, the availability of an artist who is effective in the desired medium.

TRADE PRACTICE IN COMMERCIAL ART WORK

The creation of an advertisement entails two types of art talent: one, the imaginative idea man who conceives the visual idea and makes the layouts; and two, an artist who does the finish art of the illustrations needed. In the larger advertising centers, agencies will have on their staffs art directors and layout men who handle internally the visualizing and layouts. They will then call in one of the many free-lance artists available in that city to do the finished art. In the case of a photographer, the agency will choose one who is best at certain types of shots—outdoor or studio, for example; some photographers are specialists on food shots, or style pictures, or whatever the agency seeks. For other illustrations, the agency has its choice of artists who are particularly good at some specialty such as men's styles, women's styles, furniture, machines, cartoons—name your needs and there will be some artists who are particularly good at it.

In smaller cities, agencies try to have on their staffs artists who are versatile enough to handle most finish art work for their clients' needs. Department stores, which have a flow of uniform kinds of work, will have their own artists on the premises.

Crayon

Wash

Pen and Ink

Pencil

DIFFERENT MEDIA

LEGAL RELEASE

Before anyone's picture can be used in an advertisement, his permission in the form of a written legal release must be obtained. This is necessary even though the person may have been paid to pose for the picture. A release is also needed to use a person's name in an advertisement.

CRITERIA FOR LAYOUTS

In looking over the final layout, we ask these questions:

> —Is it arresting?
> —Is it clear?
> —Is it orderly?
> —Is the most important idea given the most important attention?
> —Does it invite reading?
> —If the trademark is needed to identify the product, is it sufficiently visible?
> —Does the layout leave the desired impression about the product?

If so, we are ready to put the ad "into production."

Rough to Finish

MILITARY BOOK CLUB

Courtesy: Doubleday & Co., Inc.
Advertising Agency: Altman, Vos & Reichberg, Inc.

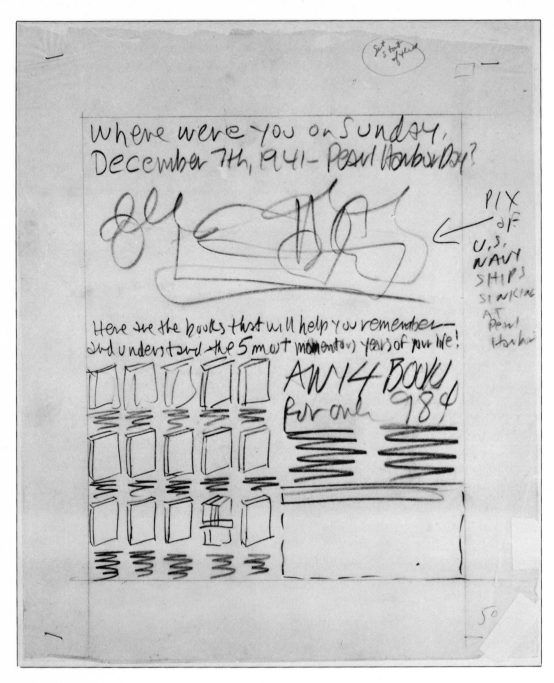

The writer's original rough idea layout

The comprehensive layout made after several intervening roughs. Note change in headline and arrangement of books.

383

Where were you at 0700 hrs 7 Dec 41?

Here are the books that will help you remember and understand World War II—the five most momentous years of your life.

PEARL HARBOR. D-Day. Anzio. Guadalcanal. Midway. Whether you were in uniform or too young to serve, the books on this page illuminate the war years as no other books can.

Would you like to know what it was like to fly a nighttime raid over Berlin? Read *Flying Fortress*. Want to discover why Eisenhower refused to let Patton push on to Berlin? Read *History of the Second World War*. Are you curious to see Admiral Yamamoto's plan to bring America to its knees? Read *Two-Ocean War*.

If you want to know *all* the bluffs, blunders, and triumphs of WWII—and WWI, and all the wars in history—join the Military Book Club. You'll get books you won't find in any other book club, at savings of 30% below the prices of publishers' editions (plus shipping & handling). Take us up on our offer. Four books—worth up to $50.00 in publishers' editions—yours for 98¢, plus shipping and handling, with a trial membership. How can you lose?
Military Book Club, Garden City, N.Y. 11530

U.S. Navy Photo above:
USS WEST VIRGINIA and
USS TENNESSEE burning after
Japanese attack on Pearl Harbor.

The Military Book Club invites you to take

Any 4 books for 98¢

if you join now and agree to accept only 4 selections or alternates during the coming year.

8755. Flying Fortress. Edward Jablonski. The B-17s and the men who flew them. 400 album photos. Pub. ed. $10.95

8714. The Two-Ocean War. Samuel Eliot Morison. Story of U.S. Navy in action from 1939 to V-J Day. Pub. ed. $15.00

1701. History of the Second World War. Basil Liddell Hart. Every major battle on land, sea, in the air. Pub. ed. $12.50

8904. Wars of America. Robert Leckie. Colonial wars to Vietnam. 2 books, counts as one. 1,000 pages. Pub. ed. $12.50

8987. The Supreme Commander. The War Years of General Dwight D. Eisenhower. Stephen E. Ambrose. Pub. ed. $10.00

8854. Iron Coffins. Herbert A. Werner. German U-boat captain's memoirs of submarine warfare in W.W. II. Pub. ed. $7.95

8995. The Battle for North Africa. John Strawson. Why did it take 3 years? Illus. Not avail. in Canada. Pub. ed. $7.95

9019. The First to Fly. Aviation's Pioneer Days. Sherwood Harris. '96 "birdmen" to WWI death machines. Pub. ed. $7.50

3590. Inside the Third Reich. Albert Speer. "I recommend . . . without reservations." N.Y. Times. Pub. ed. $12.50

8961. The War in the Air. The Royal Air Force in World War II. Anthology ed. by Gavin Lyall. Illus. Pub. ed. $7.95

8813. Strategy. 2nd Rev. Ed. B. H. Liddell Hart. Classic book on warfare. Strategists from 490 BC to Hitler. Pub. ed. $10.00

8730. Mao Tse-Tung on Guerrilla Warfare. Transl. by Gen. Samuel B. Griffith. Communist "handbook." Pub. ed. $4.95

2428. The Rising Sun. John Toland. Inside Imperial Japan. Over 60 rare photos. 2 books, counts as one. Pub. ed. $12.95

8912. Fiasco: The Breakout of the German Battleships. John Deane Potter. 1942 "Armada" succeeds. Why? Pub. ed. $6.95

The Military Book Club offers its own complete, hardbound editions, sometimes altered slightly in size to fit special presses and save members even more.

The finished advertisement embodying changes made in comprehensive layout.

VOLVO

The idea layout—rough but quite explanatory.

Carrying out a rough lay-
out idea sometimes involves
more than art work.

ARE YOU IN THE MARKET FOR A HARDTOP?

Every Volvo has six steel pillars holding up the roof. Each one is strong enough to support the weight of the entire car.

Of course, this kind of strength isn't built into a Volvo just so it will hold up a lot of cars.

Volvos are built strong so they'll hold up a lot of years. Exactly how many we can't guarantee. But we do know that in Sweden Volvos are driven an average of eleven years.

Are you sure you're in the market for a hardtop? Or is what you really want a hard top?

The finished advertisement.

FRENCH LINE

An artist tries different ways of expressing a mood.

On the inside, we're all French. Lovers of life and food and fun. The way people were meant to be.

Let out your Frenchman on an uninhibited French vacation. Cruises that take you where you want to go. But take you there French. All the way.

And who but the French can delight your senses with French cuisine (every meal a feast). French service (legions of staff to pamper you shamelessly). And especially French fun (the liberated way to play. Outdoors like the Riviera. Indoors like Paris).

A word of warning: once let out, your Frenchman may refuse to go back in.

Transatlantic Cruise Vacations
The adventurer's vacation package: 5 days exploring the world's largest, most luxurious cruise ship, the S.S. France. 3 days safari to London or Paris. Then 5 more days of wildlife on the France. From $582.

Caribbean Cruises
Two ways to discover your own special island: *The S.S. France from New York,* for elegant pleasure-lovers. From $445. *The S.S. Antilles from San Juan,* for informal camaraderie. From $255.

The Ultimate Cruise
On the Ultimate Ship, the S.S. France. 33 days indulging your sensual French self. While discovering St. Thomas, Bahia, Rio de Janeiro, Dakar, Canary Islands, Málaga, Sicily, Naples, Cannes and Madeira. Feb. 14. From $1490.

Mediterranean Cruises
The French way to savor the world's most magnificent sea. Aboard the S.S. France.

Corsican Resorts
French fun ashore. Three beautiful hotels just south of the French Riviera. Sail, hunt, fish, mountaineer on a still unspoiled island. From $8, including all meals and wine.

Is your Frenchman clamoring for release? Then take him along to your travel agent. Or write us.

Inside every American, there's a Frenchman trying to get out.

French Line®

555 Fifth Avenue, New York, N.Y. 10017 Tel. 363-3940

SAFETY INFORMATION: The S.S. FRANCE and S.S. ANTILLES, registered in France, meet International Safety Standards for new ships developed in 1960 and 1948, respectively, and both meet 1966 fire safety requirements.

The finished advertisement

1. What is the difference between visualization and layout?

2. Name, and illustrate with examples from present advertising, several ways in which the visualization of an idea may relate to the headline.

3. Find several examples from current advertising which you think have excellent visualization. Explain why you consider the visualization excellent.

4. Discuss the major guides to developing an effective layout.

5. From current advertising, find three examples reflecting what you consider to be excellent layouts. Explain why you consider them excellent.

6. Discuss the particular layout problems of small advertisements. From current advertising can you find three examples of small ads you consider to be excellent layouts?

7. Distinguish among the following types of layouts: rough, comprehensive, and mechanical.

8. From current advertising find examples of the use of three different artists' media.

9. What are some of the questions to be asked in judging the final layout?

Reading Suggestions

Art Directors of New York, *Annual of Advertising Art*. New York: Reinhold Publishing Company, annually.

Berrien, Edith Heal, *Visual Thinking in Advertising*. New York: Holt, Rinehart & Winston, Inc., 1963.

de Lopatecki, Eugene, *Advertising Layout and Typography*. New York: The Ronald Press, 1952.

Diamond, Daniel S., "A Quantitative Approach to Magazine Format Selection," *Journal of Marketing Research*, November, 1968, pp. 376–383.

"The Measurement and Control of the Visual Efficiency of Advertisements," New York: Advertising Research Foundation, Inc., 1965.

Industrial Marketing, "A Lesson for the Artist: Function of Layout is Simple as 1, 2, 3," January 1972, pp. 21–25.

Taylor, Robert C., and R. D. Peterson, "A Textbook Model of Ad Creation," *Journal of Advertising Research,* February 1972, pp. 35–41.

Turnbull, Arthur T. and Russel N. Baird, *The Graphics of Communication*. New York: Holt, Rinehart & Winston, Inc., 1964.

17

Print Production

THERE IS SOMETHING WONDERFUL about the way in which typed copy, a tissue layout, and a picture are transmuted into a finished advertisement reproduced millions of times. This is the area of print production.

Just as an architect must be familiar with building materials and methods in designing a house, so anyone concerned with the final appearance of an advertisement should have a basic understanding of typography, the principal typesetting methods, the major printing processes, and the means of organizing production.

TYPOGRAPHY

Typefaces

The first step in translating the headline and copy into type is the selection of a typeface. Every typesetter issues a book showing the styles he has to offer—all of which serve to baffle the uninitiated. The typefaces most used, however, belong to one of three major classes: *Old Style Roman, Modern Roman,* and *Contemporary.* A fourth style, *Text,* preceded the others historically, and is important because its features help to explain the others. A fifth style, *Script,* is often useful for special effects.

 Text Letters. The art of writing was kept alive during the Dark Ages by monks who prepared ecclesiastical manuscripts with wide reed pens, creating a style of lettering that we now call *Text.* When Gutenberg printed his Bible, it was done in hand-carved letters contrived to simulate the manuscripts. Although seldom seen today, except on proclamations, diplomas, and other ceremonial announcements, Text is shown here because the way the strokes are ended influenced succeeding type designs.

 Old Style Roman. During the Renaissance, type designers sought inspiration from the simplified form of lettering carved on the Roman stone monuments. The monument cutters marked the top and bottom of all their letters with a little bar called a *serif,* which is an important clue in type design. Freehand versions of the old Roman letters were designed in the seventeenth century by Claude Garamond, and in the eighteenth century by William

Caslon and John Baskerville. These designs have not only survived to be used today, but have given rise to many others in the same spirit, called *Old Style Roman,* or just *Old Style.* The chief characteristics of Old Style are that (1) there is only a slight variation between the thick and thin strokes, and (2) the serifs are blunt, often oblique, a vestige of the Text style of gracefully ending each letter.

Modern Roman. In the never-ending urge to create new typefaces, Bodoni of Parma, and Didot independently in France, late in the eighteenth century developed another version of a Roman letter, called *Modern Roman,* or just *Modern.* It differs from Old Style insofar as (1) there is a decided contrast between the thicks and thins, and (2) the horizontal serifs are cut sharply as if by a pointed tool, rather than drawn gracefully by a pen.

Contemporary. A form of letter that is in widespread use today is called *Contemporary,* because its designers did not seek inspiration from the past. Its distinguishing features are that (1) the weight of the letters, with few exceptions, is uniform throughout, and (2) the letters have either no serifs at all (and are called *sans serif*), or square (or block) serifs. Contemporary faces are also referred to as *block* letters.

Script. This refers to type designed to simulate the hand lettering of an artist by pen or brush. Used mainly for headlines, slogans, title pages, it is not good in small sizes for blocks of copy.

Typefaces are often named after their designers. Type foundries give their new faces names of their choice.

Even master type experts can do wonders while confining themselves to any of four typefaces, which are recommended to the uninitiated: Caslon, Bodoni, Garamond, and any contemporary sans serif. (Every printer has the last under different names.)

Type Measurement

The point. When Benjamin Franklin opened his print shop in Philadelphia, he ordered his type from Pierre Simon Fournier, a Frenchman credited with being the founder of the point system. With <u>72 points to the inch,</u> type can be measured much more precisely than with an ordinary ruler. It is measured in points from the top of the ascenders to the bottom of the descenders. However, the point number given for a type refers to the *total size of the metal bearing the type*—not the letter size. Therefore, the actual print of a 72-point letter as it appears on the page is less than one inch.

Typefaces up to 18 points in size are generally referred to as *text type*—"text" in this sense meaning the body copy. Type of 24 points and larger is called *display type.*

SIZE of type   8 POINT

SIZE of type   10 POINT

SIZE of type   12 POINT   *text type*

SIZE of type   14 POINT

SIZE of type   18 POINT

SIZE of type   24 POINT

SIZE of type   30 POINT

SIZE of type 36 POINT

                                            display type

SIZE of type 42 POINT

SIZE of type 48 POINT

ascender

letter
size

descender

The size of type is determined by the height of the face or body (not letter size alone) and includes the ascenders, descenders, and the metal shoulder. A "point" measures ⅟₇₂ of an inch.
SET IN 72 PT. CASLON NO. 540

The pica. The width of the line to be set is stated in terms of *picas,* of which there are six to the inch. "Pica" is the name originally given to 12-point type; its letter M was selected as a unit of width, because it is a square letter. Hence picas are sometimes called *pica-ems,* or just *ems* (of crossword fame). An *en* is half the width of an em.

When lines are set in even width, right and left, they are said to be *justified,* and one just specifies the width once for all type to be set. This paragraph is set 28 picas wide.

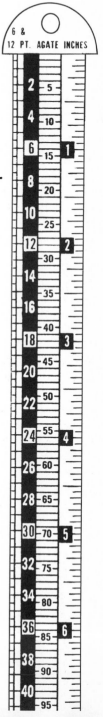

The agate line. In newspaper advertising, and in small-space magazine advertising, the depth of space (height of the ad) is measured in terms of *agate lines,* of which there are 14 to an inch.

To recap:

—The *height (size) of type* is expressed in *points.*

—The *width of a line of type* is measured in *picas*—six to the inch.

—The *depth of space* in which type is set is measured in *agate lines*—14 to the inch.

Type Font

For any given face and size of type, a *font* consists of all the letters of the alphabet, numerals, and the usual punctuation and decorative marks; it also includes all these characters in capitals ("caps") and lowercase ("l.c."), roman, italic, and small caps ("s.c."). A complete font of 11-point Garamond follows:

This is roman Garamond, capitals and lowercase (cap/l.c.).

And this is italic Garamond, initial cap and lowercase.

THIS IS ALL CAPS, IN GARAMOND ITALIC.

THIS IS CAP AND SMALL CAP IN GARAMOND.

1 2 3 4 5 6 7 8 9 0   !@#$%¢&*( )-__:," '?/

Italics. Italicized lettering was introduced in 1501 by Aldus Manutius, a Venetian printer and publisher, and named by him in honor of Italy. It imitated the slanting script of Italian handwriting.

Roman. This second, quite different, meaning of "roman" refers to the standard form of a typeface, the way in which the face was originally designed.[1] It is often used simply to distinguish copy that is not set italic. Used in this sense, the word is not capitalized.

---

[1] We meet here again the use of a word with two different meanings. Sorry, but that's the way it is.

THE BODONI family of type
BODONI BOOK

THE BODONI family of type
BODONI BOOK ITALIC

THE BODONI family of ty
BODONI

THE BODONI family of t
BODONI ITALIC

THE BODONI family of
BODONI BOLD

THE BODONI family of
BODONI BOLD ITALIC

THE BODONI fami
ULTRA BODONI

THE BODONI fam
ULTRA BODONI ITALIC

A family of type retains its basic resemblance and characteristics through all its sizes. The display lines of the Bodoni family are all set in 30 point. Note the variety of weight and color available in an individual family of type. Note also the difference of character measure or width of each face.

Caps and lowercase. In the days of hand-setting, capital letters were kept in a case above the one containing the "small" letters. Thus, "small" letters became known as "lowercase." Capital letters are sometimes referred to as "uppercase," although not often.

Leading. There is a small amount of space between typeset lines, because the type character is slightly smaller than the metal block on which it is cast. This difference between the size of the character and the metal is called a "shoulder." When lines are set without any extra space between them, they are said to be set "solid." Very often, however, additional space is desirable, and the compositor accomplishes this in one of two ways: (1) he sets the characters on a larger piece of metal, thus increasing the shoulder and the space between lines; or (2) inserts thin metal strips between lines, called *leads* (pronounced "leds"), which are measured in points. A leading is specified by adding its value in points to the size of the type: 11-point type set with 2 points of space between the lines would be noted as "11 on 13," or simply "11/13." This paragraph is set 11/13.

Type families. From a single design of type, a number of variations are possible. Each one retains, however, an essential characteristic of the original. The different variations of a single type face are referred to as its "family," and go well with each other within an advertisement where some variation is desired.

Making Type Readable

The first principle of good typography is that *if copy is important enough to be printed, it must be readable.* What makes type readable? To find an answer, Paterson and Tinker tested the speed with which 33,000 persons read various combinations of type. They found that the readability of type depends on three things: (1) size of type, (2) leading, and (3) measure.[2] Specific measurements are summarized in the accompanying chart of "safety zones" for setting type, based on that study.

---

[2] D. G. Paterson and M. A. Tinker, *How to Make Type Readable* (New York: Harper and Row, Publishers, 1940).

SAFETY ZONES FOR SETTING TYPE

	MINIMUM WIDTH	MAXIMUM WIDTH
6 point	14 picas, solid	28 picas, leaded 1 or more points 36 picas, leaded 2 or more points
8 point	14 picas, solid	28 picas, leaded 1 or more points 36 picas, leaded 2 or more points
10 point	14 picas, leaded 1 or more points	31 picas, leaded 1 or more points Between 19 and 31 picas, leaded 2 points
12 point	17 picas, solid	33 picas, leaded 1 or more points

The lines you are now reading are set in 8-pt. solid (8/8) Garamond, 28 picas wide (x 28). There is no leading between the lines, and if you are still reading them, you are a diligent reader, because ordinarily a reader would have stopped before this. It is hard to read this size type in this leading. It takes more than size of type to make a readable passage.

The lines you are now reading are also set in 8-pt. type, just like the paragraph above, but they have 2-point leading (8/10). It still isn't fun to read a long passage in 8-pt type, but notice how much easier it is to read this paragraph. This has been set this way to show the effect of *leading* in making type readable.

These lines are still set in 8-pt. type, leaded 2 points (8/10), as above, but they have been set only 16 picas wide (x 16) instead of 28 picas, to show the importance of width of line in making type readable. In all these instances, the size of the type is the same; the difference is in the leading and the width of the line.

TESTS HAVE ALSO SHOWN THAT A LINE OF TYPE SET IN CAPITAL LETTERS is harder to read than a line of type set in lowercase letters, or Caps and Lowercase letters. CAPITAL LETTERS SHOULD BE USED SPARINGLY. Used too often, they defeat their purpose.

To make an advertisement with a lot of copy readable, you might start it with an initial letter as above. Use one family of type for captions and occasional subcaptions, and set the copy into two or more columns to avoid too wide a column for the size type and leading. Remember the lesson of newspapers: Narrow columns make for easy reading of even small type.

Type fitting. Fitting of type means determining the size of type in which copy should be set. For the production man specifying type, there are many published sets of tables available. For the writer to judge how much copy he should write to fit a predetermined amount of space, here is a simple method: Look through a magazine or newspaper for an ad with copy set in the size in which you would like to see your copy set. Count the number of *characters* (not words) per square inch; each space and punctuation mark counts as a character. Figure how much space you have for copy in terms of square inches, and the number of characters you can have. On an elite typewriter you have 12 characters to the inch; on a pica typewriter, 10. Set your line width in even inches on the typewriter; you will then know how many lines to type.

Advertising typographers. When an advertiser plans to spend a considerable amount of money on space, he wants his advertisement to have fine typography—better than what an individual publisher could provide in what is known as publication setting, or "pub set." He may have his copy set by an *advertising typographer,* who specializes in type composition only

The headline tells the story

On this page we have examples of four families of type, with the headline set in 24-point type of the family, and the body copy set in 10 point on 12 of the same family. You need not go outside a family to have an interesting, harmonious ad. Note how the number of words per line varies; see where the last word of each paragraph falls. Novices are in the company of master typographers when they stay within one type family per advertisement. The sign of a real amateur is trying to use too many faces in one advertisement.

This paragraph has been set in Caslon.

The headline tells the story

On this page we have examples of four families of type, with the headline set in 24-point type of the family, and the body copy set in 10 point on 12 of the same family. You need not go outside a family to have an interesting, harmonious ad. Note how the number of words per line varies; see where the last word of each paragraph falls. Novices are in the company of master typographers when they stay within one type family per advertisement. The sign of a real amateur is trying to use too many faces in one advertisement.

This paragraph has been set in Bodoni.

The headline tells the story

On this page we have examples of four families of type, with the headline set in 24-point type of the family, and the body copy set in 10 point on 12 of the same family. You need not go outside a family to have an interesting, harmonious ad. Note how the number of words per line varies; see where the last word of each paragraph falls. Novices are in the company of master typographers when they stay within one type family per advertisement. The sign of a real amateur is trying to use too many faces in one advertisement.

This paragraph has been set in Garamond.

The headline tells the story

On this page we have examples of four families of type, with the headline set in 24-point type of the family, and the body copy set in 10 point on 12 of the same family. You need not go outside a family to have an interesting, harmonious ad. Note how the number of words per line varies; see where the last word of each paragraph falls. Novices are in the company of master typographers when they stay within one type family per advertisement. The sign of a real amateur is trying to use too many faces in one advertisement.

This paragraph has been set in Futura.

(not printing). Typographers set the type for most national advertising. Most local advertising is set by the newspapers, without cost to the advertiser.

Copy sent to the typographer or newspaper carries the type specifications, marked right on the copy. They include:

   a. Type size and leading
   b. Type face (by name)
   c. Width of line (in picas)

COPY READY FOR THE ADVERTISING TYPOGRAPHER

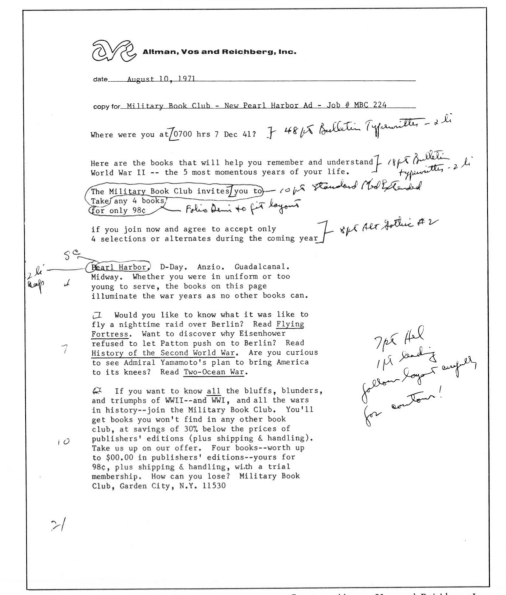

"Printer's Shorthand," used in correcting the type proofs of advertisements. The marks come in pairs, one written in the body of the proof, the other in the margin.

ℰ	Dele, or delete: take it out.
ᓇ	Letter reversed—turn.
#	Put in space.
⌒	Close up—no space.
∨∧	Bad spacing: space more evenly.
wf	Wrong font: character of wrong size or style.
tr	Transpose.
¶	Make a new paragraph.
□	Indent; or, put in an em-quad space.
⊏	Carry to the left.
⊐	Carry to the right.
⊓	Elevate.
⊔	Depress.
×	Imperfect type—correct.
↓	Space shows between words—push down.
⫽	Straighten crooked line.
‖ =	Straighten alignment.
stet	Restore or retain words crossed out.
⌒	Print (æ, fi, etc.) as a ligature.
t see copy	Words are omitted from, or in, copy
⑦	Query to author: Is this correct?
caps	Put in capitals.
sc	Put in SMALL CAPITALS.
lc	Put in LOWER CASE.
rom	Put in roman type.
ital	Put in italic type.
bf	Put in bold face type.

MAJOR TYPESETTING METHODS

Now we move on to the methods of setting type. There are basically four ways of setting type, each serving some special purpose:

1. *Hand-setting*
2. *Machine-setting*. Freshly molded by machine. Also referred to as "hot metal type."
3. *Photocomposition*
4. *"Cold type."* Typewriters with special typefaces and carriages.

Hand-setting

Hand-setting, the oldest method, affords the greatest possible latitude in designing a page of text or display matter. Each character in every headline, every phrase, sentence, and paragraph, is molded separately and set by the compositor's hand; by this painstaking method, he picks letters out of a case and assembles them in a metal holder (a composing stick), according to the style, size, and arrangement specified in the layout.

Not used for great quantities of reading matter, it is limited generally to formal announcements and title pages of brochures or books, or where special faces are specified for dignity or expression of an unusual thought. It is the slowest and least automated of all typesetting methods. This is known as *Foundry type*.

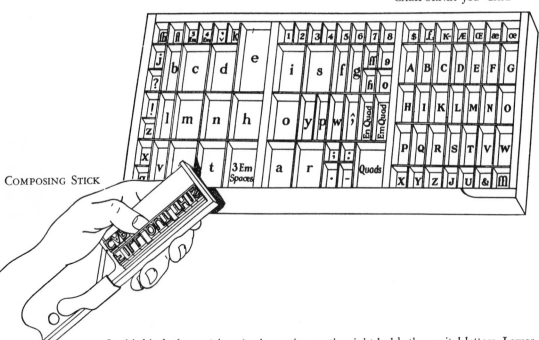

CALIFORNIA JOB CASE

COMPOSING STICK

In this kind of case (above), the section on the right holds the capital letters. Lower-case letters, figures, punctuation marks, and spacing material occupy the middle and left sections. Characters are so arranged in the case that common letter combinations are close together. . . . Cases such as these hold three or four such fonts.

From David Hymes, *Production in Advertising and Graphic Arts* (New York: Holt, Rinehart & Winston, Inc., 1966).

ELEMENTS OF A TYPE LETTER

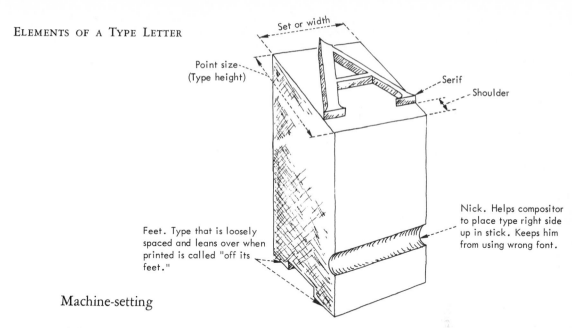

Set or width

Point size
(Type height)

Serif

Shoulder

Feet. Type that is loosely
spaced and leans over when
printed is called "off its
feet."

Nick. Helps compositor
to place type right side
up in stick. Keeps him
from using wrong font.

Machine-setting

A line at a time.   Imagine a man sitting before a machine at a keyboard like that of a typewriter. As he operates the keyboard, there is humming and clicking within the machine. In a few moments there appears a bar of metal, up to about five inches long, and type high.

Were you to pick it up, it would feel hot. Were you to look along its edge, you could read the original copy molded onto the bar. The Linotype is really a molding machine, with a pot of molten, or "hot," metal within it. The letters are molded from brass matrices which drop into their proper places with the touch of the operator at the keyboard. After the complete line has been set, it moves to the molding area where the line of type is molded. Once done, the matrices are returned mechanically to the storage magazine. The lines follow each other out of the machine, neatly stacked, ready for the next step in printing. They are collected in a tray or "galley," each exactly the same width, or "justified," by the machine.

LINOTYPE COMPOSITION

This type has been molded by
a machine, a line at a time.

Courtesy, Mergenthaler Linotype Company.

405

Just how this seeming miracle is performed can most readily be understood by seeing a Linotype in operation at a newspaper or printing plant, and such a visit would be rewarding to anyone sufficiently interested. Most newspapers, books, and reading matter in advertisements are set by Linotype.

The advantages of Linotype are that (1) it sets type rapidly, and (2) it is easier and faster to handle a line slug than individual letters of type. The chief disadvantage of the Linotype is that if you want to change a single letter, you have to recast the entire line. When the slugs have served their purpose, they are thrown back into the pot of molten metal; no need to return individual letters to the typecase, as for hand-set type.

TYPE

In the left foreground is a block of Linotype, each line set separately. In the right foreground are some units of Foundry, a "hand set" type, each letter or figure being separate. In the background are examples of type molded a line at a time on a Ludlow machine.

Courtesy, New York *Daily News*

A letter at a time. The Monotype consists of two machines—one produces what looks like a roll of punch cards; the other is fed into the second machine, a miniature type foundry. In contrast to the Linotype, which casts letters a line at a time, the Monotype casts letters one at a time, separately. They are assembled by the line, but each letter is separate. Even though you still face major resetting with a substantial deletion or insertion, you can

MONOTYPE COMPOSITION

This type has been molded by machine, but each letter is separate. Note how the type accommodates itself to the irregular plate of the illustration.

Courtesy, Lanston Monotype Machine Company

change a letter or word in a line without resetting the whole line. The compositor can vary the line width as he goes along, a fact that makes Monotype setting advantageous for setting type around an illustration, or for tabular data, or for technical and mathematical material.

Hand-set, machine-molded. The Ludlow method of setting type is used chiefly for headlines in newspapers, magazines, and ads. It is a combination of hand-setting and machine-casting. Any size line can be set. *Matrices* of the type (rather than the type itself) are assembled by hand and set into a casting machine, and within a few seconds the line of type is cast. This system provides an unlimited number of characters, and because it provides newly molded type for each job, the letters print cleanly and sharply. Lines are cast into slugs 22½ picas long, and longer lines are made in multiples.

Photocomposition

Now we come to photocomposition, which, in the opinion of many, will become the dominant way of setting advertising type, and in the opinion of some now working in the field, may become a way of the future for printing books. The system involves the computer, photography, and a special television system.

In photocomposition, an operator types all the copy on a machine that converts it into computer tape. He also types the instructions as to the size of the type and the line width, and any other typographical instructions to be followed. The tape then will control the entire operation. The photography comes in the form of a film, holding the complete font of one face of type. Obviously these letters are very small. The first surprise in photocomposition is to learn that this is all the type needed for anything set up to 18 points, because the type can be magnified to that size and then enlarged to any size! An operator can have an inventory of 1,500 fonts on six 6-inch shelves!

THE PHOTOCOMPOSITION PRINCIPLE

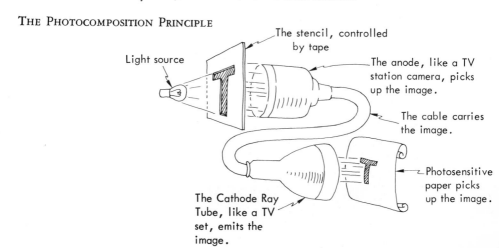

Light source

The stencil, controlled by tape

The anode, like a TV station camera, picks up the image.

The cable carries the image.

Photosensitive paper picks up the image.

The Cathode Ray Tube, like a TV set, emits the image.

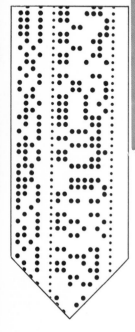

Photocomposition tape, containing all copy and type instructions.

A NORMAL...	**A** CONDENSED...	**A** EXPANDED...	**A** BACKSLANTED...
A ITALICIZED...	**A** ENLARGED...	A REDUCED...	**A**^A IN VARYING
A^A HEIGHTS...	^A**A** WIDTHS...	**A**A AND DEGREES OF SLANT!	**A**A
*A*A**A**	**A**ᴬₐ	**A**A**A**	**A**^A_A

The array of letters on the left demonstrate the flexibility of a film font. The type below, set on a photocomposition device, would otherwise have to be hand-drawn.

Courtesy, Visual Graphics Corporation

Perfectly Connected Scripts EVERY TIME!

The selected film font—really a stencil through which light can pass—is set in the machine. When everything is ready, the computer tape turns on a light in front of the film, lighting up each selected letter in turn, and moving across the width of the line at incredible speed. The light is picked up by an anode tube, as in a TV studio, which changes the light into electronic impulses, corresponding to the shape of the letters. These are carried to a cathode-ray tube like the picture tube in your TV set, which turns the electronic impulses back into picture form; except that here, it shoots the electrons directly onto photosensitive paper, which develops or prints the letters right on the paper. The result is a rapidly made print of the copy with more sharpness and less cost than by metal type. Prints can also be made on transparencies, instead of on paper, for some printing processes.

The Photo Typositor produces display type photographically from film fonts such as this one, which contains a complete alphabet of a particular type style in negative form.

Courtesy, Visual Graphics Corporation

Because photocomposition is such a radical development, anyone who has been working with hot-metal typography will become aware of the great differences in handling the two. For example, there are no standard sizes, as in hot metal typography; the letters can be made any size you want, within limits. It is necessary to use the type book of the photocompositor in choosing type, and not a hot-metal catalog. You can do all kinds of tricks with the type —all from one little film. You can make it taller or shorter, wider or thinner; you can give it perspective; make it lean forward or backward; and do all the things for which, in the past, you had to have an artist hand-letter the effect you sought. It is versatile, indeed.

The latest generation of such equipment can set the whole advertisement (photograph and copy together) from layout, and, if necessary, transmit such information over long distance by cable. There are several systems each operating by one or more principles common to existing methods.

"Cold Type"—Typesetting Typewriters

Typewriters that can type in a variety of faces and produce camera-ready copy represent the *cold type* family. The simplest machines, such as the IBM Electromatic and the various automatic electric typewriters, may or may not be able to justify copy and usually offer only one typeface and size. More complicated devices (such as VariTyper, Lithotype, and IBM Selectric) offer a greater selection of faces but are not automated. The most sophisticated forms are almost completely automated.

Computerized coldtype is used commonly for catalogs, directories, and indexes, which have to be reprinted and updated regularly. They are brought up to date with a corrections tape, saving the need for resetting everything.

THE MAJOR PRINTING PROCESSES

Most advertising is printed by one of three major printing processes:

1. *Letterpress:* printing from a raised surface *(relief printing)*

2. *Offset* lithography: printing from a plane surface *(planograph printing)*

3. *Rotogravure printing:* printing from a depressed surface *(intaglio printing)*

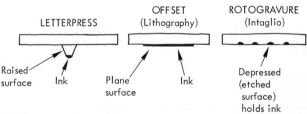

Letterpress Printing

The easiest way to understand the principle of letterpress printing is to look at the type bars of a typewriter. There each letter stands out in relief above the surface of the type bar. When the key is touched, only the letter in relief strikes the ribbon and transfers its design to paper. That's printing from relief type, called *letterpress printing.* This is the only process that uses type directly.

Letterpress printing is the most versatile form of printing, and most widely used. Most printers are equipped to produce it. Letterpress printing gives sharp reproductions. It can print full-strength colors and blacks that are really black. It can provide a high degree of fidelity to the original in color printing. In letterpress printing, the advertiser must supply the photoengraving plates of any illustrations, as we will discuss later.

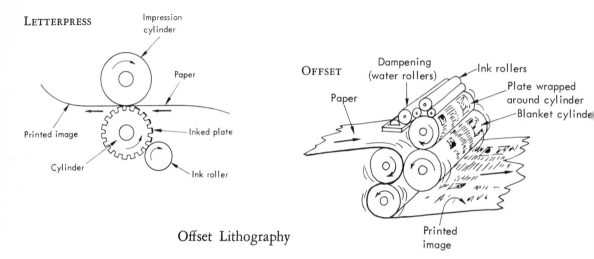

Offset Lithography

To explain the principle of lithography, skipping many details, a photographic negative is made of the advertisement. Through this negative, then, light is flashed onto a photosensitive plate. After being flushed with chemicals, the exposed (or printing) areas on the plate become capable of transferring ink to paper, while the unexposed (nonprinting) areas are not. When ink is passed over the *whole* plate, only the ink-receptive areas print.

That's *direct lithography,* which was the original form of lithography, and which is still used for printing posters, labels, and packaging. The most used form, however, is *offset lithography,* colloquially known as just *offset.* It gets its name from the fact that the roller of ink does not touch the paper, but prints on a rubber-blanketed roller, which in turn offsets the ink to the paper.

The chief advantages of offset are that it gives photographs a soft effect, that it can print photographs on rough paper, that it requires little makeready time and expense, that it has low plate-making costs—all handled by the printer—and that it can handle sheets up to 52 x 74 inches in size. Offset and letterpress are in direct price competition on many jobs. In offset printing, the advertiser must supply the material for the finished ad as it is to appear. The offset house makes all the plates of any illustrations, or at the advertiser's order, obtains them from firms that specialize in making negatives from advertisers' copy.

Rotogravure Printing

Have you ever passed your finger over an engraved calling card and felt the raised dried ink? That card was printed from a plate in which the printing area was etched by hand. When ink was applied to the face of the plate, and the excess wiped off, ink remained in the etching, and, when a card was pressed against it, was transferred to the card. That form of printing, from a sunken design, is called *intaglio printing*.

Rotogravure also works on the intaglio principle. Here the plate is not etched by hand, but by a photographic-chemical process. The etching is only one to two thousandths of an inch deep; nevertheless, it is an etching.

Platemaking for rotogravure. Hymes reports that it takes 24 steps to prepare a rotogravure plate for printing.[3] We skip from the early steps, when the advertisement is photographed and the negative transferred to a sensitized copper roller, to the final steps, when the plate has been etched and inked and

---

[3] David Hymes, *Production in Advertising and Graphic Arts* (New York: Holt, Rinehart & Winston, Inc., 1966), p. 187.

ROTOGRAVURE

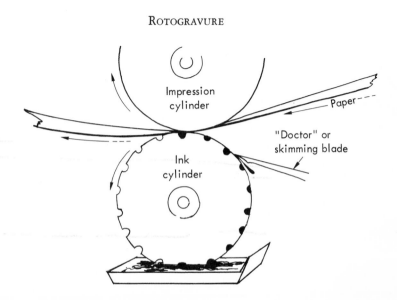

Impression
cylinder

Paper

"Doctor" or
skimming blade

Ink
cylinder

the excess wiped off. The ink in the etching is transferred to paper pressed against it. The original subject has been reproduced by rotogravure.

In rotogravure you are dealing with heavy copper rollers; you cannot readily make changes. But once the plate has been made, you can print 500,000 copies, and even millions, at a very low cost per unit. Therefore, rotogravure is widely used by catalog houses and the Sunday newspaper supplements, and for long-run direct-mail work.

In rotogravure, as in offset, the printer makes all the plates, working from precise original copy supplied by the advertiser, or, at the advertiser's order, from firms that specialize in making negatives from advertisers' copy.

Silk-Screen Printing

Even though the silk-screen process does not rank in importance with the three major ones, it is very useful for printing runs under 5,000, as for store displays and bus cards, calling for flat colors and simple line work. It is a method of printing with a squeegie, forcing the ink through a screen in which a stencil forms the area where the ink is to go. A different screen or set of stencils is used for each color. With each screen, you can print with solid colors or fluorescent colors, but not with graduated tonal values.

Since you can print on any kind of surface—paper, cardboard, glass, or metal—silk-screen printing is widely used for display cards for stores and for transit.

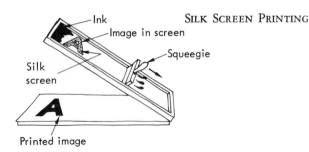

SILK SCREEN PRINTING

PHOTOENGRAVING

When an advertisement is to be printed by letterpress, the advertiser must supply all plates of the illustrative material in the form of photoengravings. The picture must stand out in relief on these plates, just as the letters of type do on a typewriter. This effect is attained by a combination of photography and chemical engraving—hence their name. The two main forms of photoengraving are (1) line plate and (2) halftones.

Line plates can be made from any illustration (preferably black and white) consisting of solid lines or solid masses, as in Illustration A. Line plates can be printed on any paper, and are the least costly form of photo-engraving.

For photographs and other illustrations with graduated tones from light to dark, halftones are needed, as in Illustration B. They are limited as to the types of paper on which they can be printed.

ILLUSTRATION A. LINE COPY

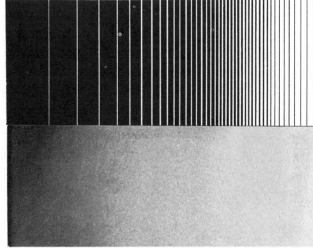

ILLUSTRATION B. HALFTONE COPY

Line Plates

Suppose you have to make a letterpress plate from a line drawing of a simple T. You would photograph it and print it on a metal surface coated with a photographic emulsion. The area where the T is printed becomes acid-resistant. The plate is dipped into a bath of acid, which eats away the metal around the T; it is left in that bath until the etching is sufficiently deep for the T to stand out high enough to be suitable for letterpress printing. The plate is removed and mounted on wood for ease of handling, and is ready to be printed. The same thing would be done to any design clearly drawn in black lines or areas. This plate is then sent to the printer, who inserts it into the space left among the standing type. Printing plates may then be made from type and engraving together.

Benday. Line plates can be made only from drawings in black line or black masses. To get the effect of a shadow, the lines can be drawn close together, but they must be sharp. Or the shadow can be drawn in solid black. The *benday process* (named after Benjamin Day, the man who created it) is designed to give a line-plate subject some variation in shades between different

THE PHOTOENGRAVING PRINCIPLE OF MAKING LINE PLATES

1. Suppose you had a flat piece of wood like this...

2. and passed a roller of ink across it...

3. and pressed paper against it...

4. the paper would come out like this.

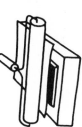

5. Now if you marked the letter Z and carved away the rest of the wood, leaving the Z raised...

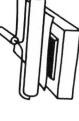

6. and passed an inked roller over the wood...

7. then pressed a piece of paper against the wood...

8. the paper would bear this imprint.

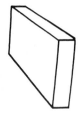

9. We begin again. This time we want to reproduce the above letter.

10. It is photographed on a metal surface coated with photographic emulsion

11. To make the T stand out, the metal surrounding it is etched away chemically instead of by tool, as in 5.

12. The result is a raised letter, as in 5.

attached to a wood block for easier handling

13. Then if you passed an inked roller over it...

14. and pressed paper against it...

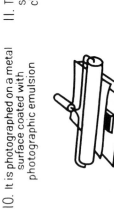

15. you will have printed the T on paper. Print as many as you want!

This is how simple black and white drawings are reproduced by line plates.

GUIDE TO LETTERPRESS PHOTOENGRAVINGS

Engraving	Specification	Advantage	Comments
Line Plates	Black & White	Prints well on any paper.	A. Least expensive engraving. B. Quickly made. C. Also known as a Line Cut. D. Not for photographs.
	Black & White Line Plate With Benday	Provide contrasting tones to a line plate subject.	A. There are different Benday patterns. B. Each Benday pattern is a uniform value of gray. C. Benday effect is specified when ordering plate but applied by engraver.
Halftones	According to Screen		
	55, 60, 65	To print photographic subject on coarse newstock.	Screen must be specified.
	85, 100, 110	For printing photographs on machine-finish paper, such as the inside pages of most magazines.	The lower a screen number, the coarser the screen, the rougher the paper on which it can be printed.
	120, 133	To print on coated paper such as magazine covers.	Up to 100 Screen is Coarse, 110 and over Fine.
	According to Finish Square Halftone	Least costly halftone engraving.	Square halftones are used for editorial pictures.
	Silhouette Halftone	Emphasizes subject by having it stand out sharply by itself without tone background.	A. To Silhouette, a photoengraver blocks out background before making the plate, otherwise it would be a square half-tone. B. There is an extra charge for Silhouette.
	Highlight Halftone	Provides pure white accents in a halftone subject.	A. Areas to be pure white are blocked out by photoengraver before making plate. B. There is an extra charge for highlights.
Halftone with Line	Combination Plate	Combines the sharpness of a line plate subject.	A. A combination plate would improve the sharpness of a label on a halftone package. B. Halftone screen must be specified.
Color Engravings	2-color Line Plates	Least expensive way to reproduce a color design by letterpress printing.	A. A separate plate is made for each color. B. Black is usually one of the colors, supported by a brighter second color. C. A color sample must be provided to printer as color inks vary.
	1 set of Duotones	Reproduces a picture in two color halftone.	A. Art work must be in color. B. Both plates are halftones, made in such a way that dots do not directly cover each other. C. One ink represents the color, supported by a Second Ink, generally Black. D. Color proofs from the photoengraver serve as a guide for printer. E. Screen must be specified.
	Set of 4-Color Process Plates	Reproduces a picture in a full range of colors.	A. Art work must be in color. B. Screen must be specified. C. Yellow, red, blue & black ink will collectively present a printed picture in full range of colors. D. A separate plate is needed for each color. E. Engravers proofs showing the progressive addition of colors serve as a guide for printer.

parts. It reminds the writer of a coloring book, where children color outlined areas in different colors, but instead of using colored crayons to color flat areas in outline form, the engraver (for letterpress) or artist (for offset) lays down a shading unit with designs of different patterns of lines and dots. Each pattern, however, is a clear line-plate subject. The result: a line plate with various designs and variations in shading.

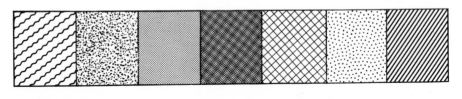

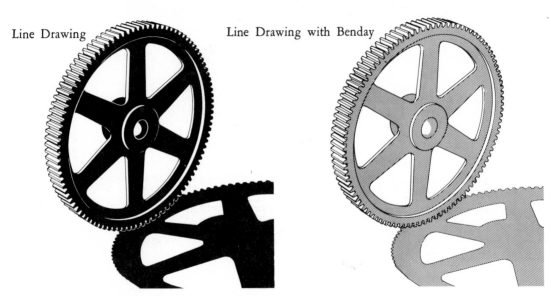

Line Drawing   Line Drawing with Benday

Line color plates.   A line plate printed in one color is referred to as a single-color plate. To produce line plates in two, three, or four colors, each extra color is marked on a separate tissue, or overlay. The artwork itself is not colored. The engraver then makes a separate set of plates for each color. Line color plates provide a comparatively inexpensive method of printing in color with effective results.

Halftone Plates

Unlike a line drawing, a photograph or painting is a blend of many black and white tones; they give form to the picture and its background.

MAGNIFICATION OF HALFTONE PLATE

Showing how it is composed of black dots of different sizes. The centers of the dots are equal distances from each other; they vary only in size.

Screening. How can these tones be converted into a form as sharp and clear as the lines and masses of a line drawing? The secret lies in a screen, which is placed in front of the lens, bearing a crosshatch of 50 to 150 hairlines per square inch, forming from 2,500 to over 25,000 little windows through which light can pass. The greater the density of the crosshatch per square inch, the smoother the appearance of the halftone.

When you look through a screened window, you are aware for the moment of the screen before you; but soon the brain adjusts to the screen, and you see the view as a whole, oblivious of the screen. But a camera has no brain to make such an adjustment. It records exactly what it sees through each of those windows. What it sees is so tiny that only a dot can come through, varying in size with the blackness of the part of the picture it is seeing. Where the picture is dark, the dots are big and close to each other; where it is light, the dots are as small as a needle point; and so, dot by dot, the camera records on a sensitized plate all the varying tones of the picture, just as they are on the original.

From that point on, the halftone is treated like a line plate; the picture in the form of dots is printed on a metallic plate, which is washed with a preparation that makes the dots acid-resistant. The plate is immersed in an acid that eats away the metal except for the dots, and before long, a plate emerges in which the dots stand out in relief. When a roller of ink is passed over them, and paper applied, the ink on the dots is transferred to the paper, producing a replica of the original picture. A halftone plate has been made and printed. If you look carefully at some newspaper ads, you will recognize the separate dots.

Choice of screens. Different types of paper reproduce differently, and screens come in a variety of sizes so that the size of the dots can be chosen that will reproduce best on the paper to be used. The number of dots per square inch is standardized. Those most frequently used are 55, 60, 65, 85, 100, 110, 120, and 133, although higher numbers are available. The higher the screen number, the more dots per square inch, and the greater the fidelity and detail in the final reproduction. But the higher the screen, the smoother the paper has to be to have all the dots strike it. That is why for newspapers, 65 screen is often used, and for magazines, 120 screen. It is mainly the paper that determines the screen.

65   110   Halftone Screens   165

The lower the number on the screen, the fewer the dots per square inch. The higher the screen, the more dots per square inch. The choice of screen depends upon the smoothness of the paper and the amount of detail required.

Halftone Finishes

The half-tone *finish* refers to the way the background of the main subject is treated. When you take a snapshot of a friend's face you will get a print of the friend's face, plus the background. If you want to make a halftone of it for printing purposes, the engraver can treat that background in a number of ways. He can leave it all in with the background screen extending to the edge of the rectangular plate. This is called a *square* halftone. He can cut away everything in the background but the face so that the face will appear sharply against the white background of the paper. This is called a *silhouette* or *outline* halftone. The square halftone is the least expensive finish; the outline halftone costs more but gives the sharpest picture of the subject. These are the forms of finish in most universal use.

Silhouette Halftone
(background cut away)

Square Halftone
(includes background)

Color halftone plates. A color reproduction can be made from half-tone copy in one of two ways. First, a halftone can be printed in black over a screen in another color. Or a halftone can be photographed twice, turning the screen on an angle the second time so that the dots for each plate fall *in between* each other rather than directly *on top* of each other. This second method is called *duotone*.

Full-color reproduction. The finest reproduction of a color print or painting is by means of a set of four color plates, representing yellow, red, blue (the primary colors), plus black. The photographer takes four separate pictures with filters; first he will use a purple filter that allows only the yellows to come through; then an orange filter for the blues; a third green one for the reds; and finally one for all shades of black. He makes a separate plate for each. Then when they are all combined by four runs through the press, they will reproduce all the colors, intensity, and values of the original. Such plates are also referred to as *four-color process plates,* or *full-color plates.*

Duplicate Plates

An advertiser may need duplicate plates of his letterpress advertisement, to send to the different publications on his schedule, to save the costly original plates, to issue reprints of his advertisements, to send to dealers for cooperative advertising, or for other purposes. He has at his disposal: (1) electrotypes, or (2) mats and stereotypes.

Electrotypes. The electrotype is the hard-working distant relative of the silver-plated spoon; they are both children of electrolysis. In the making of an electrotype, the original plate is pressed into wax, forming an exact mold. The mold is sprayed with graphite, making it a conductor of electricity. It is connected to an electric wire and suspended in a bath. Facing it in the bath is a bar of copper connected to the second wire of this circuit. When the current is turned on, there is a migration of ions from the copper bar to the wax mold, soon covering it completely and forming a hard shell. Shortly, out comes the whole wax mold with its face of copper. The wax behind that copper shell is removed, and in its place hot metal is poured. When this has cooled, there emerges a metal plate bearing an exact duplicate of the original plate. That is an electrotype (*electro*).

The Making of Electrotypes

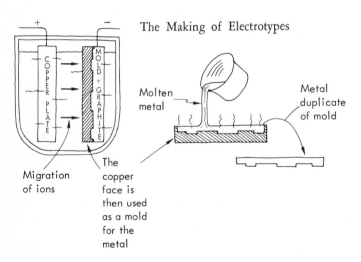

Migration of ions

The copper face is then used as a mold for the metal

Molten metal

Metal duplicate of mold

Wax-mold electros serve for most purposes. When especially fine reproduction is required, lead and plastic molds may be used, with nickel facing instead of copper. When many duplicate plates have to be made, an especially hard plate called a *pattern plate* is made, from which all the other electros are made, sparing the original.

A disadvantage of an electro is its cost, as well as the expense of shipping a heavy plate. For newspaper printing, mats are less expensive.

How a Full-Color Reproduction

is made,

through the use of

Four Color Halftone Plates

Yellow

Red

Yellow and Red

Blue

Yellow, Red, and Blue

Black

Yellow, Red, Blue, and Black

How a Full-Color Reproduction

is made,

through the use of

Four Color Halftone Plates

The mat. The least costly form of duplicate letterpress plate, and the one in widest use for newspaper advertising, is a *mat* or *matrix*. The mat, however, is only one half of a two-step operation. It is made by pressing a plate of the ad into dampened papier-mâché. When dried, the papier-mâché forms a hard matrix, from which it gets its name. When molten metal is poured into the mat and hardened, a metal replica of the original plate is formed, called a *stereotype* (or *stereo*).

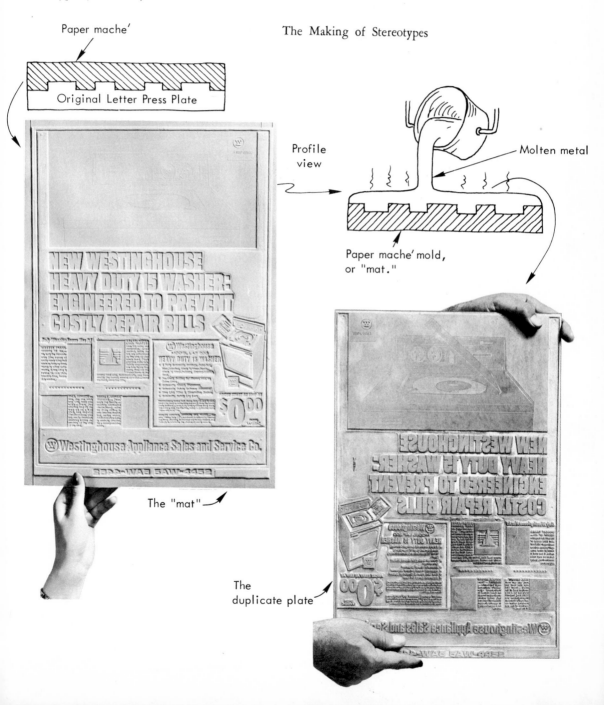

The Making of Stereotypes

Paper mache'

Original Letter Press Plate

Profile view

Molten metal

Paper mache' mold, or "mat."

The "mat"

The duplicate plate

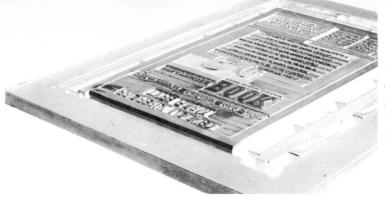

A Printing Form

In the center are various units of type, with the photoengravings prepared for the advertisement. On the outside is a strong rigid, metal frame or form. The matter to be printed is held in place by a series of wedges which are tightened. The form is then placed on a press for printing.

Courtesy, International Assn. of Electrotypers & Stereotypers, Inc.

One does not print from a mat; someone must make a stereo.

It so happens that newspapers use mats for the curved plates they need to fit the rollers of their presses. As a result, they can accept the advertiser's mat and make a stereo of this (no charge to advertisers). Mats are widely used for newspaper advertising by national advertisers; also for distribution to dealers for local advertising. Stereo reproduction is not as sharp as that of electros, but it is well suited to newspaper reproduction, and less expensive than electrotype. The number of times a mat can be used is limited.

Mats for newspapers tend to shrink, a factor that must be provided for in ordering. For better reproduction, there are stronger and sharper mats made, called *dry mats, coated mats, plastic mats,* and other patented mats. They are less sharp than electros, and cost less to make and ship.

Making Offset Plates

For both line and halftone copy, the printer needs a mechanical layout. The main plate-making advantage to offset printing is that text and line art may be handled together by the printer. If the advertising agency so elects, it can supply final-size prints of all line art, pasted into the proper position with the text. The printer can then shoot the entire mechanical with one click of the shutter. Usually, however, the agency will prefer to supply the mechanical with only the text in place and the art in oversized form, to be reduced photographically and then positioned by the printer according to instructions.

Paper

We now move from printing processes and plates to the next dimension of print procedure: paper.

For publication advertising, the creative and production directors must know on what kind of paper the advertisement will be printed, in order to plan their artwork and plate needs. In direct-mail advertising, they have the additional responsibility of selecting the paper.

The three chief categories of paper used in advertising are:

1. Writing paper
2. Book paper
3. Cover stock

Writing paper. This is the paper most used for office letter-writing and in direct mail. The kind most frequently met is *bond paper,* which is specified whenever printed matter requires permanence and durability. Letterpress and offset reproduce well on bond, and both are equally economical. Offset, however, is a better choice than letterpress when halftones are required.

Book papers. This represents the widest classification of papers used in advertising, with many variations. Chief among these are:

—*News stock.* The least costly book paper, built for a short life, porous so it can dry quickly. Takes line plates well, also halftones of 55, 60, 65 screens, provided the artwork has sharp contrasts.

—*Antique finish.* This refers to a paper with a mildly rough finish. It is soft paper. It cannot take halftones, but is widely used for offset.

—*Machine finish.* Most books and publications are printed on machine-finish paper, which takes halftones up to 110 screen well. It is the workhorse of the paper family.

—*English finish.* Here is a book paper that has a higher degree of smoothness than machine finish. It can take halftone screens up to 133 screen.

—*Coated.* This is a paper that is given a special coat of clay, and then ironed. The result is a heavier, smoother paper. It can take 150-screen halftone very well, and is therefore frequently used in industrial catalogs, where fine sharp reproduction is important and that will be used over a period of time.

WHY DIFFERENT SCREENS?

On the rough surface paper (at top) a coarse screen halftone is used so that a greater proportion of dots actually touches the paper. On smooth paper (at bottom) a greater proportion of dots from a fine screen can touch the surface, improving fidelity of reproduction.

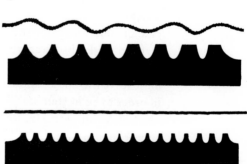

Cover paper (cover stock). Here is a strong paper, highly resistant to rough handling, used not only for the cover of booklets, but sometimes by itself in direct-mail work. Although it has many finishes and textures, it is not adaptable for halftone printing by letterpress, but reproduces tones very well in offset.

There are many other types of papers used for many purposes, but writing, book, and cover are the chief ones in advertising. In any given situation, the printer will submit samples of paper suitable for a given job.

Basic Weights and Sizes

Paper comes off the machine in large rolls. It is then cut into large sheets in a number of different sizes. In that way, many pages can be printed at one time. Paper is sold by the ream of 500 sheets, and its grade is determined by weight. To meet the problem of trying to compare the weight of paper cut to different sizes, certain sizes have been established for each class as the basic ones for weighing purposes. These are:

For writing paper	17 x 22 inches
For book paper	25 x 38 inches
For cover stock	20 x 26 inches

Hence, no matter how large the sheet may be into which the paper has been cut, its weight is always given in terms of the weight of that paper when cut to its basic size. Thus one hears a writing paper referred to as a 20-pound paper, a book paper referred to as a 70-pound paper, a cover stock identified as a 100-pound cover.

Paper has to be selected in relation to the method of printing and the plates to be used, or vice versa.

PLANNING THE WORK

In order that the creative and the production work may move with the necessary precision, a time schedule is planned at the outset. The *closing date* is the date or time when all material must be in the hands of the publisher. The advertiser works backwards along the calendar to determine when the work must be begun in order to meet that date (as in figuring out what time you must leave the house, allowing time for driving delays and parking difficulties, in order to be in your seat for the kickoff).

As an example, let us take a four-color letterpress advertisement to appear in a magazine, for which the closing date is October 1. We then plan a production schedule like this:

Production Schedule

In order to reach publication by closing date	October 1
Plates must be shipped by electrotyper by	September 26
Engravings must go to the electrotyper by	September 22
Engraver should deliver final proof	September 17
Engraver should have first proof	September 12
Material should go to photoengraver	August 24
Art and mechanical layout should be ready by	August 17
Type and mechanical layout should be ordered on	August 11
Finished artwork should be delivered by	August 10
Finished artwork should be ordered by	July 21
Creative work (art and copy) should be approved by	July 20
Creative work should start by	July 1

A PRODUCTION SCHEDULE

This form is for use in planning the preparation of an advertisement. The date when it is due at the publishers is first entered (near bottom in form). The date when electrotype is due is next filled in, and so on up the column. The work of the entire organization is thus scheduled.

PRODUCTION ORDER

Client: Product: Req'n:

Medium: Issue: Size: No. Colors:

Title:

Ad. No.:

PRODUCTION SCHEDULE   JOB No. _____

	DUE DATE	DATE MET	REMARKS
Establishment of Idea			
O.K. of Idea, if necessary			
Rough Sketch (Estimate $_____)			
Copy			
O.K. (Rough, Copy and Estimate)			
*Finished Art Work			
*Client's O.K.			
*Engraving			
*Type Setting			
*Client's Final O.K.			
*Electrotyping			
*Delivery to Publisher			

*These dates established by Mechanical Department when making out order. All other dates established by Production Manager.

Estimate $_____ Rough $_____ Outside $_____ Inside $_____ Revise $_____

In the case of an advertisement for a weekly magazine section of a newspaper with a closing date 12 days prior to the time of publication, the entire schedule would have to be proportionately compressed. In a newspaper advertisement, the work would pass along with even greater dispatch—six hours from idea to approved proof, if necessary—as any department store advertising production manager knows only too well.

REVIEW OF PRINT PRODUCTION

It may be helpful to review some of the more important technical terms we have recently encountered.

We discussed three basic forms of printing—letterpress (from *raised* surface), offset lithography (from *flat* surface), and gravure (from *etched* surface). The form of printing affects the way material is prepared for publication.

Typography deals with the style (or face) of type in which the copy is set. Typefaces come in related designs called *families*. The *size* of type is specified in *points* (72 to the inch). The *width of the line* in which type is to be set is measured in *picas* (6 to the inch).

These are the chief ways of setting metal type: by *hand;* by *Linotype* (type cast one line at a time); by *Monotype* (type molded in separate letters and set by machine in line width); and by *photocomposition* (type reproduced electronically on sensitized paper).

If you plan to use illustrations for letterpress work, you will have to order *photoengravings*. The two chief classes are *line plates* (for sharp black-and-white artwork), and *halftones* (for photographic-type artwork). In the case of line plates, you can apply different patterns of shading to different areas by means of benday. In the case of halftones, you have to specify the *screen,* which depends chiefly upon the smoothness of the paper's surface; the rougher the paper, the coarser the screen. You also have to specify how you want the background treated. This treatment is referred to as its *finish*. The chief finishes are *square* (includes everything), and *outline* or *silhouette* (everything cut away except the subject itself).

Once a photoengraving is made, you can order *duplicate plates*. For newspaper purposes, you can order a *mat* and send it to the paper, where a *stereotype* of it can be cast for use in reproducing the advertisement (the least costly way). You can also have *electrotypes* for magazines.

For offset and gravure processes, no separate plates need to be ordered. The material is forwarded to the publisher as it is to appear.

In all production work, a most important element is timing.

1. What is meant by:
   a. a serif
   b. upper case letter; lower case letter. (Draw an example of each.)
   c. leading
   d. font
   e. family of type
   f. halftone finish

2. What are the chief things to strive for in typography?

3. There are three elements to be considered in making type readable. What are they? *size, leading measure (width)*

4. When do you measure by points? How many to the inch? When do you measure by picas? How many to the inch? *6*

5. What is meant by "hot type"?

6. What are the chief methods of setting type? *hand. machine photo comps. cold-type*

7. What is the basic technical difference between letterpress, offset, and rotogravure printing?

8. What is the chief advantage or use of each?

9. How does material sent to the printer for offset and rotogravure differ from that sent for letterpress printing? *on R. printers makes all plates*

10. What is the chief difference between a halftone and line plate in regard to: (1) the art work they can best reproduce, (2) the paper on which they can be printed?

11. What is the relation between a mat and a stereo?

12. What are the chief types of paper used in advertising? *WRITING PAPER BOOK PAPER COVER STOCK*

Reading Suggestions

Arnold, Edmund C., *Ink on Paper, A Handbook of the Graphic Arts.* New York: Harper & Row, Publishers, 1963.

Bahr, Leonard F., *ATA Advertising Production Handbook.* 4th edition. New York: Advertising Typographers Association of America, Inc., 1969.

Bockus, William, Jr., *Advertising Graphics.* New York: The Macmillan Company, 1969.

Hymes, David, *Production in Advertising and the Graphic Arts.* New York: Holt, Rinehart & Winston, Inc., 1966.

Melcher, Daniel, and Nancy Larrick, *Printing and Promotion Handbook.* New York: McGraw-Hill Book Company, 1966.

Pocket Pal, "A Brief History of Printing and Paper." New York: International Paper Company, 1966. Also in Kleppner and Settel, *Exploring Advertising,* p. 166.

Schlemmer, Richard M., *Handbook of Advertising Art Production.* Englewood Cliffs, N. J.: Prentice-Hall, Inc., 1966.

18

The Television Commercial—
Creation and Production

CREATING THE TELEVISION COMMERCIAL

A GOOD FIRST STEP in creating the commercial is to decide exactly what you want the viewer to remember about your product after the commercial is over. That is the sales message. All else is technique.

The sales message is usually agreed upon before the commercial is started. If not, we have to determine the chief service this product can render in meeting some problem of the viewer—whether it's giving the family more variety in meals, or getting a better shave faster—and then determine the special way in which this product can help meet that problem. The art then is to present that story as interestingly as possible in 30 seconds, the time for most commercials. (In writing commercials, the picture is called *video;* the spoken parts, *audio*.)

Once that is determined, a writer can use all the imagination and skill at his command in the technique he uses, provided only that it holds the viewer's attention at the outset, and that when the commercial is over, the viewer comes away with the message *about the product* that was originally agreed upon. The test of a good commercial is not having the viewer say, "That's a good commercial," but rather "That's a good product."

Types of Structure

With the aid of pictures (video) and sound (audio), a writer has many ways of telling his story—even in 30 seconds, which is the most popular length of non-network commercials. Among the many approaches that Book and Cary offer are the following guidelines. They are all predicated upon trying to develop a single idea, clearly and logically.

Story line Telling a story that involves tension at the outset and leads to a logical conclusion.

429
*The
Television
Commercial—
Creation and
Production*

Problem-solution Based on predicament or problem, enlightenment, as by a friend, happy results, with aid of product (often called *slice of life*).

Chronology Tells message through series of related scenes, one growing out of another.

Special effects Strives for a mood that relates to product and its uses.

Testimonial Matching your product with believable celebrity, competent to pass judgment on such product.

Spokesman A radio commercial illustrated by a moving picture of the product and announcer.

Demonstration Don't try to fool the viewer.

Suspense Begin the suspense immediately, build it carefully, end with clarity and relevance that reward the reader.

Analogy Make certain that the analogous example is one that is familiar and understandable to most viewers.[1]

In addition to the items above, there is animation, which can tell its story with charm and humor, and many other structures that are constantly being developed.

Styles in commercials, as in movies, have their waves of popularity, representing constant challenges to the writer to develop fresh patterns.

Writing the Commercial

The commercial is usually written in double columns, with the audio on one side and the video on the other. In presentation of the commercial to a client, it is often sketched out, sequence by sequence, on a series of layout forms called a *storyboard*. The storyboard gives the advertiser a visual idea of what is planned, and provides agency and producer a base for the meeting of minds, and for estimating. In creating the commercial, Bellaire offers the following suggestions:

1. The video and the corresponding audio should relate. Don't be demonstrating one sales feature while talking about another.
2. While the audio should be relevant to the video, don't waste words by describing what is obvious in the picture. Rather, see that the words interpret the picture and thereby advance the thought.

---

[1] Albert C. Book and Norman D. Cary, *The Television Commercial* (New York: Decker Communications, Inc., 1970).

THE SINGER COMPANY
60-SEC TV COMML
"THE SINGER STRETCH"
SF-SM-0086

REVISED

AS RECORDED: Jan. 18, 1971

VIDEO

1. OPEN ON CLOSE SHOT WOMAN PUTTING
BABY IN PLAYPEN. AS SHE STRETCHES TO
PUT BABY DOWN, SHOULDER SEAM OF BLOUSE
SPLITS IN SYNC. SHE REACTS, SHOWING
SEAM SPLIT.

1.A. FREEZE FRAME

2. ZOOM BACK OR CUT TO SEE WOMAN BENDING
TO PICK UP BABY'S BOTTLE OR TOY FROM FLOOR
NEAR PLAYPEN. SFX IN SYNC WITH BENDING
MOTION.

2.A. FREEZE FRAME

3. CUT TO WOMAN PREPARING SANDWICHES.
SEE LITTLE GIRL TUGGING AT WOMAN'S SLEEVE.

3.A. FREEZE FRAME

4. DISS TO CU SINGER "S" ON 750 MACHINE.

5. ZOOM BACK TO BEAUTY SHOT OF MACHINE.

6. ECU NEEDLE SEWING STRETCH STITCH.
SUPER WOMAN ON LADDER
STRETCHING OUT ARMS TO HANG DRAPES.

7. AS SHE STRETCHES ARM TO EXTREME ...

8. ZOOM IN TO CU UNSPLIT SHOULDER SEAM
ON OUTSTRETCHED ARM.

9. DISS TO FINGER ON STITCH SELECTOR
DIAL.

10. PULL BACK OR DISS TO FULL MACHINE
SHOT. FINGER ON DIAL. "SINGER" NAME
VISIBLE.

11. CUT TO CU FINGER MOVING STITCH
SELECTOR DIAL.

AUDIO

SOUNDS: BABY, MOTHER TALKING TO BABY

SFX: RIPPING SOUND

SOUNDS OF CHILDREN OR MUSIC UNDER.

SFX: RIPPING SOUND

ANNCR: (VO)
Sometimes it's like the whole world
is trying to pull you apart.

SFX: RIPPING SOUND

But now

there's a way to really hold things
together.

BG MUSIC STARTS UP, THEN UNDER
Do the Singer Stretch!
MUSIC EFFECT: STRETCHING SOUND

Sew stitches that stretch ...

and hold! With

One Touch Sewing -- on the

newest Golden Touch & Sew machine.
By Singer.

One touch and you choose
your stitch ...

THE ORIGINAL SCRIPT

One page of the original script for a Singer sewing machine commercial. Translation: *Freeze* = hold; *CU* = close-up; *ECU* = extra close-up; *Zoom* = move camera
closer to subject, making it larger; *SFX* = sound effects.

JWT
420 LEXINGTON AVENUE
NEW YORK 17

CLIENT: THE SINGER COMPANY
PRODUCT: SEWING MACHINES
TITLE: "SINGER STRETCH"
CODE NO.: SFSM0086
JO# 409448

DATE: 2/27/71
LENGTH: 60 SECONDS

1. (MUSIC & SFX)

2. (MUSIC)

3. MOTHER: (VO) Oh!

4. (MUSIC & CHILDREN UNDER) MOTHER: (VO) Oh!

5. ANNCR: (VO) Sometimes it's like the whole world is trying to pull you apart.

6. But now there's a way to really hold things together.

7. (MUSIC UP & UNDER) Do the Singer Stretch!

8. Sew stitches that stretch... and hold!

9. With One Touch Sewing

10. —on the newest Golden Touch & Sew machine. By Singer.

11. One touch and you choose your stitch...

12. Only Singer brings you these 9 kinds of stretch stitches.

13. And stretch stitches hold when regular stitching breaks.

14. (MUSIC)

15. Do the Singer Stretch!

16. Stretch your budget with One Touch Sewing

17. on this Golden Touch & Sew machine.

18. At your Singer Sewing Center.

19. It sure helps hold your world together.

20. (MUSIC UP & OUT)

PHOTOSCRIPT OF FINISHED COMMERCIAL

A photoscript consists of photographs taken from the finished commercial, usually corresponding to the key items on the script or storyboard.

Courtesy: The Singer Company
Advertising Agency: J. Walter Thompson

1.
SHE (FADES UP)...and
don't forget to buy
milk for the kids
while I'm at...

2.
the hospital.
<u>Light n' Lively.</u>

3.
HE: (MUMBLES)
Milk, right.

4.
SHE: Not just milk.
Light n' Lively low
fat milk.

5.
HE: You buy this for
the kids, too?

6.
99% fat free?

7.
SHE: Of course, it's
got more protein and
calcium. And it's
convenient for you.

8.
HE: (LOOKS UP
      PUZZLED)

9.
SHE: You'll only
have to remember
one kind.

10.
VO: The one kind to
remember. Light n'
Lively low-fat milk:
20% more milk protein
and calcium from
Sealtest.

N·W·AYER & SON INC.

CLIENT: SEALTEST FOODS

PRODUCT: LIGHT N' LIVELY MILK

TITLE: "PREGNANT"

LENGTH: 30 SECONDS

THE ORIGINAL STORYBOARD

Going off to the hospital to have a baby is the imaginative, completely plausible
springboard for telling the story of Sealtest Light N' Lively Low Fat Milk.

1. SHE: (FADES UP) ... and don't forget to buy milk for the kids ...

2. while I'm at the hospital. Light n' Lively.

3. HE: (MUMBLES) Milk, right.

4. SHE: Not just milk. Light n' Lively low fat milk.

5. HE: You buy this for the kids, too? SHE: Um huh.

6. HE: 99% fat free?

7. SHE: Of course, it's got more protein and calcium.

8. And it's convenient for you. (SHE DRINKS) HE: (LOOKS UP PUZZLED)

9. SHE: You'll only have to remember one kind.

10. VO: The one kind to remember.

11. Light n' Lively Low-Fat Milk: 20% more milk protein and calcium.

12. From Sealtest.

PHOTOSCRIPT OF FINISHED COMMERCIAL

Showing how closely the final script matched the original.

Courtesy: Sealtest Foods
Advertising Agency: N. W. Ayer & Son, Inc. New York

3. Rely on the video to carry more than half the weight. Being a visual medium, television is more effective at showing than telling.

4. Use short, everyday words in the audio. *Sentences should be short, sentence structure uncomplicated. No more words should be used than necessary to round out the thought conveyed by the picture.*

5. Avoid static scenes. Provide for camera movement and changes of scenes.

6. Don't cram the commercial with too many scenes lest the viewer become confused. A scene should seldom be less than four seconds long.

7. Superimpose in lettering the basic theme line over scenes in the commercial, including the final scene, if practical.

8. Be sure that transitions are smooth from scene to scene. Conceiving the commercial as a flowing progression makes it easier for the viewer to follow. Proper use of opticals [discussed later] can add to the smoothness.

9. Television is a "medium of closeups." Avoid long shots. Even the largest television screens are too small for extraneous detail in the scenes of the commercial.

10. When timing the commercial, don't just read it. Act it out. The action usually requires more time than the words indicate. A good rule is purposely to time the commercial short, as it invariably runs a few seconds longer in actual production.[2]

TELEVISION PRODUCTION

The task of converting a script and storyboard into a commercial that is ready to go on the air is the province of television production. In charge of each project is a *television producer,* completely responsible for the commercial from the time it is approved until the time it is shipped to the stations. To understand the nature of this effort, we first become acquainted with the chief elements involved in producing a commercial, along with the procedures that prevail.

Forms of Commercial Production

Commercials can be produced on *films* or on *videotape;* a small percentage are delivered by an announcer (*live*).

---

[2] Arthur Bellaire, *TV Advertising, A Handbook of Modern Practice* (New York: Harper & Row, Publishers, Inc., 1959), pp. 75–76. Copyright, 1959, by Arthur Bellaire.

Films. Most commercials are shot on color film. Films represent the oldest form of showing motion pictures in color, and because of that, there is a vast pool of highly skilled talent available for all phases of film commercials. Even artists who had been making documentaries and television specials have moved over to the making of commercials. And for the same reason, there are many experienced cameramen and other technicians available in the making of films.

435
*The
Television
Commercial—
Creation and
Production*

Films give a picture a soft quality. They are very versatile; they can be used for distant shots, mood shots; they can be used for animations. In films, you can reshoot a sequence, and then select the best shots in making up your final film.

Thirty-five mm. films are the professional size used, along with videotape, by national and top regional advertisers. Great advances have been made in 16 mm. film, however. It is much less expensive than 35 mm. film and is often used for test commercials. It is widely used by regional and local advertisers.

Videotape. Often called just *tape,* this represents a method by which picture and sound are recorded on one- or two-inch magnetic tape. It is a newer process than film. Some regard tape as more brilliant and realistic than film, its audio quality better. Its chief advantage is that it can be played back immediately, permitting the work to be checked at once, and retakes made, if necessary, while the actors and staff are all assembled. There is a big saving of time in the editing, too, with computerized editing cutting the time of that operation by as much as 90 percent. Commercials shot on film can be put on videotape, at a great saving in time, without loss of quality. Commercials can be recorded in the morning, and if necessary duplicates (*dubs*) can be sent out that night.

Tapes cost somewhat more than film prints, but whereas a film can safely be replayed up to 25 times, a tape can be replayed a seemingly endless number of times, preserving the reproduction quality. The cost is about the same as for film; the big advantage is speed.

Live. A commercial that is broadcast directly by a local personality, and not from film or tape, is a *live commercial.* Not many are being used today. They are chiefly used on a station that offers a live news show, by a popular personality. In such instances, the station supplies and specifies all the facilities and directions—how many cameras on the stage, the size of the stage, even the talent involved. The producer's main responsibility is to see that all props, artwork, and products are in the correct hands, and to supervise the rehearsal. And, most important, to make sure that any props or products used for a demonstration work properly. They have been known not to.

Since a live commercial is not prerecorded, it may be desired to make a record of it when broadcast. That can be done with a *kinescope*—a filmed recording of live images and sounds emanating from a television monitor, made for future use, or merely as a record.

Opticals

Opticals are any variations of the picture that can be achieved during or after the shooting. The number of such effects is endless. The reader will recognize from his own viewing experience the most common forms:

The most used effect is the *cut,* where one scene abuts the next.

The *dissolve* is an overlapping effect—one scene fading out as the next one fades in, usually indicating a passage of time.

To *freeze* a picture is to hold it still on a frame.

To *zoom* is to change rapidly from a long shot to a closeup, maintaining the subject or scene in focus.

To *superimpose* is to place one scene, or lettering, over another.

Opticals also include any special artwork, titles, or credits that may be superimposed over a scene.

The Sound Track

The sound track of a commercial can be recorded at the time of production of a film or tape job, as in the case of people speaking or singing their parts in perfect synchronization, or in recording a live orchestra. But often the sound is recorded before or after the actual production.

When the sound track is recorded in advance, the film or tape is shot to fit the sound track—a technique used when somebody or something has to move or dance to a specific beat. It also gives assurance that the scene being shot will not be too long or too short. The post-shooting technique for recording sound is used when the commercial has been edited, and a music or sound-effect or voice track is desired to highlight certain scenes or eventual optical effects.

The various sounds are mixed together into one *final sound track,* which will be joined to the final film, or tape.

The Union Scale

One of the first facts of life of which one becomes aware in television production is that it is a highly unionized business, with rate schedules spelled out for every step.[3] To show how complex and sometimes amusing

---

[3] The chief unions involved are the American Federation of Television and Radio Artists (AFTRA), the Screen Actors' Guild (SAG), and the American Federation of Musicians (AFM).

these provisions might be, we have the instance of a young woman hired as a background performer for a swimming-pool scene. She gets paid a daily rate as a swimmer. If, prior to shooting, she is called upon to get into a bathing suit to see how she looks, there is a fitting fee. If she uses her own suit, there is a wardrobe maintenance fee. Having makeup or oil applied to more than 50 percent of her body calls for an extra fee. For diving she gets paid a fee the rate of which depends on how high the board is.

437
*The
Television
Commercial—
Creation and
Production*

It costs much more to have an announcer seen on the screen as he speaks than if he speaks his lines offscreen. There is one rate for a group singer who sings four bars or less; a higher rate for singing five bars or more. For such reasons, a producer is careful in deciding how many actors he needs, and precisely what he really needs each for.

Residual fees. In addition to a flat payment for services rendered based upon time charges, a performer is paid a fee, called a *residual,* on network commercials, every time the commercial is shown. In spot, he receives one residual payment every 13 weeks, the amount depending upon the number of cities in which the spots are shown. A producer has to plan the commercials so that a minimum number of residual charges are incurred.

The Production Studio

The making of a commercial usually takes place in a film studio or tape studio, and in a sound-recording studio. The appointment of a studio for a commercial entails more than the rental of a place to shoot the picture and a projection room to show it on a screen. It includes the services of a staff, headed by a studio director and a cameraman (the chief reason many producers will select a particular studio). It also includes the services of a team of electricians and other needed technicians. Studios are equipped to do the editing, although separate editing services are available.

Most studios are in Los Angeles, New York City, and Chicago, cities where there is also the greatest concentration of talent. Advertisers who use studios in the other cities, however, have one great advantage—their costs are usually much lower. Studio time is costly. (In smaller cities, the local station may do the production for local advertisers.)

THE MAKING OF A COMMERCIAL

The producer. When an advertiser approves a budget for television advertising, many wheels start to turn; the chief decision is the appointment of a producer. He will be responsible for the commercial from the time it is approved until the time it is ready to go on the air. Large agencies have a number of producers on a staff assigned to various accounts. Many producers also work on a free-lance basis.

The script and storyboard. A writer and an art director will be assigned as a team to create the commercials on a project that may range from a 10-second local station break to the full sponsorship of a network special, the latter entailing six minutes of commercials. The producer may be asked to sit in with the writer and art director to consult on the practicability of various ideas discussed.

The estimate. The producer's first real work begins with getting an estimate of costs. He may send the storyboards to three studios for estimates of their part of the work, considering, in each instance, the quality of their work and their skill.

A TV PRODUCTION ESTIMATE

Courtesy:
J. Walter Thompson Company

The estimate is designed to cover all costs of the storyboard as presently planned. But invariably ideas and suggestions, including those of the advertiser, arise in the course of the work. For all changes made, a supplementary estimate of costs will be submitted for approval. Strict adherence to this procedure can save much unpleasantness later.

439
*The
Television
Commercial—
Creation and
Production*

There is a wide range in the costs of commercials. There are many opportunities for saving money in production, and for getting better effects at no more cost. A knowledgeable advertiser reviewing a storyboard may ask questions such as those cited by H. C. Robinson, of the Liggett & Myers Company, who said:

> . . . There are many things, too, which reveal themselves in a storyboard which a well-educated advertiser might care to relate to costs. For example: Are there enough people or too many people employed in the commercial to make it work creatively? What are the union scales for these people? Are there any overscale? If so, why? What optical effects are indicated? Do they enhance or detract from the selling message? Should more be added? What about music? Will it be an original music track? What kind of musical effect is planned? How many musicians are contemplated? The sets? Are they to be constructed from scratch or rented? Is ample time allowed for the construction? Where is the commercial to be shot? In a studio or on location? To what extent is travel involved? Weather?
>
> All these questions (and there are many more) need not be discussed at each storyboard session, but they should be somewhere in the mind of the advertiser who reviews the board initially. As a matter of fact, if the commercial is properly planned and if we have a TV commercial cost-oriented advertiser, the answers to most of the questions are apparent in reviewing the storyboard.
>
> I must mention here that overtime often makes commercials cost more than they should. There are many people and many events which might cause unnecessary overtime. The important thing is that the man who pays the bills should be aware of what does or does not, can or cannot, cause this expenditure.[4]

The preproduction meeting. The most important meeting in the life of the commercial is the preproduction meeting, called by the producer. It will include the director of the studio selected for the job, and whichever of his assistants he asks to join the meeting: the director, a representative of the advertiser who has authority to make decisions, the agency's account executive, the writer, the art director, and anyone else the producer deems important enough to be present.

---

[4] H. Copland Robinson, "Controlling the Cost of Television Production," in *The Advertising Budget* (Association of National Advertisers, Inc., © 1967), p. 100.

The purpose of the meeting is to review the storyboard, panel by panel, and resolve all questions of handling and detail, as action, scenery, camera angle, lighting. The age and type of the actors will be decided, and the type of announcer. The casting director will know the type of talent to select, usually working through a talent agency, which sends up candidates for screening. The musical scoring will be planned. Everyone is to understand exactly what effects are desired, and what he is to do.

Television Commercial Estimate

Agency _____ Estimate # _____ Date _____

Brand _____ Studio _____

Description _____

_____

*PRODUCTION	$_____		*PRODUCTION	
			Preparation	$_____
CONTINGENCY	_____		Set Const., Strike	_____
TALENT + P&W	_____		Set Dressing	_____
MUSIC	_____		Props, Materials	_____
RECORDING	_____		Studio Rental	_____
ARTWORK	_____		Shooting (# Days ___)	_____
COLOR CORRECTION	_____		Overtime Hours (___)	_____
WARDROBE	_____		Location Rental, Exp.	_____
PROPS	_____		Crew	_____
PHOTOSTATS	_____		Crew Travel**	_____
MISCELLANEOUS	_____		Director's Fee	_____
Net Total	$_____		Camera Equipment	_____
AGENCY COMMISSION	_____		Lighting Equipment	_____
SALES TAX	_____		Sound Equipment	_____
PAYROLL TAX	_____		Special Equipment	_____
AGENCY TRAVEL***	_____		Wardrobe	_____
			Hairdresser	_____
GROSS TOTAL	$_____		Makeup	_____
			Raw. Stock (+ Process)	
			(# Ft. _____)	_____
LOCATION TRAVEL			Animation	_____
			Editing	_____

LOCATION TRAVEL

	Crew**	Talent	Agency***	Other
# People	_____	_____	_____	_____
# Days	_____	_____	_____	_____
Air Fare $	_____	$_____	$_____	$_____
Per Diem $	_____	$_____	$_____	$_____
Other $	_____	$_____	$_____	$_____
Totals $	_____	$_____	$_____	$_____

Total $_____

Rec., Transfer, Mix	_____
Contract Requirmts.	_____
Optical Costs	_____
Editorial Labor	_____
Other	_____
Net Total	$_____
Studio Markup (___%)	_____
Total Studio Bid	$_____

TALENT

# On-Camera	_____	$_____
# Off-Camera	_____	_____
# Extras	_____	_____
6½% P&W		_____
Total		$_____

WEATHER CONTINGENCY: $_____ Per Day

Remarks _____

Agency _____ _____ Date _____

Client Approval _____ Date _____

A DETAILED PRODUCTION ESTIMATE

Giving item for item estimates of the many elements that could go into TV production. Just reading the list of elements alone gives an idea of the potential complexity of producing a TV commercial.

Casting and props. The producer may already have in mind whom he wants for the different parts in the commercial; he may call a model studio and specify his needs or preferences from their model book. The models for speaking parts will be given a screen test, reading portions of their parts, and a choice will be made. Many large agencies have a casting director for this task. Meanwhile, the studio property man will be getting scenery and props together. If shooting has to be done at an outside location, arrangements will be made.

Composer and musicians. If music has to be written for the script, a composer will be called in. Arrangements also will have to be made for any musicians needed.

Rehearsals and filming. Depending on the commercial, rehearsals can be short and simple, or long and involved.

The producer and director will usually call a rehearsal if there is any question at all regarding the spoken parts and action asked for in a script.

441
The
Television
Commercial—
Creation and
Production

J. WALTER THOMPSON COMPANY

PRODUCTION SCHEDULE FOR SIXTY-SECOND 35MM COLOR TELEVISION COMMERCIAL

Client approves final script and storyboard	Friday, August 4, 1972
Bids	Monday - Thursday August 7 - August 10
Client approves budget	Friday - August 11
Pre-production, Casting	Monday - Friday August 14 - August 25
Shoot	Monday - Tuesday August 28 - August 29
Edit	Wednesday - Thursday **August 30** - August 31
Client approves rough cut	Friday - September 1
Record music	Friday - September 8
Client approves answer print	Friday - September 15
Ship air prints to stations	Friday - September 22

Courtesy:
J. Walter Thompson Company

Generally, all rehearsals take place prior to the day of shooting, with a minimal crew, to save time and money. On the actual shooting day, a full (and expensive) crew is required.

Rehearsals often reveal things that do not work. For example, one may discover that the copy is too long or too short, or that the performers may need cue cards to help them memorize and deliver their lines, or a change in the set is needed.

The rehearsal is a good time to check the products and packaging to see if they are in the proper shape to meet the client's standards. It is also a good time to decide on the most attractive angles from which to shoot the products.

The producer, director, and cameraman decide on the style of lighting desired, ranging from soft and delicate to hard and harsh, depending upon the needs of the script.

Some commercials involve many setups and scenes, complete with a large cast. Often a first rehearsal is called for in such commercials, followed the next day by a full-scale dress rehearsal. Performers have to be paid for wardrobe and costume fittings and rehearsals, but it is still an enormous saving in the long run not to waste the time and money on the actual shooting day.

The shooting day is the director's and the cameraman's day. If all has been properly planned in advance, the producer can keep his attention on whether the production is on course, and not have to worry about details. The studio, the director, and his assistants are really responsible for the shooting day and its schedule, from early makeup and hairdressing calls to the mechanics of lighting, shooting, and recording sound. Depending on how much time is required to complete a commercial, the shooting day can range from eight hours to all hours, but after eight hours the overtime charge goes into effect.

Processing and editing. The film is processed in a day or two and is screened as a first, or uncorrected, print, called *rushes* or *dailies.*

Scenes are selected from the dailies, cut up, and edited into a smooth-flowing work print known as a *rough cut.*

The rough cut is screened for the advertiser and agency for approval.

From the approved rough cut, an optical house makes negatives that contain all the optical effects.

Meanwhile, the sound has been recorded.

A composite print is made of picture, opticals, and sound, called an *answer print.*

The answer print is corrected for color, quality, density and synchronization of sound. The approved answer print becomes the *master print.* Duplicate prints of this are ordered for distribution to the stations scheduled. The commercial is ready to go on the air!

"Theme" NPS:60

ANNCR: We know you have pride in yourself and in what your country can be.

We know you have a brain and your own ideas.

We know you'd like to share these ideas with hundreds of young men and women from all parts of this country.

We know you'd like to further your education, learn a skill,

have opportunity for advancement, and thirty days vacation a year.

We also know you put a price on these things. The price is your individuality.

And you question the Army's willingness to pay this price. Today's Army is willing to pay this price.

We're committed to eliminating unnecessary formation...skin-head haircuts... ...signing out...

signing in...and "make work" projects. in Today's Army, you'll find more mature personnel policies at every level.

If you'd like to serve yourself, as you serve your Country,

Today's Army wants to join you

Today's Army wants to join you.

CALL FREE
800-243-6000
IN CONNECTICUT 1-800-942-0655

SPONSORED BY THE UNITED STATES ARMY

For the location of your nearest Army representative, call 800-243-6000, toll-free.

THE ARMY GOES TO TV

Television enables the U.S. Army to present in the short space of one commercial the many facets of its story, to get volunteer enlistments.

Courtesy: Department of the Army
Advertising Agency: N. W. Ayer & Son, Inc.

ANNOUNCER: We made this special pan to make a point.

Half is coated with TEFLON. Half isn't.

Let's cook some scrambled eggs

and see what happens.

And now let's wash.

The TEFLON side even starts off cleaner because almost nothing sticks to it.

See, the TEFLON side really is easier to clean.

But the other side...

well, you get the point.

Get cookware certified TEFLON II and be on the winning side.

An End-Product Advertiser Uses TV

Television provides a good opportunity to demonstrate the advantages of pots lined with Teflon II.

Courtesy: du Pont
Advertising Agency: N. W. Ayer & Son, Inc.

Courtesy: American Association of Advertising Agencies

Photoscripts.   After a commercial has been made, advertisers often have a photoscript made, consisting of the actual pictures made from the original script or storyboard. This provides them with a printed record of the commercial. It also is useful for sales promotion and publicity purposes.

Retail TV Production

The problems of TV production for retail stores are quite different in many respects from those of the national advertiser, which we have chiefly been discussing. How resourcefully retailers handle their special TV production needs is discussed in Chapter 27—"Retail Advertising."

1. Give a brief definition, explanation, or description of the following:

   a. Video
   b. Audio
   c. Storyboard
   d. Opticals
   e. Wipe
   f. Freeze
   g. Superimpose
   h. Sound track
   i. Residual
   j. A rush
   k. Rough cut
   l. Master print

2. Describe the three ways of physically broadcasting a commercial. What are the advantages and limitations of each?

3. What is the responsibility of a TV producer?

4. The book offers nine guidelines to the creation of the commercial. How many can you describe? Can you cite any recent commercials you have seen that fit into these categories?

5. What are some of the suggestions for writing the commercial that were discussed?

6. What is meant by television production?

7. Describe the usual way of producing a commercial with a musical background.

8. What is discussed at a pre-production meeting?

9. Which commercials have most impressed you recently? What were their unique features? What were the products advertised? What did they tell you about the products? Would you say the commercials did a good selling job?

Reading Suggestions

Bellaire, Arthur, *The TV Commercial Cost Control Handbook.* Chicago: Crain Communications, Inc., 1972.

Bellaire, Arthur, *TV Advertising.* New York: Harper & Row, Publishers, 1959.

Book, Albert C., and Norman D. Cary, *Television Commercial.* New York: Decker Communications, Inc., 1970.

Cimbalo, Guy, *A New Approach to Television Advertising.* New York: Lion House Publishing Co., 1966.

Diamant, Lincoln, *Television's Classic Commercials—The Golden Years 1948–1958.* Hastings House, Publishers, Inc., New York, 1971.

Galanoy, Terry, *Down the Tube.* Chicago: Henry Regnery Company, 1970.

Hilliard, Robert L., *Writing for Television and Radio.* New York: Hastings House, Publishers, Inc., 1967.

McMahan, Harry W., "BST: A Way To Get Your Creative Problems Out of the Revolving Door," *Advertising Age,* June 14, 1971, pp. 78–80.

Media/Scope, "What Is the Best Length for a T.V. Commercial?" October 1964, p. 63 ff.

National Association of Broadcasters, *The Television Code,* current ed.

Robinson, H. Copland, "Controlling the Cost of Television Production," in *The Advertising Budget.* New York: Association of National Advertisers, 1967.

Ross, Wallace A., *Best TV & Radio Commercials.* New York: The International TV Commercials Study Foundation, 1971.

Wainwright, Charles A., *The Television Copywriter.* New York: Hastings House, 1966.

## 19

The Radio Commercial—
Creation and Production

WRITING THE COMMERCIAL

THE BEGINNING OF an effective radio commercial is agreement between management and writer about the specific sales message to be left with the listener. Once that is clear, the whole world of radio imagery and technique is open to the writer.

He has freedom to think in terms of place and people; there are no stage or scenery costs here. He sees in his mind something happening somewhere, or some action taking place with which the listener can identify himself, with the aid of any sound to set the stage—a car door slamming, a phone ringing. He can picture 80,000 people at a bowl game, with a ten-second roar of a crowd.

Elements of Effective Radio Commercials

In a major research project (the *Yankelovich Report,* sponsored by the ABC Radio Network), four key elements were isolated that proved to be crucial in differentiating effective commercials (those that stimulate buying interest) from the less effective ones. Briefly stated, they are:

1. *Meaningful content*
   The listener must have the feeling that he has gained some informational reward out of listening. This information does not have to be new or startling—it may simply reinforce something already known.

2. *Stimulation of product-plus associations*
   This refers to the ability of a commercial to arouse thoughts and feelings that relate to the commercial's central message. A spaghetti-sauce commercial should get the listener to thinking about spaghetti for dinner rather than the size of the tomatoes in his garden.

3. *Identification by the listener*

Identification can be established in many ways—the use of dialogues in which the product is discussed, a straightforward presentation of the product's advantages, or a unique piece of music that instantly identifies the product to the listener.

4. *Good fit with listener's expectations*

Commercials scoring well in the results fitted in with the ideas, feelings, and images the listener had already built up about the product. The commercial must be believable.

The Radio Advertising Bureau offers the following guidelines for good radio copy writing:

—Know what you are writing about.

—Talk about customer benefits—what is in it for the customer, not for the advertiser.

—Write action words, rather than passive ones.

—Omit unnecessary words.

—Mention the advertiser's name as often as possible.

—Keep the message simple.

The commercial should be built around a single idea; the tendency is to try to crowd in more. The first eight seconds are the crucial ones, for in that time something must be said that makes the listener feel he wants to continue paying attention. Most effective commercials are intimate, relaxed, cheerful. Whatever style is used should be maintained throughout the commercial, to leave a sharp, single impression with the listener.

Timing of Commercials

The number of words in a commercial varies with the context and the delivery needs. The average count is:

10 seconds	25 words
20 seconds	45 words
30 seconds	65 words
60 seconds	125 words

After the commercial is written, it is well to read it normally, to catch tongue twisters, insure normal flow, and time it exactly.

Sixty-second commercials are often created to include a 10-second tag ending by the announcer directing listeners to go to a local dealer, with name and address given; including also, at times a musical logo at the beginning and end.

Musical Commercials

Commercials are often set to music especially composed for them, or adapted from a familiar song. A few bars of distinctive music, if played often enough, may serve as a musical identification of the product (a *musical logotype*), usually ten seconds.

Jingles are popular ways of making a slogan that rhymes memorable —provided the slogan contains a real selling message.

This brings us to the question of musical rights. A melody is in the *public domain,* available for use by anyone, without cost, *after* the copyright has expired. (A copyright runs for 28 years, and is renewable once for 28 years.) Many old favorites and classics are thus in the public domain and have been used as themes by advertisers. In using a tune in the public domain, however, one runs the risk of using the same tune already being used by many others.

Popular tunes that are still protected by copyrights are available only by agreement with the copyright owner. The result may be a good familiar tune, but it may be costly.

An advertiser can have an original tune created by a composer. This becomes the advertiser's own property and gives the product its own musical personality.

COMMERCIAL CATEGORIES

In their study to suggest a convenient classification system for radio commercials, Ross and Landers drew upon the library, containing over 10,000 commercials, of the Radio Advertising Bureau.[1] Their list follows:

1. *Product Demo*—Communicating how a product is used, or what purposes a product serves.
2. *Voice Power*—Use of a unique voice adding special qualities to the copy. May blend in other sounds or music, but the power of the commercial is essentially in casting of the voice.
3. *Electronic Sound*—Through synthetic sound-making machines or through devices that alter sound, commercial attempts to establish original product–sound associations.
4. *Customer Interview*—A spokesman for the product plus a customer, discussing the merits and advantages of the product or service. Often the most rewarding interviews are those done spontaneously.

---

[1] Wallace A. Ross and Bob Landers, "Commercial Categories," in *Radio Plays the Plaza* (New York: Radio Advertising Bureau, 1969), p. 29.

5. *Humorous Fake Interview*—Variation of the customer interview in humorous fashion. Has the advantages of preplanning plus the interest an interview generates.

6. *Hyperbole or Exaggerated Statement*—Use of exaggeration, extreme understatement or overstatement to arouse interest in legitimate, often basic product claims that might otherwise pass unnoticed. Can often be a spoof.

7. *Sixth Dimension*—Compression of time, history, happenings into a brief spot. Can often be a sequential narrative ultimately involving listener in future projections.

8. *Hot property*—Commercial that latches on to a current sensation. Can be a hit show, a performer, or a song. Hit is adapted for product.

9. *Comedian Power*—Established comedians do commercials in their own unique style. Has advantages of humor and inferred celebrity endorsement.

10. *Historical Fantasy*—Situations or historical characters are revived to convey product message.

11. *Sound Picture*—Sound used to help put the listener into a situation by stimulating his imagination. Sounds are usually easily recognizable to facilitate listener involvement.

12. *Demographics*—Commercial appeals particularly to one segment of the population (an age group, interest group, etc.) through use of music, references.

13. *Imagery Transfer*—Spots reinforce effects of other media through use of musical logos, or other sound associations identifiable with a particular campaign for a particular product.

14. *Celebrity Interview*—Famous person provides celebrity endorsement of the product in informal manner.

15. *Product Song*—Music and words combine to create musical logo as well as to sell product. In style of popular music with orchestration.

16. *Editing Genius*—Many different situations, voices, types of music, sounds combined in a series of quick cuts to produce one spot. Every cut contributes in some way to strength of message.

17. *Improvisation*—Copywriter conceives situations that might be good backdrop for a product and then allows performers to work out the dialogue extemporaneously. Requires postediting of tapes to make spot cohesive.

In addition to the commercial types above, there are of course *Straight Copy*—text read by station announcer—and *Ad Lib from Fact Sheet.*

The following examples of effective radio commercials reveal the flexibility in the creation of commercials:

CLIENT: Madison Laboratories   LENGTH: 60 sec.

PRODUCT: Binaca

AGENCY: D'Arcy-MacManus-Internaco, Inc.

TITLE: "TOGETHER"

BINACA MUSIC AND LYRIC

FADE MUSIC UNDER ANNOUNCER. (VERY BRIGHTLY)

ANNCR.:

How many things people do close together?

TEMPO   Well, there's working ... studying ... celebrating ...
INCREASING
        dating ... dancing ... picnicking ... partying ... nibbling

        ... necking ... hugging ... playing ... fighting ... making

        up ... teasing ... flirting ... kissing ... and ....

being together!

For all those reasons, you need Binaca! Binaca: fresh breath

you carry anywhere ... Because Binaca's in, bad breath is out!

Think of the things you do together ... now, think how Binaca

can help!

MUSIC UP

A commercial that quickly sets the stage for a series of situations. Note the economy and choice of words with which each is described. A problem and solution commercial in which the reader is involved.

CLIENT: Getty Oil Company   LENGTH: 60 sec.

PRODUCT: Getty Premium Gasoline

AGENCY: DKGinc.

TITLE: "GORILLA"

(SFX: CAR DRIVING)   (SFX: GORILLA SNORTING IN BACKGROUND)

1ST: Ah, this is crazy. The zoo should have given us a truck.

          Who ever heard of transporting a gorilla in a car?

2ND: Don't worry. He's chained down good and tight. Just don't

          drive past the Empire State Building.

1ST: You just keep feeding him those bananas and we're all right.

2ND: Look at him eat. I'd rather clothe him than feed him.

1ST: Look at this gas gauge. Didn't I give you money to fill it up?

2ND: Yeah, but I had to buy a crate of bananas. I only had two

          dollars left for gas.

(SFX: CAR COMING TO A CHOKING HALT)

1ST: Ah, now you done it. No gas and a car full of gorilla.

A commercial that combines humor, dialogue, and surprise to lead into the main
message, delivered straight by announcer, and leaves the listener smiling. To see
the contribution a commercial concept can make in delivering a sales story, just
try reading the announcement by itself and see what attention it would hold.

2ND: (NERVOUSLY) Ooooohhh. . . .

1ST: Alright, take it easy. We're just out of gas.

2ND: We're out of bananas too.

(COL. BOGEY MARCH MUSIC)

ANNOUNCER: These days a couple of bucks worth of gasoline

doesn't seem to take you very far.

But one will take you further than the rest.

Getty Premium.

At Getty we sell only Premium gasoline.

Over 100 octane.

But we sell it for a few cents less per gallon than

most other major premiums.

So at Getty, you get more gas for your money.

(SFX: HONKING HORNS)

1ST: You stay with the gorilla. I'll go for gas.

2ND: You stay with the gorilla. I'll go for bananas.

CLIENT: Pepsi-Cola Company   LENGTH: 60 sec.

PRODUCT: Pepsi-Cola

AGENCY: Batten, Barton, Durstine, & Osborne, Inc.

TITLE: B. J. THOMAS SINGS FOR PEPSI-COLA

LYRICS

There's a whole new way of living. Pepsi helps supply the drive. It's
got a lot to give to those who like to live 'cause Pepsi helps 'em come
alive. It's a Pepsi generation comin' atcha going strong. Put yourself
behind a Pepsi. If you're livin', you belong. You've got a lot to live
and Pepsi's got a lot to give. You've got a lot to live and Pepsi's got
a lot to give.

Here is a commercial that uses contemporary music with a catchy tune, and a popular singer. The lyrics are sharp, crisp, and directed toward the theme idea, "You've got a lot to live and Pepsi has a lot to give" . . . directed to the younger age group in appeal, language, and music.

RADIO PRODUCTION

453
*The Radio
Commercial—
Creation and
Production*

There are two ways of delivering a radio commercial: live and prerecorded. They may be combined.

The live commercial. A live commercial is one delivered directly in person by an announcer or by a station personality. It can be delivered from a prepared script or from a *fact sheet* supplied by the advertiser, in which the speaker can deliver the commercial in his own way, with his own warmth and personality and enthusiasm. Sometimes a musical introduction, or a musical sign-off with the brand name (a musical logotype) is used.

A Fact Sheet used for stations with popular local announcers, as a guide for delivering the commercial in their own style.

```
                                        MIRACLE WHITE

                                        Non Polluting Detergent

                                        (contains no phosphates)
                        FACT SHEET      (no NTA)
                                        (no enzymes)

...NEW MIRACLE WHITE POWDERED DETERGENT IS NON POLLUTING

...IT IS A NEW BREAKTHROUGH FORMULA that contains none of the polluting
   phosphates that stimulate the growth of algae and weeds that choke out
   healthy plant life and eventually destroy sources of life-giving oxygen.

...NOW!  Wash without regret!

...NEW!  Powerful formula has bleach, borax and brighteners to give you a clean,
   bright wash the first time and every time!

...IT CONTAINS NO ENZYMES!

...IT IS SAFE!  Its unique sudsing formula gives you powerful yet safe cleaning
   results for all your washables without fear of damaging fabrics or washing
   machine.

...MIRACLE WHITE NON POLLUTING DETERGENT IS BIODEGRADABLE...especially formulated
   to actually destroy itself by bacterial action.  No foam remains to impair
   rivers, lakes or septic tanks.

...MIRACLE WHITE NON POLLUTING DETERGENT is effective in both cold and hot
   wash water for a clean and bright wash.

...MIRACLE WHITE promises you a clean, bright wash the first time, you must
   be satisfied 100% with the NON POLLUTING DETERGENT or receive double your
   money back, details are on the package.

...Now you can wash without regret.
```

Courtesy: Beatrice Foods Company
Advertising Agency: Spot Radio Advertising

The advantage of a live announcer is that he may have a popular following; listeners tend more readily to accept what he tells them. A disadvantage in having him ad lib is that he may not stick to the script, or may omit some important selling points. For a large national campaign where personalities' capabilities are not all known, or where a complete control of the commercial content is desirable, advertisers usually prefer to use a prerecorded commercial, which they produce and supply.

Prerecorded commercial. A prerecorded commercial can be as simple as the delivery of one announcer, or as complex as having more than one announcer, with a singer and sound effects and orchestra.

For making a radio recording, a radio producer will be assigned. His first task will be to set up an estimate and get a budget approved. His continuing responsibility will be to keep within that budget. He will select a recording studio, a casting director if he feels he needs one, and a musical director and an orchestra, if they are needed. The musical director may write his own music and arrangements, or may select the music from one of the musical libraries. The whole operation can be greatly simplified, depending on budget and complexity of the script.

A recording studio will be hired by the day or half day, or several days, depending on how many commercials are to be produced. A cast is selected, gathered, and rehearsed. When the producer feels they are ready, the commercial is acted out and recorded on tape.

The music and sound may be taped separately, and then mixed with the vocal tape by the sound-recording studio. When all this has been done, a *master tape* of the complete commercial is produced.

Duplicates. A popular way to make duplicates of a commercial is by playing the master tape on a reel of ¼-inch *tape*. Such tape recordings have an exceedingly long life. They are often cased in a tape cartridge for the increasing number of stations that operate with such cassettes.

Another form of duplicate is made by recording the master record on an acetate record, referred to as an *acetate* dub or just an *acetate*. This is a comparatively soft record, made one at a time, useful when a record is needed quickly, but each acetate is good for no more than 50 playings.

The most popular form of record is a *pressing,* also known as an electric transcription (e.t.), or just *transcription*. Here the master tape is played onto a *master duplicate record*. This is very hard—over a thousand duplicate records can be pressed into it—hence the name. These records are very sharp, can be played an infinite number of times, and are very economical when a quantity of duplicates is needed.

Thus we have three forms of duplicate commercials, all made from the master tape—the *tape,* or cartridge cassette; the *acetate,* fast if only a few are wanted for short runs; and the *pressing,* a most serviceable record for large schedules.

Review Questions

1. Give a brief definition or explanation of:
   a. tag ending
   b. musical logotype
   c. jingle
   d. public domain
   e. sound picture
   f. transcription

2. Describe the key elements that, as research shows, differentiate effective from less effective radio commercials.

3. Cite examples from current radio commercials for any six of the specific classifications of radio commercials that are mentioned in the text.

4. Discuss the comparative advantages and disadvantages of pre-recorded commercials, live straight copy commercials, and ad lib commercials from a fact sheet.

5. Describe the three forms of duplicate commercials.

6. Which recent radio commercials have impressed you most favorably? What were the unique features of the commercials? What did they advertise? What did they say about its product?

Reading Suggestions

Advertising Age, "Impressible Radio Enters Phase Four: A New Dimension in Commercials," January 8, 1968, pp. 49–50.

Felsenthal, Norman, G. Wayne Shamo, and John R. Bittner, "A Comparison of Award-Winning Radio Commercials and Their Day-to-Day Counterparts," *Journal of Broadcasting,* Summer 1971, pp. 309–315.

Hilliard, Robert L., *Writing for Television and Radio.* New York: Hastings House, Publishers, Inc., 1967.

Ross, Wallace A., *Best TV & Radio Commercials.* New York: The International TV Commercials Study Foundation, 1971.

V
THE ADVERTISING CAMPAIGN

20

Trademarks
Packaging

TRADEMARKS

NEVER BEFORE HAS A good trademark been so important as in this age of self-service. The trademark directly affects the distinctiveness of the product, and therefore the ease with which it is remembered, and its sales. The trademark often becomes the most important asset of a company, growing more valuable each year. A whole body of law has been developed to protect this property against infringers. Getting legal protection is the province of the attorney. However, it begins right with the creation of the trademark itself. Hence, in creating or considering a trademark, it is important to understand some of the basic legal ground rules.

WHAT IS A TRADEMARK?

A trademark is any symbol, sign, word, name, or device, or combination of these, that tells who makes a product or who sells it, distinguishing that product from those made or sold by others. Its purpose is to protect the public from being deceived, and the owner from unfair competition and the unlawful use of his property.

A trademark invariably consists of, or includes, a word or name by which people can speak of the product—"Do you have *Dutch Boy* paint?" That word or name is also called a *brand name*. A trademark may, but does not have to, include some pictorial element.

A *trade name,* on the other hand, is the name under which a company does business. *General Mills,* for example, is the trade name of a company making a cake mix whose trademark (not trade name) is *Betty Crocker.* The terms *trademark* and *trade name* are often confused.

A product can have several trademarks, as *Coca-Cola* and *Coke.*

Chief among the basic legal requirements of a trademark are the following:

1. *The trademark must be used in connection with an actual product.* The use of a design in an advertisement does not make it a trademark, nor does having it on a flag over the factory. It must be applied to the product itself, or be on a label or container of that product. If that is not feasible, it must be affixed to the container or dispenser of it, as on a pump at a gas service station.

2. *The trademark must not be confusingly similar to trademarks on similar goods.* It should not be likely to cause the buyer to be confused, mistaken, or deceived as to whose product he is purchasing. The trademark should be dissimilar in appearance, sound, and significance. *Cycol* was held to be in conflict with *Tycol,* for oil; *Air-O* was held in conflict with *Arrow* for shirts; *Canned Light* was held in conflict with *Barreled Sunlight* for paint, because of such possible confusion.

The two products involved need not be identical. The marks will be held in conflict if the products are sold through the same trade channels, or if the public might assume that a product made by a second company is a new product line of the first company. So-Soft *tissues,* for example, was held in conflict with Snow & Soft *paper napkins* for this reason. BIG BOY! powder for *soft drinks* was held in confusion with BIG BOY *stick candy.*

3. *A trademark must not be deceptive.* A trademark must not indicate a quality not in the product; it must not be misdescriptively deceptive. Words that have legally been barred for this reason include *Lemon* soap that contained no lemon, *Half-Spanish* for cigars that did not come from Spain, *Nylodon* for sleeping bags that contained no nylon.

4. *A trademark must not be descriptive.* "I have often noticed," the head of a baking company might say, "that people ask for fresh bread. We will call our bread *Fresh;* that's our trademark. How nice that will be for us!" But when people ask for "fresh bread," they are describing the kind of bread they want, not specifying the bread made by a particular baker. To prevent such misleading usage, the law does not protect trademarks that are merely descriptive, such that any producer might apply them to his product. This includes words that describe the nature, quality, structure, merits, or uses of a product. *Aircraft* for control instruments and *Computing* for a weighing scale were disallowed as trademarks for being descriptive. The misspelling or hyphenating of a word, such as *Keep Kold* or *Heldryte,* does not make a nondescriptive word out of one that, if spelled correctly, would be descriptive of the product. However, although a word must not literally be descriptive, it may *suggest* certain qualities, and we will touch upon this matter shortly.

TRADEMARKS

A word alone, even if set in a standard type, can be a trademark. Often it is formed into a design, or combined with one, to add distinctiveness and memorability.

FORMS OF TRADEMARKS

Dictionary words.   Many trademarks consist of familiar dictionary words used in an arbitrary, suggestive, or fanciful manner. *They must not be used in a descriptive sense* to describe the nature, use, or virtue of the product. Good

461

examples of dictionary words that meet the foregoing requirements are *Dial* soap, *Glad* plastic bags, *Sunbeam* toasters, *Shell* oil, and *Rise* shaving cream. The advantage of using words that can be found in the dictionary is that you have so many from which to choose. The public will recognize the words; the task is to get them to associate it with the product; but if you have done that, the chances of protection against infringement are good. (A problem may arise with a manufacturer who has not had trademark experience and who asks, "But what has that to do with my product?")

Coined words. The most prolific source of trademark ideas is words made up of a new combination of consonants and vowels. *Kodak* is the classic forerunner of this school of thinking. We also have *Kleenex, Xerox, Norelco, Exxon*—the list is long. The advantage of a coined word is that it is new; it can be made phonetically pleasing, pronounceable and short. Coined words have a high rank for being legally protectable, but to create one that is distinctive is the big challenge. (One drug company tried using a computer to create coined words for its many new products. They were distinctive, but just not pronounceable.)

When coining a word from a root word associated with a product, there is always the danger that the basic word selected is so obvious that others in the field will likewise use it, with the result that there is a confusion of similar names. In one issue of the *Standard Advertising Register*, there were fifteen trademarks beginning with *Flavor* or *Flava*. We also have *Launderall, Laundromat, Launderette; Dictaphone, Dictograph.* But think of a fresh root concept, and you have the makings of a good trademark.

Personal names. These may be the names of real people, such as *Elizabeth Arden;* fictional characters, like *Betty Crocker;* historical characters, as in *Lincoln* cars; mythological characters, as in *Ajax* cleanser. A surname alone is not eligible as a new trademark; others of that name may use it. However, names like *Lipton's* tea, or *Heinz* foods, or *Campbell's* soups have been in use so long that they have acquired what the law calls a "secondary meaning"; that is, through usage the public has recognized them as representing the product of one company only. But a new trademark can have no secondary meaning.

Geographical names. A geographical name is really a "place" name: *Nashua* blankets, *Palm Beach* cloth, *Pittsburgh* paints. These names are old trademarks, and have acquired secondary meaning. The law does not look with favor on giving one man the exclusive right to use a geographical name in connection with his new product as against others making similar goods in that area. However, a name chosen because of the fanciful connotation of a geographical setting, rather than to suggest it was made there, may make it eligible for protection, as with *Bali* bras.

Initials and numbers.   This refers to trademarks such as *RCA* television, *AC* spark plugs, *J&B* whisky, *A.1* sauce. Fortunes and years have been spent in establishing these trademarks; hence they are familiar. In general, however, initials and numbers are the hardest form of trademark to remember and the easiest to confuse and to imitate. One issue of the *Standard Advertising Register* listed the following numerical trademarks: No. 1, No. 2, 2 in 1, 3 in 1, 4 in 1, 5 in 1, No. 7, 12/24, No. 14, 77, and 400.

Pictorial.   To reinforce their brand name, many advertisers use some artistic device, as distinctive lettering (called a *logotype*), or a design, insignia, picture, or other visual device.

CREATING THE TRADEMARK

The use of a word for a trademark generally gives the owner the right to express the idea in a variety of ways, as with a picture or symbol (such as the trademark *Green Giant* for frozen and canned vegetables, and a picture of a green giant for the same purpose). The total design can then be carried on labels, cartons, packing cases, warehouse signs, and gasoline service stations, both here and abroad. A trademark word or name is more apt to get quick recognition if it is always lettered in a uniform style; this unit is called a *logotype*. A test of a design is whether it is distinctive enough to be recognized immediately in any size.

Creative Goals of a Trademark

Among the qualities desired of a trademark are the following:

Distinctive.   Since the purpose of a trademark is to identify a product, the overall attribute that a trademark should possess is that it be *distinctive*. The trade directories are full of trademarks that play it safe and follow the leader, with the result that one directory listed 89 *Gold*s or *Golden*s, 75 *Royal*s, 95 *National*s, and 134 *Star*s! The quest for distinction also applies to designs, where the use of circles, ovals, and oblongs are commonplace.

Simple, crisp, short.   Good examples: *Sanka* coffee, *Ajax* cleansers, *Ritz* crackers, *Silex* percolators.

Easy to pronounce, and in one way only.   The makers of *Sitroux* tissues changed their name to *Sitrue;* the makers of *Baume Bengué* changed it to *Ben Gay.* To help customers pronounce *Suchard,* the makers created a charming trade character called *Sue Shard,* and changed the name too. These companies made the best of their old trademarks. But there should be no doubt about the pronunciation of a new trademark.

Conveying an apt suggestion.   Although a trademark cannot get legal protection if it literally describes the uses, qualities, or advantages of a product, it may *suggest* such attributes, as in the case of *Downy* fabric softener, *Band-Aid* bandages, *Accutron* watch, *Bisquick* biscuit mix. The suggestive trademark is a most popular form. It calls upon imagination to create it, and it invokes the imagination of the buyer.

The great problem with suggestive trademarks is that they may so easily go over that vague boundary that divides them from being descriptive. Even experienced advertisers have this problem. The Sun Oil Company spent upward of $30 million over a six-year period advertising its brand of gasoline called *Custom Blended,* only to have the courts finally rule that it was a descriptive term that any gasoline company could use.

Usable design.   If a design is used, will it be usable and identifiable when reduced to small black-and-white size? It takes a long time for the public to associate a company name with a design; hence many are meant to be used in connection with the product or company name, to help reinforce the identification.

Having no unpleasant connotations, here or abroad.   A trademark should be avoided if it can be punned unpleasantly. It should not be offensive abroad. The makers of an American car discovered its name meant "sudden death" in one Oriental country where they had been trying to do business.

Having reviewed all the desirable attributes of the trademark, we come back to the first question: Is it distinctive?

What "Registering" a Trademark Means

In the United States, the first to use a trademark for a certain category of goods has the exclusive right to it for those goods and for other goods that people might think he made or sold. To let the world know he is using a trademark, and to help establish the date he began using it, he can register it in Washington with the Patent Office, which has a record of over a half million trademarks. Registration is not obligatory (except for certain gold and silver products). Federal registration applies only to goods sold in interstate commerce. However, if, within five years, another man can prove, by means of old ads or bills of sale, that he had been using the trademark prior to the time when it was registered by another, he would have the rights to that trademark over the man who had registered it. Nevertheless, most firms apply

The Dow Chemical Company issued these instructions to all who have anything to do with its advertising.

big S, small t, y, r, o, f, o, a, m.

(Please)

That's the way we spell Styrofoam®. Always with a cap S. Styrofoam is a registered trademark for the specific brand of polystyrene plastic foam made only by The Dow Chemical Company. So it deserves the initial cap.

Like all trademarks, Styrofoam should be used correctly. This avoids confusing people about the true source of a product.

Please, hit that capital S when typing Styrofoam or mark it UC on proofs. We'd be most grateful. The Dow Chemical Company, Midland, Michigan.

for federal registration. There is also state registration for those seeking limited protection only.

Once a trademark has been registered, it should carry a notice to that effect wherever it appears, such as ® next to the trademark, or "Registered, U.S. Patent Office" or "Reg. U.S. Pat. Office," or some similar notice. When a trademark is repeatedly used in an ad, some firms put the registration notice on only the first time it appears, to reduce the possibility of typographic "bugs."

PUTTING A LOCK ON THE TRADEMARK

We now meet a paradoxical situation, in which the owner of a successful trademark suddenly discovers that anyone can use it—all because he failed to take certain precautionary steps to guard his claim. This problem arises when the public begins using a trademark to describe a type of product, rather than just a brand of that type of product. Originally, *Thermos* was the trademark owned by the Aladdin Company, which introduced vacuum bottles. In time, people would ask, "What brands of thermos bottles do you carry?"

The day the iceman lost his cool.

When the Frigidaire refrigerator came along, the iceman's wife took a fancy to it.

Naturally, the iceman just wouldn't warm up to the idea. A refrigerator to replace his icebox? Never.

But thank goodness, the little lady prevailed. One day even she got her Frigidaire refrigerator.

You know, Frigidaire is much more than a famous name.

It's a name that's been giving you the very best in benefits for years and years.

We were first to give you the convenience of an all-in-one refrigerator-freezer.

We did away with the messy chore of defrosting by inventing the Frost-Proof refrigerator.

Today, every Frigidaire refrigerator comes with a Power Capsule that has only three moving parts. Fewer parts can mean less expense and inconvenience over the life of your refrigerator.

During Frigidaire Week, if you decide to buy our 3-door refrigerator, No. FPCI 3-200 VT, you'll get an automatic icemaker for free. You only pay for the installation. Offer ends Aug. 31, 1972. Before you decide to buy just any refrigerator remember...

Every refrigerator is not a Frigidaire.

To Protect a Great Name

An advertisement in the retentive stage, working to reenforce the exclusiveness of the name, and the reputation of the "Frigidaire" refrigerator.

The courts held that "thermos" had become a descriptive word that any manufacturer of vacuum bottles could use, and was no longer the exclusive trademark of the originator. *Victrola, cellophane, nylon, escalator, aspirin,* and *linoleum,* each of which started off as the trademark of one company, but then it became generic—a word that is public property because their owners failed to take certain simple steps to put a "lock" on their property.

The steps to "putting a lock" on the ownership of a trademark are these: (1) Always make sure the trademark word is capitalized, or set it off in distinctive type. (2) Always follow the trademark with the generic name of the product, thus: Glad *disposable trash bags,* Kleenex *tissues,* Windex *glass cleaner.* (3) Don't speak of it in the plural as, say, three Kleenexes; rather, say three Kleenex tissues. (4) Don't use it in a possessive form—not Kleenex's new features, but the new features of Kleenex tissues—or as a verb—not "Kleenex your eyeglasses," but "Wipe your eyeglasses with Kleenex tissues." This is a legal matter but the advertising man's responsibility to carry out in the advertisements.

HOUSE MARKS

Up to now we have been speaking of trademarks that identify specific products. We now speak of the *house mark,* the primary mark of a firm that makes a large and changing variety of products. Here the house or firm mark is usually used with a secondary mark: *du Pont* (primary), Lucite, Dacron, Zerone (secondary); *Kellogg's* (primary), Special K, Product 19 (secondary).

Many companies create a design to go with their house mark. This design alone can appear on everything from a calling card to the sides of a truck, and on the sides of shipping cases going overseas. It can become an international identification. But it takes time to establish a design; hence companies often use their name along with the house mark.

This brings us to a major marketing-policy decision as to how, if at all, the relationship of all the company's products should be presented to the public. We quote from a report on the subject issued by the 4 A's:

> This is a question of policy. What may be logical for one advertiser may not be at all suitable for another. The food field offers a good example of the two philosophies at work.
>
> General Foods aims to have each of its many brands stand on its own advertising feet. In their early days they were acquiring companies at the rate of one every three months . . . in virtually every case, each was already established as an advertiser. For many years there was not family identification in the advertising. Then "A Product of General Foods" was included in small type, and more recently there has been an attempt toward family identification through the General Foods Test Kitchen. . . .

HOUSE MARKS

On the other hand, California Packing has too many products to attempt to establish brand names for each. Consequently all are carried under the house mark, *Del Monte*. They feel that the quality reputation established for the overall mark rubs off on each product. They also point out that this philosophy makes their trademark generically invincible. Who would ask for "a can of Del Monte"?

Some follow a mixed course. National Biscuit has some 200 cookie and cracker packages in its line, a good many of which feature their own brands. Yet all carry the *Nabisco* trademark—usually shown on a corner of the package.

In some cases the association of brand and company is deliberately omitted from advertising, usually because of product competition within the company's line itself. This is a common occurrence with these companies.

This also applies when such associations reflect unpleasantly on the product or corporate image. A food company making fertilizer, for instance. The Quaker Oats "Q" trademark is not seen in connection with Puss-in-Boots cat food.

Or when the association is meaningless. The *Gillette* mark is not used in advertising Paper-Mate pens.

Thus we see that a consideration of trademarks goes deep into management problems regarding the entire policy of marketing a variety of products made under the control of one company.[1]

A SERVICE MARK

SERVICE MARKS; CERTIFICATION MARKS

People who render *services,* as an insurance company, an airline—even Weight Watchers—can protect their identification mark by registering it in Washington as a *service mark.* There is also registration for *certification marks,* whereby a firm certifies that a user of his identifying device is doing so properly. Teflon is a material sold by du Pont to kitchenware makers for use in lining their pots and pans. *Teflon* is du Pont's registered trademark for its nonstick finish. *Teflon II* is du Pont's certification mark for Teflon-coated cookware that meets du Pont's standards. Advertisers of such products may use that mark. The Wool Bureau has a distinctive label design that it permits all manufacturers of pure-wool products to use. These marks are all registered as certification marks. They have the same creative requirements as trademarks—most of all, that they be distinctive.

---

[1] American Association of Advertising Agencies, *Trademarks—Orientation for Advertising People*, pp. 22–23. © 1971. Published by permission.

A CERTIFICATION MARK

The Woolmark label on this blanket means that you're getting a quality-tested product made of the world's best... pure wool.

PURE WOOL®

PACKAGING

WE NOW MOVE ON to packaging. The package is the most conspicuous identification a product can have, and a major factor in its success.

The average supermarket carries about 8,000 items. It is an ever-changing panorama, with new products, improved products, and new package designs constantly appearing on the scene. This is the arena in which consumer products have to fight—first, to be selected by the store buying committee to get on the shelf, and second, to be plucked off the shelf by the shopper. Many people are involved in packaging decisions, and the advertising director is one of them.

BASIC REQUIREMENTS

From the consumer's viewpoint. With all the changes in packaging taking place, certain basic requirements never change. The package must protect its contents from spoilage and spillage, leakage and evaporation, and from other forms of deterioration, from the time it leaves the plant until the time the product is used up. (How long that might be is an important consideration.) It must fit the shelf of the refrigerator or medicine cabinet in which that type of product is stored. (Recently, the Vaseline bottle, which had been round for generations, was redesigned as a rectangular bottle, to save room in the crowded medicine chest.) Cereal boxes must fit pantry shelves. If the package is meant to be set on a dressing table, it should not tip easily, spilling its contents. The package should be comfortable to hold, and not slip out of a wet hand. (Note how shampoo bottles usually provide a good grip.) It should be easy to open without breaking a fingernail, and to reclose for future use. It should be attractive.

EVOLUTION OF THE COCA-COLA BOTTLE

The first Coca-Cola bottle (1900) had a rubber stopper which popped when opened—believed to be the origin of the word "Pop" for a soft drink.

Courtesy: *Modern Packaging Encyclopedia*

469

From the store operator's viewpoint. The store manager has additional criteria for judging a package. It must be easy to handle, store, and stack. It should not take up more shelf room than any other product in that section, as might a pyramid-shaped bottle. Odd shapes are suspect; will they break easily? Tall packages are suspect; will they keep falling over? The package should be soil-resistant. Does it have ample and convenient space for marking? The product should come in the full range of sizes and packaging common to the field.

For products bought upon inspection, as men's shirts, the package needs transparent facing. (Puritan Shirts even included a plastic hanger for the store's use.) The package can make the difference in whether a store stocks the item.

Small items are expected to be mounted on cards under a plastic dome, called *blister cards,* to provide ease of handling and to prevent pilferage. Often these cards are mounted on a large card that can be mounted on a wall, making profitable use of that space. And at all times, the buyer judges the attractiveness that a display of that product will add to the store.

There are factors other than packaging that may cause a product to be selected, but poor packaging may relegate that product to a poor shelf position. Moving a product from floor level to waist level has increased sales of a product by as much as 80 percent.[2] Good packaging can make that much difference.

PACKAGING THINKING

Packaging ideas may be generated by men who perceive a marketing need that could be filled better by a fresh packaging application, or who see in a new packaging material or method of design the opportunity to develop a new packaging idea. We discuss a few of these ideas to reveal the range of marketing possibilities opened by packaging thinking.

Packaging ideas based on changing life-styles. "The sixties saw a major thrust toward convenience packaging," reports *Modern Packaging Encyclopedia,* "when the ever-busier consumer was better able to afford time- and labor-saving features in packaged goods. The need was answered by an irresistible trend toward single-trip packaging, opening closures, and unit-of-use disposable packages." And as for the seventies, it adds, "kitchen-ready, oven-ready, table-ready quick service, and carry-out are terms that will describe much of packaging's largest opportunities." [3]

---

2 Walter P. Margulies, *Packaging Power* (New York: World Publishing Company, 1970), p. 8.

3 *Modern Packaging Encyclopedia* (New York: McGraw-Hill, Inc., 1971), p. 11.

In this connection, the makers of Kraft cheese had this to say about the housewife, in a trade-paper advertisement:

1. She's more concerned than ever about food costs.
2. She often doesn't serve all of a package at one meal.
3. She hates throwing away partially opened packages because they won't reseal.

When what's left in the package won't keep until the next time she needs it, she's lost money. That hurts. Especially nowadays.

That's why Kraft never stops working to give her packages that continue to protect even after they're opened.

Kraft American singles are just one example of what's been done to cut her food waste down. Each slice is individually wrapped. Many Cracker Barrel Cheeses have their own plastic bag that reseals protectively. Kraft Grated Cheeses come with shaker tops. And Kraft was among the first to use twist-off caps on jelly and preserve jars.

Family Circle magazine reported that in 1970, over a million people under 30 lived by themselves, an increase of 133 percent in eight years.[4] Obviously, their buying needs differ from those of a family, and that fact is reflected in the way goods are created and packaged for their special needs. And now packages containing "The Weight Watcher's Lunch" have been added to the roster of packaged goods.

Packaging ideas that make the product. Here we have the famous "bug bomb" of World War II, which came into civilian use in 1947 for insecticide sprays. In 1969, 2.4 billion pressurized containers were sold, but only 100 million, or less than 4 percent, were for insecticides. One and a third billion pressurized units were used for body sprays, ranging from hair sprays to sprays for athlete's foot; 600 million units were for household sprays, such as cleansers; 225 million were for paint coatings and finishes; 88 million were for foods; and 1.7 billion for other uses—a tremendous convenience in many fields, born of a packaging idea.[5]

The roll-on applicator used for antiperspirants created a new way of applying a product. Aluminum trays, introduced in 1950, created the TV dinner, by making it possible to heat and serve meat, vegetables, and other frozen foods in their containers—all packaging ideas.

Packaging ideas based on sizes and forms. It is always good to survey all the products in a field to see if you are not overlooking a size or a good

---

[4] *Family Circle,* November 1971, p. 6.
[5] *Modern Packaging Encyclopedia,* p. 18.

way of presenting the product. Among the forms to consider are single packs, standard packs in a wide range of sizes, and multipacks, for carrying six or more bottles or cans. A package can be made so attractive that the user of the product will want to keep the container afterward for his own use—for example, a handy, stylized plastic box for small items, or a graceful decorative plastic bowl for margarine that can be used for serving nuts and popcorn.

Packaging ideas based on new materials and methods. One of the prolific sources of packaging ideas is the technical improvements in packaging capability. We have stretchable "shrink" plastics to cover odd-shaped products. We have high-speed heat-sealed plastic packages holding powdered soup and drinks, nuts, candies—a feat of moisture control as well as of automation. The first to use any such development has a competitive advantage.

Tin cans, which are really tin-plated steel, have seen many changes. They are lighter in weight and have thinner walls than those of some years ago. Since 1965, a tin-free steel has been used. And new aluminum cans have been moving in on the field. In 1970, more than 4 billion aluminum containers, including all types, were produced. Every time some technical improvement is made in the manufacturing of packages, a new packaging idea is on its way.

 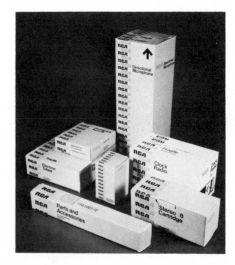

CREATING ONE PACKAGE DESIGN FOR 12,000 PRODUCTS

The above represents the answer to a challenge to bring a unified look to RCA's 12,000 products, of many sizes and shapes, for homemakers and aerospace scientists, which would convey RCA consistently and avoid a profusion of symbols. The final design aligns the new RCA logotype and other information horizontally and vertically in a modern design. The basic colors were red, black, and white.

Courtesy: Lippincott & Margulies, Inc.

Packaging ideas based on better closures and reuse features. If there is any one packaging goal on which everyone in the packaging field may be said to be working, it is improvement of the closure of packages. Many a customer has been lost because of the difficulty of opening a package. It is a never-ending quest. Kleenex first offered a package from which you could pull one tissue at a time. Aluminum-foil rolls and wax paper now come in boxes with a cutting edge. Some medicinals now come in bottles that are hard for children to open—the opposite of making a package easy to open, for a good cause. Even the conventional tube of toothpaste (a form that has resisted all change) was improved by putting on a wide cap that would not disappear down the drain. The search for the ideal closure goes on.

* * *

These are some of the forces from which new packaging ideas arise. For an up-to-the-minute exhibit of such ideas, a visit to a supermarket can be most enlightening.

DESIGNING A NEW PACKAGE

We have now come to the moment of decision in the creation of a new package for a product. Package design embraces the entire physical presentation of the package—its size and shape, the materials of which it is made, the closure, the outside appearance of its total area, the labeling.

OLD AND NEW

This is more than a change in package. It reflects a basic design change that had to be adaptable to all the packages on the next two pages.

Courtesy: Lippincott & Margulies, Inc.

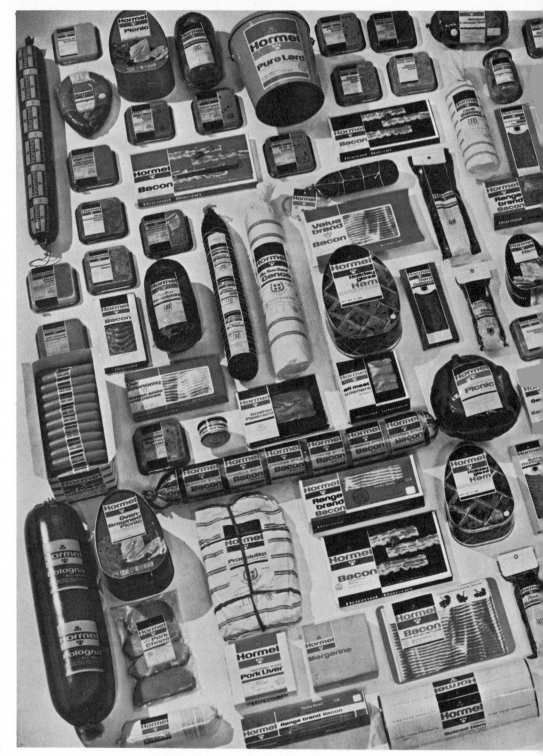

RESTYLING AN ENTIRE LINE

Though you see close to 100 packages here of different sizes and shapes, you immediately see a unified harmony of packaging, with each package clearly identified.

Courtesy: Lippincott & Margulies, Inc.

Walter P. Margulies, a foremost package designer, stresses the fact that a package is not a thing alone. It is something that must fit into the marketing goals of a company; it is a projection of a corporate image. Often it is related to existing products of a company; if not, it may be the forerunner of a line, and must be designed so that its design is expansible to embrace future products. Package thinking is first of all marketing thinking, and embraces questions such as:

—How much emphasis should be placed on the brand name? On the product name?

—Toward what segment of the market should the product's basic appeal be aimed?

—In what way will the packaging system best communicate product appeal?

—Should the graphics try to convey the size, shape, color, in-use applications? If so, how?

—In dealing with a food product, is it advisable to include recipes on the package? Which ones? Should they be changed in accordance with the seasons?

—Are all package panels being used to their best advantage? Will they effectively sell the product regardless of the way the package is stacked on the supermarket shelf?

—Can the basic design be extended to logically encompass other items in the manufacturer's line? Is it flexible enough to permit the addition of new products at some future date?

—Is there ample space for the inclusion of extra copy to announce special sales offers?

—What about price marking? Has a specific place been set aside where the product can be priced easily by the retailer so as not to mar the total look of the package?

—Is the design flexible enough to permit the addition of new products?

These are but a mere handful of the multitudinous factors that have to be taken into consideration by those whose job it is to launch a new package.[6]

TIME FOR A CHANGE?

We now jump ahead a number of years and perhaps many millions of dollars in sales for the product we so wisely trademarked and packaged, and whose merits have earned it many repeat customers. "What's this?" someone exclaims

---

[6] Reprinted by permission of The World Publishing Company from *Packaging Power* by Walter P. Margulies. Copyright © by Walter P. Margulies.

some morning. "You want to make changes in our good-luck package?" There is no clock of package life that says whether or when you might want to consider a change. But there are certain telltale market indexes that say it may be time to review the situation. Among them Margulies cites the following:

1. Innovation in physical packaging
2. Exploiting a reformulated product based on a meaningful formula change
3. The force of competitive action
4. Repositioning your product
   General Foods learned that the image of the decaffeinated Sanka brand was that of a castrated bean. The coffee-loving public avoided it. To reposition Sanka, the yellow label, which, according to research, suggested weakness, was replaced with a dominantly brown label, "very strong." And the statement "97 percent caffein-free" was given a less significant spot on the label
5. When effective ads force a shift in tactics
   Only when a theme has established itself as distinctive and long-lived
6. When changing consumer attitudes force a shift in marketing tactics
7. Upgraded consumer taste in graphic design
8. Changing retail selling techniques
9. When unrecognized home use determines a new marketing posture

As against these reasons for considering a change, Margulies offers the following reasons for not changing:

1. Don't change because of a new brand manager's desire to innovate.
2. Don't change to imitate your competition.
3. Don't change for physical packaging innovation only.
4. Don't change for design values alone.
5. Don't change when product identification is strong.
6. Don't change if it may hurt the branding.
7. Don't change if it will weaken the product's authenticity.
8. Don't change if it will critically raise the product's price.

"A decision to stay with the status quo," he adds, "is as important as the one to innovate." [7]

However, F. Kent Mitchel, vice-president and director of marketing

---

[7] *Ibid.*, pp. 62–67.

services of General Foods, had this to say. "The company is constantly testing new packaging for products which could turn an old product into a new one at much less cost than starting from scratch." [8]

When a package is to be changed, it is often done on a gradual basis, changing only one element at a time, so that old customers will not suddenly feel that this is no longer the product they have known and trusted.

Package design has become so important that a specialized field of package designers has developed.

TESTING THE DESIGN

A number of sophisticated devices have been developed to test various aspects of package design. The polariscope indicates which of several designs is most legible under the poorest illumination. An angle meter tests which design is most legible when approached from an angle, which is the way most packages are first seen when one is walking through a shopping aisle. The tachistoscope is a machine that tests which design, or part of a design, is most legible in a quick moment of viewing.

Packages are also subjected to consumer tests, to see how well open-

[8] *Advertising Age,* November 8, 1971, p. 1.

A PACKAGE TEST

When it was planned to modernize the Droste Cocoa package, the two new packages on the right were tested against the two old packages on the left. Interestingly enough, the research showed that people preferred the old packages.

Courtesy: Royal Droste Factories
Research: Richard Manville Research Inc.

ing devices work, and to get consumer reaction to the package as a whole. Raphael cites one of the consumer tests for the easy-opening tab on beer cans. It was found that women did not have the strength in their fingers to open the first version, and the tab was altered.[9] In order to improve the image of a brand of margarine, it was decided to wrap the sticks in parchment, the way butter is usually wrapped, and it is generally accepted that comparison with butter is the criterion by which the quality of margarine is judged. Before actual production of the parchment-wrapped stick, an in-home comparison test was made between sticks of margarine wrapped in foil and in parchment. The test revealed there was an overwhelming preference for the margarine *wrapped in foil!* As a result, the manufacturer cancelled an expensive order for parchment wrapping, which, if used, would have hurt sales.

Proposed new packages are usually tested not only against alternate designs, but with the packages of competitive products.

LEGAL ASPECTS OF PACKAGING

There are federal and state laws regarding packaging and labeling which make it mandatory, for various products, to include certain information on the package regarding size and content. The Fair Packaging and Labeling Act of 1966 says:

> Informed consumers are essential to the fair and efficient functioning of a free economy. Packages and their labels should enable consumers to obtain accurate information as to the quality of the contents and should facilitate value comparisons. Therefore it is hereby declared to be the policy of the Congress to assist consumers and manufacturers in reaching these goals in the marketing of goods.

This is a most far-reaching law affecting packaging and labeling. The Food and Drug Administration is responsible for enforcing the law as it affects foods, drugs, cosmetics, and other devices. The Federal Trade Commission has jurisdiction over "other consumer commodities."

In 1970 the FDA regulations placed on the manufacturer the burden of submitting data on the safety of food, including the packaging material with which it may come into contact. In about 25,000 words the regulations spell out the exact labeling requirements, including the descriptive words that may be used, and how quantities and volume must be stated; also the exact size and placing of type, and the background colors.

The Federal Trade Commission has rules about packages designed

---

[9] Harold J. Raphael, *Packaging: A Scientific Marketing Tool* (East Lansing, Mich.: Michigan State University Book Store, 1969), p. 165.

to prevent misrepresentation. For example, no package may say "Economy Size" or "Jumbo Size" unless it has available one other smaller size. In addition the FTC has rules regarding the labeling statements of a variety of products; also the enforcement of the Health Warning on cigarette packages. The Alcohol Tax Unit of the Treasury Department has its mandatory labeling requirements on alcoholic beverages.

The chief contribution the advertising man can make regarding the mandatory requirements on a package is to make certain the package and label have been approved by an attorney.

THE WASTE-DISPOSAL PROBLEM

I was astonished to discover that as recently as 1965, when the preceding edition of this book went to press, the subject of pollution did not loom into sufficient importance to be mentioned in the text. Today pollution is the chief subject of concern discussed at all the meetings of the industry. It is a major topic at women's clubs. "It will come as a shock and a surprise to most packagers and suppliers," said a report by *Modern Packaging,* which had made a study of 500 consumers in 38 states, "that the general public does not share their belief in the utility and necessity of packaging. In fact, the public blames packaging for an enormous—and unjustified—share of today's waste disposal problem. . . . Most people believe that packaging accounts for 50 percent or more of their solid wastes. (The true figure is about 15 percent.)" [10]

The industry is deeply involved in problems of recycling and other waste-disposal techniques. It is particularly concerned about those plastics that are not biodegradable (that is, that will not decompose and join the soil). What further restraints on packaging will the law invoke? What disposal problem might a proposed new container represent? Will people change their attitude towards packaging? If so, how? And how will it affect their buying habits? These are questions that remain to be answered.

Review Questions

1. Define a trademark. What is its purpose?

2. Give a brief definition or description of the following:
   a. trade name
   b. coined word
   c. secondary meaning
   d. house mark

3. What are the important legal requirements to keep in mind in creating a trademark?

4. At times you will see the same trademark used for two different products (Esquire Shoe Polish, Esquire Hosiery). How is this possible?

---

[10] *Modern Packaging,* March 1971, pp. 38–41.

5. What are the chief criteria from the advertising viewpoint for creating or selecting a trademark?

6. Explain what is meant by the registration of trademarks. Can you use a trademark which has not been registered?

7. What are the basic requirements of a package from the consumer's viewpoint? From the retailer's?

8. Can you cite several examples where packaging ideas "made" the product?

9. In your own words, discuss how packaging is related to marketing thinking.

10. Discuss some of the conditions favoring and not favoring a change in a successful package.

11. Describe some of the approaches used in testing packages.

12. In what ways do you think ecological concerns affect packaging?

13. Find three examples of current advertising where the emphasis is on the package.

Reading Suggestions

American Association of Advertising Agencies, *Trademarks—Orientation for Advertising People.* New York: 1971.

Barlow, C. Wayne, *Corporate Packaging Management.* New York: American Management Association, Inc., 1969.

Business Management, "Packaging: Why You Must Plan for the Future," April 1967, pp. 50–60.

Business Week, "The Power of Proper Packaging," February 20, 1965. Excerpted in Kleppner and Settel, *Exploring Advertising,* p. 254.

Diamond, Sidney J., "Protect Your Trademark by Proper Usage," in *Exploring Advertising,* ed. by Kleppner and Settel. Englewood Cliffs, N.J.: Prentice-Hall, Inc., 1970.

Gardner, David M., "The Package, Legislation, and the Shopper," *Business Horizons,* October 1968, pp. 53–58.

Guss, Leonard M., *Packaging Is Marketing.* New York: American Management Association, Inc., 1967.

Levitt, Theodore, "Branding on Trial," *Harvard Business Review,* March–April 1966, pp. 21–38.

Margulies, Walter P., *Packaging Power.* New York: World Book Company, 1970.

Marquette, Arthur F., *Brands, Trademarks and Good Will.* New York: McGraw-Hill Book Company, 1967.

Modern Packaging Encyclopedia. New York: McGraw-Hill, Inc., annual.

Raphael, Harold J., *Packaging: A Scientific Marketing Tool.* East Lansing, Mich.: Michigan State University Book Store, 1969.

Sales Management, "The Name is the Game," May 1, 1969, pp. 55–58.

Sarnoff, Robert W., "Anatomy of a New Trademark," *Saturday Review,* April 13, 1968. Also in Kleppner and Settel, *Exploring Advertising,* p. 248.

21

The Dealer Program

A SALESMAN FOR A new spray oven cleaner walks into a store.

"Good morning," he says. "I have a new spray oven cleaner I would like to show you."

"Have enough oven cleaners."

"But this one is different—it does a much better job than anything now on the market."

"Never heard of it."

"Soon this advertising campaign will appear, and when it does, you will have many calls for this cleaner—it's such a fine product."

"Well, maybe so. Just as soon as I get any calls for it, I'll call you."

What is the salesman supposed to say?

Here is another problem: The salesman of a well-known product is called in by the buyer of a chain carrying his goods.

"We have just completed an analysis of all items in your category, and we are planning to drop those making the poorest showing; we just haven't got room for them all. You are on the list to be dropped unless you do something to change the sales picture quickly. Have you any plans?"

In both instances, the salesman is faced with the problem of presenting a program through which the dealer can expect fast sales action. Creating and producing such programs, as a part of the basic sales presentation, is standard operating procedure for any advertiser selling through distributors. These projects are variously known as *promotions, dealer programs, merchandising plans,* and *sales-promotion plans.*

merchandising~ effort to get dealer to buy

FORMS OF DEALER PROGRAMS

The most frequent forms of dealer programs are:

—Point-of-purchase advertising   —Coupons and sampling

—Premiums   —Deals

—Contests   —Cooperative advertising

Displaying Merchandise Is Not a New Idea

These are often used in different combinations with each other. How important they can be in a company's sales operation is revealed in a report by the Nestlé Company, producers of a long line of food products, that in 1970 spent $23 million in major media, and an additional $10 million in promotion.[1]

POINT-OF-PURCHASE ADVERTISING

The effective use of point-of-purchase advertising is based on an understanding of:

1. The shopping habits of the consumer
2. The needs of the store manager

---

[1] *Advertising Age,* November 1, 1971, p. 70.

3. Forms of displays

4. The display idea

5. Getting the display used

The Shopping Habits of the Consumer

Over a number of years, du Pont has made a most extensive survey of the buying habits of the consumer. Their latest report, based on 7,147 shoppers, 345 supermarkets, and 95,262 purchases, showed that 49.9 percent of all purchases made were of items that the shopper did not have in mind upon entering the store. Unplanned purchases are often called impulse purchases (which the writer regards as an oversimplification of the mental process whereby a person becomes ready to make what may seem a totally spontaneous decision). Incidentally, the average shopper visits the supermarket two or three times a week, and spends 26 minutes shopping.[2]

In another study of consumer reaction to point-of-purchase material in seven types of retail outlets, 60 percent reported the material was an aid in shopping; in supermarkets the figure was 73 percent.[3]

The Needs of the Store Manager

The *Progressive Grocer* conducted a test of the effects of 734 displays over an eight-week period, based on sales of 360 grocery items in five super-

---

[2] *7th du Pont Consumer Buying Habits Study,* copyright 1965 by E. I. du Pont De Nemours & Company, Inc.

[3] "Consumer Reaction to Point of Purchase Advertising in Seven Major Types of Retail Outlets," Point of Purchase Advertising Institute, 1971.

The formula below determines net profit space yield of item x

1	Handling cost per case (suggested by McKinsey-General Foods 1963 study)	$ .42
2	Cases sold per average week	2
3	Total product handling costs	$ .84
4	Exposure space used 12" x 18"	1.5 sq. ft.
5	Occupancy cost @ $.10 per sq. ft. (based on Supreme's overhead)	$ .15
6	Weekly dollar sales of item ($6 per cs x 2)	$12.00
7	Gross profit dollars @ 20%	$ 2.40
8	Total "net" profit yield (Gross dollars minus occupancy and handling costs)	$ 1.41
9	Profit yield per square exposure foot	$ .94

The Arithmetic of Shelf Space

Courtesy:
Chain Store Age, Supermarkets Magazines

COMPARISON OF SALES

Normal Sales vs. Use of Displays

	DISPLAY UNIT SALES	NORMAL UNIT SALES	% INCREASE	DISPLAY $ SALES	NORMAL $ SALES	% INCREASE
Coffee, Tea, Cocoa	4,904	879	458%	$ 4,303	$ 891	383%
Crackers & Cookies	13,112	2,226	489	4,677	781	494
Desserts	5,466	301	1,716	576	41	1,296
Jams, Jellies, Spreads	3,761	288	1,206	1,219	173	603
Paper Products	4,937	1,064	364	1,426	345	314
Prepared Foods	16,026	944	1,598	1,914	177	979
Salad Dressing, Mayonnaise	1,919	379	406	866	168	415
ALL DISPLAYS (WITHOUT PRICE CHANGES)	57,587	10,052	473%	$18,832	$3,581	425%

Source: Progressive Grocer, *January 1960, pp. 4–7. This is partial list.*

markets. The report shows that the sales of products on which there was no variable except the display increased by 425 percent in dollar income during that period.[4] No wonder the manufacturer keeps hearing a voice from his sales department saying, "What we need are some good displays!"

But the store manager constantly hears a louder voice, saying "Beat last year!" Displays are only one element of the profit-making structure. In determining which items he will promote with point-of-purchase advertising, the retailer uses the following criteria.

—The product returns a good dollar volume.

—The display has an exciting promotional theme (often a projection of one used in the mass media).

—The display is well adapted for the store—not too large nor too small.

—The promotion promises to sell related items.

—The promoted item carries a good markup.

—The promotion fits the retailer's own schedule of promotions.[5]

---

[4] *Progressive Grocer,* January 1960, pp. 4–7.

[5] From "The Value of In-store Support," The Point of Purchase Advertising Institute, Inc., 1971.

The anatomy of a storewide

During the run of the merchandising test, Del Monte offered its annual storewide promotion to the trade, an effort that included a wealth of in-store display material and a major consumer promotional effort.

Tables show how the featured Del Monte products reacted to store wide activity in markets that made full use of the program compared to those that did not participate. Each type of product featured was analyzed by brand so that, for the first time, the net selling productivity of this promotional activity could be established.

All stores in the test panel enjoyed the benefits of the same retail and manufacturer advertising and promotion. However, pairs of stores were assigned varying levels of in-store participation to test the selling effect of maximum use versus minimum use of point-of-purchase and decorative storewide material.

On the average, featured products sold 153% more units in stores that made full use of the manufacturer-supplied materials. The conclusion is that while outside promotion can give promise of increased sales, the potential can die at the store's front door if there is no follow-through inside.

Fruit cocktail

	% Change of product movement in participating stores	% Change of product movement in non-participating stores
Del Monte Brand	+ 105%	+ 36%
Brand "A"	+ 24%	+ 9%
Brand "B"	− 27%	+ 14%
Net results:	**Net results:**	
Unit sales + 58%	Unit sales + 9%	
Dollar sales + 59%	Dollar sales +26%	

Catsup

	% Change of product movement in participating stores	% Change of product movement in non-participating stores
Del Monte Brand	+ 820%	+ 77%
Brand "A"	+ 8%	+ 6%
Brand "B"	− 11%	+ 20%
Net results:	**Net results:**	
Unit sales + 51%	Unit sales + 28%	
Dollar sales + 60%	Dollar sales + 30%	

Green peas

	% Change of product movement in participating stores	% Change of product movement in non-participating stores
Del Monte Brand	+ 374%	+ 95%
Brand "A"	− 75%	− 8%
Brand "B"	− 50%	+ 50%
Brand "C"	+ 25%	0%
Net results:	**Net results:**	
Unit sales + 150%	Unit sales + 34%	
Dollar sales + 148%	Dollar sales + 33%	

Tuna

	% Change of product movement in participating stores	% Change of product movement in non-participating stores
Star-Kist Brand	+ 293%	+ 15%
Brand "A"	+ 6.5%	+ 17%
Brand "B"	− 18%	− 5%
Brand "C"	+ 23%	+ 12%
Net results:	**Net results:**	
Unit sales + 16%	Unit sales + 7%	
Dollar sales + 23%	Dollar sales + 7%	

Green beans

	% Change of product movement in participating stores	% Change of product movement in non-participating stores
Del Monte Brand	+ 351%	+ 48%
Brand "A"	+ 11%	+ 75%
Brand "B"	− 230%	− 32%
Brand "C"	+ 45%	+ 8%
Net results:	**Net results:**	
Unit sales + 233%	Unit sales + 28%	
Dollar sales + 192%	Dollar sales + 5%	

Fruit punch

	% Change of product movement in participating stores	% Change of product movement in non-participating stores
Del Monte Brand	+ 314%	+ 79%
Brand "A"	+ 60%	+ 17%
Brand "B"	+ 25%	− 5%
Net results:	**Net results:**	
Unit sales + 123%	Unit sales + 21%	
Dollar sales + 122%	Dollar sales + 27%	

Courtesy: *Grocery Mfr. Magazine*, May 1971

REPORT OF STOREWIDE POINT-OF-PURCHASE TEST

A survey among operators of key stores in seven different types of retail outlets asked how point-of-purchase material can be made more acceptable. The answers indicated a preference for displays that are simple and easy to use, that are not too big for the location for which they are planned, that have a novel idea and good artwork, and that arrive two or three weeks ahead of the time at which they are to be used.[6]

Aspects of in-store support. *Grocery Mfr.* magazine joined in making controlled merchandising tests with a panel of A&P stores, "to put the calipers on in-store techniques—and directly measure their value." We quote some of their findings:

---

[6] "The Combination for Display Utilization at the Retail Level," a report by Louis Harris and Associates, Inc. (Point of Purchase Advertising Institute, Inc.), 1963.

FLOOR STAND DISPLAY

This floor-stand display became the Maybelline Eye Fashion Center, designed to provide 127 product facings in minimum space, for easy customer selections.

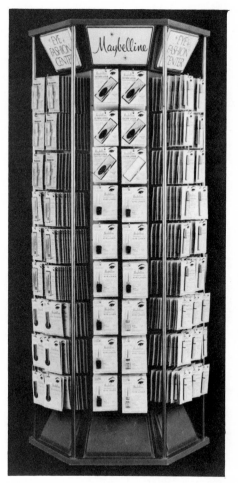

Courtesy: POPAI

In general, the tests demonstrated the selling power of the heavily traveled front-of-store position, with second place going to first-aisle and back-aisle locations.

Highly promoted advertised special-priced products and those with a strong consumer franchise [i.e., consumer following] fare well even if displayed at locations with less than optimum shopping traffic. However, impulse products and "low profile" items need to be placed at the heavily traveled locations to make displays pay off.

When a special display of the merchandise is made (as in a basket) and if it is featured in retail ads or is special-priced, the chances are that the shelf sales will be relatively unaffected and might even inch up during the display period. However, in every case for products without any advertising or price promotion, shelf movement declined during the display period (though the total sales for the period are

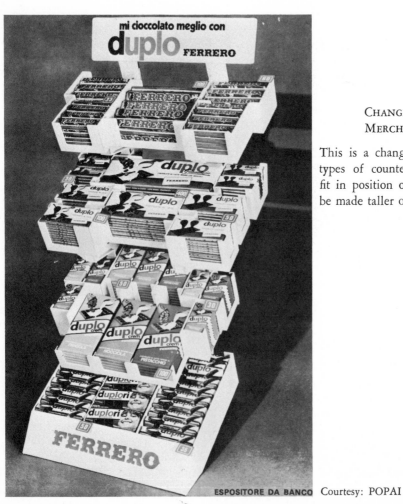

ESPOSITORE DA BANCO Courtesy: POPAI

CHANGEABLE COUNTER MERCHANDISING STAND

This is a changeable display for various types of counters. Interchangeable trays fit in position on the display, which can be made taller or shorter.

much higher). For an unadvertised canned drink item, normal shelf movement dropped from a normal rate of 27 to 19 during the first week of the display and 23 for the second week; meanwhile the display sold 156 units in the two-week period.

Unless it is a fast-moving seasonal item, the effective life of a display is brief; beyond the second week it is counterproductive in valuable space.[7]

The information above applies particularly to grocery chains and supermarkets. In the case of hardware stores, displays are usually smaller and stay up longer. In shopping centers where hard goods are sold, the displays are usually more descriptive of the products, and stay up longer.

Forms of Displays

Displays are designed to take advantage of all dimensions and areas of an establishment, and include outside signs, window signs, floor displays (including *jumble displays*), counter displays, shelf displays (*shelf extenders*), wall displays, overhead signs, and cards holding merchandise, for check-out counters.

Permanent signs. These include the signs in front of a gas station, or the clock in a soda parlor, or a glass sign of an expensive watch in a jeweler's window. Displays can also be *illuminated*. The illuminated ones, of course, get more attention, and are reserved for good spots in good outlets (as for a back bar). Illuminated displays are usually designed to be effective even when not plugged in.

Motion displays. In a succession of tests, displays with motion were favored by 70 percent of the dealers, were given 88 percent of the prime in-store locations (compared with 47 percent for nonmotion displays), and produced an 83 percent average gain above normal shelf sales.[8]

Permanent merchandise trays, racks, and cases. The dealer welcomes displays occupying little counter or floor space, and that hold or dispense merchandise and provide a self-service feature. This may be an open-face stand from which merchandise such as paintbrushes, phonograph records, furniture polish, floor wax, and pocket-size books can be picked right out. For small, costly items such as watchbands, displays may be designed so that they show the goods to the customer, but are accessible only from the dealer's side of the counter, in a pilferproof arrangement.

---

[7] *The Value of In-store Support,* published by *Grocery Mfr. magazine,* 1971.
[8] Report of Point-of-Purchase Advertising Institute, Inc., 1965.

The Display Idea

The heart of the display, however, is its selling idea, designed to generate purchases. Here, the creative man can think in terms of three dimensions, and, subject only to outer-size limitations and need for construction simplicity and cost, he has the world of shapes and materials with which to work. Among the directions on which he can embark are ideas such as these:

The product itself. The most important display piece in a store is the product itself, and any idea that focuses attention on it is helpful. The solution may be a large stack of the packaged product on the floor, with a sign stating an advantage and the price. Or the merchandise can be tumbled in a large box from which the shopper is invited to pick one (a relic of our childhood grab-bag days, no doubt), likewise with a sign stating an advantage.

The current advertising theme. Point-of-purchase advertising is a projection of the current advertising theme, whatever it may be. The challenge is to reduce it to its simplest elements, then dramatize it in three dimensions.

Tie-in with other products. This form of display idea suggests the promotion of other products, related to the one advertised, that the store also sells. A display of beer suggested pretzels and potato chips. Kellogg's Corn Flakes displays featured appetizing dishes of Kellogg's with berries and other fruit on sale in the store.

Storewide promotion. Some displays are based on a storewide promotion, as Back-to-School, Cook-Out, Spring Cleaning, Fall Festival, and Vacation Needs. Here, the manufacturer provides thematic point-of-purchase material that can apply to all departments in the store, with special emphasis, of course, on his own products.

Tie-in with national advertising. For the smaller independent stores, window displays based on the national advertising theme may be particularly helpful in reminding the passerby that here is the place to get the product he saw advertised.

Demonstrating the product. Often the display can invite the shopper to try out features of the product for himself, by pressing a button, looking through an opening, or turning a knob. This is especially good for new types of products.

get rich on peanuts

...and pretzels
...and potato chips
...and Holland House

Get faster returns on your inventory investment by using a Holland House display to sell related high profit items. It's a terrific way to remind your Holland House customer to stock up on her collateral entertaining needs.

So this year, put it all together with Holland House and find yourself getting rich on peanuts. And other related items like snacks, dips, chips, anchovies, cheeses, straws, pretzels, popcorn. And maybe even caviar.

NUTS

POTATO CHIPS

Holland House
COCKTAIL MIX

Follow the leader

SHOWING HOW DISPLAY CAN HELP OTHER SALES

This trade paper advertisement for Holland House Cocktails shows dealers how by using this display they can also increase the sale of pretzels and potato chips. Purpose: to get them to use the display.

Getting Displays Used

There is great waste in the issuance of displays; the problem is in getting them used. There must be a plan, and the retailer should know about it in advance. The chief burden for getting the cooperation of the store manager in using the manufacturer's displays is upon the manufacturer's salesman who calls upon that store or chain. Many salesmen will also go to extra effort to make sure that the display is put to good use and stays up as long as possible. Many displays are not used in department stores and chains because they are not in accordance with promotion and/or merchandising policy. In many cases all that is needed is tailor-making the displays somewhat to fit the store's requirements.

Having Displays Made

There are firms that specialize in creating and manufacturing different types of displays—made of cardboard, metal, wood, plastic, or glass. Some will combine these facilities, or subcontract parts of the work. These firms will usually submit their ideas in design and dummy form, along with a total production estimate, on speculation. There are many firms that serve as consultants and brokers in the sale of displays, supplying the idea, and if they get the order, having it produced through various manufacturers. Either of these procedures always requires a clear understanding in advance about the conditions for doing business. For example, take the case of a firm submitting an idea that is desired, but whose production cost is too high. Perhaps arrangements can be made to give them the order for the first run at their price, and open the field to competition for the reruns. But whatever the deal, it must be made before any work is done.

Most large firms that have a continuing stream of display requirements have their own creative display departments, which create the idea. The manufacturing is then processed through the advertiser's purchasing department.

PREMIUMS

A premium, as the term is used in advertising, is an item offered as an inducement to buy the advertised product. Such an item offered without extra charge is called a *free giveaway*. Or it may be offered upon proof of purchase and payment of a charge; this is called a *self-liquidating premium*, or *self-liquidator*.

A free giveaway premium may be handed to the person *directly*, when he makes his purchase; for example, a gas-station attendant might hand out glasses to people who buy a set amount of gas. Or the premium might be packed in the packages that are purchased, as might a plastic measuring cup

Stainless spoon offer from 'TOTAL'.

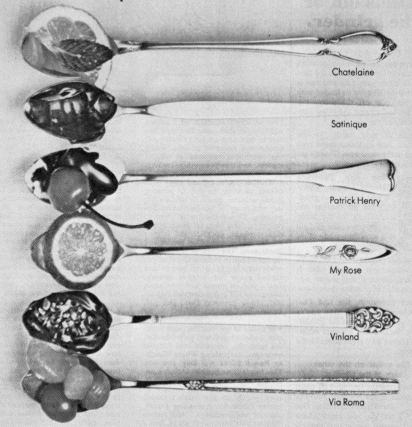

Chatelaine

Satinique

Patrick Henry

My Rose

Vinland

Via Roma

A set of six beautiful iced-drink (or whatever!) spoons
in Oneida Community stainless, as featured in the Betty Crocker Coupon Catalog.

Summer's here! And whether you serve your guests tall, refreshing iced drinks or fancy desserts, you'll be glad you have a set of these lovely, practical stainless Oneida spoons. They're designed for us exclusively by Oneida silversmiths, and the patterns you can choose from are pictured above.

Any set of these solid stainless spoons can be yours for only $2.50 and one proof of purchase from specially marked boxes of Total. (You'd expect to pay more than $6.00 in stores for a set of six iced-drink spoons of this quality!)

So pick up a box of Total today. Then send for your set of spoons, and have a long, cool summer!

Featuring a Self-liquidating Premium

packed in a can of coffee. This is called an *in-pack* premium. Sometimes this enclosure is a coupon that can be redeemed. The premium might be affixed to the outside, as might a towel that goes with a box of detergent; this is called an *on-pack* premium. Or a double package can be planned, to hold both the advertised product and the premium.

Self-liquidating premiums usually require a proof of purchase to be mailed in, along with money to cover the set charge.

The Use of Premiums

The purpose of a premium is to get an immediate and demonstrable increase in sales. It can be used to introduce new products. It can be used in a local territory where strong competitive pressure has developed; it can be used on a national basis. It can be used to increase the unit of sale, or to get traffic into a showroom. It can be used to offset seasonal slumps and to attract heavy users.

To introduce Fresca, the Coca-Cola Company offered a free phonograph record with proof of purchase of two cartons of Fresca, and distributed 500,000 records. To build traffic for all its dealers, the Armstrong Cork Company offered for $1 an album of records of all the songs in its TV showing of *Brigadoon,* to all people who would go to a dealer and pick up an order blank; over 750,000 people visited dealers. General Mills made a national broadcast offering a comic book for proof of purchase of two boxes of Wheaties, and had over 7,200,000 requests for their comic book.

Premiums are not indicated, however, for a product that is bought only occasionally, like tires, or for products bought only when a special need arises, like a cough preparation. Premiums are not helpful when the sales of a company have been steadily going down. The cause for such a decline is far more critical than can be offset by premiums.

The types of premiums used most in 1971 were games, toys, sporting goods, general kitchenwares, and appliances. The biggest users of premiums were manufacturers of health and beauty aids, gasoline, meat products, soft drinks, and appliances.[9]

What Makes a Good Premium?

The more of the following qualities a premium has, the better:

—It should have glamor or be useful.
—It should be something of which the consumer seldom has too many.

---

[9] *Incentive Marketing,* August 1971.

—It should not be on sale elsewhere.

—It should represent a real value in quality and price.

—It should not compete with another product regularly in the store, unless it is a part of the advertiser's family of products.

—It should be simple to handle and to mail.

The trend in premiums is to offer products of better quality and higher price.

A symposium of the Premium Advertising Association made the following suggestions:

1. Give complete specifications about your premium in the advertising. Give sizes, colors, and any other details that will help visualize what you are offering.

2. Deliver premiums as quickly as possible; this applies especially to children's premiums.

3. If you charge anything at all for your premium, be sure that your customer will feel that his money was well spent.

4. Be sure that premiums offered to children are such as have the approval of the parents.

5. If it is necessary that a coupon be filled out in order to get a premium, provide room enough for writing in an average name and address.

Often different premium offers will be tested in different markets to determine which holds the most promise.

But premiums have their problems, too. An in-pack premium in a package of food must meet the requirements of the Food and Drug Administration, to make sure it does not impair the foodstuff. In-pack coupons must meet the regulations of the Federal Trade Commission. On-pack premiums are not favored by the trade on account of pilferage. The physical work of handling premium mail and fulfillment is usually done by firms specializing in this work.

There is one guide that should be followed in advertising premiums. *The advertising must so clearly and correctly describe and picture the premiums, and must state the terms so clearly, that the person receiving it will not be disappointed.* This applies to prompt delivery, too. If a child, especially, has been disappointed, the whole family feels his sadness.

Legal aspects. A variety of federal and state laws may bear upon a premium offer. Everything should be cleared by an attorney first. The biggest legal problem in the advertising of premiums is the use of the word *FREE.* A free offer is one to which no cost is attached. If a product is given free with the purchase of another one, the price of the other product must be its regular

A Study in Premium Offers

ADVERTISER	PREMIUM	TERMS
Beech Nut (baby food)	Terry-cloth bib	25¢ and 3 labels
General Foods (Gaines Gravy Train)	Vinyl tablecloth	75¢ and 2 labels
Gillette (Right Guard)	Traveler's bag	$6.95 and label
Kraft Dinner line items	Teflon-coated cook-ware (12 pieces)	$25 and 6 labels
Lever Bros. (Rinso)	Hosiery	$1 and 2 labels
Nestlé (chocolates)	Candy dish	$2 and label
Sunmaid Raisin Growers (raisins)	Fielder's glove	$5.50 and seal
Shulton (Old Spice toiletries)	3 literary classics	$2.95 and proof of purchase
3M Company (freezer tape)	Knife for frozen food	$1 and label
Planters (peanuts)	Booklet—*Appliance Cooking for All Seasons*	25¢ and label

Source: Incentive Marketing, *1971 issues.*

price; it may not be increased to absorb some of the cost of the free item. All conditions of purchase to obtain the free item must be stated conspicuously in conjunction with the word *FREE* at the outset. A "free" offer is not to be allowed in a trade area for more than six months in a twelve-month period, according to F.T.C. regulations.

Fulfillment firms. The physical work of handling premiums, including opening the mail, verifying payment, packaging, addressing, and mailing, is often handled on a fee basis by firms who specialize in "premium fulfillment." They also handle contest responses and prizes.

Premiums as Trade Incentives

Premiums are also used as incentives for salesmen to reach certain sales goals, and to dealers for ordering certain quotas of goods that they are then to support with special displays and featuring. Giving premiums to salesmen and the trade falls within the province of the sales department, but any advertising man sitting in the council that is establishing an entire sales and advertising promotion should be aware of them. They are referred to as the *incentive* end of the premium business.

Somewhere in every discussion of a consumer promotional plan, the idea of a contest is sure to come up. A Coca-Cola "Tour the World" contest brought in 9,250,000 entries. Not too many firms can embark on a contest of such magnitude, but the fact that the public responds in such numbers gives contests a perennial place for consideration in major advertising plans.

In a highly competitive, highly advertised field, a contest may be a welcome change of pace from head-on competitive claims. It brings fresh interest in the product to its present customers. It reaches out for new ones. It may be run locally to meet competition; it may serve as a test before expanding the program regionally or nationally. It may generate new interest among dealers by bringing traffic into the store.

A Contest
Involving Use of Product

Worcestershire a winner tonight.

Then enter your recipe in Lea & Perrins contest.

10 First Prizes– one for each of these categories.

1. SEAFOOD   5. POULTRY
2. MEATS   6. SOUPS
  [LAMB, VEAL,]   7. SALADS
  [BEEF, PORK]   8. VEGETABLES
3. EGGS   9. APPETIZERS
4. CHEESE   10. "YOU NAME IT"

Let yourself go in the kitchen with Lea & Perrins Worcestershire Sauce. It can make almost any recipe into a winner. Have fun experimenting with your own favorite recipes and you'll see. You can bring out the flavor of all kinds of foods, from chicken to carrots, from salmon to squash. And add a subtle difference to every dish.

Try it. Then send us your own original ways to use the original Worcestershire Sauce. There are 10 First Prizes—one for each of the ten categories. And you can enter any or all, with as many recipes as you like.

There are 50 runner-up prizes, too. And everybody who enters wins a free copy of the Lea & Perrins "Exciting Ideas" Cookbook: 77 things to worcestershire—and every one a winner.

PRIZES
First Prize in each category:
A Minutemaster Microwave oven by Litton Industries. Cuts cooking time by 75%. Lightweight, portable, cooks clean and cool.

Five Runner-Up Prizes in each category:
Ronson's Superflexible "Quintisserie"—a five-in-one unit. Broils, grills, fries, griddles and roasts. Holds roasts or turkeys up to 25 pounds.

200 Honorable Mentions:
A Certificate of Merit from Lea & Perrins acknowledging you as a member of the "Be Original" Culinary Club.

Everybody Wins: The Lea & Perrins "Exciting Ideas" Cookbook.

CONTEST RULES:

1. Entries must be original recipes using Lea & Perrins Worcestershire Sauce, and will be judged on the basis of originality, appeal, consumer usefulness and accuracy.

2. Each recipe must be written legibly in ink, or typed, on one piece of paper.

3. Each recipe must (a) bear name and address of contestant, (b) indicate category title and number in which it is competing, (c) list ingredients and exact measurements in order of use, and (d) give complete directions for combining and completing, including pan size, time and temperature for cooking.

4. Multiple entries are encouraged in any or all categories. Entries must be postmarked by July 31, 1972.

5. Employees of Lea & Perrins, Inc., Creative Marketing Management, Creative Food Service, Inc., their respective advertising agencies and their families may not participate. All entries will become the property of Lea & Perrins and may be altered or advertised without further permission; none will be returned.

6. Judging will be conducted by Creative Food Service, Inc., an independent judging firm. Decision of the judges is final. In case of duplicate winners, duplicate prizes will be awarded.

7. Liability for Federal, state and other taxes is the sole responsibility of winners. This contest is subject to all Federal, state and local regulations.

8. Winners will be announced and notified by mail on or about December 1, 1972, and agree to participate in publicity, advertising and other materials related to the contest, at the sole discretion of Lea & Perrins, Inc.

MAIL ENTRIES TO:
LEA & PERRINS
"ORIGINAL RECIPE" CONTEST
P.O. BOX 560
MONTCLAIR, N.J. 07042

COUPONS

Each offers cash inducement to buy product.

As in the case of premiums, contests are of no help if the sales of a company have steadily been declining. Something more basic needs correction.

Forms of Contests

There are vogues in forms of contests. In 1950, the fourth edition of this book reported, "Most contests are for trademarks and slogans." In 1966, the fifth edition reported that 65 percent of all contests were for sweepstakes, and 23 percent for completion questions, such as "Why I like . . ." In 1971, *Incentive Marketing* magazine reported, "84 percent of all contests are for sweepstakes." Completion questions were not even mentioned.

A contest may provide a theme for the whole advertising and sales-promotion program, including the dealer promotion. It must be planned well in advance.

Legal Aspects

Contests are subject to federal and state laws.

The Federal Trade Commission is directly interested, especially in the way winners are selected. The U.S. Postal Service prohibits the use of mail for any lottery, which is defined as "a plan for distribution of things of value by lot or by chance among people who have given consideration." The key words here are "have given consideration"; therefore there must be no payment of any kind required to get into a sweepstakes, where the winners are drawn by lot. (If, however, the contest requires some manifestation of talent, as writing your ideas about something, this is not considered a lottery. Such contests, however, are harder and slower and more expensive to judge.)

Among other details that are important are the statement of the expiration date, notice of how the winners are to be notified, and a clause, "Void where prohibited by law," to meet the problem of state laws.

The first man to call to your side in discussing contests is your lawyer.

Handling Contest Replies

There are firms that specialize in handling the physical details of contests (called *contest fulfillment*), including receiving entries, selecting and notifying winners, and handling other details incident to the contest.

SAMPLING

A sample of a product is one of the best ways of convincing a person of its merits. Sampling is used most frequently for new low-priced products with a fast repeat sale, like cosmetics, toothpaste, and foods. Sampling usually coincides with mass-media advertising taking place in an area at the same time.

Sampling is usually done by door-to-door delivery by distributing firms in various markets geared to handle such assignments, or through the mail (the expensive way).

A trade practice has developed whereby an entrepreneur assembles minipacks of different products, puts them up in one wrapping, and sells them through the stores. To the consumer, it is good value; to the store, it is a full markup; to the advertiser, it is an economical way of getting distribution for his sample. Again, the value of the contents lies in the reputation the products have built through their usage and advertising.

A question often arises about taking money away from the advertising fund to put it into sampling. We quote this excerpt from the report of an anonymous "Brand Manager" writing of his experience in *Advertising Age:*

> Seems as though our sampling program was going great guns for a hair preparation I then worked on. As we expanded across the country, we were capturing a 20% to 25% share of market within four to six months of introduction. . . .
>
> About halfway across the country, we learned that a competitor was coming into the marketplace shortly, and so we decided to expand more rapidly than we originally planned. Unfortunately, advertising and promotion dollars were not easy to come by. . . .
>
> So I recommended to management what turned out to be a big mistake.
>
> I suggested we cut back our sustaining area advertising budget to a bare-bones minimum in order to turn up the money for sampling in the expansion markets. Moreover, I recommended that our introductory advertising budget be substantially less in expansion areas than in the half of the country we had already introduced in, in order to turn up needed funds for sampling.
>
> The results were depressing, if not catastrophic. We missed our share objective by 20% in the expansion areas! We did some consumer research to try to ascertain why. The answer was simple: Although men tried a sample of our product, they were not convinced of its superiority, in the way they had been in the original half of the country we introduced in. The reason: We did not have sufficient advertising support to make the sample serve as a see-for-yourself validation of our advertising claims. The men tried our product without knowing what to look for.
>
> I'll never sacrifice one element in the marketing mix for another in the future—without testing the premise first.
>
> Moral: Don't ask promotion to substitute for advertising.[10]

---

[10] Reprinted with permission from the January 18, 1971, issue of *Advertising Age.* Copyright 1971 by Crain Communications, Inc.

We are all familiar with the coupons issued by advertisers of grocery and cleaning items and other preparations—5¢ off, 10¢ off, 20¢ off the price of a package presented at the shopping center. Think of this as a massive sampling campaign, supported by the advertising done in behalf of those products. It attracts new users, brings back into the fold those who have strayed from the product, and reinforces the attitude of present users as to the desirability of the product.

The extent of couponing may be surprising. It is estimated that over 800 companies distribute about 10 billion coupons per year, of which roughly 1 billion are redeemed, for a saving to the consumer of about $100 million. (Although the redemption averages 10 percent, that from direct mail is 15 percent.) [11]

Coupons are distributed in a number of ways. Many are contained in the packages consumers buy (subject to FDA regulations in the case of foods). They may be sent by mail, but because of the high postage costs, it is now common to share in a joint mailing of coupons with a number of noncompetitive products. Often, coupons are issued through magazines; many advertisers have the coupon appear as a special insert in connection with their ads. Coupons appear in the daily newspaper (low response rate), and in the Sunday supplements. The great swing for the distribution of coupons, in the light of the postal increases, has been to the special loose newspaper supplement.

DEALS

There are two types of deals: *consumer deals* and *trade deals.*

Consumer deals. A consumer deal is a plan whereby the consumer can save money in the purchase of a product. It may be a direct price reduction, of which the cents-off deal is the most familiar form. Or it may be a merchandising deal, where three bars of soap are wrapped together and sold at a reduced price, or when a package of a new member of the family is attached to a package of the present product, at little or no extra cost—an effective way of introducing a new product.

In a study of price deals, Hinkle reports:

—The closer deals are to each other, the less effective they are. Brands which deal frequently encourage even regular customers to stock up and wait for the next deal.

—The majority of annual price reductions occur in high-volume periods, but off-season deals are more effective.

---

[11] Report in *Printers' Ink,* March 25, 1966, p. 42.

—Dealing is more effective for newer brands than for old.

—Deals are as much as two to three times more effective when a brand's advertising share level is maintained.

—Deals are fruitless for products whose sales have been going off steadily. "An assessment should be made of the more basic corrective measures." [12]

Deals may provide the theme for a strong local advertising campaign. Cents-off deals must meet Federal Trade Commission requirements.

Trade deals. A trade deal is a special discount to the retailer for a limited period of time. It may entail a minimum purchase; it may be a sliding scale of discounts depending on the size of the purchase. It may be in connection with a consumer merchandising deal, offering a discount on the purchase of a given number of consumer deals and size assortments. It may include the counter displays to help sell the product to the consumer. All trade deals are subject to the restrictions of the Robinson-Patman Act, which we shall discuss later in the book.

Trade deals are extensively advertised in the trade papers.

There is a division of opinion on the efficacy of deals. After analyzing over a hundred different Scott promotions, James D. Stocker, advertising manager of the Scott Paper Company, reported, ". . . much to our surprise, less than 15 percent of these forcing promotions actually paid for themselves in terms of new permanent business." [13]

COOPERATIVE ADVERTISING

Cooperative advertising is that placed in the local media by a retailer or local distributor for which he is reimbursed by the national advertiser. The repayment may be 100 percent, 50 percent, based on the volume of business, or whatever terms are agreed upon. But *whatever the terms are, they must be available to all other distributors in the market on the same proportionate basis.* That is the crux of the federal Robinson-Patman Act, which governs cooperative advertising, and which is enforced by the Federal Trade Commission. (We discuss this at greater length in the final chapter of this book.)

Usually the national advertiser will provide mats for the newspaper advertising, videotape for television, scripts and recordings for radio, and printed matter for any direct mail, in each instance allowing room for the

[12] *Harvard Business Review,* July–August 1965, pp. 75–84.

[13] James D. Stocker, "The Effects of the Growth of Advertising Volume in Merchandising Policies," address before AAAA Eastern Annual Conference, New York City, November 1962.

dealer's name. It is estimated that over 50 percent of all department-store newspaper advertising is cooperative. In such instances, the store may not use the advertiser's mats; it may use the cooperative allowance for the store under its own logotype. Or it may use mats of different manufacturers in creating a full-page advertisement over its own name, called an *omnibus* advertisement. It may then charge each manufacturer a pro rata share of the total cost of the whole advertisement.

The idea for cooperative newspaper advertising was originally spawned by the fact that in many papers the local rate was much lower than the national rate, so that even if the national advertiser reimbursed the retailer 100 percent, he might still be getting the space at a lower rate than if he placed it directly at national rates.

The retailer might also be disposed to provide room for store displays for the product, if it is advertised over his name; and also to make sure the item is in stock if a special cooperative ad on it is run.

Among the advantages of cooperative advertising to the retailer are that it helps defray part of his selling costs. He gets the local prestige of the additional advertising. Furthermore, the space used by a manufacturer's cooperative advertising may help him earn a better rate for all his advertising. The disadvantage is that even if the store has to pay only 50 percent of the cost, that sum may not be justified by the profits on the sale of that product, or the manufacturer's ads may not meet the special style of the store.

What's the catch to all this? There are a number.

In the first place, some newspapers are going on the single-rate basis; hence the potential saving between national and local rates is decreasing. There are often difficulties and disparities for the advertiser in the store's billing procedure. Stores may not use the manufacturer's mat; rather, they may prepare an advertisement in the store style, charging the manufacturer the production cost, and changing the image of his advertising. His advertisement may be placed in the weaker paper in town to help the store earn a quantity discount there. As a result, the manufacturer may lose strict control over the format of the advertising, as well as over the choice of media.

NEW WESTINGHOUSE HEAVY DUTY 15 WASHER ENGINEERED TO PREVENT COSTLY REPAIR BILLS

...me a rugged, two-fisted washer that's ...e-free—one that can take big loads as well ...ail loads and get them thoroughly clean." ...s what we found in survey after survey on ...women want most in an automatic washer. ...th these objectives in mind, our engineers ...to work and developed the new "Heavy ...15"—our most thoroughly tested automatic ...r in 25 years.

Tested 138,000 Hours

...its porcelain top right down to its massive ...bottom, the new "Heavy Duty 15" Laundro-...Automatic Washer has been checked, re-checked and tested through and through to minimize the chance of costly repairs. That's what it takes to build a trouble-free, heavy duty washer. There just isn't any other way.

New Trouble-Free Transmission

We built the transmission (the cause of costly repair bills) half again as large as those found in other automatics. We tested it part for part, hour after hour to make sure it won't break down. Then we developed a new heavy duty suspension system and tested it for months with the toughest off-balance wash loads possible. Result: no shimmy, shaky antics.

Big 15 Pound Capacity

To handle today's big wash loads, we de... the "Heavy Duty 15" to tackle 15 pounds ... toughest wash. And believe us, it can. To... it, we tested our big sturdy agitator with... of the hardest wash loads we could drea... (sheets, shag rugs) to make sure it coul... the strain and get clothes thoroughly clea... tested it for delicate things too, and it was a... gentle about it.

Our "Heavy Duty 15" is rugged and depen... Good reason for putting yourself on a solid f... with one soon—at your Westinghouse de...

You can be sure if it's Westinghouse

DEALER ADVERTISING BACK OF NATIONAL ADVERTISING

To get dealer support back of this national consumer magazine advertisement, an extensive cooperative advertising program was prepared, shown on the following pages.

THE DEALER MERCHANDISING PROGRAM

This was the first page of a 12-page newspaper-size dealer bulletin,
listing the advertising and other dealer aids to be used concurrent
with the appearance of the national advertising.

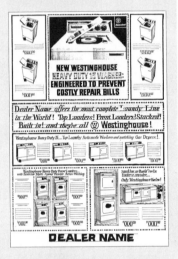

A page from a portfolio offering variety of mats and suggestions for cooperative newspaper advertising.

1. Define briefly each of the six most frequent forms of dealer programs.

2. Discuss the guidelines the retailer should use in deciding what items warrant point-of-purchase promotion.

3. Describe some of the evidence that in-store promotional support pays off for the retailer.

4. Describe the major kinds of selling ideas from which good displays can grow.

5. Based on visits to supermarkets, department stores, and drugstores, what current display ideas strike you as particularly effective? Why?

6. Distinguish between give-away and self-liquidating premiums.

7. What are the characteristics of a good premium?

8. What are the principal benefits to the advertiser of conducting a contest?

9. Define sampling, and describe how its use can be integrated with media advertising.

10. Describe the role played by cents-off coupons. In what different ways are coupons distributed?

11. Distinguish between consumer deals and trade deals.

12. Define cooperative advertising, and discuss its advantages for the manufacturer and for the retailer. Its disadvantages.

13. From current advertising, find an example of a contest being promoted in media advertising. Of a coupon offer in media advertising. Of cooperative advertising.

Reading Suggestions

Anny, "A Premium User's Nightmare," May 10, 1968. Also in Kleppner and Settel, *Exploring Advertising,* p. 258.

Business Week, "A P.O.P. Art Form that Turns Shoppers On," January 8, 1972, p. 36ff.

Davidson, John R., "FTC, Robinson-Patman and Cooperative Promotional Activities," *Journal of Marketing,* January 1968, pp. 14–17.

Everett, Martin, "One Small Step for Co-op Advertising," *Sales Management,* April 3, 1972, pp. 23–27.

Grocery Manufacturer, "The Value of In-Store Support," 1971.

Hinkle, Charles L., "The Strategy of Price Deals," *Harvard Business Review,* July–August 1965, p. 75.

Long, Durwood, "Selectivity: Key to Effective Sampling Techniques," *Advertising and Sales Promotion,* November, 1971, pp. 38–41.

Nelson, Robin, "Marketing Incentives Are on the Rise Again," *Marketing/Communications,* November, 1971, pp. 26–29.

Offenhartz, Harvey, *Point-of-Purchase Design.* New York: Reinhold Book Corp., 1968.

Point-of-Purchase Advertising Institute, *Trade Practices and Current Procedures among Buyers and Sellers of Point-of-Purchase Advertising Materials.* New York: 1967.

Seipel, Carl-Magnus, "Premiums—Forgotten By Theory," *Journal of Marketing,* April 1971, pp. 26–34.

Sorenson, Douglas, "Three Views of Cooperative Advertising," *Journal of Advertising Research,* December 1970, pp. 13–19.

22

Appraising
Ads and Campaigns

With all the money being invested in advertising, it is not surprising that much thought and much money is being spent in seeking to appraise the effectiveness of advertisements. Every advertiser would like to know which of the ideas submitted for his approval is best for his purpose. Every advertiser welcomes proof of how effective is the campaign he is currently running. For these purposes, various research methods have been developed, and new ones are constantly appearing.

We have *pretesting* of ads and *post-testing* of ads. Pretesting of ads (sometimes called *copy-testing*) usually means ranking a series of alternate advertisements before embarking on a major advertising expenditure. Post-testing of ads means appraising the effects of advertisements after the launching of a major expenditure, to see what can be learned for the next round. The differences are more in purpose than in technique.

The form of advertising where the sales results per dollar of advertising expenditure can be traced with the greatest exactitude is mail order and other forms of direct-response advertising. Where every printed advertisement carries a coupon or enclosed order form, identifying the source of the order, and where every TV commercial soliciting direct response gives an address or phone number by which those replies can be traced, an advertiser knows exactly how much business was produced for every dollar spent. By means of split-run tests (which we will discuss further in the chapter on Direct-Response Advertising), a direct-response advertiser can also test two different coupon advertisements appearing in alternate copies of a publication, giving him a numerical basis for judging which ad is the better. Direct-response advertising is indeed the most scientific form of advertising.

But measuring the effectiveness of national advertising represents a more complex problem. The national advertiser knows what his sales are, day by day, but many influences besides advertising may have helped produce those sales. Even before his product got on the shelf from which a housewife bought it, someone had to convince the store's buying committee to stock it, and much of the effectiveness of the advertising depends upon the success of the sales department in getting that distribution.

As a product gets more costly, the role of the personal salesman becomes also more important in closing the sale. Automobile advertising tells about the car and also tries to get the prospective buyer to go to the dealer, who will be responsible for the consummation of the sale. Thus an ad for the Renault car, headlined "Last year over four million people bought front wheel drive. Shouldn't you at least test one?" was targeted to get the reader to go to the showroom. An ad for Carrier air-conditioning units concludes, "Only a Carrier dealer can help you decide. To find the one nearest you, look in the Yellow Pages." After presenting its attractive Caribbean tours, an airline advertises, "Ask your travel agent for our Caribbean tours brochure, or phone us." Every household-appliance advertisement urges the reader to see a demonstration of the new model at the dealer's. The advertising is designed to interest the person sufficiently in the product so he will get in touch with the dealer.

The sales of a product may also have been helped by deals and promotions, price changes, and sales-department drives; they may have been retarded by the weight of advertising by competition, and *their* deals and promotions. How does one properly credit advertising for sales when it is only one part of the marketing mix in a competitive market?

ADVERTISING GOALS VS. MARKETING GOALS

Many men have sought an approach to the problem of appraising national advertising in the light of all these outside influences. Much of the discussion on the subject in recent years centers around a report, by Russell H. Colley, prepared for the Association of National Advertisers.[1] The thesis of this study is that *it is virtually impossible to measure the results of advertising, unless and until the specific results sought by advertising have been defined.* When asked exactly what their advertising is supposed to do, most companies have a ready answer: to increase their dollar sales, or to increase their share of the market. But these are not *advertising* goals, Colley holds; they are *total marketing* goals. Obviously, national advertising alone is not intended to accomplish this task, but rather the use of it as part of the total marketing effort. The first step in appraising results of advertising, therefore, is to define specifically what the company expects to accomplish through advertising. The report defines an advertising goal as "a specific communication task, to be accomplished among a defined audience to a given degree in a given period of time."

As an example, the report cites the case of a branded detergent. The *marketing goal* is to *increase the share of industry from 10 to 15 percent.* The *advertising goal* is set as *increasing among the 30 million housewives* who own automatic washers the number who identify brand X as a low-sudsing deter-

[1] Russell H. Colley, *Defining Advertising Goals for Measured Advertising Results* (Association of National Advertisers, Inc., 1961).

gent that gets clothes clean. This represents a specific communication task that can be performed by advertising, independent of other marketing forces.

The report speaks of a marketing communications spectrum ranging from an *unawareness* of the product to *awareness, comprehension, conviction,* and *action,* in successive steps; and the way to appraise advertising, according to this view, is by its effectiveness in the communications spectrum, leading to sales.

DIFFERENCES OF OPINION

Researchers differ on judging the effectiveness of national advertising on a communications yardstick rather than just by sales. A report on the subject by the Marketing Science Institute says:

> In general, total sales are not considered a valid measure of advertising effectiveness, because of the presence of other influencing variables. Sales as a criterion may have some validity if advertising is the most prominent variable, or, in the case of mail-order advertising, when it is the only variable.[2]

On the other hand, there are those who "deplore the general acceptance of measures of advertising short of sales or purchases; they frown on communications measures as the sole criterion."[3] Yet even these critics concede that the effectiveness of communications in general is more readily measurable, and for a given expenditure is more reliable, than sales alone.

APPRAISING THE INDIVIDUAL ADVERTISEMENT

To appraise advertising in terms of its communications effectiveness, research patterns such as the following have been developed:

> *Awareness*
> Was the advertisement seen?
> Was it linked to the advertiser?
> *Recognition tests* (of print advertisements) and *recall studies* (for television commercials) are the most frequently used methods of testing individual and combination ads along these lines.

---

[2] Patrick J. Robinson, ed., *Advertising Measurement and Decision Making* (Boston: Allyn & Bacon, Inc., 1968), p. 66.

[3] *Ibid.,* p. 67.

Knowledge and understanding

What specific points did the ad communicate?

What miscommunication may have occurred?

Copy playback testing is most often used to examine these aspects of individual ads.

Attitudes

Did the ad improve the consumer's favorable attitude toward the brand?

Brand preference and *attitude shift* studies are the most frequent techniques used to assess the impacts of ads on attitudes.

Action or trial

What sales or inquiry action did the ad generate?

Comparison testing is widely used here.

Awareness

Readership tests. The first step toward judging the effectiveness of a print advertisement in delivering a message is to judge how many people saw it and read it. In the 1930's, Dr. Daniel Starch began the first service to appraise the readership of ads in the more prominent magazines, and this led to the widely known "Starch Reports" of today—a continuing research operation.

An interviewer carrying a copy of the latest issue of the magazines being surveyed calls on households per a selected sample, and asks the person to be interviewed which magazine he or she has recently read. If the answer is one of the publications being surveyed, the interviewer opens his copy, and asks the person to go through it page by page, to point out which advertisements he remembers having seen, which he looked at carefully, and which he read. For this information, the advertisements are rated as follows:

"Noted"   —An advertisement that a person has previously seen in the issue being studied.

"Associated"   —An advertisement read by a person who not only "noted" it but also saw or read some part of it that clearly indicated the brand or advertiser.

"Read-Most"   —An advertisement in which a person read half or more of the written material.

These reports are made weekly or monthly for the magazines studied.

On the following report, the key figures are the "Seen associated" figures in the first and second columns on the left. Among men, the automotive ads ranked highest. Among women, food, clothing accessories, and household furnishings ranked high; automotive ads ranked low—confirming the facts that a person's total interest in an ad depends upon his interest in the product.

STARCH ADVERTISEMENT READERSHIP SERVICE
Current Issue Report

63 ADS

MEN READERS

PAGE	SIZE & COLOR	ADVERTISER	% NOTED	% SEEN-ASSO.	% READ MOST	$ NOTED	$ SEEN-ASSO.	$ READ MOST	NOTED Ratio	NOTED Rank	SEEN ASSO. Ratio	SEEN ASSO. Rank	READ MOST Ratio	READ MOST Rank
		AUTOMOTIVE CARS AND TRUCKS												
24	1PBWB	VOLKSWAGEN	52	50	20	84	81	32	221	1	253	1	400	1
68	2P4C	RAMBLER	61	59	10	38	37	6	100	30	116	21	75	37
92	2P4C	CHEVROLET	61	59	10	38	37	6	100	30	116	21	75	37
118	1PBW	HARLEY DAVIDSON	28	23	10	52	43	19	137	9	134	11	238	9
121	1P4CB	MERCURY	46	46	7	49	49	7	129	13	153	6	88	33
		BOOKS AND MAGAZINES												
113	1/2P2C	SPORTS ILLUSTRATED	17	16	11	47	44	30	124	15	138	10	375	2
		CLOTHING MEN												
54	1P4C	ARROW SHIRTS	44	39	10	54	48	12	142	7	150	8	150	18
		CLOTHING WOMEN												
16	1P4CB	CHEM ACRILAN HARPER	20	7	1	21	7	1	55	55	22	62	13	60
94	1P4CB	CHEMSTRAND NYLON	20	11	5	21	12	5	55	55	38	57	63	47
		CLOTHING ACCESSORIES												
2	1PBWB	BULOVA WATCHES	28	20	2	45	32	3	118	20	100	31	38	54
8	1P4C	PRINCE GARDNER	27	21	7	33	27	9	87	43	84	43	113	26
46	1P4CB	LORD BUXTON WALLETS	38	31	16	40	33	17	105	24	103	26	213	11
59	1P4C	TRIFARI JEWELRY	24	15	7	29	18	9	76	48	56	52	113	26
82	1/2P4C	KREMENTZ JEWELRY	18	12	5	37	25	10	97	35	78	45	125	25
		FOOD												
43	1P4C	CAMPBELLS SOUPS	27	24	2	33	29	2	87	43	91	38	25	56
86	1P4C	WHITMAN CANDIES	31	27	6	38	33	7	100	30	103	26	88	33
109	1P4C	CONTADINA PASTE	12	8	1	15	10	1	39	60	31	59	13	60
130	1P4C	CANADA DRY	27	24	6	33	29	6	87	43	91	38	75	37
		HOUSEHOLD FURNISHINGS												
1	1PBW	G E PRODS	27	23	5	50	43	9	132	10	134	11	113	26
12	1/2P4CB	UNIVERSAL PRODS	20	18	5	36	32	9	95	37	100	31	113	26
21	1PBW	MAYTAG DRYER	13	9	1	24	17	2	63	52	53	52	25	56
21	1/2P2BW	NECCHI SEW MACHINE	19	16	4	31	24	3	82	47	75	46	38	54
23	1PBW	WESTINGHOUSE OFFER	35	30	6	35	30	4	92	39	94	37	88	33
60	1P4C	FRIGIDAIRE WASHERS	8	5	1	10	6	1	26	63	19	63	13	60
67	1P4C	SINGER PRODS	14	8	1	17	10	1	45	59	31	59	75	37

WOMEN READERS

ADVERTISER	% NOTED	% SEEN-ASSO.	% READ MOST	$ NOTED	$ SEEN-ASSO.	$ READ MOST	NOTED Ratio	NOTED Rank	SEEN ASSO. Ratio	SEEN ASSO. Rank	READ MOST Ratio	READ MOST Rank
AUTOMOTIVE CARS AND TRUCKS												
VOLKSWAGEN	25	21	7	44	37	12	100	30	103	31	120	21
RAMBLER	37	20	4	25	20	3	57	54	56	54	30	52
CHEVROLET	32	27	3	22	18	2	50	58	50	55	20	61
HARLEY DAVIDSON	20	9	3	40	18	4	91	36	50	55	40	48
MERCURY	30	25	3	35	29	3	80	46	81	42	30	52
BOOKS AND MAGAZINES												
SPORTS ILLUSTRATED	7	4	1	21	12	3	48	61	33	62	30	52
CLOTHING MEN												
ARROW SHIRTS	35	29	8	47	39	11	107	26	108	27	110	28
CLOTHING WOMEN												
CHEM ACRILAN HARPER	55	42	13	64	49	15	145	14	136	17	150	15
CHEMSTRAND NYLON	46	35	13	53	41	15	120	20	114	24	150	15
CLOTHING ACCESSORIES												
BULOVA WATCHES	45	37	4	79	65	7	180	8	181	8	70	41
PRINCE GARDNER	32	25	13	43	33	17	98	33	92	35	170	11
LORD BUXTON WALLETS	37	30	13	37	30	15	84	41	83	41	150	15
TRIFARI JEWELRY	62	52	23	82	69	31	186	5	192	7	310	2
KREMENTZ JEWELRY	50	41	13	112	92	29	255	2	256	2	290	5
FOOD												
CAMPBELLS SOUPS	62	57	9	82	76	12	186	5	211	5	120	21
WHITMAN CANDIES	37	35	5	49	47	7	111	22	131	20	70	41
CONTADINA PASTE	37	30	5	49	40	7	111	22	111	26	70	41
CANADA DRY	35	29	8	47	39	11	107	26	108	27	110	28
HOUSEHOLD FURNISHINGS												
G E PRODS	46	39	15	92	78	30	209	4	217	4	300	3
UNIVERSAL PRODS	39	33	9	76	64	14	173	10	178	10	100	31
MAYTAG DRYER	24	23	7	48	46	14	109	24	128	21	140	19
NECCHI SEW MACHINE	34	27	3	126	100	26	286	1	278	1	260	6
WESTINGHOUSE OFFER	41	37	9	82	74	18	186	6	206	6	180	10
FRIGIDAIRE WASHERS	24	17	4	32	23	5	73	47	64	50	50	47
SINGER PRODS	43	41	9	57	55	12	130	16	153	21	120	21

This report covers full run advertisements. Regional and split run ads are omitted.

Note: Wherever duplicate cost ratios appear they have been given the same rank number. Ranks are not reported for issues having less than 25 advertisements.

Notes: * Less than one half of one percent.
□ Read Most Score for Advertisements with less than 50 words.
☆ Size approximate.
** Not Applicable

C COATED STOCK
G GATEFOLD
I ISLAND
S SPECIAL POSITION
INSERT

A PAGE FROM A STARCH READERSHIP REPORT

The Starch Reports are used by advertisers to learn how well their advertisements do in getting attention and in being read, in comparison with other advertisements in the same issue of a magazine.

Courtesy: Daniel Starch and Staff

Among men, a one-page, black-and-white ad for Volkswagen had the greatest number of readers per dollar—81. In the same issue, a Mercury four-color bleed ad had only 49 readers per dollar. A Necchi Sewing Machine ad got 100 readers per dollar among women, compared with a Singer products ad that received only 55 readers per dollar.

These reports must be compared over a period of time to draw any final conclusions about the ad's ability to get attention. They give no clue to the further reaction of the people to the advertisements; that calls for other types of research.

The testing method Starch used is called *aided recall*. There is another testing method called *unaided recall*. These two methods are widely used in TV research: "Did you watch the Chrysler program last night?" (Aided recall) "What programs did you watch last night?" (Unaided recall)

Television-viewing research. Television advertisers interested in knowing how well their commercials are listened to, and how well people who viewed the commercial remember the product and got its message, are users of *day-after recall* studies. Names are systematically drawn from the telephone directory, and the interviewer will call with questions such as these:

1. Determining that respondent was in the program audience—"Were you watching TV last night between _____ and _____ o'clock?" . . . "Please tell me if you saw any part of the _____ program on Channel _____ between _____ and _____ o'clock last night." . . . "What was the program generally about?"
2. Unaided recall of ad—"While watching that program, what commercials do you remember seeing?"
3. Aided recall (aid can be at several levels)—"Did you see a commercial for [product]?" "Did you see a commercial for [brand]?"
4. Content of the commercial (after recall)—"What do you remember about the [brand] commercial?" . . . "Anything else?" . . . "What other thoughts about [brand] were in the commercial?"

The chief usefulness of such tests is in learning not merely what percentage of viewers remember seeing the commercial, but what percentage of these carried away the message about the product that the advertiser was trying to convey. The two tests are frequently combined.

Knowledge and Understanding

Playback. One of the most useful and used forms of communications testing is that of the playback—having a reader or viewer tell you in his own words what message the advertisement delivered to him. What a reader or consumer gets from an ad is often different from what the advertiser had intended to convey. The question is: What message comes through?

On the following page we have the report of a playback on a Scott Family Placemat ad. The captions read:

New Scott Family Placemats
So much like cloth it's hard to believe they're disposable
Thrifty enough to use every day!

That, obviously, was the message the ad was designed to deliver. Yet notice how these qualities ranked below two other attributes of the product that appealed more to the reader.

The value of all playback testing is not only to see clearly how the desired message came through, but, when it did not come through, to figure out why.

New Scott Family Placemats
So much like cloth it's hard to believe they're disposable!

Most practical placemat ever for kids. Drinks up spills. Just use 'em and toss 'em away. New Scott Plastic Cups are great for youngsters too.

Lovely as cloth for entertaining. Cushioned to insulate and protect against scratches. A variety of colors to coordinate with Scott Family Napkins.

Perfect for informal living. Great for TV snacks and "drop in" guests. / are always fresh and handy—no wiping, no washing, no ironing.

Beautiful designs and colors. These thrifty new Scott paper placemats dress up any table. Look for them wherever Scott products are sold.

Thrifty enough
to use
every day!

3 quilted thicknesses of special absorbent paper

SCOTT MAKES IT BETTER FOR YOU

Scott Family Placemats

		% Respondents
One or more sales points		100
Variety of designs, colors, patterns		89
With flowers	26	
Blue, aqua	11	
With stripes	11	
Attractive, beautiful		71
Disposable		66
Economical, inexpensive		47
Thrifty, thrifty enough to use every day	24	
New		42
Thick, heavy		37
3 thicknesses	24	
Saves work, time		34
Saves washing, laundry	18	
Saves ironing	11	
Absorbent		32
Like cloth		26
Variety of uses, for any occasion		24
For snacks, TV snacks	11	
Dresses up the table, brightens, improves		21
Use for company, entertaining		18
Practical		16
Good for children		16
Strong, sturdy, durable		11
Convenient, handy		11
Good quality, best		11
"Scott makes it better for you"	3	

*   *   *   *   *   *

Descriptive Mentions:	
Reference to blue mat/boy at table illustration	42
Reference to pink flower/pink mat illustration	26
Reference to yellow mat/mat on tray illustration	26
Reference to package/package in cart illustration	16
Mention blue border	1
Favor to product (excluding users)	94
Disfavor to product	3
Favor to ad	13
Disfavor to ad	1
Average number of ideas per respondent	5.7

What is the message the advertisement really delivers? This research was designed to find out what impression and specific facts about the product the advertisement left with the reader.

Courtesy: Scott Paper Company
Advertising Agency: J. Walter Thompson Company
Research: Gallup & Robinson, Inc.

Sharpening the focus. It is easy enough, in testing mail-order ads, to decide which ad is the best of a series; you count the orders from a split-run test. But how do you decide which is the "best" ad to run out of four ads being considered for use in national advertising? You have to set up measurable yardsticks in terms of exactly what message about the product you wish the advertisement to deliver.

THE KELVINATOR TEST

Here is how Kelvinator handled the problem in selecting the advertisement for a campaign theme for their refrigerator; from among four different ones which they produced and tested:

GOAL OF ADS: The ads were tested in terms of the *interest* they had for a housewife, and how much *conviction* they carried.

Observe, this was not a test of which ad the housewives "liked best," but of which ads interested them the most, and left them feeling most convinced of the claims made.

METHODS: This was planned as a paired comparison test. Five completely finished ads were used. One was a control ad that had been pretested. Four hundred interviews with women were arranged and completed, divided equally among Hartford, Indianapolis, Wichita, and Atlanta. In each city, each woman was shown the control ad and only one of the test ads, and asked questions that revealed which ad was more interesting and which more convincing, so that each ad was exposed to a total of 100 women in different cities, each compared with the same control ad. Compare the figures for the best scores and the poorest. (Can you figure out the reasons?)

Attitudes

The degree of a person's change in attitude toward a product can be measured. Usually it takes a number of ads over a period of time to change an attitude toward a product, but some change can take place even after one ad, and this change lends itself to testing.

Various methods have been set up for testing attitude changes within the span of a single TV commercial. In one theater testing plan, women are invited to watch a thirty-minute film program, which includes commercials other than the ones being tested. They will be awarded a shopping bag of products, and before the test begins, are asked to choose the products they would like. After the film showing, they are again asked to prepare a list of what they would like. (The amount of the products is large enough to warrant thoughtful consideration of the brands.) By comparing the "pre-" to "post" preferences, the relative effectiveness of the commercial can be weighted. This test can be repeated with other groups, with alternate commercials.

Attitude changes are much more readily observed after exposure to a series of ads in an advertising campaign. We shall treat their measurement further when we discuss campaign evaluation.

Hidden-offer tests. Often a national advertiser who has a long copy story would like to know which ad, or which publication, gets the best readership. One technique is to offer something valuable or interesting to the reader. To make sure that a casual reader did not see only this free offer and send in for it, it will be set just like the rest of the copy, at its end, without a caption to call attention to it. This is referred to as a *hidden offer*. Its purpose is not to get as many responses as possible, but to get as many as possible from the people who read all the way through the ad. In this way you may get a clue as to the ranking of media by running the same ad in different media. Or you can get a clue as to ranking of ads if you run different ads in the same medium. The important point to keep in mind is that this is merely a comparative test of ads or media, not a test of the total effectiveness of the ads.

Action or Trial

The role of coupons in a national advertisement. You see many advertisements with coupons that say in substance, "See your dealer or send coupon for brochure." These are not advertisements for direct-response selling, because the sales are made by the dealer. They are national advertisements, with a coupon tie-in idea that may provide leads for dealers. How do you appraise the effectiveness of such advertisements?

You may have two ads for the same proposition. Ad A brings in more coupons than ad B. But the dealers get more calls after ad B runs. Both dealer and advertiser are happier with ad B than with ad A. Hence the coupon count is no reliable index. Coupon responses to national advertisements, however, are useful in appraising media that use the same ad. They are also useful in comparing different pieces of copy in one medium as in the "hidden offer" test.

Before-and-after Sales Tests

Sometimes you may be able to create a completely controlled sales situation in which you can test an advertising idea on a before-and-after sales-test basis. A good example is provided in the following test by Kress to judge the effectiveness of a point-of-purchase end display for use in supermarkets:

The research covers a four-week period within the three stores. During that time, 19 items and their substitute products were studied under various selling situations.

The test of each particular product was carried on in three segments.
1. Test period number one (the normal week)
   a. The test product is sold from its normal shelf position at the regular price and is not promoted.
   b. Its substitute products are also sold from their normal shelf positions at regular prices and receive no promotion.
2. Test period number two (the display week)
   a. The test product is given special promotion and display. In some cases the test product is also placed on sale.
   b. Its substitute products are sold from their normal shelf positions at regular prices with no promotion.
3. Test period number three (the third week)
   a. The test product is once again sold from its normal shelf position at its regular price and is not promoted.
   b. The substitute products are sold from their normal shelf positions at regular prices and are not promoted.

The results. The results of the various display weeks are condensed into a single display week in this study. The normal week is used as the base period. The results of the display week and the third week are compared with it.

Effect on the sale of all items on display. Unit sales of all items increased an average of 772 percent and dollar sales increased 673 percent when the test products were sold from end-display racks. Every product tested in this study had at least a 100 percent increase in unit sales from its normal weeks' sales. The percentage increases range from a high of 5,841 percent for canned cherries to a low of 115 percent for cereals.[4]

---

[4] George J. Kress, *The Effect of End Displays on Selected Food Products Sales,* abridged ed. A study at the Graduate College of The State University of Iowa, for the Point-of-Purchase Advertising Institute, Inc., 1961.

APPRAISING CAMPAIGNS

We are now speaking of appraising a whole nationally advertised campaign, rather than just an individual advertisement. For determining how effective a job it is doing, we again refer to the communications spectrum, except that we now apply a different yardstick and different measurement research techniques. The chief questions in which we are now interested are:

> *Awareness*
> Do consumers know my company or brand?
>
> *Knowledge and understanding*
> What major characteristics are associated with the company or brand?
>
> *Attitudes*
> How does my company or brand measure up in terms of consumer preference?
>
> *Action—Sales*
> How many consumers have tried or are using the brand? What sales were generated by the campaign?

Awareness

The first step in the learning process is to be aware of something; therefore it is logical that the first step in the evaluation of a campaign is to find out how many people already recognize the name of the product or company advertising. This is particularly appropriate for new products. However, most large, well-known advertisers do not even stop to ask this question, but proceed directly to asking about problems of greater interest to them. Other advertisers combine such questions with further questions, such as the areas we now discuss.

Knowledge and Understanding

Now we move on to ask not only whether the person recognizes the brand or company name we are talking about, but what it stands for, if anything, in his mind. What has its advertising said to him? This is the benchmark—the standard of comparison. Then, after the campaign has been run, another research among a matched group measures the difference in these categories. This is the measure of the degree to which the advertising has delivered its message.

We have an interesting report of a research in the awareness of a company and knowledge of its message, conducted for the Weyerhaeuser Company, which had long been advertising in magazines, and now added television to its schedule. The company wanted to know what the TV advertising was doing in getting the company and its story better known. They ran a control test before the TV advertising began, and again after it had been running for six weeks, with the following results. (This was only one part of the total research.)

	PERCENTAGE-POINT CHANGE BEFORE-AND-AFTER INTERVIEWS	
	CONTROL (BEFORE TV PROGRAM)	TV PROGRAM (AFTER)
Recognition of Weyerhaeuser Co.	.9	15.2
Recall of any Weyerhaeuser advertising	2.1	11.4
Share recalling message who associated it with Weyerhaeuser	2.6	18.8

Stephen A. Greyser, Cases in Advertising and Communications Management *(Englewood Cliffs, N.J.: Prentice-Hall, Inc., 1972), p. 205.*

The impact of the television advertising was traceable in measurable terms.

Reeves cites a research covering the degree of penetration of the messages of different campaigns for packaged-goods products; the degree of penetration ran from 1 to 78 percent. This report includes two advertisers, each spending $10 million a year, who changed their stories at the same time. One year later, one of these had registered his new message with 44 percent of all the people in the United States. The advertising of the other registered with only 1.8 percent of the people.[5]

An example of deeper evaluation of a campaign, in terms of the delivery of a message, is offered by the Haag Drug Company, of Indianapolis. Haag sought to overcome the competition of discount houses by virtue of their wide variety of merchandise. They ran a saturation television schedule of spots for six weeks on three Indianapolis stations and another in Fort Wayne. The spots had a simple idea: Show that Haag carries 25,000 different items. The creative concept was to film a small boy laboriously counting them, one by one, with various humorous angles. (He loses count at 8,019 and starts over, and so on.)

When the campaign concluded, interviewers asked passersby, *How many items would you expect to find stocked by a drugstore?* Thirty out of 100 persons replied—unaided—"25,000." Asked *What drugstore did you have in mind?* 63 percent replied, "Haag's." And 58 percent volunteered the information that they had seen the firm's commercials.

A check survey in a Haag market where no television ad appeared showed that the average respondent guessed 5,000 to 6,000 as the number

---

[5] Rosser Reeves, *Reality in Advertising* (New York: Alfred A. Knopf, Inc., 1961), p. 13.

of items in a drugstore. In the market with the television ad, even when respondents didn't give the exact figure of 25,000, the guesses were much higher—from 10,000 to 27,000. Thus the campaign was regarded as having fulfilled its communications objective.[6] This case also proves the usefulness of making tests at the communications level, when direct reaction in the form of sales cannot readily be traced.

Some advertisers wish to probe deeper than just about having their message understood; they would like to know how well it is believed and accepted.

The Abex Company is a large manufacturer of industrial control equipment. It began in 1902 as the American Brake Shoe and Foundry Company; that name was changed in 1943 to the American Brake Shoe Company. But the company greatly diversified the range and scope of its activities, with many divisions under their own names, and in 1966 it became the Abex Company, to give itself a chance for a better image of its many activities. The company was particularly interested in telling the story of its new status to financial analysts and other members of the business community, and it launched an advertising campaign in *Time, Newsweek, The Wall Street Journal,* and in other media in the chief metropolitan financial centers. There were three main points it sought to convey in its ads, as quoted below. The table opposite is the result of one part of an extensive research, designed to find out how effective the advertising was in delivering the message. This advertising represented the Spring half of a one-million-dollar campaign. Wave 1 represents the report made before the advertising campaign started. Wave 2 represents the report after the advertising had run for ten weeks. The difference in the figures is a measure of the effectiveness of the advertising in telling the story.

The research method used was as follows: 402 analysts in three different cities, names scientifically selected for sampling purposes, were interviewed by phone just before the advertising began. (Wave 1) The same steps were taken with a matched group of analysts in the same cities at the end of this Spring flight of advertising. (Wave 2) This is known as a *matched-set comparison test.* The findings in this test were as follows: the differences between Wave 2 and Wave 1 reflect the impact of the advertising.

Attitudes

But even if an advertisement clearly conveys an advertiser's message, and even if that message is received and understood, it may nevertheless result in "no sale." In a school-committee election campaign, an extensive advertising program was mounted in behalf of a group of "reform" candidates campaigning jointly. On the morning after the election, in which all the reform candidates lost, a campaign worker lamented, "I guess we didn't get

---

[6] *Television Age,* March 1, 1965, p. 40.

	Wave 1	Wave 2
A company that has product applications in many different fields:		
True	38%	46%
Not very true	3	2
Not at all true	—	1
Don't know	18	19
Unfamiliar with Abex	47	32
A company that is active in the advancement of modern technology:		
True	26%	35%
Not very true	5	7
Not at all true	*	3
Don't know	22	23
Unfamiliar with Abex	47	32
A company that is broadening its scope of operations:		
True	35%	48%
Not very true	1	1
Not at all true	*	*
Don't know	17	19
Unfamiliar with Abex	47	32

* Less than 0.5%.
Source: Stephen A. Greyser, Cases in Advertising and Communications Management *(Englewood Cliffs, N.J.: Prentice-Hall, Inc., 1972), p. 501.*

our message across." A trained researcher would perhaps disagree, saying, "The group had got its message across—only too well—but the voters had rejected it." It is important to recognize that the *reception* of an idea is not the same as the *acceptance* of that idea as a premise for buying the product or proposal.

However, in the case of a company, advertising can generate a favorable attitude toward it—the basis of most institutional advertising. Although there is no definite proof that a person's favorable attitude toward a product is an assurance that he will buy it, nevertheless, measurements of changes in attitude are widely sought by advertisers as an index of how effective their advertising is in predisposing a person more favorably to the product or company. These studies are of particular interest to heavy advertisers, and to corporations concerned with their public image.

The most common way of gathering overall attitude information is to ask respondents to rate a company or brand on an opinion scale. "Very favorable" to "very unfavorable" opinions on a multipoint scale can be given. Typically, ratings for several companies or brands would be gathered to mask the identity of the interested firm.

Another approach to attitude and brand-preference measurement is to ask simply, "If you were buying a brand of [product], which one would you buy?"

The wisest way to use attitude tests is to repeat them with a matching sample over a period of time to indicate trends.

Action—Sales

Experimental sales-test patterns. As mentioned earlier, some prominent researchers do not agree that communications measures are appropriate for assessing advertising. They cite instances where communications measures went up, yet sales went down, and vice versa.[7] This school of advertising research argues that trying to measure advertising's effects on sales means trying to isolate those effects. They advocate the use of *experiments* to try to do this. These experiments involve using control areas, using several cities, rotating the treatments being tested through each set of experimental areas, and practicing rigorous mathematical analysis. While admitting that designing and carrying out such experiments is difficult and expensive, they believe this is the most reliable route and is particularly appropriate for large-budget advertisers.

---

[7] See especially Charles Ramond, "Must Advertising Communicate to Sell?" *Harvard Business Review,* September–October 1965, p. 148.

REGIONS / CITIES	PRODUCTS TESTED				
	"DESSERT TOPPING"	"SEASONED COATING MIX"	"READY-TO-EAT CEREAL"	"GROUND COFFEE"	"PACKAGED PRE-COOKED RICE"
EAST					
PITTSBURGH	1/3 MAG.	1/3 MAG.	ALL TV	ALL TV	ALL MAG.
CLEVELAND	ALL TV	ALL TV	1/3 MAG.	1/3 MAG.	ALL TV
CENTRAL					
CHICAGO	1/3 MAG.	ALL TV	ALL TV	NOT TESTED	ALL TV
DETROIT	ALL TV	1/3 MAG.	1/3 MAG.	NOT TESTED	ALL MAG.
WEST					
SAN FRANCISCO	1/3 MAG.	ALL TV	ALL TV	1/3 MAG.	ALL TV
LOS ANGELES	ALL TV	1/3 MAG.	1/3 MAG.	ALL TV	ALL MAG.

Market Test Design

Source: "A Major Advertiser Tests the Effectiveness of General Magazines and Television," booklet published by *Life, Look,* and *Reader's Digest,* New York.

An outstanding example of such controlled research was provided by General Foods in its test to compare magazines and television in the effectiveness of delivering advertising messages. The result affected a basic media policy decision involving millions of media dollars. Five products were used in the test; one served as a control used in all the other tests. Six cities were involved, representing matched pairs in three different parts of the country. The accompanying chart shows the test pattern. Its allocation of media is worth studying.

Although General Foods did not publish the report of its findings, the fact is that they doubled their magazine investment from six to twelve million dollars following their report. Magazines were credited with getting a higher degree of correct product identification, and delivered more of the sales story, than did television. (This was a turn in the tide for magazines, which long had been losing business to TV.)

Martin Mayer reports another test by a "major food advertiser" who tried four radically different campaigns in a large number of test regions. Four results were measured for each campaign—sales, display space, consumer attitude, and competitive activity. The cost of the research was over $100,000, and it too took a year, "but the company plans to use the most successful campaign until the cows come home." [8]

Store sales tests. An advertiser who is not prepared to spend the money or time on such sophisticated appraisals may nevertheless get reasonable answers on a more modest scale if he has a new campaign, or if he wishes to test campaigns in different matched markets. He can arrange to get an actual inventory count of the sale of his product in a number of stores in different test markets through methods largely developed by the A. C. Nielsen Company. They have arranged with such stores to have someone make an actual count of products on the shelf as well as in inventory, and also to learn how many new goods were received during the week. By keeping a running record of such sales, the advertiser can relate them to the current advertising activity, especially if it represents a new program. In all such instances, a rate-of-sales count must be taken before the new advertising starts to run, to provide a basis of comparison.

Consumer usage surveys. These surveys are made by direct interviews with housewives in their homes, asking specifically which brands of products in different categories they are using now, and which they had previously used. A similar test survey is made among a matched group of such housewives in the same community at periodic intervals, to provide a base of comparison.

---

[8] Martin Mayer, *The Intelligent Man's Guide to Sales Measure of Advertising* (New York: Advertising Research Foundation, Inc., 1965), p. 6.

Use of cable television. A landmark development in research has been the use of cable television, pioneered by AdTel. Briefly, it is based on the fact that in many cities throughout the country, thousands of homes get their television reception via cable. In some cities, cable companies not only relay the programs of distant TV stations, but can cut in with their own programs.

AdTel began by selecting one typical test city in which about 50 percent of the homes had cable television. It set up a panel of 2,000 subscribers who agreed to keep a diary of their purchases which they reported each week (for which they were compensated).

The large advertisers for whom AdTel conducts the tests either already have a TV schedule in that market or they can add it to their list. AdTel is able to cut in on the advertiser's own program, replacing their regular commercial with the test commercials, Test Ad A being transmitted to half the homes on the panel, and Test Ad B to the other half. The subscribers just see the test ads as regular commercials. From their purchase-diary entries over a period of time, it is possible to compare actual sales to the subscribers who saw Ad A with those to the subscribers who saw Ad B.

The ability of this system to divide a market into two homogeneous test areas, equally subject to the factors that can foul up the usual tests between two different markets, getting a weekly diary report of purchases, has been expanded to other test cities. It is also being used to check rate of repurchase, and alternative promotional efforts, like sampling and couponing; also to test different levels of expenditure to determine the optimum from the profit viewpoint. An advantage to advertisers is that it keeps tests of new products away from the eyes of competitors.

Use of Tracking Measures

Some consumer packaged-goods advertisers use a set of "tracking" measures of awareness, trial, and usage to appraise the effectiveness of their advertising. "Trial" refers to people who once tried the product, whether or not they are using it now. "Usage" refers to people who are using it now.

Measuring consumer trial and usage of a brand is not too difficult; you conduct a consumer survey. Connecting that trial and usage to advertising alone is usually more difficult. But this information, in conjunction with awareness data, can provide helpful diagnosis of different elements of the marketing program, including advertising. Tracking these three factors is particularly valuable in the instance of new products.

1. From the trends in the percentage of consumers who are aware of the product or brand, an advertiser learns about the impact of his advertising, particularly of the spending level and media plan, and to some extent the memorability of the message.

2. From the trends in the percentage of consumers who have tried the product or brand, an advertiser learns about the motivating impact of his advertising message. Does it convince the consumers to buy *once?* In addition, he may have distribution problems, if trial figures are substantially behind awareness figures.

3. From the trends in the percentage of consumers who are users of the product or brand, an advertiser learns about the caliber of the product itself. If the gap between trial and usage is very wide, it signals that people have tried it, but *not* liked it.

OTHER RESEARCH METHODS

Because of the amount of money resting on decisions made with the aid of research, men are continually exploring new paths of enlightenment, including the following:

Mathematical models. Researchers are using the computer to develop mathematical models that will relate advertising investment to a series of resultant consumer reactions, such as being aware of the product, buying it, and repurchasing it. One model, developed by the New York advertising agency of Batten, Barton, Durstine & Osborn, applies particularly to repetitively purchased consumer goods, and tries to estimate the sales level or share of market necessary to justify a particular advertising spending level, and to predict the likelihood of success for a new product.

Physiological measures. These refer more to the rating of ads than of campaigns, or more specifically to the impact of the visual image of the ad. One measure is of the eye pupillary response to an ad; the other a skin galvanometer response to the reading of an ad.

The foregoing measures are still basically experimental. They do illustrate, however, the extent to which advertising researchers try to apply scientific insights from nonadvertising fields to the continual search for ways to identify effective advertisements and campaigns.

RESEARCH GUIDELINES

Conditions conducive to research. "As a rule of thumb, in judging whether measurement of results is possible and how comprehensive such measurements can be, the following axioms may be helpful," said the National Industrial Conference Board. To the report, which follows, the writer has added some comments in italics:

1. The more important advertising is to the sale of a product, the easier it is to appraise results.
   Where advertising plays a minor role in the marketing mix, as in the case of raw materials, even a 100 percent improvement in advertising will not add too much weight to the buying decision.

2. The faster the turnover of a product, the easier it is to appraise the results of advertising.

   The shorter the period of time elapsed between the appearance of an advertisement and the need to make a decision, the better. Fast turnover means early decisions. The price risk of such purchases is usually low.

3. The fewer selling methods employed in moving a product, the easier it is to appraise the advertising.

   The results of the end advertising to the consumer by a synthetic-yarn manufacturer who sells to the weaver of the fabric, who sells to a suit manufacturer, who sells to a department store, are much harder to trace than the results of a mail-order ad.

4. The less complex the market is (and the less intense the competition), the easier it is to appraise advertising results.[9]

   The more competitive a market is, the more business will be done other than by advertising—through deals, promotions, and price changes, obfuscating the effects of advertising and the ability to measure it.

How much testing?   The desirability of conducting extensive testing is a function, first, of the importance of advertising to the company. When advertising is very important to the overall marketing program and a lot of money is spent on it, then extensive research on evaluating ads and campaigns is warranted and necessary. Thus, most major consumer-goods marketers devote much more energy and research money to testing ads than do industrial advertisers.

A second major factor influencing the extent of advertising testing is how major a change in the advertising program is being contemplated. The greater the change, the greater the need for a wide testing base and for in-depth studies. When a previous campaign is being extended with only minor variations, however, partial evaluation will usually suffice.

Resumé of methods.   There is no one form of advertising research; it is many things, depending upon the object of the research. But it would be well to begin all research by asking:

—What is the object of the research?

—if the research provides the information sought, what will be done about it?

—In what terms of measurement will the findings be reported?

—What results must that which is being researched attain to make its performance acceptable?

---

9 Wolfe, Brown, Thompson, *Measuring Advertising Results* (New York: National Industrial Conference Board, Inc., 1962), p. 9.

We have touched, in the course of this chapter, upon many different methods of research for various purposes. It may be opportune to bring them together here:

Paired comparison—split run
> This is used in publication advertising for direct-response advertisers. Two different ads appear in alternate copies of a single publication in the same space. The ads are judged by their coupon responses.

Matched-set comparison
> Conducting a test with two groups matched demographically. Each is shown a different advertisement (or commercial) and interviewed. Responses to each ad are compared.

Sales tests
> Goods actually sold, measured in units or dollars, on a before-and-after basis.

Readership tests
> "Did you read this publication? Did you see this ad? What do you remember about it?" (Aided recall) "What ads do you remember having seen?" (Unaided recall)

Recall tests
> (TV) "Were you watching television last night? What programs did you watch?" (Unaided recall) "Remember any of the commercials?"

> "Did you see the Dodge program last night? Do you remember what the commercial said?" (Aided recall.)

Hidden-coupon offer
> An offer for something worthwhile, free or for a small charge, made in the body of an advertisement at the bottom of the copy and without any display line to call attention to it, designed to reach only those who have read the entire ad. Used for making comparative tests of readership; not an index of how good the ad is.

Bench marks and trend lines. Before-and-after advertising studies of awareness, message delivery, attitudes, or sales imply that at least two measurement points are involved—before and after. Most large advertisers go much further; they conduct such studies on a continuous basis, in order to provide a regular trend line of whatever elements are under examination. Such trend-line studies enable the executives to trace the effects of the advertising in respect to the questions for which the research was designed, and to react promptly to adverse trends.

The importance of bench marks, the "before" or control figures, cannot be overemphasized. May the trends following the bench marks of any research you do go up . . . up . . . up. . . .

1. What are the differences in methods between pretesting and post-testing of ads?

2. What factors tend to make it difficult to isolate the sales effects of advertising for most national advertisers?

3. Describe the basic idea behind Colley's approach to evaluating advertising. What method is favored by men who don't agree with this?

4. What is meant by the communications spectrum?

5. What are the chief problems associated with controlled sales experiments to assess advertising campaigns?

6. Explain what is meant by each of the following:
   a. split run test
   b. aided recall
   c. unaided recall
   d. playback
   e. hidden offer
   f. benchmarks and trend lines
   g. matched sample

Reading Suggestions

Axelrod, Joel N., *Choosing the Best Advertising Alternative.* New York: Association of National Advertisers, Inc., 1971.

Barton, Roger, "Are Awareness, Attitude, and Behavior Related?" *Media/Scope,* January 1968. Excerpted in Kleppner and Settel, *Exploring Advertising,* p. 111.

————, *Handbook of Advertising.* New York: McGraw-Hill Book Company, 1970.

Business Week, "Why Business Is Spending Millions to Learn How Customers Behave," April 18, 1964. Also in Kleppner and Settel, *Exploring Advertising,* p. 260.

Campbell, Roy Hilton, *Measuring the Sales and Profit Results of Advertising: A Managerial Approach.* New York, The Association of National Advertisers, Inc., 1969.

Colley, Russell H., *Defining Advertising Goals for Measured Advertising Results.* New York: Association of National Advertisers, Inc., 1965.

Freeman, Cyril, "How to Evaluate Advertising's Contribution," *Harvard Business Review,* July–August 1962, p. 137.

Gordon, Howard L., "Yes, Virginia, Research Helps Make Better Advertisements," *Journal of Marketing,* January 1967, pp. 64–66. Also in Kleppner and Settel, *Exploring Advertising,* p. 273.

Haskins, Jack B., *How to Evaluate Mass Communications.* New York: Advertising Research Foundation, 1968.

Mayer, Martin, *The Intelligent Man's Guide to Sales Measures of Advertising.* New York: Advertising Research Foundation, 1965.

Palda, Kristian S., "The Hypothesis of a Hierarchy of Effects: A Partial Evaluation," *Journal of Marketing Research,* February 1965, pp. 13–25.

Palda, Kristian S., *The Measurement of Cumulative Advertising Effects.* Englewood Cliffs, N.J.: Prentice-Hall, Inc., 1964.

Ramond, Charles K., "Must Advertising Communicate to Sell?" *Harvard Business Review,* September–October 1965, p. 148.

Robinson, Patrick J., Homer Dalbey, Irwin Gross, and Yoram Wind, *Advertising Measurement and Decision Making.* Boston: Allyn and Bacon, Inc., 1968.

Schwartz, David A., "Measuring the Effectiveness of Your Company's Advertising," *Journal of Marketing,* April 1969, pp. 20–25.

Smith, Gail, "How GM Measures Ad Effectiveness," *Printers' Ink,* May 14, 1965. Also in Kleppner and Settel, *Exploring Advertising,* p. 277.

Starch, Daniel, *Measuring Advertising Readership and Results.* New York: McGraw-Hill Book Company, 1966.

Twedt, Dik W., "How to Plan New Products, Improve Old Ones, and Create Better Advertising," *Journal of Marketing,* January 1969, pp. 53ff.

Wells, William D., Seymour Banks, and Douglas J. Tigert, "Order in the Data," in *Changing Marketing Systems,* ed. by Moyer, Reed. Chicago: American Marketing Association, 1968. Also in Kleppner and Settel, *Exploring Advertising,* p. 289.

Wheatley, John J., *Measuring Advertising Effectiveness: Selected Readings.* Homewood, Ill.: Richard D. Irwin, Inc., 1969.

Young, Shirley, "Copy Testing Without Magic Numbers," *Journal of Advertising Research,* February 1972, pp. 3–12.

23

The Complete Campaign

WE ARE NOW READY to take a new product and place it on the market. By asking questions, we bring together many of the elements we have discussed. The answers will influence the steps we take.

THE PRODUCT

Does the product work? The first questions include, "Is the product a good one? Has it passed all the government tests for such a product? Is it technically sound? If it is mechanical, will it work properly in the hands of the average consumer? If the product is chemical, is it effective under the normal conditions of use?

A well-known grocery company with a bakery division produced a frozen doughnut that won over competition in severe taste tests. The company had good standing with the trade, and the product received good distribution and was launched with a sizeable TV schedule. The first reports of movement off the shelves were encouraging, but before long, widespread complaints came in about the taste; the doughnuts came back from all sides. The product had to be withdrawn from the market. What went wrong? Much time was spent trying to get the answer. Finally they traced the source of the trouble: the tests had been made when the doughnuts came fresh from the freezer, but when they were sold through the trade there was a time lag in delivery, on the grocers' shelves, on the trip home, and in the buyer's freezer until they were served. In that interval there was a change in the chemistry of the doughnut, resulting in a bad flavor.

Is the product in step with the times? Here we speak of the social climate, which affects our ideas of the kinds of values we seek in products. On this subject, Guy M. Minard, Chairman, Kimberly-Clark Corporation, said:

> In addition to constantly studying and re-evaluating the consumer and his desires, manufacturers are also taking a penetrating look at themselves. Their own role in society is subject to the same forces of rapid change.
>
> Until recently, that role has been built almost entirely on a masterful ability to produce and distribute economic goods and services in ever-

increasing amounts. . . . It was natural to assume that business could continue to live up to its highest calling simply by giving more and more goods to more and more people.

However, today's consumer will tell you in very convincing terms that quantity is not enough, and that quality of goods and the side effects of production and distribution also are important. Individual demands must be dealt with—demands having to do with unit pricing, packaging, product safety, advertising claims, warranties, quality control, and other issues such as the handling of by-products of production which result in pollution and disposal problems. . . .[1]

We are aware of the constant changes in tastes and styles. What is the trend for this type of product? Is it being replaced by something better? Or because of changes in living styles? Or technology? (You may recollect the report that sales of spray starch have been going down ever since drip-dry synthetic fabrics came along.) Is it part of an increasing trend, or of a waning one? Is there any economic or legislative threat that might affect the ability to produce and sell this product? (As this is being written, detergents with phosphates are being banned from Chicago.)

Apropos of the entry of the Ralston Purina Company into the health-food market, *Advertising Age* has this to say:

> While health foods have been recording a slow, but consistent, growth for nearly a decade, consumer interest in such products has accelerated recently due to a combination of social and environmental pressures. One of the strongest of these pressures is the new food attitudes of many young people which lead them to raise questions about some aspects of modern food chemistry and to seek more natural foods.[2]

Of every new product, one should ask, "Is time with it or against it?"

Positioning the product. The decision regarding what you want your product to be known and used for is one of the most important in its success. In one of its own house ads, Ogilvy & Mather, advertising agency, had this to say on the subject:

> The most important decision you will ever make about your advertising is: "How should I position my product?"
>
> Should you position Good Seasons Salad Dressing as a gourmet's delight, for people who appreciate its subtle blend of herbs and spices? Or as a product which competes with bottled salad dressings?

---

[1] Guy M. Minard, "Business and the Consumer: A Value Gap," from *The Presidents Forum, Winter 1971,* published by The Presidents Association. Reprinted by Kimberly-Clark Corporation. Neenah, Wisc.

[2] *Advertising Age,* July 31, 1972, p. 2.

Should you position Shake'n Bake as a new flavor for chicken? Or as an easier way to get old-fashioned "fried-chicken" taste?

The results of your advertising will depend less on how it is *written* than on how it is *positioned*. It follows that the positioning must be decided before the advertising is created.

We positioned Hershey's *oldest* product, Hershey's Milk Chocolate Bar, as the market leader. Familiar, warm, friendly, "the great American chocolate bar."

We positioned Hershey's *newest* product, their new Rally Bar, as "the Hershey-covered hunger-stopper." [3]

Not all advertising men agree that positioning is *the* most important element in the success of a product, but none would deny that it is one of the most important of these elements.

What's the differential? We appraise the product from the viewpoint of the user. What is its reason for existence as far as the consumer is concerned? Why should he buy it? What values does it offer that other products are not already offering? What is its unique advantage? How important is that point of difference in enabling the product to serve better the purpose for which a person would buy it?

Not only should the product have a *significant* differential, but that feature should be *conspicuous,* or lend itself to demonstration or dramatization. One of the reasons we don't see more brand advertising of salt is that few companies have succeeded in establishing a differential, as has Morton's salt, with its ability to flow freely in wet weather.

The Ralston Purina Company went into the frozen-food business, on which they had built up a volume of $9 million, but were losing money, so they gave it up. In reporting on this, the *Gallagher Report* said, "Marketing Me-Tooism Invites Disaster. Lack of product originality reason for failure of Ralston Purina venture into frozen foods." [4]

Edgar Griswold, Hunt-Wesson's new products director, said, in discussing Hunt-Wesson's new product development, that

(1) Only products substantially different from existing ones would be introduced, (2) substantial value must be added (the new item should not resemble the raw commodity from which it was derived), (3) it must be different enough so that consumers would not mistake it for another brand, and (4) recognizing the shortened life cycle, dollars invested should be returned within a year.[5]

---

[3] Advertisement in *Advertising Age,* July 10, 1972, p. 9.

[4] *The Gallagher Report,* June 8, 1972, p. 2.

[5] Based on a paper for Conference Board, New York, October 1972, by Edward M. Krakauer, Vice President of Consumer Marketing, Hunt-Wesson Foods, Inc., read by Edgar Griswold. *Advertising Age,* October 16, 1972, p. 3.

The costliest form of advertising is that in which the producer expects the uniqueness of the advertising to make up for the lack of uniqueness in the product. If a proposed new product does not represent a significant, demonstrable differential, management might better be advised to put its advertising money into product research and development.

THE TRADEMARK AND THE PACKAGE

The first step in grooming a product for marketing to the consumer is to give it a trademark. It should meet the requirements previously discussed (Chapter 20)—that it be distinctive, short, simple, easy to pronounce, and that it meet all legal requirements for registering, including those of not being descriptive, confusingly like other trademarks, nor deceptive.

Is the product to be trademarked one of a family of existing products, or is it to be the beginning of a family of products? That may affect its choice.

Likewise, we ask if the package is to be one of a family of packages. Are its sizes right to meet the demands of the market, with possibly a size for the "singles" buyer? Does it take advantage of the latest technology in the field? Does it represent a pollution problem? Is it important to feature the house name in addition to the trademark? Does it contain all the mandatory information called for by the law? The package design must meet the competition of other products in its class. It can be pretested before making a final selection, to see how it compares with the packages of competition, and to see also how various designs compare with each other, to select the best one.

PRICING THE PRODUCT

There are many elements that go into setting a price. If this represents a new type of product in the pioneering stage, there is no base for price comparison. It could well be on the high side if it is really unique. The task is to establish the product quickly, before imitators and other competitors move in. Products in the competitive stage usually move into established price ranges for goods of that type and quality.

IN WHAT STAGE IS THE PRODUCT?

If the product is a new type of product in the pioneering stage, how large is the potential sale for it? How much educational work will have to be done to create interest in this kind of product? How much in sales will be needed to defray developmental costs? Can the product be protected by patents in order to prevent competitors from quickly moving in (which they will do as soon as the product shows signs of success)? If not, does the company have sufficient resources to move swiftly in order to get distribution and establish the product before competition gets going?

Lestoil was a new-formula cleaning product that was introduced by a small company in New England, where it proved very effective and successful, overtaking many established cleansers. The plan was to do a thorough merchandising job in New England and move into other markets. When Lestoil was ready to enter other markets, they found that other preparations like Lestoil, produced by well-known companies, were already there, and dealers had no interest in Lestoil, which was not then known in those markets.

If the product is in the competitive stage, does it fit into a category that can support a profitable market? What is the total volume of business being done at this time? Is it growing or waning? How many competitors are there, and how strong are they? What are their weaknesses? In some fields, a few companies do most of the business, and a large list of others scramble for the rest. Would this be one of those fields? What share of the market would one hope to get? Is there some idea or plan that would make it possible for a newcomer to make a place for himself despite the priority and the advertising of others?

SELECTING THE TARGET MARKET

Is there any part of the country that especially favors this type of product? Is there any overlooked ethnic group that might offer opportunities for marketing efforts? Who buys the product? Men, women, or children? Who makes the decision to buy in a household? What are their significant demographic characteristics? Is it sex? Age? Income level? Home ownership? Or what do these prospects have in common that would enable one to identify them as a group? In addition to considering buyers in general, it may be desirable to aim for the *heavy users* of the product. If so, the message and the medium can be focused on a specific audience. Cereal manufacturers love homes with lots of children; soft-drink manufacturers love homes with high school teenagers.

HOW IS THE PRODUCT TO BE DISTRIBUTED?

Will it be sold through the usual retail trade channels, or will it be by exclusive distributorships, or house-to-house salesmen? In the first case, the advertising will be designed to get people to go to any dealer for the product, as is the case for most nationally advertised goods. In the second case, the advertising may be focused on encouraging the prospect to go to the distributor's showroom for demonstration (as in the case of a car), or getting in direct touch with him otherwise. If it is to be sold at home by a salesman, as in the case of encyclopedias, it may call for direct-response advertising to get leads.

What Is the Seasonal Factor?

Are sales affected by the season, as with sunburn preparations, for example? Then the schedule can begin in the South in the winter, and move to the North. Or anti-freeze, for another example; this might start in the North and move south. Soft drinks sell all year round, but the peak sales are in the summer. Advertising schedules for seasonal products usually begin before the advent of the season.

What Shall be the Creative Strategy and Theme?

In a broad sense, we know that if a product is a new type of article in the pioneering stage, we will have to stress the great advantage now available that was never available in any form before. We will have to help people convince themselves that this product really works, with stress on seeing a demonstration or on a trial offer.

Featuring a Competitive Advantage

The problem here was quickly to impress the differential of this watch —its ability to run even in deep water. Good thinking began with the naming of the watch. The headline is specific—not "deep water" but under 333 feet of water." The headline is selective— "For the Man who Dares the Depths." The visualization is arresting and simple, immediately telling that this watch is meant to be in the water.

This Bulova Oceanographer runs under 333 feet of water. For the man who dares the depths.

Even if your normal depth is 12 inches, you get a reassuring margin of safety when your watch is tested to keep out moisture 333 feet down. At that depth, the water presses on every square inch of watch surface with a weight of 144 lbs.

At *your* depth, our Oceanographer won't even know it's under water. But suppose you get *out* of your depth and go coral diving some day? The Oceanographer will automatically tell you what that day is. And its date.

And the luminous dial will still be giving you the right time that night. That's another reason for owning this extraordinary watch: You never know when you'll have an extraordinary day.

Bulova. These days the right time isn't enough.

Oceanographer "Q," $95. Other Oceanographer watches from $55. Available at fine jewelry and department stores. Bulova Watch Company, Inc.

If the product is in the competitive stage, we will seek the chief distinctive advantage that this product offers that the other products do not have. We look for that advantage that is of significant service to the user; we seek to present it as dramatically and conspicuously as we can, only making sure that when a person buys a product it will make good on our claim.

If a product attains a top-of-market share and is in the retentive stage where it is chiefly concerned with a holding action, we know it will have to fight off brand substitutes (Coca-Cola, "It's the real thing"; Lea & Perrins sauce, "Many imitations, no substitutions"; Frigidaire refrigerators, "Not every refrigerator is a Frigidaire"). But the real problem here is not to stand still in that stage, not to rely on continued loyalty of your customers to your product, but to go after new markets with new uses, or else to improve greatly the product, or add more products to the line.

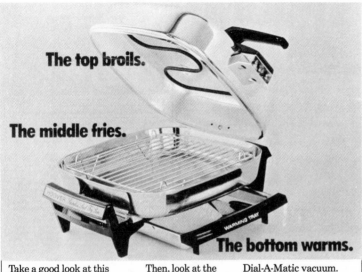

The top broils.

The middle fries.

The bottom warms.

Take a good look at this Hoover fry pan.
Look at it three ways.
Look at the broiler lid. With it, you can broil steaks, chops and hamburgers. Anywhere. Including at the table. And the broiler unit is removable when you don't need it.
Look at the deep 12" x 12" frying surface. Big enough to cook a roast. It's completely immersible, too.

Then, look at the warming tray in the bottom. That means you keep bacon, potatoes, mushrooms, at perfect eating temperature while you're cooking the eggs, broiling the steak or whatever.
So, why settle for a fry pan that's just a fry pan?
The Hoover fry pan does more than fry. A lot more.
Giving you something extra is typical of Hoover products.
For example, the Hoover

Dial-A-Matic vacuum.
It's really two cleaners in one. An upright for carpets, with our famous beats-as-it-sweeps-as-it-cleans action. Flip a switch and it's a canister for walls, drapes, furniture or anything that's dusty.
Of course, we don't always give you two or three appliances in one.
But we always try to give you more appliance for your money.

**Hoover.
Helping you has made us
a household word.**

MOVING OUT OF THE RETENTIVE STAGE

"Hoover," a household word for vacuum cleaners, here presents a new product to take advantage of its reputation. It gives the frying pan chief emphasis, and minor selling space to the vacuum cleaner. Note deft hook-up: "Giving something extra is typical of Hoover products."

In addition to these broad problems that affect the product, depending upon the stage in which it finds itself, it is reasonable to expect that every product will have its own special selling problems, ranging from apathy to active prejudice. We are now called upon to establish the specific strategy that will get action despite, or perhaps because of, these obstacles. The following examples might illustrate this facet of advertising thinking.

To increase the uses of a product. Here we come to a widely used strategy for increasing sales for a product that is already well known. This can be done *by increasing the variety of uses of the product.* Food advertisers are constantly showing new recipes. A ScotTowel advertisement said, "Nothing wraps up like a strong absorbent towel," with suggestions for seven different uses. Mothers are told why children and teenagers should have four glasses of milk daily. The makers of Dixie cups designed a wall bracket for their cups, to be installed in the bathroom, in order to keep colds caused by the common family bathroom glass from spreading by having paper cups accessible at all times.

To increase the quantity purchased. The unit of purchase may be increased by offering larger-sized packages—frequently called gift size, family size, economy size, or by some similar designation. (There is an FTC ruling on size designations.) A package can also be made to hold several units of the advertised product. Soft drinks and beer are offered in carrying cases of six and eight bottles or cans. Golf balls are offered to you in a wrap of three, and in a box of twelve. Packaging an assortment of related products is another familiar method of increasing the sale of the items included, as in cereals.

Libby's pictures an appetizing assortment of dishes prepared with a dozen of their canned and frozen foods, in an advertisement urging women to have a shelf full of Libby's "to be ready for all occasions."

A variant of the technique of increasing the quantity purchased was the advertising of Band-Aid bandages, designed to increase the quantity used, saying:

> Protect your child a little longer with a Band-Aid adhesive bandage. It heals better if it's protected a little longer.

To increase length of buying season. Campbell's Soups endeavored to offset the summer slump in soups by saying, "Summer suppers are better with one hot dish. Make it chicken vegetable soup." The tea industry introduced an iced-tea mix to popularize tea as a summer drink as well as a winter favorite, by making it easy to prepare. It was even offered as a diet drink for those who didn't want to increase their sugar intake.

Turkey has long been a traditional favorite for the Thanksgiving–New Year holiday season. However, the turkey growers of California embarked on a campaign to make turkey an all-year favorite. "Make your summer barbecue more fun," said one of its advertisements, giving the specific directions of a "patio chef" for barbecuing the turkey.

Advertising is indicated for lengthening the buying season of a product when it can be stored, used, shipped, and otherwise enjoyed in a season other than the customary one. If the business continues to be highly seasonal despite efforts to straighten out the dip, it may be wise to expand the line to include new products that are in season when the present product is out of season.

To attract a younger generation. When the Bible reported, "There arose a new king over Egypt, which knew not Joseph," it spoke of a problem that continually faces every business today. The popularity of a product can decay as its present faithful customers die off, and as a new generation that may not have the same respect for the name grows up. Accordingly, advertising is often planned to make customers of the new generation that is appearing on the buying scene.

GOING AFTER NEW GENERATION

Typewriters are in the competitive stage for office use, but Smith Corona decided to go after a new generation—teenagers—with pioneering advertising addressed to parents. And when parents decide to give a typewriter, the chances are good that Smith Corona will be their first choice.

"Younger generation" is a comparative term. The distributors of Dewar's Scotch whisky realized that its reputation and high price had made it a long-time favorite among men who were now middle-aged. They prepared a special campaign addressed to those in their late twenties and early thirties—to them, the "younger generation." They ran campaigns to both audiences at the same time in different magazines.

To feature a promotional idea. Among the areas of thinking that are always available is that of a promotional idea—a premium offer, a contest, a cents-off coupon offer, a sampling campaign. This way of thinking is opportune when it is desired to give the product an intensive sales push, or to meet the promotion of a competitor.

A CAMPAIGN BUILT AROUND A PROMOTIONAL IDEA

Sometimes you look outside your product for a service you can render, such as offering free a whole month of menu ideas and recipes, computerized for the individual family, based on its size and the family income. Over 1,300,000 requests were received. The total sales effect was a great sales boost for the entire Hunt-Wesson line.*

* Source: Direct communication from advertiser.

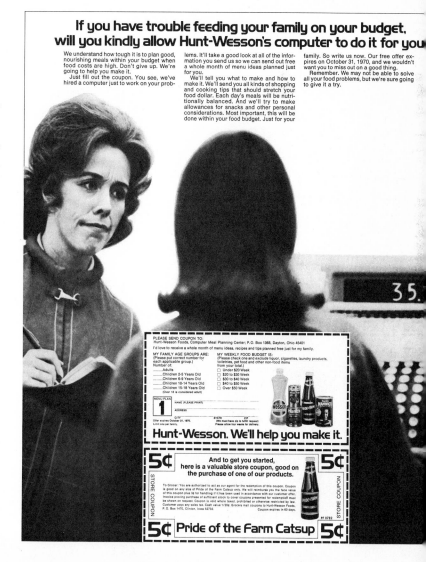

To secure acceptance of a subordinate product or process; to reach the end user. Campaigns are often addressed to the consumer by the manufacturer who makes the raw material used in the finished product that the consumer buys.

Celanese is a fiber made by Fiber Industries, Inc., who make the fiber into cloth and sell the cloth to dress manufacturers, who sell their dresses to retail stores, who sell their dresses to their customers—the end users. Fiber Industries convinced eighteen garment manufacturers to make clothes of Celanese, and had each manufacturer send them his best style. Then they ran a triple-page (gatefold) magazine advertisement showing each of these styles with the manufacturer's name and listing the stores in the various cities throughout the country where the styles were sold. All this resulted in their selling Celanese to the dress manufacturers, who sold more dresses because of that total advertising effort.

Movies without movie lights.

Four things Kodak did to make them possible:

Kodak has built four special features into the XL movie cameras that let in up to 6 times as much light as cameras without these features: **ONE.** An extra-fast *f*/1.2 Ektar lens. **TWO.** An enlarged shutter opening that lets in extra light. **THREE.** A special exposure control that doesn't block the light. **FOUR.** A viewing system that doesn't steal the light.

Just drop in a cartridge of high-speed Kodak Ektachrome 160 movie film and you're ready for movies without movie lights. This film is four times faster than Kodachrome II movie film.

See the Kodak XL movie cameras at your photo dealer's. From less than $120. The XL55 (shown) with power zoom is less than $215.

Prices subject to change without notice.

Kodak XL movie cameras. Ektachrome 160 movie film.

PRODUCT NEWS PROVIDES
CAMPAIGN IDEA

You don't have to look far for a campaign theme when an improvement in a product is as noteworthy as this. Observe clear promise headline: concise, specific copy.

To create "merchandising packages" of a variety of services.   To increase flights on their planes, airlines advertise entire "packaged tours," including plane fare, hotel accommodations, meals, and sightseeing, to various parts of the world, for varying lengths of stay, all for a set price (except extras, of course). This strategy of making your product part of something bigger, offered as a unit, is particularly good in the service field.

To turn a disadvantage into an advantage.   A classic example of the triumph of capitalizing on a disadvantage was shown some years ago in the drive-yourself car field, in which Hertz dominated at the time, followed at a distance by a lot of smaller companies. Among them was Avis, which ranked second to Hertz. "We are Number Two," they said proudly, "we have to try harder." And their "We try harder" slogan was quickly picked up as a plausible reason for expecting better service, eliciting a warm response from those who also were trying hard to get ahead. By positioning themselves as Number Two, they pulled their image way above the host of other drive-yourself companies in the field.

The situations cited above are just a handful of examples to present the thinking about advertising campaigns in terms of strategy.

CREATING THE ADVERTISEMENTS AND COMMERCIALS

Up to now we have been discussing *what* to say. Now we deal with *how* to say it. To summarize all that was said on the subject in the discussion of creating advertisements: Have sharply in mind what you want to communicate; then say it in as fresh, interesting, and clear a way as you can. Try at least three different ways of doing this before you select the one to use. In the case of TV and radio commercials, begin with the ending, and let your imagination loose on how to get there.

SELECTING THE MEDIA

He who deals with media deals with money. He allocates funds to different media in different proportions. His decisions determine the number of messages that will be delivered per dollar, to whom, and how often; his judgment directly affects the cost/profit ratio of a marketing program.

There is great opportunity for creative and courageous media selection, not always following the crowd in choice of media, use of space or time, and timing. There is also great variability in what a media man can get for his dollars in the purchase of time and space.

GETTING THE BUDGET AND CAMPAIGN APPROVED

In presentation of an advertising proposal to top management for approval, it has been found wise to set out with a statement of the company's *marketing* goals. They may be to launch a new product, to increase sales by X percent, to increase its share of the market by Z percent—or whatever the marketing target may be. Next follows a description of the philosophy and strategy of the advertising, with the reasons for believing that the proposed plan will help attain those objectives. Not until then are the advertisements or the commercials presented, along with the media proposal and the plans for coordinating the entire effort with that of the sales department. What are the *reasons* for each recommendation in the program? On what basis were these dollar figures arrived at? On what research were any decisions based? What were the results of preliminary tests, if any? What is competition doing? What *alternatives* were considered? What is the total cost? And finally, how may the entire program help contribute to the company's return on its investment? These questions are the kind that those who control the corporate purse strings like to have answered when they are asked to approve a total advertising program.

PREPARING AND SCHEDULING THE ADVERTISING

Once the budget and campaign are approved, we come to the task of actually producing the advertisements and the commercials, and all the trade promotional material, and buying the space and time. The biggest problem at this juncture of the effort is invariably coordination and timing, and these call for good advance planning.

PRESENTING THE CAMPAIGN TO THE SALES FORCE

The sales force always looks forward to the annual announcement of the company's newest plans and may gather for the event at a convention-like meeting at the home or branch office. There, everything may be set up on a stage under wraps, with all the excitement characteristic of the launching of a new venture; finally, the new product and the new advertising campaign are unfurled to view.

Sometimes the launching of a new campaign is done with the aid of a closed-circuit television presentation from the home office to the different branch-office meetings, to which the dealers might be invited. At other times, the men are all brought in, along with the main distributors, and given a theatrical presentation with music—as with the automobile companies and makers of household utilities. Or it can all be done on a modest scale; the men are called in to the sales manager's office, and the advertising manager tells of the advertising program.

Usually a kit of the various advertising material will be prepared, with which the salesmen are able to show all the details of the new campaign to the dealers on whom they will call.

APPRAISING THE RESULTS

The Big Day comes! The campaign is released. The advertising is released. The tension of getting up the campaign is released . . . but not for long. Soon the question comes up, "How are we doing?" For this purpose we have available a variety of appraisal plans. The chief lesson to be derived from all appraisal efforts is this: before spending any money on advertising, lay down the ground rules as to exactly what the advertising is supposed to accomplish, make sure these goals are reasonable, then test the results against that bench mark.

SUMMARY OF THE STEPS

The steps in preparing an actual national campaign for a consumer product may be outlined in the following manner. (The sequence does not follow the previous discussion exactly, but has been rearranged for convenience in surveying the entire problem.)

1. Develop a product that offers good value.
2. Create the trademark.
3. Design the package.
4. Determine who can use it. Where are they? What are they like? Who are the heavy users?
5. Position the product.
6. Determine the selling price.
7. Determine the method of distribution.
8. Establish the advertising strategy and theme.
9. Set the appropriation; get it approved.
10. Prepare the advertisements and commercials.
11. Choose the media; prepare schedules; order the time and space.
12. Create the dealer tie-in plan.
13. Present the complete campaign to the salesmen and distributors.
14. Release the advertising to the public.
15. Appraise the results.

Fitting the Image to the Times
Northwestern Mutual Life Insurance Company

A case report on a complete campaign

IN 1971, THE Northwestern Mutual Life Insurance Company undertook a complete reappraisal of its advertising program. The company, seventh largest life insurance firm in the country, wanted to examine not only the specifics of its advertising program (target audiences, media, message strategy, and the like), but also general questions such as why the company should advertise at all, and what its advertising goals should be.

BACKGROUND

Over recent years, Northwestern's advertising apparently had not generated the identity that company executives considered appropriate for the seventh largest life insurance company. More specifically, the 1970 Gallup National Insurance Index survey showed that NML ranked 34th in awareness (of 55 major life insurance companies studied). Moreover, although policyowners held strong positive reactions to the company, to *non*-policyowners the company was "something of an unknown." In addition, there was some executive dissatisfaction with recent campaigns.

Traditionally, NML's advertising sought to develop a quality image for the company, with the aim of preselling the company's name and values. It had been recognized that the actual selling of policies was *not* a realistic objective for the company's advertising.

The company's past advertising had been aimed at "prime prospects" —upper-income, well-educated men, initially those in the 35–45 age bracket, later 25–45. News weeklies, later supplemented by *Sports Illustrated* (for younger men), had been the national media; magazines—and news magazines particularly—were chosen because of their ability to reach the desired audiences efficiently and to establish frequency within a limited budget.

The most successful past campaign had been the 20-year "Karsh campaign," which featured quality people in the ads with a distinguished appearance of the ads themselves. This campaign was seen as "very merchandisable" by the field force. But times changed, and the Karsh campaign's

---

Courtesy of Northwestern Mutual Life Insurance Company, Richard S. Haggman, Superintendent of Advertising.

emphasis on older business figures as authorities may well have been "out of joint" with the tenor of the late 1960's. The "faces" and "individuals" campaigns followed, also illustrated here; neither of these generated agent enthusiasm. On three measures of reactions to advertising—ad readership scores, public identification of the company, and agent enthusiasm—none of the campaigns scored high on *all three*.

Northwestern Mutual Life policyowner for 38 years. Mr. Oelman today has eleven policies with NML.

KARSH, OTTAWA

ROBERT S. OELMAN, *Chairman and Chief Executive Officer, The National Cash Register Company, Dayton, Ohio*

"Don't ignore the asset value life insurance offers you."

"Everyone recognizes the protection value of life insurance. It's so dramatic, in fact, that many people don't give attention to another big advantage—the dollar reserves life insurance creates. □ To my mind, its ever-growing cash values are a vital family asset. They're basic to security planning . . . a solid base for financial well-being. A ready source of help for emergencies, education, retirement—you name it." □ Your money does more for you at Northwestern Mutual Life—NML. Cash values grow fast. The dividend rate has gone up steadily: 13 times in 16 years. □ NML operating expenses are low. They run about one-third less, as a percentage of premiums, than the average of the 14 other largest life insurance companies. Ask the NML agent for the full story. It can pay you. Northwestern Mutual Life—Milwaukee.

NML

21-900 (68-4)

This statement and photograph appeared in an advertisement. Those who appear in the program do so voluntarily and in the public interest and receive no remuneration.

One of the Famous "Karsh" Portrait Series that Ran for 20 Years

An exploration with company and advertising agency people of the question, "What is advertising supposed to do for the company?" revealed several major roles for NML's advertising. First, particularly from those associated with the field selling effort, advertising is seen as a *sales support,* a door-opener, a preselling tool that sets the stage for a more favorable reception for the agent. Related to this is a second major role—namely, to instill a *favorable image* for the company among its selective prospect groups. A third is to *reinforce "warm feelings"* on the part of present owners. From these (especially the first two), and also from the level of spending, emerges a fourth role—to sustain and improve the morale of the agents.

No one, however, claimed a direct selling role for advertising. Perhaps for this reason, advertising was called into question by some as possibly a waste of resources. Yet a number of arguments were put forth as to why it was important to advertise:

—Because competitors do it

—Because NML is a major national firm in a major industry

—Because agents like it (especially when they like the ads)

—Because it's an efficient way to communicate the company's favorable characteristics to many prospects simultaneously

—Because we don't know what would happen if we stopped

At this point, the company's focus shifted to what it saw as a more meaningful question: "How can we *maximize the usefulness* of our advertising program?" An attempt was made to articulate the shorter- and longer-term roles of advertising on prospects and on current owners, and also on agents. Some of these impacts were more sales-oriented than others. In chart form, these shorter- and longer-term impacts were stated as:

| | IMPACTS | |
GROUP	SHORT-TERM	LONGER-TERM
Prospects	Door-opener via name identification and favorable image (Awareness is achievable in short to medium term)	Same, with increasing image favorability (Specific attributes take longer to "build" than does awareness)
Current owners	Reinforce feeling of "right" decision and strengthen pride of ownership Reach those current owners not similar to "prime" prospects (among "target audiences")	Retain pride of ownership and enhance likelihood of purchase of more insurance and other products from NML; advertising supplements experience
Agents	Merchandisability; morale uplift	Same, plus make it easier to recruit new agents

Consumer research had shown that Northwestern's name was *not* recognized, nor was the company distinctively identified (commensurate with size and performance), by consumers in its prospect group. Among policyholders themselves, the company was seen clearly and favorably; indeed, group interviews with policyowners reaffirmed the view of company executives and data from past policyowner studies that policyowners were enthusiastic about the company. But among groups of non-policyholders who were demographically equivalent to the owners' group, NML was "something of an unknown." More specifically, among non-policyowners, recall of NML advertising was low, and believability of the identifying sentence, "World's largest company specializing in individual life insurance," was not only low, but was *resisted*. In the absence of knowledge of the company, this claim was incomprehensible, and the non-owner's intellectual resolution was to refuse to believe it *could* be true.

In trying to define for itself the company's distinctive characteristics, executives sought to find unique, real differentiating elements not being emphasized by other insurance companies. This, in short, would provide an identity for NML both supportable and preemptible (vs. competition).

In fact, company executives believed that *superior performance* was a documentable, unique attribute, using traditional industry-wide criteria. Their hope was, first, that a meaningful "translation" of this superiority could be developed—meaningful to policyowners and non-owners. Second, they hoped a distinctive creative execution of the theme could be developed.

TARGET AUDIENCES

The principal group to whom the company's advertising had been addressed was *prospective buyers*. These were further defined into "prime prospects"— well-educated men, 21–35, in upper and middle social classes and in occupations similar to those of present policyowners. (This represents only about 5 percent of the public.) It was agreed that prospective- and present-owner publics were the most salient audiences for advertising, and that a successful job with these groups would lead the agents to react very favorably too. Fortunately also, there is considerable overlap, in terms of national media, in reaching prospective- and present-owner audiences, since the demographic characteristics of the former have been defined largely in terms of the latter.

Several basic questions were raised about target audiences: Within the prospect group, were there subgroups to whom more emphasis should be given? Was there more about the *non*-demographic aspects of prospects that might help communicate to them? Was enough being done to reinforce the company's image with present owners? Were there additional audiences to whom advertising should be aimed?

The company concluded that:

—Greater relative emphasis than in the past be put on reaching prospects *not* among the "primes," since the field force focused almost entirely on the primes.

—More work be done to get insights into the qualitative nature of prospects (within the key demographic groups).

COMMUNICATING IDENTITY AND IMAGE (MESSAGE)

In exploring (not deciding) specific directions for the content of a new campaign, executives considered several background elements, based on research and impressions:

—Life insurance advertising still focuses in large part on the need for life insurance and on selling achievements of agents; yet consumer research (including the Yankelovich industry study) indicates that most consumers seem to recognize the need for insurance, and that they feel "threatened" by really good salesmen.

—In the context of the 1970's, consumers *want* to feel that they are capable of being good judges of, and wise buyers of, insurance; buying insurance is one of the important financial commitments that today's consumer wants to make on what he sees as rational grounds.

—There are clear emotional connotations of insurance (e.g., "care of loved ones"), but the buying decision is seen as one involving careful consideration (compared with buying a brand of canned peas).

The implications for insurance advertising were seen as pointing to advertising that should include objective, rational criteria on which a consumer can confidently base a buying decision for insurance (for example, performance appraisal criteria). Further, consumers seem to want information that removes, or reduces, the "mystery" from assessing life insurance. And consumers are also likely to seek reassurance that they are making—or have recently made—a good decision.

Thus, research for the new campaign was to focus on how to communicate—believably and meaningfully—what constitutes excellence, how to recognize it, and that Northwestern has it. The company thought there was believable and meaningful *evidence of superiority* in terms of such traditional industry criteria as low lapse rate and high repeat-purchase rate (indications of consumer satisfaction), favorable mortality experience (arising from NML's practice of accepting only "selected risks"), high investment return, and low operating cost. Northwestern's "family" relationships with its policy-owners was considered by executives an additional positive element for prospective use in developing the campaign. However, they recognized the need to have prior consumer assessment of both the content and execution of specific proposed advertising messages. Such research would be carried out with policyowners and non-owners, since each group is an important audience for the advertising; each was thought to have a rather different perspective on the company.

REACHING THE TARGET AUDIENCES (MEDIA)

NML had traditionally emphasized magazines in its media plan. This was viewed as making excellent sense, in the light of the positive attributes of magazines for insurance advertising. (Competition uses magazines heavily also.)

The principal arguments for the kinds of magazines NML has used are as follows:

—*Selectivity* (efficiency of ad spending directed to NML's traditional demographic targets)

—*Continuity* (sustaining the message, given the total budget dollars)

—*Susceptibility to a story* (permitting a longer message for the reader to chew on)

—Basically *serious mood* (and the resultant setting for a serious message)

—*Merchandisability* (via reprints)

Two major questions about magazine advertising at this point are these: *First,* is it a "tired medium" for NML's communication with its target audience(s); that is, is there a certain sameness that will affect *any* new message? *Second,* since some competitors are in television, is there a need for NML to "play the glamor game" too? Are there specific advantages in TV for NML?

On the first point, executives agreed that a meaningfully different (in the consumer's own view) *message* could overcome any sameness in the medium. But in the second area, the arguments were more complex. On the one hand, the dramatic impact of TV, its creative possibilities, its presumed morale impact on the agents (and executives) as an "active medium," and its use by some competitors made its serious consideration necessary. Counterbalancing these, there were several major arguments against TV:

—Its low efficiency in reaching NML's traditional target demographic groups

—The high "start-up" cost of achieving the meaningful frequency in TV necessary for visibility (probably $1.5 million or more)

—The need for a "pool" of several commercials, the production cost of which is likely to be over $100,000

—The need for some "maintenance budget" in print (which would add to the *total* budget)

The agreement was that TV should be undertaken if a sufficiently dramatic and creative use of the medium could be developed, if a "creative" TV media buy (such as news or special events) could markedly reduce the inherent inefficiencies of the medium in reaching target audiences, and if executives were excited enough about the campaign to be willing to make a major additional budget investment in the initial year's program.

ADVERTISING SPENDING LEVELS

What more, if any, should the company spend on advertising?

NML's 1971 (national) advertising outlay of some $800,000 represented about double the expenditure of ten years before. However, advertising dollars as a percentage of total premium income had increased only marginally in ten years. On the other hand, compared with competition, on the basis of advertising per total premium income, NML *underspent* by several hundred thousand dollars the estimated national media budget of other major mutual companies, and most other life insurance companies as well. Executives saw a need to increase the budget if a new and exciting campaign were developed, in order to "spend enough to be visible," to achieve some critical mass of advertising spending in order to make any meaningful impact. This would be particularly relevant for TV: To get into TV at all was *not* seen as desirable unless one were willing to spend well over $1 million in the medium. They agreed to consider increasing NML's "basic" level of national advertising spending by $250,000 or so, closer to the proportionate level of major mutual companies, and to make a major additional advertising investment of up to $500,000 for a one-year or two-year period for an "exciting" campaign, especially if it called for the use of TV. A modest reduction in present spending while a new campaign was being developed would help support the added budget later.

DEVELOPING THE NEW CAMPAIGN

After the company and agency executives had completed their review of past and present advertising, they moved forward to try to develop a new advertising campaign. In the course of their work on the advertising content, the

unusual media opportunity arose—namely, partial television sponsorship of
the 1972 Summer Olympics. Although expensive (over a million dollars), the
TV Olympic sponsorship would provide an exciting setting for the new campaign. It also measured up well on reaching the target demographic groups,
particularly the "non-prime" prospects whom the company wanted to reach
through its advertising. Finally, the Olympic sponsorship was seen as highly
exciting and merchandisable to and by the agents. Thus, the decision was made
to go into TV with the Olympics.

At this point, work continued on the campaign itself. Using the interview information from policyowner and non-owner groups, seven major
themes were developed by Northwestern's advertising agency, the Chicago
office of J. Walter Thompson Company.

1. *Theme:* We Recognize Your Money Is Precious to You

   Expressions
   Because You've Got More to Do With Your Money Than Just
       Buy Life Insurance
   We Make Life Insurance a Little Easier to Live With
   Why Put More Money into Life Insurance Than You Really
       Have To?
   Isn't It Nice to Get a Little More Than You Pay For?
   We Treat Your Money like It's Still Your Money. Because It Is.

2. *Theme:* We Recognize Your Time Is Precious to You

   Expressions
   Invest Your Time as Wisely as You Invest Your Money
   A Visit From a Life Insurance Agent Doesn't Have to Be like a
       Visit from Your Mother-In-Law

3. *Theme:* We Are 100 Years Old, The 7th Largest Life Insurance
   Company, but Only the 34th Best Known

   Expressions
   Not the Best Known . . . Just The Best
   The Great Unknown
   The Best-Known Company You Never Heard Of
   Northwestern Mutual Life. It's Time You Heard About Us

4. *Theme:* Service to You as an Individual

   Expressions
   The Personal Life
   It's Your Life. It's Your Company.
   We're Different Because You Are

5. *Theme:* Creative Living

   Expressions
   Insure as Creatively as You Live
   Creating a Better Life Through Insurance
   The Good Life

6. *Theme:* We Recognize That You Are Unsure of Your Own Competence as a Life Insurance Buyer

   Expressions
   After We Tell You What You Need to Know, You Tell Us What You Need to Buy
   The Less You Know About Life Insurance, the More You Need Northwestern Mutual
   People Making Life Insurance Work for People
   We've Simplified the Business of Life

7. *Theme:* There Is a Difference in Life Insurance Companies

   Expressions
   Not All Life Insurance Companies Are Alike
   If Anybody Can Change Your Mind About Life Insurance, It's Probably Us

THEME TESTING

Among these themes, careful company and agency consideration selected 1, 3, and 6 for development into full-blown ads for consumer testing. Three ads were prepared—and modified in order to "give the themes an even chance" in further group interviews with policyowners and non-owners; all those interviewed were in the demographic target groups.

The interviews yielded the following highlights:

1. Being a little-known company, NML needs to tell people who it is before going into detail about what it has to offer. The "you never heard of" theme works well. It sets a tone of modesty and humility, while credibly communicating NML's steadfast adherence to the rule of quality above quantity—since 1888, when everyone knows quality and pride in workmanship really did exist. Given this prologue, the fact that NML is seventh largest serves as proof positive that it really has put its customers first, and left it to word of mouth to take care of growth. "Seventh largest" in the context of this commercial says that service and strict adherence to quality have paid off, and implies stability. Admission of the fact that NML is an unknown suggests humility and integrity. The use of a little-known announcer will reinforce the communication of straightforward integrity; if NML tried to borrow fame from a well-known announcer, it would be regarded as dishonest.

2. People agree that life insurance is hard to buy, and they don't know the right way to go about it. People are willing to believe that NML agents are equipped to help, but they still think the agent will strive to maximize his commissions, and will only provide the information that suits his purposes. There is considerable skepticism that the company actually has control over its agents. Non-policyowners particularly question the idea of

agents being solely interested in the consumer's interest. Dividend performance, stability, and flexibility are important things to know about, but determining the correct size and type of policy, and thus avoiding getting oversold, is the central consumer problem in buying life insurance. Although some people *doubt that NML agents will produce as promised,* they are willing to give NML a try. The agent had really better deliver, because many say they will be especially alert for any signs of pushiness or deception.

People have some trouble with the theme, "You have more to do with your money." Life insurance is not considered one of the best investments or provisions you can make for the future. It may be one of the safest and most necessary investments, but not the best.

"Efficient," in terms of just the right amount of coverage, is right on target. As before, most people believe the agent will try to sell all the coverage he can, but they seem willing to be shown that NML is different. ". . . just the right amount of coverage. Not too much. Not too little. But based on what you can honestly afford . . . today," works right at their central concern, and does it very well.

3. "The best-known company you never heard of" seems to be an effective identifying statement. It is important to have one.

THE MEDIA SCHEDULE

It was decided to buy participation in the 1972 Olympics program on the ABC National network for two weeks, from August 25 to September 11. The schedule included 46 spots, both 30- and 60-second. Ten commercials were used, telling the NML story along the lines that tested out best. The total cost, including production, came close to $1,250,000.

BENCH-MARK STUDY

Along with the development work on the new campaign, the company also planned a two-stage research study to help assess the impact of the campaign. The research was to be conducted with a national sample of college-educated men in the 20–40 age range. The questionnaire focused on *awareness* of various major insurance companies, *preference* (in terms of having a policy with them or calling them if considering a policy), *desirability* of particular attributes of insurance companies (such as size, low expenses, and so on), *recall of advertising* for various companies, and ratings of NML on particular attributes.

The same study was planned to be conducted both before the Olympics and shortly after. In this way, the company thought it could assess the impact of the Olympics campaign on its target group's awareness of and attitudes toward NML and the advertising.

NORTHWESTERN MUTUAL LIFE INSURANCE COMPANY
1972 SUMMER OLYMPICS

"Size Seven"--One of Ten Commercials Produced for the Olympics

RAY: I was just down the street talking to Tom Armstrong about his new boy.

He pulled out about a hundred snapshots of him and the little guy's only six weeks old.

Hmmph . . . you know it's kind of funny how when a man has his first baby, he starts thinking about the future and protection.

Anyway, Tom asked me if I'd recommend any life insurance companies. "Sure," I said, "Northwestern Mutual Life."

You know what he says to me? No, I was thinking of one of the big ones. So I came back with "Well, how does size seven feel, Tom!"

Well, he looked puzzled. So I told him, "Northwestern Mutual is the seventh largest life insurance company in America and it's over a hundred years old."

Then he wants to know how come they're number seven and he never heard of them. So I tell him it's simple.

They've been too busy making sure their life insurance is the best around to spend much time talking about it.

ANNCR: Northwestern Mutual Life . . . The Quiet Company . . . that people have been talking about for over 100 years.

Photoscript of a TV Commercial Stressing "The Quiet Company" Theme

Working with the group-interview information, the agency's creative group continued its efforts to develop the TV commercials for the Olympics. One aim was to come up with a strong "memory peg" for company identification. The line that emerged was, "The quiet company people have been talking about for over 100 years." This line was seen as capitalizing on the company's longevity but indicating that the viewer might not have heard about NML.

The final commercials themselves continued to emphasize the non-pushy nature of the NML agent, in a way that did not stretch the believability of the viewer. The age, size, and stability of NML was underscored, as was the company's concern for selling the "right" amount of insurance for the consumer.

RESULTS

Initial reactions to the Olympics campaign were well beyond those anticipated. Television audiences for the Olympics were substantially higher than expected. Awareness of Northwestern immediately after the campaign leaped from its previous low rankings to the level of other major insurance companies. Recall of the commercials themselves was over twice the norm. Correct association of "The Quiet Company" with Northwestern was well above the level achieved by comparable advertising budgets of other advertisers. Northwestern Life's agents were enthusiastic and a flood of favorable mail came into the company from agents and policyholders alike.

Bisquick

A case report on giving new life to an old product

THIS IS THE STORY of General Mills' Bisquick—old and new—a story that embraces 38 years of consumer packaged goods marketing experience with the product. It's the story of the rebirth and revitalization of a declining brand.

BACKGROUND

Bisquick had originally been introduced as a biscuit mix in grocery stores on the West Coast in 1934. Bisquick's principal "reason for being" in this period was its special formulation for biscuit baking; also, Bisquick included the shortening in the box. The original Bisquick included flour, shortening, sugar, salt, leavening, and dry milk in the package. Thus it offered biscuit-baking convenience to consumers.

As the product's acceptance grew and consumers' experience with it increased, Bisquick became a variety baking mix. This variety characteristic was not a result of reformulation specifically designed for variety end-product uses. Rather, it happened—as General Mills–Betty Crocker marketing executives learned, and promoted the fact—that consumers were using the original product for a variety of baking end products, principally biscuits, pancakes, shortcakes, waffles, and dumplings.

Until the mid-1950's, Bisquick's annual volume continued to grow. However, after it reached a peak in 1955, a decline set in. By 1965 its sales had fallen substantially from the all-time high of 1955, although Bisquick was still a profitable product for the company. The decline was viewed by marketing executives as resulting principally from the entrance into the market of more convenient specialty baking-mix items.

PRODUCT AND MARKET ANALYSIS LAUNCHED

In the face of this situation, the marketing organization of General Mills initiated a thorough and complete product and market analysis of Bisquick. This analysis began with the recognition that biscuits, pancakes, and short-

---

Courtesy General Mills, Inc., James S. Fish, Vice-president, Advertising and Marketing Services.

cakes continued to be the mainstay baking items for which Bisquick was used.
It also recognized that despite the volume generated by these end-product
bakings, little true homemade-biscuit-baking consumption was being penetrated by Bisquick's convenience mix. For instance, in the southern part of the
United States, where 70 percent of all biscuits are consumed, Bisquick had
virtually no penetration and did an insignificant proportion of its volume
relative to the biscuit market potential. Bisquick had been considered in 1965
the best of the variety baking mixes, but had never delivered a product that
the Southern housewife, in particular, found acceptable for basic biscuit
bakings.

The potential of penetrating the biscuit market with a reformulated
Bisquick product was so significant that considerable research effort was ex-
pended in the South to determine what constituted a good Southern biscuit.
Key characteristics of good Southern biscuits were lightness, tenderness,
fluffiness, and moistness. With this information, and with considerable market-
potential and financial-implication data developed, General Mills' product research was directed to develop a reformulated Bisquick product that would
provide the consumer with a superior-quality end-product biscuit—superior to
all other ways of making biscuits. This biscuit from Bisquick obviously would
have to be lighter, more tender, more fluffy, and more moist, with better
overall taste and texture than any other homemade-recipe biscuit could be.

RESULTS IN THE SOUTH

In 1966, New Bisquick was launched into three Southern markets, in test, to
determine the viability of penetrating the Southern "scratch" market. The
reformulated product was viewed just as though it were one of General Mills'
new-product introductions. The Bisquick test-market experience in the South
was outstandingly successful: In its first full year in test, the product delivered
25 percent more volume than it had in the preceding (pretest) year. Further,
in the second year, an additional 18 percent volume increase was generated.
At that point, the overall results for the brand showed an increase of 45 percent in deliveries, 20 percent in consumer market share, and 42 percent in per
capita consumption of New Bisquick. There had also been a jump of 14 percent in sales of the entire product category, reflecting the fact that the "scratch"
part of the market had indeed been penetrated. Bisquick's test had clearly
been successful, and on the strength of these results, the brand was rolled
into the entire southern United States.

NORTHERN EXPANSION

The success of New Bisquick in the South raised the question to management
of whether New Bisquick should be introduced into the North. The old formulation's brand situation in the North, although not similar to its former one

You can
make all these
from
one package of

NEW, FAMILY SIZE BISQUICK!

TWO 10" PIZZAS

BATCH OF BISCUITS

TWO LARGE WAFFLES

SHORTCAKE FOR 6

VELVET CRUMB CAKE FOR 8

18 PANCAKES

COFFEE CAKE FOR 10

12 DUMPLINGS

NOW BISQUICK COMES IN *THREE* SIZES!

You get a full fifteen cups of Betty Crocker's most versatile mix in this new Family Size Bisquick. Enough to make all the good things shown above, from one box! (You don't have to stop with these, either. Directions for many other tasty treats on the package!) How *else* could you make so many good things so easily?

Save time, trouble *and* money with new Family Size Bisquick. It's not only thrifty but extra convenient. Bigger size means less chance of running out!

THE OLD

This advertisement appeared in 1963, when Bisquick was featured as a variety baking mix. Sales were going down, and the new size package was introduced, but the sales still kept going down.

560

NOW A COMPLETELY NEW BISQUICK! MAKES BISCUITS LIGHTER, FLUFFIER THAN SCRATCH or your money back

New Bisquick Buttermilk Biscuit Mix is here. With four good reasons to stop making scratch biscuits:

1) You get a special, lighter flour stores don't sell. So your biscuits turn out lighter than scratch.

2) You get a livelier leavening stores don't sell. So your biscuits turn out fluffier than scratch.

3) You get an almost-instant formula far easier than scratch. Just add water and 3 minutes' fixing time.

4) You pay no more than you'd pay for the best scratch biscuits.

You'll say new Bisquick biscuits are lighter, fluffier, better eating than your favorite scratch biscuits. Or, your money back. If not completely satisfied, mail box top (with price mark) to General Mills, Inc., Box 200, Minneapolis, Minn.

P.S. New Bisquick also makes delicious pancakes, waffles, shortcake—and other favorite bakings.

Proved lighter than scratch biscuits made at Athens, Georgia... in actual weighings.

THE NEW

This is not merely a new ad, but an announcement of a new formulation of Bisquick, targeted to the home-made biscuit market, leading to the best sales record the brand ever had.

in the South, still reflected opportunity for growth, particularly in terms of percentage of homes penetrated.

Consumer-usage studies showed that *pancake baking* in the North was considerably greater on an index basis than it was in the South. This end product seemed to offer an excellent opportunity to improve volume in the North for the New Bisquick . . . *if* the product could perform. Again, extensive research was done to confirm that New Bisquick made pancakes lighter than the best "scratch" pancake recipes. With this confirmed, New Bisquick was introduced into several Northern test markets in 1968.

The test-market program was similar to that employed in the South, but with the advertising focused on the product's superiority for pancakes. The scale as symbol of New Bisquick's superiority appeared in all promotion and product support. Test results again were successful: New Bisquick's volume in the test markets grew 6 percent, against a goal of 5 percent. In view of this success, New Bisquick was extended to full national distribution.

RETROSPECTIVE

By the early 1970's, it was clear that New Bisquick's introduction, South and North, had made a significant positive impact on volume. In 1971 and 1972, the brand enjoyed its best years and is continuing to operate at high marketing levels.

Three conclusions can be drawn with application to consumer packaged-goods marketing:

1. Established products can be revitalized and reintroduced, given sufficient market-research information and market analysis to identify potential.
2. Thorough, defined market research and market testing can generally be translatable to expansion-area business. While there are always wiggles in the data, the general direction of market research is translatable to expansion areas if the research reflects actual test-market experience over time.
3. Marketing is an evolutionary process in terms of planning, not static. This is demonstrated in Bisquick's current volume-level performance, four to five years after its initial reintroduction.

1. What would be the chief technical questions you would ask about a new product presented to you for your marketing and advertising proposals?

2. Products in the pioneering, competitive, or retentive stage require different kinds of advertising approaches. What direction or approach would you take if you were called upon to advertise different products in each one of the stages?

3. Select three of the specific selling problems described in the chapter. For each, discuss a particular current advertisement or commercial that illustrates an approach to overcoming that problem.

4. Describe the areas you, as advertising manager, would cover in a presentation to top management for approval of your advertising program and budget.

5. Without looking at the summary in the text, review the steps in preparing a new consumer product for market. (Then compare your list with the text.)

6. The Northwestern Mutual Life Insurance Company case describes a company's review and redevelopment of its advertising. Based on this case:
   a. What were the roles of advertising at Northwestern?
   b. Who were the target audiences?
   c. What were the pros and cons of magazines and TV?
   d. What did the company mean by "spending enough to be visible" in its budgeting?
   e. How did the group interviews help in developing the ads themselves?
   f. What advertising research was planned to assess the new campaign?

7. From the standpoint of marketing strategy, the text draws three conclusions about the Bisquick case report. Discuss information in the case that supports each of the three points.

8. Based on your analysis of the Bisquick case:
   a. What were the main factors leading to Bisquick's product reformulation?
   b. How did marketing research contribute to the success of New Bisquick in the South? in the North?
   c. "Revitalizing a brand means treating it like a new product." Discuss.

Reading Suggestions

Association of National Advertisers, *Perspectives in Advertising Management.* New York: 1969.

Barton, Roger, ed., *Handbook of Advertising.* New York: McGraw-Hill Book Company, 1970.

Glatzer, Robert, *The New Advertising: Great Campaigns from Avis to Volkswagen.* New York: Citadel, 1970.

Greyser, Stephen A., *Cases in Advertising and Communications Manage-* *ment.* Englewood Cliffs, N.J.: Prentice-Hall, Inc., 1972.

Miller, T. J., "When You Move into a Fluid and Growing Industry," *Advertising and Sales Promotion,* September 1967, p. 45ff. Also in Kleppner and Settel, *Exploring Advertising,* p. 74.

Rice, Craig S., *How to Plan and Execute the Marketing Campaign.* Chicago: Dartnell Corp., 1966.

VI
ADVERTISING
MANAGEMENT

## 24

The Advertising Agency

THE ADVERTISING AGENCY HAS long played an important role not only in the ever-changing advertising scene, but in American industry; and more recently, in world industry.

Just what does an agency do? How does it operate? What is its role today in relation to advertisers and to media? To understand these matters, it is well to begin at the beginning.

HISTORY

Early Days

It is not generally known that the first Americans to act as advertising agents were the colonial postmasters, according to Lee, who reports:

> In many localities, advertisements for Colonial papers might be left at the post offices. In some instances the local post office would accept advertising copy for publication in papers in other places; it did so with the permission of the postal authorities. . . . William Bradford, publisher of the first Colonial weekly in New York, made an arrangement with Richard Nichols, postmaster in 1727, whereby the latter accepted advertisements for the *New York Gazette* at regular rates.[1]

Space Salesmen

In 1841, Volney B. Palmer of Philadelphia went into the business of soliciting advertisements for newspapers, as a sales agent on a commission basis. Newspapers at that time had difficulty in getting out-of-town advertising. Palmer contacted publishers, offering to get them business for a 50 percent commission, but he often settled for less. There was no such thing as a rate card, or a fixed price for space or commission. "A first demand for $500

---

[1] James Melvin Lee, *History of American Journalism,* rev. ed. (Boston: Houghton Mifflin Company, 1933), p. 74.

by the papers might be reduced before the bargain was struck to $50." [2] (Today we call that "negotiation.") Soon there were more agents, offering various deals.

Wholesalers of Space

In the 1850's, George P. Rowell of Philadelphia became a wholesaler, buying a big block of space from publishers at a very low rate for cash (most welcome), less agent's commission. He would then sell it in small "squares"—one column wide—at his own retail rate. He next contracted with 100 newspapers to buy one column of space a month, and sold space in his total list at a fixed rate per line for the whole list. "An inch of space a month in one hundred papers for one hundred dollars." Selling by list became widespread. Each man's list, however, was his private stock-in-trade. (The original media package deal.)

The First Rate Directory

In 1869, Rowell shocked the advertising world by publishing a directory of newspapers with their card rates, and with his own estimates of their circulation. Other agents accused him of giving away their trade secrets. Publishers howled, too, because his estimates of circulation were lower than their claims. Nevertheless, he offered to provide advertisers an estimate of space costs based on those published rates for whatever markets they wanted. This was the beginning of the media estimate.

The Open Contract

In 1875, N. W. Ayer & Son of Philadelphia (successors to Rowell) made the startling proposal to bill the advertiser for what they actually paid the publishers, plus a fixed commission, provided the advertiser placed all his business through the agency. This "open contract" was a big step toward a client–agency relationship. In 1901, the Curtis Publishing Company announced it would allow commissions only to agencies that charged the full card rates. This was the beginning of the "no-rebating" provision in regard to agency commission that prevailed in the agency–media field for over 50 years.

The "Full-Service" Agency Emerges

A number of free-lance writers appeared on the scene in the late 1870's, writing the advertisements for advertisers, and also for agencies who hoped to sell more advertising space as a result. Around the 1880's, two of

---

[2] Frank Presbrey, *The History and Development of Advertising* (Garden City, N.Y.: Doubleday Doran & Co., 1929), p. 263.

Earnest Elmo Calkins
580 Park Avenue
New York
21

Dear Mr. Kleppner:

You perhaps do not realize what a disorganized muddle advertising was in the 1880's and 1890's. Most agencies merely placed copy furnished by clients. The rate cards were farces. The average agent simply bartered with the medium, magazine or newspaper, as to cost, beating it down to the lowest possible amount by haggling.

I consider my greatest contribution as being the first agency to recognize that advertising was a profession, to be placed on a much higher plane than a mere business transaction of placing advertising -- with the copy, the art work, the plan as the important part. I wrote my first advertising while still living in my home town, won a prize for an ad, wrote copy for local business men, worked a year as advertising manager for a department store, and received an offer from Charles Austin Bates, who was the first man to make a business of writing advertising copy. There I met Ralph Holden, and from that association sprang the name of the old firm of Calkins and Holden. I am now more than 96 years old.

Cordially,

Earnest Elmo Calkins

AN HISTORIC LETTER

"All of this I have seen, and part of which I have been." A letter from Earnest Elmo Calkins, one of the pioneers in the advertising agency business, written three months before his death in 1964.

the agencies, Calkins & Holden of New York and N. W. Ayer & Son of Philadelphia, went a step further: They put writers on their staffs, along with artists, and offered advertisers a comprehensive advertising service, including preparation of a plan, creating the advertisements, producing them, and placing them—the emergence of what is called today a "full-service" agency.

The advertising agency has been a great and continuing force for the use and application of advertising. It provides a team with a variety of experiences in meeting marketing problems through advertising, and in creating advertising. For a new advertiser, it provides a place to which an experienced advertiser can turn for a coordinated operation that can swing into action quickly.

1900–1917

There was a great ferment taking place in advertising in the decades before World War I. The advertising industry was getting itself organized. The American Association of Advertising Agencies was formed to help improve the operation and effectiveness of agencies and advertising. Advertisements revealed greater and more imaginative communications skills. Advertising became more closely identified with marketing. Research departments appeared in agencies. Agency commissions paid by the media were generally standardized at 15 percent for publications, 16⅔ percent for outdoor advertising.

The *Saturday Evening Post* was the prime advertising medium during this period.

1919–1945

This period saw the end of World War I, ten years of boom, an economic crash in 1929, a depression that lasted until World War II, and a postwar boom. Among the highlights that affected the agency business were these:

In the 1920's:

—Automobile production and advertising set new highs.

—Much advertising for electric refrigerators, electric shavers, air conditioning, washing machines, and other appliances.

—Radio arrived.

The 1930's, and into the 1940's:

—Radio gave a great lift to agencies, otherwise sharing in the depression. By 1942, agencies billed more for radio ($188 million) than for newspapers ($144 million).[3] Agencies also produced many of the radio shows.

---

[3] *Printers' Ink,* Compilation Advertising Statistics since 1935. Published 1968.

—It was an age of trying to make advertising more effective through research. George Gallup, of Gallup Poll fame, was research director of Young & Rubicam. The first Starch Reports appeared; and the first radio-listening research, Hooperatings.

—Agencies competed for business with services—research, sales promotion, merchandising. One agency even had a test kitchen for its food clients. . . . Then came World War II.

1945–1956:

—This was the post– World War II period, with consumers avid for the goods they had not been able to get during the war; with manufacturers anxious to use their expanded production facilities and new technologies for peacetime products. The GNP moved to new highs, as did disposable income. Television emerged as an explosive new advertising medium. Between 1946, the first year after the war, and 1956, the volume of advertising tripled—from $3,364 million in 1946 to $9,905 million in 1956.[4] And agencies grew in number and volume, and in services rendered. The multiplicity of these services becomes one of the elementary discussions of the agency compensation system in the 1960s.

Why do we pick 1956 as a focal date for advertising agencies? Because that was the year of the Department of Justice "consent decrees" that changed the compensation structure of the agency business, as we shall shortly see.

THE AGENCY BUSINESS TODAY

There are about 5,770 advertising agencies in the United States today, doing an annual business of about $7 billion, and employing about 75,000 people. This analysis of the composition of these agencies is illuminating:

GROUP	NUMBER OF AGENCIES	BILLINGS * (IN BILLIONS)	NUMBER OF EMPLOYEES
A	200 (4%)	5.2 (70%)	40,000
B	1,300 (23%)	1.7 (22%)	22,000
C	4,200 (73%)	.56 (8%)	13,000

* The total dollar amount of business placed by its clients.

In other words, 1,500 agencies do 92 percent of the business. The other 4,200 agencies do 8 percent. The largest agency of all, the J. Walter Thompson Company, does a world business of over $774 million annually. On the other hand, the 4,200 agencies in Group C average less than a half million dollars

[4] *Ibid.*

in billings per year. Half of these do less than $100,000 per year, representing the many one- and two-man shops handling mostly the varied advertising needs of local advertisers.[5]

The Work of a Full-service Agency

When an agency is assigned an account, it will usually conduct research to determine whether the product is positioned to best advantage in the minds of the public, or whether it should be repositioned. As an example: In the case of instant decaffeinated coffee, should it be presented as an instant coffee that is also decaffeinated, or as a decaffeinated coffee that helps you sleep, which incidentally is instant? Each presentation appeals to a different audience. The agency will make a study of the people who would be the best customers, decide upon the point of most significance about the product as against competition, create a dramatic way of presenting that quality, and submit the proposed ads and commercials for approval. Along with these, it will offer a media proposal covering consumer and dealer plans. When the ads have been approved, the agency will produce the material, ship it to the media, see that it runs properly, bill the advertiser for time or space and production, pay the media, and pay the vendors.

In addition, the full-service agency may be equipped to offer a series of collateral services as needed—such as research, sales promotion, merchandising (including premium buying), computer softwear, and research and development. These may be available to clients and nonclients alike on a negotiated-fee basis.

The Organization of an Agency

Many of today's agencies were started by two entrepreneurs, one a creative man, the other an account man. At first they may have handled all the functions of an agency themselves, but soon they would have to round out their organization to handle the basic areas of full-service agency responsibility. For the sake of clarity we will assign a title to the man in charge of each area (this varies with the agency): for example, *account management director, creative director, media director, research director,* and *administrator.* We trace the development of the agency by first tracing the work of these men.

The account management director. He is responsible for the relationship between the agency and the client. He is indeed a man of two worlds

---

[5] U.S. Department of Commerce, *1967 Census of Business, Advertising Agencies,* advance report BC61 (A) SSI (issued June 1970) and report BC67 SAI.

—that of the client's business, and that of advertising. He must, of course, be knowledgeable about his client's business and problems—his profit goals, his marketing problems, his advertising objectives. He is responsible for helping to formulate the basic advertising strategy recommended by the agency, for seeing that the proposed advertising prepared by the agency is on target, then for presenting the total proposal—media schedules, budget, rough advertisements or storyboards—to the client for approval. He then makes sure the agency produces the work to the client's satisfaction.

As the business grows and he has several accounts under his wing, he will appoint an *account executive* to become the continuing contract on one or more accounts and to get approvals of specific advertisements and estimates. The account executive must be a skillful communicator and follow-up man. His biggest contribution is to keep the agency ahead of the client's needs.

As billings increase, more account executives are added. In time, an *account supervisor* may be appointed to supervise and back up the work of several account executives. The organizational growth of an agency consists chiefly of the multiplication of such operational staff units. But the account management director will continue in his overall review of the account handling, and maintain his contacts with his counterpart at the advertiser's office.

The creative director. He is responsible for the effectiveness of the advertising produced by the agency; on this, the success of the agency depends. He must set the creative philosophy of the agency, its standards of craftsmanship. He has to generate a stimulating environment that inspires writers and artists to do their best work, and in turn inspires the best men to seek work there.

At first, the writers and artists will work directly with him, but as the business grows, various creative directors are assigned to various accounts, reporting to the head creative director.

There will also be the *Print Production Department* and the *TV Commercials Production Department.* (There are variations in agencies as to the separateness or togetherness of the print and television creative and production operations.)

To keep the work flowing on schedule from department to department, and to meet all closing dates without overtime, are the functions of the *Traffic Department.*

The media director. This person is responsible for the philosophy and planning of the use of media, for the selection of specific media, and for ordering space and time. As the agency grows, he may have a staff of media buyers, divided by media (print or TV or radio), accounts, or territory. He will have an estimating department and an ordering department, as well as

ADVERTISING AGENCY ORGANIZATION CHART

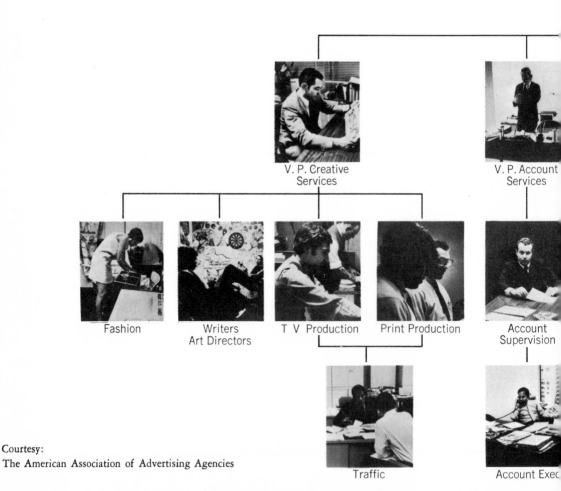

V. P. Creative
Services

V. P. Account
Services

Fashion

Writers
Art Directors

T V Production

Print Production

Account
Supervision

Traffic

Account Exec

Courtesy:
The American Association of Advertising Agencies

574

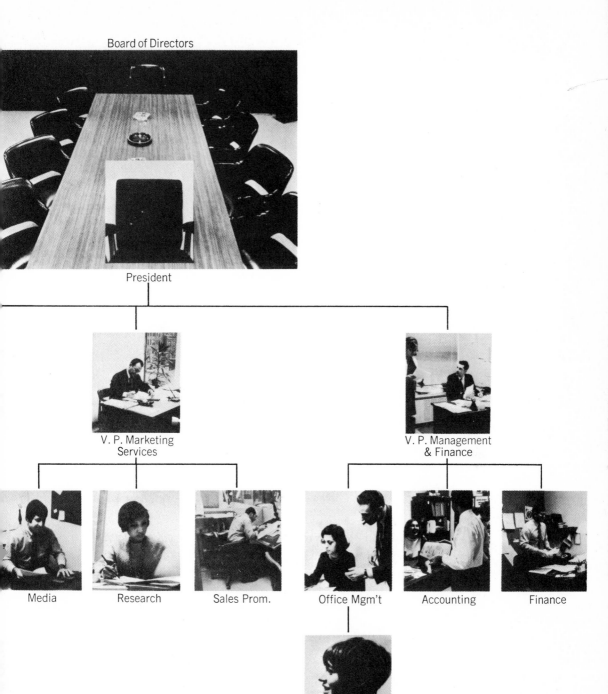

Board of Directors

President

V. P. Marketing
Services

V. P. Management
& Finance

Media

Research

Sales Prom.

Office Mgm't

Accounting

Finance

Personnel

one to handle the residual-payment records and other business records related to media. He may work with independent media services in the planning and purchase of media, especially TV and radio time, as we will shortly describe.

The research director. Early in its work, the agency will require research to define its marketing and copy goals; later research will also be used to appraise the effectiveness of its advertising after it has appeared. The agency may work through an outside research consultant and organization. In some agencies, research and media planning are coordinated under one man.

The administrative director. Like all businesses, an advertising agency needs an administrative head to take charge of financial and accounting control, office management, and personnel (including trainees).

The plans board. Many large agencies will have a plans board, called by various names, consisting of the senior members of the different departments, who review all new campaign proposals before they are submitted to the client, to make sure that the strategy represents the best thinking of the agency. In smaller agencies, the heads of the agency usually keep close supervision of the output.

THE AGENCY COMMISSION SYSTEM

Can anyone open an office and call himself an advertising agency? Yes, and we have already seen how many one- and two-man shops regard themselves as agencies. But an agency will not get a commission for the advertising it places in media unless these media "recognize" it. (Newspapers pay no commission on local advertising, which they handle directly at a low rate.) To get recognition, a new agency usually must show that it has business to place; it should demonstrate competence in advertising; and it should meet the financial requirements of the media's credit departments. Every medium decides for itself whom it will recognize as an accredited agency. At first the agency may apply directly to that local or trade medium with which it wants to place some business. Or the agency can apply for nationwide recognition among media by applying to their respective national trade associations, who perform the credit-checking function for their members.[6] Upon the association's recommendation, its members usually recognize the agency and allow it commission on the business it places.

---

[6] American Newspaper Publishers Association (ANPA), for most newspapers. Periodical Publishers Association (PPA), for most consumer magazines. American Business Press (ABP), for most trade and industrial publications. Agricultural Publishers Association (APA), for most farm papers.

Let us say an agency gets approval to insert a page advertisement in a magazine at $1,000 for the space. The advertisement appears. The magazine will bill the agency $1,000 less 15 percent agency commission, or $850 net. In addition, the magazine may offer a 2 percent cash discount on the $850, or $17, for prompt payment. The agency then bills the advertiser $1,000 and passes on the $17 publisher's cash discount on the cost of the space, for prompt payment by the advertiser.[7] The same procedure applies to newspapers, which also allow 15 percent. Television and radio allow 15 percent, but do not, as a rule, allow a cash discount. Outdoor allows 16⅔ percent agency commission.

The agency commission applies only to the cost of space or time. It does not apply to the cost of producing the material for print for the ads, or the production of commercials. The agency usually bills production expenses at actual net cost plus a service charge of 17.65 percent (which is 15 percent on the gross), subject to prior agreement with the client.

THE CONSENT DECREES

Up to 1956, the media associations who granted agency recognition required an agency seeking such recognition to agree not to rebate any part of its commission to the advertiser. In that year, the Department of Justice held that any media owner could legally make such requirement individually, but for a group of publishers, joining through their association to agree to impose such restriction was price-fixing, and that was illegal.

As a result of this action, the trade associations involved signed consent decrees in 1956, agreeing in substance not to intervene in any deal the advertiser and agency saw fit to make with each other.[8] Since then, the field has been wide open between advertiser and agency to work out whatever arrangement they see fit.

AGENCY COMPENSATION

The action of the Department of Justice came just about the time that a number of large advertisers were becoming restive with the entire philosophy of the advertising-agency compensation structure. They felt that the system whereby the agency got its chief income from the media the advertiser used was not logical. It did not recognize that there could be a difference in the cost to the agency of handling two accounts of the same size. As an alternative,

---

[7] The agency does not give a discount of its 15 percent commission, as that represents a payment for services for which cash discounts are not customary.

[8] The American Association of Advertising Agencies likewise signed such a consent decree, agreeing not to make a no-rebating stipulation a requisite for membership.

they suggested that the total agency compensation for handling the account be separately negotiated between the advertiser and the agency, and that the commissions the agency gets on that account be credited to the advertiser. (Before the consent decrees, that would have been called "rebating," and not sanctioned.)

The fee idea was not new. Industrial and medical agencies, whose commissions on the low-cost trade-paper space were not adequate compensation for their work, had long worked on a minimum-fee basis. Even advertisers who had been on the "commission" system invariably paid a service charge on production and other special services, so that as a practical matter, there has always been a separate agreement between agency and advertiser as to how the agency was to be paid. It wasn't until the early 1960s that a prominent agency announced it agreed to handle a major account on a completely free basis. Negotiated fee arrangements are more common now, varying widely in what the agency is to do for how much.

"If any generalizations can be made regarding the comparative costs of agency service under fees and commissions," said the Association of National Advertisers in its report on the subject, they would be these:

> Savings to advertisers are most likely to occur under a fee arrangement when the advertising budget is concentrated in mass media, the advertiser's creative or service needs are limited, and/or the client is largely self-sufficient in marketing. When these conditions are not present, the converse is more likely to be the case.[9]

THE FULL-SERVICE HOUSE AGENCY

A full-service house agency, referred to just as a "house agency," is one that is owned by an advertiser and does all the work of an independent full-service agency. Such an agency can handle the advertising of other firms, too. In the early years of the century, there were many house agencies: Procter & Gamble used to have one—the Procter & Collier Company of Cincinnati—but like many other early advertisers, they gave up this practice in favor of independent agencies.

The chief reason an advertiser has a house agency is to save a part of the 15 percent commission from which the agency derives its income. The advertiser also seeks the additional profit that he believes might accrue from a more efficient total operation. Full-service house agencies have, on the whole, not worked out well. To save a part of the 15 percent, advertisers have often

---

[9] New York Association of National Advertisers, Inc., *Fee Methods of Agency Compensation*, p. 65. Copyright 1969.

sacrificed what they were getting for the 85 percent. In the world of independent agencies, skilled men who prove their talent move up rapidly in
compensation. The house agency is drawn into the slower and smaller com-
pensation-raise policy of the large corporation. As a result, house agencies
generally cannot attract and hold the best creative talent. Their work tends
to become inbred because of lack of contact with the problems of other advertisers. Many advertisers who have acquired recognized full-service agencies have given up such house agencies and gone back to the independents.

THE IN-HOUSE AGENCY

Four developments in the late 1960's gave birth to another new structure in
advertising—the *in-house agency*. First was the pressure by large advertisers
for ways to save money in their total advertising operation and to improve
the special type of service they needed.

Second was the quest for creative talent wherever an advertiser could
find it. Sometimes advertisers found fine work being turned out by a small
agency, which they could retain on a fee basis, just for that work. Soon there
appeared on the scene men who got together to form just a creative service,
generally called a *boutique*. Among them were men who had made their mark
in big agencies; also, while working for agencies, did moonlighting on other
assignments.

The third factor was that numerous agencies made some of their
services available on an *à la carte basis* (also called a *modular* basis). Some
agencies would offer to place the ready-made ads (prepared by the advertiser) for a percentage of the 15 percent commission they received from the
media.

The fourth development was the appearance of *independent media
services*, especially in the field of television and broadcasting, prepared to
handle as much of the total media operation as an agency or advertiser desired.

Thus an advertiser could, if he wished, buy his creative work from a
creative service, buy his media through a media service, and place his advertising through a recognized agency that would charge only a small part of its
commission for clearing the ads.

But it takes internal coordination and a considerable amount of skill
to handle such an internal operation—which is referred to as an *in-house
agency* to distinguish it from the *full-service house agency* or the full-service
outside agency. Such an arrangement is suitable, if at all, for large advertisers
only, as it takes a sizable appropriation to warrant the cost of hiring talent
capable of handling such an operation, and to keep it busy full time.

Advertisers using an in-house agency may do so on some of their projects, as in the case of a new product on which they wish to keep fingertip control, and continue to use independent agencies on other assignments, either on a full-service or à la carte basis.

Two Views on Agency Operations

What the new breed of marketers wants is to be able to move fast, to avoid endless meetings, to make their advertising more attuned to their dealers and their salesmen. Companies such as Monsanto and Thom McAn Shoes switched to free-lance creative services partly to get faster action; they churn out a lot of different ads and they need quick results.

—From an editorial in *Advertising Age,*
September 9, 1971, p. 12.

Western Electric Company, a wholly owned subsidiary of the American Telephone and Telegraph Company, invited three agencies to solicit its account. "Only full-service agencies were in the running," explained Mr. John F. Rhame, Director of Advertising. "We want things available right there when we want them."

—*New York Times,* April 22, 1971, p. 69.

Competing Accounts

The relationship between client and agency is a professional one. The agency will share many of the client's confidences, often including plans for new products. Therefore, a full-service agency will not, as a rule, accept the advertising of products in direct competition with those it is currently handling. This has led to many conflicts in this age of conglomerates, when a client may buy a company one of whose products competes with one the agency is presently handling. When two agencies consider merging, the first question is, Will any of their accounts conflict? This subject also presents a problem in dealing with free-lance creative services.

The Agency of Record

Large advertisers will have a number of agencies handling the advertising of their various divisions and products. To coordinate the total media buy, and the programming of products in a network buy, the advertiser will appoint one agency as the *agency of record.* It will make the corporate media contracts under which other agencies will issue their orders, keep a record of all the advertising placed, and transmit management's decisions as to the allotment of time and space in a schedule. For this service, the agencies involved pay a small part of their commissions to the agency of record.

In the 1920's, Lynn Ellis, an advertising management consultant, saw the problem of middle-size agencies that had no branch offices to handle the regional problems of their clients. He organized a group of such agencies— one in each main advertising center—into a "network," to help each other on any problem in their respective areas, and to exchange ideas, experiences, and facilities. The success of this plan has prompted the formation of other agency networks.

INTERNATIONAL AGENCY OPERATIONS

Virtually every large American agency has branch offices in the lands where their clients conduct their international business; there are such branches in 88 countries throughout the world. A report of the five leading agencies whose stock is publicly owned disclosed that in 1971 profits on their international operations averaged 44 percent of their total profits.[10]

Having branch offices also serves as a defensive step for agencies. If an agency does not have a foreign office to serve an overseas client, that advertiser will turn to the branch office of an agency that does have such facilities, opening the door to that competitive agency to take over the main American part of the billings—the largest of all.

However, setting up a foreign office involves more than setting up a branch office within the United States. Each land is a different market, with its own language, buying habits, ways of living, mores, business methods, marketing traditions, and laws affecting business. In recognition of this, most American agencies wishing to operate abroad make some financial arrangement with a successful agency, purchasing a majority or minority interest. On the question of manning such an operation, *Business Week* reports:

> Strong local management is a necessity, not only because natives know consumer likes and dislikes far better than most foreigners, but because the once-popular idea of sending Americans to "show them how it's done" seldom works out in practice.[11]

Instead of trying to staff the foreign agency branch with some of their own personnel, American agencies usually appoint a top management man at the head of the overseas branches, then regularly gather the key members of their international offices at the main office for an intensive seminar on the philosophy and operation of the agency, for them to carry back and adapt as they see fit.

---

[10] Loeb, Rhoades & Co. (New York), Industry Survey, May 1972.
[11] *Business Week*, September 12, 1970, p. 81.

Review Questions

1. Give a brief description or explanation of the following:
   a. full service agency
   b. collateral services
   c. traffic department
   d. plans board
   e. agency recognition
   f. 1956 consent decree
   g. fee system
   h. agency of record
   i. agency network

2. What were the steps taken by N. W. Ayer & Son, and the Curtis Publishing Company, that placed the advertising agency in a new role?

3. Discuss the primary functions of a full-service advertising agency?

4. Describe the major responsibilities of the account management director. Of the creative director. Of the media director.

5. Define agency commission and explain how the system works. What is and is not included?

6. Distinguish between the house agency, the in-house agency, and the independent agency.

Reading Suggestions

Advertising Age, "The Centennial of the J. Walter Thompson Company," December 7, 1964.

American Association of Advertising Agencies, *A Handbook for the Advertising Agency Account Executive.* Reading, Mass.: Addison-Wesley Publishing Company, Inc., 1969.

Barton, Roger, ed., *Handbook of Advertising Management.* New York: McGraw-Hill Book Company, Inc., 1970.

Calkins, Earnest Elmo, *Modern Advertising.* New York: Appleton-Century-Crofts, 1905.

Gerson, Irving B., *Tomorrow's Advertising "Agency."* Chicago: Gerson, Howe & Johnson, Inc., 1970.

Hower, R. M., *The History of an Advertising Agency,* rev. ed., Cambridge, Mass.: Harvard University Press, 1949.

King, William R., "A Conceptual Framework for Ad Agency Compensation," *Journal of Marketing Research,* May 1968, pp. 177–180. Also in Kleppner and Settel, *Exploring Advertising,* p. 310.

Loomis, Carol J., "Those Throbbing Headaches on Madison Avenue," *Fortune,* February 1972, p. 103ff.

Lowndes, Douglas, *Marketing: The Uses of Advertising.* Elmsford, N.Y.: Pergamon Press, Inc., 1969.

Television Age, "Agency Presidents View the Next Ten Years," June 3, 1968, pp. 21–22. Excerpted in Kleppner and Settel, *Exploring Advertising,* p. 318.

Weiss, E. B., "The Shape of the Agency Business Beyond 1980," *Advertising Age,* June 26, 1972, p. 61. This is the first in a series of ten monthly feature articles on the future of advertising.

Wyman, S., and Herbert Maneloveg, "Agency Service: A la Carte or Full Fare," *Advertising Age,* February 7, 1972, p. 49ff.

25

The Media Services

ONE OF THE MOST significant changes in advertising in many years has been the development and acceptance of media services, which appeared on the scene in the late 1960's.

BACKGROUND

The most ephemeral thing in television and radio is commercial time. To a television or radio station, commercial time that isn't sold today is income lost forever. A newspaper can adjust the number of its pages to the amount of advertising scheduled; so can a magazine within limits. But TV and radio stations have no such flexibility; they must be on the air for the licensed period of time. Mindful of this fact, time buyers, holding an extensive schedule in their hands, have long been approaching stations, offering to buy "if the price is right." It might be a lower rate for the entire schedule; it might be more spots per dollar; it might be getting a greater proportion of spots in desirable time at the same price as spots in less desirable time periods.

To the station it meant the assurance of some income for time that might otherwise be lost. To the advertiser, it meant getting more for his TV and radio dollar. The prowess of an agency's media operation was judged by the way it could stretch the advertiser's dollar. The name of the game was negotiation.

The media-buying services grew out of this long-followed trade practice.

THE MEDIA SERVICES APPEAR

There had long been an industry created by entrepreneurs who had developed a plan for acquiring large blocks of radio and television time at low prices, through a barter arrangement (which we will discuss later), and selling that time below card rates. They came to the advertiser from the time-selling side. But in the 1960's, a new breed of men came into the field—most of them former senior executives of large agencies—who set up independent media

I.   1. PRODUCT _____   2. Date: _____

3. Budget: $ (M) _____   4. Advertising Period: Start date _____ ;   End date _____

II. 5. PURPOSE OF PLAN (Check where applicable):

a) _____ Introduction   b) _____ Annual   c) _____ Heavy-Up   d) _____ Weight test   (_____ hi; _____ low)

4) _____ Other (pls. explain): _____

_____

III. 6. MARKETING OBJECTIVES (Pls. describe briefly the two or three objectives you feel should govern the product's strategy e.g.
a) Where advertised must use competive pressure;
b) Color a must):

a) _____

b) _____

c) _____

IV. AUDIENCE (Pls. check primary and secondary audiences by categories shown):

	Primary Audience	Secondary Audience
7. Sex	: ____ Female _____ Male	_____ Female _____ Male
8. Age (Yrs)	: ____ to 6; _____ 6-11; _____ 12-17; _____ 18-35; _____ 36-49; _____ 50+	_____ to 6; _____ 6-11; _____ 12-17; _____ 18-35; _____ 36-49; _____ 50+
9. Income ($M)	: ____ Under 5. _____ 5.-9.9 _____ Over 10	_____ Under 5. _____ 5.-9.9 _____ Over 10
10. Region*	: ____ NE ____ EC _____ WC _____ S _____ P	_____ NE _____ EC _____ WC _____ S _____ P
11. County Size*	: ____ A _____ B _____ C _____ D	_____ A _____ B _____ C _____ D

*Nielsen

V. GEOGRAPHIC SALES   (Pls. first show percent of product's sales by its sales territories, secondly your best estimate of
how percents would fall if best potentials by sales territories could be realized.)

							% Tot.
12. Territories:	____	____	____	____	____	____	100.0
13. % Sales:	____	____	____	____	____	____	100.0
14. % Potentials:	____	____	____	____	____	____	100.0

A MEDIA PLANNING DATA SHEET

Showing the key questions involved in creating a media plan.

584

VI. <u>SEASONAL SALES</u> (Pls. repeat same procedure as in V):

			1st				2nd				3rd				4th	Grand
	J	F	M	Tot.	A	M	J	Tot.	J	A	S	Tot	O	N	D	Tot.	Total

15. % Sales: __ __ __ __ __ __ __ __ __ __ __ __ __ __ __ __

16. % Potential: __ __ __ __ __ __ __ __ __ __ __ __ __ __ __ __

VII. <u>COPY</u> (Pls. check copy lengths and sizes available for consideration):

TV %	Radio %	Mags. %	Newsp. %	Outdr. %
60″	60″	P-4C	ROP	24
30″	30″	P-BW	Color	30

Other ___ __   _____ __   _____ __   _____ __   _____ __

VIII. <u>MEDIA</u>

18. Reach & Frequency (Pls. check the relationship of reach to frequency you feel most pertinent to this product):

_____ Reach more important _____ Reach less important _____ Reach and frequency equal

19. Competition (Pls. list share of market, advertising budgets and distribution among major media of product and its three largest competitors):

	Mkt. Share	Ad. Bud. $M	TV Net	TV Spot	Radio	Mags	Newsps	Outdr	Other	Total
Prod.	•	•								100.00
A.	•	•								100.00
B.	•	•								100.00
C.	•	•								100.00

IX. 20. OTHER CONSIDERATIONS (Pls. check other items which must be considered in constructing this media plan):

a. _____ corporate network support

b. _____ ethnic and/or special market support

c. _____ coupon and/or sampling promotion support

d. _____ others

SIGNED: _____
                                CLIENT

SIGNED: _____
                                VMI PARTNER

Courtesy: Vitt Media International, Inc.

services, performing whatever part of the total media operation an advertiser or agency might require—planning, scheduling, negotiating, verifying. The chief service featured by most of them was at the pocketbook level, in negotiating the purchase of time on behalf of the advertiser . . . and thus the independent media services were born.

The heads of the media services believed they could save the advertiser money by operating with an experienced staff of negotiators and media technicians, concentrating on media function only. They also felt they might be able to save agencies money in handling some phases of their own media operations. Upon their ability to make good on this challenge rests the survival and success of the independent media service.

The advent of these services was also in response to the quest of some advertisers to retain specialists to handle their work, operating on an in-house-agency basis. Some advertisers also saw that competition in media negotiations would result in the best rates for the advertiser—and media services represented competition to the agency's media department.

How Media Services Function

A media service is retained by an advertiser or an agency at *one or both* of two points in time:

1. *When initial media planning is being done.* The service may develop the plan for the agency or advertiser, or the service may counsel them in the development of the plan from its specialized knowledge of media usages and media rates.
2. *When the media plan is ready to be executed, and the media buying is ready to be done.* If the media service has developed the plan, then after approval by the agency or advertiser, it proceeds to purchase the media schedules according to the specifications. If the plan has been developed by the agency or advertiser, the media service reviews the specifications of the plan and agrees to accept responsibility for purchase of media schedules that will meet the specifications.

After the media buys have been made, the media service provides the agency or advertiser with summaries of the media schedules purchased and estimates of the audience delivered. Generally, the media service will also verify schedule performance (by means of television or radio-station affidavits or print-media checking copies), check on preemptions and make-goods, and pay the media. Some of the media services will also provide the agency or advertiser with a "post-buy analysis," documenting the audience delivery of the media schedule according to syndicated research-service measurements of the media schedule as it ran. Generally this is what agencies do also; the media services try to do it better.

There is no standard method of compensation. Each service makes its own arrangements with the advertiser or the agency, based on the services it is to perform. The media still pay the agency commissions. Two arrangements are current examples of methods being followed: One is a set fee based on total billings; another is an incentive arrangement, such as the following: The fee the buying service earns comes out of dollars saved. This means all specifications and objectives must be met prior to a fee's being earned. An example of an incentive arrangement is as follows:

1. Once all objectives have been met for budgeted dollars, the first 5% of all dollars saved reverts to the buying service.
2. The next 10% of all dollars saved reverts to the client.
3. Thereafter, all dollars saved are split 50-50.
4. The agency commission is paid on gross media cost.

RELATIONSHIP OF MEDIA SERVICES TO AGENCIES

Although the specialized skill offered by media services is sometimes employed by advertisers, frequently advertising agencies avail themselves of the media services to augment their own media staff.

In those instances, use of outside media services can also reduce their nonmedia servicing and overhead costs. To the small-to-medium agency, a media service may also be helpful in case of a sudden increase in the work load. Some have found that they can use the media services to buy more effectively than they can do themselves.

Where the media service is retained on an incentive basis by the advertiser who also retains an agency, the agency generally receives full agency commission on gross media costs.

WORKING WITH MEDIA SERVICES

Grey Advertising agency, which has used independent media services in connection with its own media operation, offers the following suggestions on using media services:

1. *Media planning must be very specific.* It must spell out all facets of the buy. It must insist on spot-by-spot reporting to avoid averaging within or between markets. The number and spread of stations to be bought must be specified. The method of estimating ratings should be agreed upon in advance. Merchandising requirements should be spelled out, and documentation of all facts and costs should be insisted upon.

2. *All post-buy analysis should examine in depth how closely the buy met all specifications* set up in the original plan, such as delivery of target audiences, achievement of estimated rating goals.

3. *All checking, including affidavits from stations, station logs, etc., must be carefully done.* Checking and evaluating should be done over an extended period of time. One flight alone is not a sufficient test.[1]

BARTER

Barter is another way for an advertiser or agency to buy time below card rates. It has nothing to do with media services; it is an alternative method, which works on a completely different principle. We discuss it in this chapter as a matter of convenience only.

Long before barter, as practiced today in the buying of television and radio time, appeared on the scene, hotels began a practice that they continue to this day, of paying for advertising space in exchange for *due bills,* which were good for the payment of rooms. They bartered their rooms for advertising space. The barter system has developed into an $80-million industry in the buying and selling of radio and television time, below card rates. The operation extends to print advertising also.

Barter in broadcasting began in the early days of radio, when cash was always tight (even as it often is today), and studios would have to spend a lot of money for equipment, and also arrange for gifts to be given away at the quiz shows. Some entrepreneurs got the idea that they would get these goods at very low cost, and barter them with the stations in exchange for blocks of time on the air—again at a very low rate—and then sell that time to advertisers below card rates. (One firm holds forth a savings of 50 to 70 percent on radio and 20 to 50 percent on television.) The Federal Communications Commission has held that bartering for broadcast time is legal.

Firms that handle barter will supply a station anything it needs in barter for time, but the chief subject of barter is program material in the form of films—a constant need of TV stations. These include Hollywood films, films of popular old TV programs, and, more important, films of current popular TV series, which the barter houses control. All of this involves no cash disbursement to the station.

Some barter houses now pay cash for blocks of spot time, virtually becoming brokers or wholesalers of time. They build up an inventory of time for sale below card rates, which they then offer to advertisers or agencies.

Of course, barter has its drawbacks. Often the weaker stations in a market go most for it. Some stations won't accept barter business from ad-

---

[1] *Grey Matter,* June 1970. Published by Grey Advertising, Inc., New York.

vertisers already on the air in the market. Much of the time is poor time (even though it is still good value at the low rate paid). Prime or fringe time is usually preemptable. Barter time is often treated by the stations like a second-class passenger. The advertiser or agency does not deal directly with the station; it deals with barter houses, who then deal directly with the station. Problems of make-goods can be sticky.

Today barter is a flourishing practice, used for many well-known products.

TRADE-OUT SYNDICATED SHOWS

Advertisers themselves have entered the field of bartering, or syndicating, their broadcast productions, meaning that they produce a TV or radio show at their own expense and include their own commercials, then offer a film or tape of that show to stations for their own use, without financial outlay. The station is then free to sell the rest of the available commercial time.

The advertiser is bartering the cost of the production for the time of his own commercials. *Advertising Age* announced that the Coca-Cola Company would barter six half-hour auto-racing specials to be sponsored in local markets by local Coca-Cola bottlers, and that the Pillsbury Company would produce two more Magic Circus one-hour specials for syndication. These would be numbers 3 and 4 in a series of one-hour telecasts starring magician Mark Wilson. The first of these specials was aired in 101 markets.[2]

The advantage to the advertiser in providing these *trade-out syndicated shows,* as they are called, which are costly to produce, is that he is assured of good spots for his own commercials, and since he is offering the station good-quality programming, he is able to obtain advertising time efficiently.

Review Questions

1. Describe what services a media service firm performs.

2. Discuss the several major reasons behind the development of media services.

3. At what points might such a service be used by an advertiser or agency?

4. Compare the guidelines suggested in the text for effectively using media services with those you might employ as an advertiser working with your own or your agency's media buying department.

5. Define and describe the barter method of buying time.

6. What are trade-out syndicated programs? What are their advantages for the advertiser? For the station?

---

[2] *Advertising Age,* December 6, 1971, p. 63.

Dannehower, Gilbert, and Sam Wyman, "The Case for the Independent Media Buying Services," *Madison Avenue,* February 1972, p. 12ff.

Manoff, Richard, "Negotiating with the Negotiators," *Media Decisions,* May 1971, p. 36.

"Media Buying, Inside and Out," *Media Decisions,* December 1969, p. 27.

"The Day of the Media Consultant," *Media Decisions,* May 1971, p. 78.

"Now They're Edging into Print," *Media Decisions,* October 1970, p. 27.

26

The Manufacturer's
Advertising Department

WHEN A MANUFACTURER FIRST decides to advertise, someone has to be made responsible for ordering the advertising, having it produced and placed, and following up on it. On that day, an advertising department has been launched; the man in charge becomes the advertising manager. The advertiser may also appoint an agency, whose function and that of the advertising department differ. Basically, the chief function of the agency is to plan, create and place advertising designed to meet the advertiser's marketing goals. The chief function of the advertising manager and his department is to direct and administer the whole advertising effort, to provide needed advertising services other than those performed by the agency, within the framework of the marketing plans of the company, and to administer the budget.

From such beginnings, large advertising departments have grown, responsible for budgets running into millions of dollars.

ORGANIZATION OF THE ADVERTISING DEPARTMENT

Each advertising department is unique, reflecting the personality of its management and its corporate planning and marketing needs. Even the titles of the chief advertising functionaries differ—advertising manager, advertising director, vice-president in charge of advertising, or vice-president in charge of marketing. In an extensive survey among its members, the Association of National Advertisers found advertising functions to be organized in certain patterns, as follows: [1]

By product	40%
By subfunction of advertising	19
By market (end-user)	18
By media	9
By geography	5
Other, or a combination of these	9

[1] The Association of National Advertisers, Inc., *The A.N.A. Advertising/Marketing Organization Study* (New York, 1967), p. 7.

Organization by product (40%). If the company has one product, the whole advertising department will be dedicated to it, under an *advertising manager* or *director*. If it has more than one product, or divisions of products, the advertising of each may be assigned to one man, often called the *brand* or *divisional advertising manager,* under the company advertising director. This structure is the most prevalent organizational form.

Organization by subfunction of advertising (19%). In this setup, the advertising department is divided into activity areas, as print media buying, TV/radio buying, television production, print production, outdoor advertising, print media, sales promotion. This arrangement is found chiefly among the very large advertisers with several agencies. Each functionary serves as an expert in his field in dealing with the agencies on those subjects.

Organization by market (end user) (18%). This refers to large producers of raw material, whose finished products end up in different marketing worlds. The Celanese Corporation has one division selling chemicals and plastics; another selling textile fibers. The Gulf Oil Company has one division selling oil, another antifreeze, another chemicals, another petroleum and specialty products. Each is a world apart, marketwise. Each has its own advertising department.

Organization by media (9%). The same as by subfunction of advertising, except limited to media.

Organization by geography (5%). The advertising function is organized according to the marketing territorial divisions. Shell Oil Company, for example, has West Coast, Midwest, and East Coast offices.

CENTRALIZED OR DECENTRALIZED CONTROL

Just what does the advertising department do? How does it relate to other departments? This brings us to the question of centralized or decentralized control.

Centralized Advertising Control

In a centralized-control advertising operation, we have an advertising manager who reports to a top marketing executive—or in a few cases (mostly large industrial firms or utilities) to the director of public relations—from whom he gets his budget, marketing directives, and information. He is responsible for the total advertising operation; in a majority of cases, this includes sales promotion. Most companies with budgets under one million dollars have centralized operations; a number above that figure do too.

The advertising manager. Perhaps the best way to see what an
advertising department of a national advertiser does is to look at it through
the eyes of the advertising manager. Here is a partial *composite* list of what
the responsibilities of different advertising managers include:

593
*The
Manufacturer's
Advertising
Department*

1. Get a budget approach.

2. Prepare an advertising plan within the budget set by management.

3. Make recommendations for an agency if one has not already been chosen. (Usually top management makes final decision.)

4. If the company plans to use modular or outside services, select the services, direct and coordinate their efforts.

5. If the company uses a full service agency, get sharp definition of work they will do, and charges; organize handling of rest of work, such as sales promotion.

6. Inform agency of all pertinent marketing data needed to make their plans on target. Guide the direction of their efforts. Tell them *what* is needed. The *how* is up to them.[2]

7. Review and pass upon plans and advertisements submitted by agency. Get final approval on new material from top management.

8. Negotiate corporate media buys for use in all the advertising divisions of the company.

9. Supervise planning and creation, also production, of sales-promotion material, including displays and printed pieces.

10. Prepare, issue, and control cooperative advertising.

11. Keep sales force informed of all forthcoming advertising.

---

[2] This dichotomy is that of Clarence Eldridge.

Advertisement, New York
Times

12. Organize, plan, and direct issuance of dealer advertising service.

13. Working with sales department, help plan sales drives.

14. See that all bills are checked; keep a strict account of funds and status of budget, including costs of jobs in work and non-cancellable commitments.

15. Build and train a staff that can grow.

16. Have plans ready for next year's proposal and budget recommendations.

The departmental organization. There are many ways and combinations of ways to organize the work within the department. We have here a series of basic schematic charts that may clarify the allocation of responsibility.[3]

Chart 1 shows a department organized by product or marketing division. A man, generally referred to as the *advertising brand manager,* may be assigned to handle each of these units; he may handle several brands.

Chart **1**

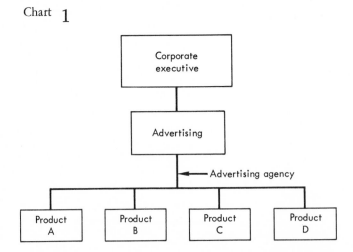

Chart 2 shows a centralized advertising and sales-promotion department organized by advertising subfunction. These subfunctions may vary, as sales promotion, publicity, art and production, exhibits and displays, but each represents specialists who work with the brand or product managers. The media department, for example, would negotiate all the deals for corporate rates from the media. This setup is found chiefly among the very large advertisers.

---

[3] Roger Barton, ed., *Handbook of Advertising Management* (New York: McGraw-Hill Book Company, 1970), pp. 4–8.

Chart 2

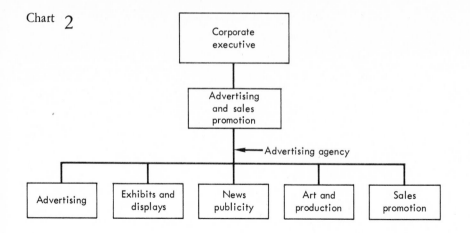

Chart 3 shows a centralized department organized by product, with supporting functional units. The brand managers get their budgets and their directives from the advertising director. Each of the advertising brand managers may avail himself of aid from the respective company departments.

Chart 3

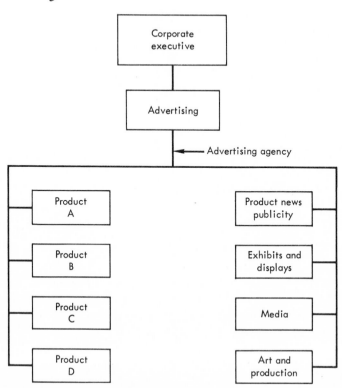

The chief feature of the centralized advertising operation is that the flow of authority is from a central top-management source to whom the advertising director is responsible.

Decentralized Advertising Control

The decentralized advertising department has a different structure. It is usually found in large companies with many marketing divisions. Each division or company will represent a separate marketing team. Each will be headed by a *product brand manager* (not to be confused with the advertising brand manager in charge of the advertising of the brand). The product brand manager is completely responsible for sales and profits. He is the one who decides what is needed for the advertising function, and he has an agency assigned to him. (Chart 4)

There is also a corporate advertising department with a staff of specialists that work with agencies and brand managers. It has a media department that makes the bulk time and space contract deals for the entire corporation. It may have a TV production department, bringing the total experiences of the company to bear on the production of commercials for any division; it will have a research department. All these departments are available to the product brand managers for advice on technical operating questions.

The pioneers in the product-manager concept (which bypasses the advertising-manager concept) are Procter & Gamble, of whose brand-manager system *Television Age* had this to say:

> The brand manager came to work closely with the account executive to give his product the greatest degree of push. Unlike salesmen, who

Chart 4

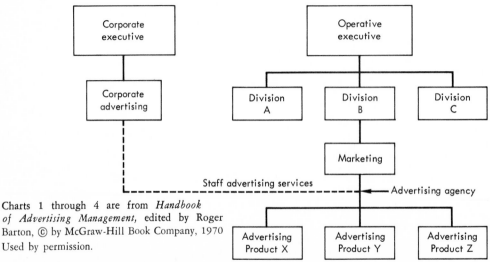

Charts 1 through 4 are from *Handbook of Advertising Management,* edited by Roger Barton, © by McGraw-Hill Book Company, 1970 Used by permission.

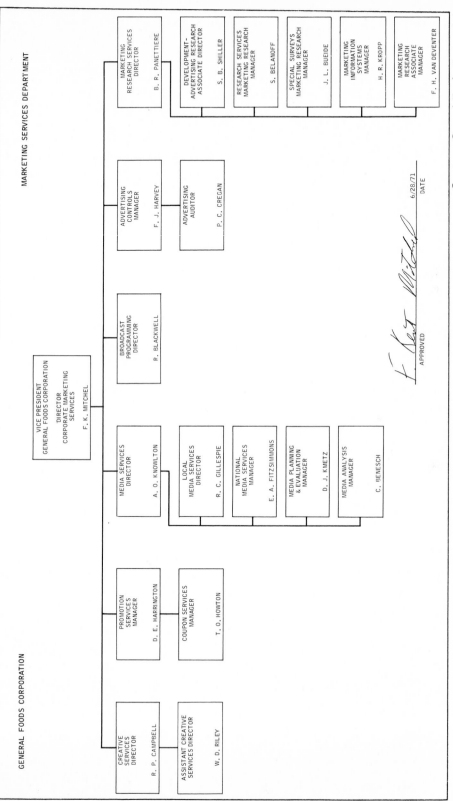

ORGANIZATION CHART, GENERAL FOODS CORPORATION, MARKETING SERVICES DEPARTMENT   Courtesy: General Foods Corporation

Each representing a specialist in some phase of the marketing activity. Available for guidance of brand managers; also coordinating all the activities of the respective areas and giving all brands the benefit of the corporate experience.

handled the full line, the brand man focused all his talent and energies on that single objective.

He's not alone. He is not only free to call on the company's other departments for help, he's expected to. As the modern P & G brand manager operates, advertising gives him the biggest boost. He makes use of all its sections: copy, art and packaging, media, sampling and couponing, and legal. He relies on market research to determine the packages, the scents, the sizes, the colors people want—on product research to improve his brand when competition begins breathing down its label—on sales to pry shelf space for it out of reluctant grocers and druggists.

The typical P & G brand manager is young, tough-minded, and a relentless competitor—whether he's going against a product being pushed by Lever or by his counterpart down the hall at P & G, or, as is often the case, both.

The brand man selects the type and extent of promotion for his product, then works out a budget. But he has to make it pay off in the test market before he's allowed to play for keeps.

From the outside, Procter & Gamble is a tremendous corporate structure that manufactures some 65 products. But from the inside, it is, in effect, 65 efficiently managed, doggedly competitive, single-product companies, each able to draw on apparently inexhaustible reserves of money, research brains, advertising talent, and sales muscle. And it all pivots on the brand managers.[4]

The Advertising Budget

"Management is called upon to make no decisions that are more important, or that can more significantly affect the health, growth, and profitability of the business," said Eldridge, "than those involving the marketing budget. In many companies whose success depends upon effective marketing programs, the cost of marketing is the largest controllable expense; in some companies the cost of marketing a product is even greater than the cost of producing it—including raw materials, labor, and packaging costs." [5]

The decision on how much to invest in advertising is an outgrowth of the total operating philosophy of the company, its long-term and short-term goals. It is based also on how important a role advertising plays in the sale of goods of an industry. It is far more important in the sale of consumer goods than for industrial goods. Within one class of consumer goods, there is a big variation between companies also, as we discussed in Chapter 3.

---

[4] *Television Age,* July 29, 1968, pp. 39–40. Reproduced by permission.
[5] Clarence E. Eldridge, *The Marketing Budget and Its Allocation in the Advertising Budget* (New York: Association of National Advertisers, Inc., 1967), p. 25.

The Federal Trade Commission issues figures of expenditures by industry, but these are poor guides in setting a budget. Different companies charge different things to advertising. Some charge samples and exhibits; some don't. Some include overhead; some don't. Furthermore, the figures are a composite of a total industry, nonadvertisers and advertisers, large advertisers and small ones. As a practical matter, mindful of all the variables, and of the other demands on the company purse strings, advertisers use a number of ways to arrive at a budget for advertising.

1. Percentage-of-sales method
2. The task method
3. Share-of-market method
4. Use of mathematical models
5. Empirical method

Percentage-of-sales method. When a company has been operating for many years, it may have built up its data of budget experience in terms of the ratio of its advertising to sales. It may take last year's dollar figure as a base for this year's advertising, projected to this year's anticipated sales. This method has tradition behind it, and it is convenient; it is subject to periodic review in the light of sales. However, it looks backward; it may be perpetuating the mistakes of yesterday. What steps are being taken in a test market to see whether the company wouldn't do better to spend a greater percentage of sales than last year? Using past percentage as a base, the company may increase the figure for the coming year to recognize the increased cost of media and production, as well as because they have more aggressive marketing plans.

The method of using a percentage of past sales as a base of consideration for next year's budget is common.

The task method. This is a method very widely used. By this method, the company gives itself a specific sales goal, asks what will have to be done to help attain that goal, adds up the cost, asks whether it can afford the risk, and says, "Let's go—but let's watch it."

In speaking of the task method, Charles W. Mortimer, who rose through the advertising and marketing ranks to the presidency of the General Foods Corporation, had this to say:

> The task method is built brick by brick; not pulled out of a hat, or divined with a willow wand. . . . It is based on a concrete estimate of the job to be done. It uses extensively past advertising experience—all that is available—but never accepts any rule of thumb or past statistical relation as a sufficient guide for expenditures without reexamination of the nature of the task and the most promising method of

accomplishing it *this* year—not *last* year. It involves constant awareness of what the competitors are doing with respect to advertising
themes and expenditures, but it does not blindly follow the competitor's program.

The only safe assumption to make in determining advertising expenditures is that each year—or campaign—involves a task that is *new* in
some important respect. Old measurements and old answers, accepted
uncritically, are not good enough.[6]

The task method represents the same spirit of enterprise, confidence
in judgment, and willingness to back up that confidence with every dollar at
their command that made most of the large advertisers of today out of the
small advertisers of years ago.

Most budgets are based on a mixture of the percentage-of-sales and
task methods.

Share-of-market method. Peckham developed the idea of setting
the budget in relation to the share of market of an old or a new product, as
follows:

First, for *new* brands:

All calculations are made in terms of its share of the market for that
type of product. If a new brand is a good product from a consumer
point of view, its share of market bears a fairly close relationship to
its advertising and promotion investment.

Advertising expenditures on a new brand must take the total advertising of the entire field into account. The advertising necessary to
introduce a new brand in the grocery field should represent a share of
advertising approximately *twice* that of the share of sales the new
product feels it can attain at the end of the two-year period. In the
toilet goods field, the advertising–share-of-sales relationship is about
one and a half to one.

As an example, let us say we have a new product in the grocery field.
The total annual business of that type of product is $30,000,000.

Two-year sales goal—10% of market, or	$3,000,000
Total annual advertising in field	4,500,000
Annual advertising need, 20%, or	900,000

Next, for *established* brands:

---

[6] Charles G. Mortimer, Jr., "How much should you spend on advertising," in
Advertising Handbook, ed. Roger Barton (Englewood Cliffs, N.J.: Prentice Hall, Inc., pp.
113–15).

Assuming that you keep your brand (and its resulting advertising appeals) strictly up to date, the best insurance of maintaining or increasing your share of market is consistently to maintain your share of advertising at a point somewhat ahead of your share of sales.[7]

The advantage of this approach is that you deal with measurable quantities. A shortcoming is held to be that it tends to keep you up with the pack, instead of encouraging you to get ahead in your profit margin.

Use of mathematical models. To apply the technology of quantitative problem solving to setting the budget, Weinberg presented an analytic approach in a 125-page report published by the Association of National Advertisers. It is too long and technical to present here, but his statement of the problem is so lucid that we quote these excerpts:

1. How can the *overall* effectiveness of a company's *past* advertising programs be measured?
2. How can the *probable* level of advertising expenditures required to attain a *desired future* marketing objective be predicted?
3. How can the expected profitability of a future advertising program be estimated?
4. What criteria may be employed to develop an optimal *long-term* advertising program (i.e., an advertising program that maximizes the company's *future* profits)?
5. What criteria may be employed to determine the point at which "diminishing returns" makes an additional increment of advertising expenditure unprofitable?

Every business operates in four environments simultaneously. These environments are as follows:

1. An economic environment
2. An internal environment
3. A competitive environment
4. An institutional environment

A company's net profits are dependent upon not less than five sets of factors:

1. The level of general economic activity, insofar as it affects total industry sales

---

[7] Based on addresses by J. O. Peckham, executive vice-president of the A. C. Nielsen Company, before the Grocery Manufacturers Association, November 12, 1963, and before the Toilet Goods Association, June 27, 1964.

2. The level of total industry sales, a share of which will represent company sales

3. The actions of the company's competitors, insofar as they will determine what share of the total industry market the company will capture

4. The actions of the company itself, insofar as they meet the actions of its competitors and insofar as they affect the company's profit–sales relation

5. The structure of tax rates, insofar as they determine that fraction of gross profits which will be available after taxes (i.e., the company's net profits after taxes)

Consider the factors outlined above. These factors reflect the four basic environments within which the company operates. In order to carry out a *truly meaningful analysis* of the *strategic impact* of advertising on the company's net profits, it is important to consider each of these factors simultaneously. Considering these factors individually or independently or not considering all the factors can often lead to erroneous conclusions regarding advertising contribution to the company's profits.[8]

This report is cited as an example of the advanced thinking in the quest to determine the optimum amount to spend on advertising.

Empirical method. This method holds that the way to determine the optimum amount to spend on advertising is to actually run a series of tests at different levels of advertising. One such test was conducted by the du Pont Company when it first introduced Teflon to the public.[9] Daytime television only was used for this test. Twelve test markets were used, in two flights of tests, spring and fall. The advertising in each market varied, from zero to one-half million dollars to one million dollars. The cost of the advertising was matched against the sales.

No difference in sales was found between the markets that had no advertising and those that had a half-million dollars in advertising, but there was a significant sales and profit effect at the million-dollar mark. The product was then introduced at that level of expenditure.

That still left the question of whether that was the optimum figure. Would increasing it continue to increase profits? Subsequent multilevel tests of higher expenditures involving 20 test markets were conducted, and in addi-

---

[8] Robert S. Weinberg, *An Analytical Approach to Advertising Expenditure Strategy* (New York: Association of National Advertisers, Inc., 1960).

[9] Malcolm A. McNiven, "Choosing the Most Profitable Level of Advertising: A Case Study," in *How Much to Spend for Advertising* (New York: Association of National Advertisers, Inc., 1969), p. 90.

tion, print media were tested along with television. The extremely high levels did not prove more profitable.

Here then was a test that proved how much was too little, how much too high, and at which point the advertising budget was most profitable. This method takes great planning, ample funds for testing, and discipline in not drawing hasty conclusions. But it shows what can be done.

Review Questions

1. Discuss the major responsibilities of the manufacturer's advertising department compared with those of its full-service advertising agency.

2. Describe some of the major patterns of company organization of the advertising function.

3. On what basis does an advertiser pay a creative group for their work?

4. Describe the job of the brand manager. How does he differ from a product advertising manager?

5. Describe and discuss each of the common methods of setting an advertising budget.

6. If you were asked how much advertising money you thought would be needed for launching a new brand of a grocery product, how would you go about getting an answer?

Reading Suggestions

Barton, Roger, ed., *Handbook of Advertising Management.* New York: McGraw-Hill Book Company, 1970.

Frey, Albert Wesley, "Approaches to Determining the Advertising Appropriation," in *Speaking of Advertising,* ed. by John S. Wright and Daniel S. Warner. New York: McGraw-Hill Book Company, 1963.

Friedman, Lawrence, "A Variable Budgeting System For Consumer Advertising," Marketing Science Institute Working Paper, 1970.

Fulmer, Robert M., "How Should Advertising and Sales Promotion Funds Be Allocated," *Journal of Marketing,* October 1967, pp. 8–11.

Kelly, Richard J., *The Advertising Budget.* New York: Association of National Advertisers, Inc., 1969.

McNiven, Malcolm, *How Much to Spend for Advertising.* New York:

Association of National Advertisers, Inc., 1969.

Media Decisions, "The New Breed in Media: The Product Manager," December 1967, pp. 13–17. Also in Kleppner and Settel, *Exploring Advertising,* p. 301.

Obermeyer, Henry, *Successful Advertising Management.* New York: McGraw-Hill Book Company, Inc., 1969.

Payne, Richard A., *The Men Who Manage the Brands You Buy.* Chicago: Crain Communications Inc., 1971.

Simon, Julian L., *The Management of Advertising.* Englewood Cliffs, N.J.: Prentice-Hall, Inc., 1971.

Stansfield, Richard, *Advertising Manager's Handbook.* Chicago: The Dartnell Corporation, 1969.

VII
OTHER WORLDS
OF ADVERTISING

## 27

Retail Advertising

THERE IS MORE MONEY spent for local newspaper advertising in the United States than for all of television advertising, or for all of magazine advertising, or for all of radio advertising. The fastest-growing classification of any medium—national or local—is local television advertising. The fastest-growing segment of radio advertising is that of local advertising,[1] and by far the greatest part of all local advertising is retail advertising, the world we enter in this chapter.

DIFFERENCES BETWEEN NATIONAL AND RETAIL ADVERTISERS

National advertising, as we have been speaking of it, refers chiefly to advertising done by a producer to get people to buy his branded goods, wherever they are sold. Retail advertising refers chiefly to that done by local merchants or service organizations, to attract customers to their local establishment for the goods and services they have to offer.

But some firms combine both activities. The outstanding example is Sears, which produces goods under its own name and trademarks, and advertises them nationwide—making it one of the largest national advertisers; Sears also has many stores which advertise under the Sears name in their respective communities, and thus are local advertisers.

Many franchise operations use national advertising to spread their reputations around the country, and local advertising to get the business of the immediate neighborhood. The fact that both forms of advertising are used by a single firm should not obscure the basic differences between national and local advertising.

In national advertising, the manufacturer says, "Buy this brand product at any store you can." The retail advertiser says, "Buy this product here. Better come early!"

In national advetrising, it is difficult to trace the sales effect of a single insertion of an ad, and to trace the effect of a series of them takes time and is difficult unless it runs exclusively in one medium. In retail advertising, a retailer can usually tell by noon the day after an ad appeared how well (or poorly) it is doing.

---

[1] 1970 figures. See p. 121.

A national advertiser speaks to a wide and distant audience. The retail advertiser works in the community in which he advertises. He knows the people, their life styles, their tastes.

A woman looks at national advertising whenever she happens to come upon it—in newspapers, magazines, television, or while listening to the radio. She reaches for her newspaper as a matter of ritual to see what is the latest that the department stores are offering in styles and values, and what the supermarkets are featuring.

The national advertiser has chiefly one product or one line of products to sell over a period of time. The retailer is faced by a relentless river of new styles and offerings he wishes to sell within a week, generating a great sense of urgency in the advertising department. It's a fast tempo.

Retail newspaper rates, as we have previously discussed, are lower than national rates—one of the factors that have given rise to cooperative advertising.

CLASSES OF RETAIL STORES

Retailing covers a wide variety of store and service operations. There is much shifting and overlapping among them. "Drug stores" sell radios, "food stores" carry garden furniture, and "discount" department stores sell food. For purposes of understanding the retail advertising problems, however, we consider the chief retailing operations to be:

      —Traditional department stores

      —Chain department stores

      —Discount stores

      —Supermarkets

      —Specialty shops

      —Catalogue merchandise stores

Each type of operation has its own pattern of merchandising and advertising operation. We consider each separately.

THE TRADITIONAL DEPARTMENT STORE

This refers to stores selling fashion apparel for different members of the family, along with general merchandise. It is arranged by departments, with individual clerks assigned to each. These stores emphasize customer service in other ways, too—with deliveries, dressing rooms with fitters' services, ease of returning merchandising, ladies' lounges, restaurants—all with a view to creating regular clientele. About 50 percent of their volume is on credit. Most of these stores began with what is now the "downtown" or "main" store, and then built branches in the suburbs.

These are the stores we usually have in mind when we say "department stores"; we label them here as *traditional department stores* to distinguish them from *chain department stores,* which have a different advertising outlook and operation, as do discount stores and specialty shops.

Types of Advertising

The kind of advertising done by a traditional department store stems directly from the kind of store the management wishes to operate, the type of trade it seeks, and the range of merchandise it plans to offer. This affects everything connected with the operation—store location, decor, degree of emphasis on latest styles, and types and price range of merchandise. It affects the advertising. All advertising of all stores has one thing in mind—to sell the specific article advertised, and to bring in store traffic, with the basic store policy as its frame of reference. Such advertising may be any of three types, or a combination of them.

Promotional advertising refers to an advertisement devoted to a specific product, such as dresses, bedspreads, lamps, china. Such advertisements reflect the efforts of a buyer to make a particularly advantageous purchase in terms of style, variety, and price. Promotional advertising can be that of individual items, or it may be devoted to goods of one particular department. Departmental advertisements are often built around a theme designed not merely to sell the particular items advertised, but to establish that department as a headquarters for such goods.

Next, there is the *advertising of sales,* including store-wide special sales events. Most stores have storewide special sales at the end of each season or on some annual or special promotional basis, such as Washington's Birthday, Anniversary Sale, Midsummer Sale. Special advertising will be prepared to move merchandise that may be growing stale, to try out new merchandise for the coming season, and above all, to generate traffic. There will also be departmental sales during the year to which advertising will be devoted.

Most traditional department store advertising is a mixture of the foregoing types.

Then there is *institutional advertising,* designed to give the whole store a lift in the esteem of the public, above and beyond its reputation for good merchandising. It may be to help some community project; it may be something the store is doing to bring pride to the community; it may be some advice to help a woman in her shopping knowledge of products. It makes no specific price offerings of merchandise.

Institutional advertising, as a rule, is a one-shot ad, created only when

A Promotional Ad

Designed to sell the specific merchandise pictured, as well as to attract buyers to the department.

A STORE-WIDE SALES AD

An Institutional Ad

Designed to get good will, rather than to sell specific merchandise.

there is something to say, or it may be a series of occasional ads devoted to an overall theme. The results are hard to trace. Most stores rely on their range of merchandise and the character of their advertising to help them establish an institutional image.

Much retail advertising is a blend of the foregoing forms.

A Typical Organizational Structure

At the head of the typical large department store will be the president, who makes the final decisions about all budgets, in addition to his other corporate responsibilities. There may be a series of senior vice-presidents, including one in charge of the merchandising of, let us say, soft goods; another in charge of the merchandising of hard goods; a third in charge of the merchandising of the budget store. The number of vice-presidents and the scope of their duties varies by the store.

Each merchandising vice-president will have under his wing a number of divisional merchandising managers, each of whom is responsible for a number of related departments headed by buyers, who are responsible for the profitability of their respective departments.

There will also be a vice-president, variously known as the publicity director, promotion director, or public relations director, who is in charge of all promotional activities, including advertising, public relations, displays, and signs. The advertising department, under him or her, will be in charge of an advertising manager.

The Department Store Advertising Department

The functional structure of most department store retail-advertising departments is something like this:

Advertising manager
  Manages total advertising operation
  Coordinates all the requests for space in a given period, and decides on space and paper for each department and each week

Copy chief
  Writers (working directly with the buyers)

Art director
  Staff artists (producing virtually all art work)

Production manager
  Staff that handles print production

Head of direct mail

Head of radio and television

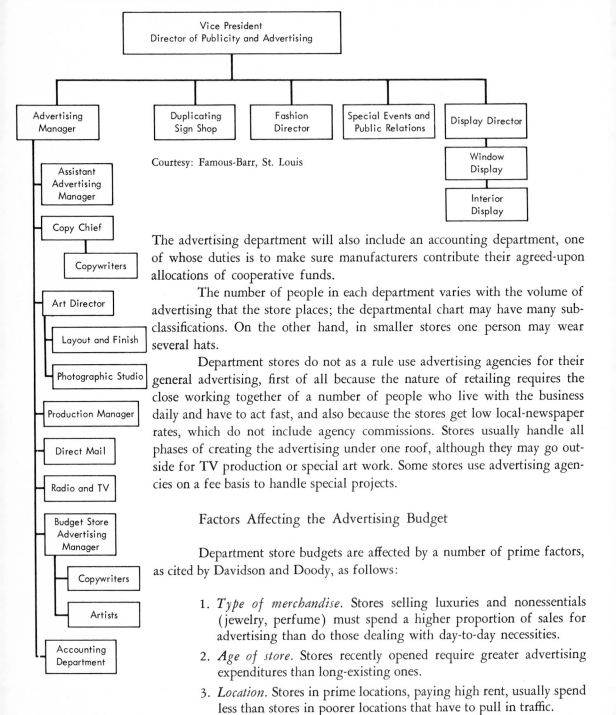

Courtesy: Famous-Barr, St. Louis

The advertising department will also include an accounting department, one of whose duties is to make sure manufacturers contribute their agreed-upon allocations of cooperative funds.

The number of people in each department varies with the volume of advertising that the store places; the departmental chart may have many sub-classifications. On the other hand, in smaller stores one person may wear several hats.

Department stores do not as a rule use advertising agencies for their general advertising, first of all because the nature of retailing requires the close working together of a number of people who live with the business daily and have to act fast, and also because the stores get low local-newspaper rates, which do not include agency commissions. Stores usually handle all phases of creating the advertising under one roof, although they may go outside for TV production or special art work. Some stores use advertising agencies on a fee basis to handle special projects.

Factors Affecting the Advertising Budget

Department store budgets are affected by a number of prime factors, as cited by Davidson and Doody, as follows:

1. *Type of merchandise.* Stores selling luxuries and nonessentials (jewelry, perfume) must spend a higher proportion of sales for advertising than do those dealing with day-to-day necessities.

2. *Age of store.* Stores recently opened require greater advertising expenditures than long-existing ones.

3. *Location.* Stores in prime locations, paying high rent, usually spend less than stores in poorer locations that have to pull in traffic.

4. *Competition.* The appropriation is affected by the amount of advertising done by competition.

5. *Store character.* Highly promotional stores tend to have higher advertising expenditures.[2]

There are many demands for the use of funds within a retail operation. In addition to funds for advertising expense, the top management must decide how much to allocate for buying expense, selling expense, display expense, and general store expense.

Once the funds for advertising have been decided upon by top management, the vice-president in charge of advertising and publicity joins in deciding how the funds are to be allocated to direct mail, radio and television, general institutional promotion, and contingencies.

But the major portion of the total budget will be devoted to newspaper advertising. These funds are then allocated to the general merchandising managers of the respective broad areas, such as hard lines, soft lines, and budget-store merchandise.

At this point there is usually a meeting of all divisional heads and buyers, along with the advertising director and publicity people, to establish long-range merchandising and advertising programs for the year, such as the annual store events. Usually this is set up in terms of a fall and winter calendar.

---

[2] William R. Davidson and Alton F. Doody, *Retailing Management,* 3rd ed. (New York: The Ronald Press Company, 1966), p. 639, excerpted.

A typical sales promotion calendar showing the variety of store-wide sales events scheduled for the period.

FALL PROMOTION CALENDAR

Month	Week	Last Year (Actual)	This Year (Planned)
August	1	Back-to School direct mailer	Back-to-school mailer
	2		
	3		
	4		
Sept.	1	Designer Week	Career Girl Fashion Show
	2	Fashion Shows	& Luncheon
	3		
	4		
	5	Storewide Clearance	Storewide Clearance
October	1		
	2	Anniversary Sale	Anniversary Sale
	3		
	4		
November	1		
	2	Xmas Catalog to Charge Customers	
	3		Thanksgiving Sale Xmas Catalog to Charge Customers
	4	Thanksgiving 3-day Sale	
December	1	Open major Xmas Shops downtown	
	2	Open Xmas shops Branch stores	Open all Xmas shops
	4		
	5	Post Xmas Sales & Clearance	Post Xmas Sale and Clearance
January	1	January White Sale Event	January White Sale Event
	2		
	3	Annual Remnant Day Sale	Annual Remnant Day Sale
	4	Warehouse Store Furniture Clearance	

Courtesy: Famous-Barr, St. Louis

These general merchandise managers will then decide how to allocate the funds among the divisional merchandise managers reporting to them.
The divisional merchandise managers supervise groups of related departments.

The Retail Advertising Schedule

Six weeks ahead.   About six weeks prior to the beginning of a given
month, the divisional merchandise manager asks his buyers to submit requests
for advertising space for specific items. He then reviews all the requests and
decides which to accept and which to reject. Although the buyer may request
a 1,200-line ad, the divisional merchandise manager may use his discretion to
increase or decrease the size of a given ad, depending on how important he
believes the ad to be, and how the ad relates to the requests of other buyers
in the division.

This whole process takes place under continuous time pressure. The
advertising department would like more lead time, because then they could
produce better ads. The buyers clamor for a shorter lead time, because this allows for more accurate interpretation of customer demand and therefore
better buying decisions.

After the divisional merchandise manager has reviewed all the buyers'
requests, and has adjusted the total month's advertising to conform to the
budget he has been allocated, he then submits his divisional advertising program for the month to the advertising manager.

The advertising manager coordinates the requests from all the divisions of the store and produces a master plan for each week of the month. This
master plan indicates which ads will run each day of the week, and it even
specifies the newspaper in which the ads are to appear. This is a very important step in the entire process, because the store management has predetermined criteria relating to the use of newspaper space by day and by
paper. For instance, a buyer may prefer to run an ad in the Wednesday evening paper; but the advertising manager may have to run it in the Thursday
morning paper in order to preserve balance by day and by paper, so that the
customer is continuously exposed to the store's advertising efforts. Everyone
concerned in the buying and selling organization gets a copy of the master
plan.

Three weeks ahead.   Three weeks before the actual running date of
an ad, the buyer submits to his divisional manager a fact sheet giving all the
information that will be needed by the advertising department. When approved by the divisional manager, it is sent to the advertising department,
along with samples or photographs of the goods to be advertised. The layout
man draws up a layout and submits it to his supervisor for approval. Using
the approved layout and the buyer's fact sheet, the copy man prepares the
necessary copy and submits it to his supervisor for approval. At this point,

311,014

Yellow Copy . . . . . to Advertising
Pink Copy . . . . to Sharpstown
Blue Copy . . . . to Pasadena
White Copy . . . . . to Department

Foley's

Advertising
FACT SHEET

Department Name . . . . **#**

This is sheet used by department store buyers to supply necessary information for the preparation of their advertisements.

**FACT SHEET DUE
IN ADVERTISING
14 DAYS IN
ADVANCE OF
RUNNING DATE!**

Date AD runs

Columns

Mail orders? Yes No

Phone orders? Yes No

Is AD part paid? . . . .

Vendor paid? . . . .

Internal load? . . . . . .

(how much, % or $. . . .)

Should item be a:
(Circle one)

Cut   Box   Liner

ART INFORMATION

Has item been
sketched or photo-
graphed before? Yes No

Attach mfs. photos if any!

**PICK UP DATE for cuts
IF OLD ART can't be
repeated . . . tell us why?**

**What credit plans
should be advertised
for this item:**
(Circle appropriate ones:)

FBA 30-day charge

Lay-away

"Few Pennies a Day"

Special terms _____

ITEM . . . .

Style or Model #. . . . .

REMEMBER: Merchandise is due with advertising request

**Has item been
Advertised Before?** Yes [ ] No [ ] When [ ]   If irregulars check here [ ]

CLASSIFICATION OF AD: [ ] A   [ ] B

IF COPY can't be repeated . . . tell us why?

What information should be in the HEADLINE?

Merchandise to be sold at: [ ] Downtown   Sharpstown [ ]   Pasadena [ ]

Comparison prices:*

Regular . . . .   Special purchase! . . . .   SELLING PRICE

Was . . . .   Compare at . . . .

*Refer to your copy of the Houston Better Business Bureau
"Advertising Answer Book."

If item is on SALE . . . what kind of a sale is it?
(Reductions from stock? Special Purchase and circumstances? Competitive action?
Seasonal promotion, etc.)

SELLING POINTS (List in order of importance)

1. . . . .

2. . . . .

3. . . . .

4. . . . .

COLORS: _____

Fabric (fiber content percentages) or material: _____

Sizes or dimensions: _____

Approved: DM . . . . **DMM** . . . .

Order your display signs now!

Courtesy: Foley's, Houston

every store has its special controls to verify the accuracy of comparative price claims.

The next step is to submit this layout to an artist who will prepare the finished artwork. The finished artwork and the copy then go to the production department. Here a typographer marks up the copy for typesetting, which is done by the newspaper. The approved copy and the finished artwork then go to the newspaper, which will set the type and rush the copy proofs back to the store to be approved by the buyer for accuracy. In the meantime, the newspaper is making the plates of the art work. The store will then receive a final proof of the completed advertisement as it is to appear in print, for final approval.

famous·barr	AUTHORITY FOR THE USE OF A VALUATION		Dept. No. _____
	FORM 790 (3-70)		Date _____
Name of Promotion _____		Please check ☐ Copy ☐ Signs ☐ Tags (____ Quan.)	

NOTE: ADVERTISING COPY, SIGNS AND HANG TAG REQUISITIONS, AND THIS FORM MUST BE APPROVED BY SERVICE REVIEW AND SUBMITTED TO THE ADVERTISING DIRECTOR NO LATER THAN TWO (2) WEEKS BEFORE THE AD IS SCHEDULED TO RUN OR SIGNS OR HANG TAGS ARE TO BE USED UNLESS SPECIAL APPROVAL HAS BEEN RECEIVED FROM THE GENERAL MERCHANDISE MANAGER OR MRS. VAN de ERVE.

Terms to be Used	Item and Substantiating Record and Information	Quantity of Mdse. on hand for event	Date of Ad	Date return to regular price	Promotion Price	COMPARATIVE PRICE					
						Regular Price	Original Price	Intermediate Markdown	If Perfect Price	Comparable Price	Other Price (please explain)

REMARKS:

My signature verifies that the above information is correct_____
(Buyer)

Divisional Merchandise Manager _____ and/or General Merchandise Manager _____ Advertising Director _____

Courtesy: Famous-Barr, St. Louis

VALUATION VERIFICATION FORM

Before a buyer can run an ad at a sale price, or make a comparative price statement, he must present such form, supporting those claims, for approval.

The ad runs. As soon as the ad appears in the local paper, the executives in the store begin to watch the advertised items for selling results. Customer comments are listened to carefully, but the most important indicator is the end-of-day sales figure. If an advertised item begins to sell rapidly, the store executives may decide to order additional quantities of the goods, on the assumption that the item will continue to sell well in the coming weeks. They may decide to repeat the same ad, often in a competing newspaper. This gives the retailer an opportunity to reach customers who do not read the first paper.

In the meantime, the manufacturer may have backed up the advertisement by holding predetermined quantities of the advertised merchandise. As soon as he gets the urgent phone call from one of the stores, he can immediately ship more goods, by air, if necessary.

An extremely successful advertisement may be repeated over a long period of time, as long as there is a demand for the goods.

Each store will have its own routine for handling the steps in between budget and appearance of an ad, but in all instances the operation is a fast-moving one, relying for its success on good coordination and good timing.

Cooperative Advertising

Although we have discussed cooperative advertising allowances in the past, chiefly from the manufacturer's point of view, it may be opportune to review some of the advantages and disadvantages from the store's viewpoint.

Chief advantages:

—It helps the buyer stretch his advertising capability.
—It may provide good artwork of the product advertised, with good copy, in mat form—especially important to the smaller store.
—It helps the store earn a better volume discount for all its advertising.

Cooperative advertising is best when the line is highly regarded and is a style or other leader in the field.

Chief disadvantages:

—Although the store may pay only 50 percent of the cost, that sum may still be out of proportion from the viewpoint of sales and profit.
—Most manufacturers' ads give more emphasis to the brand name than to the store name.

A DEPARTMENT STORE COOPERATIVE AD

Featuring nationally advertised appliances of different manufacturers, at an attractive price.

Manufacturers' ads cannot have the community flavor and the style of the store ads. Retail stores get far more offers for cooperative advertising than they can possibly use. However, if the merchandise is what the buyer wants, and if the price is right, he will seek a cooperative advertising allowance.

CHAIN DEPARTMENT STORES

We next meet the chains of department stores that each operate under one name—such as Sears, Montgomery Ward, J.C. Penney. These may be national or regional in scope. They concentrate on the middle-range price level and good quality of all the goods they handle. They tend to go in for the "solid" type of styles, rather than high fashion, and carry a higher percentage of durables than do the traditional department stores. Most of their products bear their own label.

| Sears | **RADIO COMMERCIAL** |

```
NATIONAL HARDWARE WEEK SALE          60 Sec. Live Version
LAWN AND GARDEN EQUIPMENT

Stock #2537, 29204-5, 3401-2, 35187,   13-3-72-32-60
        28533-36, 60055-56-57

ANNCR:   National Hardware Week is Sears greatest hardware sale
         event of the Spring.  So, if you've been looking for
         an excuse to buy that special power tool, or get started
         on home improvement...stop looking!  Come to Sears
         National Hardware Week Sale.  You'll find fabulous
         savings for the professional, the home craftsman...
         there's something for everyone.  You'll see terrific
         values on power tools, hand tools, paints, electrical
         needs, work clothes, plus many home improvement items
         on sale during Sears National Hardware Week.  And you
         can charge your purchase on Sears Revolving Charge or
         use Sears Easy Payment Plan.  Save big during Sears
         National Hardware Week Sale...save on such values as...
         great items from the Suburban Shop.  Lawn and garden
         tractors, roto-spaders, gas chain saws and gable roof
         lawn buildings...plus Sears exciting new shredder-bagger
         that shreds leaves, hedge and tree trimmings for easy
         disposal without burning.  Stop by the Suburban Shop now
         during Sears National Hardware Week Sale and save on
         spring lawn clean-up and gardening values.  Sears,
         Roebuck and Company, _____.
                                 (address)
                                                              46
```

Courtesy:
Sears, Roebuck & Co.

Because they control their own production, they can plan all their merchandise programs, including special sales and special offerings, well in advance. All the advertising material for each part of the year is prepared centrally—including newspaper ads, radio scripts, TV spots, store signs, and direct mail. It is then available directly from the home office, or from the regional office, upon requisition by the store. In such operations, the merchandising manager may decide to feature children's apparel during the 30-day period before Easter—and all the advertising will be prepared for that event. Stores located in warmer climates may decide to run this particular children's ad four weeks prior to Easter, while stores in the northern states may prefer to run the ad ten days prior to Easter. Once this decision is made, the advertisement has to be positioned in the local papers, signs and in-store displays have to be requisitioned, and salespeople must be advised so they will be knowledgeable about the advertised goods.

Although chains may be national, the stores are billed at the local rate—the rule being that if an ad appears over one name, it is so eligible.

DISCOUNT STORES

The fastest-growing form of retail outlet is the general merchandise discount store, whose volume is now 50 percent greater than that of department stores, with the difference in sales between them ever widening. Chief among such mass merchandisers are K Mart (Kresge), Gibson Products (Zayre), and Woolco (Woolworth). A discount store is one whose only claim to patronage is low price. These stores operate on a smaller markup than do department stores, with low-cost mass-buying of a limited variety of numbers in a line, and fast turnover for their profit. Many shoppers who go to a department store for their latest apparel will go to a discount store to buy those staples where the best price is the inducement.

Some discount stores specialize in one line, as in the case of a furniture store that uses a warehouse full of furniture as its showroom; a buyer can select his furniture and take it right out in his own car, if he can carry it, or he can arrange his own trucking if needed. There is no waiting for deliveries, the buyer can see exactly what he is getting, and the prices are the lowest in the area, as a result of the low operating costs.

Discount stores will have highly streamlined, tight-budget, central advertising departments, operating on a tight time basis. Newspapers, TV, mailers, and radio are all used.

SUPERMARKETS

The largest type of retailing operation in the United States is the supermarket, which in 1970 did a volume of $63 billion, compared with discount stores

($24 billion) and department stores ($16 billion).[3] Their chief advertising activity centers around their weekly food specials, which fill the newspapers Wednesdays and Thursdays. Many are heavy users of radio and TV, also.

Most of these stores are parts of regional or national chains, and their advertising as well as merchandising activity comes from a central office. In the case of one large regional chain, the main office handles the buying and scheduling of media, handling the paper work involved in the cooperative advertising, and the creation of the print ads and commercials, chiefly through their own staff of writers and artists, and radio and TV producers. Of all the areas of advertising where work is done under pressure, none involves more pressure than getting out the weekly newspaper advertisements. The advertising department is often one of the subgroups representing marketing services, along with sales promotion and store design and decoration.

The Quest for the Steady Customer

Although price is the main feature in discount stores and supermarkets, the fact is that no store could survive if people came in to buy only the very low-priced special advertised. And no store could reduce its overhead and improve its margin of profits over the years if it did not develop a following of shoppers who would automatically drive to the store any time they planned any shopping, and do most of their shopping there.

The best way of acquiring such a steady following is by earning the reputation of being a reliable store where you get good value for the money. One technique for helping this image is used by Hills Supermarket, who interspersed their supermarket price ads with institutional ads such as the one on page 625, "All about roast beef," which was followed by similarly informative ads such as "All about chicken," "All about veal," "All about peaches." Each offered an informative leaflet on the subject.

In his letter on this campaign, George Pittel, vice-president of Hills Supermarkets, reported:

> For the first six months of the campaign, we ran a full page of the institutional ad each week, along with the regular price ad. After the first six months, we ran an ad once every two weeks for about four months, and then once every three weeks.
>
> Within two weeks of the start of the campaign, there was a 3% increase in sales, a slight increase in customer count, and an 8% increase in the average customer sale. The sales increase continued the next four months and averaged between 8% and 10%, with about a 10% increase in the average customer sale. An increase in average customer sales means people are buying more at your store, and that is significant.
>
> We distributed about 4,000,000 brochures covering about 26 subjects.

---

[3] *Discount Merchandiser,* June 1971.

A Typical Supermarket Advertisement

Featuring low prices of nationally advertised brands and of the store's own house brands.

Rib Roast, explained.

Do you know what a "First Cut Rib Roast" is? Do you know what texture the meat should be? And what color the fat should be? And how much marbling to look for?

Don't you think you should know what makes a tasty, juicy, tender, easy-to-carve Rib Roast, tasty, juicy, tender and easy to carve?

We do. And we're going to tell you.

Rib Roast, what is it?

Rib Roast, also known as Standing Roast, also known as the "King of Roast Beef," can't help but make you the Queen of your table. That's because Rib Roast is one of the finest, most flavorful cuts of beef you can treat the family's tastebuds to. It's tender because it comes from one of the choicest parts of the steer. The sixth through the twelfth rib.

The rib eye, why look at that?

If you want to spot a good rib, just look a rib eye in the eye. The rib eye, that's the part in the center with all the meat.

So, what should you see when you look at the rib eye? Meat that looks firm, fine-grained, and velvety-textured. A sure sign you're getting quality Rib Roast our butchers say. With all the quality flavor and tenderness in every last rib.

At Hills, we never cover a rib eye with a label. On either side. That way, you can always get a good look at your Rib Roast. From either side.

Fat and marbling, what about it?

Don't be surprised if you see a lot of marbling running through the meat. A Rib Roast has even more marbling than roast beef. Which is what makes Rib Roast so super tender and juicy and flavorful and easy to carve.

The fat should look firm and white to creamy white.

Which is about perfect, our butchers say.

Firm white fat. Plenty of marbling. Now you know your Rib Roast will cook evenly. Without getting dried out in the least.

Ribs, how many?

A Rib Roast starts out with 7 full ribs. At Hills, we cut this into a 3-rib roast and two 2-rib roasts. A "First Cut Rib Roast" is the first 3 ribs. It may cost you a little more, but that's because you're getting more solid rib eye and less waste.

Want a full 7-rib roast? A club steak? A nice succulent rib steak? How about a Newport roast? With the top of the rib ground into some of the most fabulous hamburger you ever tasted?

At Hills, you can have it. If you don't see it in the case, just stick your head behind the counter. Ask to speak to one of our butchers. He'll be happy to cut a Rib Roast for you. Special. Any time and any way you want it. Exactly to your taste.

Government inspected?

If you buy a whole rib at Hills you may see two government stamps alongside the Hills stamp. (Sometimes they're lost in the trimming.) But we thought you might like to know that our Rib Roasts are all inspected by the government. They're all U.S. Government Graded. And they're all inspected for quality and wholesomeness by the U.S. Department of Agriculture.

More information.

Now you know what the best Rib Roast looks like. Now you know you can come into Hills and buy the best.

And when you come to Hills, we have an informative brochure on Rib Roast waiting for you. It'll tell you the exact time to cook a rare Rib Roast, a medium rare Rib Roast or a well done Rib Roast (what a pity!). It'll tell you how much you should buy, how to store it, what goes with it. (Want some easy carving instructions for your husband? You'll find them in our brochure.)

As for anything more you might want to know about excellent Rib Roast, buy ours and let your mouth tell you the rest.

hills
We dare to make
you a smarter shopper.

AN INSTITUTIONAL SUPERMARKET AD

One of a series designed to help the housewife become a more knowledgeable shopper, to have more confidence in the store, and to feel friendlier toward it.

Reactions to this campaign from the consumers were glowing, and the file of letters received is voluminous. Whenever we ran one of these ads we placed the item on sale at a reduced price. We found that we were enjoying about a 10% increase in the sale of the item over the normal sale in the past.

Although our campaign ended in 1971, our sales have continued at a good rate, staying at an increased level of about 8% and 10% from the time we started. Our objective was to create a new image and confidence in Hills, and this was definitely achieved.

Management was extremely happy with the idea and the results.[4]

SPECIALTY SHOPS

Many stores feature one class of merchandise—women's apparel, household appliances, TV and radio, hardware. Most of these are independently owned and cater strictly to the local trade. Since their chief service to the community is to have a wide range of needed goods, their advertising is usually confined to holidays and an annual sales event, at which time they use newspapers, circulars, radio. There are television production firms that prepare syndicated TV commercial tapes, which stores can use on television for a series of short flights during the year to sell the establishment to the viewers—as, for example, a series of films for jewelers, to advertise jewelry and gifts toward the holiday and wedding seasons. Similarly, there are syndicated services available for use in newspaper advertising. The whole ad, with art work, is prepared in mat form, with room for the local merchant's name. Often such stores will use a local agency to prepare the advertising on a fee basis, or possibly a freelance advertising man can be helpful.

CATALOG MERCHANDISE STORES

The history of retailing tells of a continual evolution in form. Innovative merchants are always emerging, always testing new ways to please the consumer. The supermarkets of the forties, the branch stores and regional shopping centers of the fifties, the discount stores of the sixties, and the furniture warehouse stores of the seventies, all attest to this continual evolution. The decade of the seventies is bringing forth a new form, the catalog merchandise showroom.

These stores are located near, but not in, shopping centers where the rents are lower than in other shopping-center areas. About one fourth of the space is devoted to displays of sample merchandise and to catalog order desks. The remaining space is devoted to warehouse facilities, in which are stocked

---

[4] Direct communication from Mr. Pittel.

large quantities of the items displayed in the front of the store, so that the customer can take an item right home with him. The customer gets lower prices because of the low real estate costs, lower display and selling costs, and lower losses from shoplifting. At the store, the customer can buy from the display room or order other merchandise from the catalog, which is the chief form of advertising. In addition, the catalog is sent out to carefully selected lists. The preparation of these catalogs, and the planning of their mailing, promises to become an important adjunct to advertising. It may be expected that, with competition, the stores will use mass media to let the consumer know of their existence, operation, and advantages.

THE RETAIL MEDIA MIX

The problem of selecting local media is a "How best to . . . ?" problem: How best to use the newspapers, radio, television, direct mail—the chief media—alone or in combination with each other, to sell merchandise and to attract store traffic.

Newspapers in Retailing

Newspapers have been around for a long time. They continue to be the backbone of retail advertising; they are part of the way of life of a large part of the population. Many a woman gets the paper, glances at the front page, especially for local news, then turns to the department store ads to see what's new, what's the latest style, even though she is not planning right now to buy a new garment. And for grocery shopping, she turns to see the latest specials the food stores are offering. Because the paper comes out daily, it permits the retailer to tell about his latest offerings in each of his many departments, as his schedule permits. Its Sunday edition, with its circulation going to the outlying reaches, brings in many mail orders from the further distances, in addition to store traffic the next day.

Newspaper supplements, which boomed into prominence late in the 1960's, have eagerly been seized by department stores for getting quick response to their ads. These loose inserts—usually about tabloid size and from eight pages up (but page size and number vary)—have also attracted direct-response advertisers, with the result that the number of supplements carried per issue threatens to become a clutter problem. Stores are watching their continued effectiveness closely.

Newspapers are a special favorite of many department store buyers, who like to see a proof of their ad before it runs, then see the ad when it runs in the paper (so they can promptly call up the advertising department if they are unhappy about it). The buyer can also post his ad in his department so that the sales staff can be informed of it.

Radio in Retailing

Two thirds of all money spent on radio is spent for local advertising.[5] Prominent among the retailers who have long used it are the discount houses and the chain stores; the traditional department stores joined in later, in terms of volume.

Radio is a newsy medium with a short closing time. Through choice of stations, programs, and type of music, a retailer can broadly reach different audiences. One station will be programmed to appeal to young people 20–25; another to the homemaker. A department store may use two or three stations with a young audience, to promote a new young men's department, and a different combination of radio stations and times to advertise a ladies' coat sale.

Radio is an effective medium for selling specific items or groups of items. Radio can be used to promote a major sale of mattresses, with a sense of urgency. "You had better take advantage of this event now, while the goods last," is the message.

Radio production costs are small; commercials can be produced quickly and be on the air overnight. Radio has proved most effective for terse commercials of a specific merchandising offering.

Thirty-two department stores, members of the Frederick Atkins, Inc., buying group, responded to a questionnaire on radio use. Here is a cross-section of replies:

Miller & Rhoads, Richmond: 49 spots a week, 52 weeks, on three stations. Extra spots added for special promotions. . . . All time segments covered, Sunday through Friday. . . . Plan to increase radio use. Commercials are prepared by the agency. They promote sales, items, store services, and image. Also tea room, buffets and charge accounts.

The Killian Company, Cedar Rapids: 18 spots per week plus flights: 50–75 for a storewide sale; 70–80 for five days for "Teen Fashion Bash" (high-school show, off premises); 10–15 for two days prior to one-day warehouse, carpet, or mattress sales; 30–40 a week prior to special events. Spots promote sales and service, events, items, image.

The Crescent, Spokane: We have found that radio is very productive in reaching the teenager and young adult. We are using radio more and more to reach the housewife during the day and the businessman going to and from work.

The Halle Bros. Company, Cleveland: Most recent successes were: Our warehouse sale. . . . On all previous sales, we used only newspaper, and traffic always dropped off at noon the day of the sale. For this sale we used radio in addition to newspaper, and traffic was heavy all day long. . . . Our store in Akron wanted to sell 150 pair of shoes in a two-day period. We used radio and sold over 300 pairs.

---

[5] See p. 121.

Porteous Mitchell & Braun Co., Portland, Maine: Two-day mattress sale advertised on radio only at a cost of $400 produced $5000 in sales.[6]

Television in Retailing

Of all retailers, the two largest users of television spots are Sears and J.C. Penney. Discount houses and supermarkets are likewise large users of television. Traditional department stores as a whole were slow in getting into television—largely, no doubt, because buyers liked the control over their ads that newspapers provide, with their proofs and tear sheets. But the rise in the use of television of these stores within five years has been spectacular, as revealed in the number of commercials used in one week in October 1965 as contrasted with that week in 1970, as follows:

	1965	1970
Sanger Harris (Dallas)	18	63
Hudson's (Detroit)	3	142
Joske's (San Antonio)	22	257
Carson Pirie Scott (Champaign)	43 *	112
Rike's (Dayton)	35	106

* Figure for 1968, when store TV began.
Source: Television Bureau of Advertising, Inc., 1972.

In connection with their TV advertising, Richard Slusher, vice-president for sales promotion of Rike's (Dayton), had this to say:

> Television on a local basis not only covers a metropolitan area, it covers a multicounty area. Television covers that area where the rapid expansion of newly developed communities requires a viable way of communication. Statistics will show that our print friends have not kept up with the moving masses. Circulation figures in most cases bear out this fact.
>
> Another advantage for television is the great ability to zero in on a specific customer. With this selectivity, you can put your message before whatever age you select: male, female, teenager, and so on. Whether it is a promotion for a single item, advertised on television only, or whether it is advertising to back up a general event in all media, we know television works—it reaches people and the message is registered!
>
> What does it cost? Let's look into some ideas related to production numbers.
>
> Television production does not have to be expensive. Excluding cities such as New York City, Chicago, and Los Angeles, television production actually can be dirt cheap.

---

[6] Radio Advertising Bureau, 1970.

There are four practical avenues of TV production:

First, there are the *in-house* production facilities, where you set up an office that will consist of approximately 1 copywriter, 1 cinematographer, and 1 coordinator. This is really the bare minimum to set up your own television production staff, plus, of course, a manager or director. With an in-house office, you can produce commercials economically and, with practice, efficiently and professionally. Of course, to commit yourself to this personnel expenditure, you must have a pretty large commitment of broadcast dollars.

The *second* avenue open to retailers is an independent film producer—probably a one- or two-man production company. In this case, you could write the copy with your existing print staff and have a creative meeting with your outside producer and arrive at a suitable shooting script. This is probably one of the more common ways of solving a retailer's production problem, since you are able to take advantage of part of your existing staff.

The *third* avenue of production is a total surrender of production to an agency or production house. In this case, you would give the raw information with some direction to purpose and result to which the proposed commercial is intended. The agency then produces the commercial from almost inception to the end product. This can be effective if you are capable of little or no input based on your experience or size of staff.

This leads to the *fourth* and final consideration of production facilities.

The television station:

Of all the people to be interested in your well-being, it is the television station. You will find that they will be more than willing to explore production possibilities with you and to service you in any way they can. This includes video taping as well as filming. Now, all of the foregoing leads to down-to-earth costs and how to get them:

First, if you are serious about participating in electronic media, you will realize that it takes a serious commitment of dollar expenditure to be effective. If you can agree to an amount of expenditure for a period of time (which is 1 year in most cases), you will certainly be able to bargain with your local television stations.

The important fact at this point is that you are committed to a certain dollar expenditure within a certain period of time. On this basis, you can explore the best or most positive production possibilities in your market. Your commitment is really your bargaining power. Of course, it becomes your responsibility to determine which avenue of production is best suited for your company. Regardless of the amount of dollars you have, whether it is $20,000 or $100,000, the station or stations that you sign a contract with will give you a certain number of spots for your money. In most cases you can work out a production package as part of the deal. It is still possible that you could get your commercials produced cheaper from an outside source. So when it's contract time, contact all your television stations, agencies, and production houses. The idea is to let each of these parties make a bid for your business, and when they realize they are in competition with someone else, you will be pleasantly surprised at how low you can get production done.

Air time vs. production costs—how do you figure that?

I have developed a formula that is simple and seems to be reasonable from the standpoint of costs vs. air time. Simply, it is a 4 or 5 to 1 ratio. That's if your commercial production for 1 spot costs you $500, you should spend about $2,000 to $2,500 minimum on air time. The number of commercials become important to reach a certain number of homes or a certain number of gross rating points. I really don't want to talk about money, because each market has different problems and different costs. A better answer would be that for each commercial you air you should have at least 20 spots. (There are exceptions, as 1-day sales, etc.)[7]

Direct mail advertising in retailing. "There's gold in them thar hills" might be said of every store with a mailing list of charge customers; for many stores, these run up into many hundreds of thousands. For these are the source of much business through direct mail.

Mass mailings of direct mail are costly. A store will venture its entire list only once or twice a year—as for an annual sale, or for Christmas shopping. It will then solicit mail orders, or more important, invite all who receive the mailing to come in before the sale is announced in the newspapers the following Sunday. (This technique has resulted in some of the biggest sale days of the year.)

But during the rest of the year, the list is not idle. It is computerized with much information on it. Creative analysis of the list can yield fertile subgroup listings. Mailings can be sent out to those who bought in one of the departments only, instead of to the entire list, using a mailing that will be of interest chiefly to them. Charge accounts with activity in the children's department indicate young families, to whom a mailing could be sent for that market. Or a list of customers who primarily buy home furnishings from a full-line department store may provide the list for a research as to why these customers shop elsewhere for apparel, so that appropriate steps might be taken to bring such customers into the apparel department. Or a letter could be written to charge customers who have not ordered in the past number of months. Just being noticed like that is great therapy for the customer who thought nobody was paying attention, and is a source of goodwill and continued business for the store.

Sears, Roebuck sends computer-written letters to customers who pay

---

[7] Television Bureau of Advertising, Inc., 1972.

their bills early, encouraging these customers to shop often in the store, and informing them of the arrival of the new season's lines, especially in the fields of their purchases.

CAREER OPPORTUNITIES IN RETAIL ADVERTISING

Of the many talents that lead to a career in retail advertising, writing ability and art talent are preeminent. Does an applicant like to write? Does he write well? Has he written for the school paper? Has he done any other kind of writing for any club? These are the questions that will be asked of him. If he shows that he does, and gets himself into an advertising department, he may find himself working on some real ads soon, under guidance, and being quickly launched into retail copywriting. From then on, depending entirely on his talent, a career in retail advertising is ahead of him.

And if an applicant likes to draw, especially figures and style subjects, his sketchbook may be very interesting to an art director. Good advertising artists are hard to find, and if an applicant proves to be one, he has a marketable talent.

Many advertising managers who came up through the creative end are now officers of the stores for which they worked.

The above may not be surprising. What may be surprising, however, is a report by Buxton. In speaking of five advertising agency men—correction, four men and a woman—who changed the advertising world in the sixties, he says: ". . . All had a solid retail experience, usually with department stores." [8]

---

[8] Edward Buxton, *Promise Them Anything* (New York: Stein & Day, 1972), p. 55.

Review Questions

1. What are the differences between retail and national advertising?

2. Generally speaking, how does the retailer evaluate the effectiveness of his advertising?

3. In department store advertising, distinguish among promotional advertising, special events advertising, and institutional advertising.

4. Why do most retailers use their own advertising departments rather than advertising agencies?

5. Discuss the major factors that affect department store advertising budgets.

6. Explain the typical roles in department store advertising of the divisional merchandise manager, the department buyer, and the advertising manager.

7. From the retailer's viewpoint, what are the advantages and disadvantages of cooperative advertising?

8. Compare advertising planning in a major chain department store with that in a large traditional department store.

9. In supermarket advertising, discuss the relative roles of featured low-priced specials and of institutional advertising.

10. Describe the major avenues of television production available to the local retailer who would like to use TV.

Reading Suggestions

Duncan, Phillips, Hollander, *Modern Retailing Management,* 8th edition. Homewood, Ill.: Richard D. Irwin, Inc., 1972.

Edwards, Charles M., Jr., and Russell A. Brown, *Retail Advertising and Sales Promotion.* 3rd ed. Englewood Cliffs, N.J.: Prentice-Hall, Inc., 1959.

Koehler, Alan, "Beware of Seven Deadly C's of Retail Newspaper Ads," *Advertising Age,* October 26, 1970, pp. 56, 58.

Rachman, David J., *Retail Strategy and Structure.* Englewood Cliffs, N.J.: Prentice-Hall, Inc., 1969, Chapter 14.

Simon, Julian L., "A Scientific Approach to Dividing the Advertising Budget," *Journal of Retailing,* Fall, 1969, pp. 37–45ff.

Sorenson, Douglas, "Three Views of Cooperative Advertising," *Journal of Advertising Research,* December, 1970, pp. 13–19.

Whitney, John O., "Better Results from Retail Advertising," *Harvard Business Review,* May–June, 1970, pp. 111–120.

28

Direct-Response Advertising

DIRECT-RESPONSE ADVERTISING IS A field in which it is very easy to confuse terms, because it represents a commingling of selling methods, media, and trade practices. Hence we begin with some definitions.

DEFINITIONS

Direct marketing. This is the all-inclusive term that has come into use comparatively recently to describe all forms of marketing in which the seller sells directly to the end user, without recourse to a retailer or dealer. It includes in-home selling, mail-order selling, catalog selling, and, when cable television gets going with its two-way communication systems, cablecasting selling.

Direct-response advertising. This describes any advertising that asks the reader for a prompt response to the advertisement, with his name and address. Typical uses of direct-response advertising are (1) selling merchandise or a service directly; (2) soliciting inquiries that will be followed up at home or in the office by a salesman, or by mail; (3) soliciting requests for a catalog (from which the recipient can subsequently order); and selling subscriptions or enrolling members in a club, for instance a book or record club.

Direct-response advertising uses a great variety of media—magazines, newspapers, television, radio, matchbook covers, paperback books, and direct mail.

Mail-order advertising. This is the form of direct-response advertising used in the marketing of goods directly from seller to buyer without recourse to a retail establishment, dealer, or salesman. Many media are used for mail-order advertising, as cited above. *Mail-order advertising,* which represents a way of selling, should not be confused with *direct-mail advertising,* representing the use of a medium.

Direct-mail advertising.   This branch of direct-response advertising is the designation of any advertising sent through the U. S. mail, or by "independent postal services," which are currently the object of experiments in various cities. Direct mail is a medium in which the reader is usually asked to return a card, order form, application blank, or even a roll of exposed film—in other words, to take some action.

Direct mail is our third largest medium of dollar expenditure, ranking behind newspaper and television expenditures, and 50 percent above magazine expenditures. Its usage has grown at a fast rate, expanding by 49.3 percent between 1960 and 1970 as compared with the average growth of all media of 64.3 percent.[1] It is estimated that 75 percent of all direct mail is used to produce direct responses.

Some large companies that operate many large book clubs and magazines spend up to $30 million per year to mail up to 30 or 40 million pieces of direct mail.

Direct-mail advertising is used for purposes other than direct-response advertising, too. It is used by retailers to announce forthcoming sales. It is used by pharmaceutical houses to tell physicians about their new products. It is used by businesses to keep in touch with customers. But the principal use of direct mail is for direct-response advertising, and it is this use of direct mail to which we address ourselves when we later discuss the medium.

UNIQUE FEATURES OF DIRECT-RESPONSE ADVERTISING

In national advertising, the reader is encouraged to buy the advertised product whenever the timing for making such purchase is right for him. Each advertisement is a cumulative reminder to do so.

In retail advertising, the reader is urged to come in early tomorrow morning for the advertised product, at which time it is hoped he will buy some other items also. But if he does not come in then, it is still hoped he will think of this store first when he does go out shopping; the ad still has some institutional value.

In direct-response advertising, the advertiser asks the reader to act *now,* to send in the coupon or order card *now,* because if he does not do it before he turns the page or throws the mailing away, the ad is considered a loss. There is no credit for cumulative effect of such advertising, or institutional value, to offset the lack of immediate response. This realization that the advertisement has only one chance and one way of being successful permeates the entire direct-response effort.

---

[1] See p. 121.

A Mail-Order Advertisement

Observe how specific is the offer, how it is presented in words and pictures, and again, how it is all spelled out in panel on right. The copy is detailed (though hard to read in this size). Accompanied by 3-way guarantee. Presenting also a variety of other offerings. At top—urge to action, with free offer. Reiterated on coupon copy below. All designed to get that signed coupon back.

Said Frank Vos, an authority on direct-response advertising, "The art of direct-response advertising is taking an order." The crux of taking an order is in planning the offer that the reader is asked to make. A substantial proportion of such advertisements offer an outright sale of a specific product.

The simplest examples of this kind of advertising are the small ads one sees in the shopping columns in the back of some magazines, or in the shopping section of Sunday newspaper supplements. It is expensive, per unit, to get an order this way; hence either the order item must be high-priced in relation to cost, to show a profit, or else the offer is a way of building a list

A DIRECT-RESPONSE ADVERTISEMENT

Designed to get expression of interest, which may serve as a lead for a salesman.

Why does World Book outsell all other encyclopedias? It's easy to understand.

Their school day doesn't end with the ringing of the bell. It continues at home . . . with every research paper they write, project they prepare, and exam they study for.

It can be a difficult time for children. World Book can make the going easier. Because World Book is designed for students. It's geared to their school curriculum. Especially suited to their study and reference needs. It's comprehensively written. And written to be understood.

World Book offers them a current and accurate reference source of information. Puts facts and figures at their fingertips. And stimulates their imaginations with meaningful articles, with maps and illustrations.

In addition, World Book encourages deeper investigation and independent research. Its Research Guide/Index . . . Volume 22 . . . not only gives them 150,000 index listings, but a 30-page section on How to Do Research. And 200 Reading and Study Guides that lead them to many important sources beyond the set.

So, is it really any wonder why . . . World Book is the encyclopedia that outsells all the others?

FREE: Reprint of World Book's new 12-page "Environmental Pollution" article.

TO: Charles Stewart, Sta. 20, Field Enterprises Educational Corp., Merchandise Mart Plaza, Chicago, Illinois 60654.

Please have a representative contact me regarding World Book. No obligation, of course.

☐ I would like a free reprint of the World Book article entitled "Environmental Pollution".

☐ I now own a 19___ World Book, and would like information on trading in my old set for the 22-volume World Book.

Name_____

Address_____

City _____ State_____ Zip_____

Phone Number_____

The 22-volume World Book Encyclopedia in the luxurious Renaissance binding is just $264 plus tax, delivered (slightly higher in Canada). Other bindings at lower prices. Monthly terms available.
041-72-11-WB

World Book
The one encyclopedia that outsells all the others.

Field Enterprises Educational Corporation. A Subsidiary of Field Enterprises, Inc. Affiliated with Field Educational Publications, Inc., and A. J. Nystrom Co.

World Book-Childcraft of Canada, Ltd.

of people to whom the advertiser can later sell kindred items by mail. Whoever responds to a mail-order offer will probably receive a package containing many "bounce-back" circulars offering other merchandise of related interest. "Bounce-back" circulars included in mail-order shipments will often produce as much as 20 to 40 percent additional immediate sales from customers. The advertiser takes this extra business into consideration when he calculates how much response he needs to made his ad pay.

Another type of direct-response advertisement is a two-step sales method. The advertisement is designed to get an expression of interest in the form of an inquiry that will be followed up as a "lead" by a salesman. This technique is frequently employed by firms selling costly products such as home study courses and multivolume encyclopedias. These may entail the need to discuss the whole matter with a personal salesman, to answer the questions a prospective buyer may have.

Another type of direct-response advertising in two steps is that in which the advertisement seeks to get inquiries for a catalog from which the recipient can then order at will.

Book-club and record-club ads utilize still another form of proposition. They offer a book buyer a great bargain now, in exchange for his promise to buy a certain number of books later. In offers of this type, the advertiser does not expect to break even on the original offer. He makes his profit on the books (or records) subsequently purchased and paid for by the new member.

DIRECT-RESPONSE COPY

Of all forms of advertising, direct-response advertising adheres most closely to a recognizable pattern. It uses strong specific promises or selective headlines, as in these instances:

15 ways to bigger pay

How to get $20
in buying power—for every
ten bucks you spend

Most women can't answer
these 22 questions about clothes.
Can you?

How to get $20 in buying power—for every ten bucks you spend!

Do you have to "know somebody" to buy at factory prices? Yes, you do. Us. Unity Buying Service.

Join us . . . and you'll *never* pay regular store prices again.

To be specific, you'll get about $2 worth of merchandise for every dollar you spend. How is this possible? *Simple.* You'll have an "in." You'll be part of a special group of people who *never* have to pay store prices . . . a privileged "inner circle" of consumers who *can save up to 50% or more on every purchase they make.*

Our organization can be described in one simple sentence: We enable you to buy nationally advertised, brand-name merchandise at DIRECT FACTORY PRICES plus a 6% service charge.

That's all there is to it. There are no "gimmicks." No strings attached.

If you want to get more for your money — actually DOUBLE your purchasing power — join Unity *now!*

As a member you can buy the things you want at *never-heard-of prices* like these . . .

- $18.85 for a nationally advertised watch listed at $41.95
- $21.95 for 7½" saw listed at $49.95
- $35.00 for a portable sewing machine selling for $99.95
- Yes, that's all you pay plus 6% service charge and shipping.

And I'm talking about savings on famous-brand merchandise. Names like Kodak, Gruen, Polaroid, Schick, Royal, Remington, Webcor, West Bend, Oster, Regina, MacGregor, Oneida — and more than 200 other nationally known manufacturers.

Unity gives you the power of numbers . . .

How can Unity offer merchandise at such exclusively low prices?

Well, suppose you could buy direct from the factory. Your cash savings would be enormous.

But you're only one person. Chances are that no manufacturer will sell directly to you. *But we represent 400,000 members — and that's a lot of buying muscle!* So we're able to buy direct at factory prices. And we sell to our members at . . . *the factory price, plus 6%, plus shipping charges. Period.*

That 6% is to help us cover our administrative costs and make a profit. No store, no matter how large, can make that statement.

Everything you buy is brand new, first quality, and fully guaranteed.

No "seconds" or "discontinued models." Every item is brand new, first quality, and in the *original factory carton.*

How much did you overpay today?

If you just bought this famous-name blender for $36.00, you overpaid by $17.10!

If you just bought this nationally advertised cookware set for $34.55, you overpaid by $19.56!

With few exceptions like bulky furniture, all items are stocked in our modern warehouse where all orders are filled and shipped promptly. Remember we are *not* brokers or agents — *we stock our merchandise.*

Everything comes with the manufacturer's full guarantee. And with our own guarantee on top of that: if you are ever dissatisfied, for any reason, with anything you buy from us, let us know within 10 days . . . we will either exchange it or give you a refund.

Prove it to yourself!

In a "nutshell" we are *promising you* up to two dollars' worth of buying power for every dollar you spend now. This may seem to be too good to be true . . . and these days, we can understand that!

So what other proof can we offer you that Unity Buying Service is *for real?* Just this: test the Service at *no risk.* Here's how: Send us the *membership application* with your $6 annual membership fee. In return, we will rush you . . .

- Our 436-page current catalog, picturing in full color most of the 10,000 items you can buy at huge discounts. This catalog will show you the manufac-

turer's suggested list price or the fair comparison price.
- FACTORY PRICE BOOK, where you'll find the Dealer Cost of every item, and, lowest of all, the Factory Price you pay plus 6% service charge.

Then start comparison shopping. Check the prices in our Factory Price Book against any store or discount house in your area. We know they can't beat us.

You can depend on UNITY BUYING SERVICE —

Unity has been in business over 10 years. We're pledged to prompt, efficient, dependable service. Maybe that's why we've become America's Number One factory buying service.

We do an annual business that runs into millions of dollars. In the last five years alone, we've sold more than $100,000,000 worth of merchandise.

Orders are processed within 48-72 hours, and shipped direct by U.S. Mail, United Parcel Service, Railway Express or insured trucking firms.

**Unity Buying Service, Inc.
Mt. Vernon, New York 10551**

No minimum purchase!

You can buy one item — 10 items — 100 items — *or nothing at all.* There is no limit, and no minimum purchase. The choice is yours.

Act now!

We print a limited number of catalogs each year. Once our supply is exhausted, we will not be able to accept new members until a new catalog is printed next year. All memberships are accepted on a first-come, first-served basis. Membership applications received too late will be returned. Mail your application *right now!*

EXTRA BONUS with one-year membership only. We will include Better Business Bureau's CONSUMER BUYING GUIDE Free. Keep this valuable book even if you cancel membership.

MAIL COUPON TO:

Unity Buying Service, Inc.
Dept. 434, Mt. Vernon, New York 10551

Yes, I'm tired of paying today's high prices. Enroll me as a member of Unity Buying Service and rush my giant colorful 436-page current catalog and confidential Factory Price Book. I understand there is no obligation to purchase anything. However, any merchandise I do decide to buy will always be shipped direct to me at low factory prices plus 6% service charge and shipping. If not satisfied with any shipment, I may return the item for exchange or refund.

CHECK ONE:

☐ I am enclosing $6 to cover one full year's membership. Include the Better Business Bureau's *Consumer Buying Guide* Free — mine to keep in any case!

☐ I am enclosing $2 to cover a three-month trial membership.

Print Name_____

Address_____ Apt. #_____

City_____ State_____ Zip_____

NO-RISK GUARANTEE: If not delighted I can cancel membership and return all membership material within 30 days for prompt refund of my membership fee.

A DIRECT-RESPONSE ADVERTISEMENT

Designed to get payment for membership in a catalog buying service.

Such headlines will be followed by an abundance of copy that is specific, factual, detailed—completely describing the proposition. It seeks to anticipate all the questions that the buyer might ask. The advertiser must convince the reader *totally*—even at the risk of losing the attention of many people who don't like to read long ads. This is probably why successful direct-response copy is usually wordier than other forms of advertising. The direct-response advertiser must convince the very tiny percentage of readers who are ready to order *now*.

Direct-response advertising abounds in devices designed to stimulate the reader to *action*. Free trial offers, special tokens to be inserted in order cards, bargain trial subscriptions to magazines, reduced-price prepublication book offers, extra gifts or merchandise for immediate orders; these are some of the tools of getting coupons back in direct-response advertisements.

The coupon. The coupon, or order card, must restate the entire details and terms of the proposition, for, when signed, it becomes a contract. Each will carry a small code (key number) to enable the advertiser to trace the medium from which the coupon came, and the advertisement. The order card itself may be IBM-punched in advance to indicate the source. The direct-response advertiser can tell instantly whether his order came from *Better Homes and Gardens* or from *Good Housekeeping,* and from which issue.

DIRECT-RESPONSE MEDIA

In national advertising, the advertiser determines who and where the people who represent his market are, and then seeks to select media to reach them. The product itself will be bought in many stores by people who never saw the advertising. To the direct-response advertiser, however, the media are his only market; he has no other means of reaching people who may be interested in his product. Or conversely, unless he has a medium for reaching people who may be interested in his product, he has no market; he has no business.

Direct-response advertisers use most of the media employed by national advertisers, but the way they use them may be different in some respects:

1. The position in which an ad runs in a magazine is very important to the direct-response advertiser. His results are usually greater if his ad appears in "the front of the book." Right-hand front pages are preferred. Back covers of a magazine are also very productive per dollar. Another good position is the page facing the third cover of a magazine.

2. All advertisements contain a coupon or order card. In magazines, the direct-response advertiser heavily uses card and order-form inserts, along with his full-page advertisements.

3. In newspapers, the direct-response advertiser goes in heavily for color pages in the Sunday magazine sections and for loose inserts. He also uses the special sections devoted to his type of product, such as gardening or travel sections. Some Sunday papers also have special mail-order pages.

4. Advertising in certain months seems to pull better for some (but not all) direct-response advertising than that in other months. The better months are July, August, September, January, and February.

5. In television, time scheduling is quite different for the direct-response advertiser than for the national advertiser, as we will discuss later.

DIRECT MAIL

Direct mail is the only medium for whose production and issuance the advertiser is wholly responsible. His audience is the list of people selected to receive the mailing. The first step in the direct-mail operation is gathering the audience, represented by lists of people.

The List

There are various ways of looking at lists. First we consider them as being either *house lists* or *outside lists*.

House lists. One's own lists are usually referred to as *house lists*. These lists may consist of the name and address of the firm's customers, or a list of prospects, or any other mailing list that the advertiser keeps and maintains. Depending on the size of the advertiser and the size of the list, the method for maintaining the list might range from a simple file of address stencils to a computer tape on which the names and addresses are recorded magnetically. Today, virtually all lists of any size are kept on magnetic tape.

House lists have to be kept up to date. Changes of address must be posted promptly and regularly. New names have to be added to the list (suitably keyed to show how they entered the list—customer, inquirer, etc.). From time to time an advertiser will send out to the list a mailing piece bearing a legend on the envelope that requests the Postmaster to return those envelopes that cannot be delivered; such names are then removed from the list.

House lists can be classified in many ways to enable selective mailings to be made to customers or prospects. The Postal Service requires that mailing lists be broken down by states and in conformance with zip code centers in order to facilitate postal handling.

The care and feeding of house lists is a big responsibility—and expense.

Outside lists. In addition to his own lists, an advertiser can use outside lists gathered from two original sources: *compiled lists* and *response-derived lists*. A *compiled list* is one that has been put together from other printed sources, such as the telephone book, trade directories, association members, club members, and other published records too numerous to mention. This compilation is usually done by list companies, who issue catalogs describing their list offerings—Beverly Hills homeowners, New York State plumbers, new Cadillac owners, high-prescription-writing physicians, and other closely identifiable groups. The larger lists can be rented for a one-time use; the smaller ones are usually purchased outright.

Large compiled lists are widely used for mass magazine-subscription mailings, "cents-off" coupon mailings, and for other broad marketing purposes. They are also extensively used for industrial direct-mail purposes.

MAIL ORDER BUYERS

Here is an unusual group of Mail Order Buyers, and Charge and Credit Card Lists arranged for your convenience by classification:

Gift Buyers
Credit Card & Charge Account Customer Files
Erudite Book & Magazine Buyers
Religious & Educational Material Buyers
Hobby & HiFi Consumer Buyers
Sporting Goods Buyers
Miscellaneous Consumer Buyers
Business Mail Order Buyers
Farmer Mail Order Respondents

Included here are the following:
1. What we are certain will be the top gift list of the "70's"— J. Carlton's Inc.
2. A dozen lists of true affluents – who buy by mail.
3. One of the key business mail order lists
4. The major farmer mail minded list
5. One of the best entries to upper income black Americans
6. Bond Store mail order & charge account customers

The data here covers name, a brief description and price per M. For detailed descriptions and the lists which seem to fit your market please request a list data card from your favorite list broker, or from one of the offices of Ed Burnett, Inc.

GIFT BUYERS
Gift Merchandise For Executives

150,000	"J. Carlton's Inc. M.O. Buyers"	30/M
15,000	New Orders Each Month	40/M

Catalogue & Item M.O. Buyers
With Average Sale of $21
Can select Buyers by size of purchase, multiple buyers, buyers this month, Catalogue Buyers, Credit Card Buyers, Direct Mail Advertising Buyers.

"Mail Order Watch Buyers"

46,000	HILTON & SILVER WATCHES	25/M

Mail order buyers of watches – average value, over $25. Males and females. 100% by mail.

M.O. Gift Merchandise Buyers
JOHN BROOKS, LTD.
A division of Missouri Petroleum

74,000	Recent Buyers	25/M
59,000	Former Buyers	20/M

This list, placed on computer by J. Carlton's Inc., is one of the best known merchandisers of gifts by mail. Average sale – over $10. 100% M.O.

Florida Citrus M.O. Buyers

69,000	"MAIL-A-MATIC"	25/M

Buyers of oranges and other food products by mail. Primarily confirmed multiple repeat buyers.

300,000	Mail Order Catalog Buyers	27.50/M

MAJESTIC DISTRIBUTORS
Buyers of Appliances, Lawn Furniture, Camping Equipment, General Catalog Merchandise. $40 Average Order

Black is Beautiful
Black Women M.O. Buyers of Wigs, Fashions, Cosmetics

356,000	"HOWARD TRESSES"	30/M

List owner must do mailing.
Not returnable.

14,000	"EWING GIFT SALES"	25/M

A small determined mail order house in the southwest, just beginning to catch on. $5 to $10 gift items. 100% Direct Mail. Doubling annually.

HIGH LEVEL CREDIT CARD HOLDERS
AND CHARGE ACCOUNT CUSTOMERS
Luxury Leather Goods
Charge Account Customers

200,000	MARK CROSS BUYERS	30/M

Families of means who buy expensive luggage and gifts at one of the most exclusive gift stores in America.

High Fashion Charge Account Customers
THE PECK AND PECK WOMAN

380,000	New Charge Accounts	25/M

Travel minded, upper income ($18,000 Med. income) college educated families who buy debonair fashions in one of America's great chains of specialty apparel stores.

720,000	Credit Cleared Charge Customers	25/M

BOND STORES CHARGE LIST
Includes over 200,000 large ticket credit mail order buyers. All active accounts within current two year span. Cleaned monthly. For M.O. selection, please inquire.

324,000	Big and/or Tall Mail Order Customers (BATMO)	25/M
	Can Select 21,000 Current Mail Order Buyers	30/M
	Can Select 110,000 Mail Order Catalog Requesters	30/M

Odd and Oversize Men – Who Regularly Buy by Mail

50,000	"RESTAURANT ASSOCIATES"	25/M

High income credit checked executives who dine at "Four Seasons" and other expense account restaurants.

25,000	Well Heeled Gardners	25/M

Mail Order Buyers & Inquirers for Greenhouses $116 Average Order – $90 Minimum
Available for the first time, customers of "PETER REIMULLER – GREENHOUSEMAN"
Adding 10,000 per year

200,000	M.O. Land Inquirers & Buyers	25/M

LEHIGH ACRES DEVELOPMENT, INC.
. . . plus 30,000 new names monthly
inquirers and installment buyers of Florida land. Average sale $2,500.
75% Male. Updated Regularly.

POLAROID CAMERA BUYERS
Two Million M.O. Respondents. . .

including hundreds of thousands of M.O. Buyers
A. By Mail Order

100,000	Mail Order Color Pack Buyers ($50 to $100)	25/M
50,000	Polaroid Copy Service Buyers (multiple copy print buyers by mail)	25/M
15,000	M.O. Christmas Card Buyers	25/M

B. Warranty Card Registrants by Mail

1,500,000	Buyers of Color Pack Cameras ($50 to $160) (can select by age or owner, and value of camera)	20/M
500,000	Buyers of Polaroid Swinger (can select by Age and Sex – 2/3 under age 30, 40% under 20)	20/M
50,000	Canadian Polaroid Buyers (can select Color Pack or Swinger Model Buyers)	25/M

ERUDITE MAGAZINE AND BOOK BUYERS

30,000	Patrons, Donors, Contributors to	25/M

AMERICAN CONSERVATORY THEATRE
San Francisco's nationally famous ACT –
virtually every culturally minded civic leader in Bay Area. Mail order oriented.

Collectors Editions of Books, by Mail
"HERITAGE CLUB M.O. BUYERS"

40,000	Club Buyers	25/M
17,000	Expires	20/M

Average purchase of elegantly bound books – $50. People of expensive taste, with means to match, willing to buy by mail

Interior Decor Magazine Buyers
"ARCHITECTURAL DIGEST"

55,000	Subscribers	25/M
30,000	Recent Expires	20/M

Average annual income – $30,000
Interested in exceptional homes, and home decor, prints, painting, sculpture.

Chess Devotees

23,000	M.O. Chess Magazine Subscribers	25/M
55,000	Prospects & Expires, Inquirers & Contestants	15/M

U.S. Chess Federation ("CHESS LIFE & REVIEW") list of chess devotees. Only publication serving chess players.

LIBERAL COMMITTED THINKERS
"CENTER MAGAZINE"

90,000	Subscribers	35/M
40,000	Expires	25/M
10,000	Trials	25/M

Subscribers & Former Subscribers to one of the leading magazines of dialogue and controversy.

Concerned Liberal Americans

40,000	"INDIVIDUALS AGAINST THE CRIME OF SILENCE"	30/M

People committed to immediate ending of Vietnamese conflict . . . contributors who permitted use of their names.

Psycholocial & Sociological Magazine Buyers

8,000	"INSIGHT SUBSCRIBERS"	35/M

A think magazine published by Interdisciplinary Studies of Men concerning insight into the mind of man. Mainly M.O. buyers.

Courtesy: Ed Burnett

PAGE FROM MAILING LIST CATALOG

Note the variety of different lists which can be bought.

Response-derived lists. Somebody else's customer list or prospect list, which is offered for rent, is referred to as a *response-derived list.* The addressee had to "send away" for something to enter the list—usually in response to a mail-order ad or a piece of direct mail. For this reason, people on response-derived lists tend to be more prone to ordering by mail, and therefore these lists are more productive than compiled lists.

Usually these rented lists do not actually come into the advertiser's possession. A third party, such as a *lettershop,* which we discuss later, undertakes to address Company A's mailing pieces with the names on Company B's list. Company A therefore never actually sees the mailing list it uses. Only those names that respond ever become known to the mailer.

The List Broker

An advertiser may also be able to rent the use of lists through a list broker, who acts as a clearinghouse and consultant. One leading list broker, the Lewis Kleid Company, describes its work this way:

> Our office registers some 9,000 different lists. We merely act as agents and negotiate the rental or exchange of names. These lists run from approximately $25 per M up to $35 per M. At the lower end of the scale we have inquiry names, contest names, premium names, and at the other end there are subscriber lists, members of record clubs, buyers of financial services, etc.
>
> Our commission (20%) is paid by the owner of the list, so that the user gains our knowledge, experience, and advice without a surcharge.
>
> It would be hard to define all the possible types of lists used for any specific mailing, since it is a matter of constant testing. For example, a magazine like *Saturday Review* would test lists of people who have bought records by mail, books by mail, people who have attended concerts, people who have been abroad, and almost any other list which has a cultural mail order qualification.
>
> With the advent of computers, almost 95% of the available lists are now being reproduced on labels and magnetic tape. The magnetic tape is used for computer letter writing and for eliminating duplication among the lists being mailed.
>
> When you rent names, it is understood that the names will be used one time. The list owner must approve the mailing piece and the mail date.

Billions of mailing-list names are rented and exchanged each year, for one-time or multiple use. Before renting the entire mailing list, direct-response advertisers will test a sample portion of a list in order to ascertain the cost per response, before proceeding with a larger use of the list.

The computer and magnetic tape make possible many refinements in mailing list selection.

Matching Lists

One of the big problems that have plagued direct-mail advertisers—and the public—is the fact that one person can be on many different computerized lists that an advertiser may use. As a result, that person will receive two or three copies of the same mailing (from different lists), which in itself is a big waste, but more important, annoys him greatly and reduces a chance of getting an order. Since most lists are on tape, especially the large ones, it is now possible to have the various tapes matched, casting out all duplicates and leaving one master tape. These duplicates are valuable; they represent people who were on two or more lists because of their purchases; they may be prime prospects for other offerings. Large mail-order houses keep a list of bad credit risks, which likewise can be checked, along with other lists, in developing the master list; they also list zip code areas that are known to be unsalable for the advertised product under consideration, and names in these areas can be removed from such a master list.

What Makes a Good Name?

There are certain people who will be more responsive to a mailing than others. Among these will be (1) customers who have recently ordered; (2) customers who order frequently; (3) customers of similar products; (4) volume buyers, (5) people who have shown interest in a related product—i.e., book-club buyers, record and tape buyers; and (6) people who have a demographic interest in a product—i.e., parents, encyclopedias; young marrieds, insurance. Direct-response advertisers get a higher response from those who are known to reply to direct mail than from those who are not so known.

Planning the Direct-mail Material

The creation and production problems of direct mail are interesting and varied. The direct-mail writer, art director, or production man is not bound by a set of publisher's rules, as in the case of magazine or newspaper advertising. Instead, he uses whatever size format he wants and whatever paper and printing processes he wishes.

Formats. A piece of direct mail may vary from a single folder, bearing the address on the outside, to elaborate color folders and booklets sent with other enclosures in a special envelope (referred to as the *direct-mail package*). There has been a steady rise in production costs, as list rentals,

addressing, printing, and, above all, postage—have all been growing costlier.
Postage is scheduled to go still higher. Ironically enough, the postage increase
has been a strong influence to come out with more elaborate packages, designed to pull more orders per thousand, as a way of overcoming the rising
costs. Therefore the trend has been toward more creative mailing pieces, often
involving computerized personalization of letters, and other devices designed
to encourage the reader to reply.

Experience has shown that any mailing that seeks an order should
include a separate order form. If money is sought, a business reply envelope
should also be included.

A letter is always advisable when an order is desired. It may be accompanied by a circular that expands upon the uses, applications, virtues, and
details of a product, but a circular alone rarely does a good job of getting
orders.

Airmail envelopes and postcards have often been effective in conveying a sense of importance and urgency for the message.

The direct-mail production manager has special scheduling problems
to solve in preparing direct-mail advertising. First of all, he has a mailing-
date deadline to meet. This date will be determined by the availability of list
rentals at a particular time, the seasonality of the offer, and the wishes of the
advertiser. Certain parts of the mailing piece are going to take much longer
to produce than others. Special-size envelopes usually require the greatest
amount of time; mechanical artwork for them must be released first.

Mechanical artwork for the circular is usually next to be released.
The order card and the letter are usually simpler, and thus they require less
time between the release of the mechanical and the delivery of the finished
work by the printer.

The mailing pieces sent to names on each list will have to be keyed
separately, so that the advertiser can tell exactly how many orders are produced by each list. The production man must determine the exact quantities
of each key, and issue precise instructions to the printer and to the lettershop.
This requires careful attention on the part of the production and traffic personnel.

The *lettershop* is a specialized business that has developed to serve
the direct-mail advertiser. This type of company takes care of the physical
handling of mailing pieces, often addressing (nowadays labels are mostly
used, addressed by computerized methods), inserting, sorting, and mailing
them.

Good lettershops can be found in all large and medium-size cities
and in many smaller ones. They perform a wide range of services for the
direct mailer, and they can save both the neophyte and the experienced advertising man much grief.

For those who are interested—one's own mailbox is a living source
of direct-mail examples.

DIRECT-RESPONSE ARITHMETIC

Most advertising men are fascinated by direct-response advertising, because it is the only form of promotion that enables an advertiser to know exactly "where he is at," to know exactly how well (or how badly) the advertisement

WORKSHEET FOR PLANNING PROFITABLE MAILINGS

Date: *Date*

PROPOSITION *Practical Mathematics* KEY *64*

1 - Price of Merchandise or Service	**$25.00**

2 - Cost of Filling the Order

a) Merchandise or Service	5.00	
b) Royalty	—	
c) Handling Expense	.75	
d) Postage and Shipping Expense	.60	
e) Premium, including Handling and Postage	.30	
f) Use Tax, if any (1 x **3** %)	.75	
TOTAL COST OF FILLING THE ORDER		7.40

3 - Administrative Overhead

a) Rent, Light, Heat, Maintenance, Credit Checking, Collections, etc. (**10** % of # 1)	2.50	
TOTAL ADMINISTRATIVE COST		2.50

4 - Estimated Percentage of Returns, Refunds or Cancellations	10%

5 - Expense in Handling Returns

a) Return Postage and Handling (2c plus 2d)	1.35
b) Refurbishing Returned Merchandise (**10** % of # 2a)	.50
TOTAL COST OF HANDLING RETURNS	1.85

6 - Chargeable Cost of Returns (**10** % of $**1.85**)	.19
7 - Estimated Bad Debt Percentage	10%
8 - Chargeable Cost of Bad Debts (# 1 x # 7)	2.50
9 - Total Variable Costs (# 2 plus # 3, # 6, and # 8)	12.59
10 - Unit Profit after Deducting Variable Costs (# 1 less # 9)	12.41
11 - Return Factor (100% less # 4)	90%
12 - Unit Profit Per Order (# 10 x # 11)	11.17
13 - Loss Per Unit Profit Due to Returned Merchandise (**10** % of # 2a)	.50
14 - Net Profit Per Order (# 12 less # 13)	10.67
15 - Cost of Mailing per 1,000	96.03
16 - NUMBER OF ORDERS PER 1,000 NEEDED TO BREAK EVEN	9.0

For additional copies of this form, contact Marketing Services Manager.
BOISE CASCADE ENVELOPES, 313 Rohlwing Road, Addison, Illinois 60101   Tel. 312, 629-5000

Form No. B-9

A MAIL-ORDER COST WORKSHEET

Showing how quotas for mailings are established.

Reprinted with permission from the Aug. 17, 1970 issue of *Advertising Age.* Copyright 1970 by Crain Communications Inc.

is working. Direct-response advertisers always know what their costs are and exactly how much business was produced from any given expenditure. They have their own special kind of arithmetic. They divide the total cost of an advertisement by the number of keyed responses received from the ad. The quotient is the advertising cost per coupon, sometimes called the *cost per order* (CPO). Experience eventually tells an advertiser how much he can afford to spend for a coupon in each of the various media or lists he uses, and still make a satisfactory profit.

DIRECT-RESPONSE TESTING

Another great advantage enjoyed by direct-response advertisers is that they can readily test any particular ad or mailing piece before spending large sums on it. They test offers and prices, headlines and copy approaches, mailing format. They use keyed coupons and mailing cards to test the pull of various magazines and newspapers. And they test small segments of larger mailing lists to decide which to rent.

Split-run tests. The most frequent and precise way of testing two or more publication advertisements is through the split-run facilities offered by many large-circulation magazines, and by some newspapers, especially in their Sunday magazine supplements. By this method, each advertisement is printed on the same press but from two different rollers. The copies are printed simultaneously, so that two identical copies come off the press and through the bindery simultaneously. Ad A is run in one copy and ad B is printed in the other. These copies are automatically intermixed as they come off the press, so that an equal number are sent to each newsstand. The same thing is done with respect to subscription circulation. Each contains a keyed coupon, and a careful count is kept of the replies from each. Split runs provide a foolproof copy-testing capability; the exposure of both ads is equal and identical, and therefore the ad that pulls the most coupons must be the better of the two, and is used further, provided it meets the cost-per-order target.

However, there are a few cautions to be observed in interpreting split-run results. First of all, the kind of people who read the magazine you use to test should be more or less similar to the circulation in which you will subsequently run the winning ad. (You would certainly not want to schedule a split-run test in *Family Circle* to determine which piece of copy to run in the entire circulation of *Playboy!*) Also, there must be a statistically significant difference between results in order for conclusions to be drawn. Small differences between the pull of ad A and ad B can usually be attributed to random factors, and must be ignored in making business decisions.

SPLIT RUN TEST AD A

Most women can't answer

these | 22 questions about clothes

Can you?

- Why should you think twice about buying a coat with a blue lining?
- What popular color seems to *irritate some males?*
- Short girls: Which two fabrics should you avoid?
- Career girls: How can you transform daytime clothes into "date-time" clothes—without leaving the office?
- Brunettes with brown eyes: What are 3 shades *you* can wear that blue-eyed brunettes can't?
- How can you dress "young" . . . without looking "silly"?
- Girls with very pale hair: What 2 colors can make you look drab and "mousey"?
- There's a model's "trick" for getting into a panty girdle—do you know it?
- If your face is round—which current hat style will flatter you most?
- Which accessories can *"double"* the size of your wardrobe—at almost no cost?
- What four "classic" styles usually *stay* in style—every year?
- Stockings are always mandatory in town—except when?
- What kind of jewelry is especially flattering to gray hair?
- Broad hips? How can you minimize this when you wear shorts?
- What type figure should never wear one-piece suits?
- What style of winter gloves is considered in poor taste?
- Blondes: Which gems complement your coloring?
- Eyeglasses: How do you choose the most glamorous frame for *your* face?
- Which three colors make you look *cool* — even when it's uncomfortably *hot?*
- How can you minimize midriff bulge, heavy arms, and other figure problems?
- What's a fast way to clean diamonds—without hurting them?
- "Swimsuit bulge": Which new miracle-fabric can help hide it—without binding?

WILL YOU RISK ONE DIME . . .
to learn these and other fashion secrets?

WHAT is your figure problem? Large hips? Too tall? Heavy arms or legs? Spreading tummy? Flat chest? Short neck? Narrow shoulders? You'll find *your* particular figure type described on pages 14 to 16 of Amy Vanderbilt's new illustrated Guide —*How To Be Well Dressed*. This new Guide shows you how to "camouflage" your figure problems—how to make the most of your figure in sportswear, "basics," career clothes, summer-and-swim wear, foundations, hats, jewelry, and much more. You'll discover how to *look better in everything you wear . . . without increasing your clothing budget!* You'll also receive the famous AMY VANDERBILT NEWSLETTER. It highlights important "inside doings" in the world of women!

Why we give you all this—for only 10¢
It's your special introduction to the Amy Vanderbilt Success Program for Women. *As a member you are not obligated to buy a thing!* Each month world famous women re-

'veal their secrets of success to YOU. Quickly you gain the poise and self-assurance that can make you more popular, more admired, more successful. Friends, neighbors (the men in your life, too) . . . all will praise the exciting new "you". You'll share "models' secrets" of fashion, glamor, hair styling, wardrobe planning and dieting . . . discover creative new cooking and decorating ideas . . . learn how to meet new people and make new friends . . . plan a dinner party . . . arrange flowers . . . buy antiques. In short — the right way to succeed at everything from handling your family budget to getting more fun out of life.

Send 10¢ now—no obligation to enroll
Mail the coupon below with only a dime.

You will receive the Fashion Guide and Newsletter, plus the Hair Care Guide. Soon after you will receive your first two monthly Success Guides for which you will be billed only $1 each, plus shipping and handling.

If not completely delighted, return your first two Success Guides within 10 days to cancel membership without obligation. But we think you'll want to stay in the program. The Fashion Guide and Hair Care Guide are yours to keep in any case. As a member, you'll receive two Success Program Guides and the current Newsletter each month at only $1 each, plus shipping and handling. You may cancel anytime. Mail coupon with 10¢ now to AMY VANDERBILT SUCCESS PROGRAM, Garden City, N.Y. 11530.

Take this New Fashion Guide
plus this New Hair Care Guide

both for only **10¢**

as a trial member of the Amy Vanderbilt Success Program for Women

NEW HAIR CARE GUIDE

If you believe that the shape of your face should determine your hairstyle, you're **wrong**. Know why? How can you use just one basic "set" to create about 80% of the hairstyles seen today? What are the 5 classic hairstyles that never go "out"—and can be updated with every fashion trend? Brunettes over 40: if your hair has turned very gray, why should you **not** re-color it in your original shade? Redheads: if the "fire" is dying out of your hair, how can you light it up again? Blondes: what can you do to prevent bleach-lightened hair from "turning color?" Wigs: which one type of wig gives you the most use? Find all the answers, and more, in this full-color 64-page guide.

The Amy Vanderbilt Success Program for Women
Dept. 17-LZY, Garden City, N.Y. 11530

I enclose my dime (to help cover shipping). Please enroll me in the Amy Vanderbilt Success Program for Women and send me Amy Vanderbilt's new Fashion Guide and Newsletter, plus the new Hair Care Guide—everything—for only 10¢. Soon after I will receive my first two monthly Success Guides with a bill for only $1 each, plus shipping and handling. I will return my first two monthly Guides within ten days if I do not want to remain a member. The Fashion Guide and Hair Care Guide are mine to keep in any case. Otherwise, continue to send me two new Success Guides each month, and bill me only $1 each, plus shipping and handling. I may cancel my trial membership anytime.

Print Name Miss
           Mrs. _____

Address _____

City _____ State _____ Zip _____

Credit reference _____

(Your telephone number, bank or department store where you have a charge account is sufficient.) Members accepted in U.S.A. and Canada only. Canadian members will be serviced from Toronto. Offer slightly different in Canada.

29-AV21C

SAFETY DIME HOLDER

1. FOLD DOWN OVER DIME
3. FOLD COIN POCKET OVER COUPON

PLACE DIME HERE

2. FOLD UP OVER DIME

DO NOT TAPE OR SEAL

SPLIT RUN TEST AD B

Which did better? (Answer at the bottom of page 650)

Courtesy: Doubleday & Co., Inc.
Advertising Agency: Altman, Vos & Reichberg, Inc.

Answer to Test on pp. 648–649: Ad B

SPLIT RUN TEST AD B

Which did better? (Answer at the bottom of page 653)

Courtesy: Record Club of America
Advertising Agency: Altman, Vos & Reichberg, Inc.

a

b

A DIRECT-MAIL TEST

These are the fronts of four folders making the same offer. One outpulled the others by far. Which? (Answer bottom of page 655).

Courtesy: Doubleday & Co., Inc.
Advertising Agency: Altman, Vos & Reichberg, Inc.

c

d

Direct-mail tests. Split-run testing is also done with direct mail. In testing ads, every other name on the list is sent mailing A; the other half of the names are sent mailing B. The order cards are keyed and the results are tabulated.

But to get *statistically meaningful differences,* you must use a big enough sample of a mailing list to produce enough responses to provide a clear answer as to which is the better ad. If mailing piece A produces fourteen orders while mailing piece B produces eleven, the result of the "test" is meaningless. And in order to make our "test beds" large enough, we have to have some idea of the percentage of response to expect. This will vary enormously by medium and by proposition.

Most direct-response advertisers expect a full-page magazine ad to pull from 0.05 percent to 0.20 percent of circulation; in other words, from one half of a response per thousand to two responses per thousand. This is a typical range of figures, but results vary enormously, of course. According to Vos, direct-mail results will usually range between 0.7 percent and 5.0 percent of names mailed—in other words, from seven orders per thousand to fifty orders per thousand. You will notice that the ratio of response per thousand between direct mail and magazine space is roughly on the order of 10 or 20 to 1. However, the same ratio applies to the cost per thousand of the two kinds of media. Therefore, many advertisers find that their *cost per order* for both space and direct mail is about the same.

The whole principle of mail-order testing comes down to these important elements:

1. Make sure that the names chosen for a direct-mail test are a fair sample of the rest of the list.

2. Make sure that the mailings that are to be compared with each other are identical in every respect except the *one* variable that is being tested. (Don't try testing several variables at a time in order to save time or money. Neither is saved.)

3. Keep accurate records of replies.

4. Do not change or attempt to improve the mailing or condition of mailing once a test has proved satisfactory. If any improvement in the mailing suggests itself, test it out before using it on the balance of the mailing. The test may show that it is no improvement at all.

5. First of all, test the *big differences* in offers or formats. Then, if you have the time, patience and money, test small refinements.

The conclusions drawn from a single mailing do not necessarily hold good for another product, another list, another season, or another offer.

Answer to Test on pp. 650–651: Ad A.

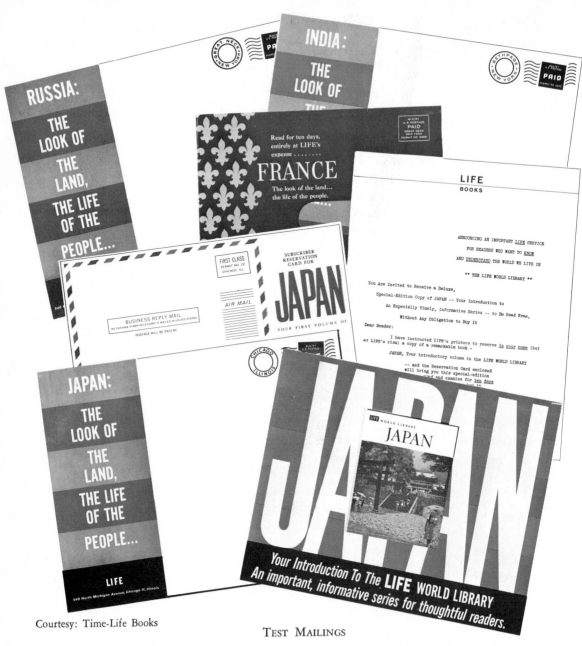

Courtesy: Time-Life Books

TEST MAILINGS

Each of these mailings consisted of a two-color letter, a four-color illustrative folder and return card, mailed in a colorful envelope. Each was devoted to a book describing a different country—India, Japan, France, and Russia. The test was to see whether the book of any one country would appeal more to readers than that of any other country.

Assuming the winner (Japan) had 100, Russia would receive a rating of 93, India 89, France 51.

Based on this test, 8 million mailings were issued the following year.

654

1. Decide general format.
2. Decide what printing process is to be used.
3. Select paper.
4. Check actual dummies with post office for weight and postage.
5. Decide on lists and size of test runs.
6. Get printing estimates.
7. Select printer; arrange for place of delivery, including envelopes.
8. Select lettershop or other mailing facility.
9. Place printing order.
10. Get proofs.
11. Get delivery.
12. Mail.

Television in Direct-response Advertising

The biggest boom in the use of television by national advertisers is by the direct-response advertisers. This industry has jumped in its use of television at the rate of 68 percent from 1970 to 1971. Direct-response TV has now passed the $50 million mark, a considerable figure for a medium that a few years ago was not considered a "direct-response medium."

Innovative marketers have found new methods of using TV that produce cost-per-thousand responses comparable to direct mail. Direct-response advertisers have found that television expands their markets by reaching prospects who were missed by traditional media. Record and book clubs, insurance companies, and direct marketers are among its biggest users.[2]

Differences in Use of TV for Direct-response Advertising

The yardstick of "cost per order" applies to television as it does to any other medium. The success of direct-response advertisers in television began when they broke away from the traditional time-buying philosophy of

---

[2] Jacob A. Evans, addressing the Mail Advertising Club of Chicago, September 8, 1971.

Answer to Test on p. 652: Ad C.

national advertisers. National advertisers want to reach as many people as possible at the lowest rate per thousand. They go by ratings, a fact that pushes them into expensive prime time. Direct-response advertisers have found there is no correlation between ratings and cost per order. And they have found that the low-cost spots produced low-cost orders.

Accordingly, they have gone for late-night shows, weekends, and other off-time periods, where the rate is low to start with. Also, at those periods they can afford the time to tell their full sales story, often using 120 seconds, as compared with the national advertiser's favorite 30-second spot. Some even use three minutes within a 15-minute program—using one minute to "set the stage," and later two minutes, giving the viewer time to get pencil and paper to take down the address, completing the sale.

TRENDS IN DIRECT-RESPONSE ADVERTISING

Direct-response advertising—and particularly direct-mail advertising—has grown greatly in recent years and will continue to grow rapidly in the years to come—despite the increased postal rates. The chief reason for this is the computer. Traditional mail-order companies now use these sophisticated electronic devices to provide them with data that makes media usage and mailing-list usage much more effective and profitable. And now other large advertisers—such as department stores and the big gasoline companies—have discovered that their computer can be much more than a supersonic accounting tool; it can also furnish them with the names and addresses of mail-order prospects, and therefore becomes an extra source of profit.

The next step may be electronic in-home ordering. Your cable-TV screen will show you a range of men's neckwear. If you see something you like, you'll simply push a few buttons on your set, the order will be received instantly and electronically, and somewhere a computer will be making this note: "Mr. Jones likes red neckties."

Review Questions

1. Distinguish among direct marketing, direct-response advertising, mail-order advertising, and direct-mail advertising.

2. In terms of consumer response, what differentiates direct-response advertising from most other advertising?

3. Explain why direct-response advertising is usually wordier than other advertising.

4. Discuss several ways in which direct-response advertisers use media, including TV, differently from most other advertisers.

5. Distinguish between house lists and outside lists; between compiled lists and response-derived lists.

6. Describe the role and functions of the list broker.

7. Discuss some of the criteria for good names for direct-response advertising.

8. Describe some of the special scheduling problems faced by the direct-mail production manager.

9. Explain how a split-run test works.

10. Discuss the main elements of conducting meaningful direct-response testing.

Reading Suggestions

Business Week. "Direct-Mail Ads Will Get More Direct," November 27, 1971, pp. 84, 86.

Hodgson, R. W., *Dartnell Direct Mail and Mail Order Handbook.* Chicago: Dartnell Corporation, 1964.

Rapp, Stanley, "How to Find Your Way Through the Treacherous Testing Maze," *The Reporter of Direct Mail Advertising,* 1967. Also in Kleppner and Settel, *Exploring Advertising,* p. 232.

Stone, Bob, "Four Assets, Four Liabilities of Today's Direct Mail," *Advertising Age,* June 1, 1970, pp. 50–51.

Stone, Bob, "Three Ways for Mail Advertisers to Boost Their Profits," *Advertising Age,* May 31, 1971, pp. 33–34.

Tobolski, Francis, "Direct Mail: Image, Return & Effectiveness," *Journal of Advertising Research,* August 1970, pp. 19–25.

29
Business Advertising

ALTHOUGH MORE MONEY IS spent on advertising to consumers than on any other form of advertising, more dollars are involved in the sales to business buyers than in those to consumers.[1]

This expenditure represents advertising directed to the distributive trades, referred to as *trade advertising,* and advertising to those who manufacture the goods, and do the building and construction, referred to as *industrial advertising.* Business advertising also includes advertising in professional journals to physicians, dentists, architects, and others who earn their living by practicing a profession; this is referred to as *professional advertising.*

TRADE PAPERS

The term *trade paper* is particularly applied to business publications addressed to those who buy products for resale, such as wholesalers, jobbers, retailers. Typical examples are: *American Druggist, Supermarket, Chain Store Age, Hardware Retailer, Jobber Topics* (automotive), *Women's Wear Daily, Home Furnishings,* whose points of view are revealed in their titles.

There is hardly a business engaged in distributing goods which does not have a special trade paper to discuss its problems. Trade papers are the great medium for reporting the merchandising news about products and packaging, prices, deals and promotions of the manufacturers who cater to their particular industries. The chain store field alone has 23 such publications. Druggists have a choice of 34, while 61 different publications are issued for grocers. There are many localized journals, as *California Food News, Illinois Beverages Journal, New England Hardware Journal, Texas Food Journal.*

Controlled Circulation

The business press includes paid circulation and *controlled* circulation. Most circulation is controlled circulation, which represents free cir-

---

[1] Philip Kotler, *Marketing Management* (Englewood Cliffs, N.J.: Prentice-Hall, Inc., 1967), p. 20.

PUBLISHER'S STATEMENT
For 6 Month Period Ending
DECEMBER 1971

BUSINESS PUBLICATIONS AUDIT OF CIRCULATION, INC.
360 Park Avenue South, New York, N.Y. 10010

No attempt has been made to rank the information contained in this report in order of importance, since BPA believes this is a judgment which must be made by the user of the report.

PROGRESSIVE GROCER

Butterick Div., American Can Company

708 Third Avenue, New York, New York 10017

OFFICIAL PUBLICATION OF   None

ESTABLISHED   1922   ISSUES PER YEAR   12

FIELD SERVED

Super markets, convenience stores and food markets; their headquarters and executives; and voluntaries, cooperatives, wholesale grocers; rack jobbers and food brokers.

DEFINITION OF RECIPIENT QUALIFICATION

The following are eligible to receive PROGRESSIVE GROCER:

Chain and independent super markets, convenience stores and food markets.
Chain executives, buyers and store supervisors.
Voluntary and co-operative headquarters, executives, buyers and store supervisors.
Wholesale grocers, executives, buyers and store supervisors.
Rack jobbers.
Food brokers.
Food associations, colleges and government food executives.

AVERAGE NON-QUALIFIED DISTRIBUTION

	Copies
☆ Advertiser and Agency	☆ 7,342
Non-Qualified Paid	–
Rotated or Occasional	–
Samples	–
All Other	6,962
(See Para. 11) . . . **TOTAL**	14,304

1. AVERAGE QUALIFIED CIRCULATION BREAKDOWN FOR PERIOD

	Qualified Non-Paid		Qualified Paid		Total Qualified	
	Copies	Percent	Copies	Percent	Copies	Percent
Single	81,296	100.0%	–	–	81,296	100.0%
Group	–	–	–	–	–	–
Association	–	–	–	–	–	–
Gift	–	–	–	–	–	–
Bulk	–	–	–	–	–	–
TOTALS	81,296	100.0%	–	–	81,296	100.0%

U.S. POSTAL MAILING CLASSIFICATION . . . . . . CONTROLLED CIRCULATION

2. QUALIFIED CIRCULATION BY ISSUES WITH REMOVALS AND ADDITIONS FOR PERIOD

1971 Issue	Qualified Non-Paid	Qualified Paid	Total Qualified	Number Removed	Number Added	1971 Issue	Qualified Non-Paid	Qualified Paid	Total Qualified	Number Removed	Number Added
July			80,630	1,732	2,436	Oct			82,267	777	1,874
August			80,104	1,741	1,215	Nov			81,757	1,687	1,177
Sept			81,170	811	1,877	Dec			81,849	669	761
						TOTALS				7,417	9,340

PUBLISHER'S STATEMENT

The interesting thing on this first page of a publisher's statement of a controlled circulation tradepaper is the record of "Qualified Circulation." To get the publication without cost a person must be eligible, as stated above; he must make a request, in writing, and annually renew the request, in writing.

#1 Sunburn Remedy...#1 Seller

Solarcaine 38.7% profit deal

Plus 5% for promotional display*- Plus 5% advertising allowance*

1971 Solarcaine Counter Unit Deal #2059

UNIT CONTAINS

	QUANTITY	ITEM	SELLS FOR
BUY:	9 Each	Lotion, 3 oz., $1.49	$13.41
	3 Each	Lotion, 6 oz., $2.19	6.57
	3 Each	Cream, 1 oz., 92¢	2.76
	2 Each	Cream, 2 oz., $1.49	2.98
	3 Each	Aerosol Spray, 4 oz., $2.19	6.57
FREE:	1 Each	Cream, 1 oz., 92¢	.92
	1 Each	Aerosol Spray, 4 oz., $2.19	2.19
	1 Each	Lotion, 3 oz., $1.49	1.49
		TOTAL RETAIL VALUE...	$36.89

SELLS FOR $36.89
COSTS $22.61 **PROFIT $14.28 = 38.7%***

Phone your favorite supplier today.

9-5/8" wide x 7" deep x 18-1/2" high.

#1 in Advertising...#1 in Net Profits!

Multi-million dollar ad campaign pre-sells Solarcaine ... and keeps the big fat profit-dollars rolling in.

Network TV. Full-color commercials on TV hits like: Marcus Welby, M.D., Love, American Style, Saturday Night At The Movies, Sunday Night Movies, The Bold Ones, other top-rated shows.
Network Radio. All 3 networks. Up

to 100 selling messages per week, network and spot, on 850 stations.

48 Leading Magazines. Full page color ads in 48 leading National Magazines, including Reader's Digest, delivering over 250,000,000 reader messages.

Full-Color Sunday Supplement Ads. Big space ads in 82 leading newspapers coast-to-coast ... selling

Solarcaine hard at the local level.

Outdoor, Skytyping. Thousands of outdoor boards in major markets. Plus SKYTYPING — reaching 15,000,000 potential customers with messages 20 miles wide above leading beach areas.

Plough, Inc.
Memphis, Tennessee 38101

A TRADE PAPER ADVERTISEMENT

Addressed to druggists, talks profits, based on a counter display of assorted Solarcaine products, at a special deal price, plus promotional display and advertising allowances. Stresses also the advertising designed to pre-sell Solarcaine to the consumer.

We've just added a third season* of Simoniz sell!

We're out there 3 seasons out of the year —not just two like everybody else. That's because we do things differently. For instance: we sell right into the fall season with a tough "Winter Protection" commercial for television, radio and print. Plus a durability story you have to see to believe—and you will see it on upcoming commercials.

Any wonder we're first in the car-wax field with Vista and Master Wax products?

SPRING, SUMMER AND *FALL ADVERTISING IN:

- RADIO
- TV (Network and Spot)
- MEN'S magazines
- SPORTS magazines
- CAR BUFF magazines
- SCIENCE & MECH. magazines

Automotive products bring husband in to grocery store:

1. He spends more
2. She spends 67% more
($8.25 VS $13.81)

Will you have it to sell when they come in to buy it?

A TRADE PAPER ADVERTISEMENT

Addressed to supermarkets, this advertisement tells what Simoniz is doing to expand the consumer buying season for its products. Stressing also that automobile products increase store traffic.

culation to a carefully selected list of those who are in a position to influence sales; furthermore, they must express in writing a desire to receive, or continue to receive, the publication in order to qualify for the list. They must also give title and function.

Circulation Audits

The leading publications belong to the Business Publications Audit of Circulation, Inc. (BPA). This organization serves in the business field the same function that the Audit Bureau of Circulations performs in the consumer field. In their audit of circulation they place particular attention upon the qualifications of all those on the controlled list, and when they last indicated they wanted the publication. Some publications have both ABC and BPA audits.

A third auditing group is the Verified Audit Circulation Company (VAC). Its standards differ somewhat from those of BPA.

The AIA Media Data Form

For many years, every publisher of a business or professional publication supplied additional data about his publication in whatever form he wished, covering such topics as he wished, to the confusion of all who tried to use such information in making media comparisons and planning schedules. Finally, through the efforts of the Association of Industrial Advertisers and with the cooperation of other interested associates, an agreement was reached as to the basic information to be given in standardized sequence and presented in a uniform way. This is referred to as the *AIA Media Data Form,* which an increasing number of publishers are using.

Many business publications—especially the smaller ones—do not offer any audit circulation report.

Trade Paper Copy

No matter what the field, all trade papers have a common editorial policy—to tell the dealer how to make more money in his operation.

An issue of a hardware dealers' magazine had articles on "Gets Four Annual Turnovers from Stock of 75 Gadgets," "New Store Front Increases Business by 30 Percent," "Contest Attracts Fishermen to Lyndale Store." The advertising likewise discusses not how good a product is—that is taken for granted—but how it will help the profit picture of the store. Among the subjects featured are news about the product, such as:

—a change in the product
—a new style of packaging of a present product
—a new display idea
—a new consumer deal

—a new store deal

—a plan for a new advertising campaign involving the retailer (couponing)

—a new promotional idea

—a new in-store suggestion for improving sales of the advertised and related products

—and any other idea that will help sales and reduce expense.

AIA Media Form

The first page of a form used by industrial publications to "assist advertisers and agencies in their media analysis by helping publishers to present information in a concise and orderly manner." Each subject is in uniform numbered sequence.

Publication Name: Progressive Grocer

REGISTERED

◆ AIA

MEDIA DATA FORM

Harold D. Hayes   DATE *May 12, 1972*
EXECUTIVE SECRETARY

MEDIA COMPARABILITY COUNCIL

This form is designed to be used in conjunction with Standard Rate and Data, (SRDS) and Canadian Advertising Rates and Data (CARD), publisher's rate card, circulation audit (or statement of circulation) and other available data. Its purpose is to assist advertisers and agencies in their media analysis by helping publishers to present pertinent information in a concise and orderly manner.

This Media Data Form is sponsored and approved by the Association of Industrial Advertisers, Association of National Advertisers, American Association of Advertising Agencies, American Business Press, Society of National Association Publications and Association of Canadian Advertisers. It may be used in conformity with the bylaws and rules of the Audit Bureau of Circulations, the Business Publication Audit of Circulation, Verified Audit Circulation Corp. and the Canadian Audit Board by member publications.

Registration of this form by the AIA Media Comparability Council **does not constitute validation of the information contained herein or endorsement of the publication by any sponsoring organization.** No attempt has been made to value-judge the items herein or place them in any rank order. Responsibility for proper use of this information rests entirely with the media planner.

1.   All information printed in this form is current as of **December 31, 1971**

2.   Publication Name: Progressive Grocer
     Street Address: 708 Third Avenue
     City, State, or Province: New York, New York   Zip: 10017
     Publishing Company: The Butterick Division, American Can Co.

3.   Is the circulation of this publication audited by ABC, BPA, VAC or CCAB?   Yes
     If Yes, by whom?   Business Publications Audit of Circulation, Inc.
     Show symbol:
     If not, explain:

Publication Name:

◆ AIA

media data form

1972

Publication Name: Progressive Grocer

NOTE TO USER: As an aid to the interpretation of information contained herein, it is suggested that the user request a copy of "Publisher's Step-by-Step Instructions." Copies are available either from the publisher or headquarters of sponsoring Associations.   Copyright 1972 AIA

INDEX: GENERAL
CIRCULATION 1- 8
UNITS & UNIVERSE .19

CIRCULATION 9-18

ADVERTISING 20-24
EDITORIAL 25-31
READERSHIP 32-35

Industrial Advertising

Every business establishment that makes something or renders a service has to buy something—raw and finished materials, machinery, tools, equipment, and possibly the materials for erecting its own buildings. It takes many men with technical skill to decide what to buy. Advertising addressed to the men responsible for buying the goods needed to make products and render services is called *industrial advertising.* Such advertising is designed to reach purchasing agents, plant managers, engineers, comptrollers, and others who have a voice in spending the firm's money for materials and equipment.

The Uniqueness of Industrial Advertising

Industrial advertising is addressed to men who have their own approach to making business decisions. For example:

1. Buying is done with a sense of professional responsibility, asking, "Will this prove to be the best choice?" A poor decision will be around to haunt all who shared in it.
2. Buyers purchase to meet predetermined specifications, not on impulse.
3. Many men may be involved in a decision—a scientist, a designer, an engineer, a production manager, a purchasing agent, a comptroller—each approaching the problem from his special viewpoint.
4. Decisions are made after many demonstrations, much inquiry, many meetings.
5. With so many individuals involved, so many actions to be taken, with so much money that may be involved, there is often a big time lag between the moment it was decided to consider a purchase and the final decision.

One may get an idea of the complexity of reaching an industrial buying decision from these cases in a report issued on the subject by Time, Inc.

An air-conditioning exhaust system—the kind found in office buildings and factories, as opposed to a room air-conditioner for home use. The process of purchasing an air-conditioning exhaust system can be very complicated. Some 16 actions were taken by six individuals within the company.

A case loader—a packaging machine used for loading small, packaged bottles into corrugated containers. Some 13 actions were taken by nine individuals or groups of individuals in middle management, top management, and purchasing.

An encoder drum—part of an electrical system needed in a Department of Defense project. Some 12 actions were taken by three individuals within the company. In addition, four suppliers were involved, as well as the U.S. government offices concerned with this project.

A desk calculator—the kind normally found in offices throughout the United States. It is a lightweight, semiportable, and highly versatile machine small enough to be placed on a desk, as opposed to a special "table" by the desk. Some eight actions were taken by four individuals or groups of individuals within the company.

Carpeting—the kind of floor covering normally found in offices and reception rooms. Some 10 actions were taken by 11 individuals within the company.[2]

It will be seen from the foregoing that anywhere from three to eleven different individuals had a say in the final buying decision. The problem is to reach all who may be involved.

The Effectiveness of Industrial Advertising

McGraw-Hill made a study to measure the effect of advertising on the cost of selling an industrial product. They gathered figures from 893 industrial companies and divided them into two groups. They ranked the companies from lowest to highest according to advertising as a percentage of sales expenses, thus dividing the "higher" from the "lower" advertisers.

Then they examined *total* selling costs (including personal salesmen), measured as a percent of total sales, of both the higher advertisers and the lower advertisers. They found that higher advertisers had total sales expenses (including advertising) that were 21 percent below that of the lower advertisers.[3]

The Arthur D. Little Company reported on the findings of 1,100 studies of the effectiveness of industrial advertising. Among the conclusions reached by the various studies are the following:

Buchen Study—companies that maintain their advertising in recession years have better sales and profits in those and in later years.

Harnischfeger Study—industrial advertising reaches purchasing influences not normally reached by the salesman.

---

[2] Based on a study conducted for *Time* magazine by Dr. Emanuel Demby, Fairleigh Dickinson University. Published courtesy of Time, Inc.

[3] "How Advertising Affects the Cost of Selling," a McGraw-Hill Research Report (New York: McGraw-Hill Book Company, 1963).

Now MOORE jig-grinds

No. 5 NC Jig Grinder shown grinding a master gage, a product of Moore's new Gage Division. The gage is used for checking out taper probe-type Coordinate Measuring Machines. Tapered grinding wheel is dressed with radius-angle attachment on Moore's self-contained Universal Wheel Dresser. This newly developed accessory is readily adaptable to all Moore Jig Grinders.

Moore Special Tool Co., which brought jig grinding to industry 30 years ago, and has pioneered every major development in jig grinding since, now introduces the Nos. 4 and 5 Jig Grinders.

The new machines, with travel on the No. 4 of 18 in. x 32 in. (450 mm x 800 mm) and 24 in. x 48 in. (610 mm x 1200 mm) on the No. 5, make it possible to jig grind larger workpiece sizes—to accuracies in the millionths.

The No. 4 and No. 5 Jig Grinders incorporate all of the construction features and ultra-accurate measuring system which have made the Moore No. 3 Jig Grinder a standard of excellence and precision throughout the world.

Both of the new machines — Standard Models — carry Moore's 10-year guarantee of accuracy.

The longer travels of the No. 4 and No. 5 Jig Grinders make the unique efficiencies of numerical control all the more significant. Both machines are available in point-to-point and continuous path NC with General Electric Mark Century* controls—as well as in standard models.

*Trademark of General Electric Co.

Shown here is a Moore No. 3 Continuous Path Jig Grinder with General Electric Mark Century Numerical Control. Many of these machines are being used in industry at as much as 10:1 time savings over conventional jig grinding.

in the largest size range

Introducing the No. 4 and No. 5

Both the No. 4 and No. 5 Precision Jig Grinders employ the same measuring system used in Moore's No. 4 and 5 Universal Measuring Machines. Repeatability of settings is ±5 millionths inch (0,15 μm). The X and Y axes have either standard inch or metric lead screws and are power-driven. Spindle housing is also power-driven.

Other features include remote control for wheel outfeed and spindle clutch, automatic clamping and unclamping on all three axes, and double-V, frictionless roller-way construction.

In longitudinal and cross travel, the greatest error in any inch is 30 millionths inch (0,8 μm). Total accumulative error in the longitudinal travel is 150 millionths inch (3,8 μm), and in the cross travel 90 millionths inch (2,3 μm).

The No. 4 and No. 5 Moore Jig Grinders can be supplied with General Electric Mark Century 7500 series Numerical Control systems for point-to-point or continuous path operation. These controls can be provided with an additional rotary axis control for angular positioning.

Moore Readout (as shown in photos) is a recommended option available in either inch and/or metric, with 0.00001 in./0,0001 mm resolution.

Write us for complete details.

Moore No. 5
Precision Jig Grinder
with 24 inch x 48 inch travel (610 mm x 1200 mm).

Moore No. 4
Precision Jig Grinder
with 18 inch x 32 inch travel (450 mm x 800 mm).

buy now or pay later

MOORE SPECIAL TOOL CO., INC.

Bridgeport, Connecticut 06607 • European Technical Center: 8005 Zurich, Switzerland

Manufacturers of Jig Borers, Jig Grinders, Universal Measuring Machines, Rotary Tables, Tool Room Products and High Precision Measuring Instruments and Gages.

American Machinist, March 6, 1972

Circle 19 on reader service card   19

Two pages of facts about Moore jig-grinds. You don't have to be an engineer to perceive that this equipment represents a heavy investment, but the ad has to convince engineers and production men that the investment is worth while for their company.

Morrill Studies—it reduces the cost per sales dollar by supplementing the salesman.

American Metal Market Study—product advertising increases the share of potential buyers who consider the brand.

Production Study—industrial advertising reaches purchasers that the salesman can't find or does not have the time to cover.[4]

INDUSTRIAL PUBLICATIONS

There are many industrial publications designed to reach the men who make the purchasing decisions for the production of goods by business enterprises. These publications may be classified as *vertical* and *horizontal*.

Vertical industrial papers are those discussing problems of a single industry. *Frosted Food Field,* for example, "is edited for management personnel in the frosted food industry . . . contains articles on frozen food distribution, processing, purchasing, merchandising, transportation, warehousing." *Mechanical Contractor* is "designed to meet the needs of the large heating, piping, plumbing, and air-conditioning contractor." Each industry will have many publications devoted to its production problems. For example, in the construction-engineering classification in the Standard Rate & Data Service, 86 publications are listed.

Horizontal publications are edited for men who have similar functions in their companies, regardless of their specific industry, as *Industrial Maintenance and Plant Operation,* published for those responsible for "maintenance and operation of industrial plants of over 50 employes," or *Purchasing,* "a news magazine for purchasing executives with titles such as purchasing agent, director of procurement, vice-president in charge of purchasing."

There are also many state publications. About 200 of the largest publications have geographic and demographic editions. About 15 publications have international editions.

Auditing reports. Most audited business publications are distributed on a controlled-circulation basis.[5] They belong to Business Publications Audit of Circulation, Inc. (BPA). Others belong to the Audit Bureau of Circulations (ABC).

PROFESSIONAL PUBLICATIONS

The Standard Rate & Data Service has a special edition for *Business Publications*. These publications include journals addressed to the professions—

---

[4] *Industrial Marketing,* June 1971.
[5] See p. 658.

physicians, surgeons, dentists, architects, and other professionals—and their editorial range varies from reporting new technical developments to discussing how to run offices more efficiently and profitably. Professional men are a most important influence in recommending or specifying the products their patients or clients will need. Much advertising, therefore, is addressed to them. The writing of copy for such publications requires training and education in the field addressed. It is a specialized arm of the advertising agency business.

Standard Industrial Classification Index (SIC)

One of the great marketing facilities enjoyed in industrial marketing and selling is the classification of all business establishments by the Bureau of the Budget. All enterprises fall into one or more of the 94 identifiable establishments. Each has a number and is always uniform. Then, by a series of additional digits, more detailed information about the plant is conveyed.

This means that industrial publications can provide an analysis of the circulation going to each classification. The advertiser can then pick the publication reaching the greatest number of the specific prospects he is seeking. This is also helpful in direct mail, in selecting prospects, as we shall again discuss.

Industrial Advertising Copy

Industrial advertising speaks to engineers and to other men who are technically trained in their calling. They read their trade or professional journals because of a constant challenge to keep informed of the latest developments affecting their field; they have to fight professional obsolescence. They read advertisements with the same critical curiosity with which they read the editorial matter. They are looking for news of products and experiences relevant to their problems, expressed in specific, factual form. They are interested in problems and their solution; they are most interested in case reports showing how some problem was successfully met. They seek confirmation or other proof of all claims made. They will read long copy, and welcome any charts or photographs that help explain matters.

Most advertisements make a strong bid to the reader to write for further information. Industrial advertising adheres closely to the copy structure discussed earlier—promise of benefit, amplification, proof, action.

Use of case histories. The case history is one of the most satisfying approaches in presenting a story to industrial advertisers. It can be used in many ways as part of an integrated promotion. These are outlined by Hofsoos as follows:

1. As a publicity release
2. As an advertisement
3. As a data or fact sheet for salesmen
4. As direct mail
5. As sales and technical literature
6. As displays and exhibits.[6]

INDUSTRIAL DIRECT MAIL

Of 615 industrial advertisers responding to a survey on direct mail conducted by the Association of Industrial Advertisers, 68 percent spent 10 percent of their budget on direct mail; 25 percent of the respondents spent 25 percent of their budget on direct mail; 5 percent spent 50 percent of their budget on direct mail; and 2 percent spent 75 percent of their budget for direct mail.

The chief purposes are to announce new products, inform of product features, obtain sales leads, and announce changes in price.[7]

The great problem in industrial direct mail is to determine who will be involved in the buying decisions of a forthcoming project. Among the steps toward arriving at a final buying decision, in which different men might join, are these:

—Determining the need
—Establishing specifications
—Preparing a list of potential buyers
—Contracting suppliers
—Evaluating suppliers
—Determining suppliers
—Placing the order
—Postpurchase evaluation [8]

One cannot always tell by their titles who are the men to contact by mail at any of these stages.

In discussing lists, National Business Lists advises:

Possibly the most crucial step in mapping out a direct-mail support program is to insure quality by the careful selection of the right

---

[6] Emil Hofsoos, *Industrial Advertising* (Houston, Tex.: Gulf Publishing Company, 1970), p. 73.

[7] Direct Mail Survey of AIA Members, Association of Industrial Advertisers, 1968, pp. 1–2.

[8] *Ibid.*

market segments. Out of the lists of four million and more names, you can carefully pick your way to the most suitable targets for your direct mail by means of several criteria.

Start with the government's *Standard Industrial Classifications* that neatly fit *all* businesses into nine major categories, each divided into hundreds of numerically designated groups, much like the Dewey Decimal System that makes it possible to find the book you want in any well-ordered library. *Manufacturing* is one of the major categories, refined into twenty groups. One of the groups is *Electrical Machinery and Equipment* (#36). In turn, this group is split into scores of specific classifications, ranging from *Welding Apparatus*

Manufacturing Firms Continued

SIC	QUANT.	PRICE	MIN QUANT	SIC	QUANT.	PRICE	MIN QUANT
□3211	84 Flat glass	$15/L	ALL	□3315	152 Steel wire drawing, nails & spikes	$15/L	ALL
				□3316	117 Cold rolled sheet, strip, & bars	$15/L	ALL
□3221	119 Glass containers	$15/L	ALL	□3317	162 Steel pipe & tubes	$15/L	ALL
□3229	306 Pressed & blown glassware, n.e.c.	$20/L	ALL				
				□3321	868 Gray iron foundries	$30/L	ALL
□3231	685 Glass products from purchased glass	$28/L	ALL	□3322	113 Malleable iron foundries	$15/L	ALL
□3241	247 Cement, hydraulic	$20/L	ALL	□3323	218 Steel foundries	$20/L	ALL
□3251	484 Brick & structural clay tile	$20/L	ALL	□3331	37 Primary smelting & refining of copper	$15/L	ALL
□3253	130 Ceramic wall & floor tile	$15/L	ALL	□3332	23 Primary smelting & refining of lead	$15/L	ALL
□3255	183 Clay refractories	$15/L	ALL	□3333	35 Primary smelting & refining of zinc	$15/L	ALL
□3259	143 Structural clay products, n.e.c.	$15/L	ALL	□3334	59 Primary production of aluminum	$15/L	ALL
□3261	54 Vitreous china plumbing fixtures, china & earthenware fittings & bathrm accessories	$15/L	ALL	□3339	78 Primary smelting & refining of nonferrous metals, n.e.c.	$15/L	ALL
□3262	35 Vitreous china table & kitchen ware	$15/L	ALL	□3341	245 Secondary nonferrous refining	$20/L	ALL
□3263	20 Fine earthenware kitchen articles	$15/L	ALL	□3351	141 Rolling, drawing & extruding copper	$15/L	ALL
□3264	70 Porcelain electrical supplies	$15/L	ALL	□3352	238 Rolling, drawing & extruding aluminum	$20/L	ALL
□3269	455 Pottery products, n.e.c.	$20/L	ALL	□3356	195 Rolling, drawing, except 3351 & 3352	$15/L	ALL
□3271	1,896 Concrete brick & block manufacturers	$30/M	1,000	□3357	256 Drawing & insulating nonferrous wire	$20/L	ALL
	1,844 Rated $10,000 & over*	add	5/M	□3361	907 Aluminum castings	$30/L	ALL
	1,745 Rated $35,000 & over*	add	7/M	□3362	573 Copper & copper alloy castings	$28/L	ALL
	987 Rated $35,000 & over	add	18/M	□3369	387 Nonferrous castings, n.e.c.	$20/L	ALL
□3272	2,459 Concrete products, except 3271	$30/M	1,000	□3391	372 Iron & steel forgings	$20/L	ALL
□3273	2,979 Ready mixed concrete	$28/M	1,250	□3392	34 Nonferrous forgings	$15/L	ALL
□3274	119 Lime	$15/L	ALL	□3399	636 Primary metal industries, n.e.c.	$28/L	ALL
□3275	117 Gypsum products	$15/L	ALL				
□3281	847 Cut stone & stone products	$30/L	ALL	□3400	25,168 Fabricated metal products, except SICS 1900, 3500, 3600 and 3700 (SIC 3411 through 3499 combined)	$23/M	3,000
□3291	311 Abrasive products	$20/L	ALL		23,963 Rated $10,000 & over*	add	5/M
□3292	157 Asbestos products	$15/L	ALL		22,436 Rated $20,000 & over*	add	7/M
□3293	266 Pipe packing & insulating materials	$20/L	ALL		20,78% Rated $35,000 & over	add	10/M
□3295	500 Minerals & earths, ground & treated	$28/L	ALL		8,058 Rated $75,000 & over	add	23/M
□3296	124 Mineral wool	$15/L	ALL		5,321 Rated $200,000 & over	add	28/M
□3297	70 Nonclay refractories	$15/L	ALL	□3411	252 Metal cans	$20/L	ALL
□3299	296 Nonmetallic mineral products, n.e.c.	$20/L	ALL	□3421	131 Cutlery	$15/L	ALL
□3300	6,352 Primary metal industries (SIC 3312 through 3399 combined)	$26/M	1,500	□3423	640 Hand & edge tools, except 3425,3541 & 3542	$28/L	ALL
	6,003 Rated $20,000 & over*	add	7/M	□3425	122 Hand saws & saw blades	$15/L	ALL
	5,782 Rated $35,000 & over*	add	10/M	□3429	993 Hardware, n.e.c.	$30/L	ALL
	2,727 Rated $75,000 & over	add	23/M	□3431	165 Enameled iron & metal sanitary ware	$15/L	ALL
	2,206 Rated $200,000 & over	add	28/M	□3432	249 Plumbing fixture fittings and trim (brass goods)	$20/L	ALL
□3312	452 Blast furnaces (including coke ovens), steel works & rolling mills	$20/L	ALL	□3433	518 Heating equipment, except electric	$28/L	ALL
□3313	45 Electrometallurgical products	$15/L	ALL				

□ List compiled from latest credit reference directories and verified by checking most recent alphabetical phone books. Names not in phone book dropped from list.
* Includes unrated firms because well over 50% would be in this category if rated. Add $8/M to exclude unrated.

Counts by state and larger cities are available on request for all lists with more than 2,000 names, but not for smaller lists.

23

Courtesy: National Business Lists, Inc.

INDUSTRIAL MAILING LISTS

A page from a catalog of a firm specializing in gathering and selling mailing lists to industrial advertisers. Note the variety.

(#3623) to *Phonograph Records* (#3652). Would your products have the same degree of application in both of those—or should you be choosing with explicit care? Why scatter your shot when you can choose the quality of prospect that means success for your sales effort? The SIC, short for Standard Industrial Classification, is an excellent weapon for that purpose.

There are other criteria that may be equally useful to you. You may want to refine your overall market by isolating businesses of different financial stature . . . or by the yardstick of number of employes.[9]

CATALOGS AND DIRECTORIES

Many industrial producers make parts and equipment that are sold through hardware supply, electrical supply, and other distributive channels. These establishments could not possibly keep on hand an inventory of all the many items for which they get occasional calls. Rather, they maintain a series of loose-leaf binders, for which manufacturers supply the pages in standardized sizes. The issuance of these pages is a large part of the advertising budget.

Every industry will have its directory and buyers' guide, with descriptions of its lines, and lists of the various companies selling its products. These directories are a responsible medium for any firm that wishes to have its name before their audiences. Thomas' Register of American Manufacturers, a distinguished comprehensive directory and catalog, even has its offerings on microfilm, in a form that can stand on a purchasing agent's desk.

BUSINESS SHOWS; PUBLICITY

One of the dependable sources of new leads for salesmen is the annual business show given by each of the many industries. All the leading sellers have booths presenting their products. All who are interested attend such shows. Another is the reaction to significant publicity; what makes such news significant and worth publicity is what it reports as a significant contribution of technology. It begins in the R&D department. But such developments do not come out every month; therefore the resourceful-minded publicity man seeks to generate some news—perhaps the issuance of a new helpful manual, or an informative film. The art lies in having something to say, not just in sending out "news" releases that no editor would accept as news from his reporters.

---

[9] *The Q Concept,* National Business Lists, Chicago, 1971, pp. 7–8.

The top executives of a company never get away from major problems. They read many publications outside those of their industry, but the problems of their own business are always in their minds. As a result, much advertising by industry appears in publications such as *Time, Newsweek, U.S. News & World Report, Forbes, Fortune,* and the *Wall Street Journal.* These advertisements usually tell of how a company licked a major problem that may apply to other companies, or present some new corporate development or facility that may benefit many companies.

Corporate Industrial Advertising—Television

The following is an excerpt from a case report on the use of television to sell expensive computers to top corporate management:

> The problem: Can television generate sales for a high-priced item aimed at a select group of businessmen?
>
> NCR, a 100-year-old company headquartered in Dayton, was a Johnny-come-lately in the computer field. In 1968, NCR introduced its century line of computers at a cost of $150 million. This brought NCR into direct competition with IBM and four other major computer makers.
>
> Could NCR convince customers that its computers would outperform already accepted models? Board Chairman Robert Oelman thought so and he set a sales goal of 5,000 computers—more than twice the number NCR had sold of its older models in the previous five years.

Advertisement, *Advertising Age*

After a thorough investigation, Ira Hays received a go-ahead to use television as an important element in his "marketing muscle" campaign. NCR bought network announcements in a golf match telecast from its home course in Dayton. Since then, CBS and NBC football, news, and news documentaries have been part of the television mix for NCR.

Last year, Ira Hayes outlined NCR's advertising goals as follows: "One: to create a new identity for NCR as an important producer of computers and related products. Two, to effect continual increase in awareness and knowledge of individual products as they apply to specific industries. And three, we want decision makers to think of us as *the* computer. . . ."

At the June '70 annual meeting, a stockholder asked Chairman Oelman if the century marketing strategy had been successful. His answer: "We already have some 2,500 orders, over 1,000 installations. And our share of market is steadily growing." And *Business Week,* June 5th, 1971, reports NCR computer sales "up sharply." [10]

CORPORATE INDUSTRIAL ADVERTISING—RADIO

Radio is used by industrial advertisers, especially at drive time, to reach their prospects. The Association of Industrial Advertisers reports:

> One advertiser concentrating with radio is Standard Oil of New Jersey. "We like to isolate markets," John Irwin, senior advisor for advertising and films, told us. "We use 11 stations in New York and 6 in Washington. We try to speak to a select audience by time period and station. We want to reach the decision makers, financial community, and government officials."
>
> Another longtime radio user is the Timken Roller Bearing Company of Canton, Ohio.
>
> Jim Oaks, Timken's ad manager, told us: "We use radio to reach select audiences in cities where the audience has an involvement with automobiles. We heavy-up in Detroit, where we run 18 spots a week aimed at automotive management, engineers, and purchasing agents. In addition, we run 12 spots a week in Pittsburgh.
>
> "To reach the industrial audience, we run 15 spots a week in Chicago, Cleveland, Milwaukee, and Moline. Our main programming is disc jockey music in morning and evening drive time. We've gotten a lot of playback from our radio spots over the years.[11]

---

[10] From presentation of Mr. Norman E. Cash, president of the Television Bureau of Advertising, before the Association of Industrial Advertisers, Palmer House, Chicago, June 23, 1971.

[11] *Media Decisions,* October 1971.

Industrial advertising is usually handled through agencies that specialize in the field, or who have men with training or experience in the sciences, engineering, chemistry, or in writing about these subjects. Such agencies are usually equipped to handle all phases of an industrial advertiser's promotion needs, including advertising, publicity, brochures, and manuals. Medical advertising to physicians has its specialized agencies and writers; sometimes such agencies are separate divisions of consumer agencies.

Budgets for industrial advertising are much smaller, as a rule, than for consumer advertising. In a questionnaire to industrial advertisers by The Gallagher Report, 163 responses were received. Their expenditures for 1971 averaged $452,700.[12] In consumer advertising, it is often possible to feel the effects of advertising on sales quickly. With the great time lag in industrial advertising between first expression of interest and final sale, with the burden of consummating that sale falling on the sales department, the direct contribution of advertising cannot easily be isolated. As Wittner pointed out, men who have come up through marketing rarely occupy the top spots in companies whose products are sold to business and industry.[13]

Which means that the full potential of advertising industrial products is yet to be experienced.

Review Questions

1. What is meant by industrial advertising?

2. Compare the major characteristics of industrial buying decisions and consumer buying decisions.

3. Distinguish between vertical and horizontal publications.

4. What is SIC? Describe its usefulness to industrial advertisers.

5. How does the nature of the industrial buying decision affect the content of industrial ads? What is the chief substance of such ads?

6. For the industrial advertiser, what is the role of (a) catalogs and directories, (b) trade shows, and (c) publicity?

7. Discuss the reasons why an industrial advertiser would undertake an advertising campaign in non-industrial magazines. In television. In radio.

8. How does the message of trade paper advertising differ from that of consumer advertising? Industrial advertising?

9. What is a B.P.A. audit?

---

[12] The Gallagher Report, Vol. XIX, No. 51852, 1971.
[13] *Media Decisions,* July, 1971, p. 60.

Business Week, "Industrial Ads: The View from the Top," May 30, 1970, p. 92ff.

Carman, James M., "Evaluation of Trade Show Exhibitions," *California Management Review,* Winter 1968, pp. 35–44.

Fox, Howard W., "A Framework of Industrial Marketing," *Baylor Business Studies* (Waco, Texas: Baylor University), November–December 1971.

Hofsoos, Emil, *What Management Should Know About Industrial Advertising.* Houston, Texas: Gulf Publishing Company, 1970.

Korn, Don, "Sales Managers Call the Shots To Get More Sell," *Sales Management,* November 29, 1971, pp. 19–24.

Messner, Fred R., *Industrial Advertising.* New York: McGraw-Hill Book Company, Inc., 1963.

Morrill, John E., "Industrial Advertising Pays Off," *Harvard Business Review,* March–April 1970, pp. 4–14.

Sales Management, "New Evidence: Industrial Ads Get Results," May 15, 1970, pp. 21–22.

Schiller, Robert D., ed., *Market and Media Evaluation.* New York: The Macmillan Company, 1969.

30

Legal and Other
Controls of Advertising

Kings: 19 mg."tar," 1.3 mg. nicotine—
100's: 20 mg."tar," 1.5 mg. nicotine av. per cigarette, FTC Report Apr.'72

Warning: The Surgeon General Has Determined That
Cigarette Smoking Is Dangerous to Your Health.

WHEN WINSTON CHURCHILL took his entrance examinations to get into
Sandhurst in 1880, he was given a choice of three essay questions: *Riding vs.
Rowing; Advertisements, Their Use and Abuse;* and *The American Civil War.*
(He chose *The American Civil War.*)[1] That the use and abuse of advertising
was up for discussion nearly a century ago reveals that today's criticisms of
advertising are not new.

The fact is that advertising is a technique; techniques have no morality
of their own, but reflect the mores of the times and the standards of their
users. When a man publishes his claims in an advertisement, he has to think
twice about what he says, because it becomes a matter of public record for
which he can be held accountable.

In most large companies, advertisements have to go through layers
of approval for accuracy before they can be released. The only reason that
advertising continues over the years to be a viable means of communication
is that most people have had satisfactory experiences with most advertised
products they have bought. There have always been some advertisers whose
products did not live up to their claims; in recent years, even some prestigious
firms have been cited by the government for making questionable claims. To
protect the public from false and misleading advertising, numerous laws have
been passed. Chief among these is the Federal Trade Commission Act, which
we discuss first. We will then touch upon some other federal and state laws
affecting advertising, as well as other steps to protect the consumer from misrepresentation in advertising.

THE FEDERAL TRADE COMMISSION ACT

When the Federal Trade Commission Act was passed in 1914, Congress held
that "unfair methods of competition are hereby declared unlawful." (For an

---

[1] Randolph S. Churchill, *Winston S. Churchill* (Boston: Houghton Mifflin Company, 1966), Vol. I, p. 129.

example of what was going on in those days, which brought on this act, the reader is referred to the Standard Oil Company activities previously cited.)[2] The law was designed to protect one businessman from another; the consumer was not in the picture.

In time, the Federal Trade Commission (FTC), the enforcing arm of the government under this act, came to consider misleading advertising as an unfair method of doing business, and in this way, the FTC became involved in protecting the consumer from misleading advertising. In 1938, the FTC's power was officially expanded by the Wheeler-Lea Amendments to the original act, to cover "unfair or deceptive acts or practices." This law also gave the FTC specific authority over false advertisements in the fields of food, drugs, therapeutic devices, and cosmetics. Today, the FTC has a wide sweep of power over advertising of products sold across state lines.

Some Basic FTC Ground Rules

Over the years, some basic ground rules for application of the FTC law to advertising have emerged, based largely on the rulings of the Federal Trade Commission and on court decisions. Important among these are the following:

Total impression. The courts have held that the overall impression that an advertisement gives is the key as to whether it is false or misleading. Thus, in one case, although the term "relief" was used in an advertisement, the net impression from the entire context was that the product promised a "cure" for the ailment. Similarly, words like "stops," "ends," and "defeats" may improperly imply permanent rather than temporary relief. If an advertisement has even a "tendency to deceive," the FTC may find it illegal.

Clarity. The statement must be so clear that even a person of low intelligence would not be confused by it. The tendency of the law is to protect the credulous and the gullible. If an advertisement can have two meanings, it is illegal if one of them is false or misleading.

Fact vs. puffery. The courts have held that an advertiser's opinion of his product is tolerated as the legitimate expression of a biased opinion, and not a material statement of fact. However, a statement that might be viewed by a sophisticated person as trade puffery can be misleading to a person of lower intelligence. Much controversy over misleading advertising hovers around the question, When is a statement trade puffery and when is it a false claim? All factual claims must be supportable. To say "This is a 17 jewel watch" is an objective statement of fact which can be verified. If the watch

---

2 See p. 15.

does not contain 17 jewels, the statement is false and misleading. To say "This is the most beautiful watch you can buy at this price" is a subjective opinion, which could be regarded as trade puffery.

The question of taste. The courts have held, "If the advertisement is not false, defendants have a constitutional right to use it even though its content and blatancy may annoy both the Federal Trade Commission and the general public. The issue is falsity. . . ." [3]

Demonstrations. Demonstrations of product or product performance on television must not mislead viewers. The FTC requires literal accuracy in nutritional ads, both audio and video.

The Campbell Soup Company discovered this when they were found guilty of deception in a TV commercial in which they put marbles in the bottom of a bowl of vegetable soup to give the impression of an amplitude of vegetables.

Exaggerations in the impression conveyed may also be found misleading. Mars, Inc., makers of Milky Way candy bar, had a TV spot showing a glass of milk magically changing into a Milky Way bar. The commercial was held misleading because it gave the impression that a whole glass of milk went into a Milky Way bar.

Guarantees. Any guarantee used in advertising must clearly and conspicuously disclose the nature and the extent of the guarantee, the manner in which the guarantor will perform, and the identity of the guarantor.

"Free." This is a popular word in advertising, along with related words, such as "Buy one—Get one free," "2 for 1 sale," "Gift," "Bonus," and "Without charge." If there are any terms of conditions for getting something free, they must be stated clearly and conspicuously with the word "free." If a purchaser must buy something to get something else free, what he buys must be at the lowest price at which it has been offered (same quality, same size) in 30 days. A "free" offer for a single size may not be advertised for six months in a market in any twelve-month period.

Lotteries. Lotteries are schemes for the distribution of prizes by chance. If a person has to pay for entering the lottery, it is held illegal by the U.S. Postal Service, and banned from the mails. If advertised in interstate commerce, the FTC also holds it illegal, and will enter to stop it. The giving of prizes in the many "sweepstakes" advertised is allowable because they do not require a person to pay money to enter.

---

[3] Judge Dawson, in FTC v. Sterling Drug, Inc., 215 F. Supp. 327, 332 (S. D. N. Y. 1963) aff'd. 317 F. 2d 669 (2d Cir. 1963).

Federal Trade Commission guidelines. The FTC, after consulting with members of over 175 individual industries, has compiled and published trade-practice rules, calling attention to practices that are illegal. These are offered as a guideline for legal operation.

Obviously the foregoing references to the laws relating to advertising are an oversimplification, designed as a guide in creating advertising, and calling attention to the danger zones. All advertisements containing any statements that would come under FTC scrutiny should be submitted to an attorney for approval before running. Honest intentions provide no shelter for an advertisement that is found misleading.

New Directions of the FTC

In the early 1970's, new directions were evident in the thrust of FTC activities. Among the practices introduced, and attitudes that were manifest, were the following:

Corrective advertising. In the past, when an advertiser had been found guilty of running advertising that the commission found false and misleading, action would result in his being obliged to sign a decree consenting to discontinue such advertising (the *consent decree*). Meanwhile, damage to the public had been done, and during the long time that the hearings required, the advertiser would continue to run the ad. Under the FTC's new Formula for Effective Relief, and in order to counteract the residual effects of the deceptive advertising, the FTC may now require the advertiser to run advertising "to dissipate the effects of that deception." This practice of corrective advertising promises to act as a meaningful deterrent to any advertiser.

Substantiation of claims. The FTC has increased its demands that advertisers make available documentation of claims relating to the safety, performance, and efficacy of their products.

Changing views on advertising content. Another view of the present attitude of the Federal Trade Commission was expressed by Gerald J. Thain, assistant director for food and drug advertising, Bureau of Consumer Protection, Federal Trade Commission. Speaking of television, he said:

> New advertising concepts have been developed during the last ten to twenty years which exploit television's unique capabilities and the consumer's vulnerability to them. Wants and desires that do not preexist may be invented, cultivated, and developed. . . . Mood advertising may associate a product with strongly held social values such

as affluence or sophistication, or it may imply benefits leading toward
the satisfaction of basic emotional needs, such as attractiveness to the opposite sex, freedom from fear, and acceptance. In neither situation is there any rational connection between the product and the inference being made, and in neither case does the advertisement provide sufficient information on the product's real attributes, such as quality and price—information conducive to a rational purchase.

The consumer, unwary of the new advertising techniques, is placed in a vulnerable and easily exploited position.[4]

Some comments regarding the statement above:

1. Television did not loom up overnight to take by surprise a vulnerable consumer. A whole generation had grown up with TV, conditioned to select stations and programs with the press of a button, and mentally to tune out commercials that did not interest them, and indeed often annoyed them. They had been reared in making instant decisions as to what they liked and what they didn't like—more so than the generation of pretelevision days was obliged to do. And they are more sophisticated and worldly-wise and critical than the pretelevision consumers, hardly more "vulnerable."

2. Why should it be wrong to enlarge a man's horizons by showing things he might not have known about, provided only that they are not harmful to health? Besides, dreams and aspirations are part of man's natural right. What's wrong with selling products that "satisfy basic emotional needs"?

3. The assumption of this article is that nothing should be bought without a "rational" fact-and-figure reason. Visit the homes of those who may express such an opinion, and you will see that each man expresses his personality in a different way—the decoration, the pictures, the books and tapes, the neatness or informality of his home, his garden—each affording him psychic satisfaction, which he denies to others as a valid basis for buying something.

4. The alarm that the consumer is "unwary of the new advertising techniques of TV" (television has been with us for over 20 years) is a regurgitation of the myth that advertising has some hypnotic power over people to make them buy things while in a trance, and that the discoverer of this secret is now going to protect people from advertising that does not meet his standards. Even television does not have the power to make a person buy something he does not want to buy, if for no other reason than that there is too much counterpressure from other advertisers.

---

[4] Address in a program of the Division of Food, Drug and Cosmetic Law in New York, on July 7, 1971, as published in *The Business Lawyer,* April 1972, p. 902.

THE ROBINSON-PATMAN ACT

Never before had the little storekeeper been at such a disadvantage in relation to the big store as just before 1936. That was the bottom of the big depression; manufacturers were hungry for business, prepared to make deep discounts and advertising allowances in exchange for a good-sized order, and these practices could drive small merchants out of business. To meet such unfair competition, the Robinson-Patman Act was passed. That law is an ever-present consideration in advertising plans today.

In brief, this law requires a seller to treat all competitive customers of a product on *proportionately* equal terms in regard to discounts and advertising allowances. This is not a law for or against advertising and promotional allowances; it simply says that *if* they are granted to one customer, they must be offered to competing customers on the same proportionate terms in relation to sales. The Federal Trade Commission, which is in charge of the enforcement of this act, offers the following examples of how the law is interpreted:

> *Example 1:* A seller may properly offer to pay a specified part (say 50%) of the cost of local advertising up to an amount equal to a set percentage (such as 5%) of the dollar volume of purchases during a specified time.
>
> *Example 2:* A seller may properly place in reserve for each customer a specified amount of money for each unit purchased, and use it to reimburse those customers for the actual cost of their advertising of the seller's product.
>
> *Example 3:* A seller should not select one or a few customers to receive special allowances (e.g., 5% of purchases) to promote his product, while making allowances available on some lesser basis (e.g., 2% of purchases) to customers who compete with them.
>
> *Example 4:* A seller's plan should not provide an allowance on a basis that has rates graduated with the amount of goods purchased, as, for instance, 1 percent of the first $1,000 purchases per month, 2 percent of the second $1,000 per month, and 3 percent of all over that.
>
> *Example 5:* A seller should not identify or feature one or a few customers in his own advertising without making the same service available on proportionally equal terms to customers competing with the identified customer or customers.

The manufacturer must also have available alternative advertising material for use by stores with varying advertising-allowance dollars. Usually, newspaper mats are available for those whose allowances permit the use of newspaper advertising. For advertisers whose dollar allowance is not big enough to run meaningful newspaper space, the manufacturer may offer the dollar equivalent in direct mail bearing the store imprint, or some other promotional offer. The enforcement of the Robinson-Patman Act has been difficult.

THE FEDERAL FOOD, DRUG AND COSMETIC ACT

Closely tied to the Federal Trade Commission Act is the Federal Food, Drug and Cosmetic Act, passed in 1938, giving the Food and Drug Administration broad power over the labeling and branding—as contrasted with the advertising—of foods, drugs, therapeutic devices, and cosmetics. The term *labeling* has been held to include any advertising of the product appearing in the same store in which the product is sold; it does not have to be physically attached to the package. In the case of one drug preparation, the package itself was properly labeled, but the stores also sold a soft-cover book on health, written by the maker of the product, in which this product was mentioned, and for which unprovable claims were made. He was in trouble with the Food and Drug Administration for false labeling and for false advertising.

It is under this law that food and drug manufacturers must put their ingredients on the labels. The latest program, as this is being written, is to require the disclosure of the percentage of seafood in seafood cocktails. The author is curious as to what kind of objections there can be to that.

OTHER FEDERAL CONTROLS OF ADVERTISING

The Federal Trade Commission also exercises control over the advertising and labeling of products under laws affecting specific industries, including:

> Wool Products Labeling Act of 1939
>
> Fur Products Labeling Act (enacted in 1951)
>
> Flammable Fabrics Act (enacted in 1953)
>
> Textile Fiber Products Identification Act (enacted in 1958)

The Alcohol Tax Unit of the U.S. Treasury Department. The liquor industry has a unique pattern of labeling and advertising under both federal and state laws. The federal laws are under the jurisdiction of the Treasury Department, for an interesting historic reason: The first American excise tax was the one levied under Alexander Hamilton, secretary of the Treasury, on alcoholic beverages. That department, through its Alcohol Tax Unit, is interested to this day in the labeling, in standards of size of bottles for tax purposes, and in the advertising of these beverages. The label must disclose the type of liquor; its proof; in the case of blends, the proportion of aged whiskies and neutral spirits; and the name and address of the distiller. It may not make any therapeutic claims and must comply with other restrictions.

Each state also has its own liquor-advertising laws for products sold within its domain. In some states you cannot show a drinking scene; in others you can show a man holding a glass, but not to his lips; in another you can picture only a bottle. In few industries does an advertising man constantly need a lawyer more than in liquor advertising.

The Securities and Exchange Commission (SEC). This is the agency of the government that has control over all advertising of public offerings of stocks or bonds. Its whole effort is to insist on the full disclosure of the truthful facts relevant to the company and the stock to be sold, so that the prospective investor can form his opinion. Its insistence on the facts that must be published—including a statement of negative elements affecting the investment—is very firm and thorough. The SEC never recommends or refuses to recommend a security; its entire concern is with the disclosure of full information. It is a criminal offense to advertise a security under SEC jurisdiction without having it registered with the SEC, unless there is an appropriate exemption (such as relatively small offerings, which at this writing means of less than $500,000).

The U.S. Postal Service. The Postal Service has the authority to stop the delivery of mail to all firms guilty of using the mails to defraud. It does so by returning to sender all such mail, rubber-stamped:

Fraudulent—Return to sender by order of Postmaster General

That is enough to put any operation out of business!

STATE LAWS RELATING TO ADVERTISING

While the pattern of the federal statutory scheme is generally one of broad language that is not essentially confined to specific industries, most states have narrower laws directed at one or more designated practices or industries. The result has been a hodgepodge of state mandates on such subjects as liquor, bedding, stockbrokers, banks, loan and credit companies, employment agents, business-opportunity brokers, and real estate brokers.

The list also includes socially disapproved services and commodities—dealing with sex and obscenity, lotteries and gambling, fortunetelling, and crime publications—and the use of state and national flags for advertising. It also covers professional and occupational advertising by lawyers, physicians, real estate salesmen, and many others.

The first basic state statute in the regulation of advertising, which still represents a landmark in advertising history, is the Printers' Ink Model Statute drawn up in 1911, attempting to punish "untrue, deceptive, or misleading" advertising. *Printers' Ink* magazine, the pioneer trade paper of advertising, has died, but its model statute, in its original or modified form, exists in 44 states.

SELF-REGULATION BY MEDIA

685
*Legal
and Other
Controls of
Advertising*

One of the oldest and most vigorous forms of control of advertising content is that of the media.

National magazines present the most striking example of the control over the advertising they accept. Publications like *Good Housekeeping* and *Reader's Digest* have rejected great numbers of unacceptable advertisements. But the *New Yorker* has reported objectionable advertising at a minimal level, for it deals mostly with national advertisers. The smaller magazines directed toward special groups are still often involved in enforcing advertising control.

Newspapers also have their codes of acceptable advertising. Most of them exercise control even over the comparative price claims made in the retail advertising they publish. A store may be asked to change a headline such as, "These are the lowest-price sheets offered," to "The lowest-price sheets we have ever offered." "The greatest shoe sale ever" will be changed to "Our greatest shoe sale ever."

The National Association of Broadcasters, to which many television stations belong, has set up codes for TV and radio. Seventy-six percent of the country's television stations, as well as all three networks, are code subscribers and follow closely the station and network code. Taste, however, is hard to define, even in a code. Radio, with 5,000 stations, presents a different problem. Only about 2,000 are code subscribers. It has been difficult to unite the radio broadcasters behind a code that, among other things, limits the amount of commercial time per broadcast hour.

The code stations do not accept liquor advertising. Their chief problem has been children's advertising, which has been severely criticized for taking advantage of children's credibility every Saturday morning. The NAB code has established clear guidelines for its members, to meet public criticism. All network programs, whether for children or not, have to be submitted to the network in advance for approval.

SELF-REGULATION BY ADVERTISERS

The problem of advertising on children's programs provides a good example of how the self-regulation of advertisers is even more rigid than the media code of the industry. The Association of National Advertisers, whose members do over 75 percent of national television advertising, has established children's-television guidelines that include specifications such as these, offered merely to show the nature of the restrictions:

Any form of presentation that capitalizes on a child's difficulty in distinguishing between the real and the fanciful should be positively guarded against.

Particular control should be exercised to be sure that:

a. Copy, sound, and visual presentation—as well as the commercial in its totality—do not mislead the audience to which it is directed on such performance characteristics as speed, size, color, durability, nutrition, noise, etc.; or on perceived benefits such as the acquisition of strength, popularity, growth, proficiency, intelligence, and the like.

b. The advertisement clearly establishes what is included in the original purchase price of the advertised product, employing where necessary positive disclosure on what items are to be purchased separately. All advertising for products sold unassembled should indicate that assembly is required.

c. A clearly depicted presentation of the advertised product is shown during the advertisement. When appropriate in assisting consumers to identify the product, the package may be depicted, provided that it does not mislead as to product characteristics or content.

d. Advertising demonstrations showing the use of a product or premium can be readily duplicated by the average child for whom the product is intended.

Self-regulation by Individual Industries

More than forty industries have established their own codes of standards of advertising practice. Most such codes relate to the local advertising of their products by their distributors or dealers or franchise owners, especially when their product has a new or servicing feature—such as air conditioning, car seat belts, water softeners. Voluntary trade codes usually prove ineffective; the associations lack the power of enforcement because of the antitrust laws, which preclude any action that might be regarded as interfering with open competition.

The Better Business Bureaus

In 1905, as we have previously mentioned, various local advertising clubs formed a national association that today is known as the American Advertising Federation. In 1911, this association launched a campaign for "Truth in Advertising," for which purpose various vigilance committees were established. These were the forerunners of the Better Business Bureaus, which adopted that name in 1916 and became autonomous in 1926. Today the movement has 122 separate bureaus operating in major cities, supported by more than 100,000 firms, and contributing over $6½ million per year. The Bureau handles about 2½ million inquiries and complaints from business and the public, and shops or investigates more than 40,000 advertisements per year for possible violations of truth or accuracy. It has also published booklets, and issues such films as "Safeguarding Your Savings," aimed at forestalling questionable advertising and selling practices. Its published service, called "Do's and Don'ts of Advertising Copy," is a standard reference work on the subject.

The Better Business Bureau has worked, until recently, chiefly at the local level. It has no legal power to enforce its findings, but has exercised its influence in the community as a force to protect the public, which also makes for good relations between the public and the local merchants. Its effectiveness has varied from one community to another. In 1971, it assumed a new responsibility and role as part of the National Advertising Review Council.

THE NATIONAL ADVERTISING REVIEW COUNCIL

In response to the many voices of different consumer groups against deceptive advertising, the chief advertising organizations formed the most comprehensive self-regulating apparatus ever established in advertising, called the National Advertising Review Council. Its chief purpose is "to develop a structure which would effectively apply the persuasive capacities of peers to seek the voluntary elimination of national advertising which professionals would consider deceptive." It concerns itself with matters of deception. It consists of the Council of Better Business Bureaus and the three leading advertising groups: the American Advertising Federation, the American Association of Advertising Agencies, and the Association of National Advertisers.

The council has two operating arms:

1. The National Advertising Division of the Council of Better Business Bureaus
2. The National Advertising Review Board

The National Division of the Council of the Better Business Bureaus has a full-time professional staff that has had a lot of experience working with advertisers on complaints. They will judge the merit of the complaint; then, if it appears valid, in personal and private contact they seek to get the advertiser to correct the deceptive item.

If that does not work, the case is passed to the National Advertising Review Board, composed of 50 individuals, from which five are assigned to a case—like a court of appeals. If they feel the action was justified and the advertiser still does not wish to correct the deceptive element, the whole matter will be referred to the appropriate government agency. The review board will publish the letter or referral, along with any statement the advertiser wishes to make.

In discussing the National Advertising Review Council, it is well to understand what it cannot do:

> It cannot order an advertiser to stop running an ad.
>
> It cannot fine him.
>
> It cannot bar him from advertising.
>
> It cannot impose a boycott of him or his product.

What it can do is to bring to bear the judgment of his peers that what he is doing is harmful to advertising, to the public, and to himself. This usually has great moral weight; in this instance, it is reinforced by the knowledge that if he declines to follow this procedure, and to accept the results of an appeal to the National Advertising Review Board, the whole matter will be referred to the appropriate government agency, and that fact will be released to the public, together with any statement the advertiser wishes to make. This step, which is unique in business self-regulation machinery, avoids any problem of violating the antitrust laws, presents the entire matter to public view, and still leaves the advertiser subject to a Federal Trade Commission ruling on his advertising.

Of the first 25 cases submitted to the council, all 25 advertisers responded to their suggestion of changing the offending advertising. A good omen.

Self-regulation by Individual Advertisers

The most meaningful of all forms of advertising self-regulation is that of the individual advertiser. It is wholly voluntary and not the result of group pressure; it reflects the policy of top management, its sense of public responsibility, and its enthusiasm to survive and grow in a competitive arena where consumer confidence is vital. Practically every sizable advertiser maintains a careful system of legal review and appraisal, backed by factual data to substantiate claims. At Lever Brothers Company, all copy developed by the advertising department and agencies is submitted first to a research and development division, where it is analyzed in the light of records and reports of experimental data. It must then be passed by the legal department, and only after these two OK's is it released for publication.

In a statement of corporate responsibility, General Mills said:

> Recognizing the power and importance of such amounts [in the advertising budget] to the corporation and to society, the company through

I. This AUTHORITY FOR THE USE OF A VALUATION must be used

   A. to justify all promotional advertising and/or sign copy including, without limitation, Famous Barr All Store events such as Anniversary Sale; Individual store or shopping center events such as Northland Days; Divisional or Departmental events such as 88¢ Sale or Dollar Day; and all Clearance events, etc.

   B. to justify all comparative prices and terms indicative of comparative prices. For example – Comparable Value, Formerly, Usually, Regularly, Originally, If Perfect, etc.

   C. whenever terms (or promotional events as in I.A. above) are used which indicate a price savings, even if a comparative price is not to be used. For example – Sale*, Save, Value, Clearance, Special Purchase, Unusual Value, etc.

NOTE: To qualify for the use of the word SALE, IDENTICAL merchandise:
1. must have been sold by us, in the recent, regular course of business, at a higher price, and
2. must return to a higher price after the promotion, or
3. must now be offered for sale by a significant competitor at a higher price. Merchandise which itself does <u>not</u> qualify for the use of the word SALE, may be advertised under an overall promotional heading, e.g., Anniversary Sale, if a qualifying term such as <u>Special Purchase</u>, precedes our selling price.

II. How to use this AUTHORITY FOR THE USE OF A VALUATION

   A. Write the NAME OF THE PROMOTION. (Refer to I.A. above.)
   B. Write the TERMS TO BE USED. (Refer to I.C. above.) If only one of the columns is to be used, write the word NONE in the second.
   C. The ITEM & SUBSTANTIATING RECORD INFORMATION column is to be used to identify the merchandise to be sold, and to substantiate the valuation.
     1. Identify the item by writing a brief description of the merchandise. A style number would be sufficient in most cases.
     2. Write the Purchase Order Number and/or Price Revision Form Number. If it is necessary to refer to specific sales-checks, refer to the item in the "Remarks" section, list the customers' names, and complete dates of sale. For example: Item 1 above, Hendricks, E. A., 3-15-67, etc.

   D. Write in the amount of MERCHANDISE TO BE ON HAND in all stores, for the promotion.
   E. In the SALE PRICE column, write the exact selling price for the item.
   F. Use one of the COMPARATIVE PRICE columns to show the comparative price, whether or not it will appear in advertising or sign copy.
     1. When the terms Sale and/or Regularly apply to an item, write the date on which the goods will return to a higher price in the appropriate column.
     2. When terms such as Originally or Clearance are used, show the dates and amounts of all intermediate price changes in the OTHER PRICE column. If there were no intermediate price changes, write in the word NONE.
     3a. The term Comparable Value may be used only with respect to merchandise of like grade and quality, offered for sale by a significant competitor at a higher price, and may NOT be used to compare with merchandise offered for sale by us. Use the "Remarks" section to justify the use of Comparable Value, write the date of comparison shopping, and the price at which the goods are offered for sale by the competitor. Both the Divisional Merchandise Manager and the General Merchandise Manager must approve the use of this term.
     3b. The term Regularly may be used only with respect to identical merchandise, previously sold by us in the immediate, regular course of business.

   G. Submit this form, with advertising, and/or sign copy and substantiating records (Purchase Order, Price Revision forms, etc.) to the Divisional Merchandise Manager and/or General Merchandise Manager.

NOTE: The MERCHANDISE OFFICE must see that substantiating records are maintained for a minimum period of two (2) years. (Sec. II., G., above.)
The COMPARISON SHOPPING GROUP maintains copies of shopping reports for a minimum period of two (2) years. (Sec. II., F., 3a. above.)
The CREDIT OFFICE maintains micro-film copies of sales checks for a minimum period of two (2) years. (Sec. II., C., above.)

   H. Send advertising and/or sign copy, together with this APPROVED form to the Advertising Department.
NOTE: The Advertising Department must maintain a file of the APPROVED <u>Authority for the use of a Valuation</u> for a minimum period of two (2) years.

NOTE: NO ADVERTISING OR SIGN COPY WILL BE ACCEPTED BY THE ADVERTISING DEPARTMENT UNLESS ACCOMPANIED BY THE NECESSARY APPROVED VALUATION FORM. SIGN ORDERS RECEIVED BY THE SIGN SHOP WHICH CONTAIN A COMPARATIVE PRICE STATEMENT WILL BE RETURNED TO THE DEPARTMENT IF THEY DO NOT BEAR THE APPROVAL STAMP OF THE ADVERTISING OFFICE.

THE CARE A DEPARTMENT STORE TAKES IN ANNOUNCING SALES PRICES   Courtesy: Famous-Barr, St. Louis

The above are the rules a buyer has to follow when he wants to offer a sale price, by any name.

Note particularly I, 1, 2, 3, and II, F. Also see p. 168.

the years has endeavored to produce advertising that is not only truthful, but also informative and educational, that renders a maximum of helpful service, and that, insofar as possible, seeks to expand markets rather than merely to take business away from competitors.

Any competitive or comparative statement to be made about any product or service must be supported. Each manager responsible for a product is also responsible for the preparation of claims and the development of adequate substantiation for them where necessary.

The Purex Corporation has rules (which are a part of the copy platform) that state:

> Purex advertising shall not claim or promise by implication any product performance or characteristic which is not fully supported by laboratory research, consumer research, or similar factual information.
>
> Comparative claims for Purex products must be clearly supported by research laboratory or consumer tests vs. competitive products. Such tests are not to be made against inferior brands, but against the best competitive products on the market.
>
> Purex management is concerned selfishly, because we recognize that without a justifiable confidence in the honesty and sincerity of an advertising message, the value of that message in selling our products is heavily discounted. . . . To contribute to still higher advertising costs through loss of consumer confidence in our advertising is unforgivable.

These statements represent the attitudes that have helped build large businesses and that have given advertising its power.

LEGAL RELEASES

Before using the name or picture of a living person in an advertisement, it is most important to get his legal release to do so. Each person is protected under the laws of privacy against such use without his written permission. In some states, such use is a misdemeanor, and in all instances it subjects the advertiser to a suit for damages. In the case of a child, the release must be obtained from the parent or guardian. Rigid house rule: No release, no picture!

COPYRIGHTING ADVERTISING

Copyrighting has nothing to do with the problems of the legal controls of advertising, which we have been discussing here. But since it is a legal subject, related to advertising, it is only appropriate to have this discussion join its legal relatives at this point.

The nature of copyrights. A copyright grants its owner for a period of 28 years, renewable once for another 28 years, the exclusive rights to print, publish, or reproduce an original work of literature, music, or art. Advertising falls into these categories. A copyright protects an "intellectual work" as a whole from being copied by another; however, it does not prevent another from using the essence of the advertising idea and from expressing it in his own way. It does not protect a concept or idea or theme, but only the expression of it.

Copyrighting policy. Many companies make it a policy to copyright all their publication advertising. Most national advertisers, however, deem copyrighting unnecessary in their publication advertising, unless it contains a piece of art or copy that they think others will use. In one issue of *Life,* eight advertisements of a half page or more carried a copyright notice; 37 did not. Retail newspaper advertising moves too fast for the advertiser to be concerned about having it bodily lifted. Direct-response advertisers often copyright their publication and direct-mail advertising, because if an ad is effective, it may be used over a long period of time, and it could readily be used, with minor changes, by another.

What may be copyrighted. To be copyrightable, an ad must contain a substantial amount of original text or picture. Slogans and other short phrases and expressions cannot be copyrighted even if they are distinctively arranged or lettered. Familiar symbols and designs are not copyrightable.

How to secure a copyright. Getting a copyright is one of the simple steps that can be handled directly by the advertiser, but it must be followed precisely.

1. Write to the Copyright Office, The Library of Congress, Washington, D.C. 20540, for the proper application form for what you plan to protect.
2. Beginning with the *first* appearance of the advertisement, the word *Copyright,* or the abbreviation *Copy.,* or the symbol © must appear with the name of the advertiser. It is good to add the year if foreign protection is planned. The three elements of this notice must appear together on all copies. *If the advertisement is published the first time without the required notice, the right to secure a copyright is lost and cannot be regained.*
3. As soon as the ad is published, two copies, with the filled-out application form and fee, should be sent to the Copyright Office.

The big pitfall in this procedure is failure to include the copyright notice in the original typographic setup of the ad. In the case of a booklet, *the notice must appear on the title page, or on the page backing it.* Many times you will see it on the back page; this is worthless.

Copyrighting vs. registration. These terms are frequently confused. You copyright an advertisement; you register a trademark, as discussed in Chapter 20.

And with this profound observation, we conclude the legal chapter.

*　　*　　*

And with this chapter, we conclude our discussion of advertising. This book has sought to capture the essence of advertising thinking in the brief moment of the long history of advertising which we call today. From the first chapter, we have seen how advertising has its roots in the history of man's desire to tell the world about what he has to sell. In our industrialized society, there are many who have products and services to offer, and there are many interested in knowing about such things, and able to buy them. In the free world there are media through which men can reach each other. As these conditions spread throughout the world, the use of advertising will grow. Techniques will change, styles of advertising will change, the forms of advertising will change. But the need for advertising will continue to grow. Hopefully, among the readers of this book are those who will help it increase its usefulness to society.

Review Questions

1. What is the Federal Trade Commission?

2. What are its criteria for considering an advertisement false and misleading?

3. What powers has the FTC over bad taste in advertising?

4. What special precautions must be observed in (a) using the word "Free!" and (b) issuing guarantees?

5. The FTC considers lotteries for use in the advertising of products illegal except on one condition. Because of what provision in the law are sweepstake contests allowed?

6. What does the Robinson-Patman Act have to say about advertising?

7. You are a manufacturer who has been allowing a flat 5 percent advertising allowance on all purchases regardless of size. A large chain says that if you will allow a 7½ percent allowance, it will increase its order by 15 percent and put on a special advertising campaign for the product. You could use the business and even at that figure make a good profit. Is there any legal reason against this? Explain.

8. Besides the FTC, what departments of the federal government are also interested in the labeling and advertising of products?

9. Broadly speaking, how do state laws affecting advertising differ from the federal laws?

10. What is the Advertising Review Board? What action can it take if an advertiser does not accept its findings, and how does this avoid anti-trust laws?

11. If you were the president of a company which spent a lot of money on advertising, what rules would you establish for the content of your advertisements?

12. What is meant by a legal release, and when do you need it?

13. What is the value of a copyright? What steps must you take to get it? When do you take those steps?

Reading Suggestions

Aaker, David A., and George S. Day, eds., *Consumerism*. Riverside, N.J.: The Free Press, 1971.

Bauer, R. A., and S. A. Greyser, "The Dialogue That Never Happens," *Harvard Business Review*, November–December 1967, p. 2ff.

Business Week, "Madison Avenue's Response to Its Critics," June 10, 1972, pp. 46–54.

Cohen, Dorothy, "The Federal Trade Commission and the Regulation of Advertising in the Consumer Interest," *Journal of Marketing*, January 1969, pp. 40–44.

Cohen, Dorothy, "Surrogate Indicators and Deception in Advertising," *Journal of Marketing*, July 1972, pp. 10–15.

Kintner, Earl W., *A Robinson-Patman Primer*. New York: The Macmillan Company, 1970.

Simon, Morton J., *The Law of Advertising and Marketing*. New York: W. W. Norton & Co., 1956.

U.S. Congress, Senate Committee on Commerce, *Advertising, 1971*. Hearing, Ninety-second Congress, First Session, on S. 1461, to Require the Furnishing of Documentation of Claims Concerning Safety, Performance, Efficacy, Characteristics, and Comparative Price of Advertised Products and Services, S. 1753, to Establish a National Institute of Advertising, Marketing, and Society. October 4, 1971. Washington, D.C.: U.S. Government Printing Office, 1971.

U.S. Congress, Senate Select Committee on Small Business, Subcommittee on Monopoly. *Advertising of Proprietary Medicines*. Hearings, Ninety-second Congress, First Session, on Effect of Promotion and Advertising of Over-the-Counter Drugs on Competition, Small Business, and the Health and Welfare of the Public. Washington, D.C.: U.S. Government Printing Office, 1971. V. 1, Pt. 1—Introduction; analgesics.

Van Den Haag, Ernest, "What to Do About Advertising," *Commentary*, May 1962, pp. 386–391. Also in Kleppner and Settel, *Exploring Advertising*, p. 25.

Wagner, Susan, *Federal Trade Commission*. New York: Praeger Publishers, 1971.

Weigand, Robert E., "The Right to Be Read," *Business Horizons*, October 1971, pp. 27–36.

P.S.

On Getting the First Job

THERE COMES A MOMENT in the life of every student of business when he must come down from the mountaintop where he has been enjoying a sightseer's view of the world and begin his personal trek upward to whatever goal he has set for himself. This brings him face to face with the problem of getting the first job. The first step is to prepare a resumé telling about your job objectives, and listing your school activities and your summer work. These are significant to a prospective employer. Jules B. Singer, in his excellent book, "Your Future in Advertising," has this to say on the subject:

> Landing a job calls for salesmanship. You are selling a commodity— yourself. You have to convince your prospective employer that you have what he needs.
>
> Sit down and try to figure out what the boss needs. If he hires you it will be because he thinks that not only will you be useful in some way immediately but that in the course of six months or a year he can train you to be even more useful. On the basis of this logic, you must sell him on the idea that you are trainable. Perhaps your school marks indicate you are very bright. Perhaps you have held summer jobs and your employer will give you an enthusiastic reference. Perhaps you were outstanding in some extracurricular activity. Think about what you have done that demonstrates your ability to learn easily.
>
> Your potential boss undoubtedly will want someone who takes initiative, who has leadership qualities, who gets along well with people, who is loyal, who will do more than the routine job. Again, sit back and think of examples to show that you have these qualities. Examples carry conviction where mere claims make little impact. When you say, "I get along well with people," no one is impressed. When you say, "I was president of my class," it demonstrates that you get along well with people. And when you can show examples of how your getting along with people enabled you to sell magazines or raise funds for a charity, you are then proving how you put this asset to use. . . . Summer jobs, things you do around the home, and any other relevant activities can be useful as demonstrations.

694

The next step is to put all this to use. Here are some of the helpful activities:

1. A personal letter to a list of employers, asking for an interview.

2. A letter about you sent to the employer by a friend of his, one of his customers, or someone you know he respects.

3. A personal call on him at his place of business.

4. Calls on people who might know about jobs, such as a banker or a newspaper editor. Obviously, such people are more accessible and more likely to be helpful in smaller towns.

5. Calls on personnel directors of large companies.

6. Calls on employment-guidance committees sponsored in some cities by advertising or sales executive clubs.

7. Calls on employment agencies.

8. Calls on the U.S. Employment Bureau.

9. Calls on school employment offices.

10. Running a situation-wanted advertisement.

11. Answering a help-wanted advertisement.

All of these methods have worked.[1]

Breaking into Advertising

ALFRED L. PLANT, VICE PRESIDENT—ADVERTISING, of the Block Drug Company, Inc., offers the following suggestions:

> There is no sure-fire way to break into advertising. Every year, however, thousands of young men and women somehow get started. Here are a few hints that might be helpful.
>
> 1. *Sell*
> Advertising is part of the selling process. So learn what interests—motivates—influences—and makes people decide to buy. The very best way is by experience. By doing it yourself and watching and listening.
>
> It doesn't matter what you sell—doorknobs or doggy-bags—the experience of selling will provide a fundamental knowledge that will stand you in good stead.
>
> 2. Get a job where you will be exposed to advertising. If possible, in an advertising department or with an agency. But don't let your

---

[1] Jules B. Singer, *Your Future in Advertising* (New York: Richards Rosen Press, Inc., 1960), Chap. XVII.

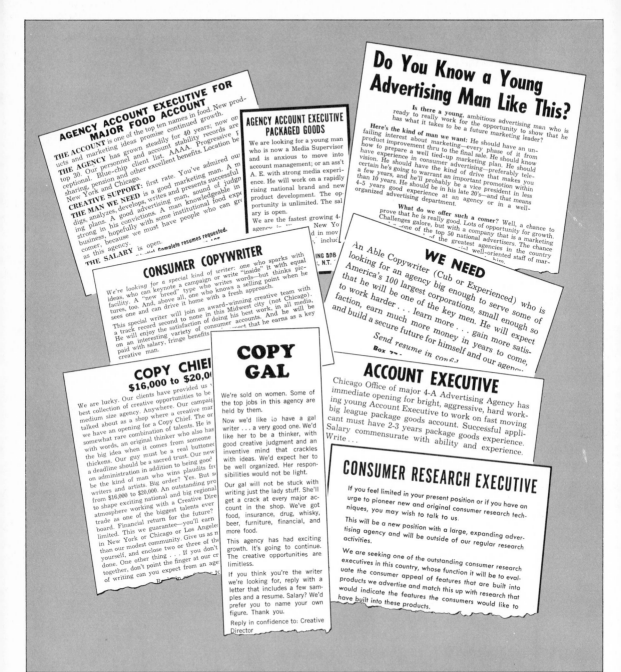

OPPORTUNITIES IN ADVERTISING

As these help wanted advertisements reveal, many opportunities begin after two to three years' experience.

pride stand in the way of starting in a lowly position if it will give you the exposure to advertising that is so essential.

This can be the gateway to a real advertising job if you are interested —ambitious—ingenious—and suitable. Many a file clerk has become a production manager; many a secretary has become a copywriter; many a mailroom boy has become an advertising manager.

3. Once you have the opportunity to be exposed to advertising, be curious and ambitious. If you are interested in copywriting, talk to some of the young copywriters. Ask them what they are doing and why they are recommending the approach they are taking. Ask if they would mind if you took a crack at writing the ad or the commercial and brought it in for their critique.

If you are interested in the film-making end, ask to see a storyboard and then talk about it and again inquire what the creative talent had in mind.

Most people are flattered when you ask for their advice and help.

4. Learn the fundamentals and mechanics of advertising. This is best done when you can work in a small agency or an advertising department where you are exposed to every facet of creating and producing advertising. Try not to get pigeonholed with one assignment, but rather move around from department to department even changing jobs if necessary to broaden your experience.

5. Learn the fundamentals of marketing. Advertising has become a tremendous, complicated business art. If you are serious about a career in advertising, devote the time, the money and your own commitment to learning your future profession both from an academic point of view and from a practical point of view.

Breaking into the Advertising Agency

Some large agencies have regular training courses in which they accept a number of college graduates each year. Other agencies may not have formal courses, but accept beginners to work in various departments. The beginning pay is usually low, but after six months to a year—when the beginner has had a chance to reveal his aptitudes—his move upward can pick up momentum. In about two years, the beginner suddenly realizes how many opportunities are open for the man with "about two years' experience." By the time he is in his late 20's or early 30's, he may well be making far more money than some of his classmates who started in other fields with higher starting salaries but slower potentials for moving up. The advertising agency world is one in which a man who reveals talent and competence is not denied the opportunity of earning good money because he is "too young" or because of seniority, as is the case in some other fields.

To the young man embarking on a career in the advertising agency, Ogilvy offers the following advice:

After a year of tedious training, you will probably be made an assistant executive—a sort of midshipman. The moment that happens, set yourself to become the best informed man in the agency on the account to which you are assigned. If, for example, it is a gasoline account, read textbooks on the chemistry, geology, and distribution of petroleum products. Read all the trade journals in the field. Read all the research reports and marketing plans that your agency has ever written on the product. Spend Saturday mornings in service stations pumping gasoline and talking to motorists. Visit your client's refineries and research laboratories. At the end of your second year, you will know more about gasoline than your boss; you will then be ready to succeed him.[2]

Sidney and Mary Edlund, in their book, "Pick Your Job and Land It!" give good advice on turning your interview into an offer:

1. Have a clear picture of what the job calls for.

2. Gather all the facts you can about the firm and its products.

3. Draw up in advance an outline of the main points to be covered.

4. Appeal to the employer's self-interest. Offer a service or dramatize your interest.

5. Back up all statements of ability and achievement with proof.

6. Prepare some questions of your own in advance. Keep etched in mind the two-way character of the interview: mutual exploration.

7. Prepare for the questions normally asked.

8. Anticipate and work out your answers to major objections.

9. Close on a positive note.

10. Send a "thank you" note to each interviewer.

11. And follow up your best prospects.

Don't necessarily do all the talking. If the employer starts talking, listen! Find out what the job is like, what he expects from you. Sometimes good listening is as effective in selling as a dictionary full of words. After the interview, follow up your conversation with a letter. Thank the man for the time he gave you. Try to use something he told you about the position to show your

---

[2] Reprinted from *Confessions of an Advertising Man* by David Ogilvy. Atheneum Publishers, 1963, pp. 151–52. Copyright © 1963 by David Ogilvy Trustee. Reprinted by permission of Atheneum Publishers, New York, and Longmans, Green & Co. Limited, London.

special aptitudes. Even if you have been given the job, it is good business to write a "thank you" note.[3]

One final word to one who may find himself doing similar work with many others in any organization: There is one sure way of standing out in the crowd and being up front when a promotion is open—be the first in the office in the morning. You will get more work done; that's a good kind of reputation to get. Some morning you will find the boss coming in with you. Some day you will *be* the boss. It has been done, and you can't lose!

---

[3] Sidney Edlund and Mary Edlund, *Pick Your Job and Land It!* (Englewood Cliffs, N.J.: Prentice-Hall, Inc. 1954), p. 277.

Appendix:
Tools of Advertising

PERIODICALS

GENERAL PUBLICATIONS

Advertising Age
  740 Rush Street
  Chicago, Ill. 60611
Journal of Marketing
  230 North Michigan Avenue
  Chicago, Ill. 60601
Madison Avenue
  866 United Nations Plaza
  New York, N.Y. 10017

Marketing
  481 University Avenue
  Toronto 2, Ontario, Canada
Media Decisions
  342 Madison Avenue
  New York, N.Y. 10017
Sales Management
  630 Third Avenue
  New York, N.Y. 10017

TELEVISION AND RADIO

Broadcasting
  1735 DeSales Street, N.W.
  Washington, D.C. 20036

Television/Radio Age
  666 Fifth Avenue
  New York, N.Y. 10020

LAYOUTS AND VISUALIZING

Art Direction
  19 West 44 Street
  New York, N.Y. 10036

Industrial Art Methods
  25 West 45 Street
  New York, N.Y. 10036

PRINT PRODUCTION

Graphic Arts Buyer
  19 West 44 Street
  New York, N.Y. 10036

Print
  19 West 44 Street
  New York, N.Y. 10036

Direct Advertising
90 Elm Street
Westfield, Mass.   01085

Direct Marketing
224 Seventh Street
Garden City, N.Y.   11534

OUTDOOR

Sign and Display Industry
2828 Euclid Avenue
Cleveland, Ohio   44115

Signs of the Times
405 Gilbert Avenue
Cincinnati, Ohio   45202

PACKAGING

Food and Drug Packaging
777 Third Avenue
New York, N.Y.   10017
Hard Goods & Soft Goods Packaging
777 Third Avenue
New York, N.Y.   10017

Modern Packaging
1301 Avenue of the Americas
New York, N.Y.   10019

SALES PROMOTION

Advertising & Sales Promotion
740 Rush Street
Chicago, Ill.   60611
Incentive Magazine
144 East 44 Street
New York, N.Y.   10017

Premium & Incentive Product News
33 West 60 Street
New York, N.Y.   10023
Sales Promotion
93 Railside Road
Don Mills, Ontario, Canada

RESEARCH

Journal of Advertising Research
Advertising Research Foundation,
Incorporated
3 East 54 Street
New York, N.Y.   10022
Journal of Marketing Research
American Marketing Association
230 North Michigan Avenue
Chicago, Ill.   60601

The Public Opinion Quarterly
Columbia University
116 Street and Broadway
New York, N.Y.   10027

INDUSTRIAL—FARM

Industrial Marketing
740 Rush Street
Chicago, Ill.   60611

AGRI Marketing (Agricultural
Marketing)
1722 West Grand Avenue
Chicago, Ill.   60622

Business Horizons
University of Indiana
Bloomington, Indiana   47401

Business Week
330 West 42 Street
New York, N.Y.   10036

Dun's Review
466 Lexington Avenue
New York, N.Y.   10017

Fortune
Time & Life Building
Rockefeller Center
New York, N.Y.   10020

The Gallagher Report
230 Park Avenue
New York, N.Y.   10017

Harvard Business Review
Soldiers Field Station
Boston, Mass.   02163

Nation's Business
711 Third Avenue
New York, N.Y.   10017

The Associations of Advertisers and Agencies

The titles of these associations reveal their general field of interest:

American Advertising Federation
1225 Connecticut Ave., N.W.
Washington, D.C.   20036

American Assoc. of Advertising
Agencies (AAAA—the 4A's)
200 Park Avenue
New York, N.Y.   10017

Association of Canadian Advertisers
(ACA)
159 Bay Street
Toronto 1, Ontario, Canada

Assoc. of Industrial Advertisers
(AIA)
41 East 42 Street
New York, N.Y.   10017

Association of National Advertisers
(ANA)
155 East 44 Street
New York, N.Y.   10017

Institute of Canadian Advertising
Suite 401
8 King Street East
Toronto 1, Ontario, Canada

International Advertising Assoc.
(IAA)
475 Fifth Avenue
New York, N.Y.   10017

Western States Advertising Agencies
Association
435 South La Cienega Boulevard
Los Angeles, Calif.   90048

MEDIA ASSOCIATIONS

These associations are a good source of information about their respective media. Any request for information should be specific.

American Business Press, Inc.
205 East 42 Street
New York, N.Y.   10017

Bureau of Advertising (Newspapers)
485 Lexington Avenue
New York, N.Y.   10017

Direct Mail Advertising Association
230 Park Avenue
New York, N.Y.   10017

Magazine Advertising Bureau of
Magazine Publishers Association
575 Lexington Avenue
New York, N.Y.   10022

National Assoc. of Broadcasters
1991 N Street, N.W.
Washington, D.C. 20036
Outdoor Advertising Institute of
America
625 Madison Avenue
New York, N.Y. 10022
Point-of-Purchase Advertising
Institute
521 Fifth Avenue
New York, N.Y. 10017
Radio Advertising Bureau, Inc.
555 Madison Avenue
New York, N.Y. 10022

Specialty Advertising Assoc.
740 Rush Street
Chicago, Ill. 60611
Television Bureau of Advertising
One Rockefeller Plaza
New York, N.Y. 10017
Traffic Audit Bureau, Inc.
708 Third Avenue
New York, N.Y. 10017
Transit Advertising Association
1725 K Street, N.W.
Washington, D.C. 20006

OTHER ADVERTISING AND MARKETING ASSOCIATIONS AND SERVICES

The Advertising Council
825 Third Avenue
New York, N.Y. 10022
An organization of advertisers, agencies, and media conducting public service advertising programs.
Advertising Research Foundation
(ARF)
3 East 54 Street
New York, N.Y. 10022
Dedicated to furthering scientific practices in research.
American Marketing Association
(AMA)
230 North Michigan Avenue
Chicago, Ill. 60601
Working to advance the science of marketing.
Audit Bureau of Circulations (ABC)
123 North Wacker Drive
Chicago, Ill. 60606
An organization devoted to verifying circulation of member consumer magazines and newspapers.
Business Publications Audit of
Circulation, Inc. (BPA)
360 Park Avenue South
New York, N.Y. 10010
An organization devoted to verifying circulation of member business publications.

Canadian Advertising and Sales
Association
900 Dorchester West
Montreal, Canada
Marketing Communications Research
Center (formerly Industrial
Advertising Research Institute)
15 Chambers Street
Princeton, N.J. 08540
Conducts research studies principally in industrial advertising.
National Better Business Bureau, Inc.
230 Park Avenue
New York, N.Y. 10017
Devoted to building and conserving public confidence in advertising and in business.
National Retail Merchants
Association
100 West 31 Street
New York, N.Y. 10001
Deals with problems of retail advertising.
Sales Promotion Executives
Association, Inc.
174 Fifth Avenue
New York, N.Y. 10010
For executives engaged in sales promotion activities.

Verified Audit Circulation Corp.
(VAC)
1801 Avenue of the Stars
Gateway West
Century City, Calif. 90067
Provides audited circulation of paid
and unpaid circulation media.

REFERENCE BOOKS

Agency Billings (special February
issue of Advertising Age)
Advertising Age
740 Rush Street
Chicago, Ill. 60611
N.W. Ayer & Son's Directory of
Newspapers and Periodicals
(annual)
N.W. Ayer & Son, Inc.
West Washington Square
Philadelphia, Penn. 19106
Editor and Publisher Market Guide
850 Third Avenue
New York, N.Y. 10022

Leading National Advertisers
(special August issue of Adver-
tising Age)
Advertising Age
740 Rush Street
Chicago, Ill. 60611
Standard Directory of Advertisers
(Classified Edition).
National Register Publishing Co.,
Inc.
5201 Old Orchard Rd.
Skokie, Ill. 60076
Survey of Buying Power (Sales
Management)
Sales Management, Inc.
630 Third Avenue
New York, N.Y. 10017

ADVERTISING INFORMATION SERVICES

Broadcast Advertisers Reports, Inc.
(BAR)
500 Fifth Avenue
New York, N.Y. 10036
Monitors television programs and
advertising in top 75 markets.
Lloyd Hall Reports (Magazine
Editorial Reports)
Lloyd H. Hall Co.
261 Madison Avenue
New York, N.Y. 10016
Provides data on editorial lineage
in leading national consumer maga-
zines.

Leading National Advertisers, Inc.
(PIB)
347 Madison Avenue
New York, N.Y. 10017
Publishes monthly cumulative report
of advertiser's schedules in national
magazines and in leading supplements. Also publishes LNA-BAR
Network Television Advertising reports and LNA-BAR Network Radio
Advertising Reports.

Media Records, Inc.
370 Seventh Avenue
New York, N.Y. 10001
Publishes monthly newspaper advertising dollar expenditures of national advertisers.

N.C. Rorabaugh Co., Inc.
347 Madison Avenue
New York, N.Y. 10017

Standard Rate & Data Service, Inc.
5201 Old Orchard Road
Skokie, Ill. 60076

Publishes complete rate cards of newspapers, consumer and farm magazines, business publications, television and radio stations, transit advertising. Also gives much helpful market data. Kept up-to-date monthly. Publishes *Standard Directory of Advertising Agencies,* which lists agencies along with the accounts they serve. Also *Standard Directory of Advertisers.*

SYNDICATED MEDIA RESEARCH SERVICES

A syndicated media research service is one which conducts regular surveys for information such as which publications people read, which stations they listen to, which advertisements they read, which programs they listen to or watch and what their reaction is to programs and commercials, what type of products they use, which brands, along with demographic information. Since they are continually working to make their output more helpful, no effort is made here to describe the specific services each offers. For latest information communicate directly with them.

American Research Bureau
4320 Ammendale Road
Beltsville, Md. 20705

Gallup & Robinson, Inc.
44 Nassau Street
Princeton, N.J. 08541

Home Testing Institute
50 Maple Place
Manhassett, N.Y.

A.C. Nielsen Company
360 North Michigan Avenue
Chicago, Ill. 60645

Alfred Politz Media Studies
300 Park Avenue South
New York, N.Y. 10010

The Pulse Inc.
730 Fifth Avenue
New York, N.Y. 10019

Schwerin Research Corporation
270 Madison Ave.
New York, N.Y. 10016

W.R. Simmons & Associates
Research, Incorporated
235 East 42 Street
New York, N.Y. 10017

Sindlinger & Co., Inc.
Winona & Mohawk Avenues
Norwood, Penn. 19074

Daniel Starch and Staff
E. Boston Post Road and
Beach Ave.
Mamaroneck, N.Y. 10544

Trendex, Inc.
200 Park Avenue
New York, N.Y. 10017

Daniel Yankelovich
575 Madison Avenue
New York, N.Y. 10022

Glossary

The following is a list of selected advertising terms with definitions drawn from authoritative sources or based upon general acceptance. In many instances this glossary does not confine itself to a definition of the terms, but indicates the practices connected with it as well.

A

AAAA (4 A's). See *American Association of Advertising Agencies.*

AAF. See *American Advertising Federation.*

ABC. See *Audit Bureau of Circulations.*

ABP. See *American Business Press.*

ACB. See *Advertising Checking Bureau.*

Account executive. That member of the agency staff who is the liaison between advertiser and agency, presenting the advertiser's problems to the agency, and the agency's recommendations and proposed advertisements to the advertiser. Is responsible for keeping in close touch with the advertiser's needs and plans, and for seeing that approved plans are carried out by the agency.

Acetate. A radio recording disc.

Across the board. A television or radio program scheduled for broadcast in the same time period on different days during the week. (Usually Monday through Friday.)

ADI. See *Area of Dominant Influence.*

Adjacency. A program or time period which immediately precedes or follows a scheduled program on a single radio or television station.

Ad lib. To extemporize lines not written into the script, or music not in the musical score. Music or lines so delivered.

Advertising. Any paid form of nonpersonal presentation and promotion of ideas, goods, and services by an identified sponsor.

Advertising agency. An organization rendering advertising services to clients.

A la carte agency. One which offers parts of its services, as needed on a negotiated fee basis; also called *modular* service.

Full service agency. One which handles the planning, creation, production and placing of advertising for advertising clients.

House agency. One which is owned and operated by an advertiser. May handle the accounts of other advertisers too.

In-house agency. An arrangement where the advertiser handles the total agency function by buying individually, on a fee basis, the respective services he needs, as creation, media services and placement.

Advertising Checking Bureau (A.C.B.). A private organization though whom most newspaper publishers send their tear sheets to national advertisers for checking purposes.

Advertising Council. The joint body of the AAAA and the ANA, and media, through which public service advertising is produced and presented.

Advertising network. A group of independently owned, non-competing advertising agencies who agree to exchange ideas and services in the interests of their clients.

Advertising Research Foundation (ARF). An association of research men devoted to furthering the use and effectiveness of marketing and advertising research.

Advertising specialty. An inexpensive gift (limit $4.00, usually much less) bearing the advertiser's name and trademark, given without cost to a selected list.

Advertising spiral. The graphic representation of the stages through which a product might pass in its acceptance by the public. The stages are *pioneering, competitive, retentive.*

Affidavit. The sworn statement of a television or radio station that a commercial appeared as stated on invoice.

Affiliate. An independent TV or radio station that agrees to carry programs provided by a network.

AFTRA. See *American Federation of Television and Radio Artists.*

Agate line. A unit measurement of publication advertising space, one column wide (no matter what the column width) and one-fourteenth of an inch deep.

Agency commission. The compensation paid by a medium to recognized agencies for services rendered in connection with placing advertising with it. Usually 15 percent. Some media also allow 2 percent of the net (85 percent) as a cash discount for prompt payment. This is passed on to the client for prompt payment.

Agency network. A voluntary affiliation of one agency in a major city to act as local office or provide local service for other members of that network. There are a number of different networks.

Agency recognition. The recognition by a medium that an organization qualifies under its terms to receive a commission for business placed.

Aided recall. A research technique that uses prompting questions or materials to aid a respondent's memory of the original exposure situation as "Have you seen this ad before?" In contrast to *unaided* recall: "Which ad impressed you most in this magazine?"

Air check. A recording of an actual broadcast that serves as a file copy of a broadcast, and which a sponsor may use to evaluate talent, program appeal, or production.

A la carte agency. See *Advertising agency.*

Allocation. The assignment of frequency and power made by the Federal Communications Commission to a broadcasting station.

Alternate sponsorship. When two TV advertisers share a single program, with one advertiser dominant one week, the other the following week. Practice quite obsolete. Most shows have a number of participating sponsors who buy up all the time.

AM. See *Amplitude Modulation.*

American Academy of Advertising. The national association of teachers of advertising in colleges and universities, and of others interested in the teaching of advertising.

American Advertising Federation (AAF). An association of local advertising clubs and representatives of other advertising associations. The largest association of advertising people. Very much interested in advertising legislation.

American Association of Advertising Agencies. A.A.A.A., The 4A's. The national organization of advertising agencies.

American Business Press, Inc., (A.B.P.). An organization of trade, industrial, and professional papers.

American Federation of Television and Radio Artists (AFTRA). A union involved in the setting of wage scales of all performers.

American Newspaper Publishers' Association (A.N.P.A.). The major trade association of daily and Sunday newspaper publishers.

Amplitude modulation (AM). The method of transmitting electromagnetic signals by varying the *amplitude* (size) of the electromagnetic wave, in contrast to varying its *frequency* (FM). Quality not as good as FM but can be heard further, especially at night. See *Frequency modulation*—FM.

A.N.A. See *Association of National Advertisers.*

Animation. Can refer to animated cartoons or to animated objects, such as packages or marionettes. May be limited animation on silent films only, or regular animation with a sound track, a costly process.

Announcement. Any TV or radio commercial, regardless of time length, within or between programs, which presents an advertiser's message or a public service message.

Announcer. That member of a TV or radio station who delivers those commercials to be de-livered live, or who introduces a taped commercial.

ANPA. See *American Newspaper Publishers' Association.*

Answer Print (TV). A composite print of the sound, music and opticals leading to a Master Print, from which duplicates are made for distribution to stations.

Antique-finish paper. Book or cover paper that has a rough, uneven surface, good for offset printing.

Appeal. The motive to which an advertisement is directed and which is designed to stir a person towards a goal involving the purchase of the product.

Applause mail. Letters of comment or appreciation received from the listening audience by radio or television stations or sponsors; fan mail.

Approach (Outdoor). The distance measured along the line of travel from the point where the poster first becomes fully visible to a point where the copy ceases to be readable. (There is long approach, medium approach, short approach, and flash approach.)

Arbitrary mark. A dictionary word used as a trademark which *connotes nothing* about the product it is to identify, e.g. *Rise* shaving cream, *Deal* soap, *Jubilee* wax.

Arbitron. The device for recording when the television in a household is on, a part of the research operation of the American Research Bureau. See *Audimeter.*

Area of Dominant Influence (ADI). A classification of the American Research Bureau showing the exclusive geographical area consisting of all counties in which the Home Market Stations receive a preponderance of total viewing hours. Used in deciding what territories to include in a market. Especially important in TV scheduling.

Area sampling. See *Sampling.*

ARF. See *Advertising Research Foundation.*

Ascap. American Society of Composers, Authors, and Publishers. An organization that protects the copyrights of its members and collects royalties in their behalf.

Ascending letters. Those with a stroke or line going higher than the body of the letter—b, d, f, h, k, l, and t—and all capitals. The descending letters g, j, p, q, and y.

Association of National Advertisers (ANA). The trade association of the leading national advertisers. Founded 1910.

Association test. A research method of measuring the degree to which people correctly identify brand names, slogans, themes.

Audience. primary. (Radio) The audience in the territory where the signal is the strongest. (Print) The readers in households which buy or subscribe to a publication.

Audience, secondary. (Radio) The audience in the territory adjacent to the primary territory which receives the signal, but not so strongly as the latter. (Print) The number of people who read a publication but who did not subscribe for or buy it. Also called pass-along circulation.

Audience, share of. The number or proportion of all TV households that are tuned to a particular station or program.

Audience composition. The number and kinds of people classified by their age, sex, income, and the like, listening to a television or radio program.

Audience flow. The TV household audience inherited by a broadcast program from the preceding program.

Audimeter. The device for recording when the television in a household is on, a part of the research operation of the A. C. Nielsen Company. See *Arbitron.*

Audio. Sound portion of a television program or commercial. See *Video.*

Audit Bureau of Circulations (A.B.C.). The organization sponsored by publishers, agencies, and advertisers for securing accurate circulation statements.

Audition. A tryout of artists, musicians, or programs under broadcasting conditions.

Audition record. A transcription of a broadcast program used by a prospective sponsor to evaluate it, generally before the broadcast.

Author's corrections, author's alterations. (Abbreviated a.a.) Alterations or changes made in proofs (called author's proofs) not due to printer's errors and so chargeable to whomever is paying for composition. Unnecessary expense for this item can be reduced by careful editing of copy before it is sent to the printer.

Availability. In broadcasting, a time period available for purchase by an advertiser.

Availability (TV). A commercial time slot that has not been sold; hence available for purchase.

B

Background. A broadcasting sound effect, musical or otherwise, used behind the dialogue or other program elements for realistic or emotional effect.

Backing up. Printing the second side of a sheet as a separate process. In fine printing it is necessary for the ink to dry on one side of the sheet before the other side is printed.

Back-to-back. Describes the situation in which two commercials

or programs directly follow each other.

Bait advertising. An alluring but insincere retail offer to sell a product which the advertiser in truth does not intend or want to sell. Its purpose is to switch a buyer from buying the advertised merchandise to buying something else.

Balloons. A visualizing device with the words of a person pictured coming right from his mouth; borrowed from the newspaper comic pages.

Balopticon (balops). A type of television animation made possible through the use of a Balopticon machine.

BAR. See *Broadcast Advertising Reports.*

Basic bus. A bus all of whose interior advertising is sold to one advertiser. When the outside is also sold, it is called a basic basic bus.

Basic network. The minimum grouping of stations for which an advertiser must contract in order to use the facilities of a radio or television network.

Basic rate. See *Open rate.*

Basic stations. TV networks are offered in terms of a list of stations which must be included. These are the Basic Stations. There is also a list of supplementing stations which may optionally be added to the list.

Basic weight. The weight of a ream of paper if cut to the standard or basic size for that class of paper. The basic sizes are: writing papers, 17 x 22 inches; book papers, 25 x 38 inches; cover stocks, 20 x 26 inches.

Battered. Type injured or broken in a form, or the damaged part of a printing plate.

BBB. See *Better Business Bureaus.*

Bearers. (1) Excess metal left on an engraving to protect and strengthen it during the process of electrotyping. (2) Strips of metal placed at the sides of a type form for protection during electrotyping.

Benday (or Ben Day). A method by which the engraver applies shaded tints in a choice of various patterns (lines or dots) to areas of artwork that otherwise would be reproduced only in solid colors or in pure white.

Better Business Bureaus. An organization launched by advertisers, and now with wide business support, to protect the public against deceptive advertising and fraudulent business methods. Works widely at local levels. Also identified with the National Advertising Review Board.

Billboard. (1) Popular name for an outdoor sign. Term not now generally used in the industry. (2) The television presentation of the name of a program sponsor plus a slogan, used at the start or close of a program, usually 8 seconds.

Billing. (1) Amount of business done by an advertising agency. (2) Name credit of talent on the air in order of importance.

Bit. A small part in a dramatic program is a bit part, and the performer who plays it is a bit player.

Bite. The depth of the etch attained in photoengraving by each separate application of the etching acid. Good bite leads to good reproduction.

Black and white. An advertisement printed in one color only, usually black, on white paper. Most newspapers are printed black and white.

Blanking Area. The white margin around a poster erected on a standard size board. It is widest for a 24 sheet poster, for example; narrower for a 30 sheet poster, and disappears with a bleed poster.

Bleed. To print and trim an advertisement so that its edges run over the edges of the outdoor board or page of a publication, leaving no margin.

Blister pack. A packaging term. A preformed bubble of plastic holding merchandise to a card. Used for small items. Also called "bubble card."

Block. (1) A set of consecutive time periods on the air; or a strip of the same time on several days. (2) Wood or metal base on which the printing plate is mounted. (3) British term for photoengraving or electrotype.

Blow-up. Photo enlargement of written, printed, or pictorial materials, as of a publication advertisement to be used as a poster or transmitted through television.

B.M.I. Broadcast Music, Inc. Chief function: to provide music to radio and television shows with minimum royalty fees, if any.

Boards (Outdoor). Term for poster panels and painted bulletins originating in the period when theatrical and circus posters were displayed on board fences.

Body copy. Main text of advertisement, in contrast to headlines and name plate.

Body type. The type commonly used for reading matter, as distinguished from display type used in the headlines of advertisements. Usually type 14 points in size, or smaller.

Boiler plate. Pages in stereotype, often including news and advertisements, that are supplied by news agencies or other syndicates to country weeklies to cut their costs of composition. Also called patent insides. Boiler plate originally meant any thin metal sheet.

Boldface type. A heavy line type, for example, the headings in these definitions.

Bond paper. The writing paper most frequently used in commercial correspondence, originally a durable quality used for printing bonds and other securities. The weight in most extensive use for letterheads is 20 lb. $(17 \times 22 = 20)$.

Book paper. A paper used in printing books, as well as for lightweight leaflets and folders, distinguished from writing papers and cover stocks. Basic size, 25 x 38.

Box top offers. An invitation to the consumer to get a gift or premium by sending in the label or box top from a package of the product (with or without an additional payment).

BPA. See *Business Papers Audit of Circulation.*

Brand name. The spoken part of a trademark in contrast to the pictorial mark; a trademark word.

Bridge. Music or sound effect cue linking two scenes in a television or radio show.

Broadcast Advertising Reports (BAR). A private service that electrically monitors all television activity in 75 markets.

Broadcast spectrum. That part of the range of frequencies of electromagnetic waves assigned to broadcasting stations. Separate bands of frequencies are assigned to VHF and UHF television, AM and FM radio.

Brochure. A fancy booklet or monograph.

Bubble card. See *Blister pack.*

Bulk mailing. When a quantity of third class mail is being sent, it must be delivered to the postoffice in bundles, assorted by state and city.

Bulldog edition. That edition of a morning paper that is printed early the preceding evening and sent to out-of-town readers on the night trains or planes. If an advertiser does not get his copy in early, he misses this edition.

Bureau of Advertising (B of A). Devoted to research and promotion of newspaper advertising.

Buried advertisement. An advertisement surrounded by other advertisements, or at the bottom corner of the page with advertisements alongside and above it. Advertisers object to having their advertisements "buried."

Buried offer. An offer for a booklet, sample, or information made by means of a statement within the text of an advertisement without use of a coupon or typographical emphasis. (Also called Hidden offer.)

Burnishing (engraving). The mechanical act of making the dark areas in a halftone appear still darker.

Business Papers Audit of Circulation, Inc. (BPA). An organization that audits business publications. Includes controlled or "qualified" free circulation.

Buying space. Buying the right to insert an advertisement in a given medium, such as a periodical, a program, or an outdoor sign; buying time is the corresponding term for purchase of television or radio broadcast privilege.

C

Cablecasting. The programming which has been originated by the CATV operator, exclusive of broadcast signals carried by the system. Goes directly from CATV studio to home by cable.

Calendered paper. A paper with a smooth, burnished surface, secured by passing the paper between heavy rolls, called calenders.

Call letters. The combination of letters assigned by the Federal Communications Commission to a broadcasting station, which serves as its official designation and establishes its identity.

Camera light. Pilot light on television cameras indicating which camera is on the air.

Camera lucinda. Familiarly lucy. A device used in making layouts enabling artist to copy an illustration larger, smaller or in the same size.

Campaign. A specific advertising effort on behalf of a particular product or service which extends for a specified period of time.

Caption. The heading of an advertisement; the descriptive matter accompanying an illustration.

Carbro. A photographic process for color printing on paper from separation negatives.

Casting off. Estimating the amount of space a piece of copy will occupy when set in type of a given size.

CATV. See *Community Antenna Television.*

Center spread. The space occupied by an advertisement on the two facing center pages of a publication.

Center-Spread (Print). An advertisement printed across the two facing middle pages of a publication bound through the center. Otherwise called *double-page spread.* (Outdoor) Two adjacent panels using coordinated copy.

Certification Mark. A name or design used upon or in connection with the products or services of persons other than the owner of the mark to certify origin, material, mode of manufacture, quality, accuracy or other characteristics of such goods or services, e.g. *Seal of the Underwriters' Laboratories, Sanforized, Teflon II.*

Chain. (1) A group of retail outlets with the same ownership, management, and business policy. (2) A regularly established system of television or radio stations interconnected for simultaneous broadcasting through the associated stations. (3) A network of television stations.

Chain break. Times during or between network programs when a broadcasting station identifies itself (2 seconds) and gives a commercial announcement (8 seconds). The announcements are referred to as *chain breaks* or ID's (for identification).

Channel. A band of radio frequencies assigned to a given radio or television station, or to other broadcasting purposes.

Chase. The iron or steel frame in which the type is locked up for the press or to make plates.

Checking copy. A copy of a publication sent to an advertiser or to his agency so that he may see that his advertisement appeared as specified.

Circular. An advertisement printed on a sheet or folder.

Circulation. Refers to the number of people a medium reaches. (1) In publication advertising: *prime* circulation is that paid for by the reader, in contrast to *pass-along* circulation. (2) In outdoor and transportation advertising: individuals who have a reasonable opportunity to observe display. (3) In TV: circulation is usually referred to in terms of audience. The measurement and verification of circulation is one of the big problems of advertising.

Class A, B, C, rates. Rates for the most desirable and costly television time usually between 6 p.m. and 11 p.m., are called Class A rates; the next most costly is Class B, and so on. Each station sets its own time classifications.

Classified Advertising. Advertising published in sections of a newspaper or magazine set aside for certain classes of goods or services, in columns so labeled. Example: Help Wanted, Positions Wanted, Houses for Sale, Cars for Sale. The advertisements are limited in size and illustrations.

Class magazines. The term loosely used to describe publications that reach select high-income readers, in contrast to magazines of larger circulations, generally referred to as mass magazines.

Clear. (1) To obtain legal permission from responsible sources to use a photograph or quotation in an advertisement or to use a certain musical selection in a broadcast. (2) To clear time is to arrange with a station to provide time for a commercial program.

Clear-channel station. A radio station that is allowed the maximum power is given a channel on the frequency band all to itself, with possibly one or two sectional or local stations far removed from it, so as not to interfere. (See *Local-channel station; Regional-channel station*).

Clear time. See *Clear.*

Clip. A short piece of film inserted in a program or commercial.

Closed circuit. Live television transmitted by cable for private viewing.

Closing date; closing hour. (1) The day or hour when all copy and plates must be in the medium's hands if the advertisement is to appear in a given issue. The closing time is specified by the medium. (2) The last hour or day that a radio program or announcement may be submitted for approval to a station or network management to be included in the station's schedule.

Clubbing offer. An arrangement whereby subscriptions to two or more different publications are offered at a reduced combination price. Considered in judging the character of the circulation of a publication.

Cluster sample. A random, or probability, sample that uses groups of people rather than individuals as a sampling unit.

Coarse-screen halftone. A halftone with a comparatively low, or coarse, screen, usually 60, 65, or 85 lines to the inch, suitable for printing on coarse paper.

Coated paper. A paper to which a coating has been applied, giving it a smooth, hard finish, suitable for the reproduction of fine halftones.

Coaxial cable. In television, the visual part is sent on AM frequency, the audio part on FM. Both frequencies are sent through the same cable, the *coaxial* cable.

Coined word. An original and arbitrary combination of syllables forming a word. Extensively used for trademarks, as Acrilan, Gro-Pup, Zerone. (Opposite of dictionary word.)

Collateral services. An agency term, to describe the non-commissionable forms of services different agencies perform, such as sales promotion, research, merchandising, new product studies. Originally these were extra services, rendered without fee in many cases, to clients. Now mostly done on a negotiated fee basis, both for clients and non-clients.

Collective mark. An identification used by the members of a cooperative, an association or collective group or organization, including marks used to indicate membership in a union, an association or other organization, e.g. Sunkist.

Color proof. Combined impressions from separate color plates.

Column-inch. A unit of measure in a periodical one inch deep and one column wide, whatever the width of the column.

Combination plate. A halftone and line plate in one engraving.

Combination rate. (1) A special space rate for two papers, such as a morning paper and an evening paper, owned by the same publisher. Applies also to any other special rate granted in connection with two or more periodicals. (2) The rate paid for a combination plate.

Comic strip. A series of cartoon or caricature drawings.

Commercial. The advertiser's message on television or radio.

Commercial program. A sponsored program from which broadcasting stations derive revenue on the basis of the time consumed in broadcasting it.

Community Antenna Television (CATV). A method whereby one antenna placed at an advantageous height can receive many stations, and from which the programs are relayed to the television sets of subscribers by means of a coaxial cable. See *Cablecasting.*

Competitive stage. The advertising stage a product reaches when its general usefulness is recognized, but its individual superiority over similar brands has to be established in order that it shall secure the preference. (Compare Pioneering stage; Retentive stage.) See *Spiral.*

Composition, (cold). Metal type, mechanically set, other than that set directly from molten metal; e.g. typewriter type. (Hand) Type already molded, picked out of its case by hand to compose the copy. (Hot) A term used to describe type molded for the needs of the copy being set in type, as by Linotype or Monotype.

Composition. Assembling and arranging type for printing. (Also called typography or typesetting.)

Comprehensive. A layout accurate for size, color scheme, and other necessary details, to show how final ad is to look.

Computerized composition. A method of composing type used for telephone directories, price and parts lists. Compresses into a few reels of punched or magnetic tape the tons of metal customers ask to be stored. Not too widely used in advertising.

Consumer advertising. Advertising directed to those people who will personally use the product, in contrast to trade advertising, industrial advertising, professional advertising.

Consumer goods. Products that directly satisfy human wants or desires, such as food and clothing; also products sold to an individual or family for use without further processing; as distinct from industrial goods.

Continuity. A TV or radio script.

Continuous tone. Shading in a negative that is not formed by screen dots.

Contract year. The period of time, in space contracts, running for one year beginning with the insertion of the first advertisement under that contract. It is usually specified that the first advertisement shall appear within 30 days of the signing of the contract.

Controlled circulation. (1) The circulation of business publications containing at least 25 per cent editorial matter, regularly issued at least quarterly, circulated free or mainly free, and addressed to individuals within a particular business industry, or profession selected as to job title, function or other characteristic relevant to the interests of the advertisers. The term is no longer used by the Business Publications Audit; qualified circulation is preferred. (2) Circulation of free suburban shopping papers to preselected areas or homes.

Convenience goods. Those consumer goods that are bought frequently at nearby (convenient) outlets, as distinct from shopping goods for which a person compares styles, quality, prices.

Conversion table. Table showing what the equivalent weight of paper stock of a given size

would be if the sheet were cut to another size.

Cooperative advertising. (1) Joint promotion of a national advertiser (manufacturer) and local retail outlet in behalf of the manufacturer's product on sale in the retail store. (2) Joint promotion through a trade association for firms in a single industry. (3) Advertising venture jointly conducted by two or more advertisers.

Cooperative mailing. A mailing to a select list comprising all the inserts of a group of non-competitive firms trying to reach the same audience. A way of reducing mailing costs.

Copy. (1) The text of an advertisement. (2) Matter for a compositor to set. (3) Illustrations for an engraver to reproduce. (4) Any material to be used in the production of a publication.

Copy approach. The method of opening the text of an advertisement. Chief forms: Factual approach. Emotional approach.

Copy platform. The statement of the basic ideas for an advertising campaign, the designation of the importance of the various selling points to be included in it, and instructions regarding policy in handling any elements of the advertisement.

Copyright. Legal protection afforded an original intellectual effort. Application blanks are procurable from the Copyright Office, Library of Congress, Washington, D. C. Copyright notice must appear beginning with first advertisement published.

Copy writer. A person who creates the text of advertisements and often the idea to be visualized as well.

Corrective advertising. To counteract the past residual effect of previous deceptive advertising, the FTC may require the advertiser to devote future space and time to disclosure

of previous deception. Began around 1967-1970.

Cover. The front of a publication is known as the first cover; the inside of the front cover is the second cover; the inside of the back cover is the third cover; the outside of the back cover is the fourth cover. Extra rates are charged for cover positions.

Coverage. (1) The portion of an area, community, or group that may be reached by an advertising medium.

Coverage (TV). All households in an area able to receive a station's signal, even though some may not be tuned in. *Grade A* coverage: those households in the city and outlying counties that receive signals with hardly any disturbance. *Grade B:* those on the fringes of the market area, receiving signals with some interference.

Cover stock. A paper made of heavy, strong fiber; used for folders and for booklet covers. Some cover stocks run into the low weights of paper known as book paper, but most cover stocks are heavier. Basic size, 20 x 26 inches.

Cowcatcher. A brief announcement preceding an advertiser's program featuring another product.

C.P.M. Cost per thousand. Used in comparing media cost. Can mean cost per thousand readers, or viewers or prospects. Must be specified.

C.P.M./P.C.M. Cost per thousand per commercial minute.

Crash finish. A surface design on paper, simulating the appearance of rough cloth.

Cropping. Trimming part of an illustration to enable the reproduction to fit into a specific space. Cropping is done either to eliminate nonessential background in an illustration or to change the proportions of the illustration to the desired length and width.

Crossplugs. In alternating sponsorship, a process which permits each advertiser to substitute one minute of commercial time from his program for one minute of his partner's program in order to maintain weekly exposure. Practice waning with decrease of alternate sponsorship.

CU. Close-up (in television). ECU is *extra close-up*.

Cue. (1) The closing words of an actor's speech and a signal for another actor to enter. (2) A sound, musical or otherwise, or a manual signal calling for action or proceeding.

Cume (abbreviation for cumulative). The unduplicated audience a program or commercial gets if played two or more times in the same environment, over a fixed period of time, usually measured in four-week spans.

Cumes. The number of unduplicated people and/or homes reached by a given schedule over a given time period. In TV this usually is four weeks. An abbreviation for cumulative audience.

Customer profile. A composite estimate of the demographic characteristics of the people who are to buy a brand and the purchase patterns they will produce.

Cut. (1) The deletion of program material to fit a prescribed period of time, or for other reasons. (2) A photoengraving, electrotype, or stereotype; derived from the term *woodcut*. In England called a *block*.

Cut-out. A printed advertisement with a design literally cut out of it used in displays; direct mail.

Cylinder press. A press with a rotating cylinder under which a flat bed containing type or plates slides forward and backward. Used for large-quantity work, or for advertisements of large size.

D

Dailies TV. See *Rushes*. (Newspapers (Daily paper), in contrast to Sunday, or weekly, paper.

Day Time TV. A loose term generally applied to the period from morning sign-on to 5 p.m.

DB. See *Delayed Broadcast*.

Dead metal. Excess metal left on an engraved plate for protection during electrotyping. Such metal portions are sometimes called bearers.

Dealer imprint. The name and address of the dealer, printed or pasted on an advertisement of a national advertiser. In the planning of direct mail, space is frequently left for the dealer imprint.

Dealer tie-in. A national advertiser's promotional program in which the dealer participates (as in contests, sampling plan, cooperative advertising plans).

Decalcomania. A transparent gelatinous film bearing an advertisement, which may be gummed onto the dealer's window. Also known as a transparency.

Deckle edge. The untrimmed ragged edge of a sheet of paper. Used for costlier forms of direct mail.

Deck panels (Outdoor). Panels built one above the other.

Definition. Clean-cut television and radio transmission and reception.

Delayed broadcast (DB). A local station's televising of a network program at a time other than at its regularly-scheduled network time. Frequently a program televised live in the East will be played by delayed broadcast tape in the Middle West and Pacific coast later at the same time period as in the East.

Delete. "Omit." Used in proofreading.

Demographic characteristics. A broad term that refers to the various social and economic characteristics of a group of households, or a group of individuals. Refers to characteristics such as the number of members of a household, age of head of household, occupation of head of household, education of household members, type of employment, ownership of home, and annual household income.

Depth interview. A research interview conducted without a structured questionnaire in which respondents are encouraged to speak fully and freely about a particular subject.

Depths of columns. The dimension of a column space measured from top of the page to the bottom, in either agate lines or inches.

Designated Market Area (DMA). This is a map by counties showing those counties in which stations of the originating market account for a greater share of the viewing households than those from any other area. Similar in concept to ARF's Area of Dominant Influence.

Diary. A written record kept by a sample of persons who record their listening, viewing, reading activities, or purchases of brands within a specific period of time. Used by syndicate research firms who arrange with a selected sample of people to keep such diaries and report weekly, for a fee.

Die-cut. An odd-shaped paper or cardboard for a direct-mail piece or for display purposes, cut with a special knife-edge die.

Diorama. (1) In point-of-purchase advertising, these are elaborate displays of a scenic nature, almost always three-dimensional and illuminated—POPAI. (2) In television, a miniature set, usually in perspective, used to simulate an impression of a larger location.

Direct advertising. Any form of advertising reproduced in quantity by or for the advertiser and issued by him or under his direction directly to definite and specific prospects by means of the mails, canvassers, salesmen, dealers, or otherwise—as through letters, leaflets, folders, or booklets.

Direct halftone. A superior type of halftone made by photographing an object itself instead of a picture of it.

Direct mail advertising. That form of direct advertising sent through the mails.

Direct Mail Advertising Association (DMAA). The national organization of users of direct response advertising.

Direct marketing. The selling of goods and services without the aid of wholesaler or retailer. Includes direct response advertising, mail order advertising and advertising for leads for salesmen. Also direct door to door selling. Uses many media, direct mail, publications, TV, radio.

Director. The person who writes or rewrites, then casts and rehearses, a television or radio program, and directs the actual air performance.

Direct process. In two-, three-, and four-color process work, color separation and screen negative made simultaneously on the same photographic plate.

Disk jockey. The master of ceremonies of a radio program of transcribed music (records).

Display. (1) Attention-attracting quality. (2) Display type is sizes larger than 14 point. Italics, boldface, and sometimes capitals are used for display; so are hand-drawn letters and script. (3) Display space in newspapers usually is not sold in units of less than 14 column lines; there is no such minimum requirement for undisplay classified advertisements. (4) Window display, interior display, and counter display are different methods of Point-of-Purchase

advertising. (5) Open display puts the goods where they can be actually handled and examined by the customer; closed display has the goods in cases and under glass.

Display advertising. (1) Advertising in a newspaper other than that carried in its classified columns. (2) Advertising on backgrounds designed to stand by themselves, as window displays, or be mounted, as a tack-on sign.

Display type. Type 14 points or larger.

Dissolve. The overlapping of an image produced by one camera over that of another, and the gradual elimination of the first image.

DMA. See *Designated Market Area*.

DMAA. See *Direct Mail Advertising Association*.

Dolly. The movable platform on which a camera is placed for TV productions when different angles or views will be needed.

Double-decker. Outdoor advertising erected one above another.

Double-leaded. See *Leading*.

Double-page spread. Two facing pages used for a single, unbroken advertisement. Also called double-spread and double-truck, or center spread if at the center of a publication.

"Down-and-under." A direction given to a musician or sound effects man playing solo in a broadcast to quiet down from his plesent playing level to a volume less than that of the lines of dialogue that follow.

Drive Time. See *Prime Time (radio)*.

Drop-in. In broadcasting, a local commercial inserted in a nationally sponsored network program.

Drop-out halftone. See *Halftone*.

Dry-brush drawing. A drawing

made with a brush using extra thick and dry ink or paint.

Dry run. Rehearsal without cameras.

Dubbing. The combining of several sound tracks for recording on film.

Dubbing in. The addition of one television film to another; as, for example, the part containing the advertiser's commercial to the part that carries the straight entertainment.

Dubs (TV). Duplicate tapes, made from a Master Print, sent to different stations for broadcast.

Due bill. (1) In a broadcast barter deal, the amount of time acquired by a film distributor, owner, or producer from a station. (2) An agreement between an advertiser (usually a hotel or resort) and a medium involving the equal exchange of the advertiser's service for time or space.

Dummy. (1) Blank sheets of paper cut and folded to the size of a proposed leaflet, folder, booklet, or book, to indicate weight, shape, size, and general appearance. On the pages of the dummy the layouts can be drawn. Useful in designing direct-mail advertisements. A dummy may also be made from the proof furnished by the printer. (2) An empty package or carton, used for display purposes.

Duograph. A two-color plate made from black and white art work. The second color is a flat color and carries no detail. Less expensive than a duotone. See *Duotone*.

Duotone. Two halftone plates each printing in a different color, and giving two-color reproductions from an original one-color plate. See *Duograph*.

Duplicate plates. Photoengravings made from the same negative as an original plate.

E

Early fringe. The time period preceding prime time. (Usually, 4:30-7:30 P.M., except in Central Time Zone where it extends from 3:30 to 6:30 P.M.

Ears of newspaper. The boxes or announcements at the top of the front page, alongside the name of the paper, in the upper right- and left-hand corners. Sold for advertising space by some papers.

Earth station. A TV receiving station designed to capture signals from satellites, for relay to broadcasting stations, or in time, possibly directly to receiving sets.

ECU (TV). Extreme-close-up in shooting a picture.

Editing (TV). Selecting the scenes from a TV film or tape for inclusion in the final.

Effective circulation (outdoor). The number of people who have a reasonable physical opportunity to see a poster. It is defined as one-half the pedestrians, one-half the automobiles, and one-fourth of surface public transportation passengers passing a poster.

Electrical transcription. A form of highfidelity recording made especially for broadcasting and allied purposes; its surface noise is very low.

Electric spectaculars. Outdoor advertisements in which electric lights are used to form the words and design. Not to be confused with illuminated posters or illuminated painted bulletins.

Electrotype. A metal facsimile of another plate made by the electrotype process. When several identical plates of a production are required, one original can be made from that. Electrotypes costs less than original plates.

Em. The square of a body of any given type face, the letter M being as wide as it is high. Usu-ally short for the 12 point Pica Em.

En. Half the width of an Em.

Enameled paper; enamel-coated stock. A book or cover paper that can take the highest-screen halftone. It is covered with a coating of china clay and a binder, then ironed under high-speed rollers. This gives it a hard, smooth finish too brittle to fold well. Made also in dull and semidull finish.

English finish (E.F.). A hard, even, and unpolished finish applied to book papers.

Engraving. (1) A photoengraving. (2) A plate in which a design is etched for printing purposes.

Equivalent weight of paper. The weight of a given paper stock in terms of its basic weight. See *Basic weight.*

Ethical advertising. (1) Advertising that comports with the standard of equitable, fair, and honest content. (2) Advertising of a preparation addressed to physicians only, in contrast to advertising a similar product addressed to the general public.

Extended covers. A cover that is slightly wider and longer than the pages of a paper-bound booklet or catalogue; one that extends or hangs over the inside pages. Also called overhang and overlap. See *Trimmed flush.*

F

Face. (1) The printing surface of type or a plate. (2) The style of type.

Facing text matter. The position of an advertisement in a periodical opposite reading matter.

Facsimile broadcasting. A process of transmitting and receiving electronically such graphic material as pictures and printed matter.

Fact sheet. A page of highlights of the selling features of a prod-uct, for use by an announcer in ad libbing a live commercial.

Fade. (TV) *Fading in* is the gradual appearance of the screen image brightening from black to full visibility. (Radio) To diminish or increase the volume of sound on a radio broadcast.

Fading. The variation in the intensity of a radio or television signal received over a great distance.

Family of type. Type faces related in design, as Caslon Bold, Caslon Old Style, Caslon Bold Italics, Caslon Old Style Italics.

Fanfare. A few bars of music (usually trumpets) to herald an entrance or announcement in broadcasting.

FCC. See *Federal Communications Commission.*

FDA. See *Food & Drug Administration.*

Federal Communications Commission. The Federal authority empowered to license radio stations and to assign wave lengths to stations "in the public interest."

Federal Trade Commission (FTC). That agency of the Federal government empowered to prevent unfair competition; also to prevent fraudulent, misleading or deceptive advertising in interstate commerce.

Field intensity map. A television or radio broadcast coverage map showing the quality of reception possible on the basis of its signal strength. Sometimes called a contour map.

Field intensity measurement. The measurement of a signal delivered at a point of reception by a radio transmitter in units of voltage per meter of effective antenna height, usually in terms of microvolts or millivolts per meter.

Fill-in. (1) The salutation and any other data to be inserted in the individual letters after they have been printed. (2) The blurring of an illustration due to the closeness of the lines or dots in the plate or to heavy inking.

Firm order. A definite order for time or space that is not cancellable after a given date known as a firm order date.

Flag (Outdoor). A tear in a poster causing a piece of poster paper to hang loose. Plant owner is supposed to replace promptly.

Flat-bed. A printing press (for letterpress printing) containing a flat metal bed on which forms of type and plates are locked for printing.

Flat proofs. Ordinary rough proofs, or stone proofs, taken of type when it is on the compositor's workbench, in contrast to press proofs made after the type has been carefully adjusted to give the best possible impression.

Flat rate. A uniform charge for space in a medium, without regard to the amount of space used or the frequency of insertion. When flat rates do not prevail, time discounts or quantity discounts are offered.

Flight. The length of time a broadcaster's campaign runs. Can be by days, weeks or months, but does not refer to a year. A flighting schedule alternates periods of activity with periods of inactivity.

FM. See *Frequency Modulation.*

Following, next to, reading matter. The specification of a position for an advertisement to appear in a publication. Also known as full position. This preferred position usually costs more than run-of-paper position.

"Follow style." Instruction to compositor to set copy in accordance with a previous advertisement or proof.

Font. An assortment of type characters of one style and size, containing the essential 26 letters (both capitals and small letters) plus numerals, punctuation marks, etc. See *Wrong font.*

Food & Drug Administration (FDA). The Federal Bureau whose authority extends over the safety and purity of foods, drugs, cosmetics; also the labeling of such products.

Foreign advertising. (1) Newspaper advertising paid for directly or indirectly by a manufacturer or national distributor (usually nonresident), as contrasted with local advertising, which is paid for by the local retailer, at a lower rate. Also known as national advertising. (2) Advertising in another country.

Form. (1) Pages of type locked in place in a strong, rectangular iron frame known as a chase. Usually holds 1, 2, 4, 8, 16, 32, or 64 pages (hence it is uneconomical to print booklets with 10, 12, 26, or 50 pages). (2) The general style of a book, as opposed to its subject.

Format. The size, shape, style, and appearance of a book or publication.

Forms close. The date on which all copy and plates for a periodical advertisement must be in.

Foundry proofs. The proofs of a typographical setup just before the material is sent to the foundry for electrotyping; identified by the heavy funeralblack border (foundry rules).

4A's. American Association of Advertising Agencies (AAAA).

Four-color process. The photoengraving process for reproducing color illustrations by a set of plates, one of which prints all the yellows, another the blues, a third the reds, the fourth the blacks (sequence variable). The plates are referred to as process plates.

Free lance. An independent artist or writer or television and radio producer, or advertising man who takes individual assignments from different accounts, but is not in their employ.

Frequency. (1) The number of waves per second that a transmitter radiates (measured in kilocycles [Kc] and megacycles [Mc]. The FCC assigns to each television and radio station the frequency on which it may operate, to prevent interference with other stations. (2) Of media exposure, the number of times an individual or household is exposed to a medium within a given period of time. (3) In statistics, the number of times each element appears in each step of a distribution scale.

Frequency modulation (FM). The method of transmitting electromagnetic signals by varying the *frequency* of the wave, in contrast to varying its *size.* See *AM—Amplitude modulation.*

Fringe Time (TV). The hours directly before and after Prime Time. May be further specified as Early Fringe or Late Fringe.

FTC. See *Federal Trade Commission.*

Full position. A special preferred position of an advertisement in a newspaper: either (1) the advertisement both follows a column or columns of the news reading matter and is completely flanked by reading matter as well, or else (2) the advertisement is at the top of the page and alongside reading matter.

Full service agency. See *Advertising agency.*

Full showing. (1) In an outdoor poster schedule, a 100-intensity showing. (2) In car cards, one card in each car of a line, or in each of the city, in which space is bought. The actual number of posters or car cards in a 100-intensity showing varies from market to market.

G

Galley proofs. Proofs on sheets usually 20 to 22 inches long, printed from type as it stands in galley trays before the type is made up into pages.

Gang. A group of plates, type pages, or the like arranged in a form for printing with a single impression; a sheet thus printed. In photoengraving, a group of repeated original set ups or negatives stripped in for multiple reproduction—especially for labels or folding boxes.

Geostationary (TV). The position of a synchronous satellite that rotates around the earth at the Equator at the same rate as the earth. Used for satellite transmission.

Ghost. An unwanted image appearing in a television picture; for example, as a result of signal reflection.

Ghosted view. An illustration giving an X-ray view of a subject.

Grain. In machine-made paper the direction of the fibers, making the paper stronger across the grain and easier to fold with the grain. In planning direct mail, it is important that the paper fold with the grain rather than against it.

Gravure. Any of the processes for printing from a metal intaglio plate. Intaglio denotes that the design on the plate is sunken below the surface, as distinct from letterpress.

Grid. A system of presenting rates that assigns various values to each time period. Higher values are assigned to non-preemptible announcements and to announcements that are telecast during peak periods. Time can be offered and sold in terms of grids.

Gross rating points. The number of rating points a program bearing a commercial has on each station in an area, multiplied by the number of times it is run

within a specified period, such as per week. See *Rating point.*

Ground bulletin (Outdoor). A painted bulletin built on the ground as opposed to one built on a roof top or a wall.

Ground waves. Those broadcasting waves (AM) that tend to travel along the surface of the earth and are relatively unaffected by the earth's curvature. See *Sky waves.*

Group discount. A special discount in radio station rates for the simultaneous use of a group of stations.

GRP. See Gross Rating Points.

Gutter. The inside margins of facing printed pages.

H

Hairline. A fine or delicate line in type, rule, or engraving; any type character that is very light throughout, or the lighter parts of modern types with serifs.

Half run. In transportation advertising, a car card placed in every other car of the transit system used. Also called a half service.

Half showing. One half of a full showing of car cards; a 50-intensity showing of outdoor posters or panels.

Halftone. A photoengraving plate, photographed through a glass screen (in the camera) that serves to break up the reproduction of the subject into dots and thus makes possible the printing of halftone values, as of photographs. Screens vary from 45 to 300 lines to the inch. The most common are 120- and 133-line screens for use in magazines; 65- to 85-line screen for use in newspapers. Square halftone—in which the corners are square and which has an all-over screen; Silhouette or outline halftone—one in which a part of the background is removed; Vignette halftone—one in which background fades away at the edges.

Surprint. A plate in which a line-plate negative is surprinted over a halftone negative, or vice versa; a Combination plate—one in which line-plate negative is adjacent to (but not upon) halftone negative; Highlight or dropout halftone—one in which dots are removed from various areas to get greater contrast.

Hand composition. Type set up by hand, as distinguished from type set up by machine. (Compare Linotype composition; Monotype composition.)

Hand lettering. Lettering that is drawn by hand, as distinguished from type that is regularly set.

Hand tooling. Handwork on an engraving or plate to improve its reproducing qualities, charged for by the hour. Unless the plate is a highlight halftone, hand tooling is needed to secure pure white in a halftone.

Haphazard sampling. See *Sampling.*

Head. Display caption to summarize contents and get attention. Center heads are centered on type matter; side heads, at the beginning of a paragraph; box heads, enclosed by rules; cut-in heads, in an indention of the text.

Head-on position. An outdoor advertising stand that directly faces direction of traffic on a highway.

Heaviside layer. A blanket of ions that encloses the earth. Bounces AM waves back at night, enabling AM stations to be heard at far distances.

Heavy-half user. This refers to those users of a product who represent 50 percent or more of the total volume sales of the product. This usually represents less than 50 percent of the total number of users of the product.

Hiatus. A break in the advertiser's broadcast schedule, usually during the summer, which permits him to resume broadcasting in that particular time spot.

Hi-Fi Color. A method of printing full color pages for newspapers by special printing plants, whereby the ad appears on one side and the other side can be left blank for the newspaper's use. Top and bottom of ad have no sharp cut-off point; ad must be designed with continuous design, like wallpaper.

"Hold." Instruction indicating what part of copy is to be reproduced; warning to stop after some preliminary operations as "Send blueprint and hold"; instruction to keep in type matter that is set up but not to be used immediately.

Horizontal publications. Business publications addressed to men representing the same strata of interest or responsibility, regardless of the nature of the company, as Purchasing, Maintenance Engineer, Business Week. See *Vertical publications.*

House agency. See *Advertising agency*

House mark. A primary mark of a business concern, usually used with the trademark of its products, as *General Mills* (house mark) and *Betty Crocker* (cake mix) (trademark); Du Pont (house mark) and Teflon II (trademark).

House organ. A publication issued periodically by a firm to further its own interests, inviting attention on the strength of its editorial content. Also known as company magazine and company newspaper.

I

Iconoscope. The special television camera that picks up the image to be sent.

ID. A TV station break between programs, or within a program, used for station identification. Usually 2 seconds, with 8 seconds for commercial, usually just the name and slogan for identification of product, hence called an ID.

Inch. The unit of advertising measurement, a space one inch deep and one column wide; a column inch.

Individual location. The location of an outdoor advertisement in which there is but a single panel, and not several adjacent ones.

Industrial goods. Commodities (raw materials, machines, et cetera) destined for use in producing other goods; also called producer goods; distinct from consumer goods.

Inherited audience. The portion of a radio program's audience that listened to the preceding program on the same station.

In-house agency. See *Advertising agency*

Insertion order. Instructions from an advertiser authorizing a publisher to print an advertisement of specified size on a given date at an agreed rate; accompanied or followed by the copy for the advertisement.

Inserts. (1) In letters or packages, an enclosure usually in the form of a little slip bearing an advertisement. (2) In periodicals, a page printed by the advertiser, or for him, and forwarded to the publisher, who binds it up in the publication. Usually in colors and on heavier stock (if the publisher permits).

Institutional advertising. That done by an organization speaking of its work, views and problems as a whole, to gain public goodwill and support, rather than to sell a specific product.

Intaglio printing. Printing from a depressed surface, such as from the copper plate or steel plate that produces engraved calling cards and announcements. Rotogravure is a form of intaglio printing. Compare letterpress and lithography.

Integrated commercial. A single TV spot in which an advertiser presents two products with the same announcer and setting. Compare with Piggyback.

Interference. The reception of an undesired radio or television program or extraneous electrical noise simultaneously with a desired program.

Ionosphere. A canopy or layer that forms in the upper atmosphere, against which AM radio signals are reflected back to earth. FM signals are not.

IP (TV). Immediate preemption rate. See *Preemption*

Island position. (1) In a publication page, an advertisement surrounded entirely by editorial matter. (2) In television, refers to a commercial isolated from other advertising by program content. (3) In point of purchase, a display arranged in the aisle of a store, separated from other displays.

Iteration. A trial and error method of getting a mathematical solution to a problem which cannot be reduced to a formula in advance. Used in determining which of a given list of media will provide the widest reach at the lowest cost.

J

Job ticket. A sheet or an envelope that accompanies a printing job through the various departments, bearing all the instructions and all records showing the progress of the work.

Judgment sampling. See *Sample; sampling.*

Junior unit. In print, a page size which permits an advertiser to use the same engraving plates for small- and large-page publications. The advertisement is prepared as a full-page unit in the smaller publication (such as Time) and appears in the larger publication (such as Home & Garden) as a "junior unit" with some editorial matter on two or more sides.

Justification of type. Arranging type so that it appears in even-length lines, with its letters properly spaced.

K

"Keep standing." Instructions to printer to hold type for further instructions after it has been used on a job. Where it may be necessary to hold type for any length of time, it is better to have an electrotype of the set-up made.

Keying an advertisement. Giving an advertisement a code number or letter so that when people respond, the source of the inquiry can be traced. The key may be a variation in the address, or a letter or number printed in the corner of a return coupon.

Key plate. The plate in color process with which all other plates must register.

Key station. The point at which a radio network's principal programs originate. There may be several.

Kinescope. Film of a live commercial or program made by photographing the television tube image, usually made in the television studio.

King-size poster. An outside transit display placed on the sides of vehicles. Size: 30" x 144". See *Queen size posters*.

Known-probability sampling. See *Sample; sampling*.

Kraft. A strong paper used for making tension envelopes, wrappers for mailing magazines, and the like.

L

Laid paper. Paper showing a regular watermarked pattern, usually of parallel lines.

Lanham Act. The Federal Trade-Mark Act of 1946, supplanting the previous Federal trademark acts.

Layout. A working drawing showing how an advertisement is to look. A printer's layout is a set of instructions accompanying a piece of copy showing how it is to be set up.

l.c. Lower-case letters.

Leaders. A line of dots or dashes to guide the eye across the page, thus:

Lead-in. In relation to audience flow, the program preceding an advertiser's program on the same station.

Leading (pronounced ledding). The insertion of metal strips (known as leads between lines of type, causing greater space to appear between these lines. The usual size is 2 points. Leaded type requires more room than type that is not leaded but set solid.

Lead-out. In relation to audience flow, the program following an advertiser's program on the same station.

Ledger. A high-grade writing paper of tough body and smooth, plated surface. Used for accounting work and for documents.

Legend. The title or description under an illustration. Sometimes called cutline.

Letterpress. Printing from a relief, or raised surface. The raised surface is inked and comes in direct contact with the paper, like that of a rubber stamp.

Limited time station. A radio station that is assigned a channel for broadcasting for a specified time only, sharing its channel with other stations at different times.

Line. A unit for measuring space one-fourteenth of a column-inch.

Lineage. The total number of lines of space occupied by one advertisement or a series of advertisements.

Line drawing. A drawing made with brush, pen, pencil, or crayon, with such shading as occurs produced by variations in size and spacing of lines, not by tone.

Line plate. A photoengraving made without the use of a screen from a drawing composed of lines or masses, which can print on any quality stock.

Linotype composition. Mechanical type setting by molding a line of type at a time. The Linotype machine is operated by a keyboard resembling that of a typewriter. (Compare Hand composition; Monotype composition.)

Lip sync. In making a movie, especially one involving singing, an actor may mouth the words without any voice, while a professional singer out of view of the camera does the actual singing.

Lip-synchronization (lip-sync). The method in television of having the voice of the performer recorded as he speaks. Requires more rehearsal and equipment and costs more than narration.

List broker. In direct mail advertising, an agent who rents prospect lists, compiled by one advertiser, to another advertiser. He receives a commission for his services.

Listening area. The geographic area in which a station's transmitting signal can be heard clearly. The area in which transmission is static-free and consistent is called the primary listening area.

Lithography. A printing process by which an image is formed on special stone by a greasy material, with the design then being transferred to the printing paper. Today, the more frequently used process is Offset-Lithography in which a thin and flexible metal sheet replaces the stone. In this process, the design is "offset" from the metal sheet to a rubber blanket, which then transfers the image to the printing paper gives soft reproduction effect.

Live. In television and radio, a program which originates at the moment it is produced, in contrast to a program which is previously taped, filmed or recorded.

Local advertising. Advertising placed and paid for by the local merchant or dealer in contrast to national, or general, advertising of products sold by many dealers.

Local-channel station. A radio station that is allowed just enough power to be heard near its point of transmission and is assigned a channel on the air wave set aside for local-channel stations. (Compare Regional-channel station; Clear-channel station.)

Local program. A non-network, station-originated program.

Local rate. A reduced rate offered by media to local advertisers that is lower than that offered to national advertisers.

Locking up. Tightening up the type matter put into a chase preparatory to going to press.

Log. A record of every minute of television or radio broadcasting. An accurate journal required by law.

Lower case (l.c.). The small letters in the alphabet, such as those in which this is printed, as distinguished from UPPER CASE OR CAPITAL LETTERS. Named from the lower case of the printer's type cabinet in which this type was formerly kept.

Logotype or logo. A trademark or trade name embodied in the form of a distinctive lettering or design. Most famous example: Coca Cola.

M

Machine-finish (MF) paper. The cheapest of book papers that take halftones well. A pa-

per which has had its pores filled ("sized") but which is not ironed. Thus it possesses a moderately smooth surface. Smoother than antique, but not so smooth as English-finish or sized and supercalendered paper.

Mail order advertising. That method of selling whereby the complete sales transaction is negotiated through advertising and the mails, and without the aid of a salesman. Not to be confused with direct mail advertising.

Makegood. (1) Print: An advertisement which is run without charge in lieu of a prior one which publisher agrees was poorly run. A print advertisement run in lieu of a scheduled one which did not appear. (2) TV, radio: A commercial run by agreement with advertiser in place of one that did not run, or was improperly scheduled. All subject to negotiation between advertiser (or agency) and medium.

Make-ready. The process of adjusting the form of type or the plates for the press to insure uniform impression. The skill and care in this work represent one of the hidden elements that serve to make a good printing job.

Make-up of a page. The general appearance of a page; the arrangement in which the editorial matter and advertising material are to appear.

Make-up restrictions. To prevent the use of freak-sized advertisements, which would impair the value of the page for other advertisers, publishers require that advertisements have a minimum depth in ratio to their width.

Mandatory copy. Copy that is required, by law, to appear on the advertising of certain products such as liquor, beer, cigarettes. Also refers to information

that, by law, must be on labels of certain products, as foods and drugs.

March issue, for example, close February 5. Second month preceding would mean that forms close January 5; third month preceding, December 5.

Market. A group of people who are able to buy a product, should they desire it.

Market profile. A demographic description of the people or the households of a product's market. It may also include economic and retailing information about a territory.

Market research. The research to gather facts needed to make marketing decisions.

Market segmentation. Designing a product to meet the needs of a particular, identifiable group, or addressing an appeal directly to them.

Mass medium. One which is not directed toward a specific audience and which is widely accepted by all types of people, as opposed to *class* medium.

Master print (TV). The final approved print of a commercial, from which duplicates are made for distribution to stations.

Matrix; "mat." (1) A mold of paper pulp, or similar substance, made by pressing a sheet of it into the type setup or engraving plate. Molten lead is poured into it, forming a replica of the original plate known as a stereotype. (2) The brass molds used in the Linotype.

Matter. Composed type, often referred to as: (1) dead matter—of no further use; (2) leaded matter—having extra spacing between lines; (3) live matter—to be used again; (4) solid matter—lines set close to each other; (5) standing matter—held for future use.

Maximil line rate. The milline rate of a newspaper computed at its maximum rate. See *Milline rate.*

Mechanical. An assembly of pictures and proofs of type, pasted in a desired arrangement (usually on a piece of cardboard), to be copied by a camera for making into a printing plate. Also called mechanical layout.

Medium. (1) The vehicle that carries the advertisement, as television, radio, newspaper, magazine, outdoor sign, car card, direct mail, and so on. (2) The tool and method used by an artist in illustrations, as pen and ink, pencil, wash, photography.

Merchandising. (1) "The planning involved in marketing the right merchandise or service at the right place, at the right time, in the right quantities, and at the right price."—American Marketing Association. (2) The promotion of an advertiser's advertising to his sales force, wholesalers, and dealers. (3) The promotion by media to the trade and the consuming public of the product advertised, by means of point-of-purchase materials, in-store retail promotions, and guarantee seals or tags.

M.F. Machine-finish paper.

Milline rate. A unit for measuring the rate of advertising space in relation to circulation; the cost of having one agate line appear before one million readers. Calculated thus:

$$\frac{1{,}000{,}000 \times \text{line rate}}{\text{quantity circulation}} = \text{milline}$$

Modern type. See *Old style type.*

Modular agency. Also called a la carte agency. See *Advertising agency.*

Monotype composition. Type set by a machine in which the individual letters are separately molded and automatically assembled into lines, as distinguished from Hand composition and Linotype composition.

Month preceding. First month preceding publication means that the closing date falls on the given day during the month that immediately precedes the publication date of a periodical.

Mortise. An opening cut through a plate, block, or base, to permit insertion of other matter, usually type.

Motivational research. A research without a questionnaire, in which the respondent is invited to talk freely on a series of selected topics relating to the advertiser's interests, or react to a situation pictured or described to him. Also called *unstructured research.*

Musical clock (radio). A broadcast format in which recorded popular music and time announcements serve as a background for numerous commercials.

N

NAD. See *National Advertising Division.*

NARB. See *National Advertising Review Board.*

National Advertising Division (NAD). The policymaking arm of the National Advertising Review Board.

National brand. A manufacturer's or producer's brand that has wide distribution through many outlets; distinct from a private brand.

National Advertising Review Board (NARB). The major organization of the advertising industry to curb misleading advertising.

National plan. The tactics in advertising campaigns of trying to get all the business that can be secured all over the country at one time. When rightfully used, it is the outgrowth of numerous local plans.

Neighborhood showing (Outdoor). Group of posters in a particular area in which an adveriser's product is available.

Nemo. Any broadcast which is not originated in the local studio.

Network. Interconnecting broadcasting stations for the simultaneous broadcasting of television or radio broadcasts.

Next to reading matter (n.r.). The position of an advertisement immediately adjacent to editorial or news matter in a publication.

Nielsen Station Index (NSI). These reports, issued by the A. C. Nielsen Company, provide audience measurement for individual television markets.

Nielsen Television Index (NTI). National audience measurements for all network programs.

Nonilluminated (also called "Regular"). A poster panel without artificial lighting.

Nonstructured interview. An interview conducted without a prepared questionnaire in which the respondent is encouraged to talk freely without direction from the interviewer.

NSI. See *Nielsen Station Index.*

NTI. Nielsen Television Index.

O

O & O stations. TV or radio stations owned and operated by networks.

Off camera. A television term for an actor whose voice is heard but who does not appear in the commercial. Less costly than being On camera.

Off-screen announcer. The effect of having the voice of an unseen speaker on a television commercial.

Offset. (1) See Lithography. (2) The blotting of a wet or freshly printed sheet against an accompanying sheet. Can be prevented by slip-sheeting. Antique paper absorbs the ink and prevents offsetting.

Old English. A style of black-letter or text type, now little used except in logotypes of trade names or names of newspapers.

Old style type (o.s.). Originally the face of roman type with slight difference in weight between its different strokes, as contrasted with modern type, which has sharp contrast and accents in its strokes. Its serifs for the most part are oblique; modern serifs are usually horizontal or vertical.

On camera. A television term for an actor whose face appears in a commercial. Opposite of Off camera. Affects the scale of compensation.

One-time rate. The rate paid by an advertiser who uses less space than is necessary to earn a time or rate discount, when such discounts are offered. Same as Transient rate, Basic rate, and Open rate.

One-way screen. A halftone with the screen in one direction only; it does not have the cross-screen that gives the dot effect. Good for odd effects. Makes tooling difficult.

Open end. A broadcast in which the commercial spots are added locally.

Open rate. In print, the highest advertising rate on which all discounts are placed. It is also called Basic Rate, Transient Rate, or One-time Rate.

Opticals. The visual effects that are put on a television film in a laboratory, in contrast to those that are included as part of the original photograph.

P

Package. (1) A container. (2) In radio or television, a combination assortment of time units, sold as a single offering at a set price. (3) A special radio or television program or series of programs, bought by an advertiser (usually for a lump sum) that includes all components all ready to broadcast with the addition of the advertiser's commercial. (4) In merchandising, a combination of products or services sold as one unit, as a Travel Package, including transportation and hotel accommodations.

Package insert. A card, folder or booklet included in a package, often used for recipes, discount coupons and ads for other members of the product family. When attached to outside of package, called package *outsert*.

Participation (TV, Radio). An announcement within a program as compared with one scheduled between programs.

Pattern plate. (1) An electrotype of extra heavy shell used for molding in large quantities to save wear on the original plate or type. (2) An original to be used for the same purpose.

Photocomposition. A method of setting type by a photographic process only. Uses no metal. Employs computer plus miniature TV system.

Photoengraving. (1) An etched, relief printing plate made by a photomechanical process—as a halftone or line cut. (2) A print from such a plate. (3) The process of producing the plate.

Photoscript (TV). A series of photographs at the time of shooting a TV commercial picture based on the original script or storyboard. (Pp. 431 & 433.) Used for keeping record of commercial, also for sales promotion purposes.

Photosetting. A method of setting hot type from computerized film or tape. Not to be confused with photocomposition.

Photostat. One of the most useful aids in making layouts or proposed advertisements. A rough photographic reproduction of a subject; inexpensive and can be made quickly (within half an hour if desired).

P.I. (Per inquiry) advertising. A method used in direct response radio and television advertising whereby orders as a result of a commercial are sent directly to the station. The advertiser pays the station on a per inquiry (or per order) received basis.

Pi or pied type. A type setup that has become disarranged.

Pica; pica em. The unit for measuring width in printing. There are 6 picas to the inch. Derived from pica, the old name of 12-pt. type ($\frac{1}{6}$ inch high), and the letter M of that series, whose width likewise is $\frac{1}{6}$ inch. A page of type 25 picas wide is $4\frac{1}{6}$ inches wide ($25 \div 6 = 4\frac{1}{6}$).

Picture resolution. The clarity with which the television image appears on the television screen.

Piggyback. A practice born before 30 second commercials came in (late 1960's) whereby an advertiser would buy a 60 second spot and play the commercial of two products on it (the second being the "piggyback"). This practice waned with the 30 second commercial. Some advertisers trying to split this with piggyback. Opposed by the industry as adding to "clutter." See *Integrated commercial*.

Pilot film (TV). A sample film to show what a series will be like. Generally specially filmed episodes of television shows.

Pioneering stage. The advertising stage of a product in which the need for such product is not recognized and must be established, or when the need has been established but the success of a commodity in filling those requirements has to be established. See *Competitive stage; Retentive stage; Spiral*.

Plant operator. In outdoor advertising, the person who arranges to lease, erect, and maintain the outdoor sign and to sell the advertising space on it.

Plate. The metal or plastic from which impressions are made by a printing operation.

Plated stock. Paper with a high gloss and a hard, smooth surface, secured by being pressed between polished metal sheets.

Platen. The part of a printing press that holds the paper and presses it against the type or plate.

Playback. (1) The playing of a recording for audition purposes. (2) The report of a viewer or reader as to what message a commercial or advertisement left with him.

Point; pt. (1) The unit of measurement of type, about $\frac{1}{72}$ inch in depth. Type is specified by its point size, as 8 pt., 12 pt., 24 pt., 48 pt. (2) The unit for measuring thickness of paper, one thousandth of an inch.

Point-of-purchase advertising. Displays prepared by the manufacturer for use by the retailers in the stores selling the manufacturer's products.

Poll. An enumeration of a sample. Usually refers to sample opinions, attitudes and beliefs.

Positioning. Deciding for what service you want the product known. Noxzema, long known as a medical cream for eczema was repositioned as a facial cream.

Poster panel. A standard surface on which outdoor posters are placed. The posting surface is of sheet metal. An ornamental molding of standard green forms the frame. The standard poster panel is 12 feet high by 25 feet in length (outside dimensions).

Poster plant. The organization that provides the actual outdoor advertising service.

Poster showing. An assortment of outdoor poster panels in different locations sold as a unit.

The number of panels in a showing varies from city to city, and is described in terms of a #100 showing, a #50 showing, a #25 showing. This identification has no reference to the actual number of posters in a showing, nor does it mean percentages. It is merely a convenient way of describing the size of different assorted packages of posters.

Posting date (outdoor). The date posting for an advertiser begins. Usually, posting dates are every fifth day starting with the first of the month. However, plant operators will, if possible, arrange other posting dates when specifically requested.

Posting leeway (outdoor). The five working days required by plant operators to assure the complete posting of a showing. This margin is needed to allow for inclement weather, holidays, etc., as well as the time for actual posting.

P.P.A. Periodical Publishers Association, a group of magazine publishers that passes on agency credit. For newspaper credit, see *ANPA.*

Pre-date. In larger cities, a newspaper issue that comes out the night before the date it carries, or a section of the Sunday issue published and mailed out during the week preceding the Sunday date.

Preemption; preemptible time. (1) The recapturing of a time period by a network or station for important news or special program. (2) By prior agreement, the resale of a time unit of one advertiser to another (for a higher rate). Time may be sold: non-preemptive (NP) at the highest rate; two weeks preemptible (lower rate) or immediately preemptible (IP) the lowest rate.

Preferred position. A special desired position in a magazine

or newspaper for which the advertiser must pay a premium. Otherwise the advertisement appears in a run-of-paper (ROP) position; that is, wherever the publisher chooses to place it.

Premium. An item, other than the product itself, given to purchasers of product as an inducement to buy. Can be free with purchase, or available upon proof of purchase and a payment (*self-liquidating*).

Primary circulation. See *Circulation.*

Primary service area. The area to which a radio station delivers a high level of signals of unfailing steadiness and of sufficient volume to override the existing noise level both day and night and all seasons of the year, determined by field intensity measurements.

Prime time. A continuous period of not less than three hours per broadcast day as designated by the station as reaching peak audiences. In television usually 7:00 P.M. to 11:00 P.M. E.S.T. (6:00 P.M. to 10:00 P.M. C.S.T.).

Prime time (radio). The time of the day when most men are going to and from work (usually 7-8:30 A.M. and 4:30-6:30 P.M., depending upon the city). Called drive time.

Prime time (TV). Refers essentially to those hours when viewing is heaviest. This varies from region to region. In the Midwest usually from 6:00 to 10 P.M. In the East and West coasts from 7 to 11 P.M. (Radio) called *Drive Time* usually 7-8:30 A.M. and 4:30 to 6:30 P.M., but varies by city.

Principal register. The main register for recording trademarks, service marks, collective marks, and certification marks under the Lanham Federal Trade-Mark Act.

Printers' Ink Model Statute.

The act directed at fraudulent advertising, prepared and sponsored by Printers' Ink, the advertising journal.

Private brand. The trademark of a distributor of products which he alone sells, in contrast to manufacturers' brands, which are sold through many outlets. Also known as private labels.

Process plates. Photoengraving plates for printing in color. Can print the full range of the spectrum by using three plates, each bearing a primary color—red, yellow, blue—plus a black plate. Referred to as 4-color plates. See *Process printing*.

Process printing. Letterpress color printing in which color is printed by means of process plates.

Producer. One who originates and presents a television or radio program.

Production. (1) The conversion of an advertising idea into an advertisement, mainly by a printing process. (2) The building, organization, and presentation of a television or radio program.

Production department. (1) The department responsible for the mechanical production of an advertisement, dealing with printers and engravers. (2) The department responsible for the proper preparation of a television or radio program.

Production director. (1) Individual in charge of a television or radio program. (2) Head of department handling print production.

Profile. (1) A detailed study of a medium's audience, broken down by size, age, sex, viewing habits, income, education and so on. (2) A study of the characteristics of the users of a product or of a market.

Program following. The television or radio program that follows a given program. Impor-

tant in deciding upon the desirability of the station and hour. See *Lead-out*.

Program opposite. The television or radio programs that are running over other stations at the same time as the given program and broadcasting to the same territory; the competition for the audience that a program experiences.

Program preceding. The television or radio program that is directly before a given program. A good "program preceding" enhances the desirability of time on the air. See *Lead-in*.

Program profile. The graphic presentation of the reactions of a group of program listeners or viewers participating in a test situation involving some type of program analyzer.

Progressive proofs. A set of photoengraving proofs in color, in which: the yellow plate is printed on one sheet and the red on another; the yellow and red are then combined; next the blue is printed and a yellow-red-blue combination made. Then the black alone is printed, and finally all colors are combined. The sequence varies. In this way the printer matches up his inks when printing color plates.

Proof. (1) An inked impression of composed type or of a plate for inspection or for filing. (2) In engraving and etching, an impression taken to show the condition of the illustration at any stage of the work. Taking a proof is pulling a proof.

Publisher's statement. The statement of circulation issued by a publisher.

Q

Quads. Blank pieces of metal (not typehigh) used by the printer to justify (or fill out) lines where the amount of type does not do so.

Quarter showing. One fourth of

a full showing in or outdoor or transportation advertising.

Queen-size poster. An outside transit advertising display placed on the sides of vehicles (usually the curb side). Size: 30" x 88". See *King size posters*.

Quota. A set goal for sales or other effort in terms of dollars, sales units, or a percentage of the total goal.

R

Radio rating point. One per cent of the homes in the measured area whose sets are tuned to that station, used for making comparisons of spot stations.

Randomization. In consumer research a method of securing random (unbiased) selection of respondents. See *Sample; sampling*.

Rate card. A card giving the space rates of a publication and data on mechanical requirements and closing dates.

Rate-holder. The minimum-sized advertisement that must appear during a given period if an advertiser is to secure a certain time or quantity discount. It holds a lower rate for an advertiser.

Rate protection. The length of time an advertiser is guaranteed a specific rate by a medium. May vary from six months to a year from the date of signing a contract.

Rating point. (1) The percentage of TV households a TV station reaches with a program, compared with the total of all TV households in that area. The percentage varies with the time of the day. A station may have a 10 rating between 6 and 6:30 P.M., and a 20 rating between 9 and 9:30 P.M. (a real hit!). (2) In the case of radio, the percentage of people who listen to a station at a certain time.

Reach. The total audience a medium actually covers.

Reading notices. Advertisements in newspapers set up in a type similar to that of the editorial matter. Must be followed by "Adv." Charged for at rates higher than those for regular ads. Many publications will not accept them.

Ream. In publishing and advertising, 500 sheets of paper (not 480). Thousandsheet counts now being used as basis of ordering paper.

Rebroadcast. A television or radio program repeated at a later hour to reach the parts of the country in a different time belt.

Recognized agency. An advertising agency recognized by the various publishers or broadcast stations and granted a commission for the space it sells to advertisers.

Regional-channel station. A radio station that is allowed more power than a local station but less than a clear-channel station. It is assigned a place on the frequency band set aside for regional channel stations. See *Local channel* and *Clear-channel*.

Register. Perfect correspondence in printing; of facing pages when top lines are even; of color printing, when there is correct superimposition of each plate so that the colors mix properly.

Registering trademark. In the United States, the act of recording a trademark with the Commissioner of Patents.

Register marks (engraving). Cross lines placed on a copy to appear in the margin of all negatives as a guide to perfect register.

Release. A legally correct statement by a person photographed authorizing the advertiser to use that photograph. In the case of minors, the guardian's release is necessary.

Relief printing. Printing in which the design reproduced is raised slightly above the surrounding, nonprinting areas. Letterpress is a form of relief printing contrasted with Intaglio printing and Lithography.

Remote control. The operation of broadcasting a program from the regular studios of the station.

Remote pickup. A broadcast originating outside the studio, as from a hotel ballroom, football field, or the like.

Repro proofs, or reproduction proofs. Exceptionally clean and sharp proofs from type for use as copy for reproduction.

Residual. A sum paid to certain talent on a TV commercial every time the commercial is run after 13 weeks, for life of commercial.

Respondent. One who answers a questionnaire or is interviewed in a research sutdy.

Retentive stage. The third stage of a product, reached when its general usefulness is everywhere known, its indivdiual qualities thoroughly appreciated, and when it is satisfied to retain its patronage merely on the strength of its past reputation. See *Pioneering stage*s *Competitive stage; Spiral*.

Retouching. The process of correcting or improving art work, especially photographs.

Reversed plate. (1) A line-plate engraving in which whites comes out black, and vice versa. (2) An engraving in which right and left, as they appear in the illustration, are transposed.

Riding the showing. A physical inspection of the panels which comprise an outdoor showing.

Roman type. (1) Originally, type of the Italian and Roman school of design, as distinguished from the black-face Old English style. Old style and modern are the two branches of the Roman family. (2) Type faces that are not italics are called roman.

ROP. See *Run-of-paper position*.

ROS. See *Run of schedule time*.

Rotary plan (outdoor). A program whereby movable bulletins are moved from one fixed location to another one in the market at regular intervals. The locations are viewed and approved in advance by the advertiser.

Rotary press. A press possessing no flat bed, but printing entirely with the movement of cylinders.

Rotogravure. The method of intaglio printing in which the impression is produced by cylinder plates chemically etched and affixed to rollers of a rotary press; useful in large runs of pictorial effects.

Rough. In the making of layouts, the first step will usually be to make a crude sketch to show basic idea or arrangement. This is called a "rough."

Rough cut (TV). A film cut and edited into a smooth-flowing work print.

Routing out. Tooling out dead metal on an engraving plate.

Run-of-paper (ROP) position. Any location in a publication convenient to publisher in contrast to preferred position.

Run-of-schedule (ROS). Commercial announcements which can be scheduled at the station's discretion anytime during the period specified by the seller. (e.g., ROS, 10 A.M.-4:30 P.M., Monday through Friday.)

Rushes (TV). The first, uncorrected prints of a commercial. Also called *dailies*.

S

Saddle stitching. Binding a booklet by stitching it with wire through the center, passing through the fold in the center pages and the backbone. Enables the booklet to lie flat. When a booklet is too thick for this method, side stitching is used.

SAG. Screen Actors' Guild.

Sales promotion. (1) Those sales activities that supplement both personal selling and marketing, co-ordinate the two, and help to make them effective; for example, displays. (2) More loosely, the combination of personal selling, advertising, and all supplementary selling activities.

Sales-promotion department. The liaison department between the sales department and the advertising department which investigates new markets, inquiries resulting from advertisements, and follows up salesmen's visits with proper letters and literature.

Sample; sampling. (1) The method of introducing and promoting merchandise by distributing a miniature or full-size trial package of the product free or at a reduced price. (2) Studying the characteristics of a representative part of an entire market, or universe, in order to apply to the entire market the data secured from the miniature part. A probability sample is one in which every member of the universe has a known probability of inclusion. A random sample is a probability sample in which names are picked from a list with a fixed mathematical regularity. A stratified quota sample (also known as a quota sample) is one drawn with certain predetermined restrictions as to the characteristics of the people to be included. An area sample (or stratified area sample) is one in which one geographical unit is selected as typical of others in its environment. In a judgment sample, an expert chooses what he considers to be representative cases suitable for study, based on his experience and knowledge of the field. A convenience or batch sample is one selected from whatever portion of the universe happens to be handy.

Satellite television. TV programs relayed from far distances by a satellite.

Saturation. A media pattern of wide coverage and high frequency during a concentrated period of time, designed to achieve maximum impact, coverage, or both.

S.C. (1) Single column. (2) Small caps.

Scaling down. Reducing illustrations to the size desired.

Scatter plan (TV). The use of announcements over a variety of network programs and stations, to reach as many people as possible in a market.

Score. To crease cards or thick sheets of paper so that they can be folded.

Screen. The finely crossruled sheet used in photomechanical plate-making processes to reproduce the shades of gray present in a continuous tone photograph. Screens come in various rulings, resulting in more, or fewer, "dots" to the square inch on the plate, to conform with the requirements of different grades and kinds of printing paper.

Script (TV). A description of the video, along with the accompanying audio, used in preparing a storyboard, or in lieu of it.

Secondary meaning. When a word from the language has long been used as a trademark for a specific product and has come to be accepted as such, it is said to have acquired a "secondary meaning," and may be eligible for trademark registration.

Secondary service area (radio). The area beyond the primary service area where a broadcasting station delivers a steady signal of sufficient intensity to be a regular program service of loudspeaker volume by both day and night and at all seasons of the year. See *Primary service area.*

SEG. Screen Extras Guild.

Segmentation. See *Market segmentation.*

Seque. (Pronounced segway; Italian, "it follows.") The transition from one musical theme to another without a break or announcement.

Serif. The short marks at top and bottom of Roman lettering. Originally chisel marks to indicate top and bottom of stone lettering.

Service mark. A word or name used in the sale of services to identify the services of a firm and distinguish them from those of others, e.g., Hertz Drive Yourself Service; Weight Watchers Diet Course. Comparable to *trademarks* for products.

Sheet. The old unit of poster size, 26 x 39 inches. The standard-size posters are 24 sheets and 30 sheets. There are also 3 and 6 sheets posters.

SIC. See *Standard Industrial Classification.*

Side stitching. The method of wire-stitching from one side of a booklet to the other. Wiring can be seen on front cover and on back. Used in thick booklet work. Pages do not lie flat. See *Saddle stitching.*

Signal. In television or radio, a reproduction of that which has been broadcast.

Signal area. The territory in which a radio or television broadcast is heard. Can be primary, where most clearly heard, or secondary, where heard subject to more interference.

Signal (TV, Radio). The communication which is received electronically from the broadcast station. One speaks of a "strong signal" or a "weak signal."

Signature. (1) The name of an advertiser. (2) The musical number or sound effect that regularly identifies a television or radio program. (3) A sheet folded ready for stitching in a book, usually sixteen pages, but with thin paper thirty-two pages; a mark, letter, or number is placed at the bottom of the first page of every group of sixteen or thirty-two pages to serve as a guide in folding.

Silhouette halftone. See *Halftone.*

Silk screen. A printing process in which a stenciled design is applied to a screen of silk or organdy. A squeegee forces paint or ink through the mesh of the screen to the paper directly beneath.

Simulation (computer). The process of introducing synthetic information into a computer for testing; an application for solving problems too complicated for analytical solution.

Simulcast. The simultaneous playing of a program over AM-FM radio. Now ruled out by FCC.

SIU. Sets in use (TV).

Sized and supercalendered paper (s. and s. c.). Machine-finish book paper that has been given extra ironings to insure a smooth surface. Takes halftones very well.

Sized paper. Paper that has received a chemical bath to make it less porous. Paper sized once and ironed (calendered) is known as machine-finish. If it is again ironed, it becomes sized and supercalendered (s. and s.c.).

Skin pack. A packaging method whereby a plastic film is pulled tightly around a product on a card. Used for "card merchandising."

Sky waves. The electromagnetic waves that shoot toward the sky from a station. During the day they all go through the Heaviside electronic layer which blankets the earth. At night the AM waves bound back at an angle; hence AM broadcasts can be received at night over vast distances. See *Ground waves.*

Slip-sheeting. Placing a sheet of paper (tissue or cheap porous stock) between the sheets of a printing job to prevent them from offsetting or smudging as they come from the press.

Slug. Notation placed on copy to identify it temporarily, and not to be reproduced in final printing.

Small caps (abbreviated **s.c.** or **sm. caps**). Letters shaped like upper case (capitals) but about two-thirds their size—nearly the size of lower case letters. THIS SENTENCE IS SET WITH A REGULAR CAPITAL LETTER AT THE BEGINNING, THE REST IN SMALL CAPS.

SMSA. See *Standard Metropolitan Statistical Area.*

Snipe. A copy strip added over a poster advertisement—such as a dealer's name, special sale price, or another message. (Also referred to as an "overlay.")

Sound effects. Various devices or recordings used in television or radio to produce lifelike imitations of sound, such as walking up stairs, ocean waves, phone bells, and auto horns.

Space buyer. The officer of an advertising agency responsible for the selection of printed media for the agency's clients.

Space discount. A discount given by a publisher for the linage an advertiser uses. Compare Time discount.

Space schedule. A schedule showing the media in which an advertisement is to appear, the dates on which it is to appear, its exact size, and the cost.

Special representative. An individual or organization that represents a medium in selling time or space outside the city of origin.

Spectacolor. Similar in purpose and method to Hi Fi color, except color pages come out with registration points to fit newspaper page; no need for continuous design.

Spectacular. An outdoor sign built to order, designed to be conspicuous for its location, size, lights, motion, or action. The costliest form of outdoor advertising.

Spiral, advertising. The graphic representation of the stages through which a product might pass in its acceptance by the public. The stages are pioneering, competitive, retentive.

Split run. A facility available in some newspapers and magazines wherein the advertiser can run different advertisements in alternate copies of the same issue at the same time. A pre-testing method used to compare coupon returns from two different advertisements published under identical conditions.

Sponsor. The firm or individual that pays for talent and broadcasting station time for a radio feature; the advertiser on the air.

Spot (TV and radio). (1) Media Use. The purchase of time from an independent station, in contrast to purchasing it via a network. When purchased by a national advertiser it is, strictly speaking, *national spot,* but is referred to as just *spot.* When purchased by a local advertiser it is, strictly speaking, *local spot,* but is referred to as *local* TV or *local* radio. (2) Creative use. The text of a short announcement.

Spread. (1) Two facing pages, a doublepage advertisement. (2) Type matter set full measure across a page, not in columns. (3) Stretching any part of a broadcast to fill the full allotted time of the program.

Spread posting dates. An advertiser can have one posting date for half the panels of his showing. Then have the other half posted on a subsequent date, say 10 or 15 days later.

Stage. See *Spiral.*

Staggered schedule. A schedule of space to be used in two or more periodicals, arranged so that the insertions alternate.

Standard Industrial Classification (SIC). The division of all industry, by the Bureau of the Budget, into detailed standard classifications, identified by code numbers.

Standard Metropolitan Statistical Area (SMSA). An allocation of territories in a metropolitan area as defined by the Bureau of the Budget, brought to county line basis. Used in sales planning and scheduling.

"Stand by." Cue that the radio program is about to go on the air.

Standby space. Some magazines will accept an order to run an advertisement whenever and wherever it wishes, at an extra discount. Advertiser forwards plate with order. Helps magazine fill odd pages or spaces.

Station breaks. Those periods of time between television programs, or within a program as designated by the program originator, that are set aside for local station identification and spot announcements called ID. Usually 8 seconds

Station clearance. See *Clear time.*

Station Satellite. A station, often found in regions of low population density, that is wholly dependent upon another, carrying both its programs and commercials. Purpose is to expand coverage of the independent station and offer service to remote areas. Nothing to do with TV from satellites.

Steel-die embossing. Printing from steel dies engraved by the intaglio process, the sharp,

raised outlines being produced by stamping over a counter die. Used for monograms, crests, stationery, and similar social and business purposes.

Stereotype. Duplicate printing plate made by casting molten metal into a Matrix or mold of wood fiber which has been made under pressure. Lacks the strength and sharpness of detail of an electrotype. Newspapers are printed from stereotype.

Stet. A proofreader's term—"Let it stand as it is; disregard change specified." A dotted line is placed underneath the letter or words to which the instructions apply.

Storecasting. The broadcasting of radio programs and commercials in stores; usually supermarkets.

Storyboard. Series of drawings used to present a proposed commercial. Consists of illustrations of key action (video), accompanied by the audio part to go with it. Used for getting advertiser approval; also as a guide in production.

Strip. (1) TV or radio. A commercial scheduled at the same time on successive days of the week, as Monday through Friday. (2) Newspapers. A shallow advertisement at the bottom of a newspaper, across all columns.

Substance No. (Usually followed by a figure, as Substance No. 16, Substance No. 20, Substance No. 24.) In specifying paper stock, the equivalent weight of a given paper in the standard size.

Supplements (newspaper). Loose inserts carried in a newspaper. Printed by advertiser. Must carry "supplement" and newspaper logotype to meet newspaper postal requirements.

Surprint. (1) a photoengraving in which a line-plate effect appears over the face of a halftone, or vice versa. (2) Print-

ing over the face of an advertisement already printed.

Sustaining program. Entertainment or educational feature performed at the expense of a broadcasting station or network; in contrast to a commercial program, for which an advertiser pays.

Sworn statement. When a publisher does not offer a certified audited report of his circulation (as many small and new publishers do not) he may offer advertisers a sworn statement of circulation.

Syndicated services (research). Reports of consumers watching TV programs, listening to radio, or reading specific publications. Sold on a subscription basis to advertisers, agencies and others interested.

Syndicated TV program. A program that is sold or distributed to more than one local station by an independent organization outside of the national network structure. Includes reruns of former network entries, and movies that are marketed to stations by specialized firms that had a hand in their production.

Syndication, Trade-out. See *Trade-out Syndication.*

T

T. Time, or times, as 1-t, 5-t, the frequency with which an advertisement is to appear.

T.A.B. See *Traffic Audit Bureau.*

Tag (TV). A local retailer's message at the end of a manufacturer's commercial. Usually 10 seconds of a 60-second commercial.

Take-one. A mailing card or coupon attached to an inside transit advertisement, which the rider is invited to tear off and mail for further information on the service or offering by the advertiser.

Tear sheets. Copies of advertisements torn from newspapers.

Telecast. A sound and pictorial image that has been sent by television.

T.F. (1) Till-forbid. (2) To fill. (3) Copy is to follow.

Till-forbid; run T.F. Instructions to publisher meaning: "Continue running this advertisement until instructions are issued to the contrary." Used in local advertisement.

Time Classifications (TV). Stations assign alphabetical values to specific time periods for easier reference while reading their rate cards. The values generally extend from A through D. In an average market, the classification might work as follows: AA and A for Prime Time; B for Early Evening and Late News; C for Day Time (afternoon) and Late Night; D for the periods from 1 A.M. until sign-off and from sign-on until noon.

Time clearance. Making sure that a given time for a specific program or commercial is available.

Time discount. A discount given to an advertiser for the frequency or regularity with which he inserts his advertisements. Distinguished from quantity discount, for amount of space used.

Tint block. Usually a solid piece of zinc, used to print a light shade of ink for a background.

To fill (T.F.). Instructions to printer meaning: "Set this copy in the size necessary to fill the specified space indicated in the layout."

Tr. Transpose type as indicated, a proofreader's abbreviation.

Trade advertising. Advertising directed to the wholesale or retail merchants or sales agencies through whom the product is sold.

Trade character. A representation of a person or animal, realistic or fanciful, used in conjunction with a trademark to help identification. May appear on packages as well as in advertising (e.g., Green Giant).

Trademark. Any device or word that identifies the origin of a product, telling who made it or who sold it. Not to be confused with trade name.

Trade name. A name that applies to a business as a whole and not to be an individual product.

Trade-Out Syndication. An advertiser will produce a TV program series in which he places his own commercials. He then offers the program without cost to stations, which can then sell remaining time to other advertisers in addition to saving program charges. Chief advantage: keeps other commercials away from his.

Traffic Audit Bureau (T.A.B.). An organization designed to investigate how many people pass and may see a given outdoor sign, to establish a method of evaluating traffic and measuring a market.

Traffic count. In outdoor advertising, the number of pedestrians and vehicles passing a panel during a specific time period.

Traffic department. The department in an advertising agency responsible for the prompt execution of the work in the respective departments and for turning over the complete material for shipment to the forwarding department on schedule time.

Traffic flow map (outdoor). An outline map of a market's streets scaled to indicate the relative densities of traffic.

Transcription. See *Electrical transcription*.

Transcription program library. A collection of transcription records from which the radio station may draw. Stations subscribe to various transcription libraries.

Transient rate. Same as one-time in buying space.

Transition time. See *Fringe time*.

Transparency. Same as decalcomania.

Traveling display. An exhibit prepared by a manufacturer of a product and loaned by him to each of several dealers in rotation. Usually based on the product and prepared in such a way as to be of educational or dramatizing value.

Trimmed flush. A booklet or book trimmed after the cover is on, the cover thus being cut flush with the leaves. Compare with Extended covers.

Triple Spotting. Three commercials back to back.

True-line. The rate per million circulation of a newspaper within a trading area (excluding outside trading area). This is in contrast to the milline rate which is its rate per million circulation based on its total circulation. Used by retail advertisers in comparing different newspaper costs measured in terms of only that part of the total circulation in which a store is interested.

TV. Television.

TvQ score. Percentage of people familiar with a network program who also consider it one of their favorites. A commercial service.

TV week. Sunday to Saturday.

25 X 38-80. Read twenty-five, thirty-eight, eighty. The method of expressing paper weight, meaning that a ream of paper 25 × 38 inches in size weighs 80 lbs. Similarly, 25 × 38-60, 25 × 38-70, 25 × 38-120, 17 × 22-16, 17 × 22-24, 20 × 26-80, 38 × 50-140.

Type face. The design and style of a type letter. Type faces are usually named after men, as, Caslon, Della Robbia, Janson, Goudy. In machine composition, the faces are known also by code numbers.

Type page. The area of a page that type can occupy; the total area of a page less the margins.

U

UHF. See *Ultra High Frequency*.

Ultra High Frequency UHF. Television channels 14-83, operating on frequencies from 470 Mc to 890 Mc.

Unaided recall. A research method for learning whether a person is familiar with a brand, slogan, advertisement or commercial without giving him a cue as to what it is. "What program did you watch last night?" See *Aided recall*.

V

VAC. Verified Audit Circulation by an auditing organization which believes every publication selling advertising should have an audit available whatever the circulation method (paid or free).

Value goal. The determination by a company of the amount and form of value it sets out to offer in a product.

Vertical publications. Those business publications dealing with the problems of a specific industry, as Chain Store Age, National Petroleum News, Textile World. See *Horizontal publications*.

VHF. Very High Frequency. The frequency on the electromagnetic spectrum assigned to television channels 2-13, inclusive. See *Ultra high frequency*.

Video. The visual portion of TV television broadcast. See *Audio*.

Videotape. An electronic method of recording images and sound on tape. Most TV shows that appear live (except sports events) are done on videotape.

Videotape recording. A system which permits instantaneous playback of a simultaneous recording of sound and picture on a continuous strip of tape.

Vignette. A halftone in which the edges (or parts of them) are shaded off gradually to very light gray.

Voice-over announcer. In television, a slide with an announcer who does not appear.

W

Wait order. An advertisement set in type ready to run in a newspaper, pending a decision on the exact date (frequent in local advertising).

Warm-up. The 3- or 5-minute period immediately preceding a line broadcast in which the announcer or star puts the studio audience in a receptive mood by amiably introducing the cast of the program, or discussing its problems.

Wash drawing. A brushwork illustration, usually made with diluted India ink or water color so that, in addition to its black and white, it has varying shades of gray, like a photograph. Halftones, not line plates, are made from wash drawings.

Wave posting (Outdoor). Concentration of poster showings in a succession of areas within the market. Usually coincides with

special promotions in each of these areas.

Wax-mold electrotype. An electrotype made from an impression taken in a sheet of wax; less expensive than lead mold. See *Electrotype*.

Wet printing. Color printing on specially designed high-speed presses with one color following another in immediate succession before the ink from any plate has time to dry.

W.F. Wrong font.

Window envelope. A mailing envelope with a transparent panel, permitting the address on the enclosure to serve as a mailing address as well.

Work-and-turn. Printing all the pages in a signature from one form and then turning the paper and printing on the second side, making two copies or signatures when cut.

Wove paper. Paper having a very faint, cloth-like appearance when held to the light.

Wrong font (w.f.). Letter from one series mixed with those from another series, or font. See if you can pick out the wrong font in this sentence.

Z

Zinc etching. A photoengraving in zinc. Term is usually applied to line plates.

Zone plan. The tactics in an advertising campaign of concentrating on a certain limited geographical area. Also known as local plan.

Zooming. The effect in television of having a subject suddenly grow bigger on the screen, like the locomotive of a train rushing right at you.

Index